"I took the A+ certification tests over the past week. I got an 812 for Hardware and 780 for the OS portion. This book was a very useful study guide. The best part of it for me was the CD-ROM. I found it very helpful to go through the end-of-chapter questions, and then go back and see what I needed to study. ...The practice exam and the bonus exams were very helpful."

St. Paul, Minnesota
A Reader from Amazon.com

"David Groth's new version of the A+ certification is the standard by which all new versions will be judged. I bought this book recently, to prep myself for the new A+ certification exam guidelines. I enjoyed the material covered on the CD as well as the end-of-section questions for reviewing subject matter. I put this book a little ahead of the Myers book for A+, and certainly ahead of the Microsoft Press A+ certification study guide."

Greg Padgett
Cedar Rapids, Iowa

"Absolutely superb! Information in the book was the key factor in my passing the A+ Core Hardware exam the first time with ease. I would recommend this book to anyone who wishes to attain the A+ Certification."

Phillip Elam
Kentucky, USA

"After deciding to get A+ certification from scratch, I bought this title and used it as my number 1 study guide. It was very complete and thorough as well as organized in a logical way. Very good for beginners. ...Overall, probably one of the best study guides out there."

A Reader from Barnes & Noble

"Make this your primary study guide. (The) *A+ Complete Study Guide, Second Edition* comes out the winner as far as I'm concerned. David Groth presents a thorough guide, logically laid out with a clear and concise synopsis of each objective. In my opinion, no one book can be all things to everyone, but this book comes closest."

Raymond Alstrom
Victoria, Texas

A+ Operating System Technologies Exam

SYBEX

OBJECTIVE   **CHAPTER**

OBJECTIVE	CHAPTER

Diagnosing and Troubleshooting

Recognize and interpret the meaning of common error codes and startup messages from the boot sequence, and identify steps to correct the problems.
    19

    Content may include the following: Safe Mode; No operating system found; Error in CONFIG.SYS line XX; Bad or missing COMMAND.COM; HIMEM.SYS not loaded; Missing or corrupt HIMEM.SYS; SCSI; Swap file; NT boot issues; Dr. Watson; Failure to start GUI; Windows Protection Error; Event Viewer—Event log is full; A device referenced in SYSTEM.INI, WIN.INI, Registry is not found

Recognize common problems and determine how to resolve them.
    17, 19

    Content may include the following: Eliciting problem symptoms from customers; Having customer reproduce error as part of the diagnostic process; Identifying recent changes to the computer environment from the user; Troubleshooting Windows-specific printing problems (Print spool is stalled; Incorrect/incompatible driver for print; Incorrect parameter)

    Other Common problems: General Protection Faults; Illegal operation; Invalid working directory; System lock up; Option (Sound card, modem, input device) or will not function; Application will not start or load; Cannot log on to network (option—NIC not functioning); TSR (Terminate Stay Resident) programs and virus; Applications don't install; Network connection

    Viruses and virus types: What they are; Sources (floppy, emails, etc.); How to determine presence

Networks

Identify the networking capabilities of Windows including procedures for connecting to the network.
    18

    Content may include the following: Protocols; IPCONFIG.EXE; WINIPCFG.EXE; Sharing disk drives; Sharing print and file services; Network type and network card; Installing and Configuring browsers; Configure OS for network connection

Identify concepts and capabilities relating to the Internet and basic procedures for setting up a system for Internet access.
    18

    Content may include the following: Concepts and terminology; ISP; TCP/IP; IPX/SPX; NetBEUI; E-mail; PING.EXE; HTML; HTTP://; FTP; Domain Names (Web sites); Dial-up networking; TRACERT.EXE

A+® Complete

Study Guide

Deluxe Edition

David Groth
Dan Newland

San Francisco • London

Associate Publisher: Neil Edde
Acquisitions and Developmental Editor: Elizabeth Hurley
Editors: Brianne Hope Agatep, Sally Engelfried, Judy Flynn, Jim Compton
Production Editors: Shannon Murphy, Liz Burke
Technical Editors: Mark Kovach, Michelle A. Roudebush, Donald Fuller
Contributors: Jarret Buse, Lisa Donald, Joseph Dreissen, Dan Haglund, Robert King, Michelle Roudebush, Charles Strother
Book Designer: Bill Gibson
Graphic Illustrators: Duane Bibby, Tony Jonick
Electronic Publishing Specialists: Judy Fung, Jill Niles
Proofreaders: Jennifer Campbell, Nanette Duffy, Dennis Fitzgerald, Leslie Higbee Light, Laurie O'Connell, Yariv Rabinovitch, Nancy Riddiough
Indexer: Rebecca R. Plunkett
CD Coordinator: Christine Harris
CD Technician: Keith McNeil
Cover Designer: Archer Design
Cover Photograph: Natural Selection Stock Photography

An earlier version of this book was published under the title *A+ Complete Study Guide, Second Edition*

Library of Congress Card Number: 2001096027

ISBN: 0-7821-4052-1

SYBEX and the SYBEX logo are either registered trademarks or trademarks of SYBEX Inc. in the United States and/or other countries.

Some screen reproductions produced with FullShot 99. FullShot 99 © 1991–1999 Inbit Incorporated. All rights reserved. FullShot is a trademark of Inbit Incorporated.

Some screen reproductions produced with Collage Complete.
Collage Complete is a trademark of Inner Media Inc.

The CD interface was created using Macromedia Director, COPYRIGHT 1994, 1997–1999 Macromedia Inc. For more information on Macromedia and Macromedia Director, visit http://www.macromedia.com.

The video portion of the CD was created and produced by Video Arts Studios, 1440 4th Avenue North, Fargo, ND 58102. For more information about Video Arts Studios and related services, please visit http://www.videoartsstudios.com, or e-mail info@videoartsstudios.com. It was filmed in David Groth's training center, Practical Training Solutions, 4745 Amber Valley Parkway, Fargo, ND 58103. For more information about Practical Training Solutions, please visit http://www.practicaltrainingsolutions.com.

The logo of the CompTIA Authorized Quality Curriculum Program and the status of this or other training material as "Authorized" under the CompTIA Authorized Curriculum Program signifies that, in CompTIA's opinion, such training material covers the content of the CompTIA's related certification exam. CompTIA has not reviewed or approved the accuracy of the contents of this training material and specifically disclaims any warranties of merchantability or fitness for a particular purpose. CompTIA makes no guarantee concerning the success of persons using any such "Authorized" or other training material in order to prepare for any CompTIA certification exam.

The contents of this training material were created for the CompTIA A+ exams covering CompTIA certification exam objectives that were current as of February 2001.

<u>How to Become CompTIA Certified:</u>

This training material can help you prepare for and pass a related CompTIA certification exam or exams. In order to achieve CompTIA certification, you must register for and pass a CompTIA certification exam or exams.

In order to become CompTIA certified, you must:

(1) Select a certification exam provider. For more information please visit http://www.comptia.org/certification/test_locations.htm.
(2) Register for and schedule a time to take the CompTIA certification exam(s) at a convenient location.
(3) Read and sign the Candidate Agreement, which will be presented at the time of the exam(s). The text of the Candidate Agreement can be found at www.comptia.org/certification
(4) Take and pass the CompTIA certification exam(s).

For more information about CompTIA's certifications, such as their industry acceptance, benefits, or program news, please visit www.comptia.org/certification

CompTIA is a non-profit information technology (IT) trade association. CompTIA's certifications are designed by subject matter experts from across the IT industry. Each CompTIA certification is vendor-neutral, covers multiple technologies, and requires demonstration of skills and knowledge widely sought after by the IT industry.

To contact CompTIA with any questions or comments:
Please call + 1 630 268 1818
questions@comptia.org

TRADEMARKS: SYBEX has attempted throughout this book to distinguish proprietary trademarks from descriptive terms by following the capitalization style used by the manufacturer.

The author and publisher have made their best efforts to prepare this book, and the content is based upon final release software whenever possible. Portions of the manuscript may be based upon pre-release versions supplied by software manufacturer(s). The author and the publisher make no representation or warranties of any kind with regard to the completeness or accuracy of the contents herein and accept no liability of any kind including but not limited to performance, merchantability, fitness for any particular purpose, or any losses or damages of any kind caused or alleged to be caused directly or indirectly from this book.

Manufactured in the United States of America

10 9 8 7 6 5 4 3 2 1

SYBEX

To Our Valued Readers:

In recent years, CompTIA's A+ program has become the most respected entry-level IT certification. Sybex is proud to have helped thousands of A+ candidates prepare for their exam, and we are excited about the opportunity to continue to provide people with the skills they'll need to succeed in the highly competitive IT industry.

It has been Sybex's mission from the start to teach exam candidates how computer technology works in the real world, not to simply feed them answers to test questions. Sybex was founded over 25 years ago on the premise of providing technical skills to IT professionals, and we have continued to build on that foundation, making significant improvements for this Deluxe Edition of Sybex's best-*selling A+ Complete Study Guide* based on feedback from readers, suggestions from instructors, and comments from industry leaders.

The most noticeable new feature is the second CD that includes professional quality video footage of the author, David Groth, performing crucial hands-on tasks in a lab environment. We've also added additional bonus exams, bringing the total number of review questions in the book and on the CD to over 1,000! We're confident that this book will meet and exceed the demanding standards of the certification marketplace and help you, the A+ exam candidate, succeed in your endeavors.

Good luck in pursuit of your A+ certification!

Neil Edde
Associate Publisher—Certification
Sybex, Inc.

SYBEX Inc. 1151 Marina Village Parkway, Alameda, CA 94501
Tel: 510/523-8233   Fax: 510/523-2373   HTTP://www.sybex.com

To those who thought I couldn't do it, and for those who thought I could.

—David Groth

For Steph, who makes everything in my life better.

—Dan Newland

Acknowledgments

Thanks first of all to you, the reader, for buying this book. You could've spent your money on any A+ book, but you chose mine. Thank you.

Thanks very much to all those who supported me while I was writing and developing this book. Thanks first to my coauthors, Dan Newland and Bob King. You can both be proud of your work here. These guys are at the top of the field in their areas. I couldn't ask for better people to work with.

A very special thanks to my wife, family, and friends for understanding when I was under deadlines and didn't have as much time as they wanted to spend with them.

Also much thanks to the all the talented people at Sybex who published this book. In particular, many thanks to my acquisitions editor, Elizabeth Hurley, for flying all the way out to Fargo for the video shoot. Also, a special thanks to Keith McNeil for lending his technical expertise to the video crew. And of course, many, *many* thanks to the fine editors who produced the book: Jim Compton, Liz Burke, Don Fuller, Stacey Corbin, and Bill Clark. As usual, everyone did a perfect job.

This book is based on much of the content from the second edition, which was an ambitious undertaking. The folks who worked on that edition should not go unrecognized for all of their hard work: Elizabeth Hurley, Shannon Murphy, Brianne Agatep, Judy Flynn, Sally Engelfried, Mark Kovach, Michelle A. Roudebush, Jill Niles, Judy Fung, Jennifer Campbell, Nanette Duffy, Dennis Fitzgerald, Leslie Higbee Light, Laurie O'Connell, Yariv Rabinovitch, Nancy Riddiough, Kara Eve Schwartz, Keith McNeil, Duane Bibby, Tony Jonick, and Rebecca R. Plunkett.

Neachan Harvey, Sybex's ever-enthusiastic and patient editorial assistant, was charged with coordinating every reprint correction for the second edition and then implementing all of them into this Deluxe Edition. What a job! It's that kind of subtle behind-the-scenes work that makes all of Sybex's books successful. Thank you, Neachan.

And we can't forget our irreplaceable video crew from Video Arts Studios in Fargo, ND. They did an excellent job of making heads and tails of our initial idea of video training material. Many kudos to our fantastic crew: Troy Parkinson, producer; Tom Tollefson, cinematographer/videographer; Marty Halgrimson, audio engineer; Phil Kerr, graphic artist; and finally Autumn Herda, avid editor. Check them out at www.videoartsstudios.com. Thanks, everyone—now we're digging where there are 'taters!

I hope all of you enjoy this book and it is useful to you. If you have questions or comments, positive or negative, please e-mail me at dgroth@practicaltrainingsolutions.com. I'm always striving to make my books better.

—David Groth

I would like to thank David for including me on this project, and the staff at Sybex for all their help and encouragement. Writing is often referred to as a lonely art, and while that is true to an extent, it is also very much a collaborative effort. Specifically, Elizabeth and Shannon did a great job of keeping the project (and me) on track, and Brianne, Judy, and Sally were spectacular at the difficult task of turning my initial drafts into a finished product.

—Dan Newland

Contents at a Glance

Contents

Introduction

Welcome to the Deluxe Edition of the *A+ Complete Study Guide!* This is a special edition of our best-selling study guide for the A+ certification sponsored by CompTIA (Computing Technology Industry Association). For this edition, we've added some really exciting material to help you prepare for your A+ exams. We've enhanced our content with even more review questions and a second CD with an instructional video. Look to these training video segments to highlight 20 of the most essential hands-on tasks you need to know to become A+ certified. The combination of reviewing the material in each chapter, referring to the instructional video when indicated, taking the chapter review practices as you go, and practicing with any of the six bonus exams will be ensure that you'll become A+ certified. It will take some work on your part, but we've created the complete toolbox for successful self-study.

This book was written at an intermediate technical level; we assume that you already know how to *use* a personal computer and its basic peripherals, such as modems and printers, but recognize that you may be learning how to *service* some of that computer equipment for the first time. The exam itself covers basic computer service topics as well as some more advanced issues, and it covers some topics that anyone already working as a technician, whether with computers or not, should be familiar with. The exam is designed to test you on these topics in order to certify that you have enough knowledge to fix and upgrade some of the most widely used types of personal desktop computers.

We've included review questions at the end of each chapter to give you a taste of what it's like to take the exam. If you're already working as a technical service or support person, we recommend you check out these questions first to gauge your level of knowledge. You can use the book mainly to fill in the gaps in your current computer service knowledge. You may find, as many service technicians have, that being well versed in all the technical aspects of the equipment is not enough to provide a satisfactory level of support—you must also have customer relations skills. We include helpful hints to get the customer to help you help them.

If you can answer 80 percent or more of the review questions correctly for a given chapter, you can probably feel safe moving on to the next chapter. If you're unable to answer that many correctly, reread the chapter and try the questions again. Your score should improve.

WARNING   DON'T just study the questions and answers—the questions on the actual exam will be different from the practice ones included in this book and on the CD. The exam is designed to test your knowledge of a concept or objective, so use this book to learn the objective *behind* the question.

What Is A+ Certification?

The A+ certification program was developed by the Computer Technology Industry Association (CompTIA) to provide an industry-wide means of certifying the competency of computer service technicians. The A+ certified "diploma," which is granted to those who have attained the level of knowledge and troubleshooting skills that are needed to provide capable support in the field of personal computers, is similar to other certifications in the computer industry. For example, Novell offers the Certified Novell Engineer (CNE) program to provide the same recognition for network professionals who deal with its NetWare products, and Microsoft has its Microsoft Certified Service Engineer (MCSE) program. The theory behind these certifications is that if you need to have service performed on any of their products, you would sooner call a technician who has been certified in one of the appropriate certification programs than you would just call the first "expert" in the phone book.

The A+ certification program was created to offer a wide-ranging certification, in the sense that it is intended to certify competence with personal computers from many different makers/vendors. There are two tests required to become A+ certified. You must pass the A+ Core Hardware Service Technician exam, which covers basic computer concepts, hardware troubleshooting, customer service, and hardware upgrading. You must also pass the A+ Operating System Technologies exam, which covers the DOS and Windows operating environments. You don't have to take the Core Hardware and the Operating System Technologies exams at the same time; you have 90 days from the time you pass one test to pass the second test. The A+ certified "diploma" is not awarded until you've passed both tests.

Why Become A+ Certified?

There are several good reasons to get your A+ certification. The CompTIA Candidate's Information packet lists five major benefits:

- It demonstrates proof of professional achievement.
- It increases your marketability.
- It provides greater opportunity for advancement in your field.
- It is increasingly found as a requirement for some types of advanced training.
- It raises customer confidence in you and your company's services.

Provides Proof of Professional Achievement

The A+ certification is quickly becoming a status symbol in the computer service industry. Organizations that contain members of the computer service industry are recognizing the benefits of A+ certification and are pushing for their members to become certified. And more people every day are putting the "A+ Certified Technician" emblem on their business cards.

Increases Your Marketability

A+ certification makes individuals more marketable to potential employers. Also, A+ certified employees may receive a higher base salary, because employers won't have to spend as much money on vendor-specific training.

What Is an AASC?

More service companies are becoming A+ Authorized Service Centers (AASCs). This means that over 50 percent of the technicians employed by that service center are A+ certified. At the time of the writing of this book, there are over 1,400 A+ Authorized Service Centers in the world. Customers and vendors alike recognize that AASCs employ the most qualified service technicians. Because of this, an AASC will get more business than a non-authorized service center. Also, because more service centers want to reach the AASC level, they will give preference in hiring to a candidate who is A+ certified over one who is not.

Provides Opportunity for Advancement

Most raises and advancements are based on performance. A+ certified employees work faster and more efficiently, thus making them more productive. The more productive an employee is, the more money they will make for their company. And, of course, the more money they make for the company, the more valuable they will be to the company. So if an employee is A+ certified, their chances of getting promoted will be greater.

Fulfills Training Requirements

A+ certification is recognized by most major computer hardware vendors, including (but not limited to) IBM, Hewlett-Packard, Apple, and Compaq. Some of these vendors will apply A+ certification toward prerequisites in their own respective certification programs. For example, an A+ certified technician is automatically given credit towards HP laser printer certification without having to take prerequisite classes and tests. This has the side benefit of reducing training costs for employers.

Raises Customer Confidence

As the A+ certified technician moniker becomes more well known among computer owners, more of them will realize that the A+ technician is more qualified to work on their computer equipment than a non-certified technician is.

How to Become A+ Certified

A+ certification is available to anyone who passes the tests. You don't have to work for any particular company. It's not a secret society. It is, however, an elite group. In order to become A+ certified, you must do two things:

- Pass the A+ Core Hardware Service Technician exam
- Pass the A+ Operating System Technologies exam

The exams are administered by Prometric and can be taken at any Prometric Testing Center. If you pass both exams, you will get a certificate in the mail from CompTIA saying that you have passed, and you will also receive a lapel pin and business card. To find the Prometric training center nearest you, call (800) 755-EXAM (755-3926).

To register for the tests, call Prometric at (800) 77-MICRO (776-4276) or register online at www.2test.com. You'll be asked for your name, Social Security number (an optional number may be assigned if you don't wish to provide your Social Security number), mailing address, phone number, employer, when and where (i.e., which Prometric testing center) you want to take the test, and your credit card number (arrangement for payment must be made at the time of registration).

Although you can save money by arranging to take more than one test at the same seating, there are no other discounts. If you have to take a test more than once in order to get a passing grade, you have to pay both times.

It is possible to pass these tests without any reference materials, but only if you already have the knowledge and experience that come from reading about and working with personal computers. But even experienced service people tend to have what you might call a 20/80 situation with their computer knowledge—they may use 20 percent of their knowledge and skills 80 percent of the time, and they have to rely on manuals, guesswork, the Internet, or phone calls for the rest. By covering all the topics that are tested by the exams, this book can help you to refresh your memory concerning topics that, until now, you might have only seldom used. (It can also serve to fill in gaps that, let's admit, you may have tried to cover up for quite some time.) Further, by treating all the issues that the exam covers (i.e., problems you may run into in the arenas of PC service and support), this book can serve as a general field guide, one that you may want to keep with you as you go about your work.

In addition to reading the book, you might consider practicing these objectives through an internship program. (After all, all theory and no practice make for a poor technician.)

Who Should Buy This Book?

If you are one of the many people who want to pass the A+ exam, and pass it confidently, then you should buy this book and use it to study for the exam. The A+ Core Hardware Service Technician exam is designed to measure essential competencies for an entry-level PC technician. The Operating System Technologies exam is intended to certify that the exam candidate has the necessary skills to work on microcomputer hardware and typically will have at least 6 months of on-the-job experience. This book was written with one goal in mind: to prepare you for the challenges of the real IT world, not just to pass the A+ exams. This study guide will do that by describing in detail the concepts on which you'll be tested.

How to Use This Book and CDs

The first CD-ROM, bound in the front of the book, contains all of the instructional video segments described earlier in the Introduction. The content is designed to enhance your understanding of all the hands-on concepts described in the book. It is intended to create visual context for objectives that measure skills such as installation, reassembly and disassembly, identifying common PC tools and interior components, and standard safety practices. These topics are discussed in their full detail within the book. As they are introduced, you will see the following icon in the margin.

When you see the film icon, pop in the CD-ROM and review the task at hand in full visual detail. You'll view each segment through an interface, using QuickTime. We've made it even easier for you by including QuickTime on the CD-ROM—no time wasted downloading! When you've completed the segment, return to the book and keep studying. Before you sit for the actual exam, you may want to watch the video in its entirety a few more times to reinforce key points and concepts.

We've also included several testing features, which you'll find in the book and on the second CD-ROM bound at the back of the book. At the beginning of the book (right after this introduction, in fact) is an assessment test for each A+ module that you can use to check your readiness for the actual exam. Take both of these exams before you start reading the book. It will help you determine the areas you may need to brush up on. The answers to each assessment test appear on a separate page after the last question of the test. Each answer also includes an explanation and a note telling you in which chapter this material appears. To test your knowledge as you progress through the book, there are review questions at the end of each chapter. As you finish each chapter, answer the review questions and then check to see if your answers are right—the correct answers appear on the page following the last review question. You can go back to reread the section that deals with each question you got wrong to ensure that you get the answer correctly the next time you are tested on the material. You'll also find 150 flashcard questions for on-the-go review. Download them right onto your Palm device for quick and convenient reviewing.

In addition to the assessment test and the chapter review tests , you'll find six sample exams. The first three exams are dedicated to the Core Hardware exam, and the second three focus on the Operating Systems Technologies exam. Take these practice exams just as if you were actually taking the A+ exams (i.e., without any reference material). When you have finished the first module, move on to the next three exams to solidify your test-taking skills for the second module. If you get more than 90 percent of the answers correct, you're ready to go ahead and take the real exam.

Additionally, if you are going to travel but still need to study for the A+ exam, and you have a laptop with a CD-ROM drive, you can take this entire book with you just by taking the CD-ROM. This book is in PDF (Adobe Acrobat) format so it can be easily read on any computer.

The Exam Objectives

Behind every computer industry exam you can be sure to find exam objectives— the broad topics in which the exam developers want to ensure your competency. The official CompTIA exam objectives are listed here.

Exam objectives are subject to change at any time without prior notice and at CompTIA's sole discretion. Please visit the A+ Certification page of CompTIA's Web site (www.comptia.org/certification/aplus/index.htm) for the most current listing of exam objectives.

The A+ Core Hardware Service Technician Exam Objectives

As mentioned previously, there are two tests required to become A+ certified: the Core Hardware Service Technician exam and the Operating System Technologies exam. The following are the areas (or "domains" according to CompTIA) in which you must be proficient in order to pass the A+ Core Module exam.

Domain 1.0: Installation, Configuration, and Upgrading

This content area deals with the installation, configuration, and upgrading of common computer Field Replaceable Units (FRUs). Most technicians spend a lot of time performing these operations. To that end, CompTIA has made sure that questions from this content area will make up 30 percent of the exam.

1.1   Identify basic terms, concepts, and functions of system modules, including how each module should work during normal operation and during the boot process.

1.2   Identify basic procedures for adding and removing field replaceable modules for both desktop and portable systems.

1.3   Identify available IRQs, DMAs, and I/O addresses and procedures for configuring them for device installation and configuration.

1.4   Identify common peripheral ports, associated cabling, and their connectors.

1.5   Identify proper procedures for installing and configuring IDE/EIDE devices.

1.6   Identify proper procedures for installing and configuring SCSI devices.

1.7   Identify proper procedures for installing and configuring peripheral devices.

1.8   Identify hardware methods of upgrading system performance, procedures for replacing basic subsystem components, unique components and when to use them.

Domain 2.0: Diagnosing and Troubleshooting

Before a technician can install or upgrade a component, he or she must determine which component needs to be replaced. A technician will normally use the skills addressed by the diagnosing and troubleshooting content areas to make that determination. Questions about these two topics together make up 30 percent of the exam.

2.1   Identify common symptoms and problems associated with each module and how to troubleshoot and isolate the problems.

2.2   Identify basic troubleshooting procedures and how to elicit problem symptoms from customers.

Domain 3.0: Preventive Maintenance

Most people don't think of computer service as a dangerous job. Most often, safety precautions are taken to prevent damage to the components. In actuality, there are a few components that can cause severe injury. This topic also covers maintenance and cleaning of computer components. Questions about these topics constitute 5 percent of the exam.

3.1   Identify the purpose of various types of preventive maintenance products and procedures and when to use and perform them.

3.2   Identify issues, procedures, and devices for protection within the computing environment, including people, hardware, and the surrounding workspace.

Domain 4.0: Motherboards, Processors, and Memory

Several of the items in these content areas give people the most problems (for example, learning the differences between all the various types of processors). This content area makes up 15 percent of the exam.

4.1 Distinguish between the popular CPU chips in terms of their basic characteristics.

4.2 Identify the categories of RAM (Random Access Memory) terminology, their locations, and physical characteristics.

4.3 Identify the most popular type of motherboards, their components, and their architecture (bus structures and power supplies).

4.4 Identify the purpose of CMOS (Complementary Metal-Oxide Semiconductor), what it contains, and how to change its basic parameters.

Domain 5.0: Printers

As we were writing this book, we asked A+ certified technicians what they thought was the hardest part of the Core Hardware exam. With a single, resounding voice they all said, "Printers!" For this reason, we have tried to make the printer section as comprehensive as possible. Although there are only two objectives here and the questions on printers make up 10 percent of the test, we have dedicated an entire chapter to printer components and operation to make sure that this area won't give you any problems.

5.1 Identify basic concepts, printer operations, and printer components.

5.2 Identify care and service techniques and common problems with primary printer types.

Domain 6.0: Basic Networking

With the explosion of the Internet into the service world, the line between a service technician and networking technician has blurred. Frequently, computers that come in for service have problems that are related to their networking hardware. An A+ certified technician should know how both the hardware and software components of networking can affect the operation of the computer. CompTIA has put basic networking concepts on the A+ Core Hardware exam, and they make up 10 percent of the total exam questions.

6.1 Identify basic networking concepts, including how a network works and the ramifications of repairs on the network.

Operating System Technologies Exam Objectives

The following are the areas in which you must be proficient in order to pass the A+ Operating System Technologies exam.

Domain 1.0: Operating System Fundamentals

This domain requires knowledge of DOS, Windows 3.*x*, Windows 95/98, Windows NT, and Windows 2000 operating systems. You will need to know the way they work, as well as the components that compose them. You will also need to know topics relating to navigating the operating systems and, in general, how to use them. Operating system fundamentals make up 30 percent of the exam.

1.1 Identify the operating system's functions, structure, and major system files to navigate the operating system and how to get to needed technical information.

1.2 Identify basic concepts and procedures for creating, viewing, and managing files, directories, and disks. This includes procedures for changing file attributes and the ramifications of those changes (for example, security issues).

Domain 2.0: Installation, Configuration, and Upgrading

This domain tests your knowledge of the day-to-day servicing of operating systems. This includes topics such as installing, configuring, and upgrading the various operating systems (DOS, Windows 9*x*, NT, and 2000). You will also be expected to know system boot sequences. These topics make up 15 percent of the exam.

2.1 Identify the procedures for installing Windows 9*x* and Windows 2000 for bringing the software to a basic operational level.

2.2 Identify steps to perform an operating system upgrade.

2.3 Identify the basic system boot sequences and boot methods, including the steps to create an emergency boot disk with utilities installed for Windows 9*x*, Windows NT, and Windows 2000.

2.4 Identify procedures for loading/adding and configuring device drivers and the necessary software for certain devices.

Domain 3.0: Diagnosing and Troubleshooting

Questions in this domain will test your ability to diagnose and troubleshoot Windows 9*x*, NT, and 2000 systems and will make up a whopping 40 percent of the test.

3.1 Recognize and interpret the meaning of common error codes and startup messages from the boot sequence, and identify steps to correct the problems.

3.2 Recognize common problems and determine how to resolve them.

Domain 4.0: Networks

This domain requires knowledge of network capabilities of DOS and Windows and how to connect to networks. It includes what the Internet is, its capabilities, basic concepts relating to Internet access, and generic procedures for system setup. Network questions make up 15 percent of the exam.

4.1 Identify the networking capabilities of Windows including procedures for connecting to the network.

4.2 Identify concepts and capabilities relating to the Internet and basic procedures for setting up a system for Internet access.

Tips for Taking the A+ Exams

Here are some general tips for taking your exam successfully:

- Bring two forms of ID with you. One must be a photo ID, such as a driver's license. The other can be a major credit card or a passport. Both forms must have a signature.

- Arrive early at the exam center so you can relax and review your study materials, particularly tables and lists of exam-related information.

- Read the questions carefully. Don't be tempted to jump to an early conclusion. Make sure you know exactly what the question is asking.

- Don't leave any unanswered questions. Unanswered questions are scored against you.

- There will be questions with multiple correct responses. When there is more than one correct answer, a message at the bottom of the screen will prompt you to "Choose all that apply." Be sure to read the messages displayed.

- When answering multiple-choice questions you're not sure about, use a process of elimination to get rid of the obviously incorrect questions first. This will improve your odds if you need to make an educated guess.

- On form-based tests, because the hard questions will eat up the most time, save them for last. You can move forward and backward through the exam. (When the exam becomes adaptive, this tip will not work.)

- For the latest pricing on the exams and updates to the registration procedures, call Prometric at (800) 755-EXAM (755-3926) or (800) 77-MICRO (776-4276). If you have further questions about the scope of the exams or related CompTIA programs, refer to the CompTIA site at www.comptia.org.

Assessment Test: Core Hardware Service Technician Exam

1. Which of the following computer components can be safely disposed of in regular trash?

   A. Monitors

   B. Printer toner

   C. Laptop batteries

   D. None of the above

2. Which of the following components is especially dangerous to repair and should only be opened by specially trained professionals?

   A. Printer

   B. Mouse

   C. Monitor

   D. Computer

3. Which of the following information is not stored on a computer's CMOS chip?

   A. Hard drive configuration

   B. Printer configuration

   C. Memory information

   D. Date and time

4. Which type of memory is typically upgraded on a computer when you are adding memory?

   A. DRAM

   B. SRAM

   C. VRAM

   D. QRAM

5. Which of the following interfaces are considered serial interfaces? (Select all that apply.)

   A. IEEE 1294

   B. FireWire

   C. USB

   D. ECP

6. Which of the following standards is commonly referred to as a FireWire port?

   A. IEEE 1294

   B. IEEE 1394

   C. ISO 1294

   D. IEEE 1666

7. Which of the following memory types offers the highest transfer rate and bandwidth rate?

   A. FPM DRAM

   B. EDO RAM

   C. DDR SDRAM

   D. RIMM

8. What is the main purpose of WRAM?

   A. It is a special type of memory designed for laptop computers.

   B. It is a specialized type of memory for video accelerators.

   C. It is a specialized type of memory for Windows accelerator cards.

   D. It is a specialized type of memory for sound accelerator cards.

9. What type of cable is used by floppy drives?

   A. 18-pin ribbon cable

   B. 21-pin ribbon cable

   C. 34-pin ribbon cable

   D. 40-pin ribbon cable

10. How much disk capacity is supported by the original IDE specification?

    A. 528MB

    B. 640MB

    C. 628MB

    D. 1.2GB

11. What type of cable is used by internal SCSI devices?

    A. 21-pin ribbon cable

    B. 34-pin ribbon cable

    C. 40-pin ribbon cable

    D. 50-pin ribbon cable

12. Which ends of a SCSI bus should be terminated?

    A. Neither end should be terminated; termination is for IDE buses.

    B. The beginning of the chain should be terminated.

    C. The end of the chain should be terminated.

    D. Both ends of the chain should be terminated.

13. Which bus feature allows devices to bypass the processor and write their information directly to main memory?

    A. DMA channels

    B. IRQs

    C. I/O addresses

    D. Bus mastering

14. Which IRQ is typically assigned to LPT2?

    A. IRQ3

    B. IRQ5

    C. IRQ10

    D. IRQ15

15. Which bus architecture is typically associated with IBM PS/2 computers?

    A. ISA

    B. EISA

    C. MCA

    D. VESA

16. What type of bus architecture is used commonly with Pentium class computers and supports 64- and 32-bit data paths?

    A. ISA

    B. EISA

    C. PCI

    D. VESA

17. What type of PCMCIA card is 5mm thick and is commonly used with modem and LAN adapters?

    A. Type I

    B. Type II

    C. Type III

    D. Type IV

18. Which of the following connector types are not typically associated with mice?

   A. Serial connector

   B. Parallel connector

   C. Bus mouse interface

   D. PS/2 interface

19. What is the maximum resolution supported by the VGA standard?

   A. 320×480

   B. 480×600

   C. 640×480

   D. 800×600

20. Which type of cable is commonly associated with parallel printers?

   A. DB-25F on the first connector and Male Centronics 36 on the second connector

   B. DB-25F on the first connector and Male Centronics 50 on the second connector

   C. DB-25M on the first connector and Male Centronics 36 on the second connector

   D. DB-25M on the first connector and Male Centronics 50 on the second connector

21. What is the primary purpose of the transfer corona assembly in a laser printer?

   A. It charges the paper so that the toner sticks to the paper.

   B. It fuses the toner to the paper.

   C. It moves the paper through the printer.

   D. It is a laser that scans the image to the printer.

22. Which of the following options offers the slowest transfer speed between a printer and a computer?

   A. Serial

   B. Parallel

   C. USB

   D. Network connection

23. Which of the following physical network topologies offers the most fault tolerance in terms of cable interruption, while balancing requirements for amount of cable required?

A. Bus

B. Ring

C. Mesh

D. Star

24. Which IEEE specification is responsible for defining fiber optic standards?

A. 802.1

B. 802.4

C. 802.6

D. 802.8

25. What is the maximum data rate that can be transmitted over UTP Category 3 cable?

A. 4Mbps

B. 10Mbps

C. 16Mbps

D. 100Mbps

26. Which DMA channel is typically assigned to the hard disk controller?

A. DMA 1

B. DMA 2

C. DMA 3

D. DMA 4

27. What will most likely happen if you leave the blank (the piece of metal or plastic that covers the space where expansion cards are placed) off the computer when an expansion card is removed?

A. More airflow will be added.

B. Less airflow will be added.

C. More static will be present in the computer.

D. Less static will be present in the computer.

28. Which universal command is used to access a computer's CMOS settings?

A. During the computer's startup, press F1.

B. During the computer's startup, press the Delete key.

C. During the computer's startup, press Control + Shift + Escape.

D. There is no universal way of accessing CMOS.

29. Which DOS command is used to create a bootable diskette that can be used for troubleshooting?

A. FORMAT A: /S

B. FORMAT A: /B

C. FORMAT A: /Q

D. FORMAT A: /T

30. Which DOS configuration file would you check if a device driver was not properly loading?

A. AUTOEXEC.BAT

B. SYSTEM.INI

C. CONFIG.SYS

D. BOOT.INI

Answers to Assessment Test: Core Hardware Service Technician Exam

1. D. Many consumer electronic components including monitors, printer toner, and batteries are considered hazardous material and should be disposed of properly. Check your local waste disposal service for more detailed disposal instructions. See Chapter 1 for more information.

2. C. The monitor is one of the most dangerous components to repair. It can retain a high-voltage charge even when it is not turned on. Monitors should only be opened by specially trained professionals. See Chapter 1 for more information.

3. B. The computer has a special chip called CMOS (Complimentary Metal Oxide Semiconductor) that saves important configuration information when the computer is turned off. This includes date and time, hard drive configuration, and memory settings as well as other options. See Chapter 2 for more information.

4. A. Dynamic Random Access Memory (DRAM) is the type of memory that is expanded when you add memory. Static Random Access Memory (SRAM) is often used for cache memory. See Chapter 2 for more information.

5. B, C. The three main types of serial interfaces are Standard serial, Universal Serial Bus (USB), and FireWire. IEEE 1294 and Enhanced Capabilities Port (ECP) are considered parallel standards. See Chapter 2 for more information.

6. B. The FireWire standard was adopted by the Institute of Electronic and Electrical Engineers in 1995 as IEEE 1394. See Chapter 2 for more information.

7. D. Direct Rambus (RIMM) is a relatively new technology that uses a fast (up to 800MHz) technology. See Chapter 3 for more information.

8. C. Windows RAM (WRAM) is a specialized memory for Windows accelerator cards. It is similar to video RAM, but it is much faster. See Chapter 3 for more information.

9. C. Floppy drive cables use a 34-wire ribbon cable with three connectors. See Chapter 4 for more information.

10. A. The original IDE specification only supported drives up to 528MB and speeds to 3.3MBps. See Chapter 4 for more information.

11. D. SCSI internal devices use a 50-pin ribbon cable. IDE devices use a 40-pin ribbon cable. See Chapter 4 for more information.

12. D. Both ends of a SCSI bus must be terminated for signals to be properly maintained. See Chapter 4 for more information.

13. A. Direct Memory Access (DMA) channels allow a device to write directly to memory. Bus mastering allows devices to write directly to each other. See Chapter 5 for more information.

14. B. IRQ5 is assigned to LPT2. Since most computers do not use LPT2, this IRQ is typically available for use with other devices. See Chapter 5 for more information.

15. C. The Micro Channel Architecture (MCA) bus was developed by IBM for their PS/2 computers as an upgrade to the ISA architecture. See Chapter 5 for more information.

16. C. Peripheral Component Interconnect (PCI) is a bus type commonly used with Pentium class computers. This bus type supports 64- and 32-bit data paths and can be used in 486 and Pentium-class computers. See Chapter 5 for more information.

17. B. Type I cards are 3.3mm thick and are commonly used for memory cards. Type II cards are 5mm thick and are used for modems and LAN adapters; they are the most commonly used cards. Type III cards are 10.5mm thick and are commonly used as PC hard disks. See Chapter 5 for more information.

18. B. Common mouse interface standards include serial connectors, bus mouse interfaces, and PS/2 interfaces. See Chapter 6 for more information.

19. C. The maximum resolution supported by VGA is 640×480. The SVGA standard supports up to 1024×768 resolution. See Chapter 6 for more information.

20. C. Parallel printer cables use a DB-25M connector to connect to the parallel port on the computer and a Male Centronics 36 connector to connect to the printer. See Chapter 6 for more information.

21. A. After the laser writes the image to a photosensitive drum, the transfer corona wire charges the paper so that the toner is pulled from the drum to the paper. See Chapter 7 for more information.

22. A. Serial is the slowest option for printer communication type. With serial connection, data is sent one bit at a time with the overhead of communication parameters. See Chapter 7 for more information.

23. D. With a physical star topology, each network device connects to a central hub. This prevents the entire network from failing in the event of a single cable segment failure. The mesh topology is technically more fault tolerant, but is not practical due to the amount of cable that would be required. See Chapter 8 for more information.

24. D. The IEEE 802 workgroup has designated 802.8 as the Fiber Optic Technical Advisory Group. See Chapter 8 for more information.

25. B. Category 3 UTP cable contains four twisted pairs of wires and has three twists per foot. It is only capable of transmitting data at 10Mbps. See Chapter 8 for more information.

26. A. DMA 1 is the default assignment for the hard disk controller. See Chapter 9 for more information.

27. B. Blanks are used to promote proper airflow to the internal components of a computer. Introducing a new hole will often result in less airflow, which could cause your computer to overheat and burn out components. See Chapter 9 for more information.

28. D. Each computer manufacturer has a specific way of accessing the computer's CMOS settings. This will vary from computer to computer. See Chapter 9 for more information.

29. A. The FORMAT A: /S command is used to create a floppy disk that has the system files installed so that the disk is considered bootable. See Chapter 10 for more information.

30. C. In a DOS environment, the CONFIG.SYS file is the main configuration file for memory management and device configuration. See Chapter 10 for more information.

Assessment Test: Operating System Technologies Exam

1. Which Windows 98 command-line utility is used to delete files and directories, even if the subdirectories contain additional files?

   A. DEL

   B. REMOVE

   C. DELTREE

   D. REMTREE

2. Which key would you use in Windows 98 to select non-contiguous files for a file action such as a copy?

   A. CTRL

   B. SHIFT

   C. ALT

   D. F5

3. Which Windows 98 utility would you use to check a disk drive for disk-related errors?

   A. Disk Cleanup

   B. Disk Manager

   C. Disk Defragmenter

   D. SCANDISK

4. What is the minimum amount of RAM a computer must have to run Windows 98?

   A. 8MB

   B. 12MB

   C. 16MB

   D. 32MB

5. Which of the following commands would you use to partition your disk drives prior to a Windows 98 installation?

   A. PARTDISK

   B. FDISK

   C. MAKEPART

   D. FORMAT

6. What is the purpose of the MSCDEX.EXE file on the Windows 98 startup disk?

   A. Memory manager

   B. Video manager

   C. Provides hard drive support

   D. Provides CD-ROM support

7. Which Windows 95 option would you use if you did not want your system checked for Plug-and-Play devices?

   A. SETUP /pi

   B. SETUP /np

   C. SETUP /-np

   D. SETUP /-npnp

8. Which of the following options best describes what happens when you install Windows 95 with the portable configuration?

   A. No networking is installed.

   B. PCMCIA support and APM support is installed.

   C. The minimum Windows 95 files are installed.

   D. The GNP components are installed.

9. Which of the following options is not an upgrade enhancement when upgrading from Windows 95 (original version, not OSR2) to Windows 98?

   A. Better Internet support through the integration of Internet Explorer

   B. Support for newer hardware such as USB, AGP, and DVD

   C. Support for the FAT32 file system

   D. DOS 6 replaced by DOS 7

10. Which Windows 98 startup file allows the rest of the operating system and its programs to interact directly with the system hardware and the system BIOS?

   A. MSDOS.SYS

   B. BIOS.SYS

   C. IO.SYS

   D. OSIO.SYS

11. Which Windows 98 utility is used to easily edit configuration files such as CONFIG.SYS and WIN.INI?

    A. MSCONFIG

    B. WINCONFIG

    C. W98CONFIG

    D. REGEDIT

12. Which Windows 98 utility would you use if you wanted to upgrade a FAT16 partition to a FAT32 partition?

    A. Disk Converter

    B. FDISK

    C. Disk Manager

    D. Disk Administrator

13. How much free disk space is required on a computer that will have Windows 2000 Professional installed?

    A. 650MB

    B. 1.2GB

    C. 1.6GB

    D. 2GB

14. You want to install Windows 2000 on a computer that has just had its hard drive formatted. What command would you use on a Windows 98 computer that had the Windows 2000 Professional CD to make Windows 2000 Startup Disks?

    A. BOOTDISK

    B. MAKEBOOT

    C. MAKEBT16

    D. MAKEBT32

15. What command would you use to install Windows 2000 Professional on a computer that needs to have the accessibility options installed?

    A. SETUP /A

    B. SETUP /H

    C. WINNT /A

    D. WINNT /H

16. Which of the following operating systems can be upgraded directly to Windows 2000 Professional? (Select all that apply.)

   A. Windows 3.1

   B. Windows 95

   C. Windows 98

   D. Windows NT Workstation 4.0

17. Which Windows 2000 boot file is used in a dual-boot configuration to keep a copy of the DOS or Windows 9x boot sector?

   A. NTBOOT.SYS

   B. NTBOOT.DOS

   C. BOOTSECT.SYS

   D. BOOTSECT.DOS

18. What file extension is associated with Microsoft Installer files?

   A. .APP

   B. .MSI

   C. .INS

   D. .DAT

19. Which of the following options provides the most reliable way to uninstall a Windows 98 application?

   A. Control Panel ➤ Windows Configuration

   B. Control Panel ➤ System Configuration

   C. Control Panel ➤ Add/ Remove Programs

   D. Delete the application files with Windows Explorer and remove any Registry entries

20. Which printer option is used to bypass printer spooling?

   A. Print Directly to Printer.

   B. Bypass Print Spooling.

   C. Disable Spooling.

   D. This option can only be set by directly editing the Registry.

21. Which of the following backup options backs up the files on a disk that have changed since the last Full backup and does not mark the files that are backed up during the session as archived?

A. Full

B. Differential

C. Incremental

D. Partial

22. Which of the following commands is not located on a Windows 98 startup disk?

A. FDISK

B. FORMAT

C. SYS

D. DELTREE

23. What command-line utility would you use to create a Windows NT Emergency Repair Disk?

A. ERD

B. MAKEERD

C. RDISK

D. MAKEDISK

24. Which of the following network protocols is not a default protocol that can be loaded with Windows 98?

A. NetBEUI

B. DLP

C. NWLink

D. TCP/IP

25. What software must be loaded on a Windows 98 client so that the computer can access other Microsoft network clients?

A. Microsoft Client for Microsoft Networks

B. Client Connect

C. TCP Connect

D. File and Print Sharing Manager

26. What UNC path would you use to connect to a folder called DATA and a share called ACCT on a computer called WS1 on a domain called ACME?

    A. \\ACME\WS1\ACCT\DATA

    B. \\ACME\WS1\ACCT

    C. \\WS1\ACCT\DATA

    D. \\DATA\ACCT\WS1\ACME

27. Which service is responsible for managing Internet host names and domain names as well as resolving the names to IP addresses?

    A. DHCP

    B. WINS

    C. DNS

    D. SMS

28. What key do you press to access Safe Mode when Windows 98 is booting?

    A. F1

    B. F2

    C. F6

    D. F8

29. Which utility would you use to troubleshoot hardware problems on a Windows 98 computer?

    A. Task Manager

    B. Device Manager

    C. SCANDISK

    D. System Services Manager

30. What command is used on Windows 98 computers to check the consistency of the Registry and to back up the Registry?

    A. REGEDIT

    B. REGEDT32

    C. SYSREG

    D. SCANREG

Answers to Assessment Test: Operating System Technologies Exam

1. C. The DEL command is used to delete files. RD is used to remove empty directories or subdirectories. DELTREE is used to delete files and directories, even if they contain files. See Chapter 12 for more information.

2. A. The CTRL key is used to select non-contiguous files, while the SHIFT key is used to select contiguous files. See Chapter 12 for more information.

3. D. SCANDISK is used to check a disk drive for errors or problems. Disk Cleanup is used to delete unneeded files. Disk Defragmenter is used to arrange data so that it is more easily accessed. See Chapter 12 for more information.

4. B. While 12MB is the bare minimum to load the operating system, Microsoft actually recommends at least 16–32MB of memory. See Chapter 13 for more information.

5. B. The FDISK utility is used to manage disk partitions. With FDISK you can create, delete, and mark the active partition. See Chapter 13 for more information.

6. D. The MSCDEX.EXE file is used to provide CD-ROM drive support prior to Windows 98 being loaded. You also need to load the proper CD-ROM driver. See Chapter 13 for more information.

7. A. The SETUP /pi switch skips the check for any Plug-and-Play devices. See Chapter 13 for more information.

8. B. When you install a portable or laptop computer and use the portable configuration, the PCMCIA support is added as well as Advanced Power Management for when the laptop is running from battery power. See Chapter 13 for more information.

9. D. When you upgrade from Windows 95 to Windows 98, DOS 7 (16-bit) is replaced by DOS32 (32-bit). See Chapter 13 for more information.

10. C. The IO.SYS file allows the rest of the operating system and its programs to interact directly with the system hardware and the system BIOS. A part of this file's code is hardware drivers for common devices (such as serial and communication ports and disk drives). See Chapter 13 for more information.

11. A. The MSCONFIG utility is used to edit configuration files easily and graphically. See Chapter 13 for more information.

12. A. The FAT32 file system offers several enhancements to the FAT16 file system. You can convert existing FAT16 partitions to FAT32 partitions through System Tools ➢ Disk Converter utility. See Chapter 13 for more information.

13. D. Windows 2000 installations require a minimum of 2GB of free disk space for the installation process. See Chapter 14 for more information.

14. B. The MAKEBOOT command is used from Windows 9*x* computers while the MAKEBT32 command is used from Windows NT or Windows 2000 computers. See Chapter 14 for more information.

15. C. Windows 2000 uses the WINNT command to start the installation process. The /H switch specifies that the accessibility options should be installed. See Chapter 14 for more information.

16. B, C, D. If the hardware requirements for a Windows 3.1 computer meet the Windows 2000 requirements you can install Windows 2000, but there is no supported upgrade path for this operating system. See Chapter 14 for more information.

17. D. If your computer has an operating system installed and you install Windows 2000 (as opposed to an upgrade), your computer will be capable of dual-booting. The previous operating system's boot information will be stored in a file called BOOTSECT.DOS. See Chapter 14 for more information.

18. B. Files used to install applications are .MSI files. Microsoft Installer files have many advantages over traditional installation processes. See Chapter 15 for more information.

19. C. The best and safest way to remove Windows applications is through the Add/Remove Programs applet within the Control Panel. See Chapter 15 for more information.

20. A. When you access a printer's properties, you can bypass printer spooling by selecting the Print Directly to Printer option. See Chapter 16 for more information.

21. B. A Differential backup does not mark the files that are backed up as archived. An Incremental backup would mark the files that are backed up as archived. See Chapter 17 for more information.

22. D. The Windows 98 startup disk is a bootable disk that contains most of the commands needed to set up the computer prior to the Windows 98 installation. However, this disk does not contain the DELTREE command by default. See Chapter 17 for more information.

23. C. The RDISK command is used in Windows NT computers to create the ERD. This disk is not bootable and is specific to the computer that it was created on. See Chapter 17 for more information.

24. B. Windows 98 does not support a protocol called DLP. See Chapter 18 for more information.

25. A. The Microsoft Client for Microsoft Networks software is used to allow the computer to access network resources located on other Microsoft computers. See Chapter 18 for more information.

26. C. Universal Naming Convention (UNC) paths specify the computer name, followed by the share name, followed by the path. See Chapter 18 for more information.

27. C. The Domain Name System (DNS) is used to resolve Internet host names or domain names to IP addresses. See Chapter 18 for more information.

28. D. When prompted during the Windows 98 boot process, press the F8 key to access Windows Safe Mode. This is useful for troubleshooting purposes. See Chapter 19 for more information.

29. B. The Device Manager utility can be used to see all of the devices and their status that are recognized by the Windows 98 operating system. See Chapter 19 for more information.

30. D. The SCANREG command is used to check and back up the Registry. It will also attempt to fix any problems it diagnoses with the Registry structure. See Chapter 19 for more information.

A+: Core Hardware Service Technician Exam

PART

I

Chapter 1

Basic Computer Service Concepts

THE FOLLOWING OBJECTIVES ARE COVERED IN THIS CHAPTER:

✓ **1.3 Identify available IRQs, DMAs, and I/O addresses and procedures for configuring them for device installation and configuration.**

Content may include the following:

- Standard IRQ settings
- Modems
- Floppy drive controllers
- Hard drive controllers
- USB ports
- Infrared ports
- Hexidecimal/Addresses

✓ **2.1 Identify common symptoms and problems associated with each module and how to troubleshoot and isolate the problems.**

Content may include the following:

- Processor/memory symptoms
- Mouse
- Floppy drive
- Parallel ports
- Hard drives
- CD-ROM
- DVD
- Sound card/audio
- Monitor/video
- Motherboards
- Modems
- BIOS

- USB
- NIC
- CMOS
- Power supply
- Slot covers
- POST audible/visual error codes
- Troubleshooting tools, e.g., multimeter
- Large LBA, LBA
- Cables
- Keyboard
- Peripherals

✓ **3.1 Identify the purpose of various types of preventive maintenance products and procedures and when to use and perform them.**

Content may include the following:

- Liquid cleaning compounds
- Types of materials to clean contacts and connections
- Non-static vacuums (chassis, power supplies, fans)

✓ **3.2 Identify issues, procedures, and devices for protection within the computing environment, including people, hardware, and the surrounding workspace.**

Content may include the following:

- UPS (Uninterruptible Power Supply) and suppressors
- Determining the signs of power issues
- Proper methods of storage of components for future use
- Determining the signs of power issues

Potential hazards and proper safety procedures relating to:

- Lasers
- High-voltage equipment
- Power supply
- CRT

Special disposal procedures that comply with environmental guidelines.

- Batteries
- CRTs
- Toner kits/cartridges
- Chemical solvents and cans
- MSDS (Material Safety Data Sheet)

ESD (Electrostatic Discharge) precautions and procedures

- What ESD can do, how it may be apparent, or hidden
- Common ESD protection devices
- Situations that could present a danger or hazard

The computers of today are complex devices. Each computer contains hundreds of individual components, and these components work together to perform specific functions inside the computer. In this chapter, we'll discuss the most common components and their functions. We'll also explain a few of the basic electronics concepts needed to service the microcomputer hardware of today. The topics are categorized as follows:

- Microcomputer electronic components
- The physics of electronics
- Tools of the trade
- Electrostatic discharge
- Safety
- Environmental concerns

The material in this chapter is introductory and is included to make sure we have all our bases covered. If you are already familiar with this material, we suggest you just skim through the chapter and answer the review questions at the end.

For complete coverage of objective 2.1, please also see Chapters 4, 6, 8, and 10. For complete coverage of objective 3.2, please see Chapter 2.

Microcomputer Electronic Components

Many of the components found in computers today are basically the same components you'd find in almost every major household appliance. Most of these components have been used since the late 1960s. For example, every television set contains resistors and transistors. Automobiles today actually contain small computers that monitor the speed of the car and make adjustments to the fuel mixture accordingly.

Analog vs. Digital

Before we discuss electronic components, we must define the words *analog* and *digital* because we will be using them throughout our discussions of computer technology.

Today's computer components use digital signals, which are signals that contain values that are discrete. *Analog* signals, on the other hand, change values over time. Consider the difference between two common types of light switches: a standard light switch and a dimmer switch. The standard light switch has only two values: on and off. As a rule, at any one time the switch will be in either one position or the other. This is similar to digital electrical signals, which have discrete values (like on and off). By way of comparison, the dimmer switch starts at *off*, but can be changed gradually to stronger and stronger intensities, up to the full *on* setting. At any one instant, a dimmer switch can have a setting almost anywhere between on and off. This is similar to an analog electrical signal, which may be on or off or somewhere in between.

Vacuum Tubes—The Old Days...

Today's computer components are the products of previous generations of trial and error. Each generation improves upon the previous era. The grandfather of today's computer components is the *vacuum tube* (Figure 1.1).

FIGURE 1.1   A vacuum tube

The vacuum tube is really nothing more than a switch. A small voltage at one pole switches a larger voltage at the other poles on or off. Because information in a computer is represented as *binary* (1s and 0s), switches are ideal—because they too have only two positions, 1 or 0.

The first electronic computers contained cabinets full of vacuum tubes. There were several problems with this. First, the tubes utilized a heating element in order to facilitate the flow of electrons between the poles. These heating elements had to be "warmed up" in order to function properly. Thus, it took several minutes to turn the computer on. Also, with several tubes in the same cabinet, the elements would generate quite a bit of heat. Unfortunately, heat shortens the life of electronic components—so each computer usually had a room full of air conditioning equipment just for keeping the tubes cool! Even so, the average temperature in these computers was greater than 100 degrees Fahrenheit.

Second, the vacuum tubes were very bulky. Computers like the first computer, ENIAC, often took up enough cabinets to fill an entire floor of a building, with the computer in one room and the air conditioning equipment in the one next to it.

Transistors—Turn Them On

If the vacuum tube is the grandfather, then the *transistor* is the parent of today's electronic components. Transistors (Figure 1.2) work in basically the same manner as vacuum tubes. A small voltage applied to one pole controls a larger voltage on the other poles. The difference between a transistor and a vacuum tube is that a transistor uses a sandwich of silicon instead of tube filled with gas to do the switching. Silicon falls into a family of elements that are neither conductor nor insulator; they're called *semiconductors*. This type of element will be either a conductor *or* an insulator depending on some condition. In the case of transistors, an electrical current will cause the silicon to be a conductor.

FIGURE 1.2   A transistor

Transistors overcame most of the limitations of vacuum tubes. They generate very little heat, and they are much smaller than vacuum tubes. With transistors, computers that fit into a single room could be made. As manufacturing techniques have become more precise, transistors have gotten smaller and smaller. Today, five million transistors can fit into an area smaller than a thumbnail.

Resistors—Keeping Electricity at Bay

Another component that is commonly used in computers is the *resistor*. As its name suggests, it resists the flow of electricity. The electricity is dissipated in the form of heat. There are two types of resistors: fixed and variable.

Fixed Resistors

Fixed resistors are used when you need to reduce the current by a certain amount. They are easily identified by their size and shape (see Figure 1.3). Their resistance level is indicated by means of colored bands painted on the resistor.

FIGURE 1.3 A fixed resistor

Fixed resistors are color coded to identify their resistance values. They are color coded rather than having their values printed right on their bodies for two reasons. First, the resistors are only ¾ inch long. Second, they're cylindrical. In other words, it is rather difficult to print on them (and the print would be difficult to read at that size anyway).

If you ever need to replace a resistor, you must replace it with a resistor of the same resistance level. The resistance level can be determined by reading the values of the colored bands. Each colored band stands for a number:

- The first two bands represent the digits of a two-digit number.
- The third band represents a multiplier.
- The presence or absence of a fourth band represents a margin-of-error factor (commonly called the resistor's *tolerance range*).

For example, say you have a resistor with the following colors (reading from left to right): red, orange, and brown. Checking the values as listed in Table 1.1, you can see that red represents the number 2, orange represents the number 3, and brown represents a multiplier of 10. The resistance is 23 times 10, which equals 230. Resistance is expressed in *ohms*, so you could express the value as 230Ω. But don't forget the tolerance value for the resistor. Because there is no fourth band in this example, the tolerance range for this value is plus or minus 20% (as noted at the bottom of Table 1.1); the true resistance of the resistor is thus somewhere between 184Ω and 276Ω.

Table 1.1 lists the colors and their associated values. Remember to always read the colors from left to right ("left" on a resistor is the side that has the three colored bands on it).

TABLE 1.1 Standard Color Codes for Resistors

Color	1st Band (Left Digit)	2nd Band (Right Digit)	3rd Band (Multiplier)
Black	0	0	1
Brown	1	1	10
Red	2	2	100
Orange	3	3	1,000

TABLE 1.1 Standard Color Codes for Resistors *(continued)*

Color	1st Band (Left Digit)	2nd Band (Right Digit)	3rd Band (Multiplier)
Yellow	4	4	10,000
Green	5	5	100,000
Blue	6	6	1,000,000
Violet	7	7	10,000,000
Gray	8	8	100,000,000
White	9	9	N/A

Note: Be sure to look for a fourth band. **If there is no fourth band**, it means the tolerance level of the resistor is not very good—it's between plus or minus 20% of the value indicated by the other bands. **If there is a fourth band**, it will be either silver or gold. Silver represents a tolerance of ±10%. Gold represents a tolerance of ±5%.

Pay special attention to the note at the bottom of the table. Tolerance bands indicate how well the resistor holds to its rated value. As we mentioned in the preceding example, if there is no fourth band, the resistor has a tolerance of plus or minus 20%. That's pretty bad. In electronics, you usually need things to be very close (like a tolerance of less than 5%). A silver band indicates a 10% variation, and a gold band indicates a 5% variation. Remember, though, this range indicates the *maximum* variation—it's possible that the resistor might be right on with its resistance value. For example, say you have the color sequence brown, green, orange, silver. The resistance would be indicated as $15 \times 1,000$, or $15,000\Omega$ (you can also express it as $15k\Omega$)—and it may very well be that this particular resistor *is* able to resist currents up to precisely that strength. However, to be safe, you need to take into account the maximum deviation from this value, which would be indicated by the fourth band color (silver in this example, which represents a ±10% variation), so this resistor might have a value of as little as $13,500\Omega$ ($13.5k\Omega$) or as much as $16,500$ ($16.5k\Omega$).

Variable Resistors

The variable resistor is also called a *rheostat* or *potentiometer*. The most common use in a computer for a variable resistor is for a volume control or brightness control. The resistance is varied between the center pole and either of the end poles (see Figure 1.4). It can be used to vary resistance directly from zero to infinity by hooking the target to one pole and the source to the center pole. Or, you can use a variable resistor to slowly vary from one source to another by hooking each source to a pole and the target to the center pole.

FIGURE 1.4 A variable resistor

Sometimes resistors are placed together into an assembly that is commonly referred to as a *resistor pack*. These resistor packs are used in some drive systems to terminate (stop) the signals being sent on the drive cable. When they perform this function, they are called *terminators*. We will discuss this type of resistor more in later chapters.

Capacitors—Storing a Charge for Later

Another commonly used component is the *capacitor*. A capacitor is used to store electrical charge. Typically used in power supplies and in timing circuits, these items are rarely the cause of failure in a system because all they do is store a charge and release it. Capacitors in a computer can be easily identified because they usually look like small metal cans or small disks with two connectors (Figure 1.5).

FIGURE 1.5 A capacitor

3.4 F

Do not touch a charged capacitor! They can hold charges of thousands of volts and can cause serious injury. Stay away from them even when power has been removed. They can retain a charge for hours after power has been removed.

Integrated Circuits (ICs)—Welcome to the 1980s

With today's manufacturing techniques, it is possible to put all of these components together into circuits that perform certain functions. In the 1970s, you might have hooked up several components on boards called circuit boards. Starting in the 80s, components were etched into pieces of silicon no larger than a dime. In order to get this small item onto a circuit board, the silicon wafer is placed into a package that has pins coming out of it. These pins are wired with tiny copper or gold wiring directly to the silicon chip. This package comes in several forms, but is generally called an *integrated circuit chip* or *IC chip*.

When we say "chip" in the computer business today, we often mean the package that the silicon wafer is housed in, not the wafer itself. From now on, when we use the word *chip*, we are referring to the IC.

There are several types of ICs, but we will cover only the most commonly used types.

Dual Inline Package

The most common package for an IC is the *Dual Inline Package*, or *DIP*. DIPs contain two rows of pins and are usually black with markings on top indicating their manufacturer and purpose. Figure 1.6 shows a Dual Inline Package IC. DIPs are commonly seen being used as memory chips, although this design is being used less and less.

FIGURE 1.6   A Dual Inline Package IC

Quad Small Outline Package

The *Quad Small Outline Package* (*QSOP*—also called a *surface mount*) is among the most commonly used types of chips today. Figure 1.7 shows an example of a QSOP package. This design has the advantage of being very compact.

FIGURE 1.7   A Quad Small Outline Package IC

Most chip manufacturers use a technology called VLSI, or Very Large Scale Integration. The idea is to integrate the functions of several small chips into one, usually larger, chip. Most often, these VLSI chips are of the QSOP type.

Single Inline Package

When a circuit needs to be removable, there are several ways of designing it. One of the first ways was with the *Single Inline Package (SIP)*. SIPs are characterized by a small circuit board with several small pins coming out of it (see Figure 1.8); the SIPs are plugged into corresponding holes or mounts in a circuit board. SIPs are not used much anymore, primarily because of the tendency of the pins to break. SIPs were often used for memory modules.

FIGURE 1.8   A Single Inline Package IC

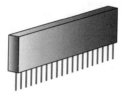

Pin Grid Array Package

Finally, when a circuit or component doesn't have to be removed often and it contains a large number of transistors, typically you use a *PGA* and a *ZIF* (Figure 1.9). PGA stands for *Pin Grid Array*, describing the array of pins used to connect the chip to the circuit board. ZIF stands for *zero insertion force*, which describes how easy it is to place a chip in this kind of socket. It is a type of socket that works with PGA chips to allow them to be mounted on a circuit board.

FIGURE 1.9   PGA Package and a ZIF socket

Miscellaneous Components

There are a few types of hardware components that don't fit well into any of the categories we've already defined. These include *jumpers*, *DIP switches*, and connectors.

And Now for the Real World...

In the past, computer service required an electronics degree, or at the very least a working knowledge of every component. Today, it is very labor intensive to troubleshoot an individual resistor or capacitor. Typically, the technician will troubleshoot a particular module or FRU (Field Replaceable Unit). Troubleshooting the logic board, hard disk, power supply, or monitor is easier than finding out which particular IC or resistor is causing the problem. This makes repair easier, faster, and cheaper. Also, it makes it easier for people to become technicians because they don't need to have electronics degrees.

It should be noted, however, that electronics experience makes troubleshooting a particular FRU easier.

Jumpers

Jumpers were developed as a way of allowing a particular device option (such as which interrupt is being used) to be both user settable and semipermanent without requiring the user to own a chip "burner." Jumpers consist of a row of pins and a small plastic cap with metal inserts. The cap can be moved by the user to cover different pairs of pins. The cap completes a circuit between those two pins, thus selecting one of the possible configuration options for that device (see Figure 1.10).

FIGURE 1.10 Jumpers and their use

A jumper (above left) can be used to make a connection between various pairs of pins in an array of pins. On some devices you may need to jumper multiple pairs, using several jumpers. This arrangement of six pins offers eight different jumper settings.

You'll often see devices with just three pins. These are common for devices that require only two settings, like on and off, or enabled and disabled.

Some cards or circuit boards have several jumpers—so when you go to configure the device, you will need to select the appropriate jumpering option. To find out which pins have to be jumpered in order to select different configuration options, consult the documentation of the device.

If you don't have the documentation, you may have to try all the different jumpering combinations to see if you can get the device configured properly:

- With a six-pin device (as shown in the top part of Figure 1.10), you have eight possible settings: all unjumpered, left pair jumpered, middle pair jumpered, right pair jumpered, left and middle pairs jumpered, left and right pairs jumpered, middle and right pairs jumpered, and all jumpered. This arrangement is common for setting the ID number or other configuration setting of a SCSI device.

- With a three-pin device (as shown in the bottom part of the figure), you are usually only concerned with setting the device to an active or inactive status. Any one of the options shown in the bottom of Figure 1.10 may mean "on"; one of the others would then be the "off" setting. (The third, perhaps in this case represented by the all-unjumpered configuration on the left, may mean "let Plug and Play determine the setting.")

Dual Inline Package (DIP) Switches

Jumpers are fine for single settings, but what if you have a number of settings that have to be user settable and semipermanent? You could use several jumpers, but in larger numbers, they were difficult to work with. Someone came up with the idea of using several *really* small switches and having the pattern of their ons and offs represent the different settings. These switches are known as DIP switches, and they can be either rocker type or slide type (see Figure 1.11).

FIGURE 1.11   DIP switches

"Rocker-type" DIP switch   "Slide-type" DIP switch

If you look carefully at Figure 1.11, you will notice that there is a little "1" imprinted on one side of the switches. When a rocker switch is depressed on that side, it is considered *on*. By comparison, when the nub of a sliding switch is sticking *up* on the side with the "1" marking, *that* indicates *on*. (Some DIP switches, by the way, are marked with a "0" to indicate the side that is the *off* position for the switch.)

Because these switches are so small, it is often easier to set them with a pen, probe, or small screwdriver than it is to set them with your fingers. If you do use your fingers, you may notice that you move more than just the switch you were intending to move.

Connectors

The last category of component that we'll discuss includes the numerous types of connectors found outside the computer. The most common type, the DB connectors, are typically designated with "DB-*n*," with the letter *n* replaced by the number of connectors. DB connectors are usually shaped like a trapezoid, as you can see in the various end-on views in Figure 1.12. The nice part about these connectors is that there is only one orientation possible. If you try to connect them upside down or try to connect a male connector to another male connector, they just won't go together and the connection can't be made.

FIGURE 1.12 DIP switches

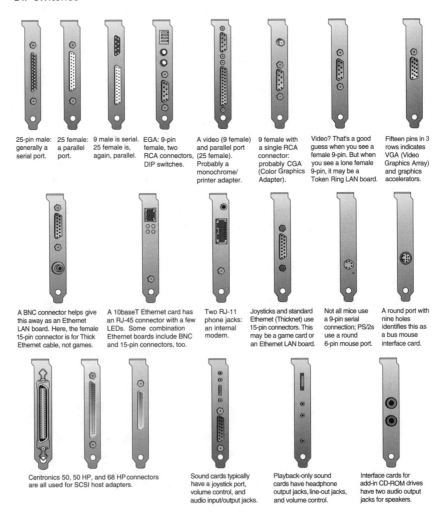

25-pin male: generally a serial port.

25 female: a parallel port.

9 male is serial. 25 female is, again, parallel.

EGA: 9-pin female, two RCA connectors, DIP switches.

A video (9 female) and parallel port (25 female). Probably a monochrome/printer adapter.

9 female with a single RCA connector: probably CGA (Color Graphics Adapter).

Video? That's a good guess when you see a female 9-pin. But when you see a lone female 9-pin, it may be a Token Ring LAN board.

Fifteen pins in 3 rows indicates VGA (Video Graphics Array) and graphics accelerators.

A BNC connector helps give this away as an Ethernet LAN board. Here, the female 15-pin connector is for Thick Ethernet cable, not games.

A 10baseT Ethernet card has an RJ-45 connector with a few LEDs. Some combination Ethernet boards include BNC and 15-pin connectors, too.

Two RJ-11 phone jacks: an internal modem.

Joysticks and standard Ethernet (Thicknet) use 15-pin connectors. This may be a game card or an Ethernet LAN board.

Not all mice use a 9-pin serial connection; PS/2s use a round 6-pin mouse port.

A round port with nine holes identifies this as a bus mouse interface card.

Centronics 50, 50 HP, and 68 HP connectors are all used for SCSI host adapters.

Sound cards typically have a joystick port, volume control, and audio input/output jacks.

Playback-only sound cards have headphone output jacks, line-out jacks, and volume control.

Interface cards for add-in CD-ROM drives have two audio output jacks for speakers.

Another type, the DIN-*n* connectors (again, the *n* is replaced by the number of connectors), are usually circular. DIN connectors were developed in Germany and became popular in the U.S. because of their small size.

For communications, there is another type, following the RJ-*n* specifications. It's a rather strange-looking connector, with a tab on the bottom and small brass connectors on top. These connectors are easy to identify—just look at the connectors on your telephone. The connector on the end of the cord that runs from the phone to the wall is an RJ-11 connector. The connector on the end of the cable that runs from your handset to your phone is the smaller, RJ-12 connector. You may have seen the type of network cable that uses an RJ-45 connector, which looks about twice as big as an RJ-11 connector.

Finally, the most unique type of connector is the Centronics connector. The 36-pin Centronics connector is used on your parallel printer cable (one end has a DB-25 connector, the other a 36-pin Centronics connector).

DB-*n* connectors are also known as D-Shell or D-Sub connectors. The terms may be used interchangeably.

Connector identifications are often given with male or female designations—*DB-9 male*, for example. Table 1.2 indicates the common uses of various connectors.

TABLE 1.2 PC Connectors

Connector	Number of Pins or Sockets	Male or Female	Common Applications
DB-9	9 pins	Male	Serial port.
DB-9	9 sockets	Female	EGA/CGA video port. (Might also be a Token Ring adapter port.)
DB-15	15 sockets	Female	If there are three rows of five, it's probably a VGA/SVGA video adapter. If it's one row of eight and one row of seven, it might be a network transceiver port or, more commonly, a joystick port.
DB-25	25 pins	Male	Serial port.

TABLE 1.2 PC Connectors *(continued)*

Connector	Number of Pins or Sockets	Male or Female	Common Applications
DB-25	25 sockets	Female	Most often a parallel port. On Macintoshes, however, this type of connector is used for the external SCSI bus.
RJ-11	4 pins	Male	Telephone wall jack phone cord.
RJ-12	4 pins	Male	Telephone handset cord.
RJ-45	8 pins	Male	10BaseT Ethernet cable.
Centronics 36	36 pins	Male	Parallel cable.
Centronics 50	50 pins	Male	SCSI connector.
PS/2	6 sockets	Female	PS/2 mouse port.
DIN-8	8 sockets	Female	Macintosh printer connector.
DIN-9	9 sockets	Female	Bus mouse port.

The Physics of Electronics

Every technician should have a basic understanding of certain physics concepts. We're sure some of you are saying, "Oh, no—not physics!" Before you get upset, however, there are only four main concepts that we have to discuss. Also, this material is not on the test, so if you don't want to read it, or if you already know it, feel free to skip ahead to the next section in this chapter.

Electricity Defined

Let's start by defining electricity. Electricity is the flow of electrons from one molecule of a substance to another. In order for electrons to flow, an element must have free electrons. Elements such as copper, iron, and zinc have free electrons, thus making them good conductors of electricity. All computer components use electricity to function.

Conductors vs. Nonconductors

We'll start with the question "Does water conduct electricity?" The standard answer is "Yes"—but technically that's an incorrect answer. We're setting you up, we admit, but it should get you thinking. Here's the scoop. If you use a multimeter (a device used to measure voltages and resistances in electronic components) to test the resistance in a bowl of pure (meaning distilled and deionized) water, you will get a reading of infinite resistance (meaning very little, if any, electricity is flowing through that bowl of water). When we follow up, then, with the question "If water doesn't conduct electricity, can you take a bath with your radio?" the answer is "Not if you don't want to get a permanent 1970s hairdo!" Why? Because the water you take a bath in *does* conduct electricity. What's happening here?

The answer is that the water you take a bath in, wash dishes in, even drink, contains impurities. It is these impurities that conduct electricity. The electrons hop from each molecule of impurity to another. The bottom line is that most metals conduct electricity, and this includes salts of metals that dissolve in water—for example, sodium chloride (table salt). Therefore, water in its *naturally occurring state* (i.e., with the impurities) *is* a conductor.

A *conductor* is any material that conducts electricity (allows it to flow readily). Copper metal is an example of a great conductor. Conversely, a *nonconductor* is a material that inhibits the flow of electricity. Paper, rubber, and most organic materials are generally considered to be nonconductors.

Dynamic vs. Static Electricity

The electricity that comes from the wall is one of two types of electricity. That kind of electricity is usually just called electricity. For the purposes of our discussion, we'll call it *dynamic electricity* because it is constantly moving. The other type is static electricity. This is the type of electricity that exists when electrons build up on a surface. For example, if you walk across a shag carpet with smooth-soled shoes in the winter, a lot of electrons are picked up from the carpet and transferred to your body—and they remain there and collect to build up a sizable charge. This charge is a *static* charge, meaning it doesn't move or flow like dynamic electricity. You'll know you're carrying this charge when you go to touch a metal doorknob because you'll feel a jolt or a "zap." This happens because, when you come into contact with a surface that has a different charge than the one you're carrying, electrons will be transferred from your body (or to it, depending on which surface has fewer electrons). The surface with fewer electrons will receive electrons in a burst that evens out the charge between the two objects. This burst is the "zap" you feel when you touch a metal doorknob.

This is important because one of these types of electricity will operate the components of an electronic circuit and the other will destroy it. Even though the amperage of static electricity is low compared to the amperage of dynamic electricity, *static electricity destroys electronic components.*

Electromagnetic Theory

Finally, electricity and magnetism have been proven to be directly related. If you run an electric current through a wire, it will produce a magnetic field around that wire. The direction of the current flow determines the direction of the magnetic field.

There is a common trick you can use to remember the relationship between the directions. It's called the "right hand rule." If you make a thumbs-up sign with your right hand and point your thumb in the direction of the current flow in the wire, the other fingers will curl in the direction of the magnetic field. Figure 1.13 illustrates this trick.

FIGURE 1.13   The "Right Hand Rule"

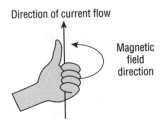

Direction of current flow

Magnetic field direction

Electromagnetic theory also says that if you intersect a magnetic field with a conductor, you will induce an electric current in the wire. Using the "right hand rule," you can see that if the magnetic field is in the direction of the fingers, then a current will be induced in the direction of the thumb. This is important because in electronics, you often have signals traveling in wires next to each other. As signals travel on the wire, they will induce spurious signals in the wires next to it. After a distance, these signals can overcome the actual signals in the adjoining wires. This is called *cross talk*, and it can be a real problem in data communications over distances longer than 3 meters (10 feet).

Another physics-related concept is the transfer of heat. Heat is the enemy of electronic components. As the temperature increases, the longevity and reliability of the component decreases. Some processors (most notably the Pentium family of processors) produce temperatures in excess of 100 degrees F. To reduce the heat, you use a very specialized device known as a *heat sink* (Figure 1.14). This device works by a process known as conduction. It works a lot like the way the fins on an air-cooled engine work. The device is made out of a heat-conducting metal, such as aluminum. As air moves throughout the inside of the computer, it will pass over the fins of the heat sink, cooling them. The heat will move toward the cooler area of the metal, thus drawing it away from the components.

FIGURE 1.14 A heat sink

Numbering Systems

Computers have often been called "number crunchers." But what numbers do they actually "crunch"? There are several different types of numbering systems in use in the computer industry today. The three major ones used by computers are decimal (base 10), binary (base 2), and hexadecimal (base 16).

Decimal Numbers

We've all used decimal numbers before. Decimal numbers are the numbers you learned to count with when you were young. The word *decimal* comes from the Latin word *decem*, meaning 10. There are 10 digits in this counting system—0, 1, 2, 3, 4, 5, 6, 7, 8, and 9.

The only time you use decimal numbers with respect to computers is when you are trying to explain things in real-world terms. Because we have used this counting system all our lives, we won't devote a lot of space to it here. Everyone knows how big 5,690 is, but do many people understand how large 5FA3 is?

Binary Numbers

Why do we need more than one numbering system? Wouldn't it be easier if computers operated in decimal mode like we do? The truth is that it is easier to store numbers as combinations of two digits, or binary numbers, than it is to store them as decimal digits. This is because every computer contains hundreds of thousands of transistors that are nothing more than simple switches, and these switches have only two positions: on and off. Computers are designed to store information as patterns of ons and offs, which are represented in binary as 1s and 0s, respectively.

Before we can discuss the details of the binary numbering system, you must understand a couple of things. First of all, the binary numbers 0 and 1 are not the same as they are in the decimal number systems. Instead, they are just placeholders. They could just have easily been called A and B. Second, we use a few special words to categorize binary numbers:

- A single digit—an individual 0 or 1—is called a *bit*.
- Eight bits associated together are called a *byte*.
- Multiple bytes associated together are usually called a *word*.

Binary numbers can have any number of digits, but because we're using binary, the number of digits will typically be a multiple of 2.

The Magic Number...

If there were such a thing as a magic number in computer science, that number would surely be the number 8, which is the number of bits in a byte. Because bytes are the real building blocks of computer information, most numbers and sizes reported by the computer are evenly divisible by 8. Notice that hexadecimal has 16 characters (16 characters = 2 times the magic number of 8).

Counting in Binary

Let's talk a little about how to count in binary.

You should recall that in a base 10 number system, each position signifies a power of 10. Because binary is base 2, all the number positions signify powers of 2. In all modern numbering systems, however, the *first* position is always reserved for numbers to the power of 0. This means you have to remember that when we talk about an 8-bit (binary) number, the highest position in the number is for values to the 7th power of 2, not the 8th power of 2. Table 1.3 shows the positions used in an 8-bit counting system.

TABLE 1.3 8-Bit Binary Positions

Position	8	7	6	5	4	3	2	1
Power of 2	2^7	2^6	2^5	2^4	2^3	2^2	2^1	2^0
Decimal value of a 1 in this position	128	64	32	16	8	4	2	1

The rightmost bit in a binary number (the digit in the 2^0 position) is called the *Least Significant Bit*, or *LSB*. The leftmost bit in a binary number (its actual power of 2 depends, of course, on how many bits are in the word) is called the *Most Significant Bit*, or *MSB*. So, in the binary number 10001000, the LSB is 0 and the MSB is 1.

Converting Binary to Decimal

Because binary numbers contain only 1s and 0s, and the 0s equal 0 no matter what position they're in, you really only have to worry about the 1s. When trying to convert a binary number, such as 10001001, to a decimal number, all you need to do is look at the positions of the 1s. As in base 10, you read the digits from MSB (left) to LSB (right). In this number, you have 1s in the 2^7, 2^3, and 2^0 positions, which means you have decimal values of 1×128, 1×8, and 1×1, respectively. When you add these numbers together, you get the decimal equivalent: 137.

A number that is all 1s would be the highest value you could have in a binary number; in an 8-bit binary word it equals the decimal number 255. It would be calculated like so:

```
(1×128) + (1×64) + (1×32) + (1×16) + (1×8) + (1×4) + (1×2) +
(1×1) = 255
```

You could use the technique above to determine the decimal value of any 8-bit binary number, by substituting 0s for 1s wherever appropriate. For example, the decimal value of the binary word 01101010 is calculated as follows:

```
(0×128) + (1×64) + (1×32) + (0×16) + (1×8) + (0×4) + (1×2) +
(0×1) = 106
```

Hexadecimal Numbers

Binary numbering systems are very easy to understand. However, it is very inefficient to represent large numbers with strings of 1s and 0s. It is more efficient to use the hexadecimal (often simply called hex) numbering system. Hexadecimal is base 16; it uses the decimal numbers 0 through 9 and the letters *A* through *F* to represent the 16 numbers. When counting in hex, you count from 0 to 9 the regular way, but instead of 10, which we're used to expressing with two digits in our common decimal number system, you use *A*. For the value of 11 you use *B*, for 12 you use *C*, and so on through *F* for the value of 15 (see Table 1.4). Although hex numbers are easily recognized by the fact that they combine letters and numbers, it is also common to see a subscript $_{16}$ or an *h* after the number to designate it as a hex number.

TABLE 1.4   Decimal, Binary, and Hex Equivalents

Decimal Number	Binary Number	Hex Number
0	0000	0
1	0001	1
2	0010	2
3	0011	3
4	0100	4
5	0101	5
6	0110	6
7	0111	7
8	1000	8
9	1001	9
10	1010	A
11	1011	B
12	1100	C
13	1101	D
14	1110	E
15	1111	F

The hexadecimal system works as follows: A binary number is broken up into groups of 4 bits. If the number of bits in the binary number is not an even multiple of 4—that is, if there aren't enough bits to make complete groups of 4 each—enough 0s are added to the left of the MSB to make a complete 4-bit group. Why break the binary number into 4-bit elements? Because a single hexadecimal digit can stand for any 1 of the 16 values that could possibly be represented by any 4-bit binary number. Each group of 4 bits is then converted from its binary value to its equivalent hexadecimal digit.

And Now for the Real World...

When you were a kid, the teacher first showed you how to do math the long way. Later, you found out how to use a calculator to figure out the problems faster. As with so many things, in computer service, anything you can do to make the service call go faster will save the customer money. (Still, you *should* know how to do it the old-fashioned way, because you may not always have access to a calculator.)

Windows comes with a tool that can help you convert decimal numbers to hex or binary numbers and back again. That tool is the Windows Calculator. When set to scientific mode, it is a great tool for doing the conversions.

To convert a decimal number to binary, start by running Calculator; in Windows 9*x* you can find it on the Start menu's Accessories folder. Set it to scientific mode by going to the View menu and selecting Scientific. Then, in the Calculator's display box, type in the decimal number you want to convert. To convert the number to binary, click the button next to the word *Binary*. To convert it to hex, just click the button next to *Hex*.

For example, if you have the binary number 01001101 (decimal number 77), you would break this 8-bit word into two groups. The first group (0100) would translate to 4 in hex, and the second group (1101) translates to D. So, this 8-bit binary number would convert to the two-digit hex number 4D. A 32-bit binary number like 01001010010010100001110000101101 converts to 4A4A1C2D (a *much* shorter number, in terms of the number of digits used to represent it).

Converting from hex to decimal works in reverse. For example, if you have a hexadecimal number like 4AC9, you start the conversion by converting each digit of the number into its 4-digit binary equivalent, like so:

4=0100
A=1010
C=1100
9=1001

So, running them together in the right order, you get 0100101011001001 as the binary conversion. To convert to decimal, you convert that 16-bit binary number into decimal as described earlier and you will come up with the decimal number 19145.

Tools of the Trade

Behind every great technician is an even greater set of tools. Your troubleshooting skills alone can get you only so far in diagnosing a problem; you also need some troubleshooting tools. And once the problem has been identified, yet a different set of tools needs to be used—to fix the problem.

There are two major types of tools: hardware and software. We'll cover the hardware category first. (We should note here that there are very few questions on the test about this material; it is only being included for background and reference information.)

Hardware Tools

Hardware tools are those tools that are "hard," meaning you can touch them, as opposed to software tools, which cannot be touched. There are several different kinds of hardware tools used in PC service today. We will discuss the most commonly used ones in this section.

Screwdrivers

The tool that can most often be found in a technician's toolkit is a set of screwdrivers. Most of the larger components in today's computers are mounted in the case with screws. If these components need to be removed, you must have the correct type of screwdriver available. There are three major types: flat blade, Phillips, and Torx.

Flat-Blade Screwdrivers

The first type is often called a flat-blade or flathead screwdriver, though most people simply refer to it as a "standard" screwdriver (Figure 1.15). The type of screw that this screwdriver removes is not used much anymore (primarily because the screw head was easily damaged).

FIGURE 1.15 A flat-blade screwdriver and screw

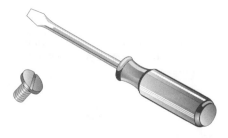

We strongly advise against using a flathead screwdriver to *pry* anything open on a computer. Computers are usually put together very well, and if it seems that you need to pry something apart, it's probably because there's still a screw or fastener holding it together somewhere.

Phillips Screwdrivers

The most commonly used type of screwdriver for computers today is the Phillips driver (Figure 1.16). Phillips-head screws are used because they have more surfaces to turn against, reducing the risk of damaging the head of the screw. More than 90 percent of the screws in most computers today will be Phillips-head screws.

FIGURE 1.16   A Phillips screwdriver and screws

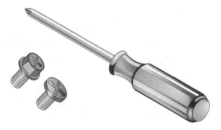

Phillips screwdrivers come in different sizes, identified by numbers. The most common size is a #2 Phillips. It is important to have a few different-sized screwdrivers available. If the wrong size is used (for example, a Phillips driver that is too pointed or too small), it can damage the head of the screw.

The Torx Screwdriver

Finally, there is the type of screwdriver you use when you're working with those maddening little screws that are found on Compaq and Apple computers (as well as on dashboards of later-model GM cars). Of course, we're referring to the Torx screwdriver (Figure 1.17). The Torx type of screw has the most surfaces to turn against and therefore has the greatest resistance to screw head damage. It is becoming more popular because people like its clean, technical look.

FIGURE 1.17   A Torx screwdriver and screw

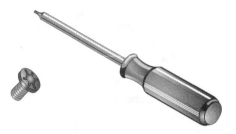

The sizes of Torx drivers are given with the designation T-*xx*, where the *xx* is replaced with a number from 1 through 20. The most common sizes are T-10 and T-15, though for some notebook computers, you will need to have much smaller Torx drivers on hand.

Several screwdrivers are available with changeable tips, like bits for a drill. The advantage is that you can easily change these screwdrivers from a flat blade to a Phillips to a Torx just by changing the bits in the driver. The bits are usually stored in the handle of this type of screwdriver.

Although it may seem convenient, don't use a multiple-bit driver that is magnetized. Magnetism and computers don't make good friends. The magnetism can induce currents in conductors and burn out components without the technician's knowledge. It could also erase magnetic disk storage media.

Needle-Nose Pliers

Another great tool to have in your toolkit is a set or two of needle-nose pliers (Figure 1.18). They are great for grasping connectors or small screws when your hands are too big. If a needle-nose is still too big for the job, a standard pair of tweezers will work as well.

FIGURE 1.18   A pair of needle-nose pliers

IC Pullers

When removing ICs from their mounting sockets, it is inadvisable to use your fingers. First of all, a static discharge could damage the pins. Also, if you pull the chip out unevenly, you may bend or break some of the pins. A pair of pliers would be even worse for this task because they multiply the force exerted by your hands into a force that can easily crush a component. It is better to use a specialized tool called a *chip puller* (Figure 1.19). This tool is usually made of spring steel and is shaped like the letter *U*. At the ends of the *U*, it has fingers that are designed to be slipped between the chip and socket. All the technician has to do is pull up on the tool and it will exert equal force on the different sides of the IC, thus safely removing the chip.

FIGURE 1.19   An IC puller

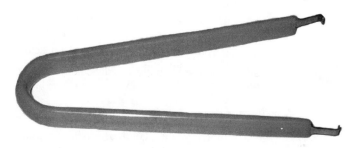

 Be careful when using an IC puller. It is possible to remove the socket as well as the chip if you pull hard enough. You may also damage the motherboard permanently.

Flashlight

Another handy tool to have is a small flashlight. You'll know how especially handy it is when you're crawling around under a desk looking for a dropped screw or trying to find a particular component in a dark computer case. Maglite makes a powerful small flashlight that runs on two AA batteries. It also fits well into a toolkit. Also, Polaroid came out with a very bright pocket flashlight to show off its five-year batteries.

Compressed Air

When you work on a computer, typically you'll first remove the case. While the cover is off, it is a good idea to clean the computer and remove the accumulated "dust bunnies." These clumps of dust and loose fibers obstruct airflow and cause the computer to run hotter, thus shortening its life. The best way to clean out the dust is with clean, dry, compressed air. If you work for a large company, it will probably have a central air compressor as a source for compressed air. If an air compressor is not available, you can use cans of compressed air, but they can be expensive—especially if several are needed. In any case, be sure to bring the computer outside before squirting it with compressed air.

Soldering Iron

One tool that is used less and less in the computer service industry is the soldering iron. You might use one occasionally to splice a broken wire; otherwise you won't have much need for it.

The soldering iron isn't used much any more because most components have been designed to use "quick disconnect" connectors to facilitate easy replacement.

Traditionally, the soldering iron was used to connect electronic components to circuit boards. The most common iron used in electronic applications is one with a narrow tip rated at 15 to 20 watts. Generally, the component was heated with the iron, then rosin-core solder (*not* acid-core) was applied to the component. The solder melted and, flowing into the joint, joined the component to the circuit board.

Wire Strippers

When soldering, it is a good idea to have a combination wire cutter/stripper available to prepare wires for connection. Stripping a wire simply means to remove the insulation from the portion that will be involved in the connection. The tool shown in Figure 1.20 is a good example of one that does both. However, the technician must be careful not to cut the wire when stripping it.

FIGURE 1.20 A combination wire cutter/stripper

Multimeters

The final hardware device we will discuss is the multimeter (see Figure 1.21). It gets its name from the fact that it is a combination of several different kinds of testing meters, including an ohmmeter, ammeter, and voltmeter. In trained hands, it can help detect the correct operation or failure of several different types of components.

FIGURE   1.21   A common multimeter

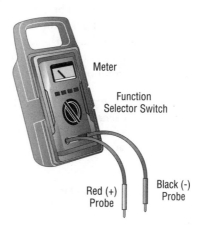

Meter

Function
Selector Switch

Red (+)
Probe

Black (-)
Probe

The multimeter consists of a digital or analog display, two probes, and a function selector switch. This rotary switch not only selects the function being tested, it also selects the range that the meter is set to. If you're measuring a battery using an older meter, you may have to set the range selector manually (to a range close to, but greater than, 1.5 volts). Newer meters, especially the digital ones, will automatically set their ranges appropriately.

WARNING

Never connect a non-auto-ranging meter to an AC power outlet to measure voltage. This action will most surely result in permanent damage to the meter mechanism, the meter itself, or both.

When measuring circuits, it is very important to have the meter hooked up correctly so that the readings are accurate. Each type of measurement may require that the meter be connected in a different way. In the following paragraphs, we will detail the most commonly used functions of the multimeter and how to make measurements correctly with them.

Measuring Resistance with a Multimeter

Resistance is the electrical property most commonly measured in troubleshooting components. Measured in ohms, resistance is most often represented by the Greek symbol omega (Ω). A measurement of infinite resistance indicates that electricity cannot flow from one probe to the other. If a multimeter is used to measure the resistance in a segment of wire and the result is an infinite reading, there is a very good chance that the wire has a break in it somewhere between the probes.

To measure resistance, the multimeter must first be set to measure ohms. This is done either through a button on the front or through the selector dial. (Assume for the rest of this book that we are using newer *auto-ranging multimeters*.) Then the component to be measured must be connected properly between the probes (see the warning and Figure 1.22). The meter will then display the resistance value of the component being measured.

WARNING   *Do not* test resistance on components while they are mounted on a circuit board! The multimeter applies a current to the component being tested. That current may also flow to other components on that board, thus damaging them.

FIGURE 1.22   Connecting a multimeter to measure resistance

Selector set to
read Ohms (Ω)

Component to be tested

Measuring Voltage with a Multimeter

There is a similar procedure to follow when measuring voltage, but with two major differences. First, when measuring voltage, you must be sure you connect the probes to the power source correctly: With DC voltage, the + must connect to the positive side and the − to the negative. (The position doesn't matter with AC voltage.) Second, you must change the selector to VDC (Volts DC) or VAC (Volts AC), whichever is appropriate, to tell the meter what you are measuring (see Figure 1.23). It should be noted that these settings protect the meter from overload. If you plug a meter into a power supply while it's still set to measure resistance, you may blow the meter.

FIGURE 1.23 Connecting a multimeter to measure voltage

Selector set to
read DC or
AC volts

Red probe (+)

Black probe (-)

Connect directly to terminals of power source

Battery

Measuring Current with a Multimeter

The final measurement that is commonly made is that of current, in amperes (amps). Again, the procedure is similar to those used for the other measurements. A major difference here is that when you connect an ammeter to measure the current that a circuit is drawing, you must connect the ammeter in series with the circuit being measured. Figure 1.24 illustrates the proper connection of a multimeter to measure current.

FIGURE 1.24 Connecting a multimeter to measure current

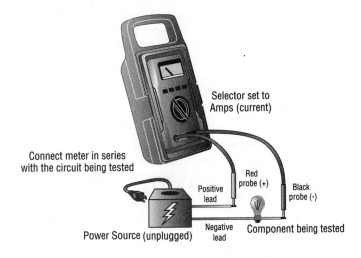

Selector set to
Amps (current)

Connect meter in series
with the circuit being tested

Positive
lead

Red
probe (+)

Black
probe (-)

Power Source (unplugged)

Negative
lead

Component being tested

And Now for the Real World...

If you ask farmers what is the most valuable tool in their toolbox, the answer is almost always "Duct tape." It is said that anything can be fixed with enough duct tape. Unfortunately, computers generally are not easily fixed with duct tape.

There *is* a tool that is invaluable when working on a computer. It can be bought from different tool vendors and is often given away at trade shows. That tool is known as a tweaker (pictured below). It is a screwdriver that is shaped like a pen and is about the same size. It has a Phillips screwdriver on one end and a flat-blade screwdriver on the other and will clip easily into a shirt pocket.

We have been able to fix several computers in a pinch with nothing more than a tweaker. We recommend that each technician run out and buy or find one immediately.

Software Tools

Hardware tools are used when major failures have occurred. However, a great portion of problems aren't related to a failing component but are due to malfunctioning or incorrectly configured hardware. You can use software diagnostics programs to troubleshoot some hardware problems. There are also programs available (usually from the component manufacturers) for configuring hardware, which relieves some or all of the task of setting jumpers or DIP switches. Finally, there are programs for testing the operation of other programs. In this section we'll look briefly at two of the most important types of software tools.

Bootable Disks

The very best software diagnostic tool for DOS machines is a bootable floppy disk: a disk that has been formatted with a version of DOS and made bootable. It belongs in every technician's bag of essentials. You create a bootable disk by typing **FORMAT A: /S** with a blank floppy in the A: drive. Diagnostic and configuration programs can also be copied onto this disk and run without the possibility of software conflicts. The advantage to this approach is that when the computer boots from a DOS bootable floppy disk, it doesn't have any drivers loaded that might conflict with your diagnostics. You can thus get real information. Also, if the machine boots successfully with a bootable disk but won't boot normally without it, this tells you that the motherboard, RAM, and major components are probably okay—which means that the problem may be the hard disk, a corrupt OS (operating system), or a device driver conflict. From this point, you can narrow the problem down.

Software Diagnostics

On the one hand are several software tools that examine the hardware, report its configuration, and identify any errors it finds. Programs like CheckIt Pro, QAPlus, and Microsoft's MSD (Microsoft Diagnostics) work in this manner. On the other hand are programs that serve mainly as reference materials. For example, some manufacturers distribute CD-ROMs that contain all of the reference material concerning their brand of computer equipment. (Toshiba, for instance, distributes a set of CD-ROMs to authorized service centers on a quarterly basis, with parts ordering information, troubleshooting flowcharts, exploded diagrams, and FRU replacement information. All of it is searchable. A very handy tool, indeed.)

Electrostatic Discharge (ESD)

ESD stands for electrostatic discharge. ESD happens when two objects of dissimilar charge come in contact with one another. The two objects exchange electrons in order to standardize the electrostatic charge between them. This charge can, and often does, damage electronic components.

The likelihood that a component will be damaged increases with the increasing use of Complementary Metal Oxide Semiconductor (CMOS) chips, because these chips contain a thin metal oxide layer that is hypersensitive to ESD. The previous generation's Transistor-Transistor Logic (TTL) chips are actually more robust than the newer CMOS chips because they don't contain this metal oxide layer. Most of today's ICs are CMOS chips, so there is more of a concern with ESD lately.

When you shuffle your feet across the floor and shock your best friend on the ear, you are discharging static electricity into the ear of your friend. The lowest static voltage transfer that you can feel is around 3,000 volts (it doesn't electrocute you because there is extremely little current). A static transfer that you can *see* is at least 10,000 volts! Just by sitting in a chair, you can generate around 100 volts of static electricity. Walking around wearing synthetic materials can generate around 1,000 volts. You can easily generate around 20,000 volts (!) simply by dragging your smooth-soled shoes across a shag carpet in the winter. (Actually, it doesn't have to be winter to run this danger. It can occur in any room with very low *humidity*. It's just that heated rooms in wintertime are generally of very low humidity.)

It would make sense that these thousands of volts would damage computer components. However, a component can be damaged with as little as 80 volts! That means, if your body has a small charge built up in it, you could damage a component without even realizing it.

Symptoms of ESD damage may be subtle, but they can be detected. One of the authors, David Groth, relates this experience:

"When I think of ESD, I always think of the same instance. A few years ago, I was working on an Apple Macintosh. This computer seemed to have a mind of its own. I would troubleshoot it, find the defective component, and replace it. The problem was that as soon as I replaced the component, it failed. I thought maybe the power supply was frying the boards, so I replaced both at the same time, but to no avail.

"I was about to send the computer off to Apple when I realized that it was winter. Normally this would not be a factor, but winters where I live (North Dakota) are extremely dry. Dry air promotes static electricity. At first I thought that my problem couldn't be that simple, but I was at the end of my rope. So, when I received my next set of new parts, I grounded myself with an antistatic strap for the time it took to install the components, and prayed while I turned on the power. Success!! The components worked as they should, and a new advocate of ESD prevention was born."

Antistatic Wrist Strap

The silver lining to the cloud described in David's story is that there are measures you can implement to help contain the effects of ESD. The first, and easiest, one to implement is the antistatic wrist strap, also referred to as an ESD strap. The ESD strap works by attaching one end to an earth ground (typically the ground pin on an extension cord) and wrapping the other end around your wrist. This strap grounds your body and keeps it at a zero charge. Figure 1.25 shows the proper way to attach an antistatic strap.

FIGURE 1.25 Proper ESD strap connection

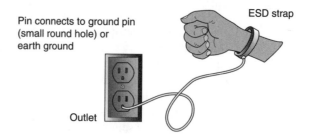

Pin connects to ground pin
(small round hole) or
earth ground

ESD strap

Outlet

An ESD strap is a specially designed device to bleed electrical charges away *safely*. It uses a 1-megaohm resistor to bleed the charge away slowly. A simple wire wrapped around your wrist will not work correctly and could electrocute you!

There is only one situation in which you should not wear an ESD strap. If you wear one while working on the inside of a monitor, you increase the chance of getting a lethal shock.

Antistatic Bags for Parts

Antistatic bags are important tools to have at your disposal when servicing electronic components because they protect the sensitive electronic devices from stray static charges. The bags are designed so that the static charges collect on the outside of the bags rather than on the electronic components. These bags can be obtained from several sources. The most direct way to acquire antistatic bags is to simply go to an electronics supply store and purchase them in bulk. Most supply stores will have several sizes available. Perhaps the easiest way to obtain them, however, is simply to hold on to the ones that come your way. That is, when you purchase any new component, it usually comes in an antistatic bag. Once you have installed the component, keep the bag. It may take you a while to gather a sizable collection of bags if you take this approach, but eventually you will have a fairly large assortment.

ESD Static Mats

It is possible for a device to be damaged by simply laying it on a bench top. For this reason, you should have an ESD mat in addition to an ESD strap. This mat drains excess charge away from any item coming in contact with it (see Figure 1.26). ESD mats are also sold as mouse/keyboard pads to prevent ESD charges from interfering with the operation of the computer. ESD charges can cause problems such as making a computer hang or reboot.

FIGURE 1.26   Proper use of an ESD static mat

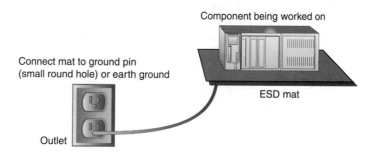

Modifying the Relative Humidity

Another preventive measure that can be taken is to maintain the relative humidity at around 50 percent. Be careful not to increase the humidity too far—to the point where moisture starts to condense on the equipment! Also, make use of antistatic spray, which is available commercially, to reduce static buildup on clothing and carpets. In a pinch, a solution of dilute fabric softener sprayed on these items will do the same.

With regard to the components, vendors have methods of protecting them in transit from manufacture to installation. Vendors press the pins of ICs into antistatic foam to keep all the pins at the same potential. Also, circuit boards are shipped in antistatic bags, discussed earlier. However, keep in mind that unlike antistatic mats, antistatic bags do not "drain" the charges away, and they should never be used in place of an antistatic mat.

At the very least, you can be mindful of the dangers of ESD and take steps to reduce its effects. Beyond that, you should educate yourself about those effects so you know when ESD is becoming a major problem.

If an ESD strap or mat is not available, it is possible to discharge excess static voltage by touching the metal case of the power supply. However, the power supply *must be plugged into a properly grounded outlet* for this to work as intended. Because it's plugged in, extra caution should be taken so that you don't get electrocuted. Also, continuous contact should be maintained to continuously drain excess charge away. As you can see, it would be easier to have an antistatic wrist strap.

Safety

As a provider of a hands-on service (repairing, maintaining, or upgrading someone's computer), you need to be aware of some general safety tips, because if you are not careful, you could harm yourself or the equipment. First, let's talk about playing it safe. Computers, display monitors, and printers can be dangerous if not handled properly.

Perhaps the most important aspect of computers that you should be aware of is the fact that they not only *use* electricity, they *store* electrical charge after they're turned off. This makes the power supply and the monitor pretty much off-limits to anyone but a trained electrical repair person. Also, the computer's processor and various parts of the printer run at extremely high temperatures, and you can get burned if you try to handle them immediately after they've been in operation. Those are just two general safety measures that should concern you. There are plenty more. When discussing safety issues with regard to repairing and upgrading PCs, it is best to break them down into five general areas:

- The computer
- The power supply
- The printer
- The monitor
- The keyboard and mouse

The Computer

If you have to open the computer to inspect or replace parts (as you will with most repairs), be sure to turn off the machine before you begin, and be sure to read the next section, which covers safety issues with the power supply.

The computer case is metal with sharp edges, so be careful when handling it. You can, for example, cut yourself by jamming your fingers between the case and the frame when you try to force the case back on.

The Power Supply

Do not take the issue of safety and electricity lightly. If you were to remove the power supply from its case (and we don't recommend it), you would be taking a great risk. The current flowing through the power supply normally follows a complete circuit; when your body breaks that circuit, your body becomes a part of the circuit.

The two biggest dangers with power supplies are burning yourself and electrocuting yourself. These usually go hand in hand. If you touch a bare wire that is carrying current, you may get electrocuted. A large enough current passing through the wire (and you) can cause severe burns. (It can also cause your heart to stop, your muscles to seize, and your brain to stop functioning. In short, it can kill you.) Electricity always finds the best path to ground. And because we are basically bags of salt water (an excellent conductor of electricity), electricity will use us as a conductor if we are grounded. Because of the way electricity conducts itself (get it?), electrical burn victims usually have two kinds of wounds: the entry wound and exit wound.

The entry wound happens at the point of contact between the conductor and the person. It's rather gruesome. The current flowing through you has enough power to boil the water in the tissues it comes in contact with, essentially cooking you from the inside out. It isn't fun. The electricity sears the tissue on its way toward whatever part of the body is closest to a ground. Then, at the point closest to a ground, the electricity bolts from the body, producing an exit wound. We hope this description will encourage you to learn proper electrical safety so you may never have to experience the pain of electrical burns.

Fire Safety

It's not often that repairing a computer is the cause of an electrical fire. You should, however, know how to extinguish one properly. There are three major classes of fire extinguishers available, one for each type of flammable substance: A for wood and paper fires, B for flammable liquids, and C for electrical fires. The most popular type of fire extinguisher today is the multipurpose, or "ABC-rated," extinguisher. It contains a dry chemical powder that will smother the fire and cool it at the same time. For electrical fires (which may be related to a shorted-out wire in a power supply), make sure the fire extinguisher will work for Class C fires. If you don't have an extinguisher that is specifically rated for electrical fires (type C), you can use an ABC-rated extinguisher.

Although it is possible to work on a power supply, it is *not* recommended. Power supplies contain several capacitors that can hold *lethal* charges *long after they have been unplugged!* It is extremely dangerous to open the case of a power supply. Besides, power supplies are inexpensive, so it would probably cost less to replace them than to try to fix them, and it would be much safer.

Current vs. Voltage—Which Is More Dangerous?

When talking about power and safety, you will almost always hear the saying "It's not the volts that kill you, it's the amps." That's mostly true. However, an explanation is in order.

The number of volts in a power source represents its potential to do work. But volts don't do anything by themselves. Current (amperage, or amps) is the actual force behind the work being done by electricity. Here's an analogy to help explain this concept. Say you have two boulders; one is 10lbs, the other 100lbs, and each is 100 feet off the ground. If you drop them, which one would do more work? The obvious answer is the 100lb boulder. They both have the same potential to do work (100 feet of travel), but the 100lb boulder has more mass, thus more force. Voltage is analogous to the distance the boulder is from the ground, and amperage is analogous to the mass of the boulder.

This is why we can produce static electricity on the order of 50,000 volts and not electrocute ourselves. Even though this electricity has a great *potential* for work, it actually does very little work because the amperage is so low. This also explains why you can weld metal with only 110 volts. Welders use only 110 (sometimes 220) volts, but they also use anywhere from 50 to 200 amps!

If you ever have to work on a power supply, for safety's sake you should discharge all capacitors within it. To do this, connect a resistor across the leads of the capacitor with a rating of three watts or more and a resistance of 100 ohms (Ω) per volt. For example, to discharge a 225-volt capacitor, you would use a 22.5kΩ resistor (225 volts times 100Ω = 22500Ω or 22.5 kΩ).

The Printer

When you attempt to repair a printer, do you sometimes think that there is a little monster in there hiding all the screws from you? Besides missing screws, here are some things to watch out for when repairing printers:

- When handling a toner cartridge from a laser printer or page printer, do not shake or turn the cartridge upside down. You will find yourself spending more time cleaning the printer and the surrounding area than you would have spent to fix the printer.

- Do not put any objects into the feeding system (in an attempt to clear the path) as the printer is running.

- Laser printers generate a laser that is hazardous to your eyes. Do not look directly into the source of the laser.

- If it's an ink-jet printer, do not try to blow in the ink cartridge to clear a clogged opening—that is, unless you like the taste of ink.

- Some parts of a laser printer (like the EP cartridge) will be damaged if touched. Your skin produces oils and has a small surface layer of dead skin cells. These substances can collect on the delicate surface of the EP cartridge and cause malfunctions. Bottom line: Keep your fingers out of where they don't belong!

The Monitor

Other than the power supply, one of the most dangerous components to try to repair is the monitor, or Cathode Ray Tube (CRT). In fact, we recommend that you *do not* try to repair monitors. To avoid the extremely hazardous environment contained inside the monitor—it can retain a high-voltage charge for hours after it's been turned off—take it to a certified monitor technician or television repair shop. The repair shop or certified technician will know and understand the proper procedures to discharge the monitor, which involve attaching a resistor to the flyback transformer's charging capacitor to release the high-voltage electrical charge that builds up during use. They will also be able to determine whether the monitor can be repaired or needs to be replaced. Remember, the monitor works in its own extremely protective environment (the monitor case) and may not respond well to your desire to try to open it.

The CRT is vacuum sealed. Be extremely careful when handling the CRT. If you break the glass, it will implode, which can send glass in any direction.

Even though we recommend not repairing monitors, the A+ exam does test your knowledge of the safety practices to use when you need to do so. If you have to open a monitor, you must first discharge the high-voltage charge on it using a *high-voltage probe*. This probe has a very large needle, a gauge that indicates volts, and a wire with an alligator clip. Attach the alligator clip to a ground (usually the round pin on the power cord). Slip the probe needle underneath the high-voltage cup on the monitor. You will see the gauge spike to around 15,000 volts and slowly reduce to zero. When it reaches zero, you may remove the high-voltage probe and service the high-voltage components of the monitor.

The Keyboard and Mouse

Okay, we know you are thinking, "What danger could a keyboard or mouse cause?" We admit that there is not much danger associated with them, but there are a couple of safety concerns you should always keep in mind.

First, the mouse usually has a cord, and you can trip over it, so make sure it's safely out of the way. Second, you could short-circuit your keyboard if you accidentally spill liquid on it. Keyboards don't function very well with half a can of cola in their innards!

Play It Safe with Common Sense

When you're repairing a PC, do not leave it unattended. Someone could walk into the room and inadvertently bump the machine, causing failure. Worse, they could step on pieces that may be lying around and get hurt. It is also not a good idea to work on the PC alone. If you should become injured, there should be someone around to help if you need it. Finally, if you're fatigued, you may find it difficult to concentrate and focus on what you are doing. There are real safety measures related to repairing PCs, so the most important thing to remember is to pay close attention to what you are doing.

Environmental Concerns

It is estimated that more than 25 percent of all the lead (a poisonous substance) in landfills today is a result of consumer electronics components. Because they contain hazardous substances, many states require that consumer electronics (televisions, VCRs, stereos) be disposed of as hazardous waste. Computers are no exception. Monitors contain several carcinogens and phosphors, as well as mercury and lead. The computer itself may contain several lubricants and chemicals as well as lead. Printers contain plastics and chemicals like toners and inks that are also hazardous. All of these items should be disposed of properly.

Remember all of those 386 and 486 computers that came out in the late 1980s and are now considered antiques? Where did they all go? Is there an "Old Computers Home" somewhere that is using these older computer systems for good purposes, or are they lying in a junkyard somewhere? Or could it be that there are folks who just cannot let go, with a stash of old computer systems and computer parts that lie in the deep dark depths of their basements.

Although it is relatively easy to put old machines away, thinking that you might be able to put them to good use again someday, it's really not realistic. Most computers are obsolete as soon as you buy them. And if you have not used them recently, your old computer components will more than likely never be used again.

We recycle cans, plastic, and newspaper so why not recycle computer equipment? Well, the problem is that most computers contain small amounts of hazardous substances (chemicals from monitor screens, chemicals from batteries, and noxious chemicals in the wiring). Some countries are exploring the option of recycling electrical machines, but most have still not enacted appropriate measures to enforce their proper disposal. However, there are a few things that we can do as consumers and environmentalists that can promote the proper disposal of computer equipment:

- Check with the manufacturer. Some manufacturers will take back outdated equipment for parts (and may even pay you for them).
- Properly dispose of solvents or cleaners used with computers, as well as their containers, at a local hazardous waste disposal facility.
- Disassemble the machine and reuse the "parts" that are good.
- Check out businesses that can melt the components down for the lead or gold plating.
- Contact the Environmental Protection Agency (EPA) for a list of local or regional waste disposal sites that will accept used computer equipment. The EPA's Web address is www.epa.gov.
- Check with local nonprofit or education organizations interested in using the equipment.
- Check out the Internet for possible waste disposal sites. Table 1.5 gives a few Web sites we came across that deal with disposal of used computer equipment.
- Check with the EPA to see if what you are disposing has an MSDS (Material Safety Data Sheet). These sheets contain information about

the toxicity of a product and whether or not it can be disposed of in the trash. They also contain "lethal dose" information.

TABLE 1.5   Computer Recycling Web Sites

Site Name	Web Address
Computer Recycle Center	www.recycles.com/
Re-Compute	www.recompute.co.uk
Re-PC	www.repc.com/

In addition to hardware recycling, there are businesses that offer to recycle consumables, like ink cartridges or printer ribbons. However, although these businesses are doing us a favor in our quest to recycle, it might not be the best way to keep up with the recycle agenda. Why? Well, we don't recommend the use of recycled ink cartridges; they may clog, the ink quality is not as good, and the small circuit board on the cartridge may be damaged. Similarly, recycled printer ribbons will lose their ability to hold ink after a while and don't last as long as a new ribbon. And, recycled toner cartridges don't operate properly after refilling. However, when you are through with the old cartridges, give them to organizations that do recycle so they can have some fresh "cores." That way, you can safely dispose of your cartridge and benefit the environment at the same time.

Remember that recycling is a way to keep our environment clean and our landfills empty. If we can take one step to recycle or redistribute outdated computer equipment, we are one step closer to having a healthier environment. However, we should not have to sacrifice quality in the process.

In particular, you should make a special effort to recycle *batteries*. Batteries contain several chemicals that are harmful to our environment and won't degrade safely. Batteries should not be thrown away; they should be recycled according to your local laws. Check with your local authorities to find out how batteries should be recycled.

Cleaning Systems

The cleanliness of a computer is extremely important. Buildup of dust, dirt, and oils can prevent various mechanical parts of a computer from operating. Because it is important, the A+ exam is going to test your knowledge of the proper way to use various cleaning products on computer systems.

Computer components get dirty. Dirt reduces their operating efficiency and, ultimately, their life. Cleaning them is definitely important. But cleaning them with the right cleaning compounds is equally important. Using the wrong compounds can leave residue behind that is more harmful than the dirt you are trying to remove!

First of all, most computer cases and monitor cases can be cleaned using mildly soapy water on a clean, lint-free cloth. Make sure that the power is off before putting anything wet near a computer. Dampen (not soak) a cloth in mild soap solution and wipe the dirt and dust from the case. Then wipe the moisture from the case with a dry, lint-free cloth. Anything with a plastic or metal case can be cleaned in this manner.

Additionally, if you spill anything on a keyboard, you can clean it by soaking it in distilled, demineralized water. In this type of water, the extra minerals and impurities have been removed and so it will not leave any traces of residue that might interfere with the proper operation of the keyboard after cleaning.

The electronic connectors of computer equipment, on the other hand, should never touch water. Instead, use a swab moistened in distilled, denatured isopropyl alcohol (also known as electronics cleaner and found in electronics stores) to clean contacts. This will take oxidation off of the copper contacts.

Finally, the best way to remove dust and dirt from the inside of the computer is to use compressed air instead of vacuuming. Compressed air can be more easily directed and doesn't easily produce ESD damage (like vacuuming could). Simply blow the dust from inside the computer using a stream of compressed air. However, make sure to do this outside so that you don't blow dust all over your work area or over yourself.

One unique challenge when cleaning computers is when you spill toner. It sticks to everything. There are two methods to deal with this. First of all, blow all the loose toner out of the printer using compressed air, being careful not to blow the toner into any of the printing mechanisms. Then, using a cool, damp cloth, wipe any remaining particles out of the printer.

Summary

In this chapter, you learned the basic computer service concepts that you will be tested for in the A+ exam. These fundamental concepts lay the foundation for the concepts throughout the rest of this book.

In the section on microcomputer components, we discussed the most common basic elements of microcomputers: resistors, capacitors, vacuum tubes, transistors, and integrated circuits. All of these components can commonly be found on the circuit boards of today's microcomputers (except maybe vacuum tubes, which are very outdated).

In addition, you learned some of science behind how certain electronics work. You learned that electricity is the flow of electrons, the difference between a conductor and nonconductor, the definition of static electricity, and the basic concepts of electromagnetic theory.

Computers use various types of numbers, including decimal, hexadecimal, and binary. We covered how to use each numbering system to count as well as how to convert between the different types.

We also discussed the different tools used to service computers as well as the proper way to use them. You learned about the types of hardware tools, including screwdrivers, multimeters, and so forth, and the different types of software tools and diagnostics, like bootable disks, used to aid a technician in servicing a computer.

Probably the most important topic in this chapter is electrostatic discharge (ESD). Electrostatic discharge is what happens when two objects of unlike charges are brought together. The charges equal themselves out by transferring electrons between the objects. The transfer of electrons from a person to an electronic component can damage sensitive electronic components during their installation. The voltage can be low enough that the person installing the component may not feel the transfer, but the damage can still occur. Symptoms of ESD include a large increase in DOA components as well as an increase in malfunctioning components.

It would not be proper to talk about servicing anything without introducing at least basic safety concepts. This chapter included a discussion of the safety precautions that must be taken when servicing computers, as well as the proper way of executing them to ensure that technicians don't inflict damage to either themselves or the computer.

The A+ exam will test your knowledge of the impact of computer service on the environment. Many chemicals used in the cleaning of computers are toxic to the environment as well as to human beings. Some of the chemicals (like lead) found in circuit boards are also toxic. These items should be treated and disposed of properly.

This chapter ended with a discussion of how to properly clean the various components of a computers system. It's important to keep in mind that dirty electronic components don't function properly, nor do they last as long as they normally would. You learned which cleaning products to use on which components; if you use the wrong one, you can actually cause more harm than good.

Key Terms

Before you take the exam, be certain you are familiar with the following terms:

analog	nonconductor
auto-ranging multimeters	ohms
binary	Pin Grid Array
bit	potentiometer
byte	Quad Small Outline Package (QSOP)
capacitor	resistor
chip puller	resistor pack
conductor	rheostat
cross talk	semiconductors
DIP switches	Single Inline Package (SIP)
Dual Inline Package (DIP)	surface mount
dynamic electricity	terminators
heat sink	tolerance range
high-voltage probe	transistor
integrated circuit (IC) chip	vacuum tube
jumpers	word
Least Significant Bit (LSB)	zero insertion force
Most Significant Bit (MSB)	

Review Questions

1. What is the resistance rating of a resistor with the markings (from left to right) red, brown, yellow, gold?

   A. 2,100 Ω ±5%

   B. 21,000 Ω ±5%

   C. 210,000 Ω ±5%

   D. 2,100,000 Ω ±5%

2. Computers and component parts use what type of signals to transmit information?

   A. Analog

   B. Digital

   C. Discrete

   D. Continuous

   E. Both B and C

   F. None of the above

3. Which electrical component resists the flow of electricity?

   A. Resistors

   B. Transistors

   C. Semiconductors

   D. Capacitors

4. Convert the following binary number to decimal: 10110101.

   A. 10110101

   B. 181

   C. 192

   D. None of the above

5. Convert this hexadecimal number to its binary equivalent: A73F.

   A. 1010011100111111

   B. 1010

   C. 1010001010010101

   D. 0100001001001100

   E. 10101011

6. What does ESD stand for?

   A. Every Single Day

   B. Electric System Degradation

   C. Electrosilicon Diode

   D. Electrostatic discharge

   E. None of the above

7. When connecting an ESD strap to an extension cord, you must connect it to _____ .

   A. The hot pin

   B. The negative pin

   C. The ground pin

   D. All of the above

8. The following components are found in today's microcomputers. (Select all that apply.)

   A. Vacuum tubes

   B. Resistors

   C. Transistors

   D. Dilithium crystals

   E. Capacitors

9. Convert the following decimal number to binary: 219.

   A. 11011011

   B. 11101101

   C. 11111111

   D. 00101001

   E. None of the above

10. How many bits are represented by a single hexadecimal digit?

   A. 1

   B. 2

   C. 4

   D. 8

11. Which type of IC package has two rows of pins, one on each side of the package?

- **A.** QSOP
- **B.** DIP
- **C.** SIP
- **D.** PGA
- **E.** ZIF

12. Which type of IC package is usually surface mounted and used for VLSI applications?

- **A.** QSOP
- **B.** DIP
- **C.** SIP
- **D.** PGA
- **E.** ZIF

13. What is the best method for preventing ESD damage?

- **A.** Antistatic mat
- **B.** Antistatic spray
- **C.** Antistatic wrist strap
- **D.** Antistatic thinking

14. Which type of screw was chosen because of its relative immunity to head damage and for its "high-tech" look?

- **A.** Phillips-head
- **B.** Flathead
- **C.** Normal
- **D.** Torx

15. How many volts does it take to damage a CMOS-based IC?

- **A.** 1
- **B.** 100
- **C.** 1,000
- **D.** 10,000

16. What is the Least Significant Bit (LSB) of the number 10100010?

- **A.** 0
- **B.** 1

17. What are two ways to configure an interrupt for a device on the motherboard?

    A. Jumpers

    B. Quads

    C. DIP switches

    D. Pin Grid Arrays

    E. Both A and C

    F. None of the above

18. What is the maximum resistance of a resistor with the following markings: red, brown, red?

    A. 2100Ohms

    B. 2020Ohms

    C. 2520Ohms

    D. 420Ohms

19. A male DB-25 port is most likely a _____ .

    A. Parallel port

    B. Serial port

    C. Joystick/game port

    D. Network port

20. Which of the following components can be used to configure an adapter card? (Select all that apply.)

    A. Software

    B. Male DB-25 port

    C. Jumpers

    D. Transistors

    E. None of the above

21. Does pure water conduct electricity?

    A. Yes

    B. No

22. Which port(s) are used for serial ports? (Select all that apply.)

    A. RJ-11

    B. DB-9

    C. Centronics 36

    D. DB-25

    E. None of the above

Answers to Review Questions

1. C. Each colored band stands for a number. The first two bands represent the digits of a two-digit number. The third band represents a multiplier. The presence or absence of a fourth band represents a margin-of-error factor commonly referred to as the tolerance range. So red would equal 2, brown equals 1, yellow equals 10,000, and gold equals ±5%. Putting this all together, take the 21 (from the first two bands) and multiply by the 10,000 of the third band. This gives you 210,000 and the tolerance is the last band, or ±5%.

2. E. Computers and component parts use signals that are both digital and discrete to transmit information.

3. A. A component that is commonly used in computers is the resistor. As its name suggests, it resists the flow of electricity.

4. B. When trying to convert a binary number to decimal, you need to look at the positions of the 1s. You read the digits from left to right. When the digits are added together, you get the decimal equivalent 181.

5. A. To arrive at this answer, convert each of the individual numerals in the hexadecimal number to its binary equivalent. A, for instance, is 1010, 7 is 0111, 3 is 0011, and F equals 1111.

6. D. ESD is a very common computer acronym. It stands for electrostatic discharge.

7. C. When connecting an ESD strap to an extension cord, you must connect it to the ground pin to ensure both your safety and the proper discharge of ESD.

8. B, C, E. Resistors, transistors, and capacitors are all very common components found in today's computers.

9. A. To arrive at the correct answer, you must start with the MSB and place a 1 in each placeholder until, added up, the placeholders equal 219.

10. C. Each hexadecimal digit is represented with 4 bits.

11. B. The DIP, or Dual Inline Package, is a type of IC package that has two rows of pins, one on each side of the package.

12. A. QSOP, or Quad Small Outline Package, is a type of IC package that is usually surface mounted and used for VLSI applications.

13. C. Of all the options listed, an antistatic wrist strap will provide you with the most ESD protection.

14. D. The Torx screw has many angles, or surfaces, in the bit head and is therefore relatively immune to head damage. This shape also gives it a very "high-tech" look.

15. B. Because CMOS chips use a thin metal oxide layer that is hypersensitive to ESD, it takes only 100 volts to damage them.

16. A. The Least Significant Bit (LSB) is always the bit on the far right. So for the number 10100010, it is 0.

17. E. An interrupt request for a device can be configured manually by either using DIP switches, which are usually much easier to set, or by or using jumpers.

18. C. Each colored band stands for a number. The first two bands represent the digits of a two-digit number. The third band represents a multiplier. The presence or absence of a fourth band represents a margin-of-error factor commonly referred to as the tolerance range. So red equals 2, brown equals 1, and red equals 100. Putting this together, take the 21 from the first 2 bands and multiply by the third, 100, to equal 2100. The tolerance range, because no fourth band is present, would be ±20%, adding another 420 for a grand total of 2520Ohms.

19. B. In most cases, a male DB-25 port will be a serial port. In some cases, you could find some specialized cards that differ, but they are rare.

20. A, C. Most adapter cards can be configured with software, which is the easiest option, or jumpers, the manual option. However, if they are software configurable, just don't lose those configuration disk. The disk are usually very specific to the manufacturer, make, and model of the card.

21. B. Pure water does not conduct electricity. This is because it contains no impurities that would actually do the conducting of electricity.

22. B, D. Most commonly, you will use DB-9 and DB-25 connectors for serial ports.

Chapter

2

PC Architecture

THE FOLLOWING OBJECTIVES ARE COVERED IN THIS CHAPTER:

✓ **1.1 Identify basic terms, concepts, and functions of system modules, including how each module should work during normal operation and during the boot process.**

Examples of concepts and modules are:

- System board
- Power supply
- Processor/CPU
- Memory
- Storage devices
- Monitor
- Modem
- Firmware
- BIOS
- CMOS
- LCD (portable systems)
- Ports
- PDA (Personal Digital Assistant)

✓ **1.2 Identify basic procedures for adding and removing field replaceable modules for both desktop and portable systems.**

Examples of modules:

- System board
- Storage device
- Power supply
- Processor/CPU
- Memory
- Input devices
- Hard drive

- Keyboard
- Video board
- Mouse
- Network Interface Card (NIC)

Portable system components:

- AC adapters
- DC controllers
- LCD panel
- PC card
- Pointing devices

✓ **1.4 Identify common peripheral ports, associated cabling, and their connectors.**

Content may include the following:

- Cable types
- Cable orientation
- Serial versus parallel
- Pin connections

Examples of types of connectors:

- DB-9
- DB-25
- RJ-11
- RJ-45
- BNC
- PS2/MINI-DIN
- USB
- IEEE-1394

✓ **3.2 Identify issues, procedures, and devices for protection within the computing environment, including people, hardware, and the surrounding workspace.**

Content may include the following:

- UPS (Uninterruptible Power Supply) and suppressors
- Determining the signs of power issues
- Proper methods of storage of components for future use

Potential hazards and proper safety procedures relating to:

- Lasers
- High-voltage equipment
- Power supply
- CRT

Special disposal procedures that comply with environmental guidelines.

- Batteries
- CRTs
- Toner kits/cartridges
- Chemical solvents and cans
- MSDS (Material Safety Data Sheet)

ESD (Electrostatic Discharge) precautions and procedures

- What ESD can do, how it may be apparent, or hidden
- Common ESD protection devices
- Situations that could present a danger or hazard

✓ **4.1 Distinguish between the popular CPU chips in terms of their basic characteristics.**

Content may include the following:

- Popular CPU chips (Intel, AMD, Cyrix)
- Characteristics
- Physical size
- Voltage
- Speeds
- On-board cache or not
- Sockets
- SEC (Single Edge Contact)

✓ **4.3 Identify the most popular type of motherboards, their components, and their architecture (bus structures and power supplies).**

Content may include the following:

Types of motherboards:

- AT (Full and Baby)
- ATX

Components:

- Communication ports
- SIMM and DIMM
- Processor sockets
- External cache memory (Level 2)
- Bus Architecture
- ISA
- PCI
- AGP
- USB (Universal Serial Bus)
- VESA local bus (VL-Bus)
- Basic compatibility guidelines
- IDE (ATA, ATAPI, ULTRA-DMA, EIDE)
- SCSI (Wide, Fast, Ultra, LVD [Low Voltage Differential])

undamentally, a computer is a lot like the human body. The human body contains a brain, organs to help the body function properly, and skin to protect the internal organs. All of the various parts of your body's internal structure work together to create a fully functional human being. Well, the microcomputer has analogous components to create a fully functional machine.

> **NOTE** For complete coverage of objective 1.1, please also see Chapters 4 and 6. For complete coverage of objective 1.2, please also see Chapters 5, 8, and 9. For complete coverage of objective 1.4, please also see Chapter 6. For complete coverage of objective 4.3, please also see Chapters 4 and 5. For complete coverage of objective 3.2, please also see Chapter 1.

The aim of this chapter is simply to take a quick look inside the computer, identify the main components, give a little historical background, and discover how everything works together. We'll cover each of the topics again in more detail in later chapters in this book, but our first chapter will serve as a useful overview. You'll be introduced to the following components:

- System boards
- CPUs
- BIOS
- Memory
- Storage
- Input/output devices
- Interfaces
- Display systems
- Power systems
- Portable systems

If you were to open any computer, you should be able to identify the components inside. As a matter of fact, the A+ exam will test your knowledge of these components and their relation to each other. Figure 2.1 shows a view of a typical

PC, its components, and their locations. We will refer back to this diagram throughout this chapter as we discuss the inner workings of the PC.

FIGURE 2.1 Typical PC components

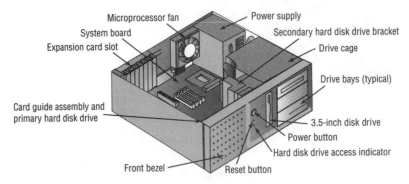

The System Board

The spine of the computer is the *system board*, otherwise known as the *motherboard* (and less commonly referred to as the *planar board*). This is the olive green or brown fiberglass sheet that lines the bottom of the computer. It is the most important component in the computer because it is the component that connects all the other components of a PC together. Figure 2.2 shows a typical PC system board, as seen from above. It is on this sheet that all other components are attached. On the system board you will find the CPU, underlying circuitry, expansion slots, video components, RAM slots, and a variety of other chips.

FIGURE 2.2 A typical system board

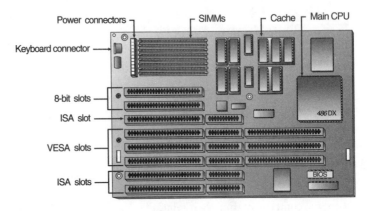

Types of System Boards

There are two major types of system boards: integrated and nonintegrated. Let's discuss the nonintegrated system boards first.

Nonintegrated system boards have each major assembly installed in the computer as expansion cards. The major assemblies we're talking about here are items like the video circuitry, disk controllers, and accessories. Nonintegrated boards can be easily identified because each expansion slot is usually occupied by one of the components we just mentioned.

Integrated system boards are called that because most of the components that would otherwise be installed as expansion cards are integrated into the motherboard circuitry. Integrated system boards were designed for their simplicity. Of course, there's a drawback to this simplicity. When one component breaks, you can't just replace the component that's broken; the whole motherboard must be replaced. Although they are cheaper to produce, they are more expensive to repair.

System Board Form Factors

Nonintegrated system boards are also classified by their form factor (design): AT, ATX, or NLX (and variants of these). The AT system boards are the same as the motherboards found in the original IBM AT. The processor, memory, and expansion slots are all in line with each other. Because of advances in technology, the same number of components that were on the original AT motherboard (now called a *"full"* AT board) were later compressed into a smaller area. This configuration is known as the *"baby"* AT configuration.

The "baby" AT is used to be the most commonly used design, but it has some fundamental problems. Because the processor and memory were in line with the expansion slots, only one or two full-length cards could be used. Also, the processor was far from the power supply's cooling fan and would therefore tend to overheat unless a heat sink or processor fan was directly attached to it. To overcome the limitations of the "baby" AT design, the ATX motherboard was designed. The ATX has the processor and memory slots at right angles to the expansion cards. This puts the processor and memory in line with the fan output of the power supply, allowing the processor to run cooler. And, because those components are not in line with the expansion cards, you can install full-length expansion cards in an ATX motherboard machine. Sales of ATX form factor boards are currently outpacing sales of the AT motherboards.

The line between integrated and nonintegrated system boards is quickly becoming blurred. Many of what would normally be called "nonintegrated" system boards now incorporate the most commonly used circuitry (e.g. IDE and floppy controllers, serial controllers, and sound cards) onto the motherboard itself.

A fairly new motherboard form factor that has been gaining popularity in the last couple of years is *NLX*. This form factor is used in "low profile" case types. What makes them unique is that the expansion slots are placed sideways on a special *riser card* (as shown in Figure 2.3) to optimally use the space.

FIGURE 2.3   An NLX motherboard

These motherboard form factors are usually found in what are known as "clone" computers (those not manufactured by a Fortune 500 PC company). Some manufacturers (e.g. Compaq and IBM) design and manufacture their own motherboard designs, which really don't conform to either standard. This style of motherboard is known as a *proprietary design* motherboard. Basically, the components are laid out differently than an AT or ATX, but it will work as a PC. The components are laid out differently than the motherboards previously discussed.

System Board Components

Now that you understand the basic types of motherboards and their form factors, it's time to take a quick look at the components found on the motherboard and their locations relative to each other. Figure 2.4 illustrates many of the following components found on a typical motherboard:

- Expansion slots
- Memory slots
- Processor slots or sockets
- Power connectors
- On-board disk drive connectors
- Keyboard connector
- Peripheral port connectors
- BIOS chip
- CMOS battery
- Jumpers and DIP switches

FIGURE 2.4 Components on a motherboard

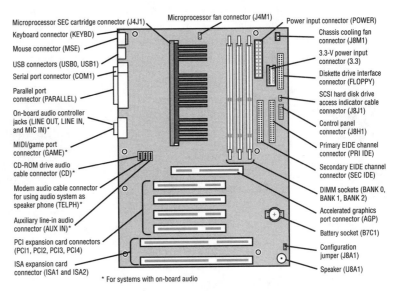

Microprocessor SEC cartridge connector (J4J1)
Keyboard connector (KEYBD)
Mouse connector (MSE)
USB connectors (USB0, USB1)
Serial port connector (COM1)
Parallel port connector (PARALLEL)
On-board audio controller jacks (LINE OUT, LINE IN, and MIC IN)*
MIDI/game port connector (GAME)*
CD-ROM drive audio cable connector (CD)*
Modem audio cable connector for using audio system as speaker phone (TELPH)*
Auxiliary line-in audio connector (AUX IN)*
PCI expansion card connectors (PCI1, PCI2, PCI3, PCI4)
ISA expansion card connector (ISA1 and ISA2)

Microprocessor fan connector (J4M1)   Power input connector (POWER)
Chassis cooling fan connector (J8M1)
3.3-V power input connector (3.3)
Diskette drive interface connector (FLOPPY)
SCSI hard disk drive access indicator cable connector (J8J1)
Control panel connector (J8H1)
Primary EIDE channel connector (PRI IDE)
Secondary EIDE channel connector (SEC IDE)
DIMM sockets (BANK 0, BANK 1, BANK 2)
Accelerated graphics port connector (AGP)
Battery socket (B7C1)
Configuration jumper (J8A1)
Speaker (U8A1)

* For systems with on-board audio

In this subsection, you will learn about the most often used components of a motherboard, what they do, and where they are located on the motherboard. For each component, there will be a picture of what it looks like so that you can identify it on any motherboard you run across. Note, however, that this is just a brief introduction to the insides of a computer. The details of the various devices in the computer and their impact on computer service practices will be covered in later chapters.

Expansion Slots

The most visible part of any motherboard is the *expansion slots*. These look like small plastic "slots", usually anywhere from 3" to 11" long and approximately ½" wide. As their name suggests, they are used to install various devices in the computer to expand its capabilities. Some expansion devices that might be installed in these slots include video, network, sound, and disk interface cards.

If you look at the motherboard in your computer, you will more than likely see one of three main types of expansion slots:

- ISA
- PCI
- AGP

Each type differs in its appearance and function, which you learn more about in Chapter 5, "PC Bus Architectures." In this chapter we will cover how to visually identify the different expansion slots on the motherboard.

ISA Expansion Slots

If you have a computer made before 1997, chances are the motherboard in your computer has a few Industry Standard Architecture (ISA) slots. They're easily recognizable as they are usually brown and have two parts, a shorter part and a longer part. Computers made after 1997 generally include a few ISA slots for backward compatibility with old expansion cards.

VL-Bus, an expansion of ISA, was designed to provide 32-bit, processor direct capabilities to ISA. You will learn more about ISA and VL-Bus in Chapter 5, "PC Bus Architectures."

PCI Expansion Slots

Most computers made today contain primarily Peripheral Component Interconnect (PCI) slots. They are easily recognizable as they are short (around 3" long) and usually white. PCI slots can usually be found in any computer that has a Pentium-class processor or higher.

AGP Expansion Slots

Accelerated Graphics Port (AGP) slots are becoming more popular. In the past, if you wanted to use high speed, accelerated 3D graphics video cards, you had to install the card into an existing PCI or ISA slot. AGP slots were designed to be a direct connection between the video circuitry and the PC's memory. They are also easily recognizable because they are usually brown, located right next to the PCI slots on the motherboard and are shorter than the PCI slots. Figure 2.5 shows an example of an AGP slot, along with a PCI slot, for comparison. Notice the difference in length between the two.

FIGURE 2.5 An AGP slot compared to a PCI slot

You will learn more about the details of the various expansion bus types and the expansion cards that go in them in Chapter 5.

Memory Slots

Memory or random access memory (RAM) slots are the next most prolific slots on a motherboard, and they contain the actual memory chips. There are many and varied types of memory for PCs today. In this chapter, you will learn the appearance of the slots on the motherboard, so you can identify them. You will learn more about the details of the different types of PC memory in Chapter 3, "PC Memory Architecture."

For the most part, PCs today use memory chips arranged on a small circuit board. These circuit boards are called *Single Inline Memory Modules (SIMMs)* or *Dual Inline Memory Modules (DIMMs),* depending on if there are chips on one side of the circuit board or on both sides, respectively. Aside from the difference in chip placement, memory modules also differ on the number of conductors, or *pins*, that the particular memory module uses. Some common examples include 30-pin, 72-pin and168-pin (the latter two are most often DIMMs). Additionally, laptop memory comes in smaller form factors known as Small Outline DIMMs (SODIMMs). Figure 2.6 shows the popular form factors for the most popular memory chips. Notice how they basically look the same, but the memory module sizes are different.

FIGURE 2.6   Different memory module form factor

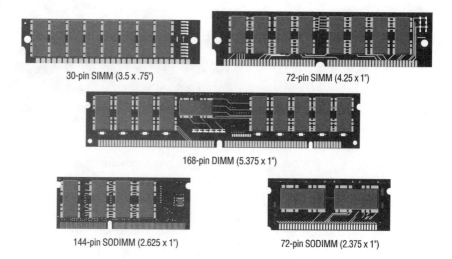

30-pin SIMM (3.5 x .75")

72-pin SIMM (4.25 x 1")

168-pin DIMM (5.375 x 1")

144-pin SODIMM (2.625 x 1")

72-pin SODIMM (2.375 x 1")

Memory slots are easy to identify on a motherboard. They are usually white, around 3" long, and placed very close together. The number of memory slots varies from motherboard to motherboard, but the appearance of the different slots is very similar. There are metal pins in the bottom to make contact with the soldered tabs on each memory module. There are also small metal or plastic tabs on each side of the slot that are used to keep the memory module securely in its slot.

Central Processing Unit (CPU) and Processor Slot

The "brain" of any computer is the *Central Processing Unit (CPU)*. This component does all of the calculations and performs 90 percent of all the functions of a computer. There are many different types of processors for computers. So many, in fact, that you will learn about them later in this chapter in "The CPU" section. Typically, in today's computers, the processor is the easiest component to identify on the motherboard. It is usually the component that has either a fan or a heat sink (or sometimes both) attached to it (as shown in Figure 2.7). These devices are used to draw away the heat a processor generates. This is done because heat is the enemy of microelectronics. Theoretically, a Pentium (or higher) processor generates enough heat that, without the heat sink, it would self-destruct in a matter of hours.

FIGURE 2.7   A processor with a fan and a processor with a heat sink

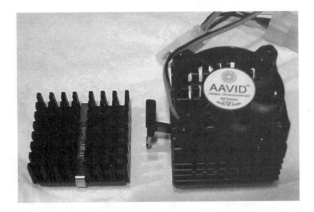

Sockets and slots on the motherboard are as plentiful and varied as processors. The three most popular are the Socket 5, Socket 7, and the Single Edge Contact Card (SECC). Socket 5 and Socket 7 CPU sockets are basically flat and have several rows of holes arranged in a square. The SECC connector is just another type of slot, but one that an Intel Pentium II or Pentium III–class processor can be inserted into (as shown in Figure 2.8). To illustrate which socket type is used for which processors, examine Table 2.1.

FIGURE 2.8   An SECC connector CPU socket

TABLE 2.1   Socket Types and the Processors They Support

Connector Type	Processor
Socket 1	486 SX/SX2, 486 DX/DX2, 486 DX4 OverDrive
Socket 2	486 SX/SX2, 486 DX/DX2, 486 DX4, OverDrive, 486 Pentium OverDrive
Socket 3	486 SX/SX2, 486 DX/DX2, 486 DX4, 486 Pentium OverDrive
Socket 4	Pentium 60/66, Pentium 60/66, OverDrive
Socket 5	Pentium 75-133, Pentium 75+ OverDrive
Socket 6*	DX4, 486 Pentium OverDrive
Socket 7	Pentium 75-200, Pentium 75+ OverDrive
Socket 8	Pentium Pro
SECC (Type I)	Pentium II
SECC (Type II	Pentium III

*Socket 6 was a paper standard only and was never actually implemented in any systems.

Power Connectors

In addition to these sockets and slots on the motherboard, there is a special connector (shown in Figure 2.9) that allows the motherboard to be connected to the power supply to receive power. Typically, there are either one or two plugs that connect into this motherboard connector. If there are two connectors, they are usually labeled P8 and P9 (as shown in Figure 2.10).

FIGURE 2.9 A power connector on a motherboard

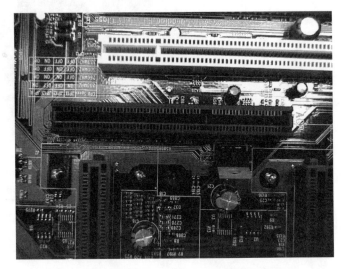

FIGURE 2.10 Power plugs that plug into the motherboard power connector

"On-Board" Floppy and Hard Disk Connectors

Almost every computer made today uses some type of disk drive to store data and programs until they are needed. You'll learn the exact details of how they work later in Chapter 4, "Disk System Architecture." Most drives need some kind of connection to the motherboard for the computer to "talk" to the disk drive. These connections are known as *drive interfaces* and there are two main types: *floppy drive interfaces* and *hard disk interfaces*. Floppy disk interfaces allow floppy disk drives to be connected to the motherboard and, similarly, hard disk interfaces do the same for hard disks. When you see them on the motherboard, these interfaces are said to be "on board," as opposed to being on an expansion card, known as "off board." The interfaces consist of circuitry and a port. Most motherboards produced today include both the floppy disk and hard disk interfaces on the motherboard.

The differences and compatibility between the different types of hard disk interfaces will be covered in Chapter 3, "PC Memory Architecture."

Keyboard Connectors

The most important input device for a PC is the keyboard. All PC motherboards contain a connector (as shown in Figure 2.11) that allows a keyboard to be connected directly to the motherboard through the case. There are two main types of keyboard connectors: AT and PS/2. The AT connector is round, about 1/2" in diameter, and has 5 sockets in the DIN-5 configuration.

FIGURE 2.11   An AT connector on a motherboard

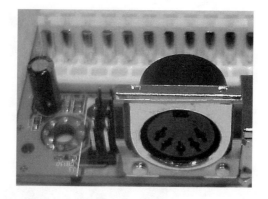

The second style, the PS/2 connector (as shown in Figure 2.12), is smaller and is more ubiquitous than the AT connector. Most new PCs that you can purchase today contain a PS/2 keyboard connector on the motherboard. Compare your PC's keyboard connector with Figures 2.11 and 2.12.

FIGURE 2.12 A PS/2 style keyboard connector on a motherboard

FIGURE 2.12 A PS/2 style keyboard connector on a motherboard

Peripheral Ports and Connectors

In order to be useful and have the most functionality, there must be a way of getting the data into and out of the computer. For this purpose, there are many different ports available. We will discuss the different types of ports and how they work later in Chapter 6, "Peripheral Devices." The four most common types of ports that you will see on a computer are the serial, parallel, Universal Serial Bus (USB), and game ports. Figure 2.13 shows an example of the two different types of *serial ports*: 9-pin and 25-pin. Figure 2.14 shows a typical *parallel port* (also called a printer port, because the most common peripheral connected to it is a printer). *Universal Serial Bus (USB)* ports look slightly different, as shown in Figure 2.15. Finally, Figure 2.16 shows an example of a *game port* (also called a *joystick port* because that's the most common device connected to it). Game ports are used to connect peripheral devices to the computer.

FIGURE 2.13 Typical 9-pin and 25-pin serial ports

FIGURE 2.14 A typical parallel port

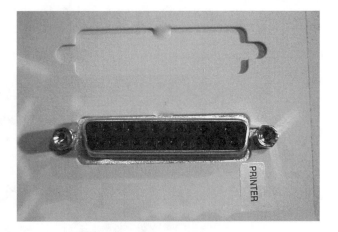

FIGURE 2.15 A typical Universal Serial Bus (USB) port

FIGURE 2.16 A typical game port

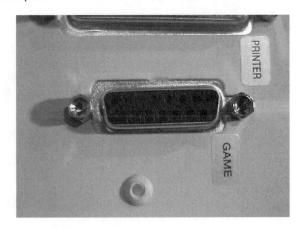

There are two ways of connecting these ports to the motherboard. The first, called a *dongle connection*, allows the ports to mounted into the computer's case with a special cable (called a *dongle*). The dongle for each port connects to the respective pins on the motherboard for that port (as shown in Figure 2.17).

FIGURE 2.17   Connecting a port to the motherboard with the dongle method

The second method of connecting a peripheral port is known as the *direct-solder method*. With this method the individual ports are soldered directly to the motherboard. This method is used mostly in integrated motherboards in non-clone machines. Figure 2.18 shows peripheral ports connected to a motherboard with the direct solder method. Notice how there is no cable between the port and the motherboard and that the port is part of the motherboard.

FIGURE 2.18   Peripheral ports directly soldered to a motherboard

BIOS Chip

Aside from the processor, the most important chip on the motherboard is the basic input/output system (BIOS) chip. This chip is a special memory chip that contains the BIOS software that tells the processor how to interact with the rest of the hardware in the computer. The BIOS chip is easily identified: if you have a "non-clone" computer (e.g. Compaq, IBM, HP, etc.), this chip will have the name of the manufacturer and usually the word *BIOS*. For example, the BIOS chip for a Compaq will say something like "Compaq BIOS" on it. For clones, the chip will usually have a sticker or printing on it from the three major BIOS manufacturers (AMI, Phoenix, and Award).

If you can't find the BIOS chip with these guidelines, look for a fairly large chip close to the CPU.

CMOS Battery

Your PC has to keep certain settings when it's turned off and its power cord unplugged. Some of these settings include:

- Date
- Time
- Hard drive configuration
- Memory

Your PC keeps these settings in a special memory chip called the Complimentary Metal-Oxide Semiconductor (CMOS) chip. Actually, CMOS (usually pronounced *see-moss*) is a type of memory chip. It is actually the parameter memory for the BIOS. But that doesn't translate into an easy-to-say acronym. So, because it's the most important CMOS chip in the computer, it has come to be called the CMOS.

To keep its settings, the memory has to have power constantly. When you shut off a computer, anything that is in main memory when you shut the computer off is lost forever. To prevent CMOS from losing its information (and it's rather important that it doesn't, actually), motherboard manufacturers include a small battery, called the *CMOS battery*, to power the CMOS memory. The battery makes comes in different shapes and sizes, but they all perform the same function.

Jumpers and DIP Switches

The last components of the motherboard we will discuss in this section are jumpers and DIP switches. These two devices are used to configure various hardware options on the motherboard. For example, some processors use different voltages (either 3.3 volts or 5 volts). You must set the motherboard to provide the correct voltage for the processor it is using. This is accomplished by changing a setting on the motherboard with either a jumper or a DIP switch. Figure 2.19 shows both a jumper set and a DIP switch. Motherboards will often have either several jumpers or one bank of DIP switches. Individual jumpers are often labeled with the moniker "JP*x*" (where *x* is the number of the jumper).

FIGURE 2.19   Jumpers and DIP switches

Jumper   "Rocker-type" DIP switch   "Slide-type" DIP switch

The CPU

Now that you've learned the basics of the motherboard, you need to learn about the most important component on the motherboard: the CPU.

The role of the CPU, or central processing unit, is to control and direct all the activities of the computer using both external and internal buses (see the subsection titled "The Bus" later in this topic). It is a processor chip consisting of an array of *millions* of transistors.

Older CPUs are generally square, with transistors arranged in a Pin Grid Array (PGA). Prior to 1981, chips were found in a rectangle with two rows of 20 pins known as a Dual Inline Package (DIP). See Figure 2.20. There are still integrated circuits that use the DIP form factor. However, the DIP form factor isn't used for PC CPUs anymore. Most CPUs use either the PGA or the SECC form factor (discussed earlier).

FIGURE 2.20   DIP and PGA

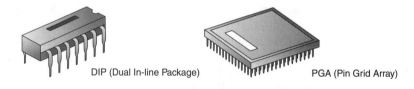

DIP (Dual In-line Package)   PGA (Pin Grid Array)

CPU Manufacturers

With the computer industry being as profitable as it is, there are many companies making CPUs for PCs today. The market leader in the manufacture of chips is Intel Corporation. Intel's competition includes Motorola, Advanced

Micro Devices (AMD), Cyrix, and IBM. When it first started making CPUs for the IBM PC, Intel shared its designs with other manufacturers, but with the introduction of the 80386 model in 1985, Intel ceased licensing its designs to other manufacturers.

Together, the Intel processors (and their compatibles) make up the bulk of the IBM-compatible personal computer processor market.

Intel Processors

When the first PC was introduced, IBM decided to go to the chip manufacturer Intel for a CPU. Since then, Intel has been the CPU supplier for almost all IBM-compatible computers.

The Intel family of PC processors started with the 8080, which found only limited use in the computer industry. The 8088 was rectangular, using a DIP array of its 40 pins. It originally ran at 4.77MHz with 29,000 transistors. It was used primarily in the IBM PC.

Next to be released was the 8086 (it was actually developed before the 8088) with a 16-bit external data bus; however, the processor used an 8-bit bus for compatibility with older systems.

After the 808*x* series came the 80*x*86 series, otherwise known simply as Intel's *x86 series*. The 80286 was the first to implement the PGA (Pin Grid Array) as described earlier in this section. It ran hotter than the 8088, with speeds from 6MHz to 20MHz. Both internal and external bus structures were 16 bits wide, and it could physically address up to 16MB of RAM.

80386

Intel introduced the 80386 in 1985. With 275,000 transistors, the 80386 represented a new generation for processors, because it was the first Intel *x*86 processor that used both a 32-bit data bus and a 32-bit address bus. The situation with the 386 was unique because up until this point Intel would license its technology to other manufacturers. As we mentioned earlier, with the 386 Intel decided to stop licensing. Not to be outdone, the other manufacturers like AMD and Cyrix came up with a chip they called the 386SX. This chip still operated internally at 32 bits (just like the full-blown 386) but had only a 16-bit external data path and a 16-bit address bus. In order to compete on the same ground, Intel then renamed its 386 to the 386DX and introduced its own version of the 386SX with similar specifications.

The 386SX had a 16-bit data path, while the 386DX had a 32-bit data path. Overall the 386 ranged in speed from 16MHz to 33MHz, used up to 4GB of memory (except the SX, which could only support 16MB of memory), supported multitasking, and was significantly faster than the 286.

80486

Intel introduced the 486DX in 1989. This processor boasted 1.25 million transistors, 32-bit internal and external data path, 32-bit address bus, an 8K on-chip cache, and an integrated math coprocessor. In 1991 Intel introduced the 486SX, as a cheaper version of the 486 processor. The only difference between the 486DX and the 486SX was that the internal math coprocessor is disabled on the SX. To add the math coprocessor to the chip, it was necessary to purchase a 487SX chip and insert it into the math coprocessor slot. Interestingly enough, this was basically a 486DX chip that, once installed, would simply disable the on-board 486SX chip and take over all processing functions from the SX chip. Figure 2.21 shows a 486 processor.

FIGURE 2.21 An Intel 486 processor

The 80486 operated at a maximum speed of 33MHz. To overcome this limitation, Intel came up with a technology known as *clock doubling*. This worked by allowing a chip to run at the bus's rated speed externally, but running the processor's *internal* clock at twice the speed of the bus. For example, they designed a chip that ran at 33MHz externally and 66MHz internally. This chip was known as the 486DX2.

Then someone came up with idea that if you can double the clock speed, why not triple it? And so you were handed the clock-tripled 486DX not long after the 486DX2 came into production. These chips were called DX4 chips (don't ask me why they used the number 4 to indicate a clock *tripled* chip; they just did).

The Pentium and Pentium Pro

Intel introduced the Pentium processor (Figure 2.22) in 1993. This processor has 3.1 million transistors using a 64-bit data path, 32-bit address bus, 16K on-chip cache, and comes in speeds from 60MHz to 200MHz. It is basically a combination of two 486DX chips in one larger chip. The benefit to this two-chips-in-one architecture is that each chip can execute instructions independently of the other. This is a form of *parallel processing* that Intel calls *superscalar*. Pentiums require special motherboards, because they run significantly hotter than previous processors. They also require the use of a heat sink on top of the processor to absorb and ventilate the heat. (The designers said that the processor would typically generate heat to the tune of 185° Fahrenheit!)

FIGURE 2.22   An Intel Pentium processor

Interestingly enough, when Intel first introduced the Pentium, it came in two versions: 60MHz and 66MHz. They were essentially the same chip; the only difference being that the 60MHz version didn't quite pass the 66MHz quality-control cut. Although they were not rated for 66MHz, the designers found that if they could slow them down a bit (to 60MHz), they ran just fine.

After the initial introduction of the Pentium came the Pentium Pro, designed to meet the needs of today's server. Released in 1995, it runs at speeds around 200MHz, in a 32-bit operating system environment using "dynamic execution." Dynamic execution performs out-of-order guesses to execute program codes.

Overdrive and MMX—The Need for Speed

Intel's 486 Overdrive processor was designed for 486 users who wanted to give their machines Pentium performance without having to pay the price for a full Pentium chip. Installing an Overdrive chip is simply a matter of replacing the existing CPU with the Overdrive CPU. Once installed, the Overdrive runs at approximately two and a half times the motherboard's bus speed. For example, if you have a motherboard with a bus speed of 33MHz, the Overdrive processor will run at approximately 83MHz. Of course, there are trade-offs to taking the Overdrive approach as opposed to making the step up to a conventional Pentium chip. First, Overdrive processors are only 32-bit processors, whereas Pentiums are completely 64-bit. Second, the Overdrive ran at least as hot as a conventional Pentium, so you had to make sure the system's ventilation could withstand the additional heat.

Another major change was the introduction of MMX technology. This version of the Pentium processor added three new features:

- It includes 57 new instructions for better video, audio, and graphic capabilities.

- It features Single Instruction Multiple Data (SIMD) technology, which enables one instruction to give instructions to several pieces of data rather than a single instruction per piece of data.
- Its cache was doubled to 32KB.

For more information on MMX technology, check out Intel's Web site, www.intel.com.

Pentium II

After the Pentium, the fastest Intel processor available was the Pentium II. The Pentium II was formerly code-named "Klamath" during its development. Speeds for this processor range from 233MHz to over 400MHz. It was introduced in 1997 amid much hoopla and some rather annoying commercials from Intel (remember the dancing clean-room technicians in their multicolored outfits?). It was designed to be a multimedia chip with special on-chip multimedia instructions and high-speed cache memory.

The most unique thing about the Pentium II compared to earlier Intel processors is that it uses a Single Edge Connector (SEC) to attach to the motherboard instead of the standard PGA package that was used with the earlier processor types. The processor is on a card that can be easily replaced. Simply shut off the computer, pull out the old processor card and insert a new one.

When released, the Pentium II was designed to be used by itself in a computer. For multiprocessor servers and workstations, Intel also released a separate processor, known as the Pentium II Xeon, based on the same Pentium II circuitry. Generally speaking, multiprocessor Pentium II servers with between four and eight processors use the Pentium II Xeon.

Celeron

When the Pentium II came out, consumers loved it. The only problem was that it was a bit too expensive for use in "low-buck" machines. To meet that market need, Intel came out with the Celeron processor. It had the computing power roughly equivalent to the Pentium II but cost less.

Pentium III

At the time this book is being written, the most current Intel processor is the Pentium III. It was released in 1999 and uses the same SECC connector as its predecessor, the Pentium II. It included 70 new instructions and was optimized for voice recognition and multimedia. Aside from faster speeds, one of the more significant features of the Pentium III was the processor serial number (PSN), a unique number electronically encoded into the processor. This number can be used to uniquely identify a system during Internet transactions. As you can imagine, Internet privacy advocates had a field day with this feature.

As with the Pentium II, the Pentium III has a multiprocessor Xeon version as well.

The Future of Intel Processors

Intel is constantly innovating. They always have at least two processors in development. These processors are given code names until the official marketing name is released. No one really knows all the features of an Intel processor until it's released (except, of course, Intel). Table 2.2 lists the code names of some of the upcoming processors in development as this book is being written.

TABLE 2.2 Upcoming Intel Processor Code Names and Descriptions

Code Name	Description
Merced	The next-generation Intel architecture. Expected in the 2000–2001 time frame, it introduces the 64-bit IA-64 instruction set jointly designed by Intel and HP, which runs *x*86 and PA-RISC software natively. Clock speeds are expected to go to 600MHz and beyond.
Willamette	Expected Late 2000–Early 2001.
Timna	Expected Late 2000–Early 2001.
Camino 2	Expected Late 2000–Early 2001.
Solano 2	Expected Late 2000–Early 2001.
Flagstaff	Expected in 2002, using two chips for the processor.

Summary of Intel Processors

Table 2.3 provides a summary of the history of the Intel processors. Table 2.4 shows the physical characteristics of Pentium (and higher) class processors.

TABLE 2.3 The Intel Family of Processors

Chip	Year Added	Data Bus Width (in bits)	Address Bus Width (in bits)	Speed (inMHz)	Transistors	Other Specifications
8080	1974	8	8	2	6,000	Used only in appliances

TABLE 2.3 The Intel Family of Processors *(continued)*

Chip	Year Added	Data Bus Width (in bits)	Address Bus Width (in bits)	Speed (inMHz)	Transistors	Other Specifications
8086	1978	16	20	5–10	29,000	Internal bus ran at 8 bits
8088	1979	8	20	4.77	29,000	
80286	1982	16	24	8–12	134,000	First to use PGA
386DX	1985	32	32	16–33	275,000	
386SX	1988	32	24	16–20	275,000	
486DX	1989	32	32	25–50	1.2 million	8KB of level 1 cache
486SX	1991	32	32	16–33	1.185 million	Math coprocessor disabled
487SX	1991	32	32	16–33	1.2 million	Math coprocessor for 486SX computers
486DX2	1991	32	32	33–66	2.0 million	
486DX4	1992	32	32	75–100	2.5 million	
Pentium	1993	32	64	60–200	3.3 million	Superscalar
Pentium Pro	1995	64	64	150–200	5.5 million	Dynamic execution
Pentium II	1997	64	64	233–450	7.5 million	32KB of level 1 cache, dynamic execution, and MMX technology

TABLE 2.3 The Intel Family of Processors *(continued)*

Chip	Year Added	Data Bus Width (in bits)	Address Bus Width (in bits)	Speed (inMHz)	Transistors	Other Specifications
Pentium II Xeon	1998	64	64	400–600	7.5 million	Multiprocessor version of Pentium II
Celeron	1999	64	64	400–600	7.5 million	"Value" version of Pentium II
Pentium III	1999	64	64	350–1000	9.5 million	
Pentium III Xeon	1999	64	64	350–1000	9.5 million	Multiprocessor version of Pentium III

TABLE 2.4 Physical Characteristics of Pentium-Class Processors

Processor	Speeds (MHz)	Socket	pins	Voltage	Cache
Pentium-P5	60–66	4	273	5V	16K
Pentium-P54C	75–200	5 or 7	320 or 321	3.3V	16K
Pentium-P55C	166–333	7	321	3.3V	32K
Pentium Pro	150–200	8	387	2.5V	32K
Pentium II	233–450	SECC	N/A	3.3V	32K
Pentium III	450–1130	SECCII	N/A	3.3V	32K

Intel "Clones" and Others

There are more than just Intel and Motorola processors out there. Among the so-called Intel "clones" were chips made by Advanced Micro Devices (AMD) and Cyrix. Table 2.5 shows some of the common processors made by AMD. Similarly, Table 2.6 shows some of the most popular Intel clone processors made by Cyrix.

TABLE 2.5 AMD Processors and Their Intel Equivalents

CPU	Clock Speed (MHz)	Intel Equivalent	Socket/Slot Type
Am486DX4-100	100	486DX4	Socket 5
Am486DX4-120	120	486DX4	Socket 5
Am5x86	75	Pentium Over-drive	Socket 5
K5 PR75	75	Pentium	Socket 5
K5 PR90	90	Pentium	Socket 5
K5 PR100	100	Pentium	Socket 5
K5 PR120	90	Pentium	Socket 5
K5 PR133	100	Pentium	Socket 5
K5 PR166	116.66	Pentium	Socket 5
K6-166	166	Pentium	Socket 7
K6-200	200	Pentium II	Socket 7
K6-233	233	Pentium II	Socket 7
K6-II	500-550	Pentium II	Socket 7
K6-III	400-450	Pentium II	Socket 7

TABLE 2.6 Cyrix Processors and Their Intel Equivalents

CPU	Clock Speed (MHz)	Intel Equivalent	Socket/Slot Type
6x86-PR120	100	Pentium	Socket 7
6x86-PR133	110	Pentium	Socket 7
6x86-PR150	120	Pentium	Socket 7
6x86-PR166	133	Pentium	Socket 7

TABLE 2.6 Cyrix Processors and Their Intel Equivalents *(continued)*

CPU	Clock Speed (MHz)	Intel Equivalent	Socket/Slot Type
6x86-PR200	150	Pentium	Socket 7
6x86MX-PR166	150	Pentium II	Socket 7
6x86MX-PR200	166	Pentium II	Socket 7
6x86MX-PR233	188	Pentium II	Socket 7

And Now for the Real World...

The surest way to determine which CPU your computer is using is to open the case and view the numbers stamped on the CPU. However, you may be able to get an idea without opening the case, because many manufacturers indicate the type of processor by using a model number that contains some combination of numbers for the processor type and speed. For example, a Whizbang 466 could be a 486 DX 66MHz computer. Similarly, a 75MHz Pentium computer might be labeled Whizbang 575.

Another way to determine a computer's CPU is to save your work, exit any open programs, and restart the computer. Watch closely as the computer returns to its normal state. You should see a notation that tells you what chip you are using. If you are using MS-DOS, you can also run Microsoft Diagnostics to view the processor type (that is, unless your computer has a Pentium, in which case it will report a very fast 486).

Processor Performance Issues

Don't forget, there's more to a chip than what meets the eye. There are several factors that affect the performance of a processor. Among them are availability of a math coprocessor, clock speed, internal cache memory, and supporting circuitry.

Math Coprocessor

The math coprocessor is used to improve the processor's number-crunching speed. It does not, however, increase the speed of simple additions and subtractions. What it does is increase the speed of calculations that involve floating decimal point operations (such as calculations for algebra and statistics). Since the introduction of the 486, the math coprocessor has been built into the processor. CPU models that preceded the 486 can add a math coprocessor as an option. (There is a special slot for it next to the CPU.)

Clock Speed

The clock speed is the frequency with which a processor executes instructions. This frequency is measured in millions of cycles per second, or megahertz (MHz). There is actually a "clock" of sorts within the CPU. This clock signal is generated by a quartz crystal, which vibrates as electricity passes through it, thereby generating a steady pulse to every component synchronized with the signal. A system cycle is generated by this pulse (called a clock "tick"), which sends a signal through the processor telling it to perform another operation. To transfer data to and from memory, an 8086 computer needed four cycles plus "wait states." Wait states allow the processor to wait for the slower speed RAM that was used in 8086-based computers. Generally speaking, the higher the MHz value, the faster the PC will be.

Cache memory

Cache memory is a storage area for frequently used data and instructions. It requires a small amount of physical RAM that can keep up with the processor. It uses this RAM for storage. The processor contains an internal cache controller that integrates the cache with the CPU. The controller stores frequently accessed RAM locations to provide faster execution of data and instructions. This type of cache is known as a *Level 1 Cache*. It is also possible to have a cache external to the CPU, called a *Level 2 Cache*. This type of cache performs the same functions as a Level 1 Cache and can speed up the perceived performance. Basically, a larger cache leads to the perception of a faster CPU.

The Bus

Finally, the processor's ability to communicate with the rest of the system's components relies on the supporting circuitry. The system board's underlying circuitry is called the bus. Although this is not the bus used to get to the mall or the football game, the idea is similar: the computer's bus moves information into and out of the processor and other devices. A bus allows all devices to communicate with each other. The bus consists of several components, including the external bus, the data bus, and the address bus.

The External Bus (System Bus)

The external bus is also referred to as the *system bus* or *expansion bus*. The expansion bus is a bus system that allows the processor to talk to another device. It is known as an external bus system because it is outside of the processor. The devices are connected through expansion cards and slots. (An expansion card is a removable circuit board that expands the capability of the computer.) We will cover bus types in more detail in Chapter 5, "PC Bus Architectures."

The Data Bus

The data bus is used to send and receive data. The larger the bus width, the more data that can be transmitted (and, therefore, the faster the bus).

> The data bus and address bus are independent of each other, but for better performance larger data buses require larger address buses. The data bus width indicates how much data the chip can move through at one time, and the size of the address bus indicates how much memory a chip can handle.

Data in a computer is transferred digitally. A single wire carries 5 volts to indicate a 1 data bit or carries zero volts to indicate a 0 data bit. Remember, computers use the binary system to transmit information. The greater number of wires allows more bits to be transmitted at the same time. For example, a 16-bit data bus width has 16 wires to transmit data, and a 32-bit data chip can transmit twice the amount of data as a 16-bit chip. A good comparison would be to the highway system. A single lane for traffic allows only one car through at a time whereas two lanes allow twice the amount of traffic to pass through at one time.

Be careful not to assume that data flows at the same speed within the processor as it does outside of the processor. Some Intel processors have an internal data bus that is greater than the external data bus. The 8088 and 80386SX are good examples of this. They are designed with an internal bus that has twice the width of the external bus. This provides for backward compatibility with other processors that do not support a wider bus.

The Address Bus

The address bus also contains a set of wires to carry information in and out of the processor, but the information the address bus sends is addressing information used to describe memory locations. This location is used for data being sent or retrieved. The address bus carries a single bit of information, representing a digit in the address, along each wire. The size of the address bus corresponds to the number of address locations. The larger the address bus, the more memory address locations that can be supported. The more memory address locations a processor can address, the more RAM a processor can use.

As an analogy, we can compare the address bus to the address of a house or its house number. If the house numbers for a street were limited to two digits, then the street could have only 100 addresses (00 to 99). For an address bus, which communicates in binary language, a limit of two digits would give four addresses (00, 01, 10, and 11). Thus, the larger the address bus, the more combinations of 0 and 1 that would be permitted to pass through at one time. Take a look back to Table 2.3. A 286 processor has a 24-bit address bus width. Using binary theory, this translates to a little over 16 million locations, which means it allows access to as much as 16MB of RAM. Using similar calculations, a 386DX with a 32-bit address bus will allow access up to 4GB of RAM.

For more information on bus types, see Chapter 5, "PC Bus Architecture."

Bus Speed

Motherboards are designed to be more or less universal. They have a processor socket or slot that can support many different processor types and speeds. The speed at which a processor can run is set via jumper, as is the speed at which the expansion bus transfers data to and from the processor. The speed of the bus and the speed of the processor are directly related.

When installing a processor into a motherboard, you must set both the processor speed and bus speed with a jumper. Typically, the bus speed is set to 66MHz, 100MHz, or 133MHz plus a multiplier. For example, when you have a 450 MHz processor, you would set the processor speed jumper to 450MHz, the expansion bus speed to 100MHz, and the multiplier to 4.5 (4.5 × 100MHz = 450MHz). Processors below 200MHz generally set their speeds without a multiplier.

Some motherboards have either processor speed jumpers or bus speed/multiplier jumpers, or both. To see which your motherboard uses, check the documentation that comes with your motherboard.

The BIOS

BIOS stands for Basic Input/Output System. The BIOS communicates between the computer and devices. The BIOS is usually stored in ROM. It was created by IBM to act as a translator to run the same operating systems on different hardware platforms. When the operating system needs to access a piece of hardware, it would now ask the BIOS, rather than just taking control of the hardware. The use of BIOS prevented programs from fighting over hardware. As long as the operating system (such as DOS) uses the BIOS for its hardware requests, it can run on different hardware platforms. The BIOS creates a standard reference point for many different types of hardware.

There are three major companies that manufacture ROM BIOS software:

Phoenix Technologies   Phoenix Technologies was the pioneer who developed BIOS in the first place. Their BIOS software supports user-defined hard drive types and 1.44MB floppy disk drives.

American Megatrends International (AMI)   AMI BIOS has been very popular. AMI not only added a more extensive diagnostic program, but, more than that, AMI produced its own system board. This provided guaranteed reliability between BIOS and computer.

Award Software   Award Software is the next largest manufacturer of BIOS software. Award took its production one step further by allowing other companies that purchase their BIOS to make modifications as needed to the software.

In 1998, Award and Phoenix Technologies merged. The new company is Phoenix Technologies. The new company will provide technical support for older products from both companies as well as produce new BIOS software.

For more information on the three ROM BIOS manufacturers, check out their Web sites: Phoenix Technologies at www.ptltd.com, AMI at www.megatrends.com, and Award Software at www.award.com.

Hardware vendors sometimes will want to include new types of hardware that the processor was never designed to talk to. In that case, a "BIOS upgrade" may have to be performed. A BIOS upgrade is the process by which the BIOS software is upgraded to a newer version. There are two ways of doing this: a PROM upgrade or by "flashing" the EEPROM. Upgrading the PROM is as simple as removing the BIOS chip on the motherboard (while the computer is off, of course) and replacing it with a new BIOS chip that contains the new version of the BIOS. "Flashing" the BIOS involves using a special piece of software to upload the new BIOS software to the BIOS EEPROM. This software can be downloaded from the BIOS manufacturer or ordered through the mail. Once the "flashing" is complete, the computer is rebooted and the new BIOS is functional.

NEVER TURN OFF A COMPUTER DURING A BIOS "flash" UPGRADE! The computer won't come back up because it doesn't have the software to boot itself. Wait for the "flash" to complete, then reboot the computer (many times the software used to "flash" the BIOS EEPROM will do this for you automatically).

Memory

"**M**ore memory, more memory, I don't have enough memory!" Today, memory seems to be one of the most popular, easy, and inexpensive ways to upgrade a computer. As the computer's CPU works, it stores information in the computer's memory. The rule of thumb is, the more memory a computer has, the faster it will operate. In this brief section I'll outline the four major types of computer memory. (Memory will also be covered in more detail in Chapter 3, "PC Memory Architecture.")

DRAM DRAM is dynamic random access memory. This is actually the "RAM" that most people are talking about when they mention RAM. When you expand the memory in a computer, you are adding DRAM chips. The reason you use DRAM to expand the memory in the computer is because it's cheaper than any other type of memory. Dynamic RAM chips are cheaper to manufacture than other types because they are less complex. "Dynamic" refers to the chips' need for a constant update signal (also called a "refresh" signal) in order to keep the information that is written there.

SRAM The "S" in SRAM stands for static. Static random access memory doesn't require the refresh signal that DRAM does. The chips are more complex and are thus more expensive. However, they are faster. DRAM access times come in at 80 nanoseconds (ns) or more; SRAM has access times of 15 to 20 ns. SRAM is often used for cache memory.

ROM ROM stands for read-only memory. It is called read-only because it can't be written to. Once the information has been written to the ROM, it can't be changed. ROM is normally used to store the computer's BIOS, because this information normally does not change. The system ROM in the original IBM PC contained the Power-On Self Test (POST), basic input-output system (BIOS), and cassette BASIC. Later IBM computers and compatibles include everything but the cassette BASIC. The system ROM enables the computer to "pull itself up by its bootstraps," or "boot" (start the operating system).

CMOS CMOS is a special kind of memory that holds the BIOS configuration settings. CMOS memory is powered by a small battery so the settings are retained when the computer is shut off. The BIOS will read information like which hard drive types are configured for this computer to use and which drive(s) it should search for boot sectors and so on. CMOS memory is usually NOT upgradable.

Storage

What good is a computer without a place to put everything? Storage media hold the data being accessed, as well as the files the system needs to operate, and data that needs to be saved. When everything is done and information needs to be stored, where should it be kept? The many different types of storage differ in terms of their capacity (how much they can store), access time (how fast the computer can access the information), and the physical type of media being used.

Hard Disk Systems

For permanent storage and quick access, the hard disk systems are used (Figure 2.23). Hard disks reside inside the computer and can hold more information than other forms of storage. The hard disk system contains three critical components: the controller, the hard disk, and the host adapter. The controller controls the drive. It understands how the drive operates, sends signals to the various motors in the disk, and receives signals from the sensors inside the drive. The drive is the physical storage medium. Hard disk systems store information on small disks (between three and five inches in diameter) stacked together and placed in an enclosure. Finally, the host adapter is the translator, converting signals from the hard drive and controller to signals the computer can understand. Some hard disk technologies incorporate the controller and drive into one enclosure. (For more information on disk types, see Chapter 4, "Disk System Architecture.")

FIGURE 2.23   A hard disk system

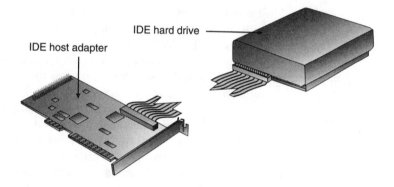

Floppy Drives

A floppy disk drive is a magnetic storage medium that uses a floppy diskette made of a thin plastic encased in a protective casing. The floppy disk itself (or "floppy," as it is often called) enables the information to be transported from one computer to another very easily. The down side of a floppy disk drive is its limited storage capacity. Whereas a hard drive can store hundreds of megabytes of information, most floppy disks were designed to store only in the vicinity of one megabyte. Table 2.7 shows the five different floppy disk drives that you may run into, with five corresponding diskette sizes supported in PC systems. (Note that the drives that offer anything less than 1.2MB are increasingly rare, as most computers today do not carry the 5 ¼" size.)

TABLE 2.7 Floppy Diskette Capacities

Floppy Drive Size	Number of Tracks	Capacity
5¼"	40	360KB
5¼"	80	1.2MB
3½"	80	720KB
3½"	80	1.44MB
3½"	80	2.88MB

CD-ROM Drives

Most computers today have a CD-ROM drive. CD-ROM stands for Compact Disk Read-Only Memory. The compact disk is virtually the same as those used in CD players. The CD-ROM is used to store data for long-term storage. CD-ROMs are read-only, meaning that once information is written to a CD, it can't be erased or changed. Also, the time it takes to access the information is a lot slower than it takes to access data residing on a hard drive. Why, then, is it so popular? Mainly because it makes a great software distribution medium. Programs are always getting larger and larger, and are requiring more and more disks to install them. So, instead of installing a program using 100 floppy disks (a real possibility, believe me), you can use a single CD, which can hold approximately 650 megabytes. (A second reason they are so popular is that CD-ROMs have been standardized across platforms, with the ISO 9660 standard.)

DVD-ROM Drives

A new type of drive is finding its way into computers: the DVD-ROM drive. You have probably heard of DVD (Digital Versatile Disk) technology in use in many home theater systems. A DVD-ROM drive is basically the same as the DVD player's drive in your home theater system. To that end, a computer equipped with a DVD-ROM drive and the proper video card can play back DVD movies on the monitor. However, in a computer, a DVD-ROM drive is much more useful. Because DVD-ROMs use slightly different technology than CD-ROMs, they can store up to 1.6GB of data. This makes them better choices for distributing large software bundles. Many software packages today are so huge they take multiple CD-ROMs to hold all the installation and reference files. A single DVD-ROM, in a double-sided, double-layered configuration, can hold as much as 17GB (as much as 26 regular CD-ROMs).

Other Storage Media

There are many additional types of storage available for PCs today. However, most of them are not covered on the A+ exam, so we'll just discuss them briefly here. Among the other types of storage are Zip drives, tape backup devices, and optical drives.

Zip Drives and Jaz Drives

Iomega's Zip and Jaz drives are detachable, external hard disks that are used to store a large volume (around 100MB for the Zip, 1 and 2GB for the Jaz) of data on a single, floppy-sized disk. The drives connect to either a parallel port or a special interface card. The major use of Zip and Jaz drives is for transporting large amounts of data from place to place. This used to be accomplished with several floppies.

Tape Backup Devices

Another form of storage device is the tape backup. Tape backup devices can be installed internally or externally and use a magnetic tape medium instead of disks for storage. They hold much more data than any other medium, but are also much slower. They are primarily used for archival storage. With hard disks, it's not "if they fail," it's "when they fail." So, you must back up the information onto some other storage medium. Tape backup devices are the most common choice in larger enterprises and networks, because they can hold the most data and are the most reliable over the long term.

Optical Drives

The final type of storage is the optical drive. Optical drives work by using a laser rather than magnetism to change the characteristics of the storage medium (typically an aluminum-coated plastic disk). Optical drives look similar to and are used for the same applications as Zip drives (e.g. archival storage and large file transport). However, optical drives can store more information and have slower access times than Zip drives.

Input/Output

Putting information into the computer involves more than just turning it on. You need a keyboard, mouse, or some other type of input device. Output devices take data from the computer and translate it to some other usable form. An A+ technician must be able to troubleshoot and fix problems with these types of devices.

Input Devices

The most important device of any computer system is the keyboard. In fact, on Macintosh systems, if a keyboard is not hooked up the computer will not start. Actually, on any computer if a keyboard is not attached, there isn't a whole lot one can do with the computer. (It can be used as a good doorstop.) On computers that do run without a keyboard (i.e., most PCs), if the keyboard is missing an error message will occur at startup (usually a "301—Keyboard Missing" error). It is the basic component used to enter information or data to the processor and storage device, so it's very important to have it connected. A standard 101-key keyboard has four separate areas:

Standard alphanumeric keys   These include the large or separately located Shift, Backspace, Tab, Enter, and Caps Lock keys.

Function keys   These are placed horizontally along the top of the keyboard, with the Escape key in the top left corner.

Numeric keypad   This set of keys has been separated to the right of the typing, cursor, and screen controls. This allows a user who is familiar with a calculator to perform with the same accuracy and speed.

Cursor and screen controls   These have also been separated, and include the Home, End, Page Up, Page Down, and Insert and Home keys. The directional keys are placed below the Home, End, Page Up, and Page Down keys.

Another device involved in the input of data is the *mouse* (or, generically, the *pointer device*, since many people use trackballs or touch pads instead of mice). The mouse changes the position of a pointer on the screen relative to the position of the mouse. It is used to select menu options and other items within Graphical User Interfaces (GUIs).

Other input devices include digitizing tablets, light pens, and touch screens. *Digitizing tablets* are most often used by artists and draftspersons. They comprise a flat "drawing" pad and a pen or plotter that interacts with electronic sensors in the pad. As the user moves the pen or plotter over the pad, the position of the pen or plotter is communicated to the computer. *Light pens* are an interactive pointing device. Attached to the computer, light pens have a photodetector in the tip that tracks the phosphors that blink on the screen. Pressing the light pen to the screen is the same as clicking a mouse button. *Touch screens* are probably the most prevalent of the non-keyboard/non-mouse input devices. They can be seen anywhere from the gift registry at the local department store to the information kiosks in shopping malls.

Output Devices

An output device gives the user a means to receive reports, communications, or the results of calculations. The most common output devices are printers, modems, and of course display systems (monitors). These devices are connected to ports in the back of the computer. The ports are either a parallel port with a standard female DB-25 connector or a serial port with a standard male DB-9 connector.

Printers

A printer is a device that converts signals from the computer into paper documents. Most printers are electromechanical devices that put either ink or toner on the paper to form the images. There are three main types of printers: dot-matrix, ink-jet, and laser.

Dot-Matrix Printers

Dot-matrix printers are the oldest type of printer, as well as the simplest. This type of printer uses an array of pins to strike an inked ribbon, which in turn makes a pattern of dots on the paper. The patterns of dots ultimately form letters and images. Dot-matrix printers are easy to use as well as very inexpensive. However, they are relatively slow and very noisy (as anyone who has tried to talk on the phone while using one can attest). The best dot-matrix printers are only "near letter quality" (letter quality is the quality found with a typewriter). They are still in use because they are the only printer that can print on carbon copy forms (invoices, receipts, etc.). Because the pins on dot-matrix printers actually strike the paper, they can make simultaneous copies when used with pressure-sensitive forms or carbon paper.

Ink-Jet Printers

Ink-jet printers spray the ink on the page instead of using an inked ribbon. The major advantages of ink-jet printers are their low cost, increased image quality, and ability to use colored ink and a variety of paper styles and sizes. However, they aren't very fast (though admittedly they are faster than dot-matrix), and the ink needs to be replaced as it runs out, which is often. Additionally, if the printer is not used for a long time, the ink can dry out, making the printer unusable until the ink is replaced. For these reasons, they are widely used with home computers and are not often found in offices.

Laser Printers

The laser printer is the most sophisticated type of printer. A laser jet printer uses lasers, electric charges, and toner (a black carbon substance similar to the lead in a pencil) to create images on paper. Laser printers have the highest image quality and speed when compared to dot-matrix and ink-jet printers. They can print at a speed of several pages per minute, which is similar to the speed of photocopiers. Laser printers are more expensive than the other types of printers. They take up more space, and their consumables (like toner) are more expensive than those used by other types of printers. However, they are very popular in offices where high capacity and quality are priorities.

For more information on printers, see Chapter 7, "How Printers Work."

Display Systems

Another important tool to use with computer systems is the monitor. It would be a little difficult to perform a calculation without being able to see the result; indeed, it's useful just to see what was input.

The first display systems were nothing more than fancy black-and-white TV monitors called CRTs (Cathode Ray Tubes). These displays were usually run from a video adapter that could also be connected to a television set. As computer technology developed, the demand for high-quality displays also developed. Soon after, technologies such as VGA, EGA, CGA, and XGA were developed and far outpaced the former CRT technology. However, each of these technologies uses some of the same concepts as the original CRT.

At the time of the writing of this book, the newest computer display technologies are liquid crystal displays (LCD). LCDs are basically the same displays being used on laptop computers, redesigned for use with desktop computers.

Modems

Modems (MODulator/DEModulators) are the devices that computers use to talk to one another over phone lines. They can be considered a type of output device because they move data out of the computer to another device. Modems work by converting digital signals (binary 1s and 0s) into analog signals (tones over a phone line), and vice versa. Modems are added to a computer either as an external device or as an expansion card installed inside the computer. Internal modems are usually less expensive than external modems, but external modems are easier to troubleshoot than internal modems because you can see the lights that indicate what is happening. For more information on modems, see Chapter 6, "Peripheral Devices."

Interfaces

Computers need ways of exchanging information with printers and other devices. These ways are called *interfaces*. There are two major types of interfaces available on computers today: parallel and serial. They differ primarily in the speed of transfer and method of connection. Let's examine each of these interfaces in detail.

Parallel Interface

The most popular type of interface available on computers today is the parallel interface. Parallel communications take the "interstate approach" to data communications. Everyone knows that interstate travel is faster, normally. This is mainly because you can fit multiple cars going the same direction on the same highway by using multiple lanes. On the return trip, you take a similar path, but on a completely separate road. The *parallel interface* (an example of one is shown in Figure 2.20) transfers data eight bits at a time over eight separate transmit wires inside a parallel cable (one bit per wire). Normal parallel interfaces use a DB-25 female connector on the computer to transfer data to peripherals.

The most common use of the parallel interface is printer communication, and there are three major types: standard, bidirectional, and enhanced parallel ports. Let's look at the differences between the three.

"Standard" Parallel Ports

The "standard" parallel port is a parallel port that only transmits data OUT of the computer. It cannot receive data (except for a single wire carrying a "Ready" signal). This is the parallel port that came with the original IBM PC, XT, and AT. This port can transmit data at 150KB/second and is commonly used to transmit data to printers. This technology also has a maximum transmission distance of 10 feet.

Bidirectional Parallel Ports

As its name suggests, the bidirectional parallel port has one important advantage over standard parallel ports: it can both transmit and receive data. These parallel ports are capable of interfacing with devices like external CD-ROM drives and external parallel port backup drives (Zip, Jaz, and tape drives). Most computers made since 1994 have a bidirectional parallel port.

Enhanced Parallel Ports

As more and more people started using their parallel ports for interfacing with devices other than printers, they started to notice that the speed wasn't good enough. Double-speed CD-ROM drives had a transfer rate of 300KBps, but the parallel port could only transfer data at 150KBps, thus limiting the speed a computer could retrieve data from an external device. To solve that problem, the Institute of Electrical and Electronics Engineers (IEEE) came up with a standard for enhanced parallel ports, called IEEE 1284. The 1284 standard provided for greater data transfer speeds and the ability to send memory addresses as well as data through a parallel port. This allowed the parallel port to theoretically act as an extension to the main bus. In addition, these ports would be backward compatible with the "standard" and bidirectional ports.

There are two implementations of IEEE 1284, ECP parallel ports and EPP parallel ports. An *Enhanced Capabilities Port* (ECP port) was designed to transfer data at high speeds to printers. It uses a DMA channel and a buffer to increase printing performance. An *Enhanced Parallel Port* (EPP port) increases bi-directional throughput from 150KBps to anywhere from 600KBps to 1.5MBps.

Serial Interface

If parallel communications are similar to taking the interstate, then serial communications are similar to taking a country road. In serial communications, each bit of data is sent one after another (single file, if you will) down one wire, and returns on a different wire in the same cable. There are three main types of serial interfaces available today: Standard serial, Universal Serial Bus (USB), and FireWire.

Standard Serial

Almost every computer made since the original IBM PC has at least one serial port. They are easily identified because they have either a DB-9 male (shown in Figure 2.24) or DB-25 male port. Standard serial ports have a maximum data transmission speed of 57KBps and a maximum cable length of 50 feet.

FIGURE 2.24   A standard DB-9 male serial port

Universal Serial Bus (USB)

Most computers built after 1997 have one or two flat ports in place of one DB-9 serial port. These ports are Universal Serial Bus (USB) ports and they are used for connecting multiple (up to 127) peripherals to one computer through a single port (and use of multi-port peripheral "hubs"). USB supports data transfer rates as high as 1.5MBps. Additionally, USB cables can be a maximum length of 5 meters.

Because of it's higher transfer rate, flexibility, and ease of use, most devices that, in the past, used serial interfaces, now come with USB interfaces. It's rare to see a newly introduced PC accessory with a standard serial interface cable. For example, PC cameras (like the Logitech QuickCam) used to come as standard serial-only interfaces. Now you can only buy them in the stores with USB interfaces.

IEEE 1394 (FireWire)

Recently, one port has been slowly creeping into the mainstream and is starting to be seen more and more on desktop PCs. That port is the IEEE 1394 port (shown in Figure 2.25), more commonly known as a *FireWire* port. Its popularity is due to its ease of use and very high (400MBps) transmission rates. Originally developed by Apple, it was standardized by IEEE in 1995 to be IEEE 1394. It is most often used as a way to get Digital Video into a PC so it can be edited with digital video editing tools. At the time of the writing of this book, many of the Apple iMac models include a FireWire port. Additionally, you can see it on many PCs and laptops.

FIGURE 2.25   A FireWire port on a PC

Power Systems

The computer's components would not be able to operate without power. The device in the computer that provides this power is the power supply (Figure 2.26). A power supply converts 110 volt AC current into the four voltages that a computer needs to operate. These are +5 volts DC, –5 volts DC (ground), +12 volts DC, and –12 volts DC (ground). By the way, you may frequently see "volts DC" abbreviated as "VDC."

Power supplies contain transformers and capacitors that carry LETHAL amounts of current. They are not meant to be serviced. DO NOT attempt to open them or do any work on them.

FIGURE 2.26 A power supply

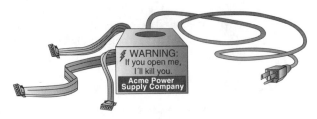

WARNING:
If you open me,
I'll kill you.
**Acme Power
Supply Company**

Power Supply Connectors

A power supply has three types of connectors used to power the various devices within the computer (Figure 2.27). Each has a different appearance and way of connecting to the device. Additionally, each type is used for a specific purpose.

FIGURE 2.27 Standard power supply power connectors

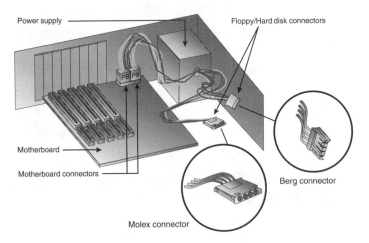

Power supply

Floppy/Hard disk connectors

P8 P9

Motherboard

Motherboard connectors

Molex connector

Berg connector

Floppy Drive Power Connectors

The first type are called *floppy drive power connectors* because they are most commonly used to power floppy disk drives. This type of connector is smaller and flatter (as shown in Figure 2.28) than any of the other types of power connectors. These connectors are also called *Berg connectors*.

FIGURE 2.28 Floppy drive power connectors

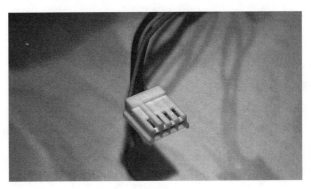

System Connectors

The next type of power connector is called the *system connector*. There are only two of these, labeled P8 and P9 (shown in Figure 2.29). They connect to the motherboard and deliver the power that feeds the electronic components on it. These connectors have small tabs on them that interlock with tabs on the power connector on the motherboard. If there are two connectors, you must install them in the correct fashion. To do this (on most systems) place the connectors side by side with their black wires together, and then push the connectors onto the receptacle on the motherboard.

While it's easy to remove this type of connector from the motherboard, the tabs on the connector make it difficult to reinstall it. Here's a hint: Place the connector at a right angle to the motherboard's connector, interlocking the tabs in their correct positions. Then tilt the connector to the vertical position. The connector will slide into place very easily.

FIGURE 2.29 Power supply system board connectors

Standard Peripheral Power Connector

The last type of connector is the *standard peripheral power connector*. This type of connector is usually used to power different types of internal disk drives. This type of connector is also called a *Molex* connector.

Specialized Power Devices

Unfortunately, it's rare for the power that comes out of the wall (what we normally call *line power*) to be consistently 110V, 60Hz. It may be of a slightly higher or lower voltage, it may cycle faster or slower, there may occasionally no power, or the worst, a 5000V spike may come down the power line from a lightning strike and fry the expensive electronic components of your computer and its peripherals.

There are three main classes of power problems that technicians have to deal with: power quality problems, problems where too much power is coming out of the wall, and problems where there is not enough. Almost every outlet has at least one of these problems. Let's examine each of these problems in detail.

Power Quality Problems and Solutions

The first type of power problem exists when the power coming out of the wall has a different frequency than normal (60Hz is considered "normal"). This type of problem manifests itself when stray electromagnetic signals get introduced into the line. This interference is called electromagnetic interference (EMI) and is usually caused by the electromagnetic waves emitted by the electric motors in appliances. Additionally, televisions and other electronic devices (including the computers themselves) can produce a different type of interference, called radio frequency interference (RFI), which is really just a higher-frequency version of EMI. However, RFI is produced by ICs and other electronic devices. If your power lines run near a powerful radio broadcast antenna or factory, they can both introduce noise into your power.

To solve these problems, companies like BEST Power Systems and APC make accessories called *line conditioners*. The function of these devices is to produce "perfect" power of 110V/60Hz. These devices will remove most of the stray EMI and RFI signals from the incoming power. They will also reduce any power overages down to 110V.

Power Overage Problems and Solutions

The most common type of power problem that causes computer damage is power overages. As the name suggests, these problems happen when too much power comes down the power lines. There are two main types of overage problems: spikes and surges. The primary difference between the two is the length of time the events last. A *spike* is a power overage condition that exists for an extremely short period of time (a few milliseconds at the most). *Surges*, on the other hand, last for much longer (up to several seconds). Spikes are usually the result of faulty power transformer equipment at power substations. Surges can come from both power equipment and lightning strikes.

A common misconception is that a power strip can protect your computer from power overage problems. Most power strips (the ones that cost less than $15.00) are nothing more than multiple outlets with a circuit breaker. There are real "surge protectors," but they usually cost upwards of $25.00. These devices have MOSFET semiconductors that sacrifice themselves in the case of a power overage. But even these aren't perfect. They are rated in terms of clamping speed (how long it takes to go from the overvoltage to zero volts) and clamping voltage (at what voltage the MOSFET shorts out). The problem is that by the time the clamping voltage is reached, some of the overvoltage has gotten through to the power supply and damaged it. After a time, the power supply will be damaged permanently.

Realistically, having a "surge protector" is better than not having one, but not by much. It's better to use a line conditioner that can absorb the overvoltage than to use a circuit breaker.

Undervoltage Power Problems and Solutions

Undervoltage problems don't cause damage to hardware, usually. More often, they cause the computer to shut down completely (or at the very least, to reboot), thus losing any unsaved data in memory. There are three major types of undervoltage problems: sags, brownouts, and blackouts.

A sag is a momentary drop in voltage, lasting only a few milliseconds. Usually, you can't even tell one has occurred. Your house lights won't dim or flicker (well, actually they will, but it's too fast for you to notice). But your computer will react strangely to this sudden drop in power. Have you ever been on the "up" side of a seesaw and had someone jump off the other end? You were surprised at the sudden drop, weren't you? Your computer will experience the same kind of disorientation when the power drops immediately to a lower voltage. A computer's normal response to this kind of "disorientation" is to reboot itself.

You've probably experienced one of the other two power undervoltage problems: brownouts and blackouts. A *brownout* occurs when voltage drops below 110 volts for a second or more. Brownouts are typically caused by an immediate increase in power consumption in your area and the lag time it takes for your power provider to respond by increasing production. You might notice when brownouts occur, because the lights in your home will dim, but not go out, then go back to full brightness a second or two later. You might also notice because your computer will reboot or the screen will flicker. (While writing this section, I have counted two brownouts. Luckily, my computer hasn't rebooted, so the voltage drop probably wasn't too bad.)

Everyone has experienced a blackout. A *blackout* occurs when the power drops from 110 volts to zero volts in a very short period of time. It is a complete loss of power for anywhere from a few seconds to several minutes. They are typically caused by a power failure somewhere in your area. Sometimes there are backup systems available, but it may take anywhere from a couple of seconds to several hours to get power available in your area again.

There are two different hardware solutions to power undervoltage conditions: the SPS and the UPS. They each take a different approach to keeping the power at 110V. In both cases you plug the units into the wall, then plug your computer equipment into the SPS or UPS. Let's look at the SPS first. SPS stands for *standby power supply*. It's called that because there is a battery waiting to take over power production in case of a loss of line voltage. The SPS contains sensors that constantly monitor the line voltage and a battery with a step-up transformer. While conditions are normal, the line voltage charges the internal battery. When the line voltage drops below a preset threshold (also called the *cutover* threshold—i.e., 105V), the sensors detect that and switch the power from the wall to the internal battery. When the power comes back above the threshold, the sensors detect the restoration of power and switch the power source back to the line voltage.

The main problem with SPSs is that they take a few milliseconds to switch to the battery. During those few milliseconds, there is NO voltage to the computer. This lack of voltage can cause reboots or crashes (rather like a brownout). An SPS is great for preventing against blackouts, but it does little for brownouts and sags. The better choice for undervoltage problems would be the *uninterruptible power supply* or UPS. The UPS works similarly to an SPS, but with one important difference. The computer equipment is always running off the battery. While the line voltage is normal, the battery gets charged. When power fluctuates, only the charging circuit is affected. The battery continues to provide power to the equipment uninterrupted. Because the equipment is constantly operating off the battery, the UPS also acts as a kind of line conditioner.

There is one main problem with UPSs: the quality of power they provide. Batteries provide DC power, and computer power supplies run on AC power. Inside the UPS is a power inverter that converts the DC into AC. It isn't perfect. AC power produces 60Hz sine waveform, whereas the inverter produces a square wave. A computer's power supply will accept these square waveforms, but it doesn't like them (see Figure 2.30). Even though this problem exists, UPS manufacturers are using more sensitive inverters that can more closely approximate the sine wave. So, a UPS should be put on every piece of computer equipment where data loss would be a problem (in other words, almost every piece of computer equipment).

FIGURE 2.30 A comparison between line power and UPS-supplied power

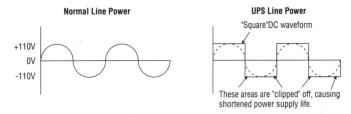

Never plug a laser printer or copier into a UPS! The large surge of power they draw when they first get turned on can burn out the inverter and battery. These devices can draw close to 15 amps when they first turn on.

Portable Computer Systems

If miniaturization trends continue, we will all soon be able to have a computer with the power of a current mainframe contained in a wristwatch or other piece of jewelry. To that end, many people have embraced the current crop of portable systems. A *portable computer* is any computer that contains all the functionality of a desktop computer system but is portable. Most people's definition of portable is defined in terms of weight and size. Just so that we can discuss things on the same level, let's define portable as less than 20 pounds and smaller than an average desktop computer.

Most portable computers fall into one of three categories: "luggable," laptop, or PDA. "Luggable" computers were the first truly portable computers, although some of their owners would beg to differ with me. Compaq computer made some of the first "luggable computers."

Laptop computers were the next type of portable computer. They contain a built-in keyboard, pointing device, and LCD screen in a clamshell design. They are also called "notebook" computers because they resemble large notebooks. Most portable computers in use today are laptop computers.

The final type of portable computer, and one that has really taken off recently, is the palmtop computer (also known as a Personal Digital Assistant, or PDA). These computers are designed to keep the information you need close to you so you have access to it whenever you need it. There are two different approaches to the PDA. Pen-based assistants are basically small digital notepads that use a stylus and handwriting interpretation software to perform operations. The Apple Newton and 3Com Palm Pilot are two examples of this type of PDA.

The other type of PDA is known as a Handheld PC (HPC). These are basically "shrunken" laptops. The HPCs run an operating system, known as Windows CE, from (whom else?) Microsoft. Windows CE is basically Windows 95 "shrunken" to fit into the limited RAM of the HPC. Instead of using a mouse to point to the icons and menus in Windows CE, the HPCs use a stylus on the touch-sensitive screen.

Portable Computer Accessories

Since portable computers have unique characteristics as a result of the portability, they have unique accessories as well. First of all, portable computers can use either of two power sources: batteries or AC power. There are many different sizes and shapes of batteries, but most of them are either Nickel-Cadmium (NiCad), Lithium Ion, or Nickel Metal Hydride (NiMH). All of these perform equally well as batteries, but NiCad batteries can only be recharged a finite number of times. After a time, they develop a "memory" and must be recharged on a special "deep charging" machine. NiMH and Lithium Ion batteries don't normally develop a memory and can be recharged many times, but they're a little more expensive.

Some of the palmtop computers can use either type of battery, but some vendors like Hewlett-Packard took a more common sense approach: they designed it to use standard AA batteries.

Most notebook computers are also able to use AC power with a special adapter that converts AC power into DC power (called an AC adapter). These can be integrated into the notebook (as on some Compaq notebooks) or as a separate "brick" with a cord that plugs into the back of the laptop.

The final accessory that is unique to portable computers is the docking station. A docking station allows a portable computer to function as a desktop computer when it is attached to it (or "docked"). The docking station usually contains interfaces and expansion ports and bays that the laptop can use only when it is docked.

Summary

In this chapter, you learned about the "nuts and bolts" of PC repair. You learned the basic components that comprise a typical PC, their functions, and how each interacts with the other components in the system.

In the first section, you learned about the main component of the PC, the System Board. Also called the motherboard or planar board, it holds all the components of the system and serves as their main attachment point. You also learned the details of the different kinds of motherboards, as well as the physical distinctions between them.

In the next section, you learned about the "brain" of the computer, the Central Processing Unit (CPU). In this section you learned what a CPU is, the various types and models of CPUs, and the differences between them. Additionally, you learned how the design of the CPU affects its performance.

The next topic you learned about was the Basic Input Output System (BIOS). The BIOS is the software hard-coded into a chip on the motherboard and manages the relationships between the hardware resources of a computer and the operating system. In this section you learned about the different brands of BIOS software and the major differences between them.

After learning about the BIOS, in the next section, you learned about memory. You learned what it is, how to locate the memory on a motherboard, what its purpose is, and what the main types of memory are. Memory is discussed in a later chapter, so continue reading the book for coverage about the different types of memory. However, in this chapter you did learn about the CMOS memory that stores the BIOS settings and that it is battery backed to save these settings when power is turned off.

Another of the computer subsystems you were introduced to in this chapter is the storage subsystem. All files and programs you need to run need to be stored somehow so that they can be loaded into memory when called upon. Data storage keeps data and programs stored for the long term so they can be kept in the computer, even when the power is turned off. In this section you learned about both fixed and removable types of storage (including hard disks, CD-ROMs, Zip disks, and CD-RW) that are available for use in a computer.

In the next section, you learned about the various kinds of input and output devices that are commonly used with computers. You learned what input devices are commonly used with computers, like mice and keyboards as well as graphics tablets. You also learned about some types of hardware used to get data out of a computer, including monitors, printers, and modems. You learned what function each component has and how each component differs from the others.

In the next section, you learned how to get the data into and out of the computer using the various interfaces commonly found on computers. Some of these interfaces include serial, parallel, USB, and FireWire. These interfaces connect input and output devices to the computer and provide the pathway for data transfers.

No computer would be able to function without some kind of power supply to convert AC current into the DC voltages (+5, -5, +12, -12 VDC) that the computer uses. In this next section, you learned about how a power supply delivers these voltages and about the connectors used to deliver those voltages. You also learned about the power problems that can, and do, occur with power supplies.

In the final section, you learned the differences between portable computer systems and desktop PC systems. The A+ exam tests your knowledge of the hardware unique to portable computers systems. You learned how these unique components work. For example, you learned how the different types of LCD displays worked. You also learned how power is supplied to portable computers through batteries and AC adapters.

Key Terms

Before you take the exam, be certain you are familiar with the following terms:

"baby" AT	Integrated system boards
"full" AT	joystick port
Berg connectors	motherboard
Central Processing Unit (CPU)	nonintegrated system boards
clock doubling	parallel port
clock tripling	parallel processing
CMOS battery	planar board
direct-solder method	proprietary design
dongle	riser card
dongle connection	serial ports
Dual Inline Memory Modules (DIMMs)	Single Inline Memory Modules (SIMMs)
expansion slots	superscalar
floppy drive interfaces	system board
game port	Universal Serial Bus (USB)
hard disk interfaces	$x86$ series

Review Questions

1. Which computer component contains all the circuitry necessary for *all* components or devices to communicate with each other?

   A. System board

   B. Adapter card

   C. Hard drive

   D. Expansion bus

2. Clock speeds are measured in _____.

   A. Ohms

   B. Volts

   C. Megahertz

   D. Milliseconds

3. What was the original name for a monitor?

   A. Video Display Unit

   B. CRT

   C. LCD

   D. Optical Display Unit

4. Which of the following is the most important input device?

   A. Mouse

   B. Digitizing tablet

   C. Keyboard

   D. Printer

5. Access time refers to what?

   A. Revolutions per unit of time

   B. Difference between the time data is requested and received

   C. Latency

   D. The time it takes to create an Access database

6. What is the maximum amount of data that can be stored on a 5¼"
    floppy disk?

    A. 360KB

    B. 1.2MB

    C. 320KB

    D. 720KB

7. The system board is also called _____.

    A. A fiberglass board

    B. A planar board

    C. A bus system

    D. An IBM system board XR125

8. The _____ is used to store frequently accessed data and
    instructions.

    A. Hard drive

    B. RAM

    C. Internal cache memory

    D. ROM

9. Which processor was introduced with 1.2 million transistors and a 32-bit
    internal and external data path?

    A. 386SX

    B. 486DX

    C. 486DX2

    D. Pentium

10. Which processor had the math coprocessor disabled?

    A. 286

    B. 486SX

    C. 486DX

    D. 387SX

11. What are the four voltages produced by a common PCs power supply?

    A. +3

    B. -3

    C. +5

    D. -5

    E. +12

    F. -12

    G. +110

    H. -110

12. Which power device would be best to attach to your computer if you were having undervoltage power problems?

    A. Surge protector

    B. UPS

    C. Line Conditioner

    D. SPS

13. If you wanted to connect a LapLink cable (a parallel data transfer cable) so that you could upload and download files from a computer, which type of parallel port(s) does your computer need to have?

    A. Standard

    B. Bidirectional

    C. EPP

    D. ECP

14. What peripheral port type was originally developed by Apple and is currently primarily used for digital video transfers?

    A. DVD

    B. USB

    C. IEEE 1394

    D. IEEE 1284

15. What peripheral port type is expandable, using a hub, operates at 1.5Mbps, and is used to connect various devices (from printers to cameras) to PCs?

    A. DVD

    B. USB

    C. IEEE 1394

    D. IEEE 1284

16. Which peripheral port type was designed to transfer data at high speeds to printers only?

    A. DVD

    B. USB

    C. IEEE 1394

    D. IEEE 1284

17. Which motherboard form factor places expansion slots on a special riser card and is used in "low profile" PCs?

    A. AT

    B. "Baby" AT

    C. ATX

    D. NLX

18. Which Intel processor type(s) use the SEC when installed into a motherboard?

    A. 386

    B. 486

    C. Pentium

    D. Pentium II

19. Which of the following can a DVD-ROM store in addition to movies?

    A. Audio files

    B. Word documents

    C. Digital photos

    D. All of the above

20. What type of expansion slot is used almost always for high-speed, 3D graphics video cards?

    A. USB

    B. AGP

    C. PCI

    D. ISA

Answers to Review Questions

1. **A.**   The spine of the computer is the system board, otherwise known as the motherboard. On the system board you will find the CPU, underlying circuitry, expansion slots, video components, RAM slots, and various other chips.

2. **C.**   Clock speed is the frequency with which a processor executes instructions. This frequency is measured in millions of cycles per second, or megahertz (MHz).

3. **B.**   The first display systems were nothing more than fancy black and white TV monitors called CRTs.

4. **C.**   The most important device of any computer system is the keyboard. It is the basic component used to enter information or data to the processor and storage device.

5. **C.**   Two factors, seek time and latency, make up the drive's access time. The average seek time plus the average latency equals the drive access time.

6. **B.**   The drives today that offer anything less than 1.2MB are increasingly rare as most computers today do not carry the 5¼" size.

7. **B.**   The spine of the computer is the system board, otherwise known as the motherboard and less commonly referred to as the planar board.

8. **C.**   An internal cache memory is a storage area for frequently used data and instructions. It requires a small amount of physical RAM that can keep up with the processor.

9. **B.**   While the 386DX was the first Intel processor to use a 32-bit data bus and a 32-bit address bus, the 486DX was the first Intel processor that used both a 32-bit internal and a 32-bit external data path.

10. **B.**   To help cut the cost of the 486DX chip, Intel created the 486SX, which disabled the internal math coprocessor.

11. **C, D, E, F.**   The four voltages that a computer needs to operate are +5 volts DC, -5 volts DC (ground), +12 volts DC, and −12 volts DC (ground).

12. **B.**   The better choice for undervoltage problems would be the UPS. The computer equipment is always running off the battery. While the line voltage is normal the battery gets charged. When power fluctuates, only the charging circuit is affected.

13. **B, C, D.**   Bidirectional parallel port can both transmit and receive data. An ECP was designed to transfer data at high speeds. EPP parallel ports provide for greater transfer speeds and the ability to send memory addresses as well as data through a parallel port.

14. C. The 1394 standard provided for greater data transfer speeds and the ability to send memory addresses as well as data through a serial port.

15. B. USBs are used for connecting multiple peripherals to one computer through a single port and support data transfer rates as high as 1.5Mbps.

16. D. IEEE 1284 standard defines the ECP parallel port to use a DMA channel and the buffer to be able to transfer data at high speeds to printers.

17. D. The NLX form factor places expansion slots on a special riser card and is used in low profile PCs.

18. D. The unique thing about the Pentium II is that it uses a Single Edge Connector (SEC) to attach to the motherboard instead of the standard PGA package.

19. D. The DVD-ROM can store many types of data as well as movies. In the computer world, data can be audio files, Word documents, digital photos, and many other things.

20. B. While technically PCI and ISA could be used for video adapters, AGP was specifically designed for the use of high-speed, 3D graphic video cards.

Chapter 3

PC Memory Architecture

THE FOLLOWING OBJECTIVES ARE COVERED IN THIS CHAPTER:

✓ **4.2 Identify the categories of RAM (Random Access Memory) terminology, their locations, and physical characteristics.**

> **Content may include the following:**
>
> **Terminology:**
> - EDO RAM (Extended Data Output RAM)
> - DRAM (Dynamic Random Access Memory)
> - SRAM (Static RAM)
> - RIMM (Rambus Inline Memory Module 184 Pin)
> - VRAM (Video RAM)
> - SDRAM (Synchronous Dynamic RAM)
> - WRAM (Windows Accelerator Card RAM)
>
> **Locations and physical characteristics:**
> - Memory bank
> - Memory chips (8-bit, 16-bit, and 32-bit)
> - SIMMs (Single In-line Memory Module)
> - DIMMs (Dual In-line Memory Module)
> - Parity chips versus non-parity chips

The most commonly misunderstood concept in PC maintenance is memory. Often confused with hard disk space, memory gives a computer its "work area." The computer uses this work area to store program instructions and data that it's working with.

In this chapter, we'll present the various types of memory that are used by PCs today. We'll also discuss approaches to recognizing problems that may be related to or solved by changing the memory settings in a customer's computer. The topics fall into the following categories:

- Physical memory
- Logical memory
- Memory optimization
- Memory troubleshooting

Physical Memory

The most important component in the computer is the memory system. When we say the word *memory*, we are most often referring to Random Access Memory or RAM. However, there are other types of memory. We will discuss them all in this chapter.

Physically, memory is a collection of integrated circuits (ICs) that store data and program information as patterns of 1s and 0s (on and off states) in the chip. Most memory chips require constant power (also called a constant *refresh*) to maintain those patterns of 1s and 0s. If power is lost, all those tiny switches revert back to the off position, effectively erasing the data from memory. Some memory types, however, do not require refresh.

Physical Memory Types

There are as many types of memory as there are IC types. Let's take a look at each type in detail.

SRAM

One type of memory is known as static random access memory (SRAM). It is called static because the information doesn't need a constant update (refresh). SRAM stores information as patterns of transistor ons and offs to represent binary digits. This type of memory is physically bulky and somewhat limited in its capacity. It can generally store only 256Kb (kilobits) per IC. The original PC and XT, as well as some notebook computer systems, use SRAM chips for their memory.

Most new computers are moving away from SRAM, to the newer, more efficient type of memory known as DRAM.

DRAM

Dynamic random access memory (DRAM) was an improvement over SRAM. DRAM uses a different approach to storing the 1s and 0s. Instead of transistors, DRAM stores information as charges in very small capacitors. If a charge exists in a capacitor, it's interpreted as a 1. The absence of a charge will be interpreted as a 0.

Because DRAM uses capacitors instead of switches, it needs to use a constant refresh signal to keep the information in memory. DRAM requires more power than SRAM for refresh signals and, therefore, is mostly found in desktop computers.

DRAM technology allows several memory units, called *cells*, to be packed with very high density. Therefore, these chips can hold very large amounts of information. Most PCs today use DRAM of one type or another.

Let's take a brief look at some of the different types of DRAM:

- Fast Page Mode (FPM)
- Extended Data Out (EDO)
- Synchronous DRAM (SDRAM)
- Double Data Rate SDRAM (DDR SDRAM)
- Direct Rambus (RIMM)

In this section you will learn about each type of DRAM and the differences between them.

Fast Page Mode (FPM)

Fast Page Mode (FPM) DRAM chips, at the time of the 486/Pentium transition, was the most common type of DRAM. Although its technical designation is FPM DRAM, because it was the most common type of DRAM, everyone just started calling it "DRAM." It allowed data to be "paged" (swapped) into memory faster than earlier versions, thus providing better performance.

Extended Data Out (EDO)

In 1995, a new type of RAM became popular. *EDO (Extended Data Out) RAM* increases performance by 10 to 15 percent over FPM DRAM by eliminating memory wait states, which means eliminating a few steps to access memory. It's usually a bit more expensive than regular DRAM.

Synchronous DRAM (SDRAM)

In the final quarter of 1996, a new type of memory, *Synchronous DRAM*, was introduced. SDRAM was developed to match the ever-increasing processing speeds of the Pentium systems. Synchronous DRAM, as its name suggests, is synchronized to the speed of the systems it will be used in (e.g. PC66 SDRAM runs at 66MHz, PC100 runs at 100MHZ, PC133 runs at 133MHz and so on). Synchronizing the speed of the systems prevents the address bus from having to wait for the memory because of different clock speeds.

If you happen to install PC133 SDRAM in a 100MHz bus, the system will function, but the 133MHz memory will only operate at the 100MHz bus speed, thus reducing overall system performance.

Double Data Rate SDRAM (DDR SDRAM)

Essentially, Double Data Rate SDRAM (DDR SDRAM) is clock-doubled SDRAM. The memory chip can perform reads and writes on both sides of any clock cycle (the "up" or start and the "down" or ending), thus doubling the effective memory executions per second. So, if you are using DDR SDRAM with a 100MHz memory bus, the memory will execute reads and writes at 200MHz and transfer the data to the processor at 100MHz. The advantage to DDR over regular SDRAM is increased throughput, thus increased overall system speed.

Direct Rambus (RIMM)

Direct Rambus is a relatively new and extremely fast (up to 800MHz) technology that uses, for the most part, a new methodology in memory system design. Direct Rambus is a memory bus that transfers data at 800MHz over a 16-bit memory bus. Direct Rambus memory models (often called *RIMMs*), like DDR SDRAM, can transfer data on both the rising and falling edges of a clock cycle. That feature, combined with the 16-bit bus for efficient transfer of data, results in the ultra-high memory transfer rate (800MHz) and the high bandwidth of up to 1.6GB/second (more than twice that of 100MHz SDRAM).

ROM

Read-only memory (ROM) is used to store information permanently for easy and quick retrieval. This type of memory chip contains transistors that are manufactured permanently in the on or off position, which is the main reason why this memory is called "read only." Once these transistors have been set, they can't be changed. Because these switches are permanently in these positions, accessing the information contained in ROMs is extremely fast.

ROMs are expensive to develop and manufacture. They are mainly used for very specialized purposes, such as storing information about how a device needs to operate. A computer's BIOS is typically stored on a type of ROM chip.

PROM

For purposes more general than those required by ROM, a type of ROM chip was developed called the Programmable ROM (PROM). The PROM is a ROM that is first manufactured with all of its circuits as logical 1s (that is, with all switches on); then, when the PROM is to be programmed, the connections that need to be set to 0 are destroyed, using a high voltage electrical pulse. This makes the settings permanent.

EPROM

The main disadvantage to ROM is that it can't be changed once it has been manufactured. To resolve this, IC developers came up with Erasable Programmable Read Only Memory (EPROM). EPROMs are erasable and able to be reprogrammed, making them more flexible than ROMs. They work by storing binary information as electrical charges deposited on the chip. These electrical deposits are *almost* permanent. They will stay until dislodged by a special-frequency ultraviolet light shone through a small window (see Figure 3.1). Exposure to this light returns the chip to its blank state. The chip can then be completely reprogrammed. These chips are usually easily identified by their small, circular windows. Some older computers, such as the IBM PC or XT, used EPROMs for their BIOS information.

FIGURE 3.1 A typical EPROM

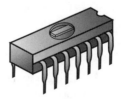

The windows in EPROM chips are used during the erasure process. When you open a computer case, make sure they are covered with a small piece of opaque material (part of a self-adhesive mailing label works well) to prevent light (either sunlight or light from fluorescent lamps) from inadvertently erasing these chips.

EEPROM

It is very inconvenient to remove an IC every time it needs to have the software it contains upgraded. It can be a real pain and *can* be dangerous. A way was needed to permit erasure of these chips "on the fly" while still maintaining their capability of keeping information intact once power is removed. Electrically Erasable PROM (EEPROM) chips were designed to solve this problem. They can be erased by sending a special sequence of electric signals to the chip while it is still in the circuit. These signals then erase all or part of the chip.

Although it might seem a good idea to use a EEPROM chip for the main memory in a computer, it would be very expensive. The primary use of this type of chip is for BIOS information; you'll see CMOS BIOS chips in most computers. The CMOS memory keeps the computer's BIOS settings while the computer is turned off. These special EEPROM chips keep their information by means of a small battery. Although the battery's charge lasts for several years, it *will* eventually lose its ability to keep the CMOS settings. It's easy to tell when this is happening, though, because the computer begins to lose its ability to keep BIOS settings when powered off.

Because the BIOS settings can eventually be lost when the CMOS battery finally loses its charge, we encourage all technicians (and PC owners in general) to record their BIOS settings (on paper or save them to a floppy) so that they may be reset if you have to replace the CMOS battery. The BIOS settings are available from the computer's Setup program, which is accessible by a special key or key combination during startup. Some computers use the Delete key, one of the function keys, or the Escape key; others use Ctrl+Alt+Esc.

Memory Chip Package Types

The memory chips themselves come in many different types of packages. The ones most frequently encountered are discussed in the following sections.

Dual Inline Package (DIP)

The first type of memory chip package is Dual Inline Package (DIP) memory (Figure 3.2), so named because the individual RAM chips use the DIP-style package for the memory IC. Older computers, such as the IBM AT, arranged these small chips like rows of caskets in a small memory "graveyard." There are typically eight chips in one of these rows, although there may be nine. If data is written to memory 8 bits at a time, why the ninth chip? The answer is that the ninth chip is used for *parity*, a kind of error-checking routine (see the following sidebar, "Parity: How Does It Work?"). Chips that have an extra chip for error checking are known as *parity chips*. Those without error checking are known as *non-parity*.

FIGURE 3.2 A DIP memory chip

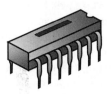

Every time a person wanted to add memory to a computer, they had to go to a computer or electronics store and buy a tube of RAM. These tubes typically contained 8–16 of these chips. The markings on the chips indicated their speed and size. A marking of AB256-80 means a 256-Kilobit chip that has an access time of 80 ns. The size was commonly given in bits or Kilobits (Kb). If you put in 256Kb chips and you put in eight of them (or nine, depending on the system), you would have added 256 Kilobytes (256KB) of RAM.

These chips were used with computers based on the 8086, 8088, and 80286 processors. The problem with the 286 processor and memory was that the processor was faster than the memory. The memory would get overrun with requests from the processor, causing serious performance problems. To solve this problem, manufacturers introduced *wait states* into their RAM. A wait state causes the processor to wait one or more clock cycles, allowing the RAM to catch up. A wait state of zero means that the processor and the memory are equally matched in speed.

Parity: How Does It Work?

Parity is a simple form of error checking used in computers and telecommunications. Parity works by adding an additional bit to a binary number and using it to indicate any changes in that number during transmission. There are two types of parity: even and odd.

- *Even parity* works by counting the number of 1s in a binary number and, if that number is odd, adding an additional 1 to guarantee that the total number of 1s is even. For example, on the one hand, the number 11101011 has an even number of 1s, so the sending computer would assign a 0 to the parity bit. On the other hand, the number 01101101 has five 1s, and so would have a 1 in the parity bit position to make the total number of 1s even. If, in the second number, the computer had checked the parity position after transmission and had found a 0 instead, it would have asked the processor to resend the last bit.

- *Odd parity* works in a similar manner. But, instead of guaranteeing that the total number of 1s is even, it guarantees that the total is an odd number.

Parity works well for detecting single-bit errors (where one bit has changed its value during transmission). But if the transmission is extremely garbled, two bits might be switched at the same time. If that were the case, the value for parity would still be valid; as a consequence, the sender would not be asked to retransmit. That's why transmissions that really need to be reliable often use another method of error checking called a *checksumming*.

Checksumming works as follows: when the sender is ready to transmit a unit of data, it runs a special algorithm against the binary data and computes what is known as a *checksum*. The sender then appends this checksum to the data being transmitted and sends the whole data stream to its intended recipient. The recipient decodes the entire data stream and runs a similar algorithm against the data portion. The recipient compares the value that it computed to the value contained in the received checksum. If the values are different, it rejects the data and asks the sender to retransmit it.

Most error checking done today uses checksumming, unless only a basic communication check is required. For example, parity is used in the case of modem communications, because these transfers are relatively slow to begin with. If modems used checksumming instead of parity, modem communications would be too slow to be a viable means of telecommunication. That's why it is necessary to set the parity to even or odd when setting up modem communications.

Single Inline Memory Module (SIMM)

The next type of RAM packaging that is commonly seen in computers is called the Single Inline Memory Module (SIMM). SIMMs were developed because DIPs took up too much "real estate" on the logic board. Someone got the idea to put several of the DIP chips on a small circuit board and then make that board easily removable. A couple of versions (there are many configurations) are shown in Figure 3.3.

FIGURE 3.3 Single Inline Memory Modules (SIMMs)

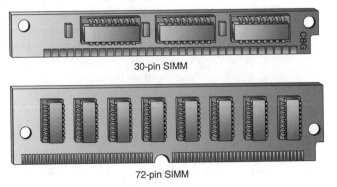

30-pin SIMM

72-pin SIMM

The first SIMMs had nine small DIP chips on them and took up less room than before, because four of them could be installed in the same space as one row of the older DIP memory chips. In order to accomplish this, the SIMMs are installed very close to each other at approximately a 45° angle. This design was also meant to prevent "chip creep"—whereby the chips that have been placed in sockets on the board start to slowly move out of their sockets (caused by the repeated heating and cooling of the system board).

An old technician's trick: If an older computer (PC or XT) is having strange, irreproducible problems, open the case and reseat all socketed chips by pressing them down securely in their sockets. Most of the time, that will solve the problem. If it does, then the problem was caused by "chip creep."

Most memory chips are 32-bit; so are several of the processors. You have a problem, however, when you have 32-bit memory chips and a 64-bit processor. To solve this, you must either install the SIMMs in pairs (always installing multiples of two—this is especially true for Pentium computers) or change to a DIMM installation (discussed next).

Dual Inline Memory Module (DIMM)

The final type of memory package is known as a DIMM (Dual Inline Memory Module). DIMMs are dual-sided memory chips that hold twice as many chips as a SIMM. (And, except for the fact that they have chips on both sides, they look just like a SIMM.) Generally, the DIMMs you'll run into will have either 72 or 168 pins. Some DIMMs are 32-bit, but more and more are 64-bit and only have to be installed one at a time in Pentium-class computers.

Specialized Memory Types

There are four major specialized applications for memory besides main memory.

Video RAM

Video memory (also called video RAM or VRAM) is used to store image data for processing by the video adapter. The more video memory an adapter has, the better the quality of image that it can display. Also, more VRAM allows the adapter to display a higher resolution of image.

Windows RAM (WRAM)

Windows RAM (WRAM) is a specialized memory for Windows accelerator cards. Developed by Samsung, it is similar to video RAM, except that it's much faster. While information is being read from one set of WRAM addresses to draw the screen, other information can be written to another set of addresses. This is faster than normal VRAM, where all addresses can only be either read from or written to. This ability of WRAM to be read from or written to simultaneously is called *dual-ported memory*.

Portable Memory

The memory styles for portable computers are many and varied. Each portable computer manufacturer comes up with their own specification for portable memory. Installing memory in a laptop usually involves removing a specially attached panel on the bottom of the laptop and installing the memory in the slot that is under the removed panel. Then you can replace the panel.

Because each laptop's memory could potentially install in completely different ways, check with the manufacturer of your laptop to determine how to upgrade the memory.

Cache Memory

When a CPU goes to get either its program instructions or data, it always has to get them from main memory. However, in some systems, there is a small amount of very fast SRAM memory, called *cache memory*, between the processor and main memory, and it is used to store the most frequently accessed information. Because it's faster than main memory and contains the most frequently used information, cache memory will increase the performance of any system.

There are two types of cache memory: on-chip (also called internal or *L1 Cache*) and off-chip (also called external or *L2 Cache*). Internal cache memory is found on Intel Pentium, Pentium Pro, and Pentium II processors, as well as on other manufacturer's chips. The original Pentium contains two 8KB-on-chip caches, one for program instructions and the other for data. External cache memory is typically either a SIMM of SRAM or a separate expansion board that installs in a special processor-direct bus.

To get the most out of cache memory, if you have the option of installing an external cache card onto your motherboard, do it. It can give you as much as a 25 percent boost in speed.

Logical Memory

Now that we have discussed the different types of physical memory, we need to talk about the logical types of memory. *Logical memory* is the way the physical memory is "put together" for the operating system. In order to use the physical memory installed in a computer, we need to organize it in some logical manner. Most people don't understand this concept. Let's reduce that number by at least one right now.

The material that follows actually covers the Memory management subsection of objective 1.1 of the Operating System Technologies exam. For instructional purposes, we feel that it makes more sense to address this topic here. For complete coverage of OS objective 1.1, please also see Part II, Chapters 12 and 14.

There is a model that helps us understand the way that memory is laid out. This model is actually called the "MS-DOS Memory Map." It was not created all at once but has evolved over time. The first computers to run DOS were based on the Intel 8088 processor. That processor could only access a maximum of 1MB (1,024KB) of memory. So, the first memory map looked like the one illustrated in Figure 3.4. This map allows us to describe how the memory is being used. It is important to remember that this memory map is also called a *stack*, because for purposes of visualizing concepts the memory blocks are stacked on top of one another.

FIGURE 3.4 The MS-DOS Memory Map

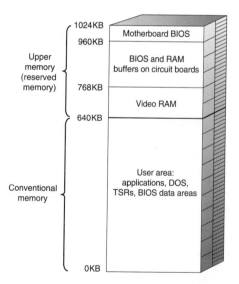

The memory map's first 1,024KB is divided up into 16 blocks of 64KB each. We will be describing the purpose of each of these blocks in the sections that follow.

The sixteen 64KB blocks are further divided into four "pages" of 16KB each. This division allows us to look in a more detailed way at how an application is using memory. Memory is allocated by the processor to those applications or devices that request it. When you need to refer to these blocks you can refer to them either by their block number (block 1, block 2, and so on), or you can refer to them as a range of hexadecimal addresses. The hexadecimal method is the most common way, since that is how the computers refer to them. These addresses are typically five-digit hex addresses, primarily because the largest five-digit hex address is FFFFF (1,048,575 decimal, corresponding to 1,048,575 bytes, or 1MB). Table 3.1 gives the blocks, their ranges in bytes, and their ranges in hexadecimal addresses.

TABLE 3.1   Memory Addresses in the MS-DOS Memory Map

Block #	Byte Range	Hex Range
1	0 to 63KB	00000 to 0FFFF
2	64 to 127KB	10000 to 1FFFF
3	128 to 191KB	20000 to 2FFFF
4	192 to 255KB	30000 to 3FFFF
5	256 to 319KB	40000 to 4FFFF
6	320 to 383KB	50000 to 5FFFF
7	384 to 447KB	60000 to 6FFFF
8	448 to 511KB	70000 to 7FFFF
9	512 to 575KB	80000 to 8FFFF
10	576 to 639KB	90000 to 9FFFF
11	640 to 703KB	A0000 to AFFFF
12	704 to 767KB	B0000 to BFFFF
13	768 to 831KB	C0000 to CFFFF
14	832 to 895KB	D0000 to DFFFF

TABLE 3.1 Memory Addresses in the MS-DOS Memory Map *(continued)*

Block #	Byte Range	Hex Range
15	896 to 959KB	E0000 to EFFFF
16	960 to 1024KB	F0000 to FFFFF

In most utilities that scan memory to find its contents, you will see memory addresses listed as hex addresses. The table above will be valuable when you're determining where a particular program or driver is resident in memory.

Conventional Memory

The first type of memory, represented as the first 640KB in the memory map, is called "conventional memory," as highlighted in Figure 3.5. It takes the first 10 blocks (00000 to 9FFFF). This type of memory is used for running programs, loading the operating system files, and loading *drivers* (see sidebar). With the old 8086 chip, this area was dedicated for user applications and data. Conventional memory turned out to be the Achilles' heel for a DOS-based system, as almost all DOS applications are written to be backward compatible, so they must support conventional memory.

FIGURE 3.5 The conventional memory area

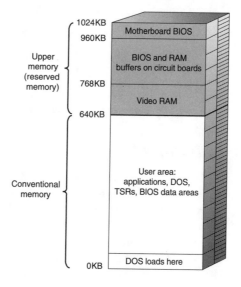

Device Drivers and Conventional Memory

Device drivers are small pieces of software that are loaded to allow the computer to talk to hardware devices. Drivers control and understand these hardware devices. For example, if you want DOS to be able to use a sound card, a driver needs to be loaded for it. When you load a driver, it is allocated memory from the conventional memory area. The problem is that your applications use this area to run in. If you have too many drivers loaded, you may not have enough conventional memory to run your programs. We will address this problem later in this chapter, in the section titled "Memory Optimization."

The first block (the first 64KB) is used for loading the DOS operating system files into memory. Also, this area contains any memory allocated to DOS disk buffers (specified by the BUFFERS= parameter in the CONFIG.SYS file). Additionally, DOS uses this area to load additional memory drivers (EMM386.EXE and HIMEM.SYS). Finally, any memory that DOS needs for system operations (input/output buffers, the processing of interrupts, and so on) is also allocated from this first 64KB area.

Besides DOS itself and drivers, there are often programs that are loaded into conventional memory and then keep a portion of themselves there after they've been terminated. This behavior can be pretty handy, as programs like e-mail software can be called up more quickly when parts of them are still located in memory. These programs are called *Terminate and Stay Resident (TSR)* programs. The following are a few examples of TSRs:

- Anti-Virus programs, because they need to stay in memory constantly
- Disk Caching programs (for example, SMARTDRIVE.EXE)
- Network protocol stacks

All of these types of programs may want to take up more memory than is available. Therefore, the developers came up with more types of memory.

Reserved Memory

If an 8088 can access 1MB of RAM, why can't you use all of it to run programs? The answer is that some devices in the computer also need RAM. Some RAM is reserved for use by some devices in the computer to store data so it can be accessed directly by the processor. This area of RAM, called "reserved memory" or "upper memory," consists of the remaining six blocks—the upper 384KB— in the MS-DOS memory map. It is highlighted in Figure 3.6.

A unique characteristic of reserved memory is that various sections of this memory area are typically allocated for special purposes. Table 3.2 lists the common uses for the reserved memory blocks and the addresses they occupy.

FIGURE 3.6   The "upper" (or "reserved") memory area

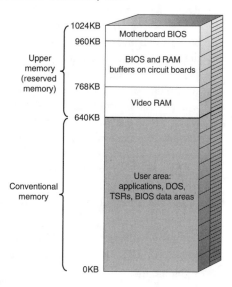

TABLE 3.2   Reserved Memory Block Usage

Address Range	Standard Usage	Notes
A0000 to BFFFF (128KB)	Video RAM	Varies according to type of video adapter used.
C0000 to CFFFF (64KB)	Available	Adapter ROMs sometimes mapped here; can also be used for EMS page frame.
D0000 to FFFFF (192KB)	Available	Adapter ROMs may also be mapped here.
E0000 to FFFFF (128K)	System ROMs	BIOS and BIOS "echo" may also be mapped here.

The first two blocks of reserved memory are usually used for accessing video RAM. When a computer needs to send information to the display, it writes it to this area. The adapter has its own memory mapped into this area. This area is only 128KB large, but some video cards have more than 1MB on them. How can the computer fit 1MB into a 128KB area? It does this through a technique known as *paging*. Paging works by taking a portion of that 1MB and accessing it by swapping it into this reserved area as data needs to be written to it.

Here's an example of how this might work: Say the processor has a large graphic to draw on the screen. It makes a call to the video card and says, "Hey, I've got some video for you," then starts writing to the video area in reserved memory. When this area is full, the video card "swaps" those full blocks for empty ones from the memory on the card. The video card takes the instructions from the "full" blocks and uses them to draw the picture on the screen. Table 3.3 shows the most commonly used memory addresses for video cards.

TABLE 3.3 Commonly Used Video Card Memory Addresses

Video Card	Memory Address Range
Monochrome Display Adapter (MDA)	B0000 to B1000 (4KB)
Color Graphics Adapter (CGA)	B8000 to BC000 (16KB)
Enhanced Graphics Adapter (EGA)	A0000 to BFFFF (128KB)
Video Graphics Adapter (VGA)	A0000 to BFFFF (128KB)
Super Video Graphics Adapter (SVGA)	A0000 to BFFFF (128KB)
Other VGA cards (super, accelerated, others)	A0000 to BFFFF (128KB)

In addition to the video adapter, other adapter cards may use the reserved memory area in the same way. These adapter cards are configured to use a particular range of memory in this area, typically in the area from C0000 to DFFFF. This area is used to map ROM memory addresses in upper memory. Additionally, some LAN cards have buffers that are mapped into this area.

Finally, the area from D0000 to DFFFF is most often used for mapping the BIOS ROM information and a copy of it, called the BIOS "shadow." This is done so that a processor can access BIOS information when it needs to. Some BIOSs have the ability to shut off the shadow, thus freeing up 64KB of upper memory.

The important concept to remember is that when you're configuring adapter cards, you can't let these memory ranges overlap. If they do overlap, you'll find that either one or the other card will work (not both), or *neither* will work. It's guaranteed, though, that the computer won't work properly.

Expanded Memory

When programs evolved and grew to the point where they were bumping up against the 640KB conventional-memory barrier, three vendors—Lotus, Intel, and Microsoft—came up with a technology to circumvent this limitation. The technology they came up with was expanded memory, or *EMS*, for *Expanded Memory System*. (It's also called LIM memory in honor of its creators.)

EMS worked by using the same type of paging technology that video cards use. Expanded memory is divided up into 16KB chunks called *pages* that are swapped into a special memory address space in reserved memory four pages at a time. The area in reserved memory that is used to hold these pages is called the *expanded memory page frame* (or *page frame*, for short—see Figure 3.7). This area normally occupies a full 64KB block in the memory map and is created when the expanded memory driver is loaded.

In the case of the original expanded memory, the actual memory was installed on a special hardware board installed in the computer, and the driver that was loaded was actually a hardware driver for the board. Incidentally, the reason that all three companies got involved is rather unique. Intel developed one of the first expanded memory boards, called the AboveBoard, which was used by people who wanted to make larger spreadsheets with Lotus 1-2-3, which ran primarily under MS-DOS (made by Microsoft). Expanded memory can be utilized on any computer from the 8088-based PC to the Pentium and higher. Depending on the motherboard you were using, you could install as much as 32MB of memory to be used as expanded memory.

Today, computers are capable of emulating expanded memory through software, because very few programs today use expanded memory. (Most computers use the next type of memory we're going to describe, *extended memory*.) The EMS emulator is a software driver called EMM386.EXE. You load it in the CONFIG.SYS file by adding the following line:

```
DEVICE=C:\DOS\EMM386.EXE
```

FIGURE 3.7 Expanded memory

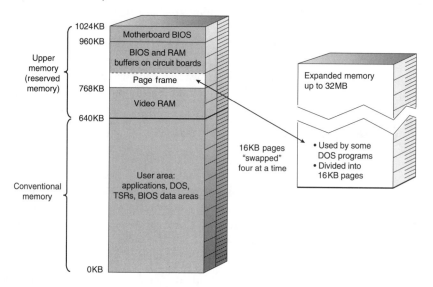

This driver also allows DOS drivers and TSR programs to be loaded into the unused portions of reserved memory by adding a second line:

```
DEVICE=C:\DOS\EMM386.EXE
DOS=UMB
```

This has the benefit of freeing up conventional memory for use by your programs and is a key concept to *memory optimization* (which will be discussed later in this chapter). If you don't need expanded memory capability, you can change these lines to turn off EMS but keep the ability to load drivers and TSRs into *upper memory blocks* (free areas in reserved memory, also called *UMBs*). To do this, your CONFIG.SYS file must have these lines:

```
DEVICE=C:\DOS\EMM386.EXE NOEMS
DOS=UMB
```

The EMS emulator (EMM386.EXE) and the DOS=UMB command were first available in MS-DOS version 5.0 (which came out in 1991). If you're trying to optimize memory on a machine that is running an earlier version of DOS, your first step should be to install the latest version of DOS.

Extended Memory

With the introduction of the 286 processor, things changed dramatically for PC memory. This processor (and all processors since then) had the capability of accessing up to 16MB of RAM (current processors can access up to 4GB of RAM). The problem was that DOS was written for the old 8086 processor and that processor could access only 1MB of RAM. In order to allow DOS programs to use all this memory, DOS would have to be rewritten to support the new processor. If this was done, the new version of DOS would not support old programs, since the old programs would not run above 1MB. Computer buyers don't like it when they buy programs that are made obsolete with the introduction of new technology. So the chip manufacturers came up with an idea to allow their new technology to be introduced.

To do this, the processor would use two different operating modes: real mode and protected mode. In *real mode*, the 286 (and above) would operate like an 8086 (only faster) and could access only 1MB of RAM. To access memory above 1MB, the processor would have to switch to *protected mode*. It is called protected mode because each program that is running is protected from other programs that may be misbehaving and taking memory away from it. For DOS programs to use this memory, a program was written to *extend* DOS for those programs that can take advantage of it. This program is called a *DOS extender*.

An example of a DOS extender is the memory driver HIMEM.SYS; it allows certain programs to switch the processor to protected mode and access the memory above 1MB. It is loaded by adding the following line to the CONFIG.SYS file:

```
DEVICE=HIMEM.SYS
```

Once HIMEM.SYS is loaded, DOS can "see" the memory above 1MB. This memory is what is referred to as *extended memory*.

Additionally, when HIMEM.SYS is loaded, DOS can place the majority of itself into the first 64KB of extended memory. This first 64KB is called the *High Memory Area (HMA)*. In order to load DOS into the HMA, you modify the CONFIG.SYS with the following two lines:

```
DEVICE=HIMEM.SYS
DOS=HIGH
```

You may have noticed that the last line is analogous to the DOS=UMB line in the last section. It is possible to have both of these lines in the CONFIG.SYS to get the greatest amount of conventional memory available, although it is easier to do them both at once, like so:

```
DEVICE=HIMEM.SYS
DEVICE=EMM386.EXE
DOS=HIGH,UMB
```

Basically, DOS can't use extended memory without the help of these extenders. However, there are several operating systems that can. These include OS/2, UNIX, and Windows NT. Programs written for these non-DOS operating systems are able to take advantage of the benefits of the 286 (and above) processor, including multitasking and access to all the memory the processor can address.

And Now for the Real World...

Most people don't understand the MS-DOS memory map. That's okay; most people don't need to. However, it is an invaluable tool for the PC technician. Several programs report problems with memory addresses in hexadecimal. This helps us understand which programs were fighting when the error occurred. Also, in order to keep most PCs running efficiently, you must get as much conventional memory as possible. To do this, it is very important you understand the different types of memory, their addressing, and how they work together in a PC.

With all of the different types of memory, you end up with a DOS memory map that looks like the one in Figure 3.8. With so many different types of memory, it is easy to get them confused. Most often, expanded and extended are juxtaposed. The easiest way to remember the difference is that expanded memory is paged and extended is not.

FIGURE 3.8   The complete MS-DOS memory map

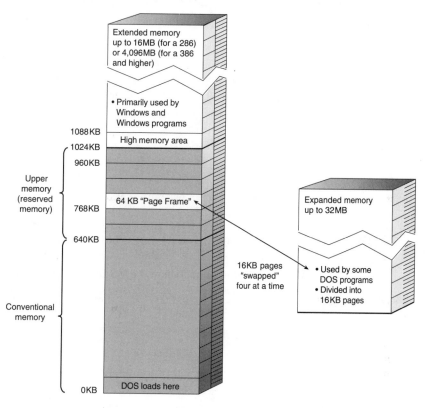

Memory Optimization

Because of the small amount of conventional memory available, the increasing number of drivers that need to be loaded, and the increasing size of the programs you need to run, it is very common to not have enough conventional memory. When people talk about memory optimization, they usually mean making as much conventional memory available as possible.

Memory optimization is one of the most important skills a technician can have. With the number of DOS applications that exist, the need for a technician to know how to optimize memory will continue to be valuable. In general, your DOS-based PCs will run best with the most possible conventional memory available. Ideally, we're talking in the neighborhood of 600KB or more free.

Step One: Determining How Much Memory You Have Available

We already understand what conventional memory is, but in order to optimize it, you must first make the determination whether or not memory optimization is needed. For DOS systems, you use the MEM.EXE program. This program allows us to determine how memory is being utilized within DOS. The syntax for the MEM command is as follows:

MEM <option>

The available options are described in Table 3.4. If you execute the command without an option, the MEM command shows how much of each type of memory is installed, as shown in Figure 3.9.

In IBM's PC-DOS, the QCONFIG.EXE program gives some of the same information as the MS-DOS MEM.EXE program, as well as information regarding fixed disks.

FIGURE 3.9 A report from the MS-DOS MEM command when executed without any options

```
C:\>mem

Memory Type          Total       Used        Free
----------------     --------    --------    --------
Conventional         640K        44K         596K
Upper                0K          0K          0K
Reserved             384K        384K        0K
Extended (XMS)       15,360K     2,240K      13,120K
----------------     --------    --------    --------
Total memory         16,384K     2,668K      13,716K

Total under 1 MB     640K        44K         596K

Total Expanded (EMS)             20M (20,463,616 bytes)
Free Expanded (EMS)              13M (13,434,880 bytes)

Largest executable program size  596K (609,968 bytes)
Largest free upper memory block   0K     (0 bytes)
MS-DOS is resident in the high memory area.
```

TABLE 3.4 MEM.EXE Command-Line Options

Option	Description
/?	The help switch. It gives basic information on the syntax of the MEM command and its usage. It shows all the switches listed in this table and their usage.

TABLE 3.4 MEM.EXE Command-Line Options *(continued)*

Option	Description
/C	The *classify switch*. When executed, gives an output similar to the one following this table.
/D	The *debug switch*. It details the usage of the first 640KB of memory (conventional memory). This switch is helpful in finding out the memory addresses of the various programs that are loaded. (Remember that MEM itself is also a program and should be listed.) An example report of MEM /D is shown a couple of pages after this table.
/F	The free memory switch. Shows all the free memory blocks in the first 640KB and their starting addresses. Also useful in optimizing memory.
/M *<module>*	The *module switch*. Shows the starting addresses of the data, program, and free memory allocated to the module you specify.
/P	The *pause switch*. When used in conjunction with the other switches, /P displays the output of the command one page at a time. When a page is displayed, the display will pause until a key is pressed. The same effect can be accomplished by piping the command's results into the MORE command (i.e., using MEM *<option>*|MORE).

A Report from the MEM /C Command

The following is the output of the MEM /C command:

```
Modules using memory below 1MB:

    Name    Total            Conventional      Upper Memory
    ------  --------------   --------------    --------------
    SYSTEM   48,880  (48K)    10,592  (10K)     38,288  (37K)
    HIMEM     1,168   (1K)     1,168   (1K)          0   (0K)
    EMM386    4,320   (4K)     4,320   (4K)          0   (0K)
    WIN       3,696   (4K)     3,696   (4K)          0   (0K)
    ----        288   (0K)       288   (0K)          0   (0K)
    vmm32   102,064 (100K)       448   (0K)    101,616  (99K)
    COMMAND   7,456   (7K)     7,456   (7K)          0   (0K)
    IBMIDECD 10,848  (11K)         0   (0K)     10,848  (11K)
    IFSHLP    2,864   (3K)         0   (0K)      2,864   (3K)
```

```
DOSKEY    4,688   (5K)          0   (0K)   4,688   (5K)
Free    627,120 (612K)    627,120 (612K)        0   (0K)
```

Memory Summary:

Type of Memory	Total	Used	Free
Conventional	655,360	28,240	627,120
Upper	158,304	158,304	0
Reserved	393,216	393,216	0
Extended (XMS)	32,347,552	95,648	32,251,904
Total memory	33,554,432	675,408	32,879,024
Total under 1MB	813,664	186,544	627,120

```
Largest executable program size         627,104   (612K)
Largest free upper memory block               0   (0K)
MS-DOS is resident in the high memory area.
```

A Report from the MEM /D Command

The following is the output of the MEM /D command:

Conventional Memory Detail:

Segment	Total	Name		Type
00000	1,024	(1K)		Interrupt Vector
00040	256	(0K)		ROM Communication Area
00050	512	(1K)		DOS Communication Area
00070	1,424	(1K)	IO	System Data
		CON		System Device Driver
		AUX		System Device Driver
		PRN		System Device Driver
		CLOCK$		System Device Driver
		A: - C:		System Device Driver
		COM1		System Device Driver
		LPT1		System Device Driver
		LPT2		System Device Driver
		LPT3		System Device Driver
		CONFIG$		System Device Driver

			COM2	System Device Driver
			COM3	System Device Driver
			COM4	System Device Driver
000C9	5,120	(5K)	MSDOS	System Data
00209	7,632	(7K)	IO	System Data
	1,024	(1K)		Relocated EBIOS data
	1,152	(1K)		Installed Device=HIMEM
	4,304	(4K)		Installed Device=EMM386
	544	(1K)		Sector buffer
	512	(1K)		BUFFERS=50
003E6	80	(0K)	MSDOS	System Program
003EB	32	(0K)	WIN	Data
003ED	288	(0K)	----	Data
003FF	256	(0K)	WIN	Environment
0040F	3,408	(3K)	WIN	Program
004E4	48	(0K)	vmm32	Data
004E7	400	(0K)	vmm32	Program
00500	288	(0K)	COMMAND	Data
00512	5,728	(6K)	COMMAND	Program
00678	1,440	(1K)	COMMAND	Environment
006D2	288	(0K)	MEM	Environment
006E4	90,464	(88K)	MEM	Program
01CFA	536,656	(524K)	MSDOS	– Free –

Upper Memory Detail:

Segment	Region	Total	Name	Type	
OC95C	1	51,968	(51K)	IO	System Data
		10,832	(11K)IBMCD001	Installed vice=IBMIDECD
		2,848	(3K)IFSHLP	Installed Device=IFSHLP
		464	(0K)		Block device tables
		4,736	(5K)		FILES=85
		256	(0K)		FCBS=4
		26,800	(26K)		BUFFERS=50
		2,816	(3K)		LASTDRIVE=`
		3,072	(3K)		STACKS=9,256
0D60C	1	272	(0K)	vmm32	Data
0D61D	1	4,688	(5K)	DOSKEY	Program
0D742	1	101,344	(99K)	vmm32	Data

```
Memory Summary:
Type of Memory       Total        Used          Free
_____    _____   _____     _____

Conventional         655,360      28,240        627,120
Upper                158,304     158,304              0
Reserved             393,216     393,216              0
Extended (XMS)    32,347,552      95,648     32,251,904

_____    _____   _____     _____

Total memory      33,554,432     675,408     32,879,024
Total under 1MB      813,664     186,544        627,120

Memory accessible using Int 15h              0    (0K)
Largest executable program size        627,104  (612K)
Largest free upper memory block              0    (0K)
MS-DOS is resident in the high memory area.

XMS version  3.00; driver version  3.95
```

Step Two: Making the Optimization Changes

Once you have determined how much conventional memory you have available (and in all likelihood found that you need to optimize your conventional memory), you must then determine how to best optimize it. If you have installed DOS with the default installation, you will have the CONFIG.SYS file shown here:

```
DEVICE=C:\DOS\HIMEM.SYS
Files=40
Stacks=9,256
SHELL=C:\DOS\COMMAND.COM /E:1024
```

The first procedure you can perform that will increase available conventional memory is to add the DOS=HIGH line to CONFIG.SYS. This has the effect of moving DOS to the HMA, thus freeing up the first 64KB block (minus a small amount to keep HIMEM.SYS and a few smaller files in conventional memory).

The next thing you can do is load some or all of your device drivers and TSRs into upper memory. This is also called loading them "high," which is a misnomer since you aren't loading them into the HMA, but rather into the upper memory area (simply the other name for reserved memory, which I guess is *higher* than conventional memory, but still, it's not in the area typically referred to as the high memory area—oh, well, I didn't come up with it). This is accomplished by doing three things:

1. Add DEVICE=C:\DOS\EMM386.EXE and DOS=UMB in your CONFIG.SYS so that DOS can manage the UMBs (upper memory blocks, discussed earlier in this chapter).

2. Make sure that you have some free UMBs. This can be done with the MEM /C command, which, in its "Memory Summary" portion (the bottom half of its report), shows the amount of upper memory available for UMBs (the row labeled "Upper") and the amount of upper memory that is already being used (the row labeled "Reserved").

3. Add something to each command that loads a driver or TSR so that it loads into the upper memory area.

The command that you use to load a driver into the upper memory area is the DEVICEHIGH=<drivername> command. You use this command in the same manner as the DEVICE= command in CONFIG.SYS. When you replace each DEVICE= line in your CONFIG.SYS with a DEVICEHIGH= command, the driver will attempt to load into the upper memory area. You can see whether this is successful by using the MEM /C command to show how much of the driver is loaded into upper memory. The driver will be displayed, along with a number in the "Upper Memory" column (in the top portion of the report) if it successfully loaded into upper memory. Additionally, if you have drivers loaded from the AUTOEXEC.BAT, you use the LOADHIGH <drivername> (or LH, for short) to load that driver or TSR into a UMB.

Additionally, you should check to see if you have a program that uses expanded memory. If you don't, you can place the NOEMS line after C:\DOS\EMM386.EXE in the CONFIG.SYS. This frees up the 64KB area being used by the page frame so it can be used for UMBs.

These memory optimization "tricks" are easy enough, but most users don't want or need to know memory optimization theory. So, both Microsoft and IBM included intelligent memory optimization utilities with their DOS operating systems (starting with version 6 of each one). The programs are MEMMAKER (by Microsoft) and RAMBOOST (by IBM). These utilities already know the theory behind memory optimization and can examine the system and determine how best to optimize the system. Each accomplishes the same ends by different means. MEMMAKER scans the CONFIG.SYS and AUTOEXEC.BAT and adds DEVICEHIGH and LOADHIGH statements to optimize memory. RAMBOOST, on the other hand, is a TSR that is constantly running. Any time you make a change to your CONFIG.SYS or AUTOEXEC.BAT, RAMBOOST detects the change, automatically reboots the computer, and automatically rearranges the drivers in upper memory to give the best possible memory configuration. It saves all its information to a file known as RAMBOOST.INI.

For more information regarding RAMBOOST or MEMMAKER, please refer to their respective user manuals.

One caution about MEMMAKER, though, is that it isn't as "smart" as we would like it to be. For example, if you had the following CONFIG.SYS:

```
DEVICE=C:\DOS\HIMEM.SYS
DEVICE=C:\DOS\EMM386.EXE
FILES=50
BUFFERS=9,256
DEVICE=C:\SB16\CTMMCD.SYS
```

MEMMAKER might optimize it to read like so:

```
DEVICE=C:\DOS\HIMEM.SYS
DEVICE=C:\DOS\EMM386.EXE NOEMS
FILES=50
BUFFERS=9,256
DOS=UMB
DEVICEHIGH=C:\SB16\CTMMCD.SYS
```

The memory usage would be more efficient after MEMMAKER had run, but there is one glaring problem. Where is DOS=HIGH,UMB? If MEMMAKER had included this statement, it would have freed up a 64KB block of conventional memory, but it didn't include it. So, while it's good at general optimization, MEMMAKER can't beat an intuitive technician with a good grasp of memory theory.

Another factor in memory optimization is the *order* in which drivers are loaded into memory. When optimizing memory, sometimes you run into a situation where you only need one or two kilobytes more of conventional memory and you've done all you can to get the most available conventional memory. The final "trick" in your bag is to change the order in which the drivers load. To do this, you load the driver that needs the most memory first. Then the next largest, and so on. Think of it this way, when you build a wall, do you put the smallest stones down first, then the largest? Or do you put the biggest first, then the smallest? Obviously, you do the latter so that your wall is stable.

Memory Troubleshooting

Very rarely does anything go wrong with the memory in a PC. However, you need to have background knowledge of *possible* memory problems in case they do occur.

It is very easy to tell when a memory error occurs, because a computer malfunctions seriously with bad memory. With a memory error, the computer will do one of two things. If the computer is already running, it will report the error and stop the program. If the error occurs during the POST (power on self-test) memory countup, the computer will not start at all. The reason the computer stops in both cases is that the computer needs reliable memory in order to function. If the computer knows the memory is unreliable, it knows it might write a 1 to memory and read back a 0. And it knows that would be bad.

There are two types of memory problems: hard errors and soft errors. We'll discuss these in reverse order.

Soft Memory Errors

Soft errors occur once and disappear after the computer is rebooted. They are usually caused by power fluctuations or single bit errors. The symptoms are typically unexplained problems with software and are not reproducible. Soft errors are like gnats: annoying little things you wish you could kill, but they don't stay in one place long enough for you to do so. However, if these errors increase in frequency, it usually indicates a hard memory error is about to occur.

Hard Memory Errors

Hard memory errors are related to a hardware failure and *are* reproducible. When a hard memory error occurs, the computer might issue either a "Parity Error" or a "201 BIOS Error" or issue a series of beeps (upon startup). For example, if you are using AMI BIOS, and the computer issues one long and three short beeps on startup (other BIOSs will use different beep codes), you have a hardware-related memory error. A table of BIOS error codes is included in Chapter 10, "Hardware Troubleshooting."

To solve a hard memory error, you must replace some memory chips. The question is always one of money. Since most computers have more than one memory chip, you must determine which chip(s) or SIMM(s) need to be replaced. One way to do this is to systematically replace one chip at a time until the memory error goes away. It may be easiest, however, to simply replace all the memory at one time, especially if memory prices stay low.

Some BIOSs have beep or error codes that indicate which chip has failed. In that case, use the manual that comes with the motherboard to determine which chip is causing the error (assuming there is a manual available)—another good argument for having documentation available.

Summary

In this chapter you learned about the way PC memory is used, the different types of memory available for a PC, the differences between them, how to optimize memory usage, and how to troubleshoot memory-related problems.

In the first section, you learned about the different types of physical memory packages. You learned about the different memory form factors, like SIMM and DIMM, as well as the different terms for the various types of memory (EDO, SDRAM, RDRAM, and ROM).

In the next section, you learned how memory is laid out with respect to the operating system. Specifically, you learned how DOS views and accesses memory. You learned that the memory is divided into four major areas: conventional, reserved, expanded, and extended. Each area is used for a specific purpose within DOS. Additionally, these memory areas are only found in DOS. Windows 95/98/ NT/2000 use a different memory scheme. They don't divide memory into discrete areas. Memory is, instead, accessed as one large "pool."

Because memory in DOS is divided into these areas and because each of these is used for more than one purpose, often there isn't enough conventional memory available to run programs properly. For this reason, it is important to know how to optimize available memory. In the next section, you learned how to optimize conventional memory both manually and using built-in tools like MEMMAKER.

The last topic you learned about in this chapter is how to troubleshoot various memory problems. You primarily learned about the two main types of memory errors: soft errors and hard errors. Soft errors are random errors that occur and that are cured by a simple reboot of the computer. They will disappear upon reboot. Hard errors are usually the result of a failed memory component. They will recur even after a reboot and usually require the replacement of memory.

Key Terms

cache memory

checksum

checksumming

Direct Rambus

DOS extender

driver

dual-ported memory

EDO (Extended Data Out) RAM

expanded memory page frame

Expanded Memory System (EMS)

extended memory

High Memory Area (HMA)

L1 Cache

L2 Cache

logical memory

memory optimization

memory refresh

page frame

page

paging

parity

pause switch

protected mode

Rambus Inline Memory Modules (RIMMs)

real mode

stack

synchronous DRAM

Terminate and Stay Resident (TSR)

upper memory block (UMB)

wait state

Review Questions

1. RAM is short for _____.

   A. Readily Accessible Memory

   B. Recently Affected Memory

   C. Random Access Memory

   D. Read and Modify

2. What type of memory stores information as patterns of transistor ons and offs to represent binary digits as physically bulky and somewhat limited in capacity?

   A. SRAM

   B. DRAM

   C. EDORAM

   D. ROM

   E. PROM

   F. EPROM

3. The most important component in the computer is the _____.

   A. Hard drive

   B. System board

   C. Peripheral ports

   D. CPU

   E. Memory system

4. Which of the following types of memory are erasable? (Select all that apply.)

   A. RAM

   B. SRAM

   C. ROM

   D. PROM

   E. EPROM

   F. EEPROM

5. Which type of memory found in desktop computers stores information as charges in very small capacitors and needs a constant refresh signal to keep the information in memory?

A. SRAM

B. DRAM

C. EDORAM

D. ROM

E. PROM

F. EPROM

6. Which switch will cause MEM.EXE to give the most detailed information about the current memory configuration?

A. /A

B. /B

C. /C

D. /D

7. Which type of ROM memory chip has a small window that allows the chip to be erased with a special ultraviolet light?

A. PROM

B. EPROM

C. EEPROM

D. APROM

8. What type of ROM memory chip is erasable using software tools and is most commonly used for BIOS chips?

A. PROM

B. ROM

C. EPROM

D. EEPROM

9. Which area of memory is used for running most DOS programs, loading drivers, and loading TSRs?

A. Conventional memory

B. Extensive memory

C. Extended memory

D. Expanded memory

10. Which of these processors was the first to access more than 1MB of RAM?

    A. 8088

    B. 8086

    C. 80286

    D. 80386

    E. 80486

11. Which processor(s) can access as much as 4GB of RAM? (Select all that apply.)

    A. 8088

    B. 8086

    C. 80286

    D. 80386

    E. 80486

    F. Pentium

12. If you are transmitting the 8-bit binary number 11010010 and are using even parity, what would the parity bit be?

    A. 1

    B. 0

    C. None

    D. A

13. What type of error-checking routine do modem communications most often use?

    A. Parity

    B. Error correction

    C. Addition

    D. Checksumming

14. A memory chip has markings of 45256–40. The last two digits after the dash mean an access time of _____.

    A. 4 ms

    B. 4 ns

    C. 40 ms

    D. 40 ns

    E. 400 ns

15. Which of the following indicate(s) a hard memory error? (Select all that apply.)

  A. 201 BIOS error

  B. 301 BIOS error

  C. One long beep, three short beeps

  D. Two long beeps, two short beeps

  E. Parity error

16. What is meant by a wait state of zero?

  A. The processor is faster than memory in terms of speed.

  B. The processor is slower than memory in terms of speed.

  C. The memory is faster than the processor in terms of speed.

  D. The processor and the memory are equally matched in terms of speed.

17. The first thing you can do to increase the available conventional memory is _____.

  A. Load all device drivers into UMBs

  B. Add `DOS=HIGH` to the `CONFIG.SYS`

  C. Remove DOS

  D. Rearrange the loading order of the drivers

18. If you don't need expanded memory, you can free up 64KB of reserved memory that can be used for UMBs by putting the _____ parameter after `C:\DOS\EMM386.EXE` in the `CONFIG.SYS` to disable expanded memory and remove the page frame.

  A. `NOEXT`

  B. `NOEXP`

  C. `NOPAGE`

  D. `NOEMS`

19. What type of memory has several chips on a small circuit board and the board is easily removable?

  A. Dual Inline Package

  B. Single Inline Memory Module

  C. Memory Package Grid Array

  D. Single Inline Package

20. Which driver must be loaded in the CONFIG.SYS to give DOS access to extended memory?

   A. C:\DOS\EXTMEM.SYS

   B. C:\DOS\UPPMEM.SYS

   C. C:\DOS\MEMORY.SYS

   D. C:\DOS\EMM386.EXE

   E. C:\DOS\HIMEM.SYS

Answers to Review Questions

1. C. As it applies to memory, RAM stands for Random Access Memory.

2. A. Of the above choices, SRAM would be the one to choose, as its storage method is to use a pattern of transistor ons and offs to represent the data. Because it's bulky and its storage method is inefficient, SRAM is not as popular anymore.

3. E. Because the computer needs a place to store instructions and data in a quickly and easily retrievable format, the memory system is the most important component.

4. A, B, E, F. Since ROM stands for read-only memory and PROM stands for programmable ROM, they automatically are incorrect answers for the question. RAM and SRAM are both monikers of short-term memory (RAM), and therefore have to be erasable to be of any use. EPROM and EEPROMs are both special types of PROMs that are Erasable Programmable (EPROM) and Electronically Erasable and Programmable (EEPROM) and therefore have the ability to be erasable and re-usable.

5. B. DRAM (Dynamic RAM) stores information in capacitors. This storage method is much more efficient and, therefore, has gained widespread popularity over SRAM. And, as the name dynamic implies, it requires a constant recharge to maintain the information.

6. D. /D signifies to run MEM.EXE in the debug mode. As such, you can think of this as a verbose mode in that it will give you the most detailed information about your memory utilization.

7. B. EPROM (Erasable Programmable ROM) is erased and reprogrammed with special ultraviolet light shone through a small window in the top of the chip. This gives this type of chip quite an advantage over PROMs.

8. D. EEPROM (Electronically Erasable PROM) is even more sophisticated than EPROM in that it can be erased and reprogrammed using software tools. This makes it an exceptional choice for BIOS chips. Software upgrade utilities are much easier to implement (and have less chance of error) than replacing an entire chip.

9. A. When the 8088 and 8086 were first produced, the programs, drivers, and TSRs were given an area of memory to run called conventional memory. This is the first 640K of memory. Later this would change, and other areas of memory would become available, but conventional memory would remain the default memory area to use.

10. C. The 80286 was the first processor to break through the 1MB barrier. It could access as much as 16MB of RAM.

11. D, E, F. As address busses expanded beyond the 24-bit capability of the 80286, this allowed them to access even more memory. With a 32-bit address bus width, the 80386, 80486, and Pentium processors can now access as much as 4GB of RAM.

12. B. Because even parity works around the concept that all bits set to 1 have to equal an even number (and in this question there are 4 bits set to 1), the parity bit would have to equal 0 to maintain that even number. However, if the above question only had 3 bits set to 1, then the parity bit would have to be set to 1, so that it would be even.

13. A. Modem communications are serial-based, so the most efficient error-checking method for them is parity. Checksumming would cause too much overhead in the transmissions.

14. D. The last two numbers on a chip generally refer to the speed of the memory; in this case it is a 40 ns chip.

15. A, C, E. Memory errors can be indicated by a beep code (each BIOS manufacturer has its own set of codes, so be sure to check the documentation that came with your motherboard) and/or by an error message that states either that there is a parity error or a 201 BIOS error.

16. D. If the memory and the processor do not run at the same speed, then wait states have to be used to make sure that one does not send more information at one time than what the other can handle. If they run at the same speed, then a wait state of 0 is used.

17. B. While A and D both offer good choices, you will not be able to perform them or gain any benefit from using them without first loading DOS=HIGH.

18. D. If you have no applications that can take advantage of expanded memory, you can disable that page frame and thereby reclaim 64KB of usable memory by adding the NOEMS switch.

19. B. The Single Inline Memory Module is a small circuit board with multiple DIPs soldered to it. Because of this, they are very easy to install and remove.

20. E. Don't let this question confuse you. EMM386.EXE grants access to the expanded memory area, but it is HIMEM.SYS that grants access to the extended memory area.

Chapter

4

Disk System Architecture

THE FOLLOWING OBJECTIVES ARE COVERED IN THIS CHAPTER:

✓ **1.1 Identify basic terms, concepts, and functions of system modules, including how each module should work during normal operation and during the boot process.**

Examples of concepts and modules are:

- System board
- Power supply
- Processor/CPU
- Memory
- Storage devices
- Monitor
- Modem
- Firmware
- BIOS
- CMOS
- LCD portable systems
- Ports
- PDA (Personal Digital Assistant)

✓ **1.5 Identify proper procedures for installing and configuring IDE/EIDE devices.**

Content may include the following:

- Master/slave
- Devices per channel
- Primary/secondary

✓ **1.6 Identify proper procedures for installing and configuring SCSI devices.**

Content may include the following:

- Address/Termination conflicts
- Cabling
- Types (example: regular, wide, ultra-wide)
- Internal versus external
- Jumper block settings (binary equivalents)

✓ **2.1 Identify common symptoms and problems associated with each module and how to troubleshoot and isolate problems.**

Content may include the following:

- Processor/Memory symptoms
- Mouse
- Floppy drive
- Parallel ports
- Hard Drives
- CD-ROM
- DVD
- Sound Card/Audio
- Monitor/Video
- Motherboards
- Modems
- BIOS
- USB
- NIC
- CMOS
- Power supply
- Slot covers
- POST audible/visual error codes
- Troubleshooting tools, e.g., multimeter
- Large LBA, LBA
- Cables

- Keyboard
- Peripherals

✓ **4.3 Identify the most popular type of motherboards, their components, and their architecture (bus structures and power supplies).**

Content may include the following:

Types of motherboards:

- AT (Full and Baby)
- ATX

Components:

- Communication ports
- SIMM and DIMM
- Processor sockets
- External cache memory (Level 2)
- Bus Architecture
- ISA
- PCI
- AGP
- USB (Universal Serial Bus)
- VESA local bus (VL-Bus)
- Basic compatibility guidelines
- IDE (ATA, ATAPI, ULTRA-DMA, EIDE)
- SCSI (Wide, Fast, Ultra, LVD [Low Voltage Differential])

All information needs to be stored somewhere. It's a simple fact of life. At your office, you may have letters, contracts, and so on that need to be stored somewhere to make them easily accessible and retrievable. This storage space needs to be large enough to hold as much information as possible, but it should also be organized for easy access to that information. Although some people simply use the top of the desk and store documents in piles, the best solution for storing paper documents at most offices is a filing cabinet.

With computers, you have various types of electronic information to store, including data files, application files, and configuration files. In this chapter, we will explain the following A+ exam topics related to information storage:

- Storage types
- Floppy disk systems
- IDE disk systems
- Small Computer Systems Interface (SCSI)

NOTE For complete coverage of objective 1.1, please also see Chapters 2 and 6. For complete coverage of objective 2.1, please also see Chapters 1, 6, 8, and 10. For complete coverage of objective 4.3, please also see Chapters 2 and 5.

Storage Types

In this section, we'll give a detailed description of each type of disk storage, starting with a brief overview of punch card and tape storage and moving into the different types of disks. Then we'll give you some tips on how to configure them and discuss their different troubleshooting techniques.

Punch Cards and Tape

Originally, computer information was contained in memory and printed to punch cards. When you wanted to retrieve the data, you ran the punch cards back into a special reader; the information was read back into memory and could then be used. This proved to be a very limited storage medium in terms of capacity and ease of retrieval. A single page of data could take several pages of punch cards. Also, the punch card order was very important. The cards had to be put into the reader in the correct order or the program wouldn't run correctly. Hopefully you kept the cards in their correct order—God forbid you dropped them on the floor or some jokester shuffled them.

Then one day, someone discovered that computer signals could be recorded with a tape recorder. When the tape was played back into the computer, the information was retrieved. This was a much more efficient storage system than punch cards. Because the tape moved in only one direction and was a single, long tape (rather than several punch cards), it reduced the possibility of getting the information out of sequence and made it easier to access the information. We've all seen movies where the computer room has massive cabinets with reels of tape moving back and forth. What you might not know is that several early personal computer systems (such as the TRS-80, the Tandy Color Computer, and the Apple II) came with cassette tape storage devices to load and store programs and data.

The major limitations of tape were in speed and precision. Tape was slow to store programs and data. Also, it was slow to access information because of its linear nature. Tape devices are described as *sequential storage* devices. With these types of devices, if a piece of information is located at the end of a tape, you have to "fast forward" through all the other information to get to the data you need. Also, the early tape mechanisms didn't have very good position locators or stepper motors. It was quite possible to start reading a tape after the information you needed had already begun, causing you to miss the start of the program or data and making it unusable.

Despite its drawbacks for most tasks you might want to undertake with a computer, magnetic tape in various forms is still a great medium for "backing up" your system—that is, recording some or all of the information stored on your hard disk and putting the recording away in case of hard disk catastrophe. Why is tape, which is not recommended for other types of information storage, recommended so often for backups? In part, it's because of the sheer amount of data it can store. Some of the cheaply available types of tape media of today can hold more than 4GB and are easily movable, removable, and insertable into their respective recorder/playback drives. Moreover, the relatively low speed of recording or playing back a backup tape is not a significant consideration for most users as it would be with other computer tasks. Most users know that they are simply performing a safety measure when they utilize a backup, so they schedule their backups to be carried out automatically when no one is using the computer anyway.

Disk Drives

To overcome the limitations of magnetic tape, magnetic disk systems were developed. Rotating stacks of disks were coated with a special substance that was sensitive to magnetism. As the disk rotated, the particles in the substance could be polarized (magnetized), indicating a 1. The unpolarized areas would indicate 0s. (We will discuss the way information is stored on a disk in the next section.) This technology is the cornerstone of most current disk storage types and hasn't changed much since its inception. These types of disk systems store data in non-linear format and are called *random access* storage devices, in contrast to tape's sequential access storage methods. The data can be accessed no matter where it is located on the disk because the read/write head can be positioned exactly over the requested data so you don't have to "fast forward" through the data that was stored before it.

There are two major types of disk systems—fixed and removable. Let's cover fixed disks first.

Fixed Disk Drives

Also known as *hard disks* and *hard drives*, *fixed disks* actually contain several disks called *platters*, stacked together and mounted through their centers on a small rod called a *spindle* (see Figure 4.1). The disks are rotated about this rod at a speed between 2,000 and 10,000 revolutions per minute (RPM). As the disks rotate, one or more *read/write heads* float approximately 10 microinches (about 1/10th the width of a human hair) above the disk surfaces and make, modify, or sense changes in the magnetic positions of the coatings on the disks. Several heads are moved together as one unit by an *actuator arm*. There is usually one head for each side of a platter. This entire mechanism is enclosed in a hard disk case. These disks are called fixed disks because the mechanism is not designed to be removed. The disk platters, though perfectly free to revolve at high RPM, are otherwise fixed in place.

FIGURE 4.1   A fixed disk

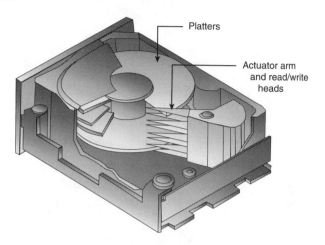

Platters

Actuator arm
and read/write
heads

Disk Organization

We must have a way of organizing this disk into usable sections. It's done by first dividing up the platters into sections as you would a pie and then further dividing this area into concentric circles, called *tracks* (see Figure 4.2). Tracks are numbered from the outside (track 0) to the inside (track 902 on a 903-track hard disk). A *disk sector* is the part of a track that falls in a particular section of the "pie slice" on the disk.

FIGURE 4.2   Disk organization

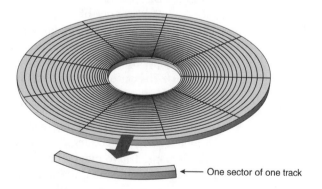

One sector of one track

If you can visualize several tracks stacked together vertically (the same tracks on each disk), you might describe that collection of tracks as a *cylinder*. In fact, that's how tracks are referred to in a discussion of the organization of disk information, because when information is read from or written to a disk, the heads read or write a sector-sized division of a track a whole stack at a time, from top to bottom (see Figure 4.3). In other words, the disks' tracks aren't treated as individual tracks on single disks; they're treated as cylinders. This amounts to quite a bit of information read or written at one time. The precise amount of information that is read at once depends on the number of cylinders, heads, and sectors, or what we call *drive geometry*.

FIGURE 4.3 Hard drive geometry

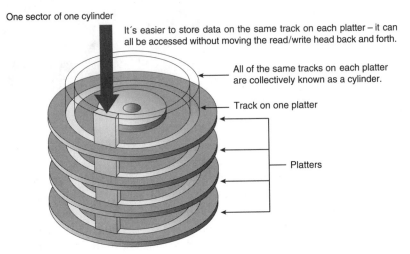

One sector of one cylinder

It's easier to store data on the same track on each platter – it can all be accessed without moving the read/write head back and forth.

All of the same tracks on each platter are collectively known as a cylinder.

Track on one platter

Platters

Disk Specifications

When a fixed disk is rated, it has several qualities that are given as specifications. Size, or capacity, is just one of the properties given. Size is determined by drive geometry. Let's quantify this by giving some values to each variable. Let's say we have 903 cylinders, 12 heads (6 platters—1 head per side, 2 sides to each platter), and 63 sectors per track. A typical fixed disk has 512 bytes per sector (that's 0.5KB/sector). The capacity of the hard disk would be 341,334KB, or 333MB (903 cyl × 12 heads × 63 sectors/track × 0.5KB/sector). These values are commonly given on the outside of a fixed disk.

Another quality that is used to gauge the performance of an individual drive is *seek time*. This value, commonly given in milliseconds (ms), is how long it takes the actuator arm to move from rest to the position where the read/write head will access information. Additionally, because the platters rotate, once the read/write is in position, it may take a few milliseconds for the target sector to move under the read/write head. This delay is known as the *latency factor*. Latency values are given in milliseconds (ms).

Because the faster a drive spins, the lower the average latency values, drives are also rated with a *spin speed*. Spin speeds indicate how fast the platters are spinning. They are stated in revolutions per minute (RPM); higher RPM values mean faster speeds and lower latency values. For example, if a disk has a spin speed of 5,000 RPM, it will be rotating at 83.34 revolutions per second. One rotation will take 1/83.34 seconds, or 11.9 ms. This value would represent the largest possible delay (i.e., the disk head is in position just after the required sector moved past it). However, disk latency values are actually only *average latency* values, because latency values are not constant. The target sector could be close, or it could be far away. So in our example, we take the largest possible latency (11.9 ms) and smallest possible latency (0 ms) and average them to get the average latency: (11.9 ms + 0)/2 = 5.95 ms.

The two factors, seek time and latency, make up the drive's *access time*. Put simply, the average seek time plus the average latency equals the drive's access time. The smaller the access time value is, the faster the drive.

Read/Write Processes

Now that we know how the drive functions and how the drives are rated, let's discuss the most important topic: how the drive stores the information. At the most basic level, the disk works by making flux transitions with an electromagnet in the read/write head to store information on the disk surface. A *flux transition* is the presence or absence of a magnetic field in a particle of the coating on the disk. As the disk passes over an area, the electromagnet is energized to cause the material to be magnetized in a small area. The process by which binary information is changed into flux transition patterns is called *encoding*.

There are many ways of converting 1s and 0s to flux transitions. The simplest way is to interpret the presence of a flux transition as a 1 and the absence as a 0. Because this was the most obvious choice, the first hard disks (ST-506, ESDI types) used this method of encoding, known as Frequency Modulation (FM), and its cousin Modified FM (MFM). This worked well until techniques for increasing the track/cylinder density became almost too successful. What happened was that tracks would be placed so tightly together that at higher speeds, the read/write heads would affect not only the track immediately under the head, but the adjacent ones as well.

To solve this problem, a technology known as *Run Length Limited (RLL)* was developed; it spaced the 1s farther apart using a special code for each byte. This method turned out to be more efficient for large drives than for small ones. RLL encoding also introduced *data compression*, a set of technologies that increased the amount of data that could be stored on the drive. Most of today's drives (IDE, SCSI, and so on) use a form of RLL encoding.

With this new type of encoding, much more data could be transferred to the computer at once, but this created a new problem. The interface would sometimes get bogged down and would stop reading in order to "catch up." This was a problem because during this pause, the platters were still rotating and the read/write heads could skip a whole bunch of sectors. To solve this problem, disk designers developed a technology known as *interleaving*.

A Question of Interleaves

Although interleaving may come up on the A+ Certification exam, the topic is almost irrelevant with the hard drives available in the last few years because the hardware technology has improved so much. Here's what you need to know for the test.

Interleaving involves skipping sectors to write the data instead of writing sequentially to every sector. This evens out the data flow and allows the drive to keep pace with the rest of the system. Interleaving is given in ratios. If the interleave is 2:1, the disk skips 2 minus 1, or 1 sector, between each sector it writes (it writes to one sector, skips one sector, then writes to the next sector). Most drives today use a 1:1 interleave, because today's drives are very efficient at transferring information. A 1:1 ratio means that the drive writes to one sector and then simply goes to the immediate next sector (skipping 1 minus 1 sectors, or 0 sectors). A 1:1 interleave ratio really means that the drive has no interleave at all.

To make it easier for the operating system to manage the storage space, the information encoded on the drive is written to groups of sectors known as *clusters*. A cluster is made up of up to 64 sectors grouped together (the actual number of sectors included in a cluster varies with the size of the hard disk). When the operating system is storing information, it writes it to a particular cluster instead of to an actual sector because it's more efficient for the operating system to keep track of clusters than sectors. The file that contains the information about where the tracks and sectors on the disk are located is known as the *file allocation table*, or *FAT*. It is contained in the outermost track (track 0) of the disk.

Why Is the FAT on Track 0?

Because advances in disk technology are constantly increasing the number of tracks, even on disks of the same size (i.e., the designers are always striving to increase the track density), if the FAT were located on the inside track, it might be in a slightly different position on one disk than on another. Also, because the outside track (track 0) is so easily accessible, the FAT is placed there so that the computer can use a simple routine to locate its operating system and disk information. Moreover, this routine never needs to change.

Formatting the Disks to Prepare Them for Use

To create the FAT, a machine at the factory performs a procedure known as a *low-level format*. This procedure organizes the disk into sectors and tracks. Once the sectors and tracks have been created, the low-level format procedure makes the FAT file and records in it the positions of the new sectors and tracks. Additionally, during this procedure, the low-level format procedure meticulously checks the disk's surface for defects. If any are found, the locations of these "bad spots" are entered into the FAT as well, so that the operating system knows not to store any information in those locations.

When an operating system is installed, it will do a *high-level format* (or operating system format) and create its own separate FAT that keeps track of where clusters are located and which files are located in which clusters. These two FAT technologies are applicable to all types of drives.

Removable Media Drives

Another type of drive system is *removable media* drives. Removable drives use technologies similar to fixed disk (fixed media) drives, except the storage medium is removable. The obvious advantage is that removable media multiplies the usefulness of the drive. With a hard disk, when the disk is full, the only two things you can do to increase space are to delete some information or get a larger drive. With removable media drives, you can remove the full disk and insert a blank one. Other than the Zip and Jaz drives discussed in Chapter 2 (and other than removable hard drives themselves), there are numerous categories of removable media drives covered on the test, as discussed in the rest of this section.

Floppy Disk Drives

The type of removable media drive that is the most often described is the floppy disk drive. It is called that because the original medium was flexible. Floppy disks are like fixed disks, but they have only one "platter" encased in a plastic shell. There are several types of floppy disk drives available in many different capacities (Figure 4.4 shows a 1.44MB 3½-inch drive), and we will discuss them in the sections to come.

FIGURE 4.4 A floppy disk drive

A floppy drive has either one or two read/write heads. Each head moves in a straight line on a track over the disk rather than on an angular path as with fixed disk systems. When the disk is placed into the drive, a motor engages the center of the disk and rotates it. This action moves the tracks past the read/write heads.

CD-ROM Drives

Another type of removable media drive is the CD-ROM drive (see Figure 4.5). These drives are slightly different from other storage media in several ways. First of all, they have a different way of reading information than magnetic media disk drives do. Because CD-ROM drives use laser light to read the information from the media, they are described as *optical drives*.

FIGURE 4.5   A CD-ROM drive

When reading information from a CD, the drive is basically reading a lot of *pits* and *lands* (lands are the spaces between the pits) in the disc surface. The pits are etched into the CD at production time. The laser reflects off the CD's surface and onto a sensor. The sensor detects the pattern of pits and lands as the disc rotates and translates them into patterns of 1s and 0s. This binary information is fed to the computer that is retrieving the data.

Another difference between magnetic media and CD-ROM drives is that CD-ROM drives are read-only devices (CD-ROM stands for Compact Disc–*Read-Only* Memory). The only way of writing to a CD-ROM is during manufacture time, where the pits are "burned" into the substrate of the disc. Once written, they cannot be erased.

The reason CD-ROMs are so popular, even though they can't be written to, is their large capacity (greater than 500MB) and easy access. They are a great choice for archival storage. Most often used for software distribution, they have really taken off in the past few years as the speed of CD-ROM drives has increased.

Recordable and rewritable CD devices are becoming popular; but strictly speaking, they are not CD-ROMs. Technically, these devices are called *rewritable compact discs*.

Finally, a CD-ROM disc has a single track that runs from the center to the outside edge, exactly the reverse of the groove on a record.

A CD-ROM uses basically the same technology as the audio compact discs in use in most homes today. When a CD-ROM is placed into a CD-ROM drive, a motor spins the CD at a specific rate. A laser that reads the CD is then activated. Because of these basic similarities, there are several compatibilities between the different compact disc technologies. For example, it is possible to play audio CDs in a computer's CD-ROM drive. Also, some computer CDs have audio tracks on them and are made to be used in either type of CD drive (home audio or computer).

This compatibility is possible because of *standards*. Standards are put together by committee (*de jure* standards) or documented simply to recognize a standard that's already in practice (*de facto* standards). CD-ROM standards are put together by several groups, the largest of which is the International Standards Organization (ISO), which has defined several standards. Table 4.1 shows the most popular CD standards and their respective applications. The compact disc standards are given as colors of books (we don't know why, they just are).

TABLE 4.1   Compact Disc Standards

CD Standard	Application	ISO Name (If Any)
Red Book	Audio CDs	CD-Audio
Yellow Book	Data Storage (CD-ROM)	ISO 9660
Green Book	CD-I (Interactive CD)	N/A
Orange Book	Write-Once CD and Magneto-Optical	N/A
White Book	CD-I Bridge	N/A

Optical Disk Drives

Another type of disk is the optical disk. An optical disk is much like a CD-ROM except that optical disks can be read from and written to (like fixed disks, except optical disks are similar to CD-ROM discs and thus a laser is used). The upside is that optical disks are removable and can hold lots of information. The downside is that they are expensive and are still slower than fixed disks.

Tape Drives

The final type of removable media drive is a tape drive (see Figure 4.6). The tape cartridge uses a long polyester ribbon coated with magnetic oxide wrapped around two spools. As the tape unwinds from one spool, it passes by a read/write head in the drive that retrieves or saves the information. It then proceeds to the other spool where it is kept until needed again.

FIGURE 4.6   A tape drive

Tape media is great for large-capacity storage, but it is agonizingly slow. The best application for tape media is for backup purposes. Current tape technology uses 4mm or 8mm Digital Audio Tape (DAT) or Digital Linear Tape (DLT) for its storage medium. With these technologies, it is possible to store up to 70GB of data on a single tape cartridge.

Disk Theory

With all of these storage technologies available, there are many to choose from. Which one is the best? The answer is, "It depends." Each type of storage has its own benefits and drawbacks. Each type of storage is ideally suited to a different application. To help understand this, a model has been developed to define the different types of storage. This model is called the "storage pyramid" and shows the relationship between the types of storage and their benefits (see Figure 4.7).

FIGURE 4.7   The "storage pyramid"

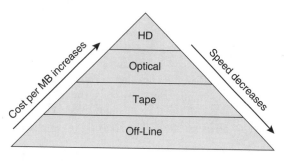

As you can see, at the bottom of the pyramid the storage types have the largest capacity but the slowest access times. Additionally, those types have the least expensive cost per megabyte.

Floppy Disk Systems

There are four major types of floppy disk drives in use today. They are usually identified by the size of the media they use and the capacity of that media. We'll cover each one and its associated configuration and troubleshooting issues. But before we do, let's discuss the four components of a floppy drive subsystem: the disk (also called the medium), the drive, the controller, and the cable.

The Medium

The floppy disk, as we have already mentioned, is the removable medium on which information is stored in a floppy disk system. There are two major types in use today, the 5¼-inch "floppy" disk and the 3½-inch "diskette" (sometimes incorrectly called a "hard floppy" or even a "hard disk"). Both are shown in Figure 4.8.

FIGURE 4.8 A 5¼-inch floppy disk and a 3½-inch diskette

5¼-Inch Floppy Disk

The 5¼-inch floppy disks are made from a polyester disk coated with iron oxide and a flexible outer covering. The disk has a large hole in the center, called the *drive hole*, that is used by the motor in the disk drive to spin the disk. In addition, there is also a 1½-inch oval window cut into the case to allow the read/write heads access to the disk media. A small round hole cut into the disk shell next to the drive hole lines up with an even smaller hole cut into the disk media. When this smaller hole spins past the slightly larger hole in the shell, it allows a light to shine all the way through the disk system. In this way, the floppy drive can tell how fast the disk is rotating by how many times in a second that hole appears.

Finally, there is a notch cut in one side of the disk. This notch is called the *write-protect tab*. When a disk is inserted into a floppy drive, a small lever places itself into this notch. When the lever is in the notch, the disk can be written to. You can "write protect" the disk (which prevents it from being written to) by covering this hole.

The 5¼-inch disks have almost completely disappeared in the last few years, replaced by the 3½-inch format, and most newer computers no longer include 5¼-inch drives.

Floppy disks and 5¼-inch disk drives aren't common in computers today. As such, you won't be tested on this topic in the A+ exam. We have included coverage in this chapter to provide you with background information.

3½-Inch Diskette

The other type of floppy disk media is not really "floppy" at all. Some people mistakenly call it a "hard disk." Its real name is a 3½-inch *diskette* (to differentiate it from a full-grown "disk," we suppose). The 3½-inch diskettes are also made from a polyester disk coated with a layer of iron oxide. This disk is enclosed in a durable, plastic case. This was an improvement over the 5¼-inch variety because the 5¼-inch floppies were easily creased or damaged. Also, the 3½-inch diskettes have a metal shutter over the media access window. Again, this was an improvement over 5¼-inch media because people often grasped the disks inadvertently by this edge of the disk, pressing their fingers onto the media and thus contaminating the disk, making it difficult to read.

Finally, there is a notch with a sliding plastic tab over it to write protect the 3½-inch disk. This is also better than 5¼-inch disks because the write-protect notch in the other disks was covered with a type of tape that could come loose in the drive and cause gum-ups.

The Drives

The next item we need to discuss is the floppy disk drives themselves. There are three items we need to discuss regarding the drives: media size, form factor, and capacity.

Media Size

Because we just covered media size in our discussion of the media, we'll just refer you to the previous paragraphs and continue on. We do want to make one note, however. You can't put a 5¼-inch diskette into a 3½-inch drive. Or vice versa. I know some of you are saying, "Thank you, Captain Obvious, for that enlightening bit of minutia." However, it has become apparent to us that not everyone seems to know this fundamental rule; we are constantly pulling folded-up 5¼-inch disks out of 3½-inch drives.

Form Factors

There are three main types of *form factors*, or drive styles, available today. A form factor usually just means the physical dimensions and characteristics. Today's floppy disk drives use either the full-height, half-height, or combo form factors. *Full-height* drives were the only ones available for the first PCs. The drives were large and bulky and usually lower in capacity than today's drives. Half-height drives take up only half the space (vertically) of full-height drives. (Captain Obvious?)

The final form factor is becoming more popular as space becomes a premium in computer cases. The *combination form factor* (or *combo*, for short) contains both 1.2MB 5¼-inch and 1.44MB 3½-inch drives in a half-height enclosure. This has the obvious advantage of having both drives in the space for one.

Capacity

The final topic in our discussion of drives is their capacity. The capacities range from 360KB to 1.44MB in various form factors. Table 4.2 details the range of capacities available today, their associated form factors, the number of sides used, and the density of the disk. Some disks use only one side of the media, whereas others use both sides. The density of a disk determines how closely the sectors and tracks can be packed. Notice how the combination of all three items relates to the capacity.

TABLE 4.2 Disk Capacities

Capacity	Form Factor	Density	Sides
180KB	5¼" FH	Single	Double
360KB	5¼" FH	Double	Double
720KB	3½" HH	Double	Double
1.2MB	5¼" FH or HH	High	Double
1.44MB	3½" HH	High	Double

You may have heard that even though some floppy disks and diskettes are rated as *single-sided*, in fact, *both* sides of a disk are *always* coated with media. Some people have taken this bit of industry knowledge and decided that it means you can actually store information on both sides of a single-sided disk. *Don't do it!* Even though the disk *might* be able to be formatted, that doesn't mean the data will stay on the disk. If the disk was rated as single-sided at the factory, you can be assured that the testing process determined that there were problems on the other side of the disk. Spend the extra 20 cents and get a disk that's rated for the drive you are using. The same holds true for formatting a low-density disk in a high-density drive and then using it in a low-density drive. These low-density disks aren't designed to have the information packed as tightly as the high-density drives save it.

The Controller

The floppy disk controller (Figure 4.9) is the circuit board that is installed in a computer and translates signals from the CPU into signals that the floppy disk drive can understand. Often, the floppy controller is integrated into the same circuit board that houses the hard disk controller. Or even better, the controller might be integrated into the motherboard in the PC. Some people might like this approach, but from a technician's standpoint, it's a nightmare. Imagine having to tell the customer that the reason their floppy drive doesn't work is because their motherboard needs to be replaced at a cost of $1,100! Wouldn't it be nicer to tell them that you need to replace the $22 floppy disk controller board?

FIGURE 4.9   A floppy controller with cable

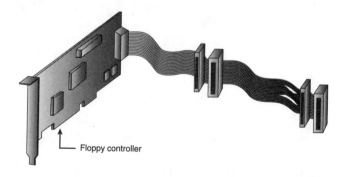

Floppy controller

A floppy controller is not a complicated device. The early controllers were large expansion boards that usually contained an Intel 8272 or Zilog 765 controller chip. As this book is being written, you can buy a card that contains the floppy controller, two serial interfaces, parallel and game interface ports, and disk interface for about $35.

The Cable

The last topic on our list of prerequisites is the floppy drive cable (shown in Figure 4.9). This cable is made up of a 34-wire ribbon cable and three connectors. One of these connectors attaches to the controller. The other two connect to the drives (one for drive A:, the other for drive B:). You can attach up to two floppy drives to a single controller. These connectors are specially made so that they can be attached to the drives in only one way.

Additionally, you might think that with 34 wires, the data would be transmitted in a parallel manner (8 bits at a time), but it isn't. Data is transmitted 1 bit at a time, serially. This makes floppy transfers slow, but usually the serial data transfer isn't the bottleneck.

The cable also has a red stripe running down one side, as shown in the detailed version in Figure 4.10. This stripe indicates which wire is for pin #1 on the controller and on the drive(s). This pin is usually marked with a small *1* or a white dot on the controller. When connecting the drives to the controller, you need to make sure that the red stripe is oriented so the wire it represents is connected to pin #1 on the drive and pin #1 on the controller. Also, you connect the drive that is going to be drive A: *after* the twist in the floppy cable for most ISA floppy systems (very important).

FIGURE 4.10 A typical floppy cable

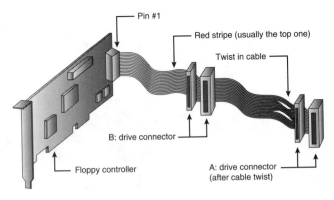

A common technician's trick to remember how to connect floppy drives is to say, "Point the red stripe toward the power cable." The problem is that this trick doesn't work with every brand of floppy drive. It could be considered a general "rule of thumb," but not a "rule to live by."

Installation and Configuration

Now that we've covered the basics, let's talk about installation, configuration, and troubleshooting. Installing floppy drives is no big trick. The first step is to connect the cable to the drive as per the aforementioned instructions. Then, install the drive in the computer by physically mounting it in the computer case and connecting the power cable. Finally, you connect the cable from the drive to the controller, as we discussed already.

With regular diskette drives, when connecting the cable to the drives, you connect the B: drive to the connector before the twist in the cable and the A: drive to the connector after the twist.

One unique situation crops up if you have a Compaq Deskpro. These computers have twists before each of the drives and the drives are reversed. The first drive on the cable, for Deskpros, is the A: drive, and the second drive is the B:. Finally, Deskpros will sometimes have a tape drive connected to the last connector on the cable, after the B: drive and on the same cable. This tape drive must be one specially made for a Deskpro.

Troubleshooting the floppy drive is also relatively simple. The most common problem after installation is a drive light that refuses to go out. This is caused by having the floppy drive cable upside down on one side. As you already know, most floppy cables are keyed so that they go on in only one direction. However, in some systems, the floppy cable might not be keyed, so you must understand the consequences of not having the cable on in the right direction. Just remember which way the red stripe goes!

In addition to the cable position, you must also set the drive type and size of the floppy drive in the CMOS setup. This is done so that the computer will know what drives are attached. If this information is wrong, most computers will detect that the wrong drive type is selected and an error will occur during bootup.

You can also troubleshoot sporadic read/write problems. More often than not, these are caused by a dirty drive. If this is the problem, it can be fixed with a floppy-disk head-cleaning kit. Another cause might be a bad floppy disk. Floppies have a finite number of uses in them and they *can* go bad. (This may come as a shock to some people who think their data is safe forever on a floppy disk.) This problem can be fixed by copying the data (if possible) from the old disk to a new one.

Also, don't forget to check the obvious things like disconnected floppy cable, power not plugged in, or disks not inserted properly. Any one of these can cause problems that most people just assume can't be the problem because it's too obvious.

Enough about floppies; let's talk about the disks that have a little more backbone: the hard disks.

IDE Disk Systems

ST-506 and ESDI drives were great drive systems in their day, but by the time the IBM AT computer came out, drive sizes were increasing beyond the capabilities of existing technologies to utilize them. The only way out was to use a technology called SCSI (pronounced "scuzzy," it stands for Small Computer System Interface—which we discuss in the next section). Although it was technologically superior, it was also, at the time, quite expensive. Two companies, Compaq and Western Digital, saw this problem and developed an alternative to SCSI.

Their idea was that if they could develop a cheap, flexible drive system, people would buy it. They were more right than they realized. That solution, known as Integrated Drive Electronics (IDE) because its major feature was a controller located right on the disk, is one of the most popular drive interfaces on the market today.

In this section, we'll discuss the theory behind IDE drive systems, as well as their configuration and installation issues.

IDE Technologies

The idea for IDE (more commonly known as AT Attachment interface, or ATA) was a simple one: Put the controller right on the drive itself and use a relatively short cable to connect the drive/controller to the system (Figure 4.11). This had the benefits of decreasing signal loss (thus increasing reliability) and making the drive easier to install.

FIGURE 4.11   An IDE drive and interface

In addition, because the controller was integrated into the same assembly as the drive, the only board that needed to be installed in the computer was an adapter that converted signals between the motherboard and the drive/controller. The board is normally called a pass-through or paddle board. (This board is often, incorrectly, called a controller. The term is incorrect because the paddle board is often integrated with a floppy controller, two serial ports, a game port, and a parallel port. In fact, this combination is normally called a multifunction interface board.) With some of today's systems, the IDE adapter is integrated into the motherboard.

The original IDE specification, in addition to being relatively simple to install, also can support drives of up to 528MB and speeds of 3.3MBps. To overcome limitations, a new technology was developed that could support drives of several gigabytes. This technology was *ATA version 2 (ATA-2)*. Also, these newer drives have data transfer rates of 11.1MBps. Because of marketing information, the general category of ATA-2 drives is known as Enhanced IDE, or EIDE.

The main limitation to IDE technologies is that they support only two drives (or four if you're using ATA-2). In order to add more drives, you must use a different technology, like SCSI. In addition, you are limited to only hard disks. To overcome this limitation, an extension to ATA-2 was developed, called the ATA Packet Interface (ATAPI). ATAPI allows other non–hard disk devices (like tape drives and CD-ROMs) to be attached to an ATA interface and coexist with hard disks.

Another update to the ATA standard is ATA version 4 (ATA-4), also known as *Ultra DMA IDE*. It can transfer data at 33MBps, so it is also commonly seen in motherboard specifications as Ultra DMA/33 or UDMA.

Installation and Configuration

Installation and configuration of IDE and EIDE devices is much easier than it is with ST-506 and ESDI systems. The basic steps for installing them are the same: Mount the drive in the carrier, connect the cable to the drive, install the drive in the computer, and configure the drive. However, IDE's cabling and configuration issues are less complex. For example, you only have a single, 40-pin cable to connect the drives to the computer. (And no, there aren't any twists in this cable.) Cabling is just a matter of connecting the drive(s) to the cable and plugging the cable into the paddle board (Figure 4.12). This is made easier because the majority of the IDE cables today are keyed so that they only plug in one way. If you happen to get one of the cables that isn't keyed, just use the red stripe trick (as discussed earlier in this chapter).

FIGURE 4.12   IDE cable installation

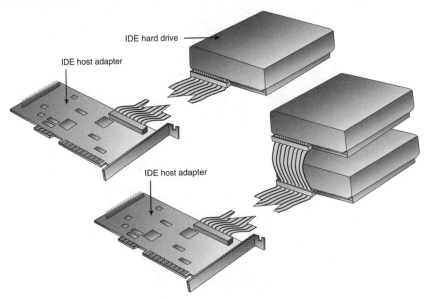

You may also want to note that some IDE drives come with only a two-connector cable, as shown at the top of Figure 4.12. If you need three connectors (for installing a second drive, as in the bottom of the figure), you may have to go to your local electronics supplier and get one.

The one situation that does complicate matters is when you have two (or more) drives in an IDE/EIDE system. Remember that an IDE drive has the controller *mounted on the drive*. If you had two drives connected, which controller would be talking to the computer and sending data back and forth? The answer is "Only one of them." When you install a second drive, you need to configure it so that the controller on one drive is active and the other drives use the controller on this drive for their instructions. You do this by setting the first drive to be the *master drive* and the others to be *slave drives*. As you might suspect, the master is the drive whose controller is used by the other drives (the slaves).

Also, most computer systems currently use ATA-2 technologies or above, which means that they can support four IDE drives. There will be a primary and a secondary IDE bus, and each will have its own master and slave drives. In these systems, you can have a primary master, primary slave, secondary master, and secondary slave drives. Which bus (primary or secondary) a device is shown as depends on the bus to which you connect the drive. From there, you can then designate each drive as master or slave as described in the next section.

Most CMOS setup programs will display all the IDE buses and which devices are connected in which positions. You can check which bus and which designation (master or slave) a device is configured for by using "View drive setup" (or similar) in your computer's setup program.

You implement the master/slave setting by jumpering a set of pins. There are several different configurations of these pins, so we'll just detail the most common. As always, check your documentation to determine which method your drive uses.

The first type is the simplest. There are two sets of pins, one labeled "master/single," the other labeled "slave" (Figure 4.13). If you have one drive, you jumper the master side and leave the slave side jumper off. If you have two drives, you jumper the master side only on the first drive (at the end of the cable) and jumper the slave side only on the other drive(s). A variant of this type uses no jumpers on either to indicate just one drive on the bus.

FIGURE 4.13   Master/slave jumpers

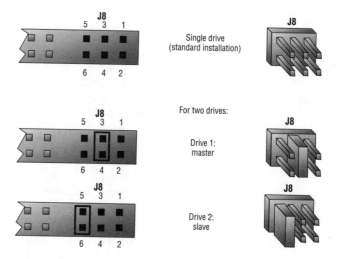

The other type commonly in use has three sets of pins labeled 1 through 6. These six pins are arranged in three rows of two, with one set labeled "master," another set labeled "slave," and the third set with no label. With one drive installed, you leave all jumpers off. With two drives installed, you set the first drive (usually located at the end of the cable) to *master* by jumpering the two pins labeled "master," then set the second drive to *slave* by jumpering the two pins labeled "slave."

If you have two drives on a bus and both are set to *master*, or both are set to *slave*, neither drive will work. In the first case (two masters), they will be fighting each other for control of the disks. In the latter case (two slaves), the disks won't know where to get their instructions from. However, if you have an EIDE interface system, you can have two masters as long as the drives are on two separate IDE buses.

Once you have the cable installed and the drives configured as either master or slave, you must tell the computer that the drives exist and what their drive geometry is. You do this by entering the BIOS's *CMOS setup program* (or the disk-based BIOS setup program for older computers). This setup program modifies the computer's settings in the CMOS memory that stores the configuration information for the computer. It is accessed by a special key or key combination at startup. Some BIOSs use Del, Esc, or one of the function keys; others use Ctrl+Alt+Esc. It should be noted that some of the newer BIOSs will auto-detect the type of drive installed in the system and automatically configure these parameters. With this type of system, you only need to accept these parameters and reboot.

If the drive you are installing is larger than 504MB (528,482,304 bytes), and most IDE drives today are, you must install it in a computer that has a BIOS that supports Logical Block Addressing (LBA). This technology allows the BIOS to access drives up to 8GB. Most BIOSes made after 1995 support this feature (although sometimes it has to be enabled).

Because each machine is different, we'll just talk in general terms. Once you have the disks installed, you enter the setup program, go to the Fixed Disk area, and enter the appropriate numbers for the number of cylinders, heads, and sectors that the drives have. You then save these values and reboot the machine. At this point, the system should recognize that there is at least one drive in the system.

There is one problem: Standard BIOS configuration of Cylinders, Heads, and Sector (CHS) information is limited to 1024 cylinders. If you are installing a drive with more than 1024 cylinders, somehow you must get the BIOS to recognize the drive's full capacity. The technology that BIOS manufacturers use to enable drive sizes larger than 1024 cylinders (approximately 600MB) is sector translation. Sector translation involves remapping the standard CHS layout of a drive in favor of a matrix that will allow the full capacity to be used. The most popular method is Logical Block Addressing (LBA). In LBA, each sector of the drive is number sequentially from the first usable sector to the last. With LBA enabled, the BIOS translates the LBA number of the data being requested into the CHS data for the drive. If you have a drive larger than 1024 cylinders, you must have a BIOS that supports LBA and it must be enabled.

You do not low-level format IDE (or SCSI) drives! IDE drives are low-leveled at the factory and should never be redone. They use a special utility to perform this delicate procedure. Performing a low-level format on an IDE or SCSI drive will render your drive unreliable, at the least (and will thus compound any problems you may have already been having). At the worst, it will make the drive completely useless by overwriting sector translation information. Once you have the drive installed and recognized by the computer, low-leveling is not necessary.

Now that your drive is installed, you can proceed to format it for the operating system you have chosen. Then, finally, you can install your operating system of choice.

And Now for the Real World...

IDE was such a popular hard disk interface that some people have adapted CD-ROM and tape devices to operate on IDE-type interfaces as well. Granted, it should be noted that an "IDE" CD-ROM may or may not coexist peacefully with an IDE hard disk. The former may reduce the performance of the latter. Some of the new Compaq computers, for example, have included a second IDE bus for the CD-ROM (it is labeled specifically for that purpose).

Small Computer Systems Interface (SCSI)

The last type of disk subsystem is probably the most flexible and the most robust. Conversely, it's probably also the most complex. In this section we'll discuss the theory behind the Small Computer Systems Interface (SCSI), the different types of SCSI, and configuration and installation issues.

As already mentioned, SCSI (pronounced "scuzzy") stands for Small Computer Systems Interface. It was a technology developed in the early '80s and standardized by the American National Standards Institute (ANSI) in 1986. The standard, which is known as ANSI document X3.131-1986, specifies a universal, parallel, system-level interface for connecting up to eight devices (including the controller) on a single, shared cable (called the *SCSI bus*). One of the many benefits of SCSI is that it is a very fast, flexible interface. You can buy a SCSI disk and install it in a Mac, a PC, a Sun workstation, or a Whizbang 2000, assuming they make a SCSI host adapter for it. SCSI systems are also known for their speed. At its introduction, SCSI supported a throughput of 5MB/sec (5 to 10 times faster than previous buses).

SCSI devices can be either internal or external to the computer. If they are internal, they use a 50-pin ribbon cable (similar to the 40-pin IDE drive cable). If the devices are external, they use a thick, shielded cable with Centronics-50 or male DB-25 connectors on it. These devices aren't always disk drives. Scanners and some printers also use SCSI because it has a *very* high data throughput.

To configure SCSI, you must assign a unique device number (often called a *SCSI address*) to each device on the SCSI bus (also sometimes call the *SCSI chain*). These numbers are configured through either jumpers or DIP switches. When the computer needs to send data to the device, it sends a signal on the wire "addressed" to that number. A device called a *terminator* (technically a *terminating resistor pack*) must be installed at both ends of the bus to keep the signals "on the bus." The device then responds with a signal that contains the device number that sent the information and the data itself.

This information is sent back to the *SCSI adapter*, which operates somewhat like a controller and somewhat like a paddle board. The adapter is used to manage all the devices on the bus as well as to send and retrieve data from the devices.

The adapter doesn't have to do as much work as a true controller because the SCSI devices are "smart" devices; they contain a circuit board that can control the read/write movement. It can also receive signals like "Get this information and give it to me." When a device receives a command like that, it is smart enough to interpret the signal and return the correct information.

Types of SCSI

The original implementation of SCSI was just called "SCSI" at its inception. However as new implementations came out, the original was referred to as "SCSI-1." This implementation is characterized by its 5MBps transfer rate, its Centronics-50 or DB-25 female connectors, and its 8-bit bus width. SCSI-1 also had some problems. Some devices wouldn't operate correctly when they were on the same SCSI bus as other devices. The problem here was mainly that the ANSI SCSI standard was so new that vendors chose to implement it differently. These differences would be the primary source of conflicts.

After a time, the first major improvement to SCSI-1 was introduced. Known as SCSI-2 (ANSI Standard document X3.131-1994), it improved SCSI-1 by allowing for more options. These options produced several subsets of SCSI-2, each having its own name and characteristics. But the most obvious change from SCSI-1 is that SCSI-2 now uses a higher-density connector (see Figure 4.14). Also, SCSI-2 is backward compatible with SCSI-1 devices.

FIGURE 4.14   A SCSI-2 connector

The first improvement that was designed into SCSI-2 was a wider bus. The new specification specified both 8-bit and 16-bit buses. The larger of the two specifications is known as Wide SCSI-2 because it's wider (Captain Obvious rides again). It improved data throughput for large data transfers. Another important change was to improve upon the now-limiting 5MBps transfer rate. The Fast SCSI-2 specification allowed for a 10MBps transfer rate, thus allowing transfers twice as fast as SCSI-1. So, Wide SCSI-2 transfers data 16 bits at a time, Fast SCSI transfers data 8 bits at a time, but twice as fast (at 10MBps).

Another option was to combine both into a blazingly fast technology known as SCSI-2 Fast-Wide. It combined the speed of Fast SCSI-2 with the bus width of Wide SCSI-2 to produce a transfer rate of 40MBps!

Finally, there is a new SCSI standard, SCSI-3 One of the feature sets is known as Fast-20 SCSI (also known to some as Ultra SCSI). Basically, this is a faster version of Fast SCSI-2 operating at 20MBps for narrow SCSI and 40MBps for Wide SCSI. Another feature set is the Ultra2 Low Voltage Differential (LVD), which increases the maximum SCSI bus length to 25 meters (82 feet) and increases the maximum possible throughput to 160MBps (on Ultra2 Wide LVD).

There are other proposed SCSI implementations, like Apple's FireWire, Fiber Channel, and IBM's SSA, all offering speeds in the hundreds of MBps range. Fibre Channel, specifically, is gaining support in the LAN arena because of its high-speed storage access and shared-media capability. The name Fibre Channel is somewhat of a misnomer because the technology will run over fiber optic cable, STP, or coaxial cable.

SCSI Device Installation and Configuration

Installing SCSI devices is rather complex, but you still follow the same basic steps as mentioned with the other types of drives (refer back to the previous types of hard disk interfaces if you're still unclear). The main issues with installing SCSI devices are cabling, termination, and addressing.

We'll discuss termination and cabling together because they are very closely tied together. There are two types of cabling:

- Internal cabling uses a 50-wire ribbon cable with several keyed connectors on them. These connectors are attached to the devices in the computer (the order is unimportant), with one connector connecting to the adapter.

- External cabling uses thick, shielded cables run from adapter to device to device in a fashion known as *daisy-chaining* (see Figure 4.15). Each device has two ports on it (most of the time). When hooking up external SCSI devices, you run a cable from the adapter to the first device. Then you run a cable from the first device to the second device, from the second to the third, and so on.

FIGURE 4.15 A "daisy chain"

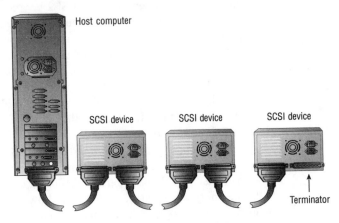

Because there are two types of cabling devices, you have three ways of connecting them. The methods differ by where the devices are located and whether or not the adapter has the terminator installed. The guide to remember here is that *both ends* of the bus must be terminated:

Internal devices only The first situation we'll discuss is one in which you have internal devices only (Figure 4.16). When you have only internal SCSI devices, you connect the cable to the adapter and to every SCSI device in the computer. You then install the terminating resistors on the adapter and on the last drive in the chain only. All other terminating resistors are removed.

FIGURE 4.16   Cabling internal SCSI devices only

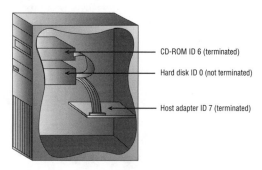

CD-ROM ID 6 (terminated)

Hard disk ID 0 (not terminated)

Host adapter ID 7 (terminated)

Some devices and adapters don't use terminating resistor packs; instead you use a jumper or DIP switch to activate or deactivate SCSI termination on such devices. (Where do you find out what type your device uses? In the documentation, of course.)

External devices only   In the next situation, you have external devices only (Figure 4.17). By external devices, we mean each with its own power supply. You connect the devices in the same manner you connected internal devices, but in this method you use several very short (less than 0.5 meters) "stub" cables to run between the devices in a daisy chain (rather than one, long cable with several connectors). The effect is the same. The adapter and the last device in the chain (the one with only one stub cable attached to it) must be terminated.

FIGURE 4.17   Cabling external SCSI devices only

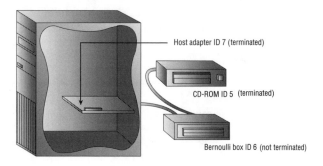

Host adapter ID 7 (terminated)

CD-ROM ID 5 (terminated)

Bernoulli box ID 6 (not terminated)

Both internal and external devices   Finally, there's the hybrid situation in which you have both internal and external devices (Figure 4.18). Most adapters have connectors for both internal and external SCSI devices—if yours doesn't have both, you'll need to see if anybody makes one that will work with your devices. For adapters that do have both types of connectors, you connect your internal devices to the ribbon cable and attach the cable to the adapter. Then, you daisy-chain your external devices off the external port. Finally, you terminate the last device on each chain, leaving the adapter *unterminated*.

FIGURE 4.18 Cabling internal and external SCSI devices together

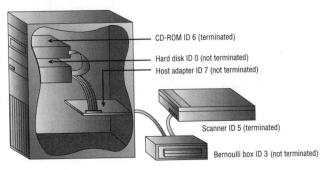

CD-ROM ID 6 (terminated)

Hard disk ID 0 (not terminated)
Host adapter ID 7 (not terminated)

Scanner ID 5 (terminated)

Bernoulli box ID 3 (not terminated)

Even though the third technique described is the technically correct way to install termination for the hybrid situation (in which you have both internal and external devices), some adapter cards still need to have terminators installed (for instance, Adaptec AHA-1542s). If you set up both internal and external devices and none of them work, you might have one of these adapters. Try enabling termination on it to see if that fixes the problem.

In addition to running the cable(s) correctly, it is important that you realize that you are limited to the number of devices you can have on the SCSI channel as well as the maximum length of the SCSI bus. Generally speaking, the faster the SCSI, the shorter the total length of the bus.

TABLE 4.3 SCSI Differences

SCSI Type	Bus Width (bits)	Max Devices	Transfer Rate (MBps)	SE (length in Meters)	LVD (length in Meters)	HVD (length in Meters)	Pins
SCSI-1	8	8	5	6	12*	25	25
SCSI-2	8	8	5	6	12*	25	50
Fast SCSI	8	8	10	3	12*	25	50

TABLE 4.3 SCSI Differences *(continued)*

SCSI Type	Bus Width (bits)	Max Devices	Transfer Rate (MBps)	SE (length in Meters)	LVD (length in Meters)	HVD (length in Meters)	Pins
Wide SCSI, aka Fast Wide SCSI	8	16	20	3	12*	25	68
Ultra SCSI	8	8	20	3	-	-	50
Wide Ultra SCSI	16	16	40	-	12*	25	68
Wide Ultra SCSI	16	8	40	1.5	-	-	68
Wide Ultra SCSI	16	4	40	3	-	-	68
Ultra2 SCSI	8	8	40	-	12	25	50
Wide Ultra2 SCSI	16	16	80	-	12	25	68
Ultra3 SCSI, aka Ultra160	16	16	160	-	12	-	68
Ultra4 SCSI, aka Ultra320	16	16	320	-	12	-	68

*NOTE: LVD was not part of these specs; however, if all devices are LVD, 12 meters applies. If any device is single ended, then length in SE column applies.

Information for this chart was obtained from the SCSI Trade Association (STA), San Francisco, CA, (www.scsita.org).

Now that you have them all correctly connected, you need to assign each device a unique SCSI ID number. This number can be assigned by jumper (with internal devices) or with a rotary switch (on external devices). You start by assigning your adapter an address. This number can be any number from 0 to 7 on an 8-bit bus, 0 to 15 on a 16-bit bus, and 0 to 31 on a 32-bit bus, as long as no other device is using that ID.

At our office, we have an 8-bit bus, so we normally set our adapter to 7 if we're using regular PC SCSI. This is because on PC SCSI, the higher the number, the higher the priority. If two devices request the bus at the same time, the device with the higher priority wins. However, if we were running PS/2 SCSI, the opposite would hold true (lower numbers, higher priority). So on PS/2s we would set our adapter to 0.

Every other device can be set to any number as long as it's not in use. However, there are some recommendations that are commonly accepted by the PC community. Remember that these are guidelines, not rules:

- Generally speaking, give slower devices higher priority so they can access the bus whenever they need it.
- Set the bootable (or first) hard disk to ID 0.
- Set the CD-ROM to ID 3.

One other note regarding setting the SCSI ID on internal devices: most internal devices use three sets of jumpers to set the SCSI ID. These three sets of jumpers represent three binary digits. The highest three-digit binary number is 111, the decimal equivalent of which is 7, or eight discrete positions (0-7). The presence of a jumper on one of these jumper sets would represent a binary "1" in that position. The absence of the same would indicate a binary "0". You set the decimal SCSI ID of a device by placing or removing jumpers on the three sets of pins so that the binary number indicated represents the SCSI ID you want the device set to. For example, if you want to set a device to SCSI ID 3, you must find out what the binary representation is. Remember from Chapter 1 that 011 is the binary representation of the decimal number 3. Therefore, you would jumper the rightmost two pins (although you should check which pins in your drive's documentation).

Now that you've got the devices cabled together and terminated correctly, you have to get the PC to recognize the SCSI adapter and its devices. The good news is that you don't have to modify the PC's CMOS settings. As a matter of fact, because SCSI devices are intelligent, you tell the PC that there is no disk installed and let the adapter handle controlling of the devices. You have two other ways of getting the PC to recognize the SCSI devices:

- If the device is going to be bootable, then you must set the card to be "BIOS enabled," meaning that the card has its own BIOS extension that will allow the PC to recognize the device without a software driver. The downside to this method is that the adapter must be configured to use an area in reserved memory for its BIOS. However, in a machine with only SCSI devices, it's the most efficient method.
- The other method, in case you haven't guessed it, is to load into the operating system a driver for the adapter. This method only works if you are booting from some other, non-SCSI device. If you must boot from the SCSI drive, you must use the preceding method. This method is commonly used when the only SCSI device attached to the computer is a scanner or CD-ROM drive.

Generally speaking, it's a bad idea to mix SCSI with any other disk technology. The only way you can make mixing work is to have the SCSI disks be secondary storage devices. It will degrade the performance of your system, however, because the boot files will be located on the first hard disk (the non-SCSI one). It will not work to have it the other way around (SCSI first, other disks second) because in that situation, their BIOSs will conflict as to who is the "boss."

Now that you have the drive installed and talking to the computer, you're almost done. At this point you can high-level format the media and install the operating system.

Remember the note about low-level formatting IDE and SCSI drives—*don't do it*!

If there are problems, double-check the termination and ID numbers. If everything looks correct, try changing ID numbers one at a time. SCSI addressing is one of those areas that is a "voodoo" art. Some things that should work don't, and some things that shouldn't work do.

Summary

Storage systems for PCs store data until is called for by the process. In this chapter, you learned about the various types of disk and storage systems available on PCs today, how they work, and the various capacities and access times for each.

In the first section, you learned to differentiate among the various types of storage. You learned about storage types used on older computer systems (storage types like punch cards and punch tape, as well as magnetic tape). These storage systems were the "grandparents" of the magnetic disks of today. In this section, you also learned how the basic types of storage work, as well as how they are laid out. You learned terms like FAT, cylinders, sectors, encoding, and interleaving.

In the next section, you learned how floppy disk storage works, the basic components of a floppy disk subsystem, and how to install and configure a floppy disk system. You learned about the different types of floppy disks available (3.5" and 5.25"), as well as the different types of drives associated with each type. You also learned about the controller and cable used to hook the floppy disk drive to the system so that data can be stored on it.

IDE disk drives are the most popular type of disk subsystem used by home PCs today. In the next section, you learned the details about this popular fixed disk system. Some of the things you learned in this section include the differences between the various types of IDE drives. You also learned how to properly configure a multiple-IDE disk system, including the concepts of multiple IDE buses and master and slave drives. Finally, you learned how to properly install and configure the different types of IDE disks.

In the last section in this chapter, you learned about Small Computer Systems Interface (SCSI) drives. SCSI drives aren't normally found in desktop PCs; they are more commonly found in servers because of their increased performance (and corresponding increased price). In this section you learned about the different types of SCSI buses. You also learned how to properly install and configure a SCSI disk, including how to properly terminate a SCSI bus and how to set the SCSI ID of a device.

Key Terms

Before you take the exam, be certain you are familiar with the following terms:

access time	low-level format
actuator arm	master drive
ATA version 2 (ATA-2)	optical drives
BIOS CMOS setup program	platters
clusters	read/write heads
cylinder	removable media
daisy-chaining	resistor pack
data compression	Run Length Limited (RLL)
drive geometry	SCSI adapter
drive hole	SCSI address
encoding	SCSI bus
FAT	SCSI chain
file allocation table	sector
fixed disks	seek time
flux transition	slave drives
hard disk drive	spin speed
hard disks	spindle
high-level format	tracks
interleaving	Ultra DMA IDE
latency	write-protect tab

Review Questions

1. Which IDE-related standard is able to transfer data at 33MBps?

   A. IDE

   B. ATA

   C. ATA-2

   D. UltraDMA (UDMA)

2. What are the most common sizes for floppy drives? (Select all that apply.)

   A. 3¼ inch

   B. 3½ inch

   C. 5¼ inch

   D. 5½ inch

3. How many devices can SCSI-1 support (including the controller)?

   A. 8

   B. 7

   C. 1

   D. 9

4. How many devices can be used by a single IDE Controller?

   A. 1

   B. 2

   C. 4

   D. 7

5. The device that converts signals from an IDE drive into signals the CPU can understand is called a _____ .

   A. Controller

   B. Host bus adapter

   C. Bus

   D. Paddle board

6. Which implementation of SCSI has a transfer rate of 20MB/sec?

    A. Fast SCSI-2

    B. Fast-Wide SCSI-2

    C. Wide SCSI-2

    D. Ultra SCSI

7. Suppose you have an internal SCSI hard drive and two external devices: a scanner and a CD-ROM drive. The scanner is the last device on the chain. Which device(s) should be terminated? (Select all that apply.)

    A. Hard disk

    B. Scanner

    C. CD-ROM drive

    D. Host bus adapter

8. The process known as _____ converts binary information into patterns of magnetic flux on a hard disk's surface.

    A. Fluxing

    B. Warping

    C. Encoding

    D. Decoding

9. What is the name for the areas that a typical hard disk is divided into (they look like the wedges in a pie)?

    A. Tracks

    B. Sectors

    C. Clusters

    D. Spindles

10. How do you low-level format an IDE drive?

    A. Enter the DEBUG.EXE program and enter **g=c800:5** at the – prompt.

    B. Run LOWLEVEL.COM.

    C. Execute FORMAT.COM.

    D. You don't; it's done at the factory.

11. Which SCSI implementation can transfer data at up to 10MBps?

    A. SCSI-1

    B. Fast SCSI-2

    C. UltraSCSI

    D. Wide Ultra2SCSI

12. How do you low-level format a SCSI drive?

   A. Enter the DEBUG.EXE program and enter **g=c800:5** at the – prompt.

   B. Run LOWLEVEL.COM.

   C. Execute FORMAT.COM.

   D. You don't; it's done at the factory.

13. Which of the following must be done when installing SCSI devices? (Select all that apply.)

   A. Terminate the first and last devices in the chain.

   B. Set unique SCSI ID numbers.

   C. Connect the first device to the connector before the twist.

   D. Set every device on the same SCSI channel to the same SCSI ID number.

14. Low-leveling a disk drive means _____ .

   A. Installing the drive in the bottom of the computer

   B. Getting a disk drive ready for the installation of an operating system

   C. Organizing the disk into sectors and tracks

   D. Organizing the disk into clusters and FATs

15. You have just replaced the floppy drive in a PC. Upon turning the computer on, you discover you can't boot to the floppy drive. The drive light turns on during power-up and stays lit until you turn the computer off. What should you do to solve this problem? (Select all that apply.)

   A. Change the drive type in the CMOS setup.

   B. Reverse the floppy drive cable.

   C. Remove the terminating resistor on the floppy drive.

   D. Move the floppy drive to the end of the floppy cable.

16. Which of the following is *not* a feature of disk drives?

   A. Rotating disks are coated with a special substance sensitive to magnetism.

   B. As the disk rotates, the particles of the substance become polarized or magnetized, indicating a 1.

   C. The unpolarized areas indicate a 0.

   D. These disk systems store data in linear format and store data in sequential access.

17. All of the following are disk specifications except _____ .

    A. Size or capacity

    B. Individual seek time

    C. Access time to perform read/write requests

    D. Spin speed

18. A typical hard drive has how many bytes per sector?

    A. 512

    B. 501

    C. 515

    D. 520

19. All of the following are means of disk organization except _____ .

    A. Tracks

    B. Heads

    C. Sectors

    D. Cylinders

20. If a typical hard disk has 903 cylinders, 12 heads, 63 sectors per track, and 512 bytes per sector, what is its capacity?

    A. 333MB

    B. 350MB

    C. 323MB

    D. 373MB

Answers to Review Questions

1. D. UDMA is able to transfer data at 33MBps. IDE and ATA are essentially the same technology and can transfer data at 3.3MBps. ATA-2 can transfer data at 11.1MBps.

2. B, C. The two sizes of drives that can be found are 3½ inch and 5¼ inch, but 3½ inch is more common now.

3. A. Including the controller card, SCSI-1 can support up to 8 devices, with address IDs ranging from 0 to 7.

4. B. Each IDE Controller can have a single master and a single slave device. Up to 2 IDE controllers are supported in most PC's.

5. D . The paddle board is the device responsible for converting signals from an IDE drive into signals the CPU can understand. It is commonly, and erroneously, called the controller card.

6. D. The Ultra SCSI, or SCSI-3, standard supports a transfer rate of 20MB/sec. This is twice as fast as the Fast SCSI-2 implementation.

7. A, B. In this example, you would want to terminate the internal hard drive, not the adapter, and terminate the scanner because it is the last device of the external chain.

8. C. Encoding converts binary information into patterns of magnetic flux on a hard disk's surface. This is how the data is written to the surface.

9. B. Although all of the options are terms that describe characteristics of the hard drive, sectors would most closely resemble pie-shaped wedges.

10. D . Low-level formatting should not *ever* be done because it is done before the drive leaves the factory. If you attempt to do so, you can render your drive unusable.

11. B. SCSI transfers data at 5MBps, Fast SCSI-2 at 10MBps, UltraSCSI at 40MBps, and Wide Ultra2SCSI at 80MBps.

12. D. Just as with IDE drives, you don't want to *ever* low-level format a SCSI drive. It can render your disk unusable.

13. A, B. To properly configure SCSI devices, the ends of the chain(s) must be properly terminated and each device must have a unique ID.

14. C. "Low-leveling" is a formatting process done at the factory that arranges the disk into the correct number of sectors and tracks. This is not something that should be done to IDE or SCSI drives because it will render them unusable.

15. A, B. One, or both, of two things need to be changed. More than likely, pin #1 is not properly connected to the ribbon cable on either the controller or the drive side of the cable. Also, it is possible that in CMOS setup, the drive is set to the wrong type and needs to be corrected.

16. D. Fixed disk drives store data randomly, so therefore, option D is not a feature of disk drives.

17. C. Generally, disk specifications are given as the capacity, the seek time, and the spin speed of the drive.

18. A. A typical hard drive has 512 bytes per sector.

19. B. Heads are a physical part of the drive system and are responsible for reading/writing the data, whereas all others are means of organizing the disk.

20. A. The way to solve this problem is to understand how the math works. Take $((903 \times 12 \times 63) \div .5) \div 1{,}024$ and the answer is roughly 333MB. The division by 1,024 is necessary to convert bytes to megabytes.

Chapter

5

PC Bus Architectures

THE FOLLOWING OBJECTIVES ARE COVERED IN THIS CHAPTER:

✓ **1.2 Identify basic procedures for adding and removing field replaceable modules for both desktop and portable systems.**

   Examples of modules:

- System board
- Storage device
- Power supply
- Processor/CPU
- Memory
- Input devices
- Hard drive
- Keyboard
- Video board
- Mouse
- Network Interface Card (NIC)

   Portable system components

- AC adapters
- DC controllers
- LCD panel
- PC card
- Pointing devices

✓ **1.7 Identify proper procedures for installing and configuring peripheral devices.**

   Content may include the following:

- Monitor/Video Card
- Modem
- USB peripherals and hubs
- IEEE-1284

- IEEE-1394
- External storage

Portables

- Docking stations
- PC cards
- Port replicators
- Infrared devices

✓ **4.3 Identify the most popular type of motherboards, their components, and their architecture (bus structures and power supplies).**

Content may include the following:

Types of motherboards:

- AT (Full and Baby)
- ATX

Components:

- Communication ports
- SIMM and DIMM
- Processor sockets
- External cache memory (Level 2)
- Bus Architecture
- ISA
- PCI
- AGP
- USB (Universal Serial Bus)
- VESA local bus (VL-Bus)
- Basic compatibility guidelines
- IDE (ATA, ATAPI, ULTRA-DMA, EIDE)
- SCSI (Wide, Fast, Ultra, LVD [Low Voltage Differential])

So far, we have discussed many key components in the average PC. However, we haven't talked about the way information travels between them. In this chapter, we'll cover the following A+ exam topics related to information flow:

- Expansion bus components
- The 8-bit expansion bus
- The Industry Standard Architecture (ISA) bus
- The Micro Channel Architecture (MCA) bus
- The Extended ISA (EISA) bus
- VESA Local Bus (VL-Bus)
- Peripheral Component Interconnect (PCI)
- Accelerated Graphics Port (AGP)
- Personal Computer Memory Card International Association (PCMCIA)

Additionally, we'll discuss the identification, installation, and configuration issues associated with each.

For complete coverage of objective 1.2, please also see Chapters 2, 8, and 9. For complete coverage of objective 1.7, please also see Chapters 7 and 9. For complete coverage of objective 4.3, please also see Chapters 2 and 4.

What Is a Bus?

Exactly what is a bus? A bus is a set of *signal pathways* that, as we have already alluded to, allow information and signals to travel between components inside or outside of a computer. There are three types of buses inside a computer: the external bus, the address bus, and the data bus.

The *external bus* allows the CPU to talk to the other devices in the computer and vice versa. It is called that because it's external to the CPU. When the CPU wants to talk to a device, it uses the *address bus* to do so. It will select the particular memory address that the device is using and use the address bus to write to that address. When the device wants to send information back to the microprocessor, it uses the *data bus*.

In this chapter, we'll focus primarily on the most common type of external bus—the expansion bus.

Expansion Bus Features

The expansion bus allows the computer to be expanded using a modular approach. Whenever you need to add something to the computer, you plug specially made circuit boards into the connectors (also known as *expansion slots*) on the expansion bus. The devices on these circuit boards are then able to communicate with the CPU and are semipermanently part of the computer.

The Connector, or Slot

The connector slots are made up of several tiny copper "finger slots," the row of very narrow channels that grab the fingers on the expansion circuit boards. These finger slots connect to copper pathways on the motherboard. Each set of pathways has a specific function. One set of pathways provides the voltages needed to power the expansion card (+5, +12, and ground). Another set of pathways makes up the data bus, transmitting data back to the processor. A third set makes up the address bus, allowing the device to be addressed through a set of I/O addresses. Finally, there are other lines for different functions like interrupts, direct memory access (DMA) channels, and clock signals.

Interrupt Lines

Interrupts are special lines that are connected directly to the processor; a device uses an interrupt to get the attention of the CPU when it needs to. It's rather like the cord you use to signal the driver when you need to get off at the next stop when you're a passenger on an actual bus. Just as you would use the "stop requested" cord to send a signal when you need the bus driver's attention, a computer device uses the *interrupt request (IRQ)* line to get the attention of the CPU.

There are several interrupt request lines in each type of bus. Lines 0 and 1 (corresponding to IRQ 0 and IRQ 1, respectively) are used by the processor for special purposes. The other lines are allocated to the various pieces of hardware installed in the computer. Not every line is used. In an average PC, there is usually at least one free IRQ line. When you configure a device for a computer, you must tell it which IRQ to use to get the attention of the processor. If two devices use the same IRQ line, the processor will get confused and neither device will work.

DMA Channels

Another feature of the bus is that it allows devices to bypass the processor and write their information directly into main memory. This feature is known as *direct memory access*, or *DMA*. Each type of bus has a different number of channels that can be used for DMA. If two devices are set to the same DMA channel, neither device will write information to memory correctly; thus, neither device will work.

I/O Addresses

Each bus type has a set of lines that are used to allow the CPU to send instructions to the devices installed in the bus's slots. Each device is given its own unique communication line to the CPU. These lines are called *input/output (I/O) addresses* and they function a lot like unidirectional mailboxes. If you want to send an invitation for people to come to a party, you write a message and address it to the mailbox of the person you want to invite. When the person receives the message, they read it and return some information, perhaps via some other method (such as a phone call). The I/O addresses (also called *I/O ports* or *hardware ports*) work in a similar fashion. When the CPU wants a device to do something, it sends a signal to a particular I/O address telling the device what to do. The device then responds via the data bus or DMA channels.

Clock Signals

Finally, each computer has a built-in metronome-like signal called a *clock signal*. There are two types: the *CPU clock* and the *bus clock*. The former dictates how fast the CPU can run; the latter indicates how fast the bus can transmit information. (In the first PCs, the CPU clock was also the clock for the bus.) The speed of the clocks is measured by how fast they "tick" and is given in millions of cycles per second, or Megahertz (MHz). The bus or the CPU can perform an operation only on the occurrence of a tick signal. Think of the clock signal as a type of metronome that keeps the processor "in time."

Bus Mastering

With DMA channels, a device can write directly to memory. But what if a device needs to read or write directly to another device (like the hard disk)? For this purpose, bus designers came up with *bus mastering*. This is a feature that allows a device to distract the CPU for a moment, "take control" of the bus, and read from or write information to the device. This feature can greatly improve performance of the device. Some buses can use several bus-mastering devices. The more bus-mastering devices, the faster the bus can operate.

Now that we have discussed the basic expansion bus concepts, we'll use these concepts to describe each of the different types of buses.

The 8-Bit Expansion Bus

The first type of expansion bus we're going to discuss is the 8-bit bus. It is also sometimes known as "You know, the first PC bus." When the first PC was developed with the Intel 8088, it only had eight data lines running from the processor to the expansion connectors. Each line carried 1 bit of data. Thus was born the *8-bit bus*. This was the most common name given to this particular bus. Some other names include the IBM PC bus, the XT bus, and the "slow bus." (Okay, that last one is a name *we* gave it, but it's true, don't you think?)

Information and Identification

The 8-bit bus is characterized by having a maximum bus clock speed of 4.77 (approximately 5) MHz, 8 interrupts (of which 6 could be used by expansion devices), 4 DMA channels, and 1 large connector with 62 tiny "finger slots" (channels) along the sides (see Figure 5.1).

FIGURE 5.1   The 8-bit bus connector

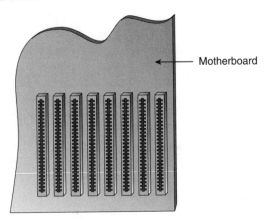

Motherboard

It is very rare to find an 8-bit bus in today's computer. If you do, it's usually just one: an 8-bit slot for a single 8-bit expansion card (Figure 5.2). The expansion cards for this size bus are easily identifiable because they have only one connector. Also, when these cards came out, Very Large Scale Integration (VLSI) had not taken off yet, so if you find an 8-bit card, it will usually be packed with resistors and other large electronics components.

FIGURE 5.2 An 8-bit bus expansion card

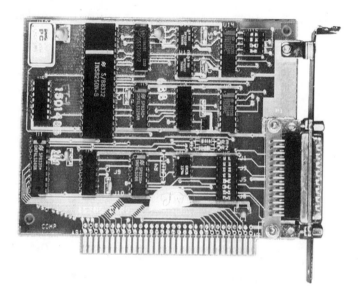

The 8-bit bus died out about the same time the 8-bit processors fell by the wayside. It wasn't efficient to try to shoehorn 32 bits or more into a bus that can only accept 8 bits at a time. Even so, some manufacturers tried to accomplish just that by placing a 386 chip on a motherboard with an 8-bit bus. What normally happened in that situation is that the computer divided the 32-bit signal into four 8-bit "chunks." It was a lot like trying to run lunchtime city freeway traffic down a side street. Every car could get through, just a lot more slowly. Also, because most processors run quite a bit faster than 4.77MHz, it was like putting the speed limit on that side street at 4.77 MPH instead of 55 MPH. Just a bit poky, don't you think?

Also, in the 8-bit bus, there were only eight interrupts and four DMA channels, most of which were being used. It made expansion of the 8-bit bus relatively difficult because there were very few choices to set expansion cards to. Tables 5.1 and 5.2 show the default uses for the eight IRQ lines and four DMA channels.

TABLE 5.1 8-Bit Bus Default IRQ Assignments

IRQ Line	Default Assignment
IRQ 0	System Timer
IRQ 1	Keyboard
IRQ 2	Available
IRQ 3	COM 2
IRQ 4	COM 1
IRQ 5	Hard Disk Controller
IRQ 6	Floppy Controller
IRQ 7	LPT1

TABLE 5.2 8-Bit Bus Default DMA Channel Assignments

DMA Channel	Default Assignment
DMA 0	Dynamic RAM Refresh
DMA 1	Hard Disk Controller (XT)
DMA 2	Floppy Controller
DMA 3	Available

Bus Configuration

Configuring your devices involves assigning system resources (that is, DMA channels, IRQs, and I/O addresses) that aren't being used by other devices. Configuration of the 8-bit bus is relatively complex, primarily because there is only one IRQ (IRQ 2) and one DMA channel (DMA 3) available. With so few system resources available, you have to decide which components will use each of the limited resources. One way to free up resources is to disable a device that you won't be using at the same time you'll be using the device you need to work with.

Each card must be separately configured to operate with the computer according to the instructions that come with the card. You set the configuration on each card using jumpers and Dual Inline Package (DIP) switches so that the settings are the way you want them. The first step in the procedure is to take the case off the computer. Next, you configure the card using the aforementioned jumpers. After that, you install the card in a free slot (assuming you have one). Finally, you boot the computer and install the software drivers to activate the card. If all was successful, the drivers will load without incident. If a conflict exists, you must repeat the entire procedure, changing one setting at a time until you get the correct setting, one that doesn't conflict with any other devices. A tedious process, to be sure.

We will cover expansion card installation in detail in Chapter 8.

The Industry Standard Architecture (ISA) Bus

The biggest shortcoming of the 8-bit bus was that it was only 8 bits wide. The design of the IBM AT processor specified a processor with a 16-bit data path. A new bus was needed for this processor because the old bus would cause the "traffic jam" scenario described earlier. The new bus design was a 16-bit bus; it was given the same name as the computer it was designed for: the *AT bus*. It was also known as the *Industry Standard Architecture (ISA) bus*.

Information and Identification

The ISA bus is easily identifiable by the presence of the small bus connector behind the 8-bit connector, as shown in Figure 5.3. This additional connector adds several signal lines to make the bus a full 16-bit bus. The other connector is a regular 8-bit bus connector. The ISA bus has eight more interrupts than the 8-bit bus and four additional DMA channels. Also, this bus can operate at nearly twice the speed of the older, 8-bit bus (ISA can run at 8MHz, and Turbo models can run as fast as 10MHz reliably). Finally, this bus can use one bus-mastering device, if necessary.

FIGURE 5.3   An ISA bus connector

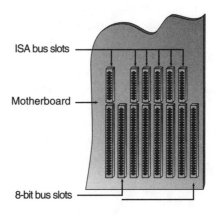

ISA expansion cards use a connector similar to the 8-bit bus but with the additional connector for the 16-bit data and address lines (Figure 5.4).

FIGURE 5.4   An ISA bus expansion card

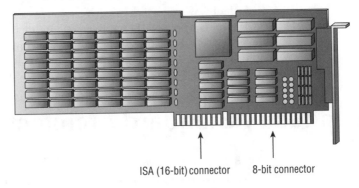

ISA (16-bit) connector   8-bit connector

One interesting thing about the ISA bus is that it is backward compatible with the older, 8-bit bus. ISA bus slots are basically 8-bit slots with the extra signal lines required to make them 16-bit on a second connector. Expansion cards made for the PC's 8-bit bus can be inserted into ISA slots and they will function properly. There is one exception, however. Some 8-bit cards have a "skirt" extending below the bus slot. This skirt will not allow the 8-bit card to be inserted all the way into the ISA slot. It is for this reason that you will sometimes have 8-bit slots mixed in with ISA slots on the same motherboards.

A major problem cropped up, however, when CPU speed outpaced the 8MHz bus speed (like the early Compaq with its 12MHz 286 processor). The computer could not use the ISA bus because that bus ran at 8MHz and the processor ran faster. Putting a 12MHz processor in this type of system would limit it to running at 8MHz, thus negating any benefits received from a faster processor.

The solution was to dissociate the CPU clock from the bus clock. This would allow the 12MHz processor to run at its rated speed and let the 8MHz ISA bus run at its rated speed. When information needed to get transferred to a component on the ISA bus, it was transferred at the 8MHz clock speed. But all other operations inside the processor happen at 12MHz.

This works well, with one exception. Some boards (like memory expansion boards) *need* to run at the processor's speed. If you put memory in an ISA board and place it in an ISA bus along with a 33MHz processor, information will get transferred from memory to the processor at 8MHz instead of 33MHz! This is a serious performance degradation. Granted, you don't find many ISA memory boards, but the potential is there. Take heart, though. This problem has been solved in a few of the other bus types (those buses that are considered to be "local" buses).

Bus Configuration

Configuring expansion cards for use in ISA buses is a little less complex than configuring 8-bit buses, mainly because there are more choices available for interrupts and DMA channels. Tables 5.3 and 5.4 list the interrupts and DMA channels that are available in an ISA system.

TABLE 5.3   ISA Bus IRQ Defaults

IRQ	Default Assignment
IRQ 0	System Timer
IRQ 1	Keyboard
IRQ 2	Cascade to IRQ 9
IRQ 3	COM 2 and 4
IRQ 4	COM 1 and 3
IRQ 5	LPT2 (usually available)
IRQ 6	Floppy Controller
IRQ 7	LPT1
IRQ 8	Real Time Clock (RTC)
IRQ 9	Cascade to IRQ 2
IRQ 10	Available
IRQ 11	Available
IRQ 12	Bus Mouse port (available if not used)
IRQ 13	Math Coprocessor
IRQ 14	Hard Disk Controller Board
IRQ 15	Available

TABLE 5.4   ISA Bus DMA Channel Defaults

DMA Channel	Default Assignment
DMA 0	Available
DMA 1	Available
DMA 2	Floppy Controller
DMA 3	Available
DMA 4	Second DMA controller
DMA 5	Available
DMA 6	Available
DMA 7	Available

Note that COM 1 and COM 3 share the same interrupt, as do COM 2 and COM 4. The pairs are differentiated by using different I/O addresses for the different COM ports. This can work without conflict. The only problem is if you connect two devices that need to use an interrupt to the COM ports that use the same interrupt (for example, a mouse on COM 1 and a modem on COM 3). When this happens, the devices will work separately, but if you try to use both at the same time (for example, use the mouse while downloading a file with the modem), they will conflict and problems will occur.

The same procedures that are used to configure the 8-bit expansion cards are used to configure ISA cards. You need to configure the card for interrupts, memory addresses, DMA channels, and I/O ports. Again, this is done using jumpers and DIP switches.

One special case exists for interrupts when configuring them. You will notice that some interrupts are "cascaded" to each other. What this means is that in an ISA system, when the computer needs to access an interrupt higher than 9, it uses IRQ 2 to get to it. This method ensures backward compatibility with 8-bit buses.

As the ISA bus and its expansion cards evolved, people got tired of setting all those jumpers and DIP switches. As the saying goes, "Build a better mousetrap and the world will beat a path to your door." Well, someone found a better way to configure ISA devices. They found that if they put the jumper positions into an EEPROM chip on the device, they could set them using a special software configuration program. Because it's so easy, this method is used to configure the settings of most ISA cards today.

There is a special case with regard to configuring ISA buses: the ISA Plug-and-Play bus. This bus consists of a standard ISA bus and a special set of BIOS extensions. The extensions examine the installed Plug-and-Play–compatible cards at start-up and set them to available settings. At least that's the theory.

The Micro Channel Architecture (MCA) Bus

Even though IBM developed the original 8-bit bus and had a hand in developing ISA, through the early part of the 1980s it steadily lost its domination of the PC market. But IBM had an ace up its sleeve. It was developing a new line of computers called the PS/2 (Personal System 2). Along with the new computer, it was developing a new bus that was supposed to be better than ISA in every way. Its higher-end models (PS/2s numbered more or less sequentially from 50 to 80) were going to incorporate this new bus. This bus used a smaller, high-density connector and was known as Micro Channel Architecture (MCA).

Information and Identification

MCA was a major step forward in bus design. First, it was available in either 16-bit or 32-bit versions. Second, it could have multiple bus-mastering devices installed. Third, the bus clock speed was slightly faster (10MHz instead of 8MHz). And finally, it offered the ability to change configurations with software rather than with jumpers and DIP switches.

The MCA bus connector is a high-density connector that looks similar to an ISA bus connector. However, the MCA bus connector has almost twice as many connectors in a smaller area and is segmented to provide for 16-bit, 32-bit, and video extension segments.

There are two easy ways to identify an MCA bus card. The first is by the connector on the card (see Figure 5.5). It looks like no other bus connector. The connectors on the card are spaced closely together. The second is by the labeling on the connector. Most MCA cards (more than 80 percent) are made by IBM. When you take an MCA card out of the package, you will notice that there are two *blue* handles on the top of the card. It's likely that the handles will display the IBM logo. Even if the cards were made by other vendors, the handles will still more than likely be blue.

FIGURE 5.5 An MCA bus expansion card

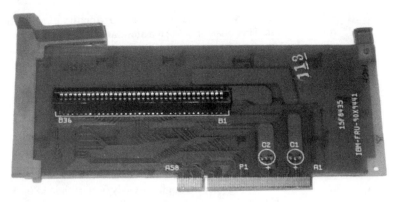

The MCA bus was a bold venture for the folks at IBM. They were hoping it would be *the* new standard for the PC bus. Unfortunately, it had a major drawback. It was *very* proprietary. Anyone who wanted to clone the MCA bus had to pay around five percent of their *gross* receipts to IBM. Although it was one of the best technically, it was more expensive. And it was incompatible with the established ISA bus architecture. It was for these reasons that many system designers chose not to "hop on the MCA bandwagon" and implemented other bus choices instead.

Bus Configuration

As we have already mentioned, one of MCA's strengths is that you can use software to configure it. Installing an expansion card in an MCA slot still involves the same concepts as installing an ISA card. You must configure the card to use an available IRQ, DMA channel, memory address, and I/O ports. To configure the options on these cards, you must use a *Reference disk* and an *option diskette* after installing the device into the computer physically.

The Reference disk is a special disk that is bootable and contains a program that is capable of sending special commands to bus devices to configure their parameters. This disk is included with the computer and is special in that it only works with one particular model of MCA bus computer.

Don't lose the Reference disk or option diskette. You can't add new devices without them. Make backup copies and use them to configure the system. Place the originals in a safe place.

Every new MCA device you can install will come with an option diskette. An option diskette contains the device-specific configuration files for the device being installed. For example, if you are going to install a sound card, the option diskette will contain settings pertaining to how the sound card needs to communicate with the rest of the computer.

Device-specific configuration files are also called ADF files because their filenames have an `.adf` extension.

Once you have a new device ready to be installed, you shut down the computer and install the board into the slot. Then, you boot the computer to the Reference disk. From the Main menu, select the option to configure the installed boards, then choose the slot number of the board you wish to configure. Because this is a new board, you will be prompted to insert an option diskette with the configuration files on it. This is where you insert the option diskette that came with the card. The files particular to the new device will be copied to the Reference disk so that the next time you need to change its settings, the files will already be on the Reference disk.

The Extended ISA (EISA) Bus

Because MCA was rather expensive and ISA was slowing down their systems, a few companies (mainly Olivetti, Compaq, AST, Tandy, WYSE, Hewlett-Packard, Zenith, NEC, and Epson, a.k.a. the "gang of nine") got together and came up with the Extended ISA, or EISA. This bus took the best parts of the other buses and combined them into a 32-bit software-configurable bus. The best part was that 16-bit ISA cards were compatible with this new bus and the standard was open.

Information and Identification

There were several new, desirable features introduced with EISA. Its creators took the best of MCA's features and added to them. As we have already mentioned, EISA has a 32-bit data path. Additionally, it has more I/O addresses, it allows expansion cards to be set up using software, there is no need for interrupts or DMA channels, and it allows for multiple bus-mastering devices. However, despite all these advances, it still uses the 8MHz clock speed of ISA (to ensure backward compatibility with ISA cards).

The bus slots (Figure 5.6) have both 16-bit and 32-bit finger slots. The 16-bit finger slots and the 32-bit finger slots alternate every other finger slot. Also, the 16-bit finger slots are located toward the top of the connectors and the 32-bit finger slots are buried deep within the connectors. The reason for all this alternating, burying, and arranging is that when you insert a 16-bit card, it will only go in halfway and make contact with the top (16-bit) connectors.

But an EISA card (Figure 5.7), because of its longer fingers, will seat all the way into an EISA slot and make full contact with the deeper, 32-bit finger slots.

FIGURE 5.6 An EISA bus connector

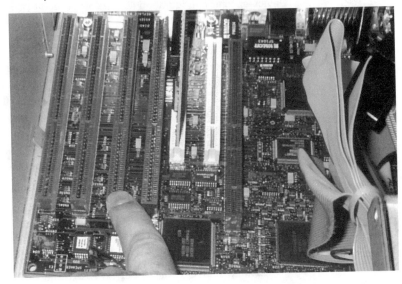

FIGURE 5.7 An EISA bus expansion card

Bus Configuration

Configuring an EISA bus is similar to configuring an MCA bus, unless you install an ISA card into an EISA bus slot. If you do that, the configuration issues for ISA apply (including interrupts, DMAs, and so forth). If you are using only EISA cards, then the steps are quite different.

First, you must select a slot number to install the card into. Obviously, the slot must not have a card already installed in it. Second, you must install the card into one of the available slots. Third, you must boot the computer. When you do this, the computer will recognize that there is a new, unconfigured card in the bus slot (very much like a Plug-and-Play ISA bus without the auto-configuration). Then, you are given the choice to run the *EISA Configuration Utility* program (or *EISA Config* for short) or to continue and ignore the new information. If you choose the latter, the next time you boot, you will be asked again.

To access the EISA configuration program on a Compaq server, press F10 when the flashing, white cursor appears in the upper-right corner of the screen at system start-up. If the cursor doesn't appear, then the EISA configuration program was not installed onto the boot sector(s) of the first hard disk. Booting to the Compaq EISA Configuration Utility disk for the first time will assist you in this process.

If you choose to configure the bus, you must have the EISA Configuration Utility disk in the A: drive so that the computer can boot to it. During the boot process, the EISA Config program will detect which card has been installed and will ask for a disk with the configuration files. These files are device specific, have the extension .cfg, and can be downloaded from the particular vendors. Also, the CFG files specific to the devices installed in the computer will be copied to the Configuration Utility disk so that you can use that disk to change the various parameters without having to have more than one disk.

Once the computer is booted, you will be running the EISA Config utility and can then pick which slot number the new card is using by selecting it from the menu. When you are viewing this portion of the configuration screen, you can change any parameters you need to. After you do so, you select the Save the Configuration Information to the BIOS option and reboot the computer. The computer now knows about the card and what resources it's using.

The high-performance and ease-of-configuration benefits offered by EISA were seen mainly in Intel 80486 and newer processors. For quite some time, EISA buses were the primary expansion bus for servers; now, however, they are quickly being replaced by the PCI bus (covered later in this chapter).

VESA Local Bus (VL-Bus)

The EISA bus had several major advantages, but it had one glaring problem: It had a maximum clock speed of 8MHz. As processors got faster and faster, the 8MHz limit was a major obstacle. What was needed was a bus that would run at the same clock speed as the processor. This type of bus is known as a *local* bus.

There are several different types of local buses. One type is a *bus slot*, usually called something like a processor direct slot. It is used for adding higher-speed expansion cards, like memory or cache cards. And because it is a local bus slot, it runs at the processor's rated speed. It is usually a single connector, and it's highly proprietary. Usually, only cards made by the computer's manufacturer will work in this slot.

Some companies took this idea and thought that they could speed up some components in the computer by putting them onto the local bus. In addition to the memory and cache cards, one of the first components to be put on the local bus was the video circuitry, because it could benefit from direct communication with the processor. Some manufacturers designed a special local-bus video card slot and designed special, high-performance cards for these slots. This approach became very popular and most companies adopted it. The problem with this approach is that the local-bus video card from one vendor would not work in a local bus slot from another vendor.

The Video Electronics Standards Association (VESA) was formed for this reason. This group made sure that cards made for one vendor's slot would work in another vendor's computer. As time passed, the slot design changed and was given a new name, the *VESA Local Bus slot* (and was also known variously as VL-Bus, VLB, or just VESA, after the group that came up with the standard). This slot was a 32-bit addition to the ISA bus and was therefore backward compatible with it.

VLB has one major drawback in that it really is just a bigger ISA bus; namely, it still has the same limitations as ISA. Configuration is still done through jumpers and DIP switches instead of through special bus-configuration programs. It's been called the "big ISA" bus because that's what it is: just a 32-bit version of ISA.

Information and Identification

Identifying a VL-Bus slot is easy, if you know what to look for. First, VESA designed this slot to be an extension of ISA. A VL-Bus slot is a regular ISA slot with the 32-bit, local bus connector added to the ISA bus connector as a third bus connector (Figure 5.8). This connector is a high-density connector that has all of its lines running directly to the processor.

FIGURE 5.8 A VL-Bus connector

The VL-Bus expansion card is also easily identifiable. The card is a bit longer than an ISA card and has one extra connector (the 32-bit, local connector). Figure 5.9 shows two typical VL-Bus expansion cards. These cards are typically used for video cards (as previously mentioned), SCSI host bus adapters, and multimedia expansion cards (sound cards, hard drive and CD-ROM controllers, and video input devices) because of the amount of throughput they need. Typically, you'll find no more than three VL-Bus connectors on a motherboard (mixed with other bus types). Any more than three and the processor wouldn't be able to keep up with the bus transfers.

FIGURE 5.9 VL-Bus expansion cards. Top: A video card. Bottom: An IDE hard drive controller.

 Because you can have only three VL-Bus slots in a PC, most vendors will mix VL-Bus slots and ISA slots (or EISA slots) on the motherboard. This approach gives the computer owner more choices for expansion.

Bus Configuration

There is very little new information we need to discuss about the configuration of VL-Bus devices. Primarily, they are ISA bus devices with an extra connector. When you configure a VLB card, you perform operations that are similar to those you perform when configuring ISA cards (moving jumpers, setting DIP switches, and so on). However, because the VL-Bus is a more modern bus, some of these cards are Plug and Play or, at the very least, software configurable.

Peripheral Component Interconnect (PCI)

With the introduction of the Pentium-generation processors, all existing buses instantly became obsolete. Because the Pentiums were 64-bit processors and most buses were of the 16-bit or 32-bit variety, using existing buses would severely limit the performance of the new technology. It was primarily for this reason that the Peripheral Component Interconnect (PCI) bus was developed.

PCI has many benefits over other bus types. First, it supports both 64-bit and 32-bit data paths, so it can be used in both 486 and Pentium-based systems. In addition, it is processor independent. The bus communicates with a special "bridge circuit" that communicates with both the CPU and the bus. This has the benefit of making the bus an almost universal one. PCI buses can be found in PCs, Mac OS–based computers, and RISC computers. The same expansion card will work for all of them; you just need a different configuration program for each.

Another advantage to PCI over other buses is a higher clock speed. PCI (in its current revision) can run up to 66MHz. Also, the bus can support multiple bus-mastering expansion cards. These two features give PCI a maximum bus throughput of up to 265Mbps (with 64-bit cards).

The final two features of PCI that we should discuss are its backward compatibility and software setup features. The PCI bus uses a chipset that works with PCI, ISA, and EISA. It is possible to have a PC that contains all these buses on the same motherboard. Also, the PCI cards are mostly Plug and Play. The cards will automatically configure themselves for IRQ, DMA, and I/O port addresses.

In some systems that are a combination of PCI and ISA, each PCI slot will be located right next to an ISA slot. When you put a card in that PCI slot, you disable the ISA slot and vice versa. Only one card will fit in a combination slot at a time.

Information and Identification

Identification of PCI bus slots is very simple. The finger slots in the bus (Figure 5.10) are packed together tightly. This connector is usually white and contains two sections. There are two versions of the PCI bus that are found in today's systems. The versions are differentiated by the voltages that they use. One uses +5.5Vdc to power the expansion cards, the other uses +3.3Vdc. When you look at the connectors for these buses, the only difference you'll see is the different placement of the *blocker* (called a key) in each connector so that a +3.3Vdc card can't be plugged into a +5.5Vdc bus slot and vice versa.

FIGURE 5.10   PCI bus connectors

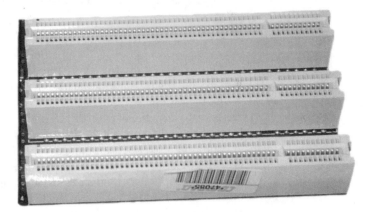

Bus Configuration

When you need to configure a PCI expansion card (Figure 5.11), you don't move jumpers or DIP switches; you simply install the card. The computer's BIOS takes care of configuring IRQ, I/O, and DMA addresses. Then you install the appropriate software so that the computer can use the device.

FIGURE 5.11   A PCI expansion card

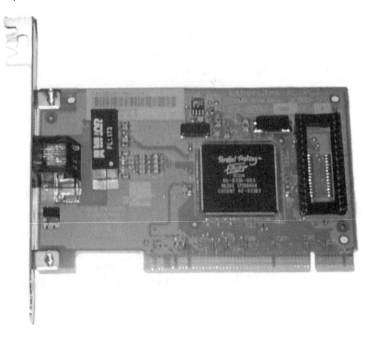

Accelerated Graphics Port (AGP)

As Pentium systems got faster, PC game players got games that had better graphics, more realism, and more speed. However, as the computers got faster, the video technology just couldn't seem to keep up, as was the case with the VL-Bus discussed earlier. VL-Bus could only run at 33MHz, and with 100 and 200MHz processors, there was a need for a faster, processor-direct, video expansion bus. The bus that was developed to meet this need was the *Accelerated Graphics Port (AGP) bus.*

Information and Identification

The AGP connector is similar in physical size and appearance to a PCI connector (as shown in Figure 5.12). But it's usually darker in color and offset from the other PCI slots to avoid confusion. The reason for the similarities is that Intel started with PCI 2.1 interface specifications to develop AGP. The bus is 32 bits wide, just like PCI. However, the similarities end there. AGP actually runs at twice the memory bus speed (as opposed to PCI, which runs at only half the memory bus speed). AGP runs at 66MHz. Additionally, in its fastest mode, AGP can transfer data at 528.6MBps! PCI is limited to 127MBps.

FIGURE 5.12 An AGP slot on a motherboard

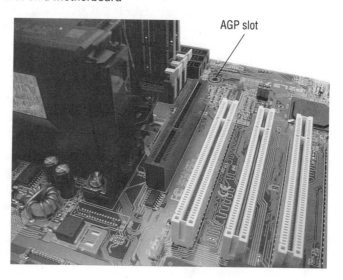

AGP slot

Bus Configuration

Configuration of an AGP expansion card is simplicity itself. Motherboards that support AGP have Plug-and-Play BIOSs that will automatically configure the card. To add an AGP card, simply power down the system, install the card in the AGP slot, and power the system back up. Once the system comes back up, the BIOS will configure the card automatically. Finally, you can install the drivers for your operating system. This step is unnecessary if you have a Plug-and-Play operating system.

PCMCIA—What Does It Stand For?

The tongue-twister *PCMCIA* stands for Personal Computer Memory Card International Association. The bus was originally designed to provide a way of expanding the memory in a small, handheld computer. The PCMCIA was organized to provide a standard way of expanding portable computers. The PCMCIA bus has been recently renamed *PC card* to make it easier to pronounce. The PC card bus uses a small expansion card (about the size of a credit card). Although it is primarily used in portable computers, there are PC card bus adapters for desktop PCs. It was designed to be a universal expansion bus that could accommodate any device.

The first release of the PCMCIA standard (PCMCIA 1, the same used in that original handheld computer) defined only the bus to be used for memory expansion. The second release (PCMCIA 2) is the most common; it is in use throughout the computer industry and has remained relatively unchanged. PCMCIA 2 was designed to be backward compatible with version 1, so memory cards can be used in the version 2 specification.

Information and Identification

As this book is being written, PCMCIA's bus width is only 16 bits, but a 32-bit version is on the way. Also, PC cards support only one IRQ (a problem if you need to install in a PC card bus two devices that both need interrupts). PC cards also do not support bus mastering or DMA. However, because of its flexibility, PCMCIA has quickly become a very popular bus for all types of computers (not just laptops).

There are three major types of PC cards (and slots) in use today. Each has different uses and physical characteristics (see Figure 5.13). Coincidentally, they are called Type I, Type II, and Type III:

- Type I cards are 3.3mm thick and are most commonly used for memory cards.

- Type II cards are 5mm thick and are mostly used for modems and LAN adapters. This is the most common PC card type found today, and most systems have at least two Type II slots (or one Type III slot).

- The Type III slot is 10.5mm thick. Its most common application is for the PC card hard disks. Developers have been slowly introducing these devices to the market.

FIGURE 5.13   PC card types by thickness

In addition to the card, there are two other components in the PC card architecture. The first one is the Socket Services software. This software is a BIOS-level interface to the PCMCIA bus slot. When loaded, it hides the details of the PC card hardware from the computer. This software can detect when a card has been inserted and what type of card it is.

The second component is the Card Services software. This software is the interface between the application and Socket Services. This is the software that tells the applications which interrupts and I/O ports the card is using. Applications that need to access the PC card don't access the hardware directly. Instead, they tell Card Services that they need access to a particular feature and Card Services gets the appropriate feature from the PC card.

This dual-component architecture allows the PCMCIA architecture to be used in different types of computer systems (that is, not just Intel's). For example, the Apple laptop computers currently use PC cards for modems and LAN interface cards, and they are based on Motorola processors.

Bus Configuration

The process for installing a PC card is different than that for any of the other bus types, mainly because this type was designed to allow the cards to be "hot swapped"—inserted or removed while the computer is powered up. This is the only bus that allows this. However, see the following warning about taking advantage of this feature.

WARNING

Even though you can remove a PC card while the power is on, *you shouldn't*! If you remove a PCMCIA card while the system is up, realize that some software may not like having its hardware ripped out from underneath it. That software will then have no hardware to talk to and it may crash the system. (As for other expansion cards, *never* remove them without shutting off the power to the computer first! If the power is on, you will certainly damage the card, the computer, or both.)

The process for installing a PC card is very straightforward. Just slip the card into an available slot, making sure the card type matches the slot type. Once the card is installed, you must install the software to use the card (Windows 9*x* will do this automatically).

You have a few items to note when installing and configuring PC cards. First, you must have the Card and Socket Services software installed before you try to physically install the card so that the computer can manage the card's resources. Second, you may have a PC card bus that supports two Type II cards or one Type III. If you do have one of these buses, you can have only one or the other situation. If you have a Type II card installed, you can't install a Type III card without removing the existing Type II. Finally, PC cards are too small to have jumpers or DIP switches, so the hardware must be configured through a software configuration program. This program can be a separate program or it can be built into the BIOS.

And Now for the Real World...

Sometimes, there is not enough memory to load all the files for Card and Socket Services. In the DOS world, the software for Card and Socket Services loads in conventional memory (or in UMBs if you so choose). With many such DOS drivers being loaded, you may run out of conventional memory and not be able to run some DOS programs.

To solve this, PC card manufacturers have come up with a piece of software called a PC Card "shim" that allows the card to be used as any other expansion card is used. In addition, it takes up less conventional memory. The only downside is that the shim might not be completely compatible with the system. Windows 9*x* incorporates this software as virtual device drivers, or VXDs.

Summary

This chapter covered the different types of expansion buses that exist. An expansion bus is used to expand the capabilities of a PC by making a computer modular. If you want to add a capability that your computer doesn't have, you just need to add a new expansion card.

In the first section, we explained exactly what a bus is. You learned about the different pathways that make up a typical paths and the difference between an internal and external bus.

In the next section, we discussed the components that make up a bus. You learned about each component and how those components work together to facilitate communication between the expansion card and the rest of the circuitry in the computer. Some of these components include the expansion slot itself, the various lines between the slot and the processor, and the bus controller. You also learned how different busses use different circuitry.

In the remaining sections in this chapter, you learned the differences between all the different types of busses as well as how to configure them. Table 5.5 shows all these differences and summarizes the details of each bus.

TABLE 5.5 Summary of Bus Types

Bus Type	Bus Width (Bits)	Maximum Speed (MHz)	Uses Bus Mastering?	Configuration
8-bit	8	4.77	N	Jumpers/DIP switches
ISA	16	8 (10 for Turbo)	N	Jumpers/DIP switches (Some cards are software configurable.)
MCA	16 or 32	10	Y	Software—Reference disk
EISA	32	8	Y	Software—EISA configuration disk
VL-Bus	32	33MHz	Y	Same as ISA
PCI	64	66MHz	Y	Software—Plug and Play
AGP	64	66MHz	N	Software—Plug and Play
PC Card	16	33	N	Software—PC Card and Socket Services

Key Terms

Before you take the exam, be certain you are familiar with the following terms:

8-bit bus	external bus
Accelerated Graphics Port (AGP) bus	hardware ports
address bus	I/O ports
AT bus	Industry Standard Architecture (ISA) bus
bus clock	input/output (I/O) addresses
bus connector slot	interrupt request (IRQ)
bus mastering	interrupts
clock signal	option diskette
CPU clock	PC card
data bus	PCMCIA
direct memory access (DMA)	reference disk
EISA Configuration Utility (EISA Config)	VESA Local Bus slot
expansion slots	

Review Questions

1. PCMCIA expansion cards need which software in order to operate? (Select all that apply.)

   A. Cardmember Services

   B. PC Card Services

   C. Modem Services

   D. Socket Services

2. ISA is an acronym for _____.

   A. InSide Architecture

   B. Industry Standard Architecture

   C. Industry Simple Architecture

   D. Internal Systems Architecture

3. EISA has a bus width of _____ bits.

   A. 32

   B. 16

   C. 64

   D. 8

4. PCI has a bus width of _____ bits. (Select all that apply.)

   A. 32

   B. 16

   C. 64

   D. 8

5. ISA has a bus width of _____ bits.

   A. 32

   B. 16

   C. 64

   D. 8

6. MCA has a bus width of _____ bits. (Select all that apply.)

   A. 32

   B. 16

   C. 64

   D. 8

7. Which of the following buses *require* a software configuration program to configure their settings? (Select all that apply.)

   A. 8-bit bus

   B. ISA

   C. EISA

   D. MCA

   E. PCI

   F. PCMCIA

8. Which of the following buses *require* the use of jumpers and DIP switches to configure their settings?

   A. 8-bit bus

   B. ISA

   C. EISA

   D. MCA

   E. PCI

   F. PCMCIA

9. Which bus signal line allows a device to request the processor's attention?

   A. I/O address lines

   B. DMA address lines

   C. Clock address lines

   D. Interrupt request (IRQ) address lines

10. Which bus signal line allows a device to send data directly to a computer's memory, bypassing the CPU?

    A. I/O addresses

    B. DMA address

    C. Clock addresses

    D. Interrupt request (IRQ) addresses

11. Which bus signal line allows the CPU to send requests to the device to send data?

    A. I/O addresses

    B. DMA address

    C. Clock addresses

    D. Interrupt request (IRQ) addresses

12. What is the maximum clock speed that an ISA Turbo bus can run reliably?

    A. 8MHz

    B. 10MHz

    C. 16MHz

    D. 33MHz

13. How many DMA channels are available in an 8-bit system?

    A. 1

    B. 4

    C. 8

    D. 16

14. You have just installed a sound card in a PC and it is not functioning correctly (it produces no sound and it hangs the computer when it tries to). After checking the settings, you find that it is set to IRQ 7, DMA 1, I/O port 300. You suspect that an IRQ conflict exists, so you check the other devices in the system. The system is using an ISA bus. Which device is the sound card conflicting with? (Assume the computer is using default settings for all devices.)

    A. A network card

    B. COM 1

    C. LPT 1

    D. COM 2

15. You have just installed a sound card in a PC and it is not functioning correctly (it produces no sound and it hangs the computer when it tries to). After checking the settings, you find that it is set to IRQ 7, DMA 1, I/O port 300. If you change the sound card from IRQ 7 to IRQ 10, will a conflict still exist? (Assume the computer is using default settings for all devices.)

    A. Yes

    B. No

16. What is the maximum bus clock speed of the 8-bit bus?

    A. 3.77

    B. 5.78

    C. 4.77

    D. 7.89

17. Which bus architecture was the first to offer configuration by software rather than by DIP switches or jumpers?

    A. 8-bit expansion

    B. ISA

    C. EISA

    D. MCA

    E. PCI

18. What is the clock speed of EISA buses?

    A. 8MHz

    B. 16MHz

    C. 32MHz

    D. None of the above

19. PCI buses were developed mainly because _____ .

   A. Pentiums were 8-bit processors

   B. Pentiums were 16-bit processors

   C. Pentiums were 32-bit processors

   D. Pentiums were 64-bit processors

20. The 8-bit expansion bus contained how many interrupts and DMA channels?

   A. 8 interrupts and 3 DMA channels

   B. 4 interrupts and 4 DMA channels

   C. 5 interrupts and 4 DMA channels

   D. 8 interrupts and 4 DMA channels

Answers to Review Questions

1. D. There are two components in the PC card architecture. The first one is the Socket Services software and the second is the Card Services software.

2. B. ISA stands for Industry Standard Architecture.

3. A. EISA supports a bus width of 32-bits.

4. A, C. PCI supports both 32-bit and 64-bit bus width.

5. B. The ISA bus is a full 16-bit bus.

6. A, B. The MCA bus was available in either 16-bit or 32-bit versions.

7. C, D, E, F. Only the EISA, MCA, PCI, and PCMCIA buses *require* a software configuration program to configure their settings.

8. A . Only the 8-bit bus *requires* the use of jumpers and DIP switches to configure its settings.

9. D. Interrupts are special lines that go directly to the processor; a device uses them to get the attention of the CPU when it needs to.

10. B. DMA channels allow a device to send data directly to computer memory, bypassing the CPU.

11. A. The I/O address bus signal line allows the CPU to send requests to the device to send data.

12. B. 10MHz is the maximum clock speed that an ISA Turbo bus can run reliably.

13. B. There are 4 DMA channels are available in an 8-bit system.

14. C. LPT 1 uses IRQ 7 by default, which conflicts with the sound card setting.

15. B . IRQ 10 is available to use as a sound card setting.

16. C. The 8-bit bus has a maximum bus clock speed of 4.77.

17. D. MCA was the first bus architecture to offer configuration by software rather than DIP switches or jumpers.

18. A. Even though EISA buses were an improvement over ISA in that they were software configurable and had a larger bus width, they still had a clock speed of 8MHz.

19. D. PCI buses were developed mainly to support the 64-bit capability of the Pentium processors.

20. D. The 8-bit bus could support only 8 interrupts and 4 DMA channels.

Chapter 6

Peripheral Devices

THE FOLLOWING OBJECTIVES ARE COVERED IN THIS CHAPTER:

✓ **1.1 Identify basic terms, concepts, and functions of system modules, including how each module should work during normal operation and during the boot process.**

Examples of concepts and modules are:
- System board
- Power supply
- Processor/CPU
- Memory
- Storage devices
- Monitor
- Modem
- Firmware
- BIOS
- CMOS
- LCD portable systems
- Ports
- PDA (Personal Digital Assistants)

✓ **1.4 Identify common peripheral ports, associated cabling, and their connectors.**

Content may include the following:
- Cable types
- Cable orientation
- Serial versus parallel
- Pin connections

Examples of types of connectors:
- DB-9
- DB-25
- RJ-11
- RJ-45
- BNC
- PS2/MINI-DIN
- USB
- IEEE-1394

✓ **2.1 Identify common symptoms and problems associated with each module and how to troubleshoot and isolate problems.**

Content may include the following:

- Processor/Memory symptoms
- Mouse
- Floppy drive
- Parallel ports
- Hard Drives
- CD-ROM
- DVD
- Sound Card/Audio
- Monitor/Video
- Motherboards
- Modems
- BIOS
- USB
- NIC
- CMOS
- Power supply
- Slot covers
- POST audible/visual error codes
- Troubleshooting tools, e.g., multimeter
- Large LBA, LBA
- Cables
- Keyboard
- Peripherals

U p to this point, we have discussed the main components of the average PC, how they work, and their service issues. But there are many kinds of components that are not directly a part of the PC. They are on the outside, or the periphery, of the computer's operations. For this reason, they fall into the category of devices known as *peripherals*. In this chapter, we will discuss the following topics:

- Input devices
- Output devices
- Computer display devices
- Other peripherals

In addition to discussing these devices, we will also discuss how to properly clean some of them.

For complete coverage of objective 1.1, please also see Chapters 2 and 4. For complete coverage of objective 1.4, please also see Chapter 2. For complete coverage of objective 2.1, please also see Chapters 1, 4, 8, and 10.

Because printers are such complex peripherals (they're also the reason for the largest percentage of service calls), they are covered pretty extensively on the A+ exam. For the same reasons, we'll skip the details concerning printers in this overall coverage of peripherals and instead devote an entire chapter to printers (Chapter 7). The topic of troubleshooting printer problems is also covered in detail in the chapter on troubleshooting (Chapter 10).

Input Devices

Let's start this chapter off by talking about some of the most commonly used peripheral devices: input devices. As their name suggests, input devices exist so that human beings can communicate with the object we call a computer. These devices interpret the intentions of their users (via a keystroke or some other movement) to tell the computer to perform some action. Without them, the computer would be of little use to us.

Keyboards

Let's begin our discussion of input devices with the most common PC input device: the keyboard (Figure 6.1). This type of device translates keystrokes into letters or numbers. The letters are then interpreted and commands are performed, depending on what was being sent. With today's PCs, the keyboard is the most important input device. There are two major types of keyboards: mechanical keyswitch and capacitive.

FIGURE 6.1 A common PC keyboard

Mechanical Keyswitch Keyboards

The first type of keyboard technology is the keyswitch type (Figure 6.2). It works by using an individual switch for each key. When you press a key, a plunger under the key cap moves down and makes a connection between two signal lines coming from the keyboard controller in the keyboard. When the connection is made, the keyboard controller sends a signal to the computer, saying, "Someone just typed an *A*." When a key is released, a spring pushes the plunger back to its original position. On a typical keyswitch keyboard, there may be more than 100 individual keyswitches.

FIGURE 6.2   How a keyswitch keyboard works

Key cap
Plunger
Return spring
Keyswitch body
Keyswitch contacts →

There are a few benefits to this type of keyboard. First, they are simple to make. Thus, they are inexpensive. Also, they are simple to service. When a key goes bad, a technician can desolder the broken keyswitch and solder in a new one.

Originally there were a few problems with this type of keyboard. The first keyboards had really "bouncy" springs. Sometimes, when a key was pressed and released quickly, the key would bounce, causing duplicate letters to appear on the screen. The first attempt at solving this problem was a mechanical one. The designers first tried to lessen the tension on the spring. That didn't work because the lessened tension increased the finger fatigue of the person typing.

Their second attempt worked better. They used an electronic technique that we call *debouncing*. It worked by having the keyboard controller constantly scan the keyboard for keystrokes. The controller registered only those keystrokes that were pressed for more than two scans, and it ignored all others (like those coming from a "bouncing" key). This technique worked and has been included in most keyboard controllers since then.

Capacitive Keyboards

The problem with keyswitch-based keyboards is that they are rather bulky. The mechanical keyswitches take up too much room to be used in laptops. Also, they require a certain minimum amount of power to operate because each switch requires a certain amount of voltage.

The solution to these problems was to take the switch out of the key. One keyboard design placed two sheets of semiconductive material separated by a thin sheet of Mylar inside the keyboard. This is one type of capacitive keyboard. When a key is pressed, the plunger presses down and a paddle connected to the plunger presses the two sheets of semiconductive material together, changing the total capacitance of the two sheets. The controller can tell by the value returned which key was pressed. The controller then sends the results (called *scan codes*) to the computer, telling it what key to display.

This keyboard has the advantages of being less complex, more durable, and even cheaper than mechanical keyswitch keyboards. One disadvantage of these keyboards—although in some ways it is also an advantage—is that you can't repair them. This can be an advantage insofar as the price for a new one (less than $40 at the time of the writing of this book) is less than the labor to repair it (around $50).

Keyboard Connectors

Keyboards have to be connected to the computer somehow. They are connected through some type of connector (Captain Obvious strikes again). This connector carries the signals from the keyboard controller to the CPU. There are two major types, identified by the type of connector they use:

- DIN-5 connector (Figure 6.3). This is also called the standard, IBM PC, or XT/AT keyboard connector.
- Mini PS/2 connector (Figure 6.4). This one is also called the PS/2-style connector because it was first used on the IBM PS/2. This style of keyboard connector has one main advantage: It's smaller.

FIGURE 6.3   An IBM PC keyboard plug and connector

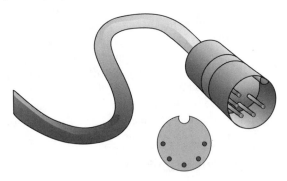

FIGURE 6.4   A PS/2-style keyboard plug and connector

Cleaning Keyboards

We think everyone who drinks pop and eats potato chips near computers should have to clean a keyboard used by such a person. When the soda dries, it leaves the syrup behind, and it's *almost* impossible to remove it from the keyboard without disassembling the keyboard. Potato chip crumbs love to stick to the syrup and complicate matters.

The easiest way to clean a keyboard is to remove it from the computer and soak it with distilled, demineralized water as soon as the spill occurs. If the spill is allowed to dry, the contaminants will be much harder to remove and disassembly of the keyboard may be required. Some people have even run their keyboards through the dishwasher (with soap and a heat-dry cycle) to clean them! This approach works when the local water supply doesn't contain very many contaminants. An easy way to tell if your water contains the type of contaminants that may be harmful to your keyboard is to look to see if water drips stain your sink; if so, your local water contains minerals or other contaminants and the dishwasher will probably do more harm than good. In any case, make sure the keyboard is *completely* dry before using it.

The other way to clean your keyboard is to disassemble it completely and use special keyboard cleaners (available in most electronic supply stores) to clean the components. This approach works well when the keyboard is extremely dirty.

The only drawback to cleaning a keyboard is that, in terms of the time that you as a professional service technician would have to spend doing it, it often costs more than the keyboard is worth. It's usually cheaper to replace a keyboard than to clean it.

Mice

For several years, operating systems were character based. They displayed information on the screen in text format and people interacted with them using command words. Then, a couple of people at the Xerox Palo Alto Research Center (PARC), intrigued with the idea that computers should be "friendly" and easy to use, started working with a *graphical user interface (GUI)*, which used pictures to represent computer entities (like files, disks, and so on). To interact with the pictures, a special device was introduced into the computer world. This device was the *mouse*. The mouse translates movements on a horizontal surface into movements of a pointer on the screen. There are two methods of making these translations: opto-mechanical and optical.

Mouse Types

The first type of mouse we'll discuss is the opto-mechanical type. This type of mouse contains a round ball that makes contact with two rollers—one for the x-axis (the horizontal) and one for the y-axis (the vertical). Moving the mouse causes the ball to roll, and because the ball is in contact with the two rollers, it causes them to turn. These rollers are connected to wheels with small holes in them (Figure 6.5). Each wheel rotates between the arms of a U-shaped optical sensor. The holes allow a light to shine through the wheel onto the optical sensor in flashes as the wheel turns. By the speed and patterns of the light pulses, the mouse senses the speed and direction it is moving and sends its interpretation of those movements to the computer and the mouse control software.

FIGURE 6.5 An opto-mechanical mouse mechanism

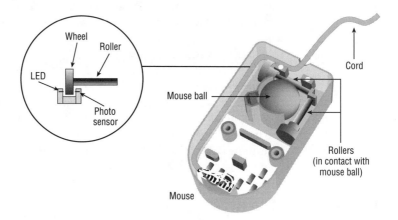

An optical mouse looks the same as any other computer mouse, except there is no mouse "ball." Instead, the optical mouse uses a special mouse pad and a beam of laser light (Figure 6.6). The beam of light shines onto the mouse pad and reflects back to a sensor in the mouse. The mouse pad has small lines crossing it that can reflect the light into the sensor in different ways. It is in this fashion that the optical mouse detects direction and speed of movements. This mouse *will not work* without the special mouse pad.

FIGURE 6.6 An optical mouse mechanism

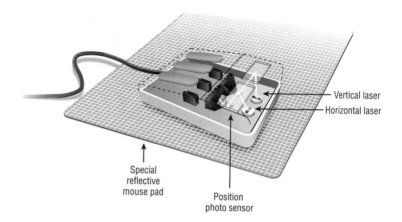

Now that we have discussed the different ways that mouse devices work, let's discuss the different ways of hooking them up to a computer.

Mouse Interfaces

Just as there are many types of mice, there are several different ways of connecting them to a PC. There are three major types of mouse interfaces: serial, bus, and PS/2. Each one has its own installation and configuration issues. Let's discuss them, in order.

Serial Mouse Interface

The serial mouse was the first major type of mouse interface, mainly because it made the most sense: Mice send position information in a stream of coordinates, and the interface that handles small, continuous streams of data best is the serial interface. All computers came with at least one serial port that the mouse could use with its female DB-9 connector. If the serial port was of the 25-pin variety, the user could plug the mouse's DB-9 connector into the adapter that was usually included with the mouse (Figure 6.7) to allow it to work. Also, installing the mouse was as simple as connecting the mouse to an available serial port and installing the mouse driver software. For these reasons, the serial mouse became very popular.

FIGURE 6.7 A serial mouse DB-9–to–25-pin adapter

One disadvantage to the serial mouse is that it uses a COM port. If the computer had only one COM port, that was it—you couldn't use any other peripheral devices. Also, if you had another COM port but it was on a shared interrupt, that other COM port couldn't be used for another communication device (like a modem) as long as data was coming into the computer on the COM port being used by the mouse. So, in a manner of speaking, a serial mouse really takes up two COM ports. For example, because COM 1 and COM 3 both share Interrupt 4, when you put a mouse on COM 1 you are also preventing the use of COM 3.

Bus Mouse Interface

To some people, the serial interface was too bulky and cumbersome. For those people, a special mouse connector was developed: the small, round PS/2 connector. This connector attached to a special, 8-bit interface card that was installed directly into the computer's bus. Thus, the signals traveled on a more direct path to the CPU. This type of mouse was called a *bus mouse* for these reasons (and because it was developed by Microsoft, primarily, it's also called the MS bus mouse). See Figure 6.8 for an example of a bus mouse connector.

FIGURE   6.8   A bus mouse PS/2 plug and connector

Although the bus mouse had a faster interface, speed wasn't really an issue. The mouse signals didn't really overload the interface. The major advantage to a bus mouse, compared to a serial mouse, was that *it didn't take up a COM port.* This allowed systems that were short on COM ports to add a mouse. The one downside was that the bus card does use an interrupt (and it can only use IRQ 2, 3, 4, or 5).

Installing a bus mouse involved three steps. First, you installed the bus card to one of the possible IRQ choices. You might have to change the IRQs on a few devices to free up one of the possible choices for the bus mouse. Once that was accomplished, you could connect the mouse to the bus mouse port. Finally, you installed the driver software for the operating system you were using.

PS/2 Mouse Interface

The bus mouse is still around; however, it has evolved to be included on the motherboard of some of today's computers. This interface uses the same connector as the bus mouse, but as already mentioned, it is not on a card but rather is hardwired to the motherboard. This interface was introduced with the IBM PS/2 series of computers and was henceforth called the *PS/2 mouse interface* (see Figure 6.9). It's essentially the same mouse as the bus mouse, except that the bus mouse uses a special expansion card with a special pin configuration, whereas the PS/2 mouse port is integrated into the motherboard.

FIGURE 6.9 A PS/2 mouse plug and connector

Installation of a PS/2 mouse is easy. Just connect the mouse to the PS/2 mouse port. (The interrupt has most likely been hardwired to IRQ 12; check your documentation to be sure.) Then you can install the mouse software and use the mouse.

Cleaning a Mouse

The largest problem with mechanical mice is that they contain moving parts. These moving parts don't like dirt and dust. The mouse is designed to move on a flat surface. Most often, the mouse ball picks up dirt and dust and deposits it on the mouse rollers. When this dirt and dust combines with the oil from your skin, it forms a substance that sticks to the mouse rollers and forms a ring around the roller.

This ring around the roller causes the mouse to rattle as it moves across the mouse pad (mainly because the ring isn't completely even). If the ring builds up too far, it may actually wedge between the mouse ball and the roller and prevent the roller from rotating. If you've ever moved a mouse and the mouse pointer appeared to have hit an invisible "wall" in the middle of the screen (that is, the pointer won't move any farther in that direction no matter how much you move the mouse), your mouse more than likely has "ring around the roller."

There's nothing you can do to prevent this condition. It is possible, however, to cure the symptoms. First, turn the mouse upside down and remove the mouse ball by rotating the retaining ring counterclockwise. Flip the mouse right side up and the mouse ball will drop out. Flip the mouse back over and locate the two rollers. The "ring around the roller" will be obvious. To clean the "gunk" from the rollers, you can use a small eyeglass screwdriver. If the gunk won't come loose, soak the deposits with a little isopropyl alcohol to loosen them. After the rollers are cleaned, the mouse will perform better and the "phantom wall" will be gone.

Other Pointing Devices

Mice are the most popular pointing devices, but they are not the only type of pointing device in common use. Why is that? The answer we'll give is in the form of a question: Have you ever tried to draw a circle with a mouse? It's downright difficult. Also, mice are too bulky to be easily used on portable computers. These are some of the reasons other pointing devices were designed.

Trackballs

A trackball is basically an opto-mechanical mouse turned upside down. Instead of moving the mouse on a table, you move the mouse ball (or, properly, the *trackball*), which otherwise remains stationary. The only other differences are that the trackball uses a bigger ball and the buttons are usually on the sides. Some manufacturers offer small, portable, clip-on versions of the trackball, which you can hold in your hand or clip onto the side of your laptop computer. Both are shown in Figure 6.10.

FIGURE 6.10   Two kinds of trackballs: a typical desktop trackball and a portable trackball

Trackballs can be connected to a computer in the same ways a mouse can be connected. More and more commonly, though, you'll see a trackball already installed into a laptop computer, right where your thumbs would hover (just below the spacebar). They fit well and the entire assembly doesn't have to move, just the trackball.

Because trackballs operate similarly to mice, they can be cleaned similarly. The trackball can be removed and the rollers cleaned in exactly the same manner.

Drawing Tablets

Another type of pointing device that is used with computers is the drawing tablet. These devices help solve the mouse circle-drawing problem. To outward appearances, the tablet is just a flat piece of plastic covered with a rubberized coating.

And Now for the Real World...

There is one laptop that does include a portable *mouse* built right into the body of the laptop. One model of Hewlett-Packard Omnibook has a small mouse that pops out of the side and can be used as a regular mouse. It's a nice compromise, and it really does work well.

You use a pen-shaped tool called a *stylus* to "draw" on the surface (sometimes a mouse-shaped device known as a *puck* might be used). As you can guess, if you do much typing at all, the drawing tablet is not really efficient as a pointing device because you have to keep picking up the stylus to use it. But it is really efficient as a drawing tool. Because they do quite a lot of drawing, graphic designers and computer-aided design (CAD) professionals use drawing tablets to make their work easier. Figure 6.11 shows a couple of typical drawing tablets.

FIGURE 6.11 Drawing tablets: one with a stylus, one with a puck

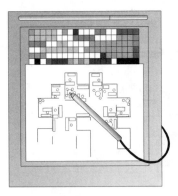
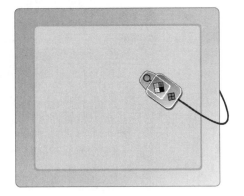

There are three major types of drawing tablets: electromagnetic, resistive, and acoustic. They differ primarily in the way that they work:

- Electromagnetic tablets have a grid of wires underneath the rubberized surface. The stylus contains a small sensor that is sensitive to electromagnetic fields. At timed intervals, an electromagnetic pulse is sent across the grid. The sensor in the stylus picks up these pulses. Because the pulses are timed, the stylus knows how long it takes to get from their point of origin in each direction to the stylus. The controller in the table translates this information into a set of x and y variables that are then sent to the computer. The computer then moves the pointer on the screen to the x- and y-coordinates on the screen corresponding to the x- and y-coordinates on the tablet.

- The resistive type of tablet has a special resistive surface instead of a grid of wires under the rubberized coating. This surface has a current induced from each of the x- and y-coordinate sides. The current gets larger as it travels along one coordinate side. The puck detects these voltages and, depending on its position, will get different voltage readings from each side. These readings are translated into x- and y-coordinate values, which are transmitted to the computer.

- The final type of drawing tablet in use today is the acoustic type. It works slightly differently than the other two models. The stylus or puck has a small spark generator inside it. There are also banks of small microphones on the x- and y-axes. When the user presses a button on the stylus, it activates the spark. The sound of the spark is picked up on the x and y microphones and the coordinates are translated into *x* and *y* values for the computer.

To clean a drawing tablet, wipe the rubberized surface with a damp cloth (no detergents!). If there is a tough stain that the damp cloth won't remove, use a cloth dampened with denatured alcohol. After removing the stain, follow with water-dampened cloth to remove any residue.

Touch Screens

The last type of pointing device we'll discuss can be found in use at many department stores: the little informational *kiosks* with screens that respond to our touch and give us information on product specials or bridal registries. Instead of a keyboard and mouse, these computer screens have a film over them that is sensitive to touch. This technology is known as a *touch screen* (see Figure 6.12). With most of the interfaces in use on touch screens, touching a box drawn on the monitor does the same thing as double-clicking that box with a mouse.

FIGURE 6.12   A typical touch screen

There are two major types of touch screens: optical and capacitive:

- Optical screens work like so: When a person uses a finger to touch the screen, it breaks light beams emanating in a grid from the sides of the screen (in front of the glass). Which light beams get broken indicates to the touch screen where the finger was, using an x-,y-coordinate notation.

- Capacitive screens work just like capacitive keyboards. There are two clear, plastic coatings over the screen, separated by a thin layer of air. When you press the coatings together in a particular spot, the controller registers a change in the total capacitance of the two layers. Based on a table that relates capacitance values to position, the screen can relay x- and y-coordinates to the computer.

Cleaning touch screens is usually just as easy as cleaning a regular monitor. With optical touch screens, the monitor *is*, in fact, a regular monitor. It can be cleaned with glass cleaner. However, if the screen has a capacitive coating, the glass cleaner may damage it. Instead, use a cloth dampened with water to clean the dirt, dust, and fingerprints from the screen.

Other Types of Pointing Devices

There are some types of pointing devices that are not mentioned on the A+ exam. One example is the *touch pad*. It uses the capacitance method to translate position to x-,y-coordinates. Its primary use is in notebook computers because it takes up very little space and doesn't have to be moved. Another pointing device commonly seen on notebooks is the *finger mouse* (or *J-mouse*, because it sticks up next to the J key on the keyboard). This device looks like a small eraser sticking up from the middle of the keyboard. When you push this "eraser," the pointer on the screen moves in the same direction. Most people either love it or hate it.

These technologies have become popular in the last few years—so much, in fact, that some keyboard manufacturers have integrated these types of pointing devices into their keyboards.

Scanners

In addition to using keyboards and pointing devices, there is another very common method of getting data into a computer. The *charge-coupled device (CCD)* was developed to allow light (and shades of light) to be converted into electrical pulses. This opened up the arena to allow a new breed of devices to input data to a computer. The largest class of these devices are scanners. *Optical scanners* (their full name) use CCDs and a light source to convert pictures into a stream of data.

Flatbed Scanners

The first type of scanner that was developed was the flatbed scanner. Named after the flat bed of glass that the item to be scanned would lie upon, they resemble the top half of a photocopier (Figure 6.13). Inside the scanner there is a motorized carriage, upon which is mounted a light source and a CCD. When you want to scan a picture into the computer, you place the item to be scanned face down on the glass that separates the item from the CCD. Then you use the software to indicate the start of the scan cycle. When this occurs, the software sends a signal to the scanner to begin scanning. The control board in the scanner turns on the light source and starts receiving data from the CCD. After scanning an entire line, the control board tells the carriage to move down slightly so the CCD can scan the next line. The carriage moves slowly down the page and the CCD scans the page one line at a time. The controller then feeds this stream of image data to the scanning software, where it is assembled, line by line, together into a picture of the item.

FIGURE 6.13   A flatbed scanner

Flatbed scanners are usually SCSI devices, therefore they need to be configured as any other SCSI device (so remember the rules of addressing and termination, especially). Sometimes, though, manufacturers include a special, proprietary interface card. In that case, configuration usually involves installing the card and simply connecting the scanner to the card with the cable provided. The downside is that this interface takes an additional IRQ address and can't be used for anything else (whereas SCSI can be used for disks and other devices). When configuring this card, use the configuration tips for the type of bus the card uses.

A dirty scanner bed (the big sheet of glass between the scanning CCD and the item being scanned) can cause image quality problems. Fingerprints show up as dark smudges in the scanned image. The scanner bed is simply glass, so you can clean it with glass cleaner.

Be careful when handling flatbed scanners. Transporting them can be dangerous because they contain a large sheet of glass. Also, never set anything sharp or heavy on the glass surface, because scratches will probably show up in the scanned image (and besides, it could shatter and cut you).

Handheld Scanners

Handheld scanners work exactly like flatbed scanners, with one exception. Instead of an all-in-one enclosure containing a carriage, controller, light source, and CCD, a handheld unit is just the controller, CCD, and light source contained in a small enclosure with wheels on it (Figure 6.14). The carriage is your hand. To start scanning, you place the item to be scanned on a flat surface and place the scanner unit at the top. You tell the software you're ready to start scanning and then press a "start" button on the scanner unit. This turns on the light source and tells the CCD to start receiving data. At the same time, you must move the scanner unit down the item being scanned. When you finish scanning, you release the start button.

FIGURE 6.14 A hand-held scanner

The major advantage of these scanners is that they produce adequate quality at less than half the price of a flatbed scanner. The major downside is that they are slow and the quality depends on how steady the hand of the operator is.

They usually use a COM port or bidirectional parallel port instead of SCSI to transfer their data. They are limited in their quality, however, and generally should not be used in graphics work.

Output Devices

We have talked about how to get data *into* a computer, so now we must discuss ways of getting it *out*. To get data out of computers, we use a class of devices known as output devices. There are two major categories: printers and computer displays.

Printers

Printers and their operation are the subject of Chapter 7 (and also about half of the troubleshooting chapter, Chapter 10), so we'll just briefly talk about the different types. There are four major types of printing devices used to get computer output into "hard" copy (paper copies). They are impact, sprayed-ink, electrophotographic (EP), and plotters.

Impact

Impact printers work by striking a form through an inked ribbon onto the paper, similar to the way a printing press works. There are two major types of impact printers: *dot matrix* and *daisy wheel*. Dot-matrix printers press a set of pins through the ribbon in patterns corresponding to the characters to be produced. Daisy-wheel printers use a wheel that has all the letters of the alphabet on different spokes. The printer's controller rotates this wheel until the spoke holding the desired letter is in place. Then, a hammer behind the wheel strikes this letter onto the inked ribbon and the paper, thus making an image.

Dot-matrix printers sacrifice quality for speed and thus produce a lower-quality image than the daisy-wheel printers. On the other hand, although daisy-wheel printers give letter-quality output, they cannot reproduce graphics. Dot-matrix printers can only achieve "near letter-quality," but they are capable of printing graphics. In addition, daisy-wheel printers are, in general, noisier. They're also generally more expensive. (Of course, you'll find that some dot matrixes are noisier than some daisy wheels, and some are more expensive.)

Today we primarily use impact printers for printing multipart carbon forms because these forms require that something strike the page to make multiple copies. No other printing technology can handle multiple-part forms (unless they print multiple copies of the same form). The quality of printout is lower with daisy-wheel and dot-matrix printers than with any other printing technology, so they are used when low-cost, fast printouts are needed and quality isn't an issue. A couple of typical impact printers are shown in Figure 6.15.

FIGURE 6.15 Typical impact printers

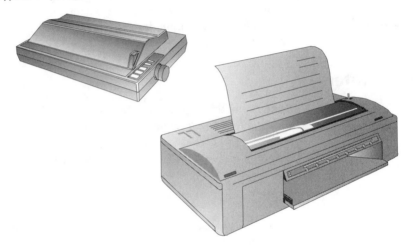

Sprayed-Ink

A sprayed-ink printer works as its name suggests. Ink is sprayed onto the page in the shape of the letters or images. There are a variety of sprayed-ink printers on the market, and they are all lumped together into this one category, but there are two basic types: ink-jet and bubble-jet. (As with the other printers mentioned in this chapter, we'll cover them in more detail in Chapters 7 and 10.) The image quality is relatively good with both types of sprayed-ink printer; better than that produced by an impact printer but not quite as good as that produced by an electrophotographic printer (discussed next). The primary advantage of sprayed-ink printers is their cost. They can offer good output at a low cost (less than that of an electrophotographic printer). They have found a niche in the SOHO (small office, home office) market as a great printer for printing letters and other small documents. A typical sprayed-ink printer is shown in Figure 6.16.

FIGURE 6.16 A typical sprayed-ink printer

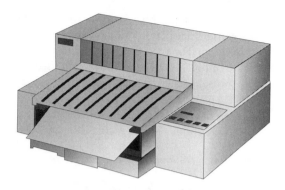

Electrophotographic (EP)

The name "electrophotographic (or EP) printer" suggests a complex image formation process. EP printers are actually more commonly known as *laser printers*, because they do use a laser (as well as high voltage and black carbon toner) to form the image on the page. Because of their complexity, these printers have a relatively high cost associated with them (about twice the cost of a sprayed-ink or impact printer). But the complexity and cost have a benefit. The images produced by EP printers are of the very best quality, and they produce these images at higher speeds (most EP printers today print at least four pages per minute).

EP printers are often found in offices and publishing firms. It's rather interesting that the first EP printers to be sold (the Apple LaserWriter and the Hewlett-Packard LaserJet) sold for more than $4,000. Today you can buy an EP printer that produces output at more than twice their resolution and speed for about one-eighth the cost.

Two typical electrophotographic printers are shown in Figure 6.17.

FIGURE 6.17 Two typical electrophotographic printers

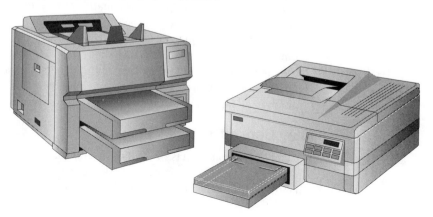

Plotters

The last type of hard copy output device isn't really a printer at all. Printers make images one line at a time and move from top to bottom during the printing process. Plotters, on the other hand, draw the image as we would, with a pen. One shape at a time. Plotters are most often used with CAD software to produce blueprints or technical diagrams. It would be quite expensive to make a printer that can print on paper as wide as these drawings require. Because a plotter uses a pen (or several pens in a holder) on a cable carrier, it is easy (and relatively inexpensive) to make a very wide plotter. A couple of typical plotters are shown in Figure 6.18.

FIGURE 6.18   Typical plotters

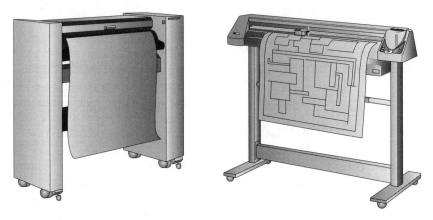

Computer Display Systems

The second way of getting information out of a computer is to use a computer display. Display systems convert computer signals into text and pictures and display them on a TV-like screen. As a matter of fact, the first personal computers actually used television screens because it was simple to use an existing display technology rather than to develop a new one. There are several different types of computer displays in use today, including the TV. All of them use either the same *cathode ray tube (CRT)* technology found in television sets (almost every desktop monitor uses this technology) or the *liquid crystal display (LCD)* technology found on all laptop, notebook, and palmtop computers.

Display Concepts

There are several aspects of display systems that make each type of display different. But most display systems work the same. First, the computer sends a signal to a device called the *video adapter*—an expansion board installed in an expansion bus slot—telling it to display a particular graphic or character. The adapter then *renders* the character for the display—that is, it converts that single instruction into several instructions that tell the display device how to draw the graphic—and sends the instructions to the display device. The primary differences after that are in the type of video adapter you are using (monochrome, EGA/CGA, VGA, or SuperVGA) and the type of display (CRT or LCD).

Video Technologies

Let's first talk about the different types of video technologies. There are four major types: monochrome, EGA/CGA, VGA, and SuperVGA. Each type of video technology differs in two major areas: the highest resolution it supports and the maximum number of colors in its "palette." Resolution depends on how many picture units (called *pixels*) are used to draw the screen. The more pixels, the sharper the image. The resolution is described in terms of the screen's dimensions, indicating how many pixels across and down are used to draw the screen. For example, a resolution of $1,024 \times 768$ means 1,024 pixels across and 768 pixels down were used to draw the pixel "grid." The video technology in this example would have used 786,432 ($1,024 \times 768 = 786,432$) pixels to draw the screen.

Monochrome

The first video technology for PCs was *monochrome* (from the Latin *mono*, meaning one, and *chroma*, meaning color). This black-and-white video (actually, they were green-and-white or amber-and-black) was just fine for the main operating system of the day, DOS. DOS didn't have any need for color. Thus, the video adapter was very basic. The first adapter, developed by IBM, was known as the Monochrome Display Adapter (MDA). It could display text, but not graphics, and used a resolution of 720×350 pixels.

The Hercules Graphics Card (HGC), introduced by Hercules Computer Technology, had a resolution of 720×350 and could display graphics as well as text. It did this by using two separate modes: a *text mode* that allowed the adapter to optimize its resources for displaying predrawn characters from its onboard library, and a *graphics mode* that optimized the adapter for drawing individual pixels for on-screen graphics. It could switch between these modes on the fly. These modes of operation have been included in all graphics adapters since the introduction of the HGC.

EGA and CGA

The next logical step for displays was to add a splash of color. IBM was the first with color, with the introduction of the Color Graphics Adapter (CGA). CGA could display text, but it displayed graphics with a resolution of only 320×200 pixels with four colors. (It displayed a better resolution—640×200—with two colors—i.e., black and one other color.) After some time, people wanted more colors and higher resolution, so IBM responded with the Enhanced Graphics Adapter (EGA). EGA could display 16 colors out of a palette of 64 with a resolution of 320 × 200 or 640 × 350 pixels.

These two technologies were the standard for color until the IBM AT was introduced. This PC was to be the standard for performance, so IBM wanted a better video technology for it.

VGA

With the PS/2 line of computers, IBM wanted to answer the cry for "more resolution, more colors" by introducing its best video adapter to date, the Video Graphics Array (VGA). This video technology had a whopping 256KB of video memory on board and could display 16 colors at 640 × 480 pixels or 256 colors at 320 × 200 pixels. It became very widely used and has since become the standard for color PC video; it's the "starting point" for today's computers, as far as video is concerned. You can get better, but your computer should use this video technology at minimum.

One unique feature of VGA is that it's an analog board. This allows the 256 colors it uses to be chosen from various shades and hues of a palette of 262,114 colors. It sold well mainly because users could choose from almost any color they wanted (or at least one that was close).

SuperVGA

Up to this point, most video standards were set by IBM. IBM made them, everyone bought them, it became a standard. Some manufacturers didn't like this monopoly and set up the Video Electronics Standards Association (VESA) to try to enhance IBM's video technology and make the enhanced technology a public standard. The result of this work was the enhancement known as SuperVGA (SVGA). This new standard was indeed an enhancement, because it could support 256 colors at a resolution of 800 × 600 (the VESA standard), or 1,024 × 768 pixels with 16 colors, or 640 × 480 with 65,536 colors.

XGA

The final development in this tale of "keeping up with the Joneses" is that IBM introduced a new technology in 1991 known as the Extended Graphics Array (XGA). This technology was only available as an MCA expansion board and not as an ISA or EISA board. It was rather like saying, "So there. You won't let me be the leader, so I'll lead my own team." XGA could support 256 colors at 1,024 × 768 pixels or 65,536 colors at 640 × 480 pixels. It was a different design, optimized for GUIs like Windows or OS/2. Also, it was an *interlaced* technology, which means that, rather than scan every line one at a time to create the image, it scanned every other line on each pass, using the phenomenon known as "persistence of vision" to produce what appears to our eyes as a continuous image.

Table 6.1 details the various video technologies, their resolutions, and the color palettes they support.

TABLE 6.1 Video Display Adapter Comparison

Name	Resolutions	Colors
Monochrome Display Adapter (MDA)	720 × 350	Mono (text only)
Hercules Graphics Card (HGC)	720 × 350	Mono (text and graphics)
Enhanced Graphics Adapter (EGA)	640 × 350	16
Video Graphics Array (VGA)	640 × 480	16
	320 × 200	256
SuperVGA (SVGA)	800 × 600	256
	1,024 × 768	16
Extended Graphics Array (XGA)	800 × 600	65,536
	1,024 × 768	256

Monitors

As we have already mentioned, a monitor contains a CRT. But how does it work? Basically, a device called an *electron gun* shoots electrons toward the back side of the monitor screen (see Figure 6.19). The back of the screen is coated with special chemicals (called *phosphors*) that glow when electrons strike them. This beam of electrons scans across the monitor from left to right and top to bottom to create the image.

FIGURE 6.19 How a monitor works

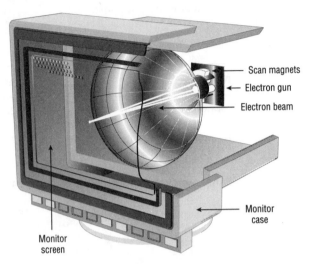

- Scan magnets
- Electron gun
- Electron beam
- Monitor case
- Monitor screen

There are two ways of measuring a monitor's quality of image: dot pitch and refresh (scan) rate. A monitor's *dot pitch* is the shortest distance between two dots of the same color on the monitor. Usually given in fractions of a millimeter (mm), it tells how "sharp" the picture is. The lower the number, the closer together the pixels are, and thus, the sharper the image. An average dot pitch is 0.28mm. Anything smaller than 0.28mm is considered great.

A monitor's *refresh rate* (technically called the *vertical scan frequency*) specifies how many times in one second the scanning beam of electrons redraws the screen. The phosphors stay bright only for a fraction of a second, so they must constantly be hit with electrons to stay lit. Given in draws per second, or Hertz, the refresh rate specifies how much energy is being put into keeping the screen lit. The standard refresh rate is 60Hz for VGA. However, some monitors have a refresh rate of 72Hz, which is much easier on the eyes (less flicker is perceived).

One note about monitors that may seem rather obvious: You must use a video card that supports the type of monitor you are using. For example, you can't use a CGA monitor on a VGA adapter.

To use a 72Hz monitor, your video card must also support the 72Hz refresh rate. Most video cards sold today support this faster 72Hz refresh rate but are configured as 60Hz out of the box. If you intend to use the 72Hz rate, you must configure the card to do so. Check the documentation that came with the card for details on how to configure it.

Liquid Crystal Displays (LCDs)

Portable computers were originally designed to be compact versions of their bigger brothers. They crammed all the components of the big, desktop computers into a small, suitcase-like box called (laughably) a *portable computer*. No matter what the designers did to reduce the size of the computer, the display remained as large as the desktop version's. That is, it did until an inventor found that when he passed an electric current through a semicrystalline liquid, the crystals would align themselves with the current. It was found that by combining transistors with these liquid crystals, patterns could be formed. These patterns could represent numbers or letters. The first application of these *liquid crystal displays* (LCDs) was the LCD watch. It was rather bulky, but it was cool.

As the LCD elements got smaller, the detail of the patterns became greater until one day someone thought to make a computer screen out of several of these elements. This screen was very light compared to computer monitors of the day. Also, it consumed very little power. It could easily be added to a portable computer to reduce the weight by as much as 30 pounds! As the components got smaller, so did the computer, and the laptop computer was born.

There are two major types of LCD displays in use in laptops today: active matrix screen and passive matrix screen. Their main differences lie in the quality of the image. Both types, however, use some kind of lighting behind the LCD panel to make the screen easier to view.

Active Matrix

An active matrix screen works in a similar manner to the LCD watch. The screen is made up of several individual LCD pixels. A transistor behind each pixel, when switched on, activates two electrodes that align the crystals and turn the pixel dark. This type of display is very crisp and easy to look at.

The major disadvantage to an active matrix screen is that it requires large amounts of power to operate all the transistors. Even with the backlight turned off, the screen can still consume battery power at an alarming rate. Most laptops with active matrix screens can't operate on a battery for more than two hours.

Passive Matrix

Within the passive matrix screen, there are two rows of transistors: one at the top, another at the side. When the computer's video circuit wants to turn a particular pixel on (turn it black), it sends a signal to the x- and y-coordinate transistors for that pixel, thus turning them on. This then causes voltage lines from each axis to intersect at the desired coordinates, turning the desired pixel black. Figure 6.20 illustrates this concept.

FIGURE 6.20 A passive matrix display

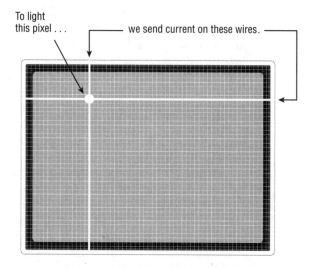

The main difference between active matrix and passive matrix is image quality. Because the computer takes a millisecond or two to light the coordinates for a pixel in passive matrix displays, the response of the screen to rapid changes is poor, causing, for example, an effect known as "submarining": If, on a computer with a passive matrix display, you move the mouse rapidly from one location to another, it will disappear from the first location and reappear in the new location without appearing anywhere in between.

In order to keep the quality of the image on an LCD the best, the screen must be cleaned often. Liquid crystal displays are typically coated with a clear, plastic covering. This covering commonly gets several fingerprints as well as a generous coating of dust. The best way to clean the LCD lens coating is to wipe it off occasionally with a damp cloth. This will ensure that the images stay crisp and clear.

Other Peripherals

In addition to all the input and output devices, we have a few categories of devices that are neither input nor output devices. Devices like multimedia devices (sound cards and CD-ROM drives) and modems don't fit well into any category, so we'll discuss them here.

Multimedia Devices

The first category of devices we'll discuss is multimedia devices. What is multimedia? The simplest answer is *multiple media*. That is, it's a way of communicating information using more than one form, such as some combination of video, pictures, sound, and text. Several devices are included in the category, including CD-ROM drives, sound cards, speakers, and microphones.

CD-ROM Drives

In Chapter 4, we discussed the way CD-ROM drives work. Let's talk a bit about the format compatibility of CD-ROM drives. Because all CD-ROM drives work in more or less the same manner, the companies that manufactured them came up with standards to allow the various types of CD disks to work in the different drives made by different vendors. The International Standards Organization (ISO) came up with several standards that specify what type of information can be saved on a CD and how it's recorded.

The first CD standard, called the Red Book standard, is the standard for recording digital audio (audio CDs that you play in your home CD player). It specifies the recording level as 16-bit, 44.1KHz, and that the entire disk will have an index of the music tracks stored on it. The Yellow Book standard defines the main requirements for data storage on a CD-ROM. This standard supports both PC (ISO9660) and Mac (HFS) file system formats as well as file system formats from other vendors (DEC and VMS).

The Green Book standard is primarily for CD-I (Compact Disk Interactive) CDs. These disks have interactive functionality written right to the CD. Orange Book is for the "writable" CDs that are only now becoming affordable for the common user.

Sound Cards

Just as there are devices to convert computer signals into printouts and video information, there are devices to convert those signals into sound. These devices are known as *sound cards*. There are many different manufacturers making sound cards, but the standard has been set by Creative Labs with their Sound-Blaster series of cards. As a matter of fact, the MPC standards specify a Sound-Blaster-compatible sound card.

When installing a sound card, usually you set the IRQ, DMA, and I/O addresses with software (although some of the older, ISA cards use jumpers). Table 6.2 details the default settings of a typical SoundBlaster sound card.

TABLE 6.2 Default SoundBlaster Configuration Settings

Parameter	Default Setting
IRQ	5
Sound Card I/O Address	220
DMA	1
MIDI port I/O Address	330

Musical Instrument Digital Interface

In addition to producing sound, sound cards have another capability that is often overlooked. The Musical Instrument Digital Interface (MIDI—usually pronounced "middy") technology incorporated into most sound cards allows PCs to talk with (and in some cases, control) musical devices. With the addition of a special adapter cable that plugs into the game port on most sound cards, a PC can use external sound modules to produce sounds. MIDI technologies are used by most electronic keyboard players and professional musicians. However, you don't need to have an electronic keyboard or external sound module to play MIDI sounds. Most sound cards include a set of ICs that incorporate some of the sound-generating circuitry found in most electronic keyboards.

Communication Devices

In this section, we will be discussing communication devices and the various types of cables they use. Before we can discuss them, however, we must explain the two major types of communication: synchronous and asynchronous.

Synchronous vs. Asynchronous Communications

When two computers want to communicate, they must first agree on the rules of communication. One of those rules concerns whether or not they are going to communicate using a synchronous or an asynchronous process. As the magician said when asked about his magic trick, "It's all in the timing." *Synchronous* communications use a clock signal that's separate from the data signal (either on a separate wire or on a completely separate cable). Communication can only happen during a "tick" of the timing signal. Synchronous communications work great when large amounts of data must be moved around quickly. However, even if there's no data, the timing signal still gets sent, which wastes bandwidth on the transmission medium.

But what if the computers had only a little data to exchange? In this case, they might use *asynchronous* transmission methods. Asynchronous transmissions don't use a constant clock signal. Instead, they add special signaling bits to each end of the data (see Figure 6.21). The bit at the beginning of the information signals the start of the data and is known as the *start bit*. The next few bits are the actual data that needs to be sent. Those bits are known as the *data bits*. Finally, you have one or more *stop bits* that indicate that the data is finished. These special "frames" of information are transmitted at irregular intervals until all the information has been exchanged.

FIGURE 6.21 An asynchronous data "frame"

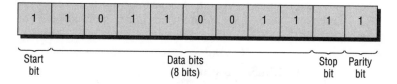

When devices for asynchronous communication are configured, both devices must agree on the number of data bits and stop bits and on whether or not parity checking should be used. If both sender and receiver aren't set to the same values, communication can't take place. The values are usually set in the software of both the sending and receiving hardware.

Modems

Modems are devices used by computers to communicate over long distances. The word *modem* is actually a partial acronym; it stands for MOdulator-DEModulator. It got this name from the way it works. When a computer wants to send data, it uses a digital signal (fluctuations in voltage, representing 1s and 0s). The problem is that these signals can attenuate (decrease in strength) over long distances. For example, if you want to transmit the binary number 10110101 as a series of voltages, you might say to both computers, "A 1 is represented by a voltage of +5.0 volts; a 0 is any voltage less than that." If you try to transmit that number over a distance of only a few feet, +5.0 volts (representing the 1s) will still be +5.0 volts when it comes out the other end of the wire. However, if you try to transmit that same number over a distance of a mile or more, after the first few hundred feet, the +5.0 voltages might drop to 4.5 volts, which of course is below +5.0 volts. This voltage will get lower as the distance gets longer. When the signals get to the other end, the number will be 00000000 because *all* the voltages will be less than +5.0 volts.

Analog signals, on the other hand, don't suffer from this problem because analog values are typically many values in a range, like sound waves. As a matter of fact, sound waves travel *very* well over long distances in wires. The sound waves are converted to pulses of voltages. Over long distances, the pulses get weaker, but the sound is just the same. It can be said, then, that analog signals are more reliable over longer distances.

Wouldn't it be great to have the best of both worlds? You can—with the modem. Modems convert digital signals into analog signals by using variations of tones to represent 1s and 0s (this is the MOdulation). The modem then sends these sounds over a phone line. At the other end, the tones are converted back into 1s and 0s (this is the DEModulation). Using two modems and a phone line, you transmit digital data through an analog medium.

The only downside to modems is that this process is relatively inefficient. Because modem communications are so sporadic, they use asynchronous communications, which have their overhead of start and stop bits. Also, today's phone lines are limited to a maximum throughput of 56Kbps.

Bits vs. Baud

The most confusing terms used to describe modem speed are *bits per second* (or *bps*) and *baud*. Actually, it's a very easy distinction. The bps value of a modem is how much data is being transmitted in one second. Baud is how many signal (tone) changes are happening in one second. Through a process known as encoding, several bits can be transmitted using only a few signal changes. Modern phone lines are limited to 9600 baud. If you increase the baud rate any higher, the modem on the other end starts to have difficulty distinguishing the individual tonal changes. However, with modern encoding techniques, it is possible to get up to 56 kilobits per second (Kbps) transmitted with 9600 baud.

There are two types of modems: internal and external. Internal modems are installed as expansion cards inside a computer. External modems have their own power supplies and connect to an external COM port with an RS-232 cable. There are advantages and disadvantages to each.

Internal modems are usually smaller and cheaper than their external counterparts. However, they are more difficult to configure. You need to configure them to use an unused COM port. Table 6.3 lists the IRQ and I/O port addresses of the standard COM ports installed.

External modems use an existing serial port, so they don't have the configuration problem with IRQs and I/O addresses. However, they don't interface directly with the computer's expansion bus, so data transfers may be slowed (especially if the modem is faster than 9600bps). If this is the case, the serial port must use a higher-speed UART (Universal Asynchronous Receiver/Transmitter). The UART is the chip that manages the serial data that's moving in and out through the serial port. If the modem is 9600bps or faster, you need to use a 16-bit UART (for example, the 16450 or 16550 model). Most computers come with 16550 UARTs, so you don't have to worry about this. However, some older computers came with the old, 8-bit 8550 UART and may need to be upgraded.

TABLE 6.3 Standard COM Port and IRQ Addresses

COM Port	IRQ Address	I/O address
COM 1	4	3F8-3FF
COM 2	3	2F8-2FF
COM 3	4	3E8-3EF
COM 4	3	2E8-2EF

And Now for the Real World...

An additional benefit of external modems is that the status lights on the modem are visible. It's sometimes helpful to know when the modem has hung up or is transmitting data. Here's a quick little guide to the common abbreviations found next to the lights on a modem:

OH   Off Hook. The modem is dialing or otherwise has the phone off the hook.

SD(TX)   Transmit Data. The modem is sending data.

RD(RX)   Receive Data. The modem is receiving data.

AA   Auto Answer. The modem is set to automatically pick up after a few rings.

Cables

Cables are used to connect two or more entities together. They are usually constructed of several wires encased together in a rubberized outer coating. The wires are soldered to modular connectors at both ends. These connectors are used to allow the cables to be quickly attached to the devices they connect. A listing of common cable types used in PCs, their descriptions, their maximum effective lengths, and their most common uses is given in Table 6.4.

TABLE 6.4 Common PC Cable Descriptions

Application	1st Connector	2nd Connector	Max. Length
Null modem	DB-9F	DB-9F	25 feet
Null modem	DB-25F	DB-25F	25 feet
RS-232 (modem cable)	DB-9F	DB-25M	25 feet
RS-232 (modem cable)	DB-25F	DB-25M	25 feet
Parallel printer	DB-25M	Male Centronics 36	10 feet
External SCSI cable	Male Centronics 50	Male Centronics 50	10 feet (total SCSI bus length)
VGA extension cable	DB-15M	DB-15M	3 feet
UTP Ethernet cable	RJ-45 Male	RJ-45 Male	100 meters
Thinnet Ethernet cable	BNC Male	BNC Male	100 meters
Telephone wall cable	RJ-11 Male	RJ-11 Male	N/A

WARNING It should be noted that some manufacturers have made cables that are much longer than the maximum length listed in the table. Although they might work, these cables may occasionally cause communication delays or dropouts and therefore should not be used. Using a 50-foot printer cable is *not* a good way to connect a computer to a printer 50 feet away. Unless you use low-capacitance cable (which might cost as much as $100), you're far better off moving the printer close enough to use a 10-foot printer cable!

One cable that deserves special mention is the *null modem cable*. It is used to allow two computers to communicate with each other without using a modem. This cable has its transmit and receive wires crossed at both ends, so when one entity transmits on its TD line, the other entity is receiving it on its RD line. The most popular application for a null modem cable is playing games, believe it or not. A null modem cable is required to play games like Doom and Descent in multiplayer mode if you aren't playing them over a network or a modem connection. It does have more useful purposes, however. For example, there are some data transfer programs (like LapLink 3, from Traveling Software) that can transfer files over a null modem cable between two computers. This can be very useful when upgrading computers.

More cables and connectors are covered in Chapter 1.

Summary

Peripherals expand the capabilities of computer systems. In this chapter, you learned about the various peripherals commonly attached to computer systems. Additionally, you learned about the technical configuration challenges that each presents. Finally, you learned the proper way to connect each peripheral to its host computer. The A+ exam will test your ability to identify the various peripherals and the cables and connectors used to connect them.

In the first section, we discussed the various types of input devices that are available for computers. We also discussed how each device is used to get data into the computer as well as exactly how each device works. Finally, we covered the basic service concepts that relate to each input device.

The next section covered the most common output devices used with computers today (e.g., monitors, printers, and modems) and how they differ from one another. You learned exactly how most of the devices work (although printers are covered in more detail in Chapter 7). You also learned how these devices are used to get output from the computer and the basic service concepts that relate to each device.

There are a number of other, miscellaneous peripherals that can be attached to a PC, such as multimedia and communications devices. As in the other sections, you learned how each device works as well as how it's commonly connected to a PC. You also learned how to install and service these devices.

Key Terms

bus mouse

charge-coupled device (CCD)

daisy-wheel printer

debouncing

dot pitch

dot-matrix printer

electron gun

graphical user interface (GUI)

graphics mode

impact printers

interlacing

laser printers

monochrome

null modem

optical scanners

pixels

PS/2 mouse interface

puck

refresh rate

stylus

text mode

trackball

Review Questions

1. "Debouncing" refers to _____ .

   A. Stopping a mouse ball from bouncing

   B. Cleaning up keyboard signals and preventing multiple characters from a single keypress

   C. Keeping the keyboard keyswitches from bouncing up and down

   D. Making sure that service customers' checks don't bounce

2. COM 1 shares an IRQ with which other COM port?

   A. COM 1

   B. COM 2

   C. COM 3

   D. COM 4

3. Which IRQ does COM 1 share with COM 3?

   A. 4

   B. 2

   C. 3

   D. 10

4. What are the two major types of mice in use today?

   A. Capacitive

   B. Resistive

   C. Optical

   D. Opto-mechanical

5. You find a cable in a box of old computer parts. It has a DB-25F connector on both ends. What kind of cable is it most likely to be?

   A. Printer cable

   B. Modem cable

   C. Null modem cable

   D. VGA cable

6. Which type of computer communication uses a separate timing signal to dictate transmission times?

   A. Synchronous

   B. Asynchronous

   C. Standard

   D. Modem

7. What are the two major types of keyboards in use today?

   A. Standard

   B. Keyswitched

   C. Capacitive

   D. Resistive

8. If a display adapter is a VGA adapter in the standard configuration, which one of the following would be the default resolution/color choice?

   A. 640 × 480 with 256 colors

   B. 640 × 480 with 16 colors

   C. 640 × 480 with 65,536 colors

   D. 1,024 × 768 with 256 colors

9. Which of the following monitors has the highest resolution?

   A. VGA 640 × 480

   B. CGA 320 × 200

   C. SVGA 800 × 600

   D. XGA 1,024 × 768

10. Which types of mouse interface technology use an interrupt (other than the ones a PC is normally using)?

    A. Bus

    B. PS/2

    C. Serial

    D. Microsoft

11. Which type of signal degrades the most over longer distances?

    A. Serial

    B. Analog

    C. Digital

    D. Parallel

12. What is the maximum practical length of a standard parallel printer cable?

    A. 6 feet

    B. 10 feet

    C. 25 feet

    D. 50 feet

13. Which type of scanner gives the best quality and highest resolution?

    A. Flatbed

    B. Handheld

    C. Photo

14. Which of the following types of output devices puts computer data on paper?

    A. Modems

    B. Monitors

    C. LCDs

    D. Printers

15. Which type of output device has the highest resolution (and therefore the best quality)?

    A. Impact printers

    B. Sprayed-ink printers

    C. EP printers

    D. Modems

16. A VGA extension cable will have _____ .

    A. DB-9F to DB9F

    B. DB-25F to DB-25M

    C. DB-15M to DB-15M

    D. DB-25M to DB25-F

17. Which LCD matrix screen works in a manner similar to an LCD watch?

    A. Active matrix

    B. Passive matrix

    C. Parallel matrix

    D. Serial matrix

18. Which type of output device draws the image with a pen one shape at a time and uses CAD software to produce blueprints or technical diagrams?

    A. Impact printers

    B. Sprayed-ink printers

    C. Electrophotographic printers

    D. Plotters

19. All of the following can be considered video technologies except _____ .

    A. EGA and CGA

    B. VGA

    C. XGA

    D. SVGA

    E. DVGA

20. Which type of mouse interface is a small, round PS/2 connector and is attached to an 8-bit interface card that is installed directly onto the computer's bus?

    A. Serial bus interface

    B. Bus mouse interface

    C. PS/2 mouse interface

Answers to Review Questions

1. B . Debouncing works by having the keyboard controller constantly scan the keyboard for keystrokes. The controller registers only those keystrokes that are pressed for more than two scans and ignores all others.

2. C. Because of the configuration of the original 8-bit bus (which supported only 8 IRQs and had only COM 1 and COM 2), when COM 3 was added later, it shared the IRQ with COM 1.

3. A. Because of the configuration of the original 8-bit bus that supported only 8 IRQs, when COM 3 was added, it had to share IRQ4 with COM 1.

4. C, D. The mice most commonly found today are the optical and opto-mechanical.

5. C. A cable with both ends having a DB-25F connector is classified as a null modem cable.

6. A. Synchronous communications uses a clock signal that is separate from the data signal; communication can only happen during a tick of the timing signal.

7. B, C. The most common types of keyboards in use today are the keyswitched and the capacitive.

8. B. This video technology had 256Kb of video memory on board and could display 16 colors at 640 x 480 pixels.

9. D. XGA could support 256 colors at $1,024 \times 768$ pixels and therefore has the highest resolution.

10. A, B. The PS/2 and bus mouse technology use a separate interrupt.

11. C. Of the signal types listed, digital is least suited for long distances because it degrades the most.

12. B. Although you can buy standard printer cables longer than 10 feet, it is not recommended that you use them because there can be problems with data loss over 10 feet.

13. A. The flatbed scanner gives the best quality and highest resolution over a handheld scanner. This is due to several reasons, such as that the scanning hardware is enclosed in a special casing and the scanning arm is moved by a motor instead of by a human hand.

14. D. Of the devices listed, printers are the only output devices capable of putting computer data on paper.

15. C. The images produced by electrophotographic (EP) printers are of the very best quality and they produce these images at higher speeds.

16. C. The VGA extension cable will have a DB-15M on both connectors.

17. A. The LCD watch was the precursor technology to active matrix LCD screens.

18. D. Plotters draw the image with a pen one shape at a time and use CAD software to produce blueprints or technical diagrams.

19. E. EGA, CGA, XGA, and SVGA can all be considered video technologies.

20. B. The bus mouse interface is a small, round PS/2 connector and is attached to an 8-bit interface card that is installed directly onto the computer's bus.

Chapter 7

How Printers Work

et's face it. We are a society that is dependent on paper. When we conduct business, we use different types of paper documents. Contracts, letters, and of course, money are all used to conduct business. As more and more of those documents are created on computers, printers will become increasingly important.

Printers are electro-mechanical output devices that are used to put information from the computer onto paper. They have been around since the introduction of the computer. Other than the display monitor, the printer is the most popular peripheral purchased for a computer, because most people need to have paper copies of the documents they create.

In this chapter, we will discuss the details of each major type of printer. We will cover the following A+ exam topics:

- Impact printers
- Bubble-jet printers
- Laser printers (page printers)
- Interfaces and print media

For complete coverage of objective 1.7, please also see Chapters 5 and 9.

Take special note of the section on laser and page printers. The A+ exams test these subjects in detail, so we'll cover them in as much detail.

Impact Printers

There are several categories of printers, but the most basic type is the category of printers known as *impact printers*. Impact printers, as their name suggests, use some form of impact and an inked ribbon to make an imprint on the paper. In a manner of speaking, typewriters are like impact printers. Both use an inked ribbon and an impact head to make letters on the paper. The major difference is that the printer can accept input from a computer.

There are two major types of impact printers: daisy wheel and dot matrix. Each type has its own service and maintenance issues.

Daisy-Wheel Printers

Although not really covered on the A+ exam, the first type of impact printer we're going to discuss is the *daisy-wheel printer*. These printers contain a wheel (called the daisy wheel because it looks like a daisy) with raised letters and symbols on each "petal" (see Figure 7.1). When the printer needs to print a character, it sends a signal to the mechanism that contains the wheel. This mechanism is called the *printhead*. The printhead rotates the daisy wheel until the required character is in place. An electromechanical hammer (called a *solenoid*) then strikes the back of the "petal" containing the character. The character pushes up against an inked ribbon that ultimately strikes the paper, making the impression of the requested character.

FIGURE 7.1 A daisy-wheel printer mechanism

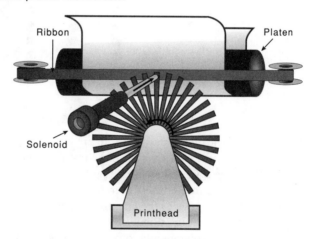

Daisy-wheel printers were one of the first types of impact printer developed. Their speed is rated by the number of *characters per second (cps)* they can print. The early printers could only print between two and four characters per second. Aside from their poor speed, the main disadvantage to this type of printer is that it makes a lot of noise when printing—so much, in fact, that special enclosures were developed to contain the noise.

The daisy-wheel printer has a few advantages, of course. First, because it is an impact printer, you can print on multipart forms (like carbonless receipts), assuming they can be fed into the printer properly. Second, it is relatively inexpensive compared to the price of a laser printer of the same vintage. Finally, the print quality is comparable to a typewriter because it uses a very similar technology. This typewriter level of quality was given a name: *letter quality (LQ)*.

Dot-Matrix Printers

The other type of impact printer we're going to discuss is the *dot-matrix printer*. These printers work in a manner similar to daisy-wheel printers, except that instead of a spinning, character-imprinted wheel, the printhead contains a row of "pins" (short sturdy stalks of hard wire). These pins are triggered in patterns that form letters and numbers as the printhead moves across the paper (see Figure 7.2).

FIGURE 7.2 Formation of images in a dot-matrix printer

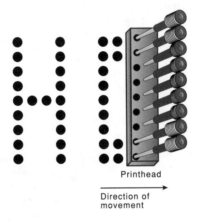

Printhead

Direction of movement

The pins in the printhead are wrapped with coils of wire to create a solenoid. Also, the pins are held in the rest position by a combination of a small magnet and a spring. To trigger a particular pin, the printer controller sends a signal to the printhead, which energizes the wires around the appropriate print wire. This turns the print wire into an electromagnet, which repels the print pin, forcing it against the ink ribbon and making a dot on the paper. It's the arrangement of the dots in columns and rows that creates the letters and numbers we see on the page. Figure 7.2 shows this process.

The main disadvantage to dot-matrix printers is their image quality, which can be quite poor compared to the quality produced with a daisy wheel. Dot-matrix printers use patterns of dots to make letters and images, and the early dot-matrix printers used only 9 pins to make those patterns. The output quality of such printers is referred to as "draft quality"—good mainly for providing your initial text to a correspondent or revisor. Each letter looked "fuzzy" because the dots were spaced as far as they could be spaced and still be perceived as a letter or image. As more pins were crammed into the printhead

(17-pin and 24-pin models were eventually developed), the quality increased because the dots were closer together. Dot-matrix technology ultimately improved to the point where a letter printed on a dot-matrix printer was *almost* indistinguishable from typewriter output. This level of quality is known as *near letter quality (NLQ)*.

Dot-matrix printers are still noisy, but the print wires and printhead are covered by a plastic dust cover, making them quieter than daisy-wheel printers. Also, dot-matrix printers use a more efficient printing technology, so the print speed is faster (typically in the range of 36 to 72cps). Some dot-matrix printers (like the Epson DFV series) can print at close to a page per second! Finally, because dot-matrix printers are also impact printers, they can also use multipart forms. Because of these advantages, dot-matrix printers quickly made daisy-wheel printers obsolete.

Bubble-Jet Printers

The next category of printer technology is one of the most popular in use today. This category of printers is actually an advanced form of an older technology known as ink-jet printers. Both types of printers spray ink on the page, but ink-jet printers use a reservoir of ink, a pump, and an ink nozzle to accomplish this. They were messy, noisy, and inefficient. Bubble-jet printers work much more efficiently.

Bubble-jet printers are very basic printers. There are very few moving parts. Every bubble-jet printer works in a similar fashion. First of all, every bubble-jet printer contains a special part called an ink cartridge (see Figure 7.3). This part contains the printhead and ink supply, and it must be replaced as the ink supply runs out.

FIGURE 7.3 A typical ink cartridge (size: approximately 3 inches by 11/2 inches)

Inside this ink cartridge are several small chambers. At the top of each chamber is a metal plate and tube leading to the ink supply. At the bottom of each chamber is a small pinhole. These pinholes are used to spray ink on the page to form characters and images as patterns of dots (similar to the way a dot-matrix printer works, but with much higher resolution).

When a particular chamber needs to spray ink, an electric signal is sent to the heating element, energizing it. The elements heat up quickly, causing the ink to vaporize. Because of the expanding ink vapor, the ink is pushed out the pinhole and forms a bubble of ink. As the vapor expands, the bubble eventually gets large enough to break off into a droplet. The rest of the ink is pulled back into the chamber by the surface tension of the ink. When another drop needs to be sprayed, the process begins again.

When the printer is done printing, the printhead moves back to its maintenance station. The *maintenance station* contains a small suction pump and ink-absorbing pad. To keep the ink flowing freely, before each print cycle, the maintenance station pulls ink through the ink nozzles using vacuum suction. This expelled ink is absorbed by the pad in the maintenance station. The stations serves two functions: to provide a place for the printhead to rest when the printer isn't printing, and to keep the printhead in working order.

Laser Printers (Page Printers)

Laser printers are referred to as page printers because they receive their print job instructions one page at a time (rather than receiving instructions one line at a time). There are two major types of page printers: those that use the Electrophotographic (EP) print process and those that use the light-emitting diode (LED) print process. Each works in basically the same way, with slight differences.

Electrophotographic (EP) Laser Printer Operation

When Xerox and Canon developed the first laser printers in the late 1980s, they were designed around the Electrophotographic (EP) process (a technology developed by scientists at Xerox). This technology uses a combination of static electric charges, laser light, and a black powdery substance called *toner*. Printers that use this technology are called EP process laser printers, or just *laser printers*. Every laser printer technology has its foundations in the EP printer process.

Let's discuss the basic components of the EP laser printer and how they operate so you can understand the way an EP laser printer works.

Basic Components

Any printer that uses the EP process contains eight standard assemblies. These assemblies are the toner cartridge, fusing assembly, laser scanner, high-voltage power supply, DC power supply, paper transport assembly (including paper pickup rollers and paper registration rollers), corona, and printer controller circuitry. Let's discuss each of the components individually before we discuss how all the components work together to make the printer function.

The Toner Cartridge

The EP toner cartridge (Figure 7.4), as its name suggests, holds the toner. Toner is a black, carbon substance mixed with polyester resins (to make it "flow" better) and iron oxide particles (to make the toner sensitive to electrical charges). These two components make the toner capable of being attracted to the photosensitive drum and capable of melting into the paper. In addition to these components, toner contains a medium called the *developer* (also called the *carrier*), which "carries" the toner until it is used by the EP process. The toner cartridge also contains the EP print drum. This drum is coated with a photosensitive material that can hold a static charge when not exposed to light (but *cannot* hold a charge when it *is* exposed to light—a curious phenomenon, and one that EP printers exploit for the purpose of making images). Finally, the drum contains a cleaning blade that continuously scrapes the "used" toner off the photosensitive drum to keep it clean.

FIGURE 7.4 An EP toner cartridge

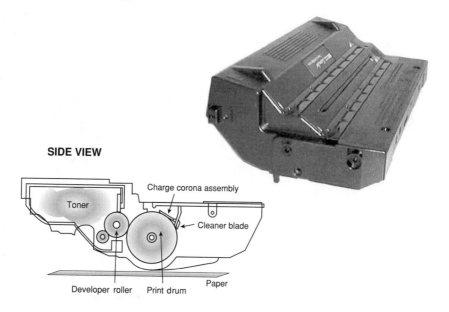

SIDE VIEW

Charge corona assembly

Toner

Cleaner blade

Developer roller   Print drum   Paper

In most laser printers, "toner cartridge" means an EP toner cartridge that contains toner and a photosensitive drum in one plastic case. In some laser printers, however, the toner and photosensitive drum can be replaced separately instead of as a single unit. If you ask for a "toner cartridge" for one of these printers, all you will receive is a cylinder full of toner. Consult the printer's manual to find out which kind of toner cartridge your laser printer uses.

The Laser Scanning Assembly

As we mentioned earlier, the EP photosensitive drum can hold a charge if it's not exposed to light. It is dark inside an EP printer, except when the laser scanning assembly shines on particular areas of the photosensitive drum. When it does that, the drum discharges, but only in that area. As the drum rotates, the laser scanning assembly scans the laser across the photosensitive drum. Figure 7.5 shows the laser scanning assembly.

FIGURE 7.5 The EP laser scanning assembly (side view and simplified top view)

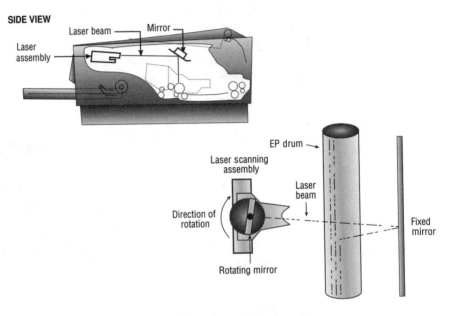

Laser light is damaging to human eyes. Therefore, it is kept in an enclosure and will operate only when the laser printer's cover is closed.

High-Voltage Power Supply (HVPS)

The EP process requires high-voltage electricity. The high-voltage power supply (HVPS) provides the high voltages that are used during the EP process. This component converts house AC current (120 volts, 60 Hertz) into higher voltages that the printer can use. This high voltage is used to energize both the corona wire and transfer corona wire.

DC Power Supply (DCPS)

The high voltages used in the EP process can't power the other components in the printer (the logic circuitry and motors). These components require low voltages, between +5 and +24Vdc. The DC power supply (DCPS) converts house current into three voltages: +5Vdc and –5Vdc for the logic circuitry and +24Vdc for the paper transport motors. This component also runs the fan that cools the internal components of the printer.

Paper Transport Assembly

The paper transport assembly is responsible for moving the paper through the printer. It consists of a motor and several rubberized rollers that each perform a different function.

The first type of roller found in most laser printers is the *feed roller*, or *paper pickup roller* (Figure 7.6). This D-shaped roller, when activated, rotates against the paper and pushes one sheet into the printer. This roller works in conjunction with a special rubber pad to prevent more than one sheet from being fed into the printer at a time.

FIGURE 7.6 Paper transport rollers

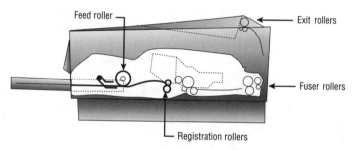

Another type of roller that is used in the printer is the registration roller (also shown in Figure 7.6). There are actually two registration rollers, which work together. These rollers synchronize the paper movement with the image formation process in the EP cartridge. The rollers don't feed the paper past the EP cartridge until the cartridge is ready for it.

Both of these rollers are operated with a special electric motor known as an *electronic stepper motor*. This type of motor can accurately move in very small increments. It powers all of the paper transport rollers as well as the fuser rollers.

The Transfer Corona Assembly

When the laser writes the images on the photosensitive drum, the toner then sticks to the exposed areas; we'll cover this in the next section, "Electrophotographic (EP) Print Process." How do you get the toner from the photosensitive drum onto the paper? Well, the *transfer corona assembly* (Figure 7.7) is charged with a high-voltage electrical charge. This assembly charges the paper, which pulls the toner from the photosensitive drum.

FIGURE 7.7 The transfer corona assembly

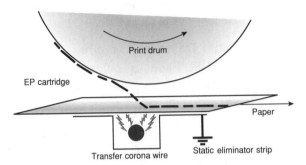

Included in the corona assembly is a *static-charge eliminator strip* that drains away the charge imparted to the paper by the corona. If you didn't drain away the charge, the paper would stick to the EP cartridge and jam the printer.

There are two types of corona assemblies, those that contain a *corona wire* and those that contain a *corona roller*. The corona wire is a small diameter wire that is charged by the high-voltage power supply. The wire is located in a special notch in the "floor" of the laser printer (underneath the EP print cartridge). The corona roller performs the same function as the corona wire, except that it's a roller rather than a wire. Because the corona roller is directly in contact with the paper, it supports higher speeds. It is for this reason that the corona wire isn't used in laser printers much any more.

Fusing Assembly

The toner in the EP toner cartridge will stick to just about anything, including paper. This is true because the toner has a negative static charge and most objects have a net positive charge. However, these toner particles can be removed by brushing any object across the page. This could be a problem if you want the images and letters to stay on the paper permanently!

To solve this problem, EP laser printers incorporate a device known as a *fuser* (Figure 7.8), which uses two rollers that apply pressure and heat to fuse the plastic toner particles to the paper. You may have noticed that pages from either a laser printer or a copier (which uses a similar device) come out warm. This is because of the fuser.

FIGURE 7.8 The fuser

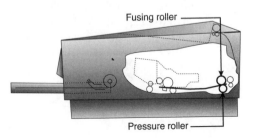

The fuser is made up of three main parts: a halogen heating lamp, a Teflon-coated aluminum fusing roller, and a rubberized pressure roller. The fuser uses the halogen lamp to heat the fusing roller to between 165 degrees C and 180 degrees C. As the paper passes between the two rollers, the pressure roller pushes the paper against the fusing roller, which melts the toner into the paper.

Printer Controller Circuitry

The final component in the laser printer we need to discuss is the *printer controller assembly*. This large circuit board converts signals from the computer into signals for the various assemblies in the laser printer, using the process known as *rasterizing*. This circuit board is usually mounted underneath the printer. The board has connectors for each of the types of interfaces and cables to each assembly.

When a computer prints to a laser printer, it sends a signal through a cable to the printer controller assembly. The controller assembly formats the information into a page's worth of line-by-line commands for the laser scanner. The controller sends commands to each of the components telling them to "wake up" and start the EP print process.

Ozone Filter

Your laser printer uses various high-voltage biases inside the case. As anyone who has been outside during a lightning storm can tell you, high voltages create ozone. Ozone is a chemically reactive gas that is created by the high-voltage coronas (charging and transfer) inside the printer. Because ozone is chemically reactive and can severely reduce the life of laser printer components, most laser printers contain a filter to remove ozone gas from inside the printer as it is produced. This filter must be removed and cleaned with compressed air periodically (usually whenever the toner cartridge is replaced is sufficient).

Electrophotographic (EP) Print Process

The EP print process is the process by which an EP laser printer forms images on paper. It consists of six major steps, each for a specific goal. Although many different manufacturers call these steps different things or place them in a different order, the basic process is still the same. Here are the steps in the order you will see on the exam:

1. Cleaning
2. Conditioning
3. Writing
4. Developing
5. Transferring
6. Fusing

Before any of these steps can begin, however, the controller must sense that the printer is ready to start printing (toner cartridge installed, fuser warmed to temperature, and all covers are in place). Printing cannot take place until the printer is in its "ready" state, usually indicated by an illuminated Ready LED light or a display that says something like "00 READY" (on HP printers).

Step 1: Cleaning

In the first part of the laser print process, a rubber blade inside the EP cartridge scrapes any toner left on the drum into a used toner receptacle inside the EP cartridge, and a fluorescent lamp discharges any remaining charge on the photosensitive drum (remember that the drum, being photosensitive, loses its charge when exposed to light). This step is called the *cleaning step* (Figure 7.9).

FIGURE 7.9 The cleaning step of the EP process

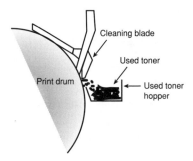

The EP cartridge is constantly cleaning the drum. It may take more than one rotation of the photosensitive drum to make an image on the paper. The cleaning step keeps the drum "fresh" for each use. If you didn't clean the drum, you would see "ghosts" of previous pages printed along with your image.

The actual amount of toner removed in the cleaning process is quite small. The cartridge will run out of toner before the used toner receptacle fills up.

Step 2: Conditioning

The next step in the EP process is the *conditioning step* (Figure 7.10). In this step, a special wire (called a *charging corona*) within the EP toner cartridge (above the photosensitive drum) gets a high voltage from the HVPS. It uses this high voltage to apply a strong, uniform negative charge (around –600Vdc) to the surface of the photosensitive drum.

FIGURE 7.10   The conditioning step of the EP process

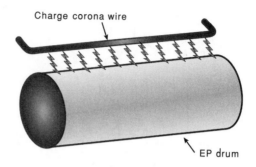

Charge corona wire

EP drum

Step 3: Writing

The next step in the EP process is the *writing step*. In this step, the laser is turned on and "scans" the drum from side to side, flashing on and off according to the bits of information the printer controller sends it as it communicates the individual bits of the image. The areas where the laser "touches" severely reduce the photosensitive drum's charge from –600Vdc to a slight negative charge (around –100Vdc). As the drum rotates, a pattern of exposed areas is formed, representing the images to be printed. Figure 7.11 shows this process.

FIGURE 7.11   The writing step of the EP process

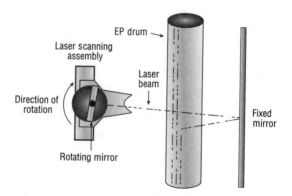

EP drum

Laser scanning
assembly

Laser
beam

Direction of
rotation

Fixed
mirror

Rotating mirror

At this point, the controller sends a signal to the pickup roller to feed a piece of paper into the printer, where it stops at the registration rollers.

Step 4: Developing

Now that the surface of the drum holds an electrical representation of the image being printed, its discrete electrical charges need to be converted into something that can be transferred to a piece of paper. The EP process step that accomplishes this is the *developing step* (Figure 7.12). In this step, toner is transferred to the areas that were exposed in the writing step.

FIGURE 7.12 The developing step of the EP process

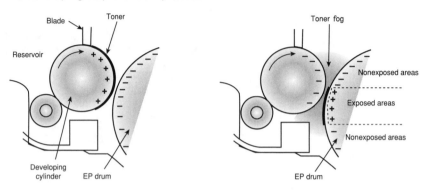

There is a metallic roller called the *developing roller* inside an EP cartridge that acquires a –600Vdc charge (called a bias voltage) from the HVPS. The toner sticks to this roller because there is a magnet located inside the roller and because of the electrostatic charges between the toner and the developing roller. While the developing roller rotates toward the photosensitive drum, the toner acquires the charge of the roller (–600Vdc). When the toner comes between the developing roller and the photosensitive drum, the toner is attracted to the areas that have been exposed by the laser (because these areas have a lesser charge, of –100Vdc). The toner also is repelled from the unexposed areas (because they are at the same –600Vdc charge and like charges repel). This toner transfer creates a "fog" of toner between the EP drum and the developing roller.

The photosensitive drum now has toner stuck to it where the laser has written. The photosensitive drum continues to rotate until the developed image is ready to be transferred to paper in the next step, the transferring step.

Step 5: Transferring

At this point in the EP process, the developed image is rotating into position. The controller notifies the registration rollers that the paper should be fed through. The registration rollers move the paper underneath the photosensitive drum, and the process of transferring the image can begin, with the *transferring step*.

The controller sends a signal to the corona wire or corona roller (depending on which one the printer has) and tells it to turn on. The corona wire/roller then acquires a strong *positive* charge (+600Vdc) and applies that charge to the paper. The paper, thus charged, pulls the toner from the photosensitive drum at the line of "contact" between the roller and the paper because the paper and toner have opposite charges. Once the registration rollers move the paper past the corona wire, the static-eliminator strip removes all charge from that "line" of the paper. Figure 7.13 details this step. If the strip didn't bleed this charge away, the paper would attract itself to the toner cartridge and cause a paper jam.

FIGURE 7.13 The transferring step of the EP process

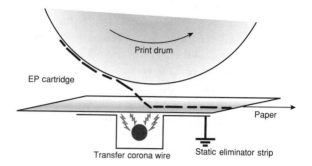

The toner is now held in place by weak, electrostatic charges and gravity. It will not stay there, however, unless it is made permanent, which is the reason for the next step, the fusing step.

Step 6: Fusing

In the final step, the *fusing step*, the toner image is made permanent. The registration rollers push the paper toward the fuser rollers. Once the fuser grabs the paper, the registration rollers push for only a short time more. The fuser is now in control of moving the paper.

As the paper passes through the fuser, the 350-degree F fuser roller melts the polyester resin of the toner and the rubberized pressure roller presses it permanently into the paper (Figure 7.14). The paper continues on through the fuser and eventually exits the printer.

FIGURE 7.14 The fusing step of the EP process

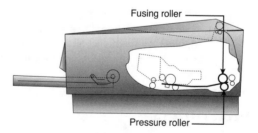

Once the paper completely exits the fuser, it trips a sensor that tells the printer to finish the EP process with the next step, the cleaning step. At this point, the printer can print another page and the EP process can begin again.

Summary of the EP Print Process

Figure 7.15 summarizes all the EP process printing steps. First, the printer uses a rubber scraper to clean the photosensitive drum. Then the printer places a uniform, negative, –600Vdc charge on the photosensitive drum by means of a charging corona. The laser "paints" an image onto the photosensitive drum, discharging the image areas to a much lower voltage (–100Vdc). The developing roller in the toner cartridge has charged (–600Vdc) toner stuck to it. As it rolls the toner toward the photosensitive drum, the toner is attracted to (and sticks to) the areas of the photosensitive drum that the laser has discharged. The image is then transferred from the drum to the paper at its line of contact by means of the corona wire (or corona roller) with a +600Vdc charge. The static-eliminator strip removes the high, positive charge from the paper, and the paper, now holding the image, moves on. The paper then enters the fuser where a fuser roller and the pressure roller make the image permanent. The paper exits the printer and the printer starts printing the next page or returns to its ready state.

FIGURE 7.15   The EP print process

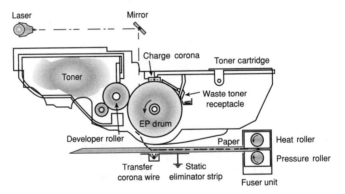

To help you remember the steps of the EP print process, in order, remember them by the first letters of each step, or CCWDTF. The most often used mnemonic sentence for this combination of letters is "Charlie Can Walk, Dance, and Talk French."

LED Page Printers

Another laser printer we're going to discuss is the LED page printer. This technology is primarily developed and used by Okidata and Panasonic. Because the A+ exam does not currently cover LED page printers, we will discuss only the differences between them and laser printers.

The two main differences between a LED page printer and a laser printer are the toner cartridges and the print process.

LED Page Printer Toner Cartridges

One problem with laser printers is that the toner usually runs out before the photosensitive drum needs to be replaced. But because they're both housed in the same replaceable unit, every time you replace the toner, you're also replacing the drum, whether it needs replacing or not. So, the designers of the LED page printers made the photosensitive drum and toner separate, replaceable items.

The main parts of the LED page printer toner cartridge are actually integrated into the printer. Additionally, the charging corona (or roller) and erasing lamps are integrated into the printer. These items cannot be replaced by the average user. An authorized service technician must remove them.

When replacing the photosensitive drum, you swing the photosensitive drum/toner cartridge out of the printer first. Then you remove the drum from its carrier and install the new one (this also replaces the waste toner receptacle).

Filling the toner hopper is fairly easy. On most LED page printers, you place the new toner cartridge over the toner hopper and lock it in place. Between the new toner cartridge and the toner hopper is a lever and door. When the lever is slid over, it opens the door and allows the toner to fall through the opening. Once all the toner is out of the cartridge and hopper, the lever is slid back, closing the door. You can then remove the cartridge and throw it away.

The LED Page Printer Process

The LED page printer uses the same process as any other laser printer, with one major exception. It uses a row of small LEDs held very close to the photosensitive drum to expose it. Each LED is about the same size as the diameter of the laser beam used in laser printers. These printers are basically the same as EP process printers, except that in the exposure step, they use LEDs instead of a laser.

There are several benefits to LED page printers over laser printers. First of all, because they use LEDs instead of lasers, LED page printers are much cheaper than a similar laser printer—they're about half the cost. Also, because the LEDs are very close to the drum, the whole printer is smaller—about two-thirds the size of a comparable laser printer. Finally, LEDs aren't as dangerous to the eye as lasers (you could probably damage your eyes if you stared at one long enough, but it's unlikely you'd do such a thing).

If they have so many advantages, why isn't everyone using them? Mainly because LED technology isn't as advanced as laser technology. The resolutions of LED page printers have yet to break the 800 dots-per-inch (dpi) mark. Another reason is that the toner system in an LED printer, although more efficient, is also messier. Because of its slight static charge, toner isn't easy to remove from surfaces.

WARNING Never ship a printer anywhere with a toner cartridge installed! If the printer is a laser printer, remove the toner cartridge first. If it's an LED page printer, there is a method to remove the photosensitive drum and toner hopper (check your manual for details).

Printer Interfaces and Supplies

Besides understanding the printer's operation, for the exam you will need to understand how the printer talks to a computer and all the items involved in that process. Also, you must understand how the different types of print media affect the print process. These two concepts will complete our discussion of printers.

Interface Components

A printer's *interface* is the collection of hardware and software that allows the printer to communicate with a computer. Each printer has at least one interface, but some printers have several, in order to make them more flexible in a multi-platform environment. If a printer has several interfaces, it can usually switch between them on the fly so that several computers can print at the same time.

There are several components to an interface, including its communication type as well as the *interface software*. Each aspect must be matched on both the printer and the computer. For example, an HP LaserJet 4L only has a parallel port. Therefore, you must use a parallel cable as well as the correct software for the platform being used (e.g., a Macintosh HP LaserJet 4L driver if you connect it to a Macintosh computer).

Communication Types

When we say "communication types," we're actually talking about the hardware technologies involved in getting the printed information from the computer to the printer. There are four major types: serial, parallel, Universal Serial Bus (USB), and network.

Serial

When computers send data serially, they send it one bit at a time, one after another. The bits "stand in line" like people at a movie theater, waiting to get in. We've already discussed serial (asynchronous) communication in Chapter 6. Just as with modems, you must set the communication parameters (baud, parity, start and stop bits) on both entities—in this case the computer and its printer(s)—before communication can take place.

Parallel

When a printer uses parallel communication, it is receiving data eight bits at a time over eight separate wires (one for each bit). Parallel communication is the most popular way of communicating from computer to printer, mainly because it's faster than serial.

A parallel cable consists of a male DB-25 connector that connects to the computer and a male 36-pin Centronics connector that connects to the printer. Most of the cables are shorter than 10 feet long.

Keep printer cable lengths to less than 10 feet. Some people try to run printer cables more than 50 feet. After 10 feet, communications can become unreliable due to cross talk (which is described in Chapter 1).

Universal Serial Bus (USB)

The most popular type of printer interface as this book is being written is the Universal Serial Bus (USB). It is actually the most popular interface for just about every peripheral. The convenience for printers is that it has a higher transfer rate than either serial or parallel and it automatically recognizes new devices.

Network

Some of the newer printers (primarily laser and LED printers) have a special interface that allows them to be hooked directly to a network. These printers have a *network interface card (NIC)* and ROM-based software that allow them to communicate with networks, servers, and workstations.

The type of network interface used on the printer depends on the type of network the printer is being attached to. For example, if you're using a Token Ring network, the printer should have a Token Ring interface.

Infrared

With the explosion of Personal Digital Assistants (PDAs), the need grew for printing under the constraints they provide. The biggest hurdle faced by PDA owners who need to print is the lack of any kind of universal interface. Most interfaces were too big and bulky to be used on handheld computers like PDAs. The solution was to incorporate the standardized technology used on some remote controls: infrared transmissions. *Infrared transmissions* are simply wireless transmissions that use radiation in the infrared range of the electromagnetic spectrum. Many laser printers (and some computers) come with infrared transmitter/receivers (transceivers) so that they can communicate with the infrared ports on many handhelds. This allows the user of a PDA, handheld, or laptop to print to that printer by pointing the device at the printer and initiating the print process.

As far as configuring the interface is concerned, very little needs to be done. The infrared interfaces are enabled by default on most computers, handhelds, and printers equipped with them. The only additional item that must be configured is the print driver on the PDA, handheld, or computer. The driver must be the correct one for the printer to which you are printing.

Interface Software

Computers and printers can't talk to each other by themselves. They need interface software to translate software commands into commands that the printer can understand.

There are two factors to consider with interface software: the page description language and the driver software. The page description language determines how efficient the printer will be at converting the information to be printed into signals the printer can understand. The driver software understands and controls the printer. It is very important that you use the correct interface software for the printer you are using. If you use either the wrong page description language or the wrong driver software, the printer will print garbage, or possibly nothing at all.

Page Description Languages

A *page description language* works just as its name says it does. It describes the whole page being printed by sending commands that describe the text as well as the margins and other settings. The controller in the printer interprets these commands and turns them into laser pulses (or pin strikes).

Life without a Page Description Language

The most basic page description language is no page description language. The computer sends all the instructions that the printer needs in a serial stream, like so: Position 1, print nothing; Position 2, strike pins 1 and 3; Position 3, print nothing. This type of description language works great for dot-matrix printers, but it can be very inefficient for laser printers. For example, if you wanted to print a page using a standard page description language and there was only one character on the page, there would be a lot of wasted signal for the "print nothing" commands.

Also, with graphics, the commands to draw a shape on the page are relatively complex. For example, to draw a square, the computer (or printer) has to calculate the size of the square and convert that into lots of "strike pin x" (or "turn on laser") and "print nothing" commands. This is where the other types of page description languages come into the picture.

The first page description language was PostScript. Developed by Adobe, it was first used in the Apple LaserWriter printer. It made printing graphics fast and simple. Here's how PostScript works: The PostScript printer driver "describes" the page in terms of "draw" and "position" commands. The page is divided into a very fine grid (as fine as the resolution of the printer). When you want to print a square, a communication like the following might take place:

```
POSITION 1,42%DRAW 10%POSITION 1,64%DRAW10D% . . .
```

These commands tell the printer to draw a line on the page from line 42 to line 64 (vertically). In other words, a page description language tells the printer to draw a line on the page, gives it the starting and ending points, and that's that. Rather than send the printer the location of each and every dot in the line and an instruction at each and every location to print that location's individual dot, PostScript can get the line drawn with fewer than five instructions. As you can see, PostScript uses more or less English commands. The commands are interpreted by the processor on the printer's controller and converted into the print control signals.

Another page description language is the Printer Control Language, or PCL. Currently in revision 5 (PCL 5), it was developed by Hewlett-Packard for its LaserJet series of printers as a competitor to PostScript. PCL works in much the same manner as PostScript, but it's found mainly in Hewlett-Packard printers (including its DeskJet bubble-jet printers). Other manufacturers use PCL, however. In fact, some printers support both page description languages and will automatically switch between them.

The main advantage to page description languages is that they move some of the processing from the computer to the printer. With text-only documents, they don't offer much benefit. However, with documents that have large amounts of graphics or that use numerous fonts, page description languages make the processing of those print jobs happen much faster. This makes them an ideal choice for laser printers. However, other printers can use them as well (e.g., the aforementioned DeskJets, as well as some dot-matrix printers).

Driver Software

The *driver software* controls how the printer processes the print job. When you install a printer driver for the printer you are using, it allows the computer to print to that printer correctly (assuming you have the correct interface configured between the computer and printer).

When you need to print, you select the printer driver for your printer from a preconfigured list. The driver you select has been configured for the type, brand, and model of printer as well as the computer port to which it is connected. You can also select which paper tray the printer should use, as well as any other features the printer has (if applicable). Also, each printer driver is configured to use a particular page description language.

If the wrong printer driver is selected, the computer will send commands in the wrong language. If that occurs, the printer will print several pages full of garbage (even if only one page of information was sent). This "garbage" isn't garbage at all, but in fact the printer page description language commands printed literally as text instead of being interpreted as control commands.

Printer Supplies

Just as it is important to use the correct printer interface and printer software, you must use the correct printer supplies. These supplies include the print media (what you print on) and the consumables (what you print with). The quality of the final print job has a great deal to do with the print supplies.

Print Media

The *print media* is what you put through the printer to print on. There are two major types of print media: paper and transparencies. Of the two types, paper is by far the most commonly used.

Paper

Most people don't give much thought to the kind of paper they use in their printers. It's a factor that can have tremendous effect on the quality of the hard copy printout, however, and the topic is more complex than people think. For example, if the wrong paper is used, it can cause the paper to jam frequently and possibly even damage components.

There are several aspects of paper that can be measured; each gives an indication as to the quality of the paper. The first factor is composition. Paper is made from a variety of substances. Paper used to be made from cotton and was called *rag stock*. It can also be made from wood pulp, which is a cheaper way of making it. Most paper today is made from the latter or a combination of the two.

Another aspect of paper is the property known as *basis weight* (or simply weight for short). The weight of a particular type of paper is the actual weight, in pounds (lb), of 500 sheets of 17-by-22½-inch paper made of that material. The most common paper used in printers is 20lb paper.

The final paper property we'll discuss is the *caliper* (or thickness) of an individual sheet of paper. If the paper is too thick, it may jam in feed mechanisms that have several curves in the paper path. (On the other hand, a paper that's too thin may not feed at all.)

These are just three of the categories that we use to judge the quality of the paper. Because there are so many different types and brands of printers as well as paper, it would be impossible to give the specifications for the "perfect" paper.

However, the documentation for any printer will give specifications for the paper that should be used in that printer.

For best results with any printer, buy the paper that has been designated specifically for that printer by the manufacturer. It will be more expensive, but you'll have fewer problems related to having the wrong type of paper for the printer. Also, the print quality will be the best it could possibly be.

Transparencies

Transparencies are still used for presentations made with overhead projectors, even with the explosion of programs like PowerPoint (from Microsoft) and peripherals like LCD computer displays, both of which let you show a whole roomful of people exactly what's on your computer screen. Actually, though, PowerPoint still has an option to print slides, and you can use any program you want to print anything you want to a transparent sheet of plastic or vinyl for use with an overhead projector. The problem is, these "papers" are *exceedingly* difficult for printers to work with. That's why special transparencies were developed for use with laser and bubble-jet printers.

Each type of transparency was designed for a particular brand and model of printer. Again, check the printer's documentation to find out which type of transparency works in that printer. Don't use any other type of transparency!

Never run transparencies through a laser printer without first checking to see if it's the type recommended by the printer manufacturer. The heat from the fuser will melt most other transparencies and they will wrap themselves around it. It is impossible to clean a fuser after this has happened. The fuser will have to be replaced. *Use ONLY the transparencies that are recommended by the printer manufacturer.*

Print Consumables

Besides print media, there are other things in the printer that run out and need to be replenished. These items are the *print consumables*. Most consumables are used to form the images on the print media. There are two main types of consumables in printers today: ink and toner. Toner is used primarily in laser printers. Most other printers use ink.

Ink

Ink is a liquid that is used to "stain" the paper. There are several different colors of ink used in printers, but the majority use some shade of black or blue. Both dot-matrix printers and bubble-jet printers use ink, but with different methods.

Dot-matrix printers use a cloth or polyester ribbon soaked in ink and coiled up inside a plastic case. This assembly is called a *printer ribbon* (or *ribbon cartridge*). It's very similar to a typewriter ribbon, except that instead of being coiled into the two rolls you'd see on a typewriter, the ribbon is continuously coiled inside the plastic case. Once the ribbon has run out of ink, it must be discarded and replaced with a new one. Ribbon cartridges are developed closely with their respective printers. It is for this reason that ribbons should be purchased from the same manufacturer as the printer. The wrong ribbon could jam in the printer as well as cause adverse quality problems.

Bubble-jet cartridges actually have a liquid ink reservoir. The ink in these cartridges is sealed inside. Once the ink runs out, the cartridge must be removed and discarded. A new, full one is installed in its place. Because the ink cartridge contains ink as well as the printing mechanism, it's like getting a new printer every time you replace the ink cartridge.

In some bubble-jet printers, the ink cartridge and the printhead are in separate assemblies. In this way, the ink can be replaced when it runs out and the printhead can be used several times. This works fine if the printer is designed to work this way. However, some people think they can do this on their integrated cartridge/printhead system, using special ink cartridge refill kits. These kits consist of a syringe filled with ink and a long needle. The needle is used to puncture the top of an empty ink cartridge. The syringe is then used to refill the reservoir. Don't use these kits! See the warning about using them for more information.

WARNING

Do not use ink cartridge refill kits! These kits (the ones you see advertised with a syringe and a needle) have several problems. First, the kits don't use the same kind of ink that was originally in the ink cartridges. The new ink may be thinner, causing the ink to run out or not print properly. Also, the printhead is supposed to be *replaced* around this same time. Just refilling it doesn't replace the printhead. This will cause print quality problems. Finally, the hole the syringe leaves cannot be plugged and may allow ink to leak out. The bottom line: *Buy new ink cartridges from the printer manufacturer.* Yes, they are a bit more expensive, but you will actually save money because you won't have any of the problems described above.

Toner

The final type of consumable is toner. Each model of laser printer uses a specific toner cartridge. The different types of toner cartridges were covered in the discussions of the different types of printers. All we would add here is to check the printer's manual to see which toner cartridge it needs.

WARNING   Just as with ink cartridges, always buy the exact model recommended by the manufacturer. The toner cartridges have been designed specifically for a particular model. Additionally, *never* refill toner cartridges, for most of the same reasons we don't recommend refilling ink cartridges. The printout quality will be poor, and the fact that you're just refilling the toner means you're *not* replacing the photosensitive drum (which is usually inside the cartridge), and it might be that the drum *needs* to be replaced. Simply replacing the refilled toner cartridges with proper, name-brand toner cartridges has solved most laser printer quality problems we have run across. We keep recommending the right ones, but clients keep coming back with the refilled ones. The result is that we take our clients' money to solve their print quality problems when all it involves is a toner cartridge, our (usually repeat) advice to buy the proper cartridge next time, and the obligatory minimum charge for a half hour of labor, even though the job of replacing the cartridge takes all of five minutes!

Summary

In this chapter, we discussed how the different types of printers work as well as the most common methods of connecting them to computers. You learned how computers use page description languages to format data before they send it to printers. You also learned about the various types of consumable supplies and how they relate to each type of printer.

The most basic category of printer currently in use is the impact printer. Impact printers form images by striking something against a ribbon, which in turn makes a mark on the paper. You learned how this type of printer works and the service concepts associated with them.

One of the most popular types of printer today is the bubble-jet printer, so named because of the mechanism used to put ink on the paper.

The most complex type of printer is the laser printer. The A+ exam covers this type of printer more than any other. You learned about the steps in the Electrophotographic (EP) process, the process that explains how laser printers print. You also learned about the various components that make up this printer and how they work together.

The final section of this chapter covered two major concepts: the interfaces used to connect printers to PCs and the consumable supplies used in them. You learned about parallel, serial, and network interfaces and how they are used and how printer supplies can affect print output quality.

Key Terms

Before you take the exam, be certain you are familiar with the following terms:

basis weight	laser printers
caliper	letter quality (LQ)
characters per second (cps)	near letter quality (NLQ)
charging corona	network interface card (NIC)
cleaning step	page description language
conditioning step	paper pickup roller
corona roller	print consumables
corona wire	print media
daisy-wheel printer	printer controller assembly
developing roller	printer ribbon
developing step	printhead
dot-matrix printer	rag stock
driver software	rasterizing
electronic stepper motor	ribbon cartridge
feed roller	solenoid
fuser	static-charge eliminator strip
fusing step	toner
impact printers	transfer corona assembly
interface	transferring step
interface software	writing step

Review Questions

1. What is the step in the EP print process that uses a laser to discharge selected areas of the photosensitive drum, thus forming an image on the drum?

   A. Writing

   B. Transferring

   C. Developing

   D. Cleaning

2. What is the correct order of the steps in the EP print process?

   A. Developing, writing, transferring, fusing, charging, cleaning

   B. Charging, writing, developing, transferring, fusing, cleaning

   C. Transferring, writing, developing, charging, cleaning, fusing

   D. Cleaning, charging, writing, developing, transferring, fusing

3. What is the most basic printer type?

   A. Impact printer

   B. Bubble-jet printer

   C. Laser printer

   D. Interfaces and print media

4. Which voltage is used to transfer the toner to the paper in an EP process laser printer?

   A. +600Vdc

   B. −600Vdc

   C. +6000Vdc

   D. −6000Vdc

5. If the static-eliminator strip is absent (or broken) in either an EP process or HP LaserJet laser printer, what will happen?

   A. Nothing. Both printers will continue to function normally.

   B. Nothing will happen in EP process printers, but HP LaserJet printers will flash a "−671 error" message.

   C. Paper jams may occur in both types of printers because the paper may curl around the photosensitive drum.

   D. Nothing will happen in HP LaserJet printers, but EP process printers will flash a "-671 error" message.

6. These particular printers are referred to as page printers because they receive their print job instructions one page at a time.

   A. Daisy wheel

   B. Dot matrix

   C. Bubble-jet

   D. Laser

7. Which of the following are possible interfaces for printers? (Select all that apply.)

   A. Parallel

   B. Mouse port

   C. Serial

   D. Network

8. Which laser printer component formats the print job for the type of printer being used?

   A. Corona assembly

   B. DC power supply

   C. Printer controller assembly

   D. Formatter software

9. Which of the following are page description languages? (Select all that apply.)

   A. Page Description Language (PDL)

   B. PostScript

   C. PageScript

   D. Printer Control Language (PCL)

10. The basis weight is the weight in pounds of 500 sheets of what size of paper?

    A. $8\frac{1}{2}$ by 11 inch

    B. 11 by 17 inch

    C. 17 by $22\frac{1}{2}$ inch

    D. $8\frac{1}{2}$ by 17 inch

11. Any printer that uses the electrophotographic process contains how many standard assemblies?

    A. Five

    B. Six

    C. Four

    D. Eight

12. Which type(s) of printers can be used with multipart forms?

    A. Bubble-jet

    B. EP process laser printers

    C. HP process laser printers

    D. Dot-matrix printers

13. LED page printers differ from EP process laser printers in which step?

    A. Writing

    B. Charging

    C. Fusing

    D. Cleaning

    E. Developing

    F. Transferring

14. What part of both EP process and HP LaserJet process printers supplies the voltages for the charge and transfer corona assemblies?

    A. High-voltage power supply (HVPS)

    B. DC power supply (DCPS)

    C. Controller circuitry

    D. Transfer corona

15. With EP process laser printers, the laser discharges the charged photosensitive drum to _____ Vdc.

    A. +600

    B. 0

    C. −100

    D. −600

16. Which impact printer has a printhead that contains a row of pins that are triggered in patterns that form letters and numbers as the printhead moves across the paper?

    A. Laser printer

    B. Daisy-wheel printer

    C. Dot-matrix printer

    D. Bubble-jet printer

17. Which printer contains a wheel that looks like a petal with raised letters and symbols on each petal?

    A. Bubble-jet printers

    B. Daisy-wheel printer

    C. Dot-matrix printer

    D. Laser printer

18. Which of the following is *not* an advantage of the daisy-wheel printer?

    A. Can print multipart forms

    B. Relatively inexpensive

    C. Print quality is comparable to a typewriter

    D. Speed

19. This printer part gets the toner from the photosensitive drum onto the paper.

    A. Laser scanner assembly

    B. Fusing assembly

    C. Corona assembly

    D. Drum

20. Which of the following is not an advantage of a Universal Serial Bus (USB) printer interface?

    A. It has a higher transfer rate than a serial connection.

    B. It has a higher transfer rate than a parallel connection.

    C. It automatically recognizes new devices.

    D. It allows the printer to communicate with networks, servers, and workstations.

Answers to Review Questions

1. A. The writing step uses a laser to discharge selected areas of the photosensitive drum, thus forming an image on the drum.

2. D. The correct sequence in the EP print process is cleaning, charging, writing, developing, transferring, fusing.

3. A. Of the types listed above, the impact printer is the most basic printer.

4. A. Because the toner on the drum has a slight negative charge (−100Vdc), it requires a positive charge to transfer it to the paper. +600Vdc is the voltage used in an EP process laser printer.

5. C. If the static-eliminator strip is absent (or broken) in either an EP process or HP LaserJet laser printer, this will cause the paper to maintain its positive charge. Should this occur, paper jams may result due to the paper curling around the photosensitive drum.

6. D. Laser printers receive their print job instructions one page at a time.

7. A, C, D. Printers can communicate via parallel, serial, and network connections.

8. C. The printer controller assembly is responsible for formatting the print job for the type of printer being used.

9. B, D. Of those listed, only PostScript and PCL are page description languages.

10. C. The basis weight is the weight in pounds of 500 sheets of 17-by-22½-inch paper.

11. D. There are eight standard assemblies in an electrophotographic process printer.

12. D. Of the choices listed, only dot-matrix printers are impact printers and therefore can be used with multipart forms.

13. A. LED page printers differ from EP process laser printers in the writing step. They use a different process to write the image on the EP drum.

14. A. The high-voltage power supply is the part of both EP process and HP LaserJet process printers that supplies the voltages for the charge and transfer corona assemblies.

15. C. With EP process laser printers, the laser discharges the charged photosensitive drum to −100Vdc.

16. C. The dot-matrix impact printer has a printhead that contains a row of pins that are triggered in patterns that form letters and numbers as the printhead moves across the paper.

17. B. The daisy-wheel printer gets its name because it contains a wheel with raised letters and symbols on each petal.

18. D. The daisy-wheel printer is much slower when compared to the dot-matrix printer and therefore speed is a *disadvantage*.

19. C. The corona assembly gets the toner from the photosensitive drum onto the paper. For some printers, this is a corona wire, and for others, it is a corona roller.

20. D. The rate of transfer and the ability to automatically recognize new devices are two of the major advantages that make USB the current most popular type of printer interface. However, it is the network printer interface that allows the printer to communicate with networks, servers, and workstations.

Chapter

8

Networking Fundamentals

THE FOLLOWING OBJECTIVE IS ARE COVERED IN THIS CHAPTER:

✓ **1.2 Identify basic procedures for adding and removing field replaceable modules for both desktop and portable systems.**

    Examples of modules:

- System board
- Storage device
- Power supply
- Processor/CPU
- Memory
- Input devices
- Hard drive
- Keyboard
- Video board
- Mouse
- Network Interface Card (NIC)

    Portable system components:

- AC adapters
- DC controllers
- LCD panel
- PC card
- Pointing devices

✓ **2.1 Identify common symptoms and problems associated with each module and how to troubleshoot and isolate problems.**

    Content may include the following:

- Processor/Memory symptoms
- Mouse
- Floppy drive

- Parallel ports
- Hard Drives
- CD-ROM
- DVD
- Sound Card/Audio
- Monitor/Video
- Motherboards
- Modems
- BIOS
- USB
- NIC
- CMOS
- Power supply
- Slot covers
- POST audible/visual error codes
- Troubleshooting tools, e.g., multimeter
- Large LBA, LBA
- Cables
- Keyboard
- Peripherals

✓ **6.1 Identify basic networking concepts, including how a network works and the ramifications of repairs on the network.**

Content may include the following:

- Installing and configuring network cards
- Network access
- Full-duplex, half-duplex
- Cabling—Twisted-Pair, Coaxial, Fiber Optic, RS-232
- Ways to network a PC
- Physical Network topographies
- Increasing bandwidth
- Loss of data
- Network slowdown
- Infrared
- Hardware protocols

magine 20 years ago working in an office with little or no computer equipment. It's hard to imagine now, isn't it? One could say that we take for granted a lot of what we have gained in technology the past few decades. Now, imagine having to send a memo to everyone in the company. Back then we used interoffice mail; today we use e-mail. This is one form of communication that only became available due to the introduction and growth of networks.

This chapter focuses on the basic concepts surrounding how a network works, including the way it sends information and what it uses to send information. This information is covered only to a minor degree by the A+ certification exam. However, if you have interest in becoming a service technician, this information will prove to be very useful, as you will in all likelihood find yourself asked to troubleshoot both hardware and software problems on existing networks. Included in this chapter is information on:

- What is a network?
- Network types
- Media types
- Connectivity devices

For complete coverage of objective 1.2, please also see Chapters 2, 5, and 9. For complete coverage of objective 2.1, please also see Chapters 1, 4, 6, and 10.

If you find that the material in this chapter interests you, you might consider studying for, and eventually taking, CompTIA's Network+ exam. It is a generic networking certification (similar to A+, only it is for network-related topics). You can study for it using Sybex's Network+ Study Guide materials available at www.sybex.com.

What Is a Network?

Stand-alone personal computers, first introduced in the late 1970s, gave users the ability to create documents, spreadsheets, and other types of data and save them for future use. For the small business user or home computer enthusiast this was great. For larger companies, however, it was not enough. The larger the company, the greater the need to share information between offices, and sometimes over great distances. The stand-alone computer was not enough for the following reasons:

- Their small hard drive capacities were inefficient.

- To print, each computer required a printer attached locally.

- Sharing documents was cumbersome. People grew tired of having to save to a diskette, then taking that diskette to the recipient. (This procedure was called "sneakernet.")

- There was no e-mail. Instead, there was interoffice mail, which was not reliable and frequently was not delivered in a timely manner.

To address these problems, *networks* were born. A network links two or more computers together to communicate and share resources. Their success was a revelation to the computer industry as well as businesses. Now, departments could be linked internally to offer better performance and increase efficiency.

You have heard the term "networking" in the business context, where people come together and exchange names for future contact and to give them access to more resources. The same is true with a computer network. A computer network allows computers to link to each other's resources. For example, in a network every computer does not need a printer connected locally to print. Instead, one computer has a printer connected to it and allows the other computers to access this resource. Because they allow users to share resources, networks offer an increase in performance as well as a decrease in the outlay for new hardware and software.

LANs vs. WANs

Local area networks (LANs) were introduced to connect computers in a single office. *Wide area networks (WANs)* came to expand the LANs to include networks outside of the local environment and also to distribute resources across distances. Today, LANs can be seen in many businesses, from small to large. WANs are becoming more widely accepted as businesses are becoming more mobile and as more of them are spanning across greater and greater distances. It is important to have an understanding of LANs and WANs as a service professional, because when you're repairing computers you are likely to come in contact with problems that are associated with the computer being connected to a network.

Local Area Networks (LANs)

The 1970s brought us the minicomputer, which was a smaller version of the mainframe. Whereas the mainframe used *centralized processing* (all programs ran on the same computer), the minicomputer used *distributed processing* to access programs across other computers. As depicted in Figure 8.1, distributed processing allows a user at one computer to use a program on another computer as a "back end" to process and store the information. The user's computer is the "front end," performing the data entry. These allowed programs to be distributed across computers rather than centralized. This was also the first time computers used cable to connect rather than phone lines.

FIGURE 8.1   Distributed processing

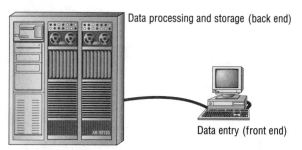

Data processing and storage (back end)

Data entry (front end)

By the 1980s, offices were beginning to buy PCs in large numbers. Also, portables were introduced, allowing computing to become mobile. Neither PCs nor portables, however, were efficient in sharing information. As timeliness and security became more important, diskettes were just not cutting it. Offices needed to find a way to implement a better means to share and access resources. This led to the introduction of the first type of PC LAN: ShareNet by Novell. LANs are simply the linking of computers to share resources within a closed environment. The first simple LANs were constructed a lot like Figure 8.2.

FIGURE 8.2   A simple LAN

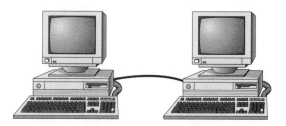

After the introduction of ShareNet, more LANs sprouted. The earliest LANs could not cover a great distance. Most of them could only stretch across a single floor of the office and could support no more than 30 users. Further, they were still simple, and only a few software programs supported them. The first software programs that ran on a LAN were not capable of permitting more than one user at a time to use a program (this constraint was known as *file locking*). Nowadays, we can see multiple users accessing a program at one time, limited only by restrictions at the record level.

Wide Area Networks (WANs)

By the late 1980s, networks were expanding to cover ranges considered geographical in size and were supporting thousands of users. Wide area networks (WANs), first implemented with mainframes at massive government expense, started attracting PC users as networks went to this whole new level. Businesses with offices across the country communicated as if they were only desks apart. Soon the whole world would see a change in its way of doing business, across not only a few miles but across countries. Whereas LANs are limited to single buildings, WANs are able to span buildings, states, countries, and even continental boundaries. Figure 8.3 gives an example of a simple WAN.

FIGURE 8.3 A simple WAN

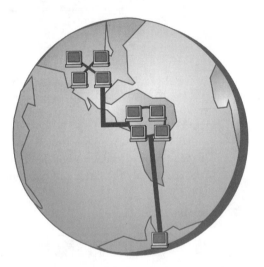

Networks of today and tomorrow are not limited anymore by the inability of LANs to cover distance and handle mobility. WANs play an important role in the future development of corporate networks worldwide. Although the primary focus of this chapter is LANs, we will feature a section on WAN connectivity. This section will briefly explain the current technologies and what you should expect to see in the future. If you are interested in more information on LANs or WANs, or if you plan on becoming a networking technician, check your local library resources or the Internet.

Primary Network Components

Putting together a network is not as simple as it was with the first PC network. You can no longer consider two computers cabled together a fully functional network. Today, networks consist of three primary components:

- Servers
- Clients or workstations
- Resources

No network would be complete without these three components working together.

Servers

Servers come in many shapes and sizes. They are a core component of the network, providing a link to the resources necessary to perform any task. The link it provides could be to a resource existing on the server itself or a resource on a client computer. The server is the "leader of the pack," offering directions to the client computers regarding where to go to get what they need.

Servers offer networks the capability of centralizing the control of resources and can thus reduce administrative difficulties. They can be used to distribute processes for balancing the load on the computers and can thus increase speed and performance. They can also offer the departmentalizing of files for improved reliability. That way, if one server goes down, then not all of the files are lost.

Servers perform several tasks. For example, servers that provide files to the users on the network are called file servers. Likewise, servers that host printing services for users are called print servers. (There are other tasks as well, such as remote access services, administration, mail, etc.) Servers can be *multi-purpose* or *single-purpose*. If they are multi-purpose, they can be, for example, both a file server and a print server at the same time. If the server is a single-purpose server, it is a file server only or print server only.

Another distinction we use in categorizing servers is whether they are *dedicated* or *nondedicated*:

Dedicated Servers   These are assigned to provide specific applications or services for the network, and nothing else. Because a *dedicated server* is specializing in only a few tasks, it requires fewer resources from the computer that is hosting it than a nondedicated server might require. This savings in overhead may translate to a certain efficiency and can thus be considered as having a beneficial impact on network performance.

Nondedicated Servers   These are assigned to provide one or more network services *and* local access. A *nondedicated server* is expected to be slightly more flexible in its day-to-day use than a dedicated server. Nondedicated servers can be used not only to direct network traffic and perform administrative actions, but often to serve as a front-end for the administrator to work with other applications or services. The nondedicated server is not really what some would consider a true server, because it can act as a workstation as well as a server.

Many networks use both dedicated and nondedicated servers in order to incorporate the best of both worlds, offering improved network performance with the dedicated servers and flexibility with the nondedicated servers.

Workstations or Client Computers

Workstations are the computers that the users on a network do their work on, performing activities such as word processing, database design, graphic design, e-mail, and other office or personal tasks. Workstations are basically nothing more than an everyday computer, except for the fact that they are connected to a network that offers additional resources. Workstations can range from a diskless computer system to a desktop system. In network terms, workstations are also known as *client computers*. As clients, they are allowed to communicate with the servers in the network in order to use the network's resources.

It takes several items to make a workstation into a client. You must install a *network interface card (NIC)*, a special expansion card that allows the PC to talk on a network. You must connect it to a cabling system that connects to another computer (or several other computers). And you must install some special software, called *client software*, which allows the computer to talk to the servers. Once all this has been accomplished, the computer will be "on the network."

To the client, the server may be nothing more than just another drive letter. However, because it is in a network environment, the client is able to use the server as a doorway to more storage or more applications, or through which it may communicate with other computers or other networks. To a user, being on a network changes a few things:

- They can store more information, because they can now store data on other computers on the network.
- They can now share and receive information from other users, perhaps even collaborating on the same document.
- They can use programs that would be too large for their computer to use by itself.

Network Resources

We now have the server to share the resources and the workstation to use them, but what about the resources themselves? A *resource* (as far as the network is concerned) is any item that can be used on a network. Resources can include a broad range of items, but the most important ones include

- Printers and other peripherals
- Files
- Applications
- Disk Storage

When an office can purchase paper, ribbons, toner, or other consumables for only one, two, or maybe three printers for the entire office, the costs are dramatically lower than the costs for supplying printers at every workstation. Networks also give more storage space to files. Client computers are not always able to handle the overhead involved in storing large files (for example, database files) because they are already heavily involved in the day-to-day work activities of the users. Because servers in a network can be dedicated to only certain functions, a server can be allocated to store all the larger files that are worked with every day, freeing up disk space on client computers. Similarly, applications (programs) no longer need to be on every computer in the office. If the server is capable of handling the overhead an application requires, the application can reside on the server and be used by workstations through a network connection.

The sharing of applications over a network requires a special arrangement with the application vendor, who may wish to set the price of the application according to the number of users who will be using it. The arrangement allowing multiple users to use a single installation of an application is called a *site license*.

Being on a Network Brings Responsibilities

You are part of a community when you are on a network, which means that you need to take responsibility for your actions. First of all, a network is only as secure as the users who use it. You cannot just randomly delete files or move documents from server to server. You do not own your e-mail, so anyone in your company's management can choose to read it. Additionally, printing does not mean that if you send something to print now that it will print immediately—yours may not be the first in line to be printed at the shared printer. Plus, if your workstation has also been set up to be a nondedicated server, you cannot turn it off.

Network Operating Systems (NOSs)

PCs use a disk operating system that controls the file system and how the applications communicate with the hard disk. Networks use a network operating system (NOS) to control the communication with resources and the flow of data across the network. The NOS runs on the server. Many companies offer software to start a network. Some of the more popular network operating systems at this time include Unix, Novell's NetWare, and Microsoft's Windows NT Server (or Windows 2000). Although several other NOSs exist, these three are the most popular.

Back in the early days of mainframes, it took a full staff of people working around the clock to keep the machines going. With today's NOSs, servers are able to monitor memory, CPU time, disk space, and peripherals, without a baby-sitter. Each of these operating systems allows processes to respond in a certain way with the processor.

With the new functionality of LANs and WANs, you can be sitting in your office in Milwaukee and carry on a real-time electronic "chat" with a coworker in France, or maybe print an invoice at the home office in California, or manage someone else's computer from your own while they are on vacation. Gone are the days of disk-passing, phone messages left but not received, or having to wait a month to receive a letter from someone in Hong Kong. NOSs provide this functionality on a network.

Network Resource Access

Now that we have discussed the makeup of a typical network, let's discuss the way resources are accessed on a network. There are generally two resource access models: peer-to-peer and server-based. It is important to choose the appropriate model. How do you decide what type of resource model is needed? You must first think about the following questions:

- What is the size of the organization?
- How much security does the company require?
- What software or hardware does the resource require?
- How much administration does it need?
- How much will it cost?
- Will this resource meet the needs of the organization today and in the future?
- Will additional training be needed?

Networks today cannot just be put together at the drop of a hat. A lot of planning is required before implementation of a network to ensure that whatever design is chosen will be effective and efficient, and not just for today but for the future as well. It is the forethought of the designer that will create the best network with the least amount of administrative overhead. In each network, it is important that a plan be developed to answer the previous questions. The answers will help decide the type of resource model to be used.

Peer-to-Peer Networks

A peer-to-peer network is a network where the computers act as both workstations and servers. An example of a peer-to-peer resource model is shown in Figure 8.4.

FIGURE 8.4 The peer-to-peer resource model

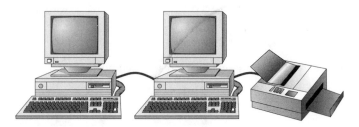

Peer-to-peer networks are great for small, simple, and inexpensive networks. In fact, this model can be set up almost immediately, with little extra hardware required. Windows 3.11, Windows 95, and Windows NT are popular operating system environments that support a peer-to-peer resource model.

There is no centralized administration or control in the peer-to-peer resource model. However, this very lack of centralized control can make it difficult to "administer" the network; for the same reason, it's not very secure. Moreover, because each computer is acting as both a workstation and server, it may not be easy to locate the resources. The person who is in charge of the file may have moved it without anyone's knowledge. Also, the users who work under this arrangement need more training, because they are not only users but also administrators.

Will this type of network meet the needs of the organization today and in the future? Peer-to-peer resource models are generally considered the right choice for companies where there is no expected future growth. For example, the business might be small, possibly an independent subsidiary of a specialty company, and has no plans on increasing its market size or number of employees. Companies that are expecting growth, on the other hand, should not choose this type of model. Although it could very well meet the needs of the company today, the growth of the company will necessitate making major changes over time. If a company chooses to set up a peer-to-peer resource model simply because it is cheap and easy to install, it could be making a costly mistake. The company's management may find that it will cost them more in the long run than if they had chosen a server-based resource model.

Server-Based Resource Model

The server-based model is better than the peer-to-peer model for large networks (say 25 users or more) that need a more secure environment and centralized control. Server-based networks use a dedicated, centralized server. All administrative functions and resource sharing are performed from this point. This makes it easier to share resources, perform backups, and support an almost unlimited number of users. It also offers better security. However, it does need more hardware than that used by the typical workstation/server computer in a peer-to-peer resource model. Additionally, it requires specialized software (the NOS) to manage the server's role in the environment. With the addition of a server and the NOS, server-based networks can easily cost more than peer-to-peer resource models. However, for large networks, it's the only choice. An example of a server-based resource model is shown in Figure 8.5.

FIGURE 8.5 The server-based resource model

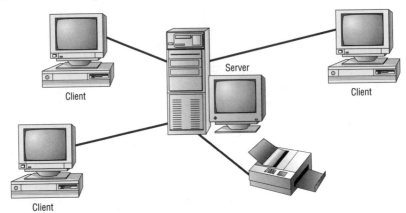

Will this type of network meet the needs of the organization today and in the future? Server-based resource models are the desired models for companies that are continually growing or that need to initially support a large environment. Server-based networks offer the flexibility to add more resources and clients almost indefinitely into the future. Hardware costs may be more, but, with the centralized administration, managing resources becomes less time-consuming. Also, only a few administrators need to be trained, and users are only responsible for their own work environment.

If you are looking for an inexpensive, simple network with very little setup required, and there is really no need for the company to grow in the future, then the peer-to-peer network is the way to go. If you are looking for a network to support many users (more than 25), strong security, and centralized administration, consider the server-based network your only choice.

Whatever you decide, be sure to take the time to plan. A network is not something you can just "throw together." You don't want to find out a few months down the road that the type of network you chose does not meet the needs of the company. This could be a timely and costly mistake.

Network Topologies

A *topology* is a way of "laying out" the network. Topologies can be either physical or logical. *Physical topologies* describe how the cables are run. *Logical topologies* describe how the network messages travel. Deciding which type of topology to use is the next step when designing your network.

You must choose the appropriate topology in which to arrange your network. Each type differs by its cost, ease of installation, fault tolerance (how the topology handles problems like cable breaks), and ease of reconfiguration (like adding a new workstation to the existing network).

There are five primary topologies (some of which can be both logical and physical topologies):

- Bus (can be both logical and physical)
- Star (physical only)
- Ring (can be both logical and physical)
- Mesh (can be both logical and physical)
- Hybrid (usually physical)

Each topology has its advantages and disadvantages. At the end of this section check out the table that summarizes the advantages and disadvantages of each topology.

Bus

A bus is the simplest physical topology. It consists of a single cable that runs to every workstation as shown in Figure 8.6. This topology uses the least amount of cabling, but also covers the shortest amount of distance. Each computer shares the same data and address path. With a logical bus topology, messages pass through the trunk, and each workstation checks to see if the message is addressed to itself. If the address of the message matches the workstation's address, the network adapter copies the message to the card's on-board memory.

FIGURE 8.6   The bus topology

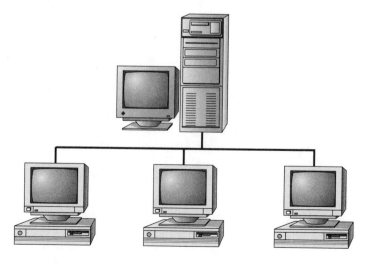

Cable systems that use the bus topology are easy to install. You run a cable from the first computer to the last computer. All the remaining computers attach to the cable somewhere in between. Because of the simplicity of installation, and because of the low cost of the cable, bus topology cabling systems (such as Ethernet) are the cheapest to install.

Although the bus topology uses the least amount of cabling, it is difficult to add a workstation. If you want to add another workstation, you have to completely reroute the cable and possibly run two additional lengths of it. Also, if any one of the cables breaks, the entire network is disrupted. Therefore, it is very expensive to maintain.

Star

A physical star topology branches each network device off a central device called a *hub*, making it very easy to add a new workstation. Also, if any workstation goes down it does not affect the entire network. (But, as you might expect, if the central device goes down, the entire network goes down.) Some types of Ethernet and ARCNet use a physical star topology. Figure 8.7 gives an example of the organization of the star network.

FIGURE 8.7   The star topology

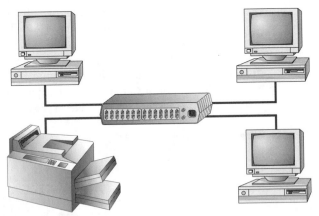

Star topologies are easy to install. A cable is run from each workstation to the hub. The hub is placed in a central location in the office (for example, a utility closet). Star topologies are more expensive to install than bus networks, because there are several more cables that need to be installed, plus the cost of the hubs that are needed.

Ring

A physical ring topology is a unique topology. Each computer connects to two other computers, joining them in a circle creating a unidirectional path where messages move workstation to workstation. Each entity participating in the ring reads a message, then regenerates it and hands it to its neighbor on a different network cable. See Figure 8.8 for an example of a ring topology.

FIGURE 8.8   The ring topology

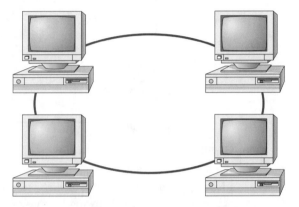

The ring makes it difficult to add new computers. Unlike a star topology network, the ring topology network will go down if one entity is removed from the ring. Physical ring topology systems don't exist much anymore, mainly because the hardware involved was fairly expensive and the fault tolerance was very low. However, one type of logical ring still exists: IBM's Token Ring technology. We'll discuss this technology later in the "Network Architectures" section.

Mesh

The *mesh topology* is the simplest logical topology in terms of data flow, but it is the most complex in terms of physical design. In this physical topology, each device is connected to every other device (Figure 8.9). This topology is rarely found in LANs, mainly because of the complexity of the cabling. If there are x computers, there will be $(x \times (x-1)) \div 2$ cables in the network. For example, if you have five computers in a mesh network, it will use $5 \times (5 - 1) \div 2$, which equals 10 cables. This complexity is compounded when you add another workstation. For example, your five-computer, 10-cable network will jump to 15 cables just by adding one more computer. Imagine how the person doing the cabling would feel if you told them you had to cable 50 computers in a mesh network—they'd have to come up with $50 \times (50 - 1) \div 2 = 1225$ cables!

FIGURE 8.9 The mesh topology

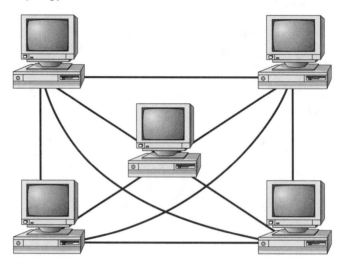

Because of its design, the physical mesh topology is very expensive to install and maintain. Cables must be run from each device to every other device. The advantage you gain from it is its high fault tolerance. With a logical mesh topology, however, there will always be a way of getting the data from source to destination. It may not be able to take the direct route, but it can take an alternate, indirect route. It is for this reason that the mesh topology is still found in WANs to connect multiple sites across WAN links. It uses devices called *routers* to search multiple routes through the mesh and determine the best path. However, the mesh topology does become inefficient with five or more entities.

Hybrid

The hybrid topology is simply a mix of the other topologies. It would be impossible to illustrate it, because there are many combinations. In fact, *most* networks today are not only hybrid, but heterogeneous (by heterogeneous I mean they include a mix of components of different types and brands). The hybrid network may be more expensive, on the one hand, than some types of network topologies, but, on the other hand, it takes the best features of all the other topologies and exploits them. Believe it or not, this is nearly the most popular topology (second only to the star topology).

Summary of Topologies

Table 8.1 summarizes the advantages and disadvantages of each type of network topology. This table is a good study aid for the A+ exam. (In other words, memorize it!)

TABLE 8.1 Topologies—Advantages and Disadvantages

Topology	Advantages	Disadvantages
Bus	Cheap. Easy to install.	Difficult to reconfigure. Break in bus disables entire network.
Star	Cheap. Easy to install. Easy to reconfigure. Fault tolerant.	More expensive than bus.
Ring	Efficient. Easy to install.	Reconfiguration difficult. Very expensive.
Mesh	Simplest. Most fault tolerant.	Reconfiguration extremely difficult. Extremely expensive. Very complex.
Hybrid	Gives combination of best features of each topology used.	Complex (less so than mesh, however).

Network Communications

You have chosen the type of network and arrangement (topology). Now the computers need to understand how to communicate. Network communications use protocols. A *protocol* is a set of rules that govern communications. Protocols detail what "language" the computers are speaking when they talk over a network. If two computers are going to communicate, they both must be using the same protocol.

There are different methods used to describe the different protocols. We will discuss two of the most common: the OSI model and the IEEE 802 standards.

OSI Model

The International Standards Organization introduced the *Open Systems Interconnection (OSI)* model to provide a common way of describing network protocols. They put together a seven-layer model providing a relationship between the stages of communication, with each layer adding to the layer above or below it.

This OSI model is just that: a model. It can't be implemented. You will never find a network that is running the "OSI protocol."

The theory with the OSI model is that as transmission takes place, the higher layers pass data through the lower layers. As the data passes through a layer, the layer will tack its information (also called a *header*) onto the beginning of the information being transmitted until it reaches the bottom layer. At this point, the bottom layer sends the information out on the wire.

At the receiving end, the bottom layer receives the information, reads its information from its header and removes its header from the information, and then passes the remainder to the next highest layer. This procedure continues until the topmost layer receives the data that the sending computer sent.

The OSI model layers from top to bottom are listed here. We'll *describe* each of these layers from bottom to top, however. After the descriptions, we'll summarize the entire model.

- Application layer
- Presentation layer
- Session layer
- Transport layer
- Network layer
- Data Link layer
- Physical layer

Physical Layer

At the bottom of the OSI model is the *Physical layer*. This layer describes how the data gets transmitted over a physical medium. It defines how long each piece of data is and the translation of each into the electrical pulses that are sent over the wires. It decides whether data travels unidirectionally or bidirectionally across the hardware. It also relates electrical, optical, mechanical, and functional interfaces to the cable.

Data Link Layer

The next layer is the *Data Link layer*. This layer arranges data into chunks called "frames." Included in these chunks is control information indicating the beginning and end of the data stream. This layer is very important because it makes transmission easier and more manageable as well as allowing for error checking within the data frames.

Network Layer

Addressing messages and translating logical addresses and names into physical addresses occurs at the *Network layer*. The Network layer is something like the traffic cop. It is able to judge the best network path for the data based on network conditions, priority, and other variables. This layer manages traffic through packet switching, routing, and controlling congestion of data.

Transport Layer

The *Transport layer* signals "all clear" by making sure the data frames are error-free. It also controls the data flow and troubleshoots any problems with transmitting or receiving data frames. This layer's most important job is to provide error checking and reliable, end-to-end communications. Secondly, it can also take several smaller messages and combine them into a single, larger message.

Session Layer

The *Session layer* allows applications on different computers to establish, use, and end a session. A session is one virtual "conversation." For example, all the procedures needed to transfer a single file make up one session. Once the session is over, a new process has begun. It enables network procedures such as identifying passwords, logons, and network monitoring. It can also handle recovery from a network failure.

Presentation Layer

The "look," or format, of the data, network security, and file transfers is determined by the *Presentation layer*. It performs protocol conversion and manages data compression. Data translation and encryption are handled at this layer. Also, the character set information is determined at this level. (The character set determines which numbers represent which alphanumeric characters.)

Application Layer

Finally, the *Application layer* allows access to network services. This is the layer at which file services and print services operate. It also is the layer that workstations interact with, and it controls data flow and, if there are errors, recovery.

Summary of the OSI Model

Figure 8.10 shows the complete OSI model. Note the relation of each layer to one another and the function of each layer. Also note that when data is sent from one computer to another, the transmission starts above the Application layer and passed down to the Physical layer. Each layer, as it receives information from the layer above, adds its own information and passes the amended packet to the next layer down. At the bottom, the Physical layer places the packet on the wire. The receiver does the exact opposite procedure. The Physical layer takes the packet off the wire, removes the Physical layer header, and transfers the information to the layer above. Each layer reads the information given to it by the transmitting counterpart layer, removes its header, and passes the remained up the stack until the data being transmitted is received by the Application layer.

FIGURE 8.10 OSI model and characteristics

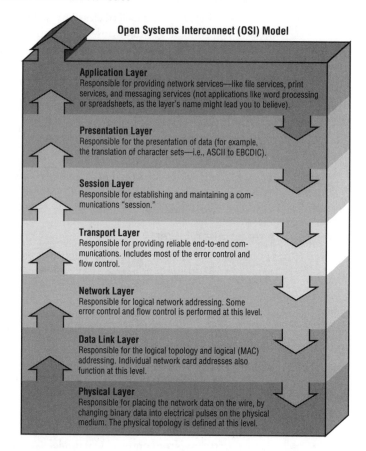

Open Systems Interconnect (OSI) Model

Application Layer
Responsible for providing network services—like file services, print services, and messaging services (not applications like word processing or spreadsheets, as the layer's name might lead you to believe).

Presentation Layer
Responsible for the presentation of data (for example, the translation of character sets—i.e., ASCII to EBCDIC).

Session Layer
Responsible for establishing and maintaining a communications "session."

Transport Layer
Responsible for providing reliable end-to-end communications. Includes most of the error control and flow control.

Network Layer
Responsible for logical network addressing. Some error control and flow control is performed at this level.

Data Link Layer
Responsible for the logical topology and logical (MAC) addressing. Individual network card addresses also function at this level.

Physical Layer
Responsible for placing the network data on the wire, by changing binary data into electrical pulses on the physical medium. The physical topology is defined at this level.

IEEE 802 Project Models

The Institute for Electrical and Electronics Engineers (IEEE) formed a subcommittee to create the 802 standards for networks. These standards specify certain types of networks, although not every network protocol is covered by the IEEE 802 committee specifications. This model breaks down into the following 12 categories:

- 802.1 Internetworking
- 802.2 Logic Link Control
- 802.3 CSMA/CD LAN
- 802.4 Token Bus LAN
- 802.5 Token Ring LAN
- 802.6 Metropolitan Area Network

- 802.7 Broadband Technical Advisory Group
- 802.8 Fiber Optic Technical Advisory Group
- 802.9 Integrated Voice/Data Networks
- 802.10 Network Security
- 802.11 Wireless Networks
- 802.12 Demand Priority Access LAN

The IEEE 802 standards were designed primarily for enhancements to the bottom three layers of the OSI model. The IEEE 802 model breaks the Data Link layer into two sublayers: a Logical Link Control (LLC) sublayer and a Media Access Control (MAC) sublayer. In the Logical Link Control sublayer, data link communications are managed. The Media Access Control sublayer watches out for data collisions, as well as assigning physical addresses.

We will focus on the two predominant 802 models that existing network architectures have been based on: 802.3 CSMA/CD and 802.5 Token Ring.

IEEE 802.3 CSMA/CD

The *802.3* CSMA/CD model defines a bus topology network that uses a 50-ohm coaxial baseband cable and carries transmissions at 10Mbps. This standard groups data bits into frames and uses the Carrier Sense Multiple Access with Collision Detection (CSMA/CD) cable access method to put data on the cable.

CSMA/CD specifies that every computer can transmit at any time. As sometimes happens, when two machines transmit at the same time, a "collision" takes place and no data can be transmitted for either machine. The machines then back off for a random period of time and try to transmit again. This process repeats until transmission takes place successfully. The CSMA/CD technology is also called "contention."

The only major downside to 802.3 is that with large networks (more than 100 computers on the same cable), the number of collisions increases to the point where there are more collisions than transmissions taking place.

An example of a protocol based on the IEEE 802.3 CSMA/CD standard is Ethernet.

CSMA/CD and Ethernet are discussed in more detail later in this chapter.

IEEE 802.5 Token Ring

The IEEE *802.5* standard specifies a physical star, logical ring topology that uses a token-passing technology to put the data on the cable. IBM developed this technology for their mainframe and minicomputer networks. IBM's name for it was Token Ring. The name stuck, and any network using this type of technology is called a Token Ring network.

In *token passing*, a special chunk of data called a *token* circulates through the ring from computer to computer. Any computer that has data to transmit must wait for the token. A transmitting computer that has data to transmit waits for a "free" token and takes it off the ring. Once it has the token, this computer modifies it in such a way that tells the computers who has the token. The transmitting computer then places the token (along with the data it needs to transmit) on the ring and the token travels around the ring until it gets to the destination computer. The destination computer takes the token and data off the wire, modifies the token (indicating it has received the data), and places the token back on the wire. When the original sender receives the token back and sees that the destination computer has received the data, the sender modifies the token to set it "free." It then sends the token back on the ring and waits until it has more data to transmit.

The main advantage of the token-passing access method over contention (the 802.3 model) is that it eliminates collisions. Only workstations that have the token can transmit. It would seem that this technology has a lot of overhead and would be slow. But remember that this whole procedure takes place in a few milliseconds. This technology scales very well. It is not uncommon for Token Ring networks based on the IEEE 802.5 standard to reach hundreds of workstations on a single ring.

The story of the IEEE 802.5 standard is rather interesting. It's a story of "the tail wagging the dog." With all the other IEEE 802 standards, the committee either saw a need for a new protocol on its own or got a request for one. They would then sit down and hammer out the new standard. A standard created by this process is known as a *de jure* ("by law") standard. With the IEEE 802.5, however, everyone was already using this technology, so the IEEE 802 committee got involved and simply declared it a standard. This type of standard is known as a *de facto* ("from the fact") standard—a standard that was being followed without having been formally recognized.

Network Architectures

Network architectures define the structure of the network, including hardware, software, and layout. We differentiate each architecture by the hardware and software required to maintain optimum performance levels. The major architectures in use today are Ethernet, Token Ring, ARCNet, and AppleTalk.

Ethernet

The original definition of the 802.3 model included a bus topology using a baseband coaxial cable. From this model came the first Ethernet architecture. *Ethernet* was originally codeveloped by Digital, Intel, and Xerox and was known as *DIX Ethernet*.

Ethernet has several specifications, each one specifying the speed, communication method, and cable. The original Ethernet was given a designation of

10Base5. The "10" in Ethernet 10Base5 stands for the 10Mbps transmission rate. "Base" stands for the baseband communications used. Finally, the "5" stands for the maximum distance of 500 meters to carry transmissions. This method of identification soon caught on, and as vendors changed the specifications of the Ethernet architecture, they followed the same pattern in the way they identified them.

After the 10Base5, came 10Base2 and 10BaseT. These quickly became standards in Ethernet technology. Many other standards (including 100BaseF, 10BaseF, and 100BaseT) developed since then. But those three are the most popular.

Ethernet 10Base2 uses thin coaxial cables and bus topology, and transmits at 10Mbps, with a maximum distance of 200 meters. If that is the case, what does the Ethernet 10BaseT use? Actually, Ethernet 10BaseT uses twisted-pair cabling, transmitting at 10Mbps, with a maximum distance of 100 meters, and physical star topology with a logical bus topology.

Token Ring

Token Ring networks are exactly like the IEEE 802.5 specification because the specification is based on IBM's Token Ring technology. Token Ring uses a physical star, logical ring topology. All workstations are cabled to a central device, called a *multistation access unit (MAU)*. The ring is created within the MAU by connecting every port together with special circuitry in the MAU. Token Ring can use shielded or unshielded cable and can transmit data at either 4Mbps or 16Mbps.

ARCNet (Attached Resource Computing Network)

A special type of network architecture that deserves mention is the *Attached Resource Computer Network (ARCNet)*. Developed in 1977, it was not based on any existing IEEE 802 model. However, ARCNet is important to mention because of its ties to IBM mainframe networks and also because of its popularity. Its popularity comes from its flexibility and price. It is flexible because its cabling uses large trunks and physical star configurations, so if a cable comes loose or is disconnected, the network will not fail. Additionally, since it used cheap, coaxial cable, networks could be installed fairly cheaply.

Even though ARCNet enjoyed an initial success, it died out as other network architectures became more popular. The main reason for this was its slow transfer rate of only 2.5Mbps. Thomas-Conrad (a major developer of ARCNet products) did develop a version of ARCNet that runs at 100Mbps, but most people have abandoned ARCNet for other architectures. ARCNet is also not based on any standard, which makes it difficult to find compatible hardware from multiple vendors. Because of its speed and compatibility limitations, ARCNet is quickly being replaced in networks.

AppleTalk

Another architecture not based on any existing IEEE 802 models is AppleTalk. AppleTalk is a proprietary network architecture for Macintosh computers. It uses a bus and typically uses either shielded or unshielded cable. There are a few things to note about AppleTalk.

First, AppleTalk uses a Carrier Sense-Multiple Access with Collision Avoidance (CSMA/CA) technology to put data on the cable. Unlike Ethernet, which uses a CSMA/CD method, this technology uses "smart" interface cards to detect traffic *before* it tries to send data. A CSMA/CA card will listen to the wire. If there is no traffic, it will send a small amount of data. If no collisions occur, it will follow that amount of data with the data it wants to transmit. In either case, if a collision does happen, it will back off for a random amount of time and try to transmit again.

A common analogy is used to describe the difference between CSMA/CD and CSMA/CA. Sending data is like walking across the street. With CSMA/CD you just cross the street. If you get run over, you go back and try again. With CSMA/CA you look both ways and send your little brother across the street. If he makes it, you can follow him. If either of you gets run over, you both go back and try again.

Another interesting point about AppleTalk is that it's fairly simple. Most Macintosh computers already include AppleTalk, so it is relatively inexpensive. It will assign itself an address. In its first revision (Phase I), it allowed a maximum of 32 devices on a network. With its second revision (Phase II), it supports faster speeds and multiple networks with EtherTalk and TokenTalk. EtherTalk allows AppleTalk network protocols to run on Ethernet coaxial cable (used for Mac II and above). TokenTalk allows the AppleTalk protocol to run on a Token Ring network.

Network Media

We have taken a look at the types of networks, network architectures, and the way a network communicates. To bring networks together, we use several types of media. A medium is the material on which data is transferred one point to another. There are two parts to the medium, the network interface card and the cabling. The type of network card you use depends on the type of cable you are using, so let's discuss cabling first.

Cabling

When the data is passing through the OSI model and reaches the physical layer, it must find its way onto the medium that is used to physically transfer data from computer to computer. This medium is *cable*. It is the network interface card's role to prepare the data for transmission, but it is the cable's role to properly move the data to its intended destination. It is not as simple as just plugging it into the computer. The cabling you choose must support both the network architecture and topology. There are four main types of cabling methods: twisted-pair cable, coaxial cable, fiber-optic cable, and wireless. We'll summarize all four cabling methods following the brief descriptions below.

Twisted-Pair

Twisted-pair is one of the most popular methods of cabling because of its flexibility and low costs. It consists of several pairs of wire twisted around each other within an insulated jacket, as shown in Figure 8.11. Twisted-pair is most often found in 10BaseT Ethernet networks, although other systems can use it.

FIGURE 8.11 Twisted-pair cable

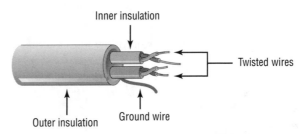

We usually break twisted-pair cabling into two types: unshielded twisted-pair (UTP) and shielded twisted-pair (STP). UTP is simply twisted-pair cabling that is unshielded. STP is the same as UTP except that STP has a braided foil shield around the twisted wires (to decrease electrical interference).

UTP comes in six grades to offer different levels of protection against electrical interference.

- Category 1 is for voice-only transmissions and is in most phone systems today. It contains two twisted-pairs.

- Category 2 is able to transmit data at speeds up to 4Mbps. It contains four twisted-pairs of wires.

- Category 3 is able to transmit data at speeds up to 10Mbps. It contains four twisted-pairs of wires with three twists per foot.

- Category 4 is able to transmit data at speeds up to 16Mbps. It contains four twisted-pairs of wires.

- Category 5 is able to transmit data at speeds up to 100Mbps. It contains four twisted-pairs of copper wire to give the most protection.

- Category 5e is able to transmit data at speeds up to 1Gbps. It also contains four twisted-pairs of copper wire, but they are physically separated and contain more twists per foot than Category 5 to provide maximum interference protection.

Each of these six levels has a maximum transmission distance of 100 meters.

Coaxial

The next choice of cable for most LANs is coaxial cable. The cable consists of a copper wire surrounded by insulation and a metal foil shield, as shown in Figure 8.12. It is very similar to the cable used to connect cable television.

FIGURE 8.12 Coaxial cable

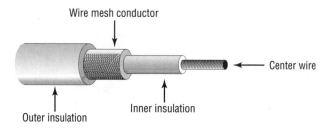

Coaxial cable comes in many thicknesses and types. The most common use for this type of cable is for Ethernet 10Base2 cabling. It is known as Thinnet or Cheapernet.

Fiber-Optic

Fiber-optic cabling has been called one of the best advances in cabling. It consists of a thin, flexible glass fiber surrounded by a rubberized outer coating (see Figure 8.13). It provides transmission speeds from 100Mbps up to 1Gbps and a maximum distance of several miles. Because it uses pulses of light instead of electric voltages to transmit data, it is completely immune from electric interference and from wiretapping.

Fiber-optic cable has not become a standard in networks, however, because of its high cost of installation. Networks that need extremely fast transmission rates, transmissions over long distances, or have had problems with electrical interference in the past often use fiber-optic cabling.

FIGURE 8.13 Fiber-optic cable

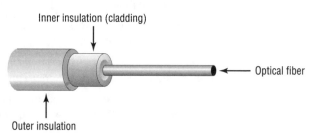

RS-232

Occasionally, networks use *RS-232 cables* (also known as *serial cables*) to carry data. The most classic example is in older mainframe and minicomputer terminal connections. Connections from the individual terminals go to a device known as a *multiplexer* that combines the serial connections into one connection and connects all the terminals to the host computer. This cabling system is seen less and less as a viable LAN cabling method, however, because LAN connections (like twisted-pair Ethernet) are faster, more reliable, and easier to maintain.

Wireless Networks

One of the most fascinating cabling technologies today—and, actually, it's one that doesn't really *use* cable—is wireless. Wireless networks offer the ability to extend a LAN without the use of traditional cabling methods. Wireless transmissions are made through the air by infrared light, laser light, narrow-band radio, microwave, or spread-spectrum radio.

Wireless LANs are becoming increasingly popular as businesses are becoming more mobile and less centralized. You can see them most often in environments where standard cabling methods are not possible or wanted. However, they are still not as fast or efficient as standard cabling methods. Also, they are more susceptible to eavesdropping and interference than standard cabling methods.

Summary of Cabling Types

Each type of cabling has its own benefits and drawbacks. Table 8.2 details the most common types of cabling in use today. As you look at this table, pay particular attention to the cost, length, and maximum transmission rates of each cabling type.

TABLE 8.2   Cable Types

Characteristics	Twisted-Pair	Coaxial	Fiber-Optic	Wireless
Cost	Least expensive	More than twisted-pair	Expensive	Most expensive
Maximum Length	100 meters (328 feet)	185 meters (607 feet) to 500 meters (1640 feet)	>10 Miles	2 miles
Transmission Rates	10Mbps to 100Mbps	10Mbps	100Mps or more	10Mbps
Flexibility	Most flexible	Fair	Fair	Limited

TABLE 8.2 Cable Types *(continued)*

Characteristics	Twisted-Pair	Coaxial	Fiber-Optic	Wireless
Ease of installation	Very easy	Easy	Difficult	Somewhat difficult
Interference	Susceptible	Better than UTP, more susceptible than STP	Not susceptible	Susceptible
Special features	Often pre-installed; similar to wiring used in telephone systems	Easiest Installation	Supports voice, data, and video at highest transmission speeds	Very flexible
Preferred uses	Networks	Medium-size networks with high security needs	Networks of any size requiring high speed and data security	WANs and radio/TV communications
Connector	RJ-45	BNC-T and AUI	Special	Dish or transceiver
Physical Topology	Star	Bus	Star (typically)	Bus or star
Other Info	Five categories of quality	RG-58 and RG-59 family; also called Thinnet and Thicknet, respectively	Requires special training to configure	Most must comply with FCC regulations

The Network Interface Card (NIC)

The network interface card (NIC) provides the physical interface between computer and cabling. It prepares data, sends data, and controls the flow of data. It can also receive and translate data into bytes for the CPU to understand. It communicates at the Physical layer of the OSI model and comes in many shapes and sizes.

Different NICs are distinguished by the PC bus type and the network for which they are used. This section describes the role of the NIC and how to choose the appropriate one. The following factors should be taken into consideration when choosing a NIC:

- Preparing data
- Sending and controlling data
- Configuration
- Drivers
- Compatibility
- Performance

Preparing Data

In the computer, data moves along buses in parallel, as on a four-lane interstate highway. But on a network cable, data travels in a single stream, as on a one-lane highway. This difference can cause problems transmitting and receiving data, because the paths traveled are not the same. It is the NIC's job to translate the data from the computer into signals that can flow easily along the cable. It does this by translating digital signals into electrical signals (and in the case of fiber-optic NICs, to optical signals).

Sending and Controlling Data

For two computers to send and receive data, the cards must agree on several things. These include the following:

- The maximum size of the data frames
- The amount of data sent before giving confirmation
- The time needed between transmissions
- The amount of time needed to wait before sending confirmation
- The amount of data a card can hold
- The speed at which data transmits

If the cards can agree, then the sending of the data is successful. If the cards cannot agree, the sending of data does not occur.

In order to successfully send data on the network, you need to make sure the network cards are of the same type (i.e., all Ethernet, all Token Ring, all ARCNet, etc.) and they are connected to the same piece of cable. If you use cards of different types (for example, one Ethernet and one Token Ring), neither of them will be able to communicate with the other (unless you use some kind of gateway device, such as a router).

Additionally, network cards can send data either full-duplex or half-duplex modes. *Half-duplex communication* means that between the sender and receiver, only one of them can transmit at any one time. In *full-duplex communication*, a computer can send and receive data simultaneously. The main advantage to full-duplex over half-duplex communication is performance. Network cards (specifically Fast Ethernet network cards) can operate twice as fast (200Mbps) in full-duplex mode than they do normally in half-duplex mode (100Mbps).

Configuration

The NIC's configuration includes things like a manufacturer's hardware address, IRQ address, Base I/O port address, and base memory address. Some may also use DMA channels to offer better performance.

Each card must have a unique hardware address. If two cards have the same hardware addresses, neither one of them will be able to communicate. For this reason, the IEEE committee has established a standard for hardware addresses, and assigns blocks of these addresses to NIC manufacturers, who then hard-wire the addresses into the cards.

Configuring a NIC is similar to configuring any other type of expansion card. The NIC usually needs a unique IRQ channel and I/O address, and possibly a DMA channel. Token Ring cards often have two memory addresses that must be excluded in reserved memory to work properly.

Drivers

For the computer to use the network interface card, it is very important to install the proper device drivers. These drivers communicate directly with the network redirector and adapter. They operate in the Media Access Control sublayer of the Data Link layer of the OSI model.

PC Bus Type

When choosing a NIC, use one that fits the bus type of your PC. If you have more than one type of bus in your PC (for example, a combination ISA/PCI), use an NIC that fits into the fastest type (the PCI, in this case). This is especially important in servers, as the NIC can very quickly become a bottleneck if this guideline isn't followed.

Refer back to Chapter 5, "PC Bus Architectures," to refresh your memory about the bus architectures mentioned in this discussion.

Performance

The most important goal of the network adapter card is to optimize network performance and minimize the amount of time needed to transfer data packets across the network. There are several ways of doing this, including assigning a DMA channel, use of a shared memory adapter, and deciding to allow bus mastering.

If the network card can use DMA channels, then data can move directly from the card's buffer to the computer's memory, bypassing the CPU. A shared memory adapter is an NIC that has its own RAM. This feature allows transfers to and from the computer to happen much more quickly, increasing the performance of the NIC. Shared system memory allows the NIC to use a section of the computer's RAM to process data. Bus mastering lets the card take temporary control of the computer's bus to bypass the CPU and move directly to RAM. This is more expensive, but can improve performance by 20 to 70 percent. However, EISA and MCA cards are the only ones that support bus mastering.

Each of these features can enhance the performance of a network interface card. Most cards today have at least one, if not several, of these features.

Media Access Methods

You have put the network together in a topology. You have told the network how to communicate and send the data, and you have told it how to send the data to another computer. You also have the communications medium in place. The next problem you need to solve is how do you put the data *on* the cable? What you need now are the *cable access methods*, which define a set of rules for how computers put data on and retrieve it from a network cable. The four methods of data access are

- Carrier Sense Multiple Access with Collision Detection (CSMA/CD)
- Carrier Sense Multiple Access with Collision Avoidance (CSMA/CA)
- Token Passing
- Polling

Carrier Sense Multiple Access with Collision Detection (CSMA/CD)

As we've already discussed, NICs that use CSMA/CD listen to or "sense" the cable to check for traffic. They compete for a chance to transmit. Usually, if access to the network is slow, it means that there are too many computers trying to transmit, causing traffic jams.

Carrier Sense Multiple Access with Collision Avoidance (CSMA/CA)

Instead of monitoring traffic and moving in when there is a break, CSMA/CA allows the computers to send a signal that they are ready to transmit data. If the ready signal transmits without a problem, the computer then transmits its data. If the ready signal is not transmitted successfully, the computer waits and tries again. This method is slower and less popular than CSMA/CD.

Token Passing

As previously discussed, token passing is a way of giving every NIC equal access to the cable. A special packet of data is passed from computer to computer. Any computer that wants to transmit has to wait until it has the token. It can then transmit its data.

Polling

An old method of media access that is still in use is polling. There aren't very many topologies that support polling anymore, mainly because it has special hardware requirements. This method requires a central, intelligent device (meaning that the device contains either hardware or software "intelligence" to enable it to make decisions) that asks each workstation, in turn, if it has any data to transmit. If the workstation answers "yes," the controller allows the workstation to transmit its data.

The polling process doesn't scale very well. That is, you can't take this method and simply apply it to any number of workstations. Additionally, the high cost of the intelligent controllers and cards has made the polling method all but obsolete.

Connectivity Devices

It's the cabling that links computer to computer. Most cabling allows networks to be hundreds of feet long. But what if your network needs to be bigger than that? What if you need to connect your LANs to other LANs to make a WAN? What if the architecture you've picked for your network is limiting the growth of your network along with the growth of your company? The answer to these questions is found in a special class of networking devices known as *connectivity devices*. These devices allow communications to break the boundaries of local networks and let your computers talk to other computers in the next building, the next city, or the next country.

There are several categories of connectivity devices, but we are going to discuss the six most important and frequently used. They are

- Repeaters
- Hubs
- Bridges
- Routers
- Brouters
- Gateways

These connectivity devices have made it possible to lengthen the distance of the network to almost unlimited distances.

Repeaters

Repeaters are very simple devices. They allow a cabling system to extend beyond its maximum allowed length by amplifying the network voltages so they travel farther. Repeaters are nothing more than amplifiers and, as such, are very inexpensive.

Repeaters operate at the physical layer of the OSI model. Because of this, repeaters can only be used to regenerate signals between similar network segments. I can, for example, extend an Ethernet 10Base2 network to 400 meters with a repeater. But I can't connect an Ethernet and Token Ring network together with one.

The main disadvantage to repeaters is that they just amplify signals. These signals not only include the network signals, but any noise on the wire as well. Eventually, if you use enough repeaters, you could possibly drown out the signal with the amplified noise. For this reason, repeaters are used only as a temporary fix.

Hubs

Hubs are devices used to link several computers together. They are most often used in 10BaseT Ethernet networks. They are also very simple devices. In fact, they are just multiport repeaters. They repeat any signal that comes in on one port and copy it to the other ports (a process that is also called *broadcasting*).

There are two types of hubs: active and passive. *Passive hubs* simply connect all ports together electrically and are usually not powered. *Active hubs* use electronics to amplify and clean up the signal before it is broadcast to the other ports. In the category of active hubs, there is also a class called "intelligent" hubs, which are hubs that can be remotely managed on the network.

Bridges

Bridges operate in the Data Link layer of the OSI model. They join similar topologies and are used to divide network segments. Bridges keep traffic on one side from crossing to the other. For this reason, they are often used to increase performance on a high-traffic segment.

For example, with 200 people on one Ethernet segment, the performance will be mediocre, because of the design of Ethernet and the number of workstations that are fighting to transmit. If you divide the segment into two segments of 100 workstations each, the traffic will be much lower on either side and performance will increase.

Bridges are not able to distinguish one protocol from another, because higher levels of the OSI model are not available to them. If it is aware of the destination address, it is able to forward packets; otherwise a bridge will forward the packets to all segments. They are more intelligent than repeaters but are unable to move data across multiple networks simultaneously. Unlike repeaters, bridges *can* filter out noise.

The main disadvantage to bridges is that they can't connect dissimilar network types or perform intelligent path selection. For that function, you would need a router.

Routers

Routers are highly intelligent devices that connect multiple network types and determine the best path for sending data. They can route packets across multiple networks and use routing tables to store network addresses to determine the best destination. Routers operate at the Network layer of the OSI model.

The advantage of using a router over a bridge is that routers can determine the best path that data can take to get to its destination. Like bridges, they can segment large networks and can filter out noise. However, they are slower than bridges because they are more intelligent devices; as such, they analyze every packet, causing packet-forwarding delays. Because of this intelligence, they are also more expensive.

Routers are normally used to connect one LAN to another. Typically, when a WAN is set up, there will be at least two routers used.

Brouters

Brouters are truly an ingenious idea because they combine the best of both worlds—bridges and routers. They are used to connect dissimilar network segments and also to route only one specific protocol. The other protocols are bridged instead of being dropped. Brouters are used when only one protocol needs to be routed or where a router is not cost-effective (as in a branch office).

Gateways

Gateways connect dissimilar network environments and architectures. Some gateways can use all levels of the OSI model, but frequently are found in the Application layer. It is there that gateways convert data and repackage it to meet the requirements of the destination address. This makes gateways slower than other connectivity devices and more costly. An example of a gateway is the NT Gateway Service for NetWare which, when running on a Windows NT Server, can connect a Microsoft Windows NT network with a Novell NetWare network.

Summary

In this chapter, you learned about the various network hardware topics that you will be tested on in the A+ exam. A few years ago, you never saw many computers with network cards come in for service. Networks were found only in offices and large companies. Now networks can be found in many homes. For this reason, the A+ exam requires that you have at least a basic understanding of network hardware.

In the first section you learned to define exactly what is a network. You also learned what components make up a network, what the network resource models are, and what a network topology is. You also learned about the OSI model and the IEEE 802 committee and their impact on networks. Finally, you learned about the various network architectures in use today.

In the next section, you learned about the different kinds of network media used to connect computers into a network. Some of these media include copper cable, fiber-optic cable, and wireless media. In addition to the different types of media, you learned about the different kinds of Network Interface Cards (NICs) used to connect computers to the network media. Finally, in this section, you learned what method of network access (e.g., contention, token passing, etc.) each major network technology uses to gain access to the network media.

In the last section of this chapter, you learned to differentiate between the different types of devices that connect to networks. These devices, called network connectivity devices, are very important to facilitating communications on a network. You learned how each device (including hubs, routers, bridges, brouters, etc.) works and how it relates to network communications.

Key Terms

Before you take the exam, be certain you are familiar with the following terms:

802.3	file locking	physical topology
802.5	full-duplex communication	Presentation layer
active hub	gateway	protocol
Application layer	half-duplex communication	resource
Attached Resource Computer Network (ARCNet)	header	router
bridge	hub	RS-232 cable
broadcasting	local area network (LAN)	serial cable
cable access methods	logical topology	server
centralized processing	mesh topology	Session layer
client computer	multiplexer	single-purpose server
client software	multi-purpose sever	site license
connectivity device	multistation access unit (MAU)	token passing
Data Link layer	network interface card (NIC)	Token Ring
de facto	Network layer	topology
de jure	network	Transport layer
dedicated server	nondedicated server	wide area network (WAN)
distributed processing	Open Systems Interconnection (OSI)	workstations
DIX Ethernet	passive hub	
Ethernet	Physical layer	

Review Questions

1. Which connectivity device transmits packets the fastest?

   A. Gateway

   B. Router

   C. Brouter

   D. Bridge

2. Which IEEE 802 standard uses a bus topology and coaxial baseband cable and is able to transmit at 10Mbps?

   A. 802.4

   B. 802.3

   C. 802.2

   D. 802.1

3. _____ is immune to electromagnetic or radio-frequency interference.

   A. Broadband coaxial cabling

   B. Fiber-optic cabling

   C. Twisted-pair cabling

   D. CSMA/CD

4. Printers, files, e-mail, and groupware can all be categorized as _____.

   A. Office equipment

   B. Peer-to-peer networking

   C. Resources

   D. Protocols

5. Which OSI layer signals "all clear" by making sure the data frames are error-free?

   A. Application layer

   B. Session layer

   C. Transport layer

   D. Network layer

6. Which topology is the easiest to modify?

   A. Star

   B. Bus

   C. Ring

   D. Token Ring

7. The _____ layer is responsible for logical addressing.

   A. Physical

   B. Data Link

   C. Network

   D. Transport

8. Which layer of the OSI model has the important role of providing error checking?

   A. Session layer

   B. Presentation layer

   C. Application layer

   D. Transport layer

9. Which type of cabling has the easiest installation?

   A. Twisted-pair

   B. Coaxial

   C. Fiber-optic

   D. Wireless

10. _____ is the type of media access method used by NICs that listen to or "sense" the cable to check for traffic and send only when they hear that no one else is transmitting.

    A. Token passing

    B. CSMA/CD

    C. CSMA/CA

    D. Demand priority

11. A physical star topology consists of several workstations that branch off a central device called a _____.

    A. Repeater

    B. Brouter

    C. Router

    D. Hub

12. A _____ links two or more computers together to communicate and share resources.

    A. Server

    B. Resource

    C. Network

    D. Client

13. Which access method asks the other workstations for permission to transmit before transmitting?

    A. CSMA/CD

    B. CSMA/CA

    C. Token passing

    D. Demand priority

14. _____ offers the longest possible segment length.

    A. Unshielded twisted-pair cabling

    B. Coaxial cable

    C. Fiber-optic cabling

    D. Shielded twisted-pair cabling

15. _____ _____ uses a thin baseband coaxial cable, bus topology, transmits at 10Mbps, with a distance up to 185 meters.

    A. Token Ring

    B. Ethernet 10BaseT

    C. Ethernet 10Base5

    D. Ethernet 10Base2

16. Which topology uses the least amount of cabling, but also covers the shortest amount of distance?

    A. Bus

    B. Star

    C. Mesh

    D. Hybrid

17. Which layer describes how the data gets transmitted over a physical medium?

    A. Session layer

    B. Data link layer

    C. Physical layer

    D. Application layer

18. What is another name for IEEE 802.3?

    A. Logic link control

    B. Token passing

    C. CSMA/CD LAN

    D. Token Ring LAN

19. What type of cabling looks similar to the cable used to connect cable television?

A. Twisted-pair

B. Coaxial

C. Fiber-optic

D. Wireless

20. What devices transfer packets across multiple networks and use tables to store network addresses to determine the best destination?

A. Brouters

B. Routers

C. Gateways

D. Bridges

Answers to Review Questions

1. D. Bridges keep traffic on one side from crossing to the other. For this reason they are often used to increase performance on a high-traffic segment.

2. B. The IEEE 802.3 standard specifies the use of a bus topology, typically using coaxial baseband cable, and can transmit data up to 10Mbps.

3. B. For those companies who wish to ensure the safety and integrity of their data, fiber-optic cable should be used, because it cannot be affected by electromagnetic or radio-frequency interference.

4. C. Resources are any items that can be used on a network by multiple people. Therefore, printers, files, and e-mail are all considered resources when they are available on a network.

5. C. It is the responsibility of the Transport layer to signal an "all clear" by making sure the data frames are error-free. It also controls the data flow and troubleshoots any problems with transmitting or receiving data frames.

6. A. The star topology is the easiest to modify. A physical star topology branches each network device off a central device called a hub, making it easy to add a new workstation.

7. C. The Network layer is responsible for logical network addressing as well as route determination.

8. D. The most important role of the Transport layer is to provide error checking. The Transport layer also provides functions such as: reliable end-to-end communications, segmentation and reassembly of larger messages, and combination of smaller messages into a single larger message.

9. A. Of the choices listed above, twisted-pair cabling is generally considered the easiest to install due to the fact that it is lighter than coaxial and doesn't require a lot of special tools or knowledge like fiber-optic cable.

10. B. CSMA/CD (Carrier Sense Multiple Access Method with Collision Detection), specifies that the NIC pause before transmitting a packet to ensure that the line is not being used. If no activity is detected, then it will transmit the packet. If activity is detected, then it will wait until it is clear. In the case of two NICs transmitting at the same time, called a collision, both NICs pause to detect, and then retransmit the data.

11. D. The hub provides the central connecting device in a star topology. All workstations must, therefore, connect to the hub in order to gain access to each other or any other resources present on the network. The one disadvantage of this is that the hub becomes a single point of failure. If the hub stops working, no one connected to the hub has network connectivity.

12. C. The purpose of a network is to link computers together so that they can communicate and share available resources such as printers, data, and applications.

13. B. CSMA/CA (Carrier Sense Multiple Access with Collision Avoidance), is slightly more sophisticated than CSMA/CD. What it will do is transmit a very small packet on the network. If it is successful, then the NIC will transmit the actual data. This initial transmission can be viewed as a "Is it OK for me to send?" message. Therefore, it is said to avoid causing collisions.

14. C. Fiber-optic cable can span distances of several kilometers, because it has higher bandwidth and much lower crosstalk and interference in comparison to copper cables.

15. D. The names of each of these tells you exactly what they are. In the case of Ethernet 10Base2, the "Ethernet" part states that it is of Ethernet architecture, the "10" means that it can transmit up to 10Mbps, "Base" signifies baseband transmission, and the "2" is the distance and, in this case, equates to the 185-meter limitation of coaxial Thinnet cable.

16. A. Due to its design, which includes a central trunk that runs the distance between the two most distant computers (as long as it does not exceed the maximum distance allowed for the cabling), a bus topology requires the least amount of cable.

17. C. The Physical layer is responsible for formatting the final packet of data for transmission (length being the most important format property, because the upper layers are not concerned with the fact that Ethernet and Token Ring packets are not the same size). Once it has done this, it is responsible for taking this digital data and transforming into electrical impulse representations and, finally, the actual transmission of the data. The Physical layer on the receiving side then has to do this in reverse: remove the signal from the wire, convert the electrical impulses to digital data, reconstruct the packet based on the proper size of that network (Ethernet or Token Ring, for example), and then pass the packet up to the Data Link layer.

18. C. As a part of the IEEE 802.3 specification, it was stated that CSMA/CD is the standard access method for Ethernet networks.

19. B. Coaxial cable and television cable are very similar in appearance. Because of this, you need to make sure you have the proper RG rating: RG-58 for Thinnet, RG-59 for Thicknet, so that you can ensure proper data transmission.

20. B. Routers are designed to route (transfer) packets across networks. They are able to do this routing, and determine the best path to take, based on internal routing tables they maintain.

Chapter

9

Installation and Upgrades

THE FOLLOWING OBJECTIVES ARE COVERED IN THIS CHAPTER:

✓ **1.2 Identify basic procedures for adding and removing field replaceable modules for both desktop and portable systems.**

Examples of modules:

- System board
- Storage device
- Power supply
- Processor/CPU
- Memory
- Input devices
- Hard drive
- Keyboard
- Video board
- Mouse
- Network interface card (NIC)

Portable system components

- AC adapters
- DC controllers
- LCD panel
- PC card
- Pointing devices

✓ **1.3 Identify available IRQs, DMAs, and I/O addresses and procedures for configuring them for device installation and configuration.**

> **Content may include the following:**
> - Standard IRQ settings
> - Modems
> - Floppy drive controllers
> - Hard drive controllers
> - USB port
> - Infrared ports
> - Hexidecimal/addresses

✓ **1.7 Identify proper procedures for installing and configuring peripheral devices.**

> **Content may include the following:**
> - Monitor/video card
> - Modem
> - USB peripherals and hubs
> - IEEE-1284
> - IEEE-1394
> - External storage
>
> **Portables**
> - Docking stations
> - PC cards
> - Port replicators
> - Infrared devices

✓ **1.8 Identify hardware methods of upgrading performance, procedures for replacing basic subsystem components, unique components, and when to use them.**

> **Content may include the following:**
> - Memory
> - Hard drives
> - CPU
> - Upgrading BIOS
> - When to upgrade BIOS

Portable systems

- Battery
- Hard drive
- Types I, II, III cards
- Memory

✓ **4.4 Identify the purpose of CMOS (Complementary Metal Oxide Semiconductor), what it contains, and how to change its basic parameters.**

Example basic CMOS settings:

- Printer parallel port—Uni., bidirectional, disable/enable, ECP, EPP
- COM/serial port—memory address, interrupt request, disable
- Floppy drive—enable/disable drive or boot, speed, density
- Hard drive—size and drive type
- Memory—parity, nonparity
- Boot sequence
- Date/Time
- Passwords
- Plug-and-Play BIOS

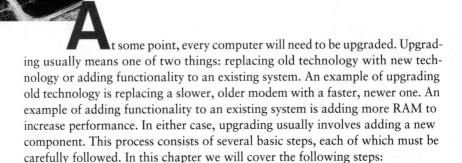

At some point, every computer will need to be upgraded. Upgrading usually means one of two things: replacing old technology with new technology or adding functionality to an existing system. An example of upgrading old technology is replacing a slower, older modem with a faster, newer one. An example of adding functionality to an existing system is adding more RAM to increase performance. In either case, upgrading usually involves adding a new component. This process consists of several basic steps, each of which must be carefully followed. In this chapter we will cover the following steps:

- Disassembly
- Inspection
- Installation and upgrades
- Reassembly

For complete coverage of objective 1.2, please also see Chapters 2, 5, and 8. For complete coverage of objective 1.3, please also see Chapter 1. For complete coverage of objective 1.7, please also see Chapters 5 and 7.

Disassembling the Computer

Disassembling a computer can be a complex operation. If you do it too quickly, you may lose parts or damage something. Further, you have to keep the reassembly process in mind as you're taking things apart, because everything you remove has to be put together again. Several steps need to be followed during the disassembly in order for the reassembly to be successful. People who take shortcuts through these steps often find themselves with "extra" parts and a computer that no longer functions.

Let's cover each step in detail, starting with the preparation of your work area.

Because portable computers often require a completely different maintenance philosophy, we'll discuss them in a separate section near the end of this chapter; they are also discussed in Chapter 2, "PC Architecture."

Preparing Your Work Area

For any work you do on a computer, you must have an adequate workspace. This could mean any number of things. First, the work area must be flat. If it's not, small parts could roll around and possibly get lost or damaged. Second, the area must be sturdy. A typical computer weighs about 25 pounds. Printers and other peripherals will add to that weight. Make sure the work surface you are using can support that weight. In addition, the area must be well lit, clean, and large enough to hold all pieces (assembled and disassembled) and all necessary tools. Figure 9.1 shows an adequate workspace for most computers.

FIGURE 9.1   A typical computer workspace

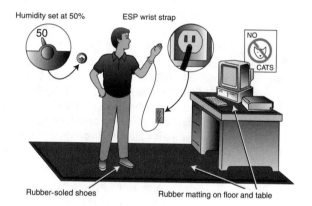

Before you begin, make sure all necessary tools are available and in working order. It may help to lay out some of the more commonly used disassembly tools such as screwdrivers and nut drivers so they can be easily found (including several antistatic bags in which to place the removed components). Also, make sure the documentation for the system you are working on is available (including owner's manuals, service manuals, and Internet resources). Three tools in particular that will be very handy aren't really tools in the traditional sense but are, rather, timesavers. They are an egg carton and a pen and notepad. An egg carton is perfect for organizing screws and small parts that might otherwise end up in the "extra parts" pile. A pen and notepad should be used to record anything that may easily be forgotten, such as cable positions, DIP switch settings, and the location from which you removed the components.

The final guideline to preparing your work area is to set aside plenty of time to complete the task. To do this, estimate the time required to complete the entire task (disassembly, installation, reassembly, and testing), and then *double it*. Too often, a technician will start a "simple" job and underestimate the time needed to complete it. When you run out of time, you must come back later to complete the job. Because of this interruption, you may forget exactly where they left off. This can lead to the "extra parts" syndrome.

Once you've prepared your work area and gathered your tools, you're ready to begin the actual disassembly of the computer. The steps are basically the same for all brands and types of computers.

Disassembly Prerequisites

Let's start by fulfilling a few prerequisites—things you need to do before you even move the computer to your work area.

1. Shut down any running programs and turn the computer off.

2. Remove all cables (*especially the power cable*) that are attached to the computer. Remember that some cables use special screws to attach them to their ports.

WARNING

That second step (removing all the cables before disassembling) is at least as important as the first. *DON'T ASSUME THAT THERE IS NO POWER TO THE COMPUTER JUST BECAUSE THE POWER SWITCH IS OFF!* Some new computers have a low power mode that, when active, makes the computer *appear* to be off. In truth, a computer in this mode is just idle and the video circuitry is shut off. If you disassemble the computer while it's plugged in or turned on, you could get *electrocuted!* Additionally, components could be damaged if inserted or removed while power is applied.

3. Remove any floppy disks from their respective drives to prevent damage to either the disk or the drive.

4. After checking once more to see that all the prerequisites have been dealt with, move the computer to the work surface.

Removing the Case Cover

Next, you are going to remove the computer's case cover. On many IBM-compatible PCs this is accomplished by removing some (but usually not all) of the screws at the back of the computer (see the warning following this paragraph) and *slowly* pulling the computer's case cover back and up to remove it (see Figure 9.2). If you pull too fast, it is possible to damage cables that may be located close to the top of the case. If the case doesn't move, check to see that all the case cover screws were removed.

WARNING Don't just start removing *all* the screws at the back of the computer! Some of these screws hold vital components (such as the power supply) to the case, and removing them will cause those components to drop into the computer. The computer's documentation should indicate which screws to remove in order to remove the case cover.

FIGURE 9.2 Removing the case cover

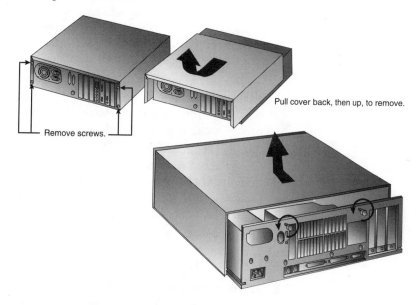

As more and more technology has become available for PCs, hardware manufacturers have begun to design systems that are easier to maintain. Many of today's PCs can be completely disassembled without a single tool. There are as many different ways to gain access to the PC internals as there are PC manufacturers. If you are unsure about how to gain access to a component on your PC, be sure to take the time to read the manual.

NOTE This move toward easier access started quite some time ago with early IBM PCs. As with many innovations, the first ones are often more a novelty than a convenience. IBM began using spring-loaded screws in their PC cases to make them easier to service. Unfortunately, 90 percent of the time the spring shot across the room and got lost. Field techs had to carry spares in their travel kit, usually right next to their screwdriver.

Removing the Expansion Cards

Once you have the case off, you will be able to see the inside of the computer. The next step in disassembly is to put on an antistatic wrist strap, plugging one end into the ground plug of an outlet. Then you can start to remove any *expansion cards*, mainly because they are the easiest things to remove at this point. There are four major steps in removing the expansion cards; to do this correctly you need to follow these steps in order:

1. Remove any internal or external cables or connectors. (You should already have removed the external ones in the prerequisite steps.) When you are removing a cable or connector, use your pen and notepad to diagram their installed positions. Also, use the pen to make identifying marks on the cables to make sure they align correctly when reinstalled.

2. Remove any mounting screws that are holding the boards in place, and place the screws somewhere where they won't be lost. If you don't have an egg carton, you can put each screw back into its mounting hole as you remove each expansion board. Just make sure to screw them in all the way, not just a couple of turns.

3. Grasp the board by the top edge with both hands and *gently* rock it front to back (*NOT* side to side). Figure 9.3 clarifies this procedure. If the expansion board doesn't come out easily, don't force it. You may damage it. Check to see that the board is not being obstructed.

4. Finally, once the board is out, place it in an antistatic bag to help prevent ESD damage while the board is out of the computer. Place the board aside and out of the way before continuing.

Repeat the procedure for each card. At the same time, be sure to note which slot it came out of since some bus types (EISA, MCA, and PCI) keep track of which slot expansion boards are installed in.

FIGURE 9.3   Removing an expansion board

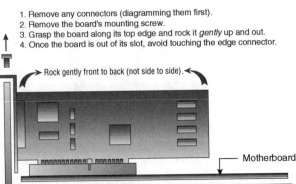

1. Remove any connectors (diagramming them first).
2. Remove the board's mounting screw.
3. Grasp the board along its top edge and rock it *gently* up and out.
4. Once the board is out of its slot, avoid touching the edge connector.

Rock gently front to back (not side to side).

Motherboard

Once again, many manufacturers have moved to a screwless design. IBM high-end servers, for instance, use a plastic tab to hold boards in place. This prevents a metal screw from falling into the case and shorting out the motherboard. If your computer still uses screws to secure expansion boards, keep a running count of the number of screws you have removed—and make sure that you can account for every screw before you plug the power cord back in!

Removing the Power Supply

The next component that should be removed is the power supply. You can easily access it with the expansion cards out of the way. Before you remove the power supply from the computer, however, you must do two things: disconnect the power supply connectors from the internal devices, and remove the mounting hardware for the power supply.

Disconnecting the connectors from the devices is a very easy process. Before removing any power connectors, note their positions and connections on your notepad (and make any marks on them to indicate their installed positions). Then, simply grasp the connector (*NOT* THE WIRES) and gently wiggle it out of its receptacle. Then, proceed to the next connector. The system board and disk drives both use power connectors. Make sure all of them are removed, including (if they exist) the cable and connector that run to the power switch at the front of the case. Figure 9.4 illustrates these procedures.

FIGURE 9.4 Removing power supply connectors

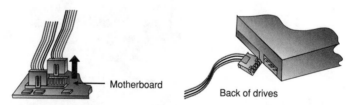

Motherboard

Back of drives

The standard PC power supply has two connectors to the motherboard. These plug into receptacles that are side by side. Document the positioning of these connectors before removing them to make it easier to put them back when you are done. If, for some reason, you get confused as to which connector goes where, the general rule is black-to-black. Grab the connectors so that the black wires are side by side, and you will be holding them the way they should be installed.

Once all the power supply connectors are disconnected from their devices, you can remove the mounting hardware for the power supply. In most PCs, you can detach the power supply from the case by removing four screws (see Figure 9.5).

FIGURE 9.5 Removing power supply screws

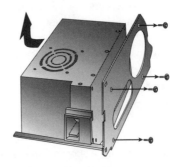

Some power supplies don't need to have screws removed; instead, they are installed on tracks or into slots in the case and need only to be slid out or lifted out.

Removing the Disk Drives

Most disk drives are installed in IBM-compatible computers with *rails* that are attached to the drives with screws. These rails allow the drive to be slid into the computer's drive bays like a drawer. The drives are then secured with at least two screws on the sides (see Figure 9.6).

FIGURE 9.6 Removing the hard drive

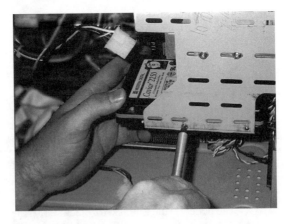

Many desktop computers (such as Compaqs, IBM PS/2s, and Hewlett-Packards) use a special drive carrier that holds the drive in place and can be easily removed without tools, thus eliminating the need for special rails. With most drives, however, you can just remove the mounting screws and slide the drive out. Consult the computer's documentation to see exactly how to remove your specific type of drive.

To remove drives from higher-end computers, you should also consult the documentation. It is possible on many higher-end machines to swap drives while the computer is still running (this is known as a *hot-swap*); to prevent damage to the drive (or maybe even other components), you will want to know the correct procedure.

Removing the Motherboard

All that's left in your computer is the *motherboard* (also known as the logic board). The only time the motherboard should need to be removed is when it needs to be upgraded or replaced. Otherwise, you should leave the motherboard in the PC's case to prevent either physical or ESD damage.

The motherboard is held away from the metal case using plastic spacers and is secured and grounded using mounting screws. To remove the motherboard, you must remove the screws holding the motherboard to the mounting brackets. Then, you must slide the motherboard to the side to release the spacers from their mounting holes in the case (see Figure 9.7).

FIGURE 9.7   Removing the motherboard

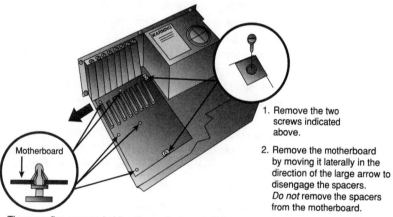

1. Remove the two screws indicated above.

2. Remove the motherboard by moving it laterally in the direction of the large arrow to disengage the spacers. *Do not* remove the spacers from the motherboard.

There are five spacers holding the motherboard off the case. A spacer is shown above, viewed from its side.

Installation and Upgrades

At some point, every computer will require the installation of a new component. Whether it's a new sound card, a memory upgrade, or the replacement of a failed component, installation is a procedure that every computer goes through in its lifetime. Throughout this section, we'll use the example of a sound card for our discussions. The installation for other types of expansion boards will follow the same basic steps.

The installation of new or replacement components in most computers is a simple process if you follow a few basic steps. These steps are very general but should cover the installation of most components.

1. Determine available resources. (If you're installing a Plug-and-Play component, you may not have to do this.)

2. Configure the new devices, using the provided instructions. (Again, with Plug and Play, you might not need to do this.)

3. Install the component and its supporting software.

4. Test the component's operation.

Determining Available Resources

If this is the first time the particular component has been installed in this computer, you must determine if there are any available resources (IRQ channels, DMA channels, memory addresses, and so on). If the part you are installing is a replacement part, you simply set the jumpers or DIP switches the same as they were on the component you removed. (You did remember to diagram these settings, right?)

The best way to determine the PC's available resources is by using hardware configuration discovery utilities. These software programs talk to the PC's BIOS as well as the various pieces of hardware in the computer and display which IRQ, DMA, and memory addresses are being used. There are numerous commercial packages that do a very good job of determining which resources are in use and which are available. Most operating systems, however, include some way of determining this information. MS-DOS, Windows 3.x, and Windows 95 included a tool named MSD.EXE. Windows 98 has a graphical utility called the Device Manager. Windows NT includes a program known as NT Diagnostics. Since all of these tools report the same type of information, we'll use MSD.EXE as our example.

One advantage of MSD.EXE over the other programs listed is that it can be included on a boot floppy. In the event that a resource conflict is preventing your system from booting properly, you can boot to the DOS floppy and troubleshoot your problem.

When you run MSD.EXE, it can display information about the computer's memory, I/O ports, IRQs that are being used, and many other PC resources that you want to see. Figure 9.8 shows the main menu that appears when you first run the program.

FIGURE 9.8 The main menu of MSD.EXE

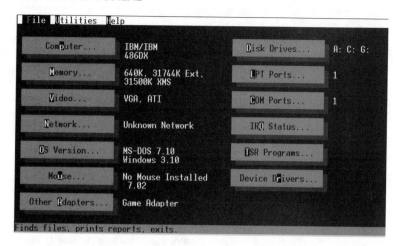

From the main menu, you can use the menu options to display information about the various resources. For example, if you want to find out if there are any IRQ channels available, press Q to bring up a screen similar to the one in Figure 9.9 (your screen may show something different).

FIGURE 9.9 MSD IRQ status screen

```
 File   Utilities   Help
┌───────────────────── IRQ Status ─────────────────────┐
│ IRQ  Address    Description      Detected         Handled By       │
│ ───  ────────   ────────────     ─────────        ──────────       │
│  0   04F6:0000  Timer Click      Yes              vmm32            │
│  1   D54C:0028  Keyboard         Yes              Default Handlers │
│  2   F000:FF33  Second 8259A     Yes              BIOS             │
│  3   F000:FF33  COM2: COM4:      No               BIOS             │
│  4   F000:FF33  COM1: COM3:      COM1:            BIOS             │
│  5   F000:FF33  LPT2:            No               BIOS             │
│  6   D54C:009A  Floppy Disk      Yes              Default Handlers │
│  7   0070:0465  LPT1:            Yes              System Area      │
│  8   D54C:0035  Real-Time Clock  Yes              Default Handlers │
│  9   F000:D218  Redirected IRQ2  Yes              BIOS             │
│ 10   F000:FF33  (Reserved)                        BIOS             │
│ 11   F000:FF33  (Reserved)                        BIOS             │
│ 12   D54C:00E2  (Reserved)       No Mouse Installed Default Handlers │
│ 13   F000:D207  Math Coprocessor Yes              BIOS             │
│ 14   D54C:00FA  Fixed Disk       Yes              Default Handlers │
│ 15   D54C:0112  (Reserved)                        Default Handlers │
│                                                                    │
│                        ▐ OK ▌                                      │
└────────────────────────────────────────────────────────────────────┘
 IRQ Status: Displays current usage of hardware interrupts.
```

As you can see, the computer in Figure 9.9 has IRQs 3, 5, 10, 11, 12, and 15 available. (You can tell this because either the IRQ Status Detected column indicates No or the Description column indicates Reserved for these IRQ channels.) If you want to install a device that requires an IRQ channel, you can set it to any of these channels and there should be no IRQ conflicts. You perform the same procedure to find out if any of the other resources are available.

Don't rely completely on the report you get from MSD if you're running it under Windows 3.*x* (or Windows 95). In that situation, MSD simply gives the information that it gets from Windows. This may be somewhat incorrect and could prove to be a problem. For best results, run MSD in DOS only (or in MS-DOS mode under Windows 95). Actually, regardless of which operating system you're using, the operating system can "color" the performance of a software diagnostic program. For this reason, it's best to always *verify* the settings the program reports against the settings as published in your computer documentation and device manuals.

Besides addressing resources, there is one other resource you need to make sure is available: physical space. There must be adequate space in the computer for the device you are installing. If you are installing a disk drive, there must be an open disk bay available. If you are installing an expansion card (for example, a sound card), you must make sure that you have an open slot available. Also, in the case of computers that use multiple bus types (ISA/PCI for example), the available slot must be of the same type as the card being installed.

Understanding Computer Resources

The various tools that you can use to discover the available resources on a PC can make installing new hardware a lot easier. Unfortunately, the tools are not much use unless you understand the information that they present. In this section, we will discuss the various resources that can be used by PC components (including that new sound card you are installing) and how those resources are used.

In general, there are four main types of PC resources that you might need to be aware of when installing a new component: interrupt request (IRQ) lines, memory addresses, direct memory access (DMA), and I/O addresses.

Interrupt Request (IRQ) Lines

IRQs, or *interrupt requests*, are appropriately named. Interrupts are used by peripherals to interrupt or stop the CPU and demand attention. When the CPU receives an interrupt alert, it stops whatever it is doing and handles the request. This is one of the techniques used to make it appear as if the computer were actually doing multiple things simultaneously (this is also known as multitasking). In reality, the CPU does one thing at a time; it just does it (and moves to the next task) so quickly that it appears as if it is handling multiple tasks simultaneously.

Each device is given its own interrupt to use when alerting the CPU. AT-based PCs have 16 interrupts available. (You wouldn't want too many things to interrupt the CPU or it would never get anything done.) Given the limited number of available interrupts, it is critical that you assign them wisely! For each of the 16 interrupts available on an AT PC, Table 9.1 lists the standard use and other uses associated with it.

TABLE 9.1 AT Interrupts

Interrupt	Most common use	Other common uses
0	System timer.	Nothing else uses (or should use) interrupt 0.
1	Keyboard.	Nothing else uses (or should use) interrupt 1.
2	None. This interrupt is used to cascade to the higher 8 interrupts (see note following this table).	Modems; COM 3, COM 4.
3	COM 2.	COM 4, network interface cards, sound cards, and just about anything else.
4	COM 1.	COM 3, network interface cards, sound cards, and just about anything else.
5	Sound card.	LPT2, LPT3, COM 3, COM 4, disk controllers on older XT-based computers.
6	Floppy disk controller.	Tape controllers.
7	LPT1.	LPT2, COM 3, COM 4, network interface cards, sound cards, and just about anything else.
8	Real time clock.	Nothing else uses (or should use) interrupt 8.
9		SCSI controllers, PCI cards, and just about anything else.
10		Secondary IDE channel, SCSI controllers, PCI cards, and just about anything else.
11		Third or fourth IDE channel, SCSI controllers, PCI cards, and just about anything else.
12	PS/2-style mouse.	Just about anything.
13	Floating point coprocessor.	None.

TABLE 9.1 AT Interrupts *(continued)*

Interrupt	Most common use	Other common uses
14	Primary IDE channel.	SCSI controllers.
15	Secondary IDE channel.	SCSI controllers, network adapters.

Interrupt 2 is a special case. In earlier (XT-based) PCs, there were only eight interrupts because those computers used an 8-bit bus. With the development of the AT, eight more interrupts were created (to match the 16-bit bus), but no mechanism was available to use them. Rather than redesign the entire interrupt process, AT designers decided to use interrupt 2 as a gateway, or cascade, to interrupts 9–15. In reality, interrupt 2 is the same as interrupt 9. You should never configure your system so that both interrupt 2 and 9 are used.

Configuring interrupts is so common that most experienced field technicians have the standards (as listed in Table 9.1) memorized.

Memory Addresses

Many components use blocks of memory as part of their normal functioning. Network interface cards, for instance, often buffer incoming data in a block of memory until they can be processed. This prevents the card from being overloaded if a burst of data is received from the network.

When the device driver loads, it lets the CPU know which block of memory should be set aside for the exclusive use of the component. This prevents other devices from overwriting the information stored there. (Of course, it also sets us up for hardware conflicts since two components cannot be assigned the same address space.) Certain system components also need a *memory address*. Some of the more common default assignments are listed in Table 9.2.

TABLE 9.2 Common Memory Address Assignments

Address	Assignment
F0000–FFFFF	System BIOS
E0000–EFFFF	In use on true IBM compatibles
CA000–DFFFF	Available on most PCs

TABLE 9.2 Common Memory Address Assignments *(continued)*

Address	Assignment
C8000–C87FF	Hard disk controller on an XT system
C0000–C7FFF	EGA/VGA display
B8000–BFFFF	CGA/EGA/VGA display
B0000–B7FFF	Monochrome display
A0000–AFFFF	EGA/VGA display
00000–9FFFF	System memory

Direct Memory Access (DMA)

When a device stores information in a memory address, this process is controlled by the CPU. In other words, if a network card needs to buffer data, it requests that the CPU write that data to its assigned memory address. Since the CPU knows which area of memory is dedicated to each device, it can help prevent any other process from overwriting the information in memory (the CPU denies any request to write to that area of memory except those that come from the proper device). Using memory addresses is a safe, stable way to for a peripheral to store data in memory, it is also rather processor intensive and inefficient.

Direct memory access (DMA) is a method used by peripherals to place data in memory without utilizing (or bothering) the CPU. As an example, a sound card can buffer music in memory while the CPU is busy recalculating a spreadsheet. The DMA peripheral has its own processor to move the data. It uses dead time on the ISA bus to perform the transfer. At the hardware level, DMA is quite complex, but the important feature to remember is that the transfer of data is accomplished without intervention from the CPU.

All DMA transfers use a special area of memory set aside to receive data from the expansion card (or CPU if the transfer is going the other direction) known as a *buffer*. The basic architecture of the PC DMA buffers are limited in size and memory location.

DMA transfers are made using a predefined DMA channel. The PC supports up to eight DMA channels, although not all are compatible with all expansion cards. Each channel is dedicated to a specific device—no DMA channel can be used by more than one device. If you accidentally choose a DMA channel that another card is using, the usual symptom is that no DMA transfers will take place (in other words, for our example, no sound would play).

Certain DMA channels are assigned to standard AT devices. Table 9.3 lists the eight DMA channels and their default assignments.

TABLE 9.3 DMA Assignments

DMA Channel	Default assignment
0	Dynamic RAM refresh
1	Hard disk controller
2	Floppy disk controller
3	Available on all PCs
4–7	Available on AT and Micro Channel PS/2 computers

I/O Addresses

I/O (input/output) addresses, also known as port addresses, are a specific area of memory that a component uses to communicate with the system. As such, they sound quite a bit like the memory addresses discussed above. The major difference is that memory addresses are used to store information that will be used by the device itself. I/O addresses are used to store information that will be used by the system. In other words, it is information waiting to be processed rather then information waiting to be prepared for processing.

A perfect example of how I/O addresses are used is the keyboard. When you type, the information (such as which letters you typed and in which order) is stored in a specific area of memory (an I/O address). The CPU knows to look at this address to find information from the keyboard. Each I/O address acts as a mail stop for information being exchanged between the CPU and a device and also acts as a reserved place to drop off data to be picked up (either by the device or the CPU depending upon which way the transfer is going). Since they are reserved for a particular device, no two devices can share an I/O address.

Certain system devices are automatically assigned an I/O address. Table 9.4 lists some of the common default assignments.

TABLE 9.4 Common I/O Address Assignments

Address	Assignment
000–0FF	Reserved for the system itself
1F0–1F8	Hard disk controller

TABLE 9.4 Common I/O Address Assignments *(continued)*

Address	Assignment
200–207	Game port
278–27F	Second parallel port (LPT2)
2F8–2FF	Second serial port (COM 2)
378–37F	First parallel port (LPT1)
3F0–3F7	Floppy disk controller
3F8–3FF	First serial port (COM 1)

Configuring New Devices

Now that you know what resources are available, you can begin configuring the device. If you installed the device without configuring it, the device probably won't work (although you might get lucky and the default settings of the card will work). There are two major steps in the configuration: reading the instructions and setting the configuration of the device.

Reading the Instructions

The saying "If all else fails, read the directions" exists because most people assume they know how to do something, even if they've never done it before. This statement is especially true for service technicians. Most technicians think that if they've installed one sound card, they've installed them all. Even worse, they won't admit that they don't know how to repair something.

It is for this reason we have instructions. Of the two steps for configuring devices, this is the most important. Every component should come with instructions (although I have certainly found some components that require you to guess how to configure them). These instructions usually have diagrams that indicate where the jumpers or DIP switches are and what positions they need to be in to set the device so that it uses the resources you specify.

When looking through the instructions for this information, you need to find the section of the installation manual that deals with configuration (you may need to look in the index or table of contents to find it). Once you find it, see if you can match the resources that you have to a set of jumper settings. For example, if you have IRQ 5 and I/O address 220 available, you need to see if your sound card can support those settings. If it can support them, find out which jumpers need to be moved. If it can't, you have to go back and pick a different set of available resources and repeat the process.

Setting the Configuration

Setting the configuration of a device on many older expansion cards involves following the instructions and moving jumpers and DIP switches.

These settings might be contained in a configuration table in the documentation. Examples of a sound card's configuration tables are shown in Tables 9.5 and 9.6. We'll assume that there are two sets of jumpers: one for the IRQ setting; another for the I/O address (labeled J1 and J2, respectively). Each set has five pairs of pins each.

TABLE 9.5 Sample IRQ Settings Table

IRQ	Jumper These Pins on Jumper J1
3	1
5 (default)	2
7	3
10	4
11	5

TABLE 9.6 Sample I/O Address Settings Table

I/O Address	Jumper These Pins on Jumper J2
220H (default)	1
240H	2
260H	3
280H	4
300H	5

If you know that you have I/O address 220H and IRQ 5 available, you can tell by the tables that you will have to jumper pin 2 on jumper J1 and pin 1 on jumper J2.

However, most expansion cards made today don't use DIP switches or jumpers. Instead, those that don't utilize Plug-and-Play technology (discussed below) use a *software setup program.* When installing a new sound card that uses a software setup program, you only set one jumper: the one that controls the I/O address setting (which is usually set to 220H for sound cards). As long as it doesn't conflict with any other devices, the software setup program can be used. Other types of expansion cards will have their own default settings (Ethernet network cards, for instance, are usually set to IRQ 3 and I/O Port 300 at the factory.) Once again, read the documentation before attempting to configure any expansion board. Some expansion cards have no physical jumpers or settings at all. These cards can be a hassle to install if the default setting conflict with hardware already in place. You usually end up taking out the old hardware, installing the new, and using the software to change its settings. Then you can place the old expansion board back.

Once you run the software setup program, it will present menu choices for each of the settings for that expansion card. You can use these menus to choose the IRQ, the DMA channel, and the memory addresses for the card.

Another type of configuration program that is used is the *Plug-and-Play* technology developed by several manufacturers, including Intel and Microsoft. This technology consists of a special BIOS that checks the configuration of every expansion card at startup. When a new card is inserted, the PC will detect that a change has occurred to the system and will configure the card to settings that, hopefully, do not conflict.

Plug and Play is a good idea, but the problem is that this technology doesn't work all of the time. Sometimes the settings the BIOS chooses *will* conflict, and these cards have no easy way of reconfiguring the settings. It is often called "Plug and Pray" because of this.

This problem manifests itself most often when the newer Plug-and-Play cards are mixed with older, legacy expansion cards in the same computer. The term *legacy* usually applies to previous-generation hardware or software (e.g., older 8-bit and ISA cards).

However, Plug-and-Play technology has become much more reliable over the last few years. As the number of legacy components dwindles, so do the number of problems. And when it works, Plug and Play beats the old system of manually configuring every device, hands down!

Installing the Component

Now that your sound card is configured, you can finally mount the device into the computer. Mounting a device usually means attaching it to the computer's case with some kind of fastener and attaching the device to an interface. In this case, it means installing an expansion card into an expansion slot and securing it with a screw.

Most expansion cards can be inserted in the same way. First of all, make sure the power is off! This step is very important because if the power is applied and you try to install a card into a slot that has power, you will most likely destroy the card, the motherboard, or both!

Second, if the place you are installing the device has a *blank* (a piece of plastic or metal that covers that space where the device is going to go), remove it. Don't throw these blanks away. If you ever want to remove a component, you will need to replace the blank so that dirt, dust, and other contaminants can be kept out. I have a small box full of blanks that I keep handy, just in case I need them when removing components.

Many technicians ignore the need for a blank when they remove a component—do not make this mistake! The most important function of a blank is to promote proper airflow over the internal components of your PC. PC manufactures have spent hours determining the proper placement of fans and air holes for their computers. Adding a new hole in the back of your computer will often result in *less* airflow rather than more as you might assume. The end result is often a computer that overheats and burns out components.

Next, align the connector on the bottom of the card with the connector on the motherboard and insert the card into its connector. You should feel a slight amount of resistance. Push the card firmly into place with an even pressure on the front and back of the card. Stop pushing when all of the card's connectors are making contact with the "fingers" in the expansion slot.

If the card doesn't go in easily, don't force it. You could break the card or the connector.

Finally, install the mounting screws to secure the device in place. In this case, you only have one screw to install, and it's located at the back of the computer. This screw will hold the metal tab on the expansion card to the computer's case. PS/2 computers have tabs that lock the board into place, so you can skip this step for PS/2 computers.

Most people would begin to reassemble the computer at this point. However, you don't want to do that just yet. I've found that Murphy's Law applies quite often when installing computer components. So leave the case off while performing the next steps: installing the software and testing the component. If something goes wrong, you won't have to remove the case again to get at the component.

Installing the Software

I've got good news and bad news. The good news is that the new component is installed. The bad news is that it doesn't work yet. You have one thing left to do before the component will be fully functional. All components require some kind of software in order to function. You must install *software drivers* so that the operating system can communicate with the new hardware component. At the same time, other *utility software* is usually installed. These utilities are what the user employs to interact with the device.

If you are installing a Plug-and-Play device, Windows 95/98 or Windows 2000 will often sense the new device and run an installation Wizard to walk you through the process of installing the device driver. If this doesn't happen, read the instructions that came with the device.

Many operating systems come with default drivers for numerous peripherals. Windows 95/98, for example, might automatically install a driver from its own CD-ROM. Do not assume that since it came with the operating system it must be the best driver. The drivers on the operating system CD-ROM are often out of date! Check the disks that came with the device or the manufacture's Web site for the latest drivers.

In our case (continuing with our sound card example), you need to install the sound card drivers and software for the sound card you just installed. Find the disks that came with the sound card (they will probably be in a white envelope inside the sound card's box). Plug all the cords back in and turn the computer on. After the computer is done booting, insert the first disk into the X: drive (where X: is whatever drive you place the disk in) and, depending on whether the program uses DOS or Windows, do one of the following:

- From a DOS prompt: type **A:INSTALL** on a command line.
- From Windows 3.*x*, select File ➤ Run, or from Windows 9*x* select Start ➤ Run, and then type **A:SETUP**.

Your installation manual will tell you which of the two methods you need to use. Follow the on-screen prompts and complete the software installation. When you finish, you may need to reboot the computer.

Testing the Components

The component should now be functional. To make sure that it's functioning properly, you need to test it. There are three ways to test components: through observation, by using software diagnostics, or, depending upon the operating system you are using, by checking with tools provided with your OS.

Observation is the simplest method of testing. It involves observing the device and seeing if the device functions as it's supposed to. For example, if your sound card is installed properly, you should be able to hear sounds when you play your favorite games. Or you should be able to play sound files with the utility that came with your sound card.

The second method of testing components is to run any diagnostics that may have come with the device. These are very simple software programs that are designed to test the functions of only that device. You can run these programs during the installation process or later.

These programs usually give their results in the form of pass/fail. For example, the diagnostic program will test the sound-generating capabilities of your sound card and return "pass" if the diagnostics found no problem with that aspect of the card. If there were problems, the diagnostics will return "fail" for the particular part of the sound card that wasn't functioning.

If you are using Windows 95/98 or Windows NT/2000, you can check for conflicts by accessing the Device Manager utility included with each operating system. Any components that are not functioning correctly will be marked with a yellow exclamation point.

As a general rule of thumb, use at least two of the three methods when testing your new component. Conflicts will often not manifest themselves until the two devices that are in conflict with each other try to access a resource simultaneously. Once you have tested the component and are confident that your computer is configured correctly, you can turn the computer off and replace the cover.

For more information on diagnostics, see Part II, Chapter 19, "Software Troubleshooting."

Reassembling the Computer

If you followed the steps under "Disassembling the Computer," you will have a computer case and several components laid out in front of you. This section deals with how to put this collection of parts together into a functioning computer. We'll cover the steps in reassembling the computer, as well as a few tips to make the job easier.

The basic rule to remember when reassembling anything is to reverse the steps you took when you took it apart. That sounds easy enough, but ask anyone who has ever taken a watch or clock apart how easy it actually is. Computers are simpler than watches, thankfully, and can be reassembled without too much trouble.

Remember to account for any screws you might have removed. At the least, there is nothing more irritating then the sound of something rolling around inside the case every time you move it. In the worst-case scenario, that missing screw could short out your motherboard!

Installing the Motherboard

The first step in reassembly is sometimes optional. If you didn't remove the motherboard during disassembly, you can skip this step. Installing the motherboard involves positioning it in the case (as shown originally in Figure 9.7) and securing it with either screws or plastic circuit board fasteners.

Once the motherboard is secured in the case, you must connect the individual connectors that run to things like the reset switch and the turbo button (if present). Figure 9.10 details this step.

FIGURE 9.10 Reconnecting the cables

Installing the Disk Drives

The next step in the reassembly of the computer is to install the disk drives. This involves mounting the drives in the case and connecting the drive cables to the adapters.

Let's discuss installing the floppy drives, CD-ROM drives, or floppy controller–based tape drives first. To install one of these devices, place it into position and secure it with at least one screw in each side. Once you finish this, connect the appropriate connector on the floppy cable to the drive and the floppy controller. Remember to orient the cable so that the red wire in the floppy cable is positioned toward pin 1. Also remember the rules for connecting floppy drives when more than one drive exists (i.e., when you have both an A: and a B: drive).

The installation of fixed disk drives follows basically the same procedure. With hard disks, position the drive (and its installation rails, if used), and secure it with at least one screw on each side. Once the drive is securely fastened to the case, connect the drive cable to the drive and to the disk adapter (or motherboard if your motherboard has an integrated disk adapter), remembering the red wire guideline mentioned above. Also, don't forget the rules for connecting disks to cables as mentioned in Chapter 4, "Disk System Architecture."

Configuring the CMOS

IDE hard disks get their configuration information from the BIOS's *CMOS* (*Complementary Metal Oxide Semiconductor*) memory. CMOS contains settings that determine how the computer is configured. These settings are user-configurable and can be accessed through the CMOS setup program by pressing some key combination at startup (such as Shift+F1 or Ctrl+Shift+Esc). For example, one setting in CMOS controls the boot sequence. The parameter is usually called *boot sequence* and can be set to either "A: C:" or "C: A:" (in most cases).

Every CMOS setup program is different and uses different commands for configuration. Usually, though, the CMOS setup program is menu driven and will present you with a list of settings that you can configure, as well as the possible settings for them. When you're done configuring, you can press Esc and the CMOS setup program will ask you to press Enter to save the changes and reboot. After rebooting, the computer will operate with the modified settings.

During the system boot, the computer checks what hardware settings are in the CMOS versus what is actually installed in the computer. If they are different, the BIOS will issue a warning and usually bring you right to the CMOS setup screen.

If you run across a computer that doesn't automatically detect an IDE hard disk when you install it, you will have to run the CMOS setup program and change the hard disk definitions. These are usually shown as a series of numbers under columns such as Cyl, Heads, and Sect. These columns and numbers correspond to the drive's cylinders, heads, and sectors (in other words, their geometry). By changing the numbers in these columns, you are changing what the BIOS "knows" about the hard disk. The numbers that must be entered in these columns can usually be found either on the back of the drive itself or in the documentation that came with the drive.

Changing the drive geometry without needing to can cause long-term data damage or loss.

CMOS is used for more than just configuring hard drive information. CMOS, working in conjunction with the system BIOS, configures the system during the boot sequence. I've mentioned that CMOS contains information about the IDE hard drives that are installed on the system, as well as information about which order boot devices should be checked for operating system files during startup. CMOS also contains the following:

- The physical resources used by parallel and serial ports, as well as any other configuration information needed for those components.
- A description of the floppy drive—its speed, density, etc.
- Memory configuration.
- The date and time.

- Any passwords that have been assigned to the hardware. Many computers require a password to complete the boot sequence.
- A list of the resources that have been reserved for use by Plug-and-Play components (and those that have been set aside for legacy equipment).
- BIOS shadowing configuration information.

Installing the Power Supply

At this point, you have the motherboard and disk drives installed. You can now install the power supply and provide power to these components. To install the power supply, hold the power supply in position and install the four mounting screws (if necessary). Then, connect the power connectors to each component (including the disk drives and motherboard) and make sure they are secure. Finally, make sure the power switch connector has been connected to the power supply.

There is a hard way and an easy way to connect the connectors labeled P8 and P9 to the motherboard. The hard way is to push the connectors straight down onto their pins. This takes considerable effort since the locking tabs are in the way. It's easier to position the connectors at a backward tilt, as shown in Figure 9.11, and then slip them down into position. They slide on much easier and you won't damage anything (including yourself).

FIGURE 9.11 Connecting power supply connectors P8 and P9

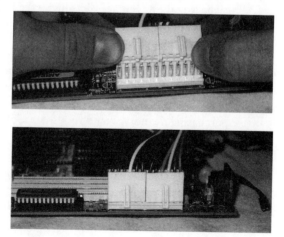

Installing the Expansion Cards

You are now ready to reinstall the expansion cards that you removed. To reinstall an expansion card, consult the diagram you made that shows the position of each expansion card and locate the slot for the card you are trying to install. Insert the card into its slot, making certain that all of the card's connectors are making contact with the expansion slot. Other than that, reinstalling expansion boards is the same as installing new ones; see "Installing the Component" earlier in this chapter for instructions.

Installing Memory

The physical act of installing memory is fairly straightforward and follows the same basic rules that have been described for installing other peripherals. There are however, a few specific differences of which you will need to be aware.

The hardest task involved in adding memory to a PC is buying the correct RAM for your computer. Memory technology has been changing at a rapid pace to match the changes in CPU and architecture. There are numerous types of RAM available, and most are not interchangeable. In other words, you must buy the correct type of memory and all of your memory must be of the same type.

Memory Types

There are two major categories of RAM on the market today: *static RAM (SRAM)* and *Dynamic RAM (DRAM)*. Static RAM is designed so that once information is placed in it, it will hold that information for as long as power is supplied to the memory chips. SRAM is usually faster then DRAM but is more expensive as well. Because of its high cost, SRAM is most often used as system cache (to take advantage of its high speed) rather than as main system memory. DRAM, unlike SRAM, must be continually rewritten in order for it to retain data. The memory is placed on a refresh circuit that rewrites the data hundreds of times per second. DRAM is relatively inexpensive and fairly fast and is used as the main memory for most modern computers. The odds are that you will be replacing or adding DRAM to your computer.

If SRAM and DRAM were the only different technologies to keep track of, purchasing memory would be a snap. Unfortunately, there are several (incompatible) types of DRAM from which you must choose:

Fast Page Mode (FPM) DRAM   Contrary to what the name implies, FPM DRAM is only slightly faster then DRAM due to a more efficient method of calling data from memory. Since other technologies are faster, FPM DRAM is not used much anymore, but it is almost universally supported on PC motherboards.

Extended Data Output (EDO) DRAM   EDO memory is slightly faster than FPM DRAM because it allows one access to begin as another finishes. EDO memory must be supported by the chipset in use on the motherboard, and you must confirm this before purchasing it. EDO memory is the most common form of DRAM in use today.

Burst EDO (BEDO) DRAM   Using a pipelining technology, BEDO DRAM is significantly faster than standard EDO memory but has gained little support in the industry.

Synchronous DRAM   SDRAM works at the same speed as the system bus, up to 100MHz. While the technology is significantly faster than other forms of DRAM memory, the speed increase is often not apparent because the system cache masks it.

Installation Concerns

Each type of memory and each system BIOS has its own peculiarities in how it supports memory. You will definitely want to read the system manual before you purchase and install your new memory. Some of the more common "rules" include:

- When installing memory, many systems require that all slots in a given memory bank be full. This means that if you have a 4-slot bank free and you want to add memory, you will have to install four memory modules.

- Do not mix memory of different speeds on your system. Many computers will not even boot if you do this. If your computer does boot, you can rest assured you'll have memory-related problems later!

- If you are installing memory of different sizes (one 64MB SIMM and two 32MB SIMMs, for instance), place the largest SIMMs in the first memory banks.

Installation Procedures

Most memory today is sold in either *SIMM (Single Inline Memory Module)* or *DIMM (Dual Inline Memory Module)* format. Each module has a governor that will prevent it from being installed incorrectly in the memory slot. (Do not force memory modules! You will break off the governor and need to have your motherboard serviced.)

Line up the module with the slot at a 45-degree angle away from the support arms. Slide the module into the slot, and stand it up. If you install it properly, you will hear a click as the module locks into place.

If you accidentally snap off the memory module lock on your motherboard, you can still use the computer. Just ensure that the memory module is firmly seated in the slot. Be aware, though, that since the memory is not locked into place, temperature changes can cause it to work its way loose over time (this is known as *chip creep*). Have the memory bank fixed at the earliest opportunity!

Installing Universal Serial Bus Peripherals and Hubs

Traditional methods for adding components to a PC usually involved removing the case and at least a couple of system reboots. These legacy methods for upgrade were also limited by the very architecture of the PC: the limit of 16 interrupts, limited DMA channels, even limited bus speed. Typical users do not understand the various rules and procedures used to install typical PC components.

With this is mind, the *Universal Serial Bus (USB)* technology was created. It has actually been around for quite some time, but it did not become popular until Microsoft included USB support in Windows 95 Second Edition.

USB offers numerous advantages over traditional peripheral architecture. By design, you can install a USB device while a computer is running, and the device will be configured automatically (without requiring that the system be restarted). The configuration is usually done without having to open the case, configure the device to use available resources, or do much more then plug the device into a USB port (and maybe supply a driver disk).

Through the use of daisy-chaining and USB hubs, a single USB port can support (theoretically) 127 devices. The USB can also moves data much faster than traditional devices do—up to 12Mbps (megabits per second).

The only real concern you might have when installing a USB device is overloading the chain. While the specifications state that 127 devices can be connected, those devices will all be competing for that 12MBps bus, and performance will suffer. This is why most modern computers come with two USB ports—it helps to split the workload.

Upgrading the System BIOS

The system *BIOS (basic input/output system)* is software (usually stored on a ROM chip) that contains all of the code required to control the keyboard, display screen, disk drives, serial ports, and various other PC components. Basically, the BIOS determines what a computer can do without accessing any outside software.

Storing the BIOS on a ROM chip ensures that it will always be available and will not be damaged by disk failure. The problem with this is that ROM is usually much slower then RAM, so many systems copy the BIOS to RAM each time the computer boots (this is known as *shadowing*).

Since the BIOS determines what devices a computer can utilize before the operating system loads, there will be times when you might need to update the BIOS to support a new component. The most common reason to upgrade the BIOS is to support hard drives that are larger than the limit imposed by BIOS code. There are two ways to upgrade system BIOS: the old way and the new way.

The old way involves ordering a replacement BIOS chip, opening the computer, removing the old chip, and inserting the new one. In some ways, this is the least nerve-racking method of upgrading, but you must be careful not to bend or break the connectors on the BIOS chip.

Most modern computers store their BIOS on an *EPROM (Erasable Programmable Read Only Memory)*. An EPROM can be updated using flash software. In many ways, this method is more dangerous than the old-fashioned method of replacing a chip. Since the flash software overwrites the information on the chip, if you make a mistake, your computer can become unbootable. You will want to follow the instructions very carefully!

Most flash software packages include the ability to back up the current BIOS before flashing the chip. *ALWAYS* take advantage of this step before performing the flash process, EVEN IF YOU HAVE USED THE SOFTWARE BEFORE! Also, do not assume that because two computers are the same make and model and were purchased at the same time, you can use the same backup as protection against errors for both machines. Manufacturers are constantly revising BIOS software. Perform the backup for every computer that you update!

Installing the Case Cover

If everything is installed correctly, you should only have the case cover and case cover screws left to install. If you have other components left, you need to double-check your work. Go back and check to see that you haven't forgotten to install a component or mounting screw.

The above reminder ("Check to see that you haven't forgotten to install a component") may seem unnecessary on the face of it, but I know that a large number of you, like most auto mechanics, will never have a completely clean workspace to start with. You probably have bits and pieces of other jobs sitting on the table you're working on right now. It's easy to lose track of which ones go with the current job and which ones you're holding onto for another project. So *do* strive to keep all the parts for one project at a time localized to just one area of your workspace; that way, you'll be able to see easily whether you've finished the job or not.

When you are ready to install the case cover, position the computer on the work surface so that it won't move. Slide the case cover onto the computer so that it rests against its mounting tabs. Insert the mounting screws and tighten them so that the cover can't move. If the cover your computer uses has locking tabs, slide them into place so that the cover is secured.

Finally, hook up all the cables (keyboard, printer, power, and mouse) and make sure they are secured. When this is finished, you are ready to power up the computer. Turn on the computer and test your handiwork.

If it doesn't power up or work correctly, you will have to troubleshoot the problem. See the sidebar for a few tips to help minimize the chances of running into a problem.

If these tips don't work, check Part II, Chapter 19, "Software Troubleshooting," for more steps.

General Reassembly Tips

There are several things that you can do to make your reassembly go smoothly. While this is by no means a comprehensive list, it does outline the most common problems when reassembling a computer.

Read the Directions   This is by far the most commonly ignored task. Everyone assumes that they know how to do something and only reads the instructions when they have problems. Besides offering the necessary warnings and guidelines, most instructions also contain a "Frequently Asked Questions" (or FAQ) list that provides answers to the most commonly asked questions. By reading the instructions before you start, you can avoid the most common pitfalls.

Take Your Time   The majority of disassembly/reassembly problems are caused by rushing. Rushing an installation may cause you to break components or to drop tools, which will cost you even more time. If you take your time, you will avoid these problems. Don't ever expect to perform a job that will "just take 10 minutes."

Check Cables for Proper Orientation   A common problem when putting a computer back together is putting a cable on upside down (this frequently happens when installing cables for floppy drives). When this happens, the computer will get erroneous signals from the device. A rule of thumb for internal cables is to orient the cable so that the red wire is toward pin 1. A common indication that the floppy cable is on upside down is that the floppy light will be on constantly.

Make Sure All Connectors Are Secure   When installing any device, make sure that the connectors are secure. After installing a device, tug *lightly* on it to make sure that the connector isn't just sitting in the slot but is actually being grasped and held by it. If the connectors aren't secure, they can cause component failure or electrical shorts (which may destroy the component, the motherboard, or both).

Portable Computers

$\mathbf{T}$he maintenance of portable computers has its own set of rules to follow. Due to the complexity of their design, most manufacturers insist that all upgrades be performed at an authorized service center. Equipment such as LCD display screens, DC controllers, video boards, or processors are often unreachable in a laptop. Most field service will involve replacing hard drives, adding memory, configuring PCMCIA cards, or adding a battery to extend useable time.

For more information on portable computers, see Chapter 2, "PC Architecture."

The following list details the areas that are most likely to need field replacement on a portable computer.

Memory   To replace or add memory to a portable computer, you follow the same rules as adding memory to any other computer. You might, however, need to read the manual for directions. There are as many ways to access memory on portable computers as there are manufacturers.

PCMCIA cards   There are three types of PCMCIA cards: Type I, Type II, and Type III. PCMCIA controller software must be installed and running in order for PCMCIA cards to be initialized into the system. If the controller software is running, PCMCIA cards will load and configure automatically. (You might be asked for a drivers disk the first time a particular card is initialized.)

Hard drives   Many portable computers have an open bay that can be used to install an extra battery, CD-ROM drive, or hard disk. Read the documentation to determine the installation process for your brand of portable computer.

Mouse   Many people, myself included, dislike the glide pad for controlling mouse actions. Luckily, most of today's portable computers have a PS/2 mouse port available. Plugging in a PS/2 mouse will usually cause the system to automatically configure the port. If a system does not have a PS/2 port, you can always add a standard serial mouse and load the appropriate drivers.

Docking Stations

As portable computers become faster and more powerful, many individuals are replacing their desktop systems with them. Unfortunately, portables often have some distinct disadvantages when used as a desktop replacement: smaller keyboards, smaller screens, fewer ports (LPT, COM, SCSI, etc.). To overcome these limitations, many people use a docking station. Most of today's laptop computers will automatically sense when they are attached to a docking station and configure themselves appropriately. On older models, you might need to load special software or (in rare cases) change a configuration parameter and reboot the computer.

Summary

In this chapter, we concentrated on the physical aspects of PC maintenance and upgrade. We discussed taking the computer apart, adding or replacing components, the configuration of those components, and the system BIOS.

We started with a discussion of the proper ways to disassemble a computer—your work area, the tools you need, and the usual methods for removing major components.

We then moved to a discussion of installing or upgrading components. We used a sound card as a specific example, but the process is about the same for adding or replacing any component to a PC. The biggest piece of this section was the discussion of PC resources—memory addresses, I/O addresses, IRQs, and DMA channels. A thorough understanding of these concepts is necessary for both real-world troubleshooting and success on the exam.

Once we covered the theory of PC resources, we moved on to the physical act of configuring expansion boards. No book can cover every technique, but we covered the most common methods used to configure components—jumpers, DIP switches, software, and Plug-and-Play technology.

We ended with a look at the system BIOS—what it does, how it can be upgraded, and how to configure it.

Key Terms

Before you take the exam, be certain you are familiar with the following terms:

BIOS (basic input/output system)	legacy
Complementary Metal Oxide Semiconductor	memory address
Direct memory access	motherboard
Dynamic RAM (DRAM)	software driver
expansion card	static RAM (SRAM)
I/O (input/output) address	Universal Serial Bus (USB)
interrupt request	

Review Questions

1. Which of the following are the most important to consider when installing new expansion cards? (Select all that apply.)

   A. ESD effects

   B. Capacity of the hard disk

   C. Position of expansion cards

   D. Removing the cover

2. All of the following are factors to consider when removing a computer case cover except:

   A. If you do it too quickly, you may lose parts or damage something.

   B. You have to keep the reassembly process in mind as you take things apart.

   C. If you take short cuts, extra parts will appear and the computer may no longer function.

   D. The computer is not a complex machine, therefore it is easy to reassemble and disassemble whenever you have a problem.

3. During which disassembly step should you take notes?

   A. Removing the case

   B. Removing the expansion cards

   C. Removing the power supply

   D. Removing the disk drives

   E. Removing the motherboard

   F. All of the above

4. You have just installed a new floppy drive. Upon powering up the computer, you discover that the floppy drive isn't working properly. The floppy drive light remains on as long as the computer is powered up. What should you check first?

   A. If the floppy drive is in the wrong position on the floppy cable

   B. If the floppy cable is installed upside down

   C. If an incorrect ribbon cable is installed

   D. If the floppy cable is defective

5. What is the first step in installing a new device?

   A. Disassembling the computer

   B. Installing software

   C. Removing the case

   D. Reading the instructions

6. At this time, *legacy* could correctly be used to refer to which types of expansion cards?

   A. 8-bit

   B. ISA

   C. MCA

   D. All of the above

7. A computer work area should contain which of the following? (Select all that apply.)

   A. An oscilloscope

   B. Assorted tools

   C. Software

   D. Antistatic wrist strap

8. When preparing the work area, all of the following should be considered except:

   A. Having a small workspace available to do all the work that has to be done.

   B. That the work area must be flat.

   C. That the area must be sturdy.

   D. That the area must be well lit and clean.

9. What is the simplest method of testing a component?

   A. Software diagnostics

   B. Hardware diagnostics

   C. Placing a multimeter across the power junction

   D. Observing the component and seeing if it operates properly

10. Place the following options in order. The correct sequence in removing expansion cards is:

    1. Once the board is out, place it in an antistatic bag to help prevent ESD damage.

    2. Grasp the board by the top edge with both hands and rock it front to back.

    3. Remove any mounting screws that are holding the boards in place and place the screws somewhere where they won't be lost.

    4. Remove any internal or external cables or connectors.

    A. 4, 3, 2, 1

    B. 1, 2, 3, 4

    C. 2, 4, 3, 1

    D. 2, 3, 1, 4

11. In removing the power supply, all of the following steps should be performed except:

    A. Disconnect the power supply connectors from the internal devices.

    B. Remove the mounting hardware for the power supply.

    C. Do not remove the connectors from the system board as the computer cannot be powered on.

    D. Note the positions of and connections before removing any power connectors.

12. Before you install a new device in a functioning computer, you should:

    A. Disassemble the computer

    B. Determine the computer's available resources

    C. Install DOS

    D. Install MSD

13. The following steps are required in removing the motherboard except: (Select all that apply.)

    A. After removing the screws, remove the motherboard from the case because of ESD discharge.

    B. Remove the screws holding the motherboard to the mounting brackets.

    C. Slide the motherboard to the side to release the spacers from their mounting holes in the case.

    D. Ensuring that you are properly grounded, remove the motherboard and place in a static-free environment.

14. Which of the following is NOT a prerequisite to disassembling a computer?

    A. Disconnecting the power cable

    B. Shutting down the computer

    C. Disconnecting the monitor and keyboard cables

    D. Disassembling the power supply

15. The installation of a new replacement component follows all of these steps except:

    A. Determining the available resources

    B. Configuring the new devices

    C. Installing the component and its supporting software

    D. Turning on the computer and letting it run

16. In reassembling the computer, the first step to perform is to:

    A. Install the motherboard

    B. Install the disk drives

    C. Configure the CMOS

    D. Install the power supply

17. All of the following are key sequences to access the BIOS except:

    A. Shift + F1

    B. Ctrl+Shift+Esc

    C. Press the Del key

    D. Press the F5 key

18. All of the following are good reassembly aids except:

    A. Read the directions.

    B. Take your time.

    C. Check cables for proper orientation.

    D. Don't worry about the connections—once you plug them in they're secure.

19. Of all the helpful reassembly hints listed below, which is the most often overlooked?

    A. Read the directions.

    B. Take your time.

    C. Check cables for proper connections.

    D. Make sure all connectors are secure.

20. All of the following steps are performed in the installation and upgrade process except:

    A. Disassembly

    B. Inspection

    C. Reassembly

    D. Preparing the work area

Answers to Review Questions

1. A, C. Whenever you remove expansion cards, ESD effects should be foremost in your mind. Therefore, always remember your ESD wrist strap. Some busses will "remember" the slot a particular card was in. Therefore, if you will be replacing it (either with itself or a new card), you should write down which slot it came out of so that you can put the replacement in the same slot.

2. D. Of all the above factors, the only untrue one is that a computer is not a complex machine. It looks deceivingly simple, until you have to return all the parts to the machine.

3. F. You should take notes during each step of disassembly. One mistake can be fatal when putting the computer back together again. Documentation is the key to success.

4. B. If the floppy drive isn't working properly, the first thing to check is to see if the cable is installed upside down. The cable usually goes in one direction, and pin 1 should always be closest to the power supply.

5. D. Reading the instructions will give you all the necessary information about installing the software and hardware items that are a part of the device.

6. D. *Legacy* is generally used as a term to describe older technology. Therefore, legacy could correctly be used to refer to 8-bit, ISA, and MCA expansion cards.

7. B, D. A computer work area should contain assorted tools needed to perform the job and an antistatic wrist strap to prevent ESD.

8. A. The work area should be large enough to work on any computer. The work area should encompass all of the above criteria except option A.

9. D. As a backup, it is generally also a good idea to run some sort of software diagnostic to confirm that there is no conflict.

10. A. The correct sequence for removing the expansion cards is:

    1. Remove any internal or external cables or connectors.

    2. Remove any mounting screws that are holding the boards in place and place the screws somewhere where they won't be lost.

    3. Grasp the board by the top edge with both hands and rock it front to back.

    4. Once the board is out, place it in an antistatic bag to help prevent ESD damage.

11. C. In removing the power supply, it is also necessary to remove the connectors from the system board (and all disk drive connectors) so that the power supply can be removed.

12. B. Before you install a new device in a functioning computer, you should determine the computer's available resources so that when installing a new device you have the necessary resources to support the device.

13. A. After removing the screws you should never remove the motherboard from the case because of ESD discharge. If you need to remove the motherboard (due to a replacement or upgrade situation), it will be necessary to remove the original motherboard so that the new one may be installed.

14. D. The step that is NOT a prerequisite to disassembling a computer is disassembling the power supply. Only a service technician who has been specially trained to operate on power supplies should attempt to disassemble one. This is due to the fact that there are many components that can be fatally dangerous to an unknowing technician.

15. D. While you will have to turn the computer on and use it sooner or later, once you get to this point you have completed the installation process (and have moved to the testing and maintenance process).

16. A. The basic rule to remember when reassembling anything is to reverse the steps you took when you took it apart. If you removed the motherboard during the last step, the first step in reassembling the computer is to install the motherboard.

17. D. The BIOS can be activated by any key except the F5 key. Generally, upon booting, your computer will display the proper key sequence for accessing your computer's BIOS.

18. D. You should always check all your cable connections to make sure they are secure before putting on the cover. This prevents having to do the same thing twice.

19. A. Reading the directions is the step most overlooked when reassembling the computer, yet it is the most important because the directions tell you everything that is required for each device.

20. D. Preparing your work area should be done prior to the actual installation and upgrade process. This process includes disassembly, inspection, installation and upgrade, and reassembly.

Chapter 10

Troubleshooting Techniques

✓ **2.1 Identify common symptoms and problems associated with each module and how to troubleshoot and isolate the problems.**

Content may include the following:

- Processor/memory symptoms
- Mouse
- Floppy drive
- Parallel ports
- Hard drives
- CD-ROM
- DVD
- Sound card/audio
- Monitor/video
- Motherboards
- Modems
- BIOS
- USB
- NIC
- CMOS
- Power supply
- Slot covers
- POST audible/visual error codes
- Troubleshooting tools (e.g., multimeter)
- Large LBA, LBA
- Cables
- Keyboard
- Peripherals

✓ **2.2 Identify basic troubleshooting procedures and how to elicit problem symptoms from customers.**

> **Content may include the following:**

- Troubleshooting/isolation/problem determination procedures
- Determine whether hardware or software problem
- Gather information from user regarding; e.g.,
  - Customer environment
  - Symptoms/error codes
  - Situation when the problem occurred

✓ **5.2 Identify care and service techniques and common problems with primary printer types**

> **Content may include the following:**

- Feed and output
- Errors (printed or displayed)
- Paper jam
- Print quality
- Safety precautions
- Preventive maintenance

troubleshooting is the process of identifying a computer problem so that it can be fixed. Until you've had the opportunity to troubleshoot several computers with several different types of customers, the only way to gain the troubleshooting skills you will rely on as a certified technician is to learn from other people's experiences. In this chapter, I'll try to summarize for you some of the experience that my colleagues and I have gained over the course of our careers as service technicians, and I'll attempt to organize these experiences by providing you with guidelines and general tips for approaching the task of troubleshooting. This chapter will cover the following A+ troubleshooting topics in detail:

- Troubleshooting methodology
- Hardware troubleshooting
- Software troubleshooting
- Printer troubleshooting

For complete coverage of objective 2.1, please also see Chapters 1, 4, 6, and 8.

Pay special attention to the last section, "Printer Troubleshooting," because there are quite a few questions on the exam that deal with printer problems.

Troubleshooting Resources

Just as an artist has paintbrushes, paints, and a vision of how things should work together, a great troubleshooter has several tools to make their job easier. And, like the artist's brushes, palette, and vision, a technician's resources can be put into service to accomplish a complex goal: the identification of a problem.

Intellectual Resources

Most technicians actually relish computer problems, because they know it's a chance to find a solution and maybe to brag to their colleagues. It can feel almost like being the first to discover a star or a comet, although very seldom do you get to name a problem or its solution (like "The Roger Smith General Protection Fault Solution" or "The Dan Jones AUTOEXEC.BAT Conundrum"). Each time a technician solves a new problem, they know that if they ever run into that problem again, they'll be able to fix it easily (or at least have a starting point for troubleshooting).

The first major resource that you can use for troubleshooting a problem is your own brain. Your brain can hold lots of information. We remember almost everything we're exposed to. For this reason, the best troubleshooters are usually the people who have been exposed to the most problems. They have seen several different types of problems and their solutions. If they run into a particular problem, they may have seen it before and can quickly fix the problem.

Service documentation is another important intellectual resource, and we might point out that it's not used as often as it should be. As soon as a new product is released, several things are released at the same time (or very shortly thereafter). These include items like the owner's manual, the buyer's guide, and (most importantly) the service and replacement parts manuals. These books can be a valuable source of troubleshooting information. They can also contain replacement parts information, such as which part(s) should be replaced when a particular component is found to be bad. Also, they usually contain exploded diagrams of the model being repaired.

The Internet, of course, has become an extremely valuable resource for troubleshooting. Almost every technology company now has a Web site. One feature of most companies' Web sites is the "knowledge base" (many have a different name for this feature), an area that contains several pieces of information that can be very valuable to technicians working with its products. First of all, the knowledge base usually contains one or more *Frequently Asked Questions (FAQ)* files. The files are summaries of the questions that technical support technicians get and their answers. Second, this is a good place to look for reports of "bugs" that have been discovered or suspected in the company's products. You may have to go to the company's support page (or some similarly purposed section of the Web site) to ask your question directly or perform a search on the knowledge base or FAQ to determine if there's a specific question or problem that relates to your situation, but in many cases, a problem you're spending time trying to solve has already been solved by someone else and reported.

Yet another intellectual resource that is seldom used, except in the most difficult cases, is a coworker. If you don't have the knowledge to troubleshoot or repair the component, a coworker might. (The reason this is the most seldom used is that people hate to admit that they don't know something. But as the saying goes, "The beginning of wisdom is 'I don't know.'")

Hardware and Software Resources

In addition to the intangible resources, you have other items you can use to troubleshoot the computer. These items fall into two categories: hardware and software.

There are several hardware resources you can use in the troubleshooting process. First, you have your computer toolkit. When troubleshooting, though, the only tools you should really need from the toolkit are the ones for removing the case, because most troubleshooting is done with the computer on and "as is." After all, you need to see what's happening before you start making changes.

See Chapter 1, "Basic Computer Service Concepts," for more information on the tools used to service a computer.

Another example of a hardware resource is a *resource discovery expansion card*. These cards, when installed into any expansion slot, will tell you what resources are being used in the computer and will indicate any possible conflicts. Several companies make these cards.

Software Troubleshooting

This section deals with a canvas that the troubleshooting artist may have to paint often: software problems. More than half of all computer problems are software related. The problems usually don't stem from the software itself, but rather the interaction of that software with other software that may be running on that machine. However, before you can start troubleshooting, you must determine if the problem is hardware related or software related. In order to determine the source of a problem (hardware or software), you have a few things you can do to narrow it down:

1. **In DOS/Windows computers, boot the computer "clean."** Booting it "clean" means starting the computer with no software drivers loading. The only things that should be in the AUTOEXEC.BAT or CONFIG.SYS (the two DOS configuration files) are the necessary memory managers and settings to get the computer up and running. Leave out sound card, CD-ROM, network, and other device drivers. You can also boot "clean" by using a bootable floppy disk (see the sidebar "Making a Bootable Diskette"). If the computer functions normally, then the problem is usually software related, although it could be a hardware problem and the device driver just enabled the device, causing the conflict to show itself.

2. **Check the operating system error messages.** Every operating system has built-in error-detection routines. These routines are designed to intercept problems and notify the user. If there is a major problem, these routines will display an error message for the software or hardware component that caused the problem. For example, when you try to print to a printer connected to your primary parallel port (LPT1) and the system returns an error like "Error writing to device LPT1," that is more than likely a hardware-related problem because a hardware device was mentioned (or alluded to) in the error message.

3. **Uninstall and then reinstall the application that's having problems.** This ensures that you have the correct version of all the application's components and that there are no missing files that may be required by the application. (For example, many applications today are intelligent enough to tell you when they're missing a necessary file to complete an operation—perhaps a spell-checker's dictionary files, or a library of programming objects, or even a file created by a coworker but stored in the wrong place on the network. The solution to this problem is very simple: If the missing file is a program file, reinstall that program from the original disks. Or, if the file is a data file, restore the data file from a backup.)

If you are using Windows 2000, you can take advantage of a new set of features known as Intellimirror. Intellimirror and its associated tools can automatically maintain applications—replacing missing files, updating INI or Registry files, or doing a complete installation—automatically!

4. **Look for ways to repeat the problem.** If it is a phantom problem, ask the user to help you out by finding a way to repeat the problem or looking for some type of pattern to the problem.

5. **Make sure you are using the latest patches.** This is especially important with machines that are on a network; having a buggy *network client* (the software that communicates with the network server and network resources) can cause a host of strange application problems. Also, make sure that all the machines running on the network are using the latest bug fixes to the application itself. You should be able to obtain these by looking on the application company's Web site.

6. **Check the Internet.** This is related to the previous point. Often software publishers will post FAQs (Frequently Asked Questions) and have a searchable knowledge base on the Internet with useful resources for troubleshooting problems with their products.

7. **Compare and isolate.** It can be difficult to determine if an application problem is caused by the software or hardware. The best troubleshooting

tools in this case are the twins, comparison and isolation. Try comparing how the application behaves on the problem machine and on a machine that you know is working fine; then remove and/or replace hardware components from the two machines to eliminate possible causes and isolate the solution.

These indicators, along with your experience, should help you narrow the problem to either a hardware or software problem.

Making a Bootable Diskette

A DOS *bootable diskette* is a valuable tool for troubleshooting. The creation process is very simple. Insert a blank 1.44MB or 720KB diskette into your floppy drive and type the following at a DOS prompt:

FORMAT *A*: /S

(You can replace *A:* with the drive letter that represents your floppy drive.) The /S parameter instructs DOS to include the DOS "system files" on the floppy after formatting it. If the disk is already formatted, you can add the system files to a disk and make it bootable by typing the following at a DOS prompt:

SYS *A*:

When the computer is done, the "System Transferred" message will appear, telling you that the computer has finished making the disk bootable. This disk, when inserted before turning the computer on, will allow the computer to be booted because it contains the smallest portion of DOS necessary to start the computer.

Windows 9*x* offers several other ways of creating a bootable diskette using graphical tools.

DOS Troubleshooting

Troubleshooting DOS problems is a fundamental skill that most technicians get several chances to practice. Understanding and being able to modify the two main configuration files of DOS—AUTOEXEC.BAT and CONFIG.SYS—can solve most DOS problems.

These topics apply to both MS-DOS and PC-DOS versions.

The DOS Configuration Files: CONFIG.SYS and AUTOEXEC.BAT

DOS is a simple operating system. It requires very few system resources to operate. It is also simple to operate. Unless you've damaged or misplaced part of DOS itself, you just type the command you want the computer to execute, and it does it. Despite the fact that it can take a lot of study to familiarize yourself with *all* the commands that DOS has to offer, you don't need to know very many of them to take advantage of its most useful capabilities. For these reasons, it stands as the most popular operating system of all time.

DOS uses two main configuration files, CONFIG.SYS and AUTOEXEC.BAT. Each file is a simple ASCII text file that contains commands and variables that set up the user environment in DOS.

- The CONFIG.SYS file is the main configuration file that DOS uses and, as such, it can be the source of several problems with DOS. The problems that are normally experienced are things like insufficient conventional memory, incorrect drivers loading, and not enough file handles. The CONFIG.SYS also has a detailed role in the logical mapping of the PC's memory. It loads memory drivers (like EMM386.EXE and HIMEM.SYS) as well as specifying the location of the DOS files (with statements like DOS=HIGH, UMB). It can also load device drivers by using lines that start with a "DEVICE=" statement.

- The AUTOEXEC.BAT, on the other hand, is a special batch file that executes automatically at system startup. This configuration file establishes the user environment and loads system drivers. Because it's a batch file, you can add statements to it that can automatically start other programs.

If either file becomes damaged or corrupt (with incorrect entries), the best two tools you have are the REM statement and backup files.

REM Statements

Let's say that the PC we're working on is inconsistently locking up. Further, let's say that you have already determined that the problem is software related, because when you boot "clean" with a boot diskette, the computer functions normally. This would mean that one of the statements in the CONFIG.SYS or AUTOEXEC.BAT is causing the problem.

In order to solve the problem, you must remove (or change) the line that is causing the problem. However, first you must find the offending line. This can be accomplished through the use of *REM statements*. The REM command is short for *remark*; by placing it at the beginning of any command line, you ensure that DOS will skip that line when running the file. The initial purpose for the REM command was to insert remarks or comments into batch files, so that the programmer or curious user could annotate what was going on in different sections of the file without requiring the computer to "run" the comment. However, you can also use it to *remove* suspect commands one at a time in order to test the effect of booting with and without them. By editing both the CONFIG.SYS and AUTOEXEC.BAT and "REMming out" one command at a time (and rebooting between each change), you can progressively eliminate statements that might be the cause of the problem.

There is another way to "step" through the CONFIG.SYS and AUTOEXEC.BAT files to determine which line is causing the problem. During the boot process, press the F8 key when you see the words, "Starting MS-DOS." This will allow you to choose whether to execute a particular line in either of these files.

Let's take a look at a sample computer problem:

The computer is randomly locking up. The CONFIG.SYS and AUTOEXEC.BAT are as follows (the lines are numbered to facilitate our discussion here; the real files would not have the numbers):

CONFIG.SYS
```
1.DEVICE=C:\DOS\HIMEM.SYS
2.DEVICE=C:\DOS\EMM386.EXE
3.DOS=HIGH
4.FILES=40
5.BUFFERS=9,256
6.DEVICE=C:\SB16\DRV\CTSB16.SYS /UNIT=0
/BLASTER=A:220 I:5 D:1 H:5
7.DEVICE=C:\SB16\DRV\DRV\SBCD.SYS /D:MSCD001 /P:220
```

AUTOEXEC.BAT
```
1.@ECHO OFF
2.SET BLASTER=A220 I5 D1 T4
3.C:\DOS\MSCDEX.EXE /D:MSCD001
4.SET PATH=C:\DOS;C:\;C:\WINDOWS;C:\MOUSE
5.SET TEMP=C:\TEMP
6.C:\WINDOWS\SMARTDRV.EXE
```

When troubleshooting a software problem the first thing I always check is the non-DOS items in either configuration file. Lines 6 and 7 of the CONFIG.SYS and line 2 of the AUTOEXEC.BAT are from a recent sound card installation. To check if one of these drivers is the problem, always start by REMming out the non-DOS items. So, if you edit both the configuration files and REM out the non-DOS items, the CONFIG.SYS and AUTOEXEC.BAT will look like so:

CONFIG.SYS
```
1.DEVICE=C:\DOS\HIMEM.SYS
2.DEVICE=C:\DOS\EMM386.EXE
```

```
3.DOS=HIGH
4.FILES=40
5.BUFFERS=9,256
6.rem DEVICE=C:\SB16\DRV\CTSB16.SYS /UNIT=0
/BLASTER=A:220 I:5 D:1 H:5
7.rem DEVICE=C:\SB16\DRV\DRV\SBCD.SYS /D:MSCD001 /P:220
```

AUTOEXEC.BAT
```
1.@ECHO OFF
2.rem SET BLASTER=A220 I5 D1 T4
3.C:\DOS\MSCDEX.EXE /D:MSCD001
4.SET PATH=C:\DOS;C:\;C:\WINDOWS;C:\MOUSE
5.SET TEMP=C:\TEMP
6.C:\WINDOWS\SMARTDRV.EXE
```

If the computer boots and operates normally with this configuration, you can assume that the problem was related to one of the non-DOS entries—that is, a driver for a peripheral (if not the peripheral itself). It should be noted that REM-ming out the statements (as we did above) would cause the devices that the statements were intended to configure to not function at all. This is not a failure, but simply the way computers work.

Sherlock Holmes said it best: "When you have eliminated the impossible, whatever remains, no matter how improbable, must be the truth." In our example, the only device drivers were for the sound card, so it's probable that the sound card was configured improperly. If you had multiple device drivers in the configuration files, you would have to test each possibility separately to find out. Troubleshooting with REM statements is a process of elimination. One by one, you must eliminate the impossible, so that you can find the improbable.

Backups

Whenever you install drivers for a hardware device, the installation program will ask you if you want it to modify the CONFIG.SYS and AUTOEXEC.BAT for you or if you would like to modify the files yourself. When the installation program modifies these files, it makes duplicates, or *backups*, of them just in case the drivers it installs cause problems. That way, if there *is* a problem, you can reboot using the backup files instead of the ones modified during the installation process.

To reboot using the backup files, first you need to rename the new CONFIG.SYS and AUTOEXEC.BAT (to anything other than those names). A good way to keep track of them is to replace the SYS and BAT filename extensions with your initials. Then you need to rename (to CONFIG.SYS and AUTOEXEC.BAT, of course) the backups that the installation process created.

Of course, before you can rename your backups to CONFIG.SYS and AUTOEXEC.BAT as directed above, you have to find them. Installation programs usually name the backup file for the CONFIG.SYS with a name like CONFIG.BAK or CONFIG.OLD, or, if you already have files with those names, by providing a numbered filename extension, like CONFIG.001 or CONFIG.002, etc. Similarly, they rename the backup file for the AUTOEXEC.BAT with a BAK, OLD, or numbered filename extension.

Since it's possible that over a matter of months a system will contain numerous backups from different installations, it can be very helpful to view the list of files according to date (in some listings this is given by clicking on the option named "Last Modified") to make it easy to find the most recently changed files—i.e., the configuration files created and modified by the problem installation.

Windows Troubleshooting

Windows problems are the most troublesome of all software-related problems, mainly because there are several components working together in Windows. If any of these components develops a problem or corruption, it can bring Windows to a screeching halt. There are three primary areas you can check for finding troubleshooting information in Windows: system resources, General Protection Faults, and the Windows configuration files.

These topics apply to Windows 3.1, Windows 3.11, and Windows 95/98.

System Resources

When Windows runs out of memory, hard disk space, or both, we say it has run out of *system resources*. Windows 3.1 has an About window (in the Windows Program Manager screen, select Help ➤ About) that can be used to check the amount of available system resources (see Figure 10.1). For optimal Windows performance, the available system resources should be above 80 percent. If they are below 80 percent you will need to add RAM, disk space, or both.

FIGURE 10.1 Windows 3.1 system resources

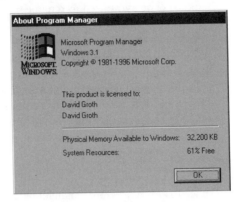

You can check the system resources in Windows 95/98 by using the Resource Meter (select Start ➤ Programs ➤ Accessories ➤ System Tools, if you have installed the Microsoft Plus! pack). The resource meter will show up as a small bar graph on your Taskbar at the bottom of the screen. If you double-click the bar graph, it will bring up a screen that shows the available system resources (similar to the Windows 3.1 statistics). Figure 10.2 shows this window.

FIGURE 10.2 Checking Windows 95 system resources

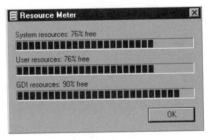

General Protection Faults

A misbehaving Windows program may overstep its bounds and try to take memory from another application. When it does this, Windows will halt the misbehaving program and display an error called a *General Protection Fault (GPF)*. This type of error is one of the most common Windows errors as well as the most frustrating. Such errors are generally the result of nonstandard programming. The programmer took shortcuts in their programming and left out the "safety nets" that would prevent a program from taking memory away from another, running program.

There is no way to make a system 100 percent GPF-free. You can, however, reduce the number of GPFs that occur by taking a couple of precautions. First of all, monitor your system resources carefully. When Windows starts running out of available memory, it means the programs that are running are tightly packed in memory. In a system with only a little space available, the likelihood is relatively great that a program will use another program's memory when it goes looking for more memory, and thus cause a GPF. (By way of comparison, when a program tries to take more memory in a system that has *plenty* of available memory, the chances are good that it will find memory that is *not* being used by some other program.) This underscores the guideline, "You can never have enough closet space or RAM."

Second, exercise some discipline: use only the "released" versions of software—the retail version, the one available commercially. Software goes through three major steps of development: Alpha, Beta, and Release. In the Alpha release, the program is intended only for testing within the software company itself, and it may not include all the features that are intended to be included in the eventual release. Also, the software at this stage will still have many errors (called "bugs") that need to be worked out. The Beta release includes all the features that will be included in the Release version, as well as the installation program (often missing in the Alpha version), and is ready for consumer testing. The features may have changed significantly between Alpha and Beta, based on the feedback generated in-house by the Alpha testers and management. There may be numerous Alpha cycles before the software is ready for outside (i.e., Beta) testing; and Betas themselves frequently undergo numerous "builds" during a Beta cycle, as platform issues and bugs are found and addressed. By the final Beta, although some of the "loose ends" may need to be tightened up, the software is basically ready. When the software is released commercially ("Final Release"), the developers consider it to be more-or-less "bug-free." There may be a few, minor bugs that crop up after the initial release, but the software will be stable for use.

NEVER use Alpha or Beta software on your computer. These software programs *are* buggy and *will* cause problems, as well as GPFs.

There are two ways of fixing the bugs that do appear after the initial release of the software. You can either use a "patch" (a type of software "Band-Aid" to fix the problem until the next release) on the software or wait until the next release of the software. Which brings us to our next tip: Try to avoid version 1.0 of any piece of software. Because this version is the first release, it will usually contain the most bugs. Wait until the software has been released for a few months and has gone through a few revisions before buying it and installing it on your computer. By Revision 1.2, most of the bugs have been worked out and the software can be considered stable.

How to Read the Version Numbers on Software

When reading the version number of most software titles, you can deduce a few things by the version number. The leftmost number in a version number indicates the major release version. Each major release introduces several new features and may completely change the way the software operates.

The first number to the right of the decimal point is the *revision number*. When a single feature (or small set of features) needs to be introduced, along with several bug fixes, a new revision of the software is released. Revision numbers increment until the software developers decide to release another major release.

Any numbers to the right of the revision number can be considered patch levels. When software is released with a second number to the right of a decimal point, it usually means that it is a bug-fix only. No new features would be released in this version.

For example, let's examine the following revision number: FURBLE 1.24. This would indicate that the software contains all the features of the first major release of the FURBLE program and is the second revision of that release and the fourth patch at that level. This software should therefore be quite stable by this stage.

It also should be noted that some vendors (mainly Microsoft) have abandoned this convention in favor of naming the software with the year it was released (i.e., Windows 95, Office 97, etc.). However, production schedules fall behind and sometimes software is released the following year.

Windows Configuration

When Windows 3.*x* programs are installed, their files are copied to the hard disk and entries are made into the Windows configuration files: the INI files and the System Registry. The entries that are made into these files control various settings and tell the program (or Windows itself) how to operate. Let's discuss each of them.

INI Files

Primarily used for Windows 3.*x* programs, *INI files* (short for initialization files) are made for each program as well as for Windows. When a new application is installed, the installation program will create an INI file that contains the new application's settings. INI files are text files that can be edited with any text editor if necessary.

The three primary INI files that Windows uses are: SYSTEM.INI, WIN.INI, and PROGMAN.INI. Each of them should be backed up before changes are made. The SYSTEM.INI has settings for the drivers that Windows uses. It is probably the most critical of the three. Changes made to this file affect Windows' resource usage as well as resource availability.

The WIN.INI controls the Windows operating environment. There are entries for the programs that Windows starts automatically, screensaver settings, desktop color schemes, wallpaper, and system compatibility information. Changes made to this file can be critical (your screen might come up in a different color, for example), and you should take care when modifying the [Compatibility] section, as that could cause problems with programs designed to run under older versions of Windows.

Finally, the PROGMAN.INI contains settings for the Program Manager. The settings control the number and file names of the program groups in the Program Manager. Changing these settings modifies which program groups appear in the Program Manager. You can also control Program Manager security (such as what menu options appear or are grayed out in the Program Manager) by modifying the [Restriction] section.

If you delete the INI file of some programs, they will create a new one with the default settings.

A problem can be tracked to an INI file if a setting was made in a Windows 3.1 program and now the program doesn't function properly or if it "GPFs" frequently. To solve this type of problem it is best to rename an old INI file to replace the corrupt one (like WINWORD.OLD to WINWORD.INI). Just like with DOS installation programs, Windows setup programs make backups of the configuration files they change and name them with .BAK or .OLD extensions or with number extensions (.001, .002, etc.). If you have a problem with a new INI file, you can rename one of the backups (preferably the most recent one) to the .INI extension to make *it* the active INI file.

The Registry

With the introduction of Windows 95, Microsoft did away with the practice of using several INI files to contain program configuration information. They introduced a special database called the *Registry* to provide a single common location for all configuration and program setting information. Every Windows 95/98 program, upon installation, will "register" itself so that Windows 95/98 knows about it. When other programs need information about what printers and devices are available in Windows 95/98, they query the Registry to get this information.

The Registry can be viewed and edited with REGEDIT.EXE. When you run this program, it presents the view shown in Figure 10.3. Each folder represents a section or "key" that contains specific information. It is within these keys that the settings for the Windows programs are kept.

FIGURE 10.3 Viewing the Registry with REGEDIT.EXE

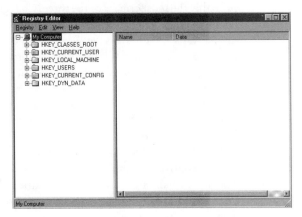

Generally speaking, you should not make changes to the Registry. Registry changes can be exceedingly complex and are not covered on the A+ core exam, so we won't devote any more space to it here.

Hardware Troubleshooting

When you're troubleshooting hardware, there are a few common problems that any experienced technician should know about. These common problems usually have simple solutions. Knowing these problems (and their respective solutions) will make you a more efficient troubleshooter.

POST Routines

The first item we're going to discuss isn't really a hardware problem, but a hardware troubleshooting aid. Every computer has a diagnostic program built into its BIOS called the *power on self-test (POST)*. When you turn on the computer, it executes this set of diagnostics. These tests go by pretty quickly, so we'll detail them here.

The POST described below is typical of IBM-brand PCs; other manufacturers have similar POSTs, but they may differ in certain aspects.

1. **The processor is tested.** POST runs checks on the CPU. If the tests fail, the system stops with no error message (usually).

2. **The ROMs are checked.** POST computes a checksum for the BIOS ROMs. If the checksums do not match, the system halts with no error message.

3. **The DMA controller is tested.** Again, if there are problems, the system halts.

4. **The Interrupt controller is checked.** If there is a problem with this component, the system will give a long beep, then a short beep, then the system will stop.

5. **The system timing chip is tested.** This is not the chip that tells time, but rather the chip that provides timing signals for the bus and processor. If this chip fails, the system will give a long beep, then a short beep, then halt.

6. **The BASIC ROMs are tested (if they exist).** Most computers since the IBM AT have not included BASIC, so this step is usually not part of their POST routines. However, on older computers, if the BASIC ROMs fail the POST test, it does another long beep, then a short beep, and then halts.

7. **The video card is checked.** At this point the system runs the diagnostics for the video card. If it fails, the system issues one long beep and two short beeps and halts. If successful, the video ROM BIOS is copied into RAM and you will usually see a message about the type of video card that the computer is using.

8. **Expansion boards are initialized.** During this part of the POST routine, any expansion boards that need to can initialize and copy their ROMs into upper memory, if necessary.

9. **RAM is counted and tested.** The system tests and counts all RAM that's installed in the machine by writing a bit to each bit of memory. If a 1 is written and read back successfully, the counter increments. A failure during this portion of the POST will generate a "201 — Memory Error" message on the screen. (Here's a free tip for you: Any POST error numbers starting with 2 are memory-related errors.)

10. **The keyboard is tested.** The keyboard controller is contacted and signals are sent to detect the presence of a keyboard. Checks for stuck keys are also made. If this test fails, a "301 — Keyboard Failure" error is generated along with a short beep. Some systems may halt, others may not. (Some systems also ask you to press the F1 key, which is kind of silly if the keyboard isn't working, huh?)

11. **The cassette interface is checked.** This is another POST routine only valid on IBM PCs and XTs. If the cassette interface doesn't work, a "131 — Cassette Interface" error is generated. The system does not halt.

12. **Test floppy drives.** The floppy disk adapter is contacted and asked to activate the drive motors of any floppy disks, in order (A:, then B:). If there are problems, a "601 — Floppy Disk" error is generated and the system will try to load cassette BASIC (if it's present, on an IBM PC or XT).

13. **Check resources and boot the computer.** The POST routine queries any remaining devices (LPT ports, serial ports, etc.), makes a short beep, and then queries the disk drives looking for an operating system. If one is found on either a floppy drive or hard disk, it is loaded and the computer is functional. If an operating system can't be found, most systems will issue an "Operating system not found" error (or something to that effect).

The POST routines are a great tool for troubleshooting. They will usually give English descriptions of any problems that they find. Some BIOS POST routines may actually give suggestions on how to fix the problem (don't expect this kind of friendliness on an IBM AT, though; it only gives cryptic error codes). Tables 10.1 and 10.2 summarize the POST beep and error codes, respectively, most often seen on computers today.

TABLE 10.1   Common POST Beep Codes

Beep Code	Problem
No Beep, system dead	Power supply bad, system not plugged in, or power not turned on
Continuous beeps	Power supply bad, not plugged into motherboard correctly, or keyboard stuck
Repeating short beep	Power supply problem
1 short beep, nothing on screen	Video card failure
1 short beep, video present, but system won't boot	Bad floppy drive, cable, or controller
2 short beeps	Configuration error (on most PS/2 systems)
1 long, 1 short	System board bad
1 long, 2 short	Video card failure

TABLE 10.2   Common POST Error Codes

Error Number	Explanation
1**	Any number starting with 1 usually indicates a system board problem.
161	CMOS battery failure.

TABLE 10.2 Common POST Error Codes *(continued)*

Error Number	Explanation
164	Memory size error. Always happens after memory has been added. Running the BIOS setup program will allow the system to recognize the memory and the error should go away.
2**	Any number starting with 2 usually indicates a memory-related problem.
201	Memory test failed. One or more portions of RAM were found to be bad. Any numbers following this error code may indicate which RAM chip is bad. See the computer's documentation for information on interpreting those codes.
3**	Any error number starting with 3 usually indicates a problem with the keyboard. Problems include a missing or malfunctioning keyboard, as well as stuck keys.
301	Keyboard error. Usually means a missing or malfunctioning keyboard or a key has been pressed too long during startup (are you resting your hand on the keyboard? is something leaning against one of the keys?). Also happens if a key remains depressed during the POST keyboard test.
4**	Monochrome video problems.
5**	Color video problems.
6**	Floppy disk system problems.
601	Floppy disk error. Either the floppy adapter or the floppy drive failed. Check to see that the floppy cable isn't on upside down and that the power to the floppy drive(s) is hooked up correctly.
17**	Hard disk problems. The hard disk geometry might not be set correctly or the disk adapter can't communicate with the hard disk.
1780	Drive 0 (C:) drive failure. The C: drive or controller isn't functioning. The disk might not be configured or the adapter isn't installed correctly.
1781	Drive 1 (D:) drive failure. The D: drive or controller isn't functioning. The disk might not be configured or the adapter isn't installed correctly.

Motherboard Problems

The motherboard's (or logic board's) functions are tested, for the most part, by the POST routines. The 1** errors and beep codes during startup indicate the biggest problems. So there are very few problems that don't show up in the POST. The occasional "phantom" problem does happen, however.

One problem becomes visible when the system constantly loses its clock. The time will reset to 12:00 on 12/01/83, for example. At the same time, you may start seeing "1780 — Hard Disk Failure" problems. When you try to reset the time, it will set correctly. But as soon as you turn off the computer and turn it back on, the time has been lost.

These symptoms indicate that the system's CMOS is losing the time, date, and hard disk settings (as well as several other system settings). The CMOS is able to keep this information when the system is shut off because there is a small battery powering this memory. Because it is a battery, it will eventually lose power and go dead.

 Some systems use a special chip called a "Dallas chip" to provide the same functionality as the CMOS, but, like the CMOS, it too will "die" eventually.

When the CMOS battery (or Dallas chip) is replaced, the system settings must be reset. But they will be retained when the power is shut off. Some people immediately think "system board problem" when the answer is a cheap little battery and 10 minutes of labor. Because of the simplicity of this repair, most service professionals replace these batteries as a courtesy service for their customers. Consider it an "outpatient" repair.

Hard Disk System Problems

Hard disk system problems usually stem from one of three causes:

- The adapter is bad.
- The disk is bad.
- The adapter and disk are connected incorrectly.

The first and last causes are easy to identify, because in either case the symptom will be obvious: the drive won't work. You simply won't be able to get the computer to communicate with the disk drive. (You can further narrow it down as to whether it's a configuration problem or not by checking to see if the drive is connected correctly. If it is, then the problem is usually a bad or misconfigured disk adapter.)

However, if the problem is a bad disk drive, the symptoms aren't as obvious. As long as the BIOS POST tests can communicate with the disk drive, they are usually satisfied. But the POST tests may not uncover problems related to storing information. For example, even with healthy POST results, you may find that you're permitted to save information to a bad disk, but of course when you try to read it back you get errors. Or the computer may not boot as quickly as it used to because the disk drive can't read the boot information successfully every time. Bad disk drives could be the cause of the problems in both of these examples, but neither one of them would be indicated by a POST test. Keep in mind, then, that a successful POST test doesn't necessarily mean a "happy" computer.

In some cases, reformatting the drive can solve the problems described in the preceding paragraph. In other cases, reformatting only brings the drive back to life for a short while. The bottom line is that read and write problems usually indicate that the drive is "going south" and should be replaced soon. Never expect a "Band-Aid"-type repair like reformatting to cover a "major trauma" problem like disk failure.

Never low-level format IDE or SCSI drives! They are low-leveled from the factory and you may cause problems by using low-level utilities on these types of drives.

Peripheral Problems

The biggest set of peripheral problems are those related to modem communications. The symptoms of these problems include the following:

- The modem won't dial.
- The modem keeps hanging up in the middle of the communications session.
- The modem spits out strange characters to the terminal screen.

If the modem won't dial, first check that it has been configured correctly, including its IRQ setting (as discussed in Chapter 6, "Peripheral Devices"). If the configuration is correct, then the problem usually has to do with *initialization commands*. These are the commands sent to the modem by the communications program to "initialize" it. These commands tell it things like how many rings to wait before answering, how long to wait between when the last keystroke was detected for it to disconnect, and at what speed to communicate.

For a while, each manufacturer had its own set of commands, and every communications program had to have settings for every particular kind of modem available. In particular, every program had commands for the Hayes line of modems (mainly because Hayes made good modems and their command language was fairly easy to program). Eventually, other modem manufacturers began using the "Hayes-compatible" command set. This set of modem initialization commands became known as the "Hayes command set." It is also known as the "AT command set," since each Hayes modem command started with the letters *AT* (presumably calling the modem to ATtention).

Each AT command does something different. The letters *AT* by themselves (when issued as a command) will ask the modem if it's ready to receive commands. If it returns "OK," that means that the modem is ready to communicate. If you receive "error," it means there is an internal modem problem that may need to be resolved before communication can take place.

Table 10.3 lists a few of the most common AT commands, their functions, and the problems that they can solve. These commands can be sent to the modem by opening a terminal program (such as the Windows Terminal or HyperTerminal [supplied with Windows 3.*x* and Windows 95, respectively], WINTERM.EXE, or ProCOMM) and typing them in. All commands should return "OK" if they were successful.

If you can't type anything, you either don't have the right COM port selected for the modem or you have half-duplex mode enabled. To address this problem, you must enter "ATF1," then press Enter. The modem should return the message "OK" and you will now be able to see your commands.

TABLE 10.3 Common AT Commands

Command	Function	Usage
AT	Tells the modem that what follows the letters "AT" is a command that should be interpreted.	Used to precede most commands.
ATDT *nnnnnnn*	Dials the number *nnnnnnn* as a tone-dialed number.	Used to dial the number of another modem if the phone line is set up for tone dialing.
ATDP *nnnnnnn*	Dials the number *nnnnnnn* as a pulse-dialed number.	Used to dial the number of another modem if the phone line is set up for rotary dialing.
ATA	Answers an incoming call manually.	Places the line off-hook and starts to negotiate communication with the modem on the other end.
ATH0 (or +++ and then ATH0)	Tells modem to hang up immediately.	Places the line on-hook and stops communication. (Note: The "0" in this command is a zero, not the letter *O*.)

T A B L E 1 0 . 3 Common AT Commands *(continued)*

Command	Function	Usage
AT&F	Resets modem to factory default settings.	This setting works as the initialization string when others don't. If you have problems with modems hanging up in the middle of a session, or failing to establish connections, use this string by itself to initialize the modem.
ATZ	Resets modem to power-up defaults.	Almost as good as AT&F, but may not work if power-up defaults have been changed with S-registers.
ATS0-*n*	Waits *n* rings before answering a call.	Sets the default number of rings that the modem will detect before taking the modem off-hook and negotiating a connection. (Note: The "0" in this command is a zero, not the letter *O*.)
ATS6-*n*	Waits *n* seconds for a dial tone before dialing.	If the phone line is slow to give a dial tone, you may have to set this register to a number higher than 2.
","	Pauses briefly.	When placed in a string of AT commands, the comma will cause a pause to occur. Used to separate the number for an outside line (many businesses use 9 to connect to an outside line) and the real phone number (e.g., 9,555-1234).
*70 or 1170	Turns off call waiting.	The "click" you hear when you have "call waiting" (a feature offered by the phone company) will interrupt modem communication and cause the connection to be lost. To disable call waiting for a modem call, place these commands in the dialing string like so: *70,555-1234. Call waiting will resume after the call is hung up.

TABLE 10.3 Common AT Commands *(continued)*

Command	Function	Usage
CONNECT	Displayed when a successful connection has been made.	You may have to wait some time before this message is displayed. If this message is not displayed, it means the modem couldn't negotiate a connection with the modem on the other end of the line, due possibly to line noise.
BUSY	Displayed when the number dialed is busy.	If displayed, some programs will wait a certain amount of time and try again to dial.
RING	Displayed when the modem has detected a ringing line.	When someone is calling your modem, the modem will display this in the communications program. You would type "ATA" to answer the call.

If two computers can connect, but they both receive garbage to their screens, it's a good chance that both computers aren't agreeing on the communications settings. Settings like data bits, parity, stop bits, and compression must all agree in order for communication to take place. When both computers have different settings it's a lot like two people from different countries trying to communicate. They can meet and shake hands, but from there they can't communicate, because they are both speaking different languages.

Keyboard and Mouse Problems

Keyboards are simple devices. Therefore, they either work or they don't. There are rarely any "phantom" problems with keyboards. Usually, keyboard problems are environmental. They get dirty and the keys start to stick. This problem is easily avoided: DON'T EAT OR DRINK NEAR THE COMPUTER. It is my personal opinion that anyone who drinks near a computer keyboard should be made to clean one that has had a soft drink spilled in it. That person will never drink near a keyboard again. The liquid works its way into the plungers under the key caps, and, instead of drying, turns into a sticky, syrupy substance that doesn't easily wash away.

To clean a keyboard, it's best to use the keyboard cleaner sold by electronics supply stores. This cleaner foams up quickly and doesn't leave a residue behind. Spray it liberally on the keyboard and keys. Work the cleaner in between the keys with a stiff toothbrush. Blow the excess away with a strong blast of compressed air. Repeat until the keyboard functions properly. If you do have to clean a keyboard that's had a soft drink spilled on it, remove the key caps before you perform the cleaning procedure. It makes it easier to reach the sticky plungers.

A friend of mine told me about his way of cleaning keyboards: Remove the electronics and then place the keyboard in a dishwasher in the rinse cycle! Then, let them air dry. I wouldn't recommend this for some of the newer, capacitive keyboards. However, this will actually work for the older keyswitch keyboards (as long as the water isn't hard enough to leave residue inside the key switches or hot enough to melt the keys). Jet-Dry, anyone? My friend actually had a part-time business—PM PM (Preventative Maintenance at night) and offered keyboard cleanup services for $20 each! (In the late '70s this was easy money!)

With mechanical keyboards, you can de-solder a broken key switch and replace it. However, most of the time, the labor to replace one key is more expensive than a new keyboard. New keyboards can be had for less than 50 bucks, so keep the one with the single malfunctioning key as a spare and replace it with a new one.

To clean the key caps on a keyboard, spray keyboard cleaner on a soft, lint-free cloth and rub it briskly onto the surface of each key. Be careful not to rub too hard; some of the cheaper keyboards use decals on their keys and you might rub them right off!

Display System Problems

Two types of video problems: no video and bad video. No video means that there is no image on the screen when the computer is powered up. Bad video means that the quality is substandard for the type of display system being used.

No Video

Any number of things can cause a blank screen. The first two are the most common: either the power is off or the contrast or brightness is turned down. It's surprising how many people get stuck on that first one. I've gotten panicked phone calls (some even from experienced technicians) that go like this: "I can't get the monitor working!" or "I don't get any video on my screen!" Usually the technicians tell me they've even checked the video card's ROM address and changed it a couple of times just to be sure. I love this part.

> Me: "Is it turned on?"

> Them: (long pause) "Oh. Never mind." <click>

Or, if they verify that it's turned on:

> Me: "Are the brightness and contrast turned down?"

> Them: "Where do I check that?"

Me: "Can you see the knobs or buttons that have a picture of a sun on one and a picture of a circle with half dark and half light on the other?"

Them: "Found 'em. Now what?"

Me: "Turn them one direction and then the other, and see if the screen gets brighter."

Them: "Okay....Oh! Wow! Cool!...Sorry about that."

If they really did check the power as well as the brightness and contrast settings, then it's either a bad video card or blown monitor. An easy way to determine which is to turn on the computer and monitor, then touch the monitor screen. The high voltage used to charge the monitor will leave a static charge on a working monitor, and it's a charge that can be felt. If there's no charge, there's a good chance the flyback transformer has blown and the monitor needs to be repaired. If there is a charge, the video card or cable are suspect.

This charge drains away fairly quickly after power-up, so this test only works immediately after power-up. Also, it's not a conclusive test, but it gives a good indication.

Be VERY careful when working with monitors! Monitors contain capacitors that store a charge used when starting up. The power in the capacitor dissipates fairly quickly, but if the timing is right (or wrong) you could end up with a nasty shock!

Bad Video

You may have seen a monitor that has a bad data cable. This is the monitor nobody wants; everything has a blue (or red, or green) tint to it, and it gives everyone a headache. This monitor could also have a bad gun, but more often than not, the problem goes away if you wiggle the cable (indicating a bad cable).

You may have also seen monitors that are out of adjustment. Their pictures don't fill the screen (size adjustment), the images "roll" (vertical or horizontal hold), or they are distorted (angle and pincushion adjustments). With most new monitors this is an easy problem to fix. Old monitors had to be partially disassembled to change these settings. New monitors have push-button control panels for changing these settings.

The earth generates a very strong magnetic field. This magnetic field can cause swirls and fuzziness even in high-quality monitors. Most monitors have metal shields that can shield against magnetic fields. But eventually these shields can get "polluted" by taking on the same magnetic field as the earth, and the shield becomes useless. To solve this problem, these monitors have a built-in feature known as the "degauss" feature. This feature removes the effects of the magnetic field by creating a stronger magnetic field with opposite polarity that gradually fades to a field of zero. A special "degauss" button activates it. It only needs to be pressed when the picture starts to deteriorate. The image will shake momentarily during the degauss cycle, then return to normal.

> The degauss feature should not be used every day. Once a month is usually sufficient if you are having color or clarity problems that get worse with time. You would only have to degauss every day if you lived in a place where high magnetic fields are a problem. If that's the situation you find yourself in, you might need to purchase a special, heavily shielded monitor for those conditions.

Floppy Drive Problems

Today the floppy drive is almost unnecessary—most applications, hardware drivers, and utilities ship on CD-ROMs. Besides, most of the things we want to back up and carry away are too large for the traditional floppy media (thus the proliferation of Zip, Jazz, and other removable media storage devices). Even so, the floppy is still a mainstay of the PC—and when you need it, it had better work!

Most floppy "drive" problems result from bad media. For some reason, people will not admit that a 10-cent floppy disk can (and will) go bad over time. Personally, I do not use a floppy disk more than twice—once to write to it and once to read from it. (Of course, being a computer geek, I've got other options for long-term storage.) Your first troubleshooting technique with floppy drive issues should be to try a new disk.

One of the most common problems that develop with floppy drives is misaligned read/write heads. The symptoms are fairly easy to recognize—you can read and write to a floppy on one machine but not on any others. This is usually caused by the mechanical arm in the floppy drive becoming misaligned so that the format it creates is not properly positioned on the disk (thus preventing other floppy drives from reading it).

There are numerous commercial tools available to realign floppy drive read/write heads. They use a floppy drive that has been preformatted to reposition the mechanical arm. In most cases, though, this fix is temporary—the arm will just move out of place again fairly soon. Given the inexpensive nature of the problem, the best solution is to spend a few dollars and replace the drive.

Sound Card Problems

Sound cards are traditionally one of the most problem-ridden components in a PC. They demand a lot of PC resources and are notorious for being very inflexible in their configuration. The most common sound card–related problems will involve resource conflicts (IRQ, DMA, or I/O address).

Luckily, most sound card vendors are quite aware of the problems and ship very good diagnostic utilities to help resolve them. Use your PC troubleshooting skills to determine the conflict, and then reconfigure until you have found an acceptable set of resources that are not in use.

BIOS Issues

Computer BIOSs don't really go bad; they just become out of date. This is not necessary a critical issue—they will continue to support the hardware that came with the box. It *does*, however, become an issue when the BIOS doesn't support some component that you would like to install—a larger hard drive, for instance.

Most of today's BIOSs are written to a Flash EPROM and can be updated through the use of software. Each manufacturer has its own method for accomplishing this. Check out the documentation for complete details.

One warning: If you make a mistake in the upgrade process, the computer can become unbootable. If this happens, your only option often is shipping the box to a manufacturer-approved service center! BE CAREFUL!

Power Supply Problems

Power supply problems are usually easy to troubleshoot—nothing happens when you flip the switch! When that happens (and it will), open the case, remove the power supply, and replace it with a new one. No one "services" power supplies anymore; replacement is so much cheaper and easier!

Be aware that different cases have different types of on/off switches. The process of replacing a power supply is a lot easier if you purchase a replacement with the same mechanism. Even so, remember to document exactly how the power supply was connected to the on/off switch. (I've spent hours trying various combinations of connections trying to get the on/off switch to work!)

Miscellaneous Problems

There are a couple of problems that really don't fit well into any category but "Miscellaneous." So, we'll cover them here.

Dislodged Chips and Cards

The inside of your computer is a fairly harsh environment. The temperature inside the case of some Pentium computers is well over 100°F! When you turn your computer on, it heats up. Turn it off, it cools down. After several hundred cycles of this, some components can't handle the stress and start to move out of their sockets. This phenomenon is known as "chip creep" and can really be frustrating.

Chip creep can affect any socketed device, including ICs, RAM chips, and expansion cards. The solution to chip creep is simple. Open the case and reseat the devices. It's surprising how often this is the solution to "phantom" problems of all sorts.

Environmental Problems

I'll never forget the time I had to work on a computer that had been used on the manufacturing floor of a large equipment manufacturer. The computer and keyboard were covered with a black substance that would not come off. (I later found out it was a combination of paint mist and molybdenum grease.) There was so much diesel fume residue in the power supply fan that it would barely turn. Also, the insides and components were covered with a thin, greasy layer of "muck." To top it all off, it *smelled terrible*!

Despite all this, the computer still functioned. However, it was prone to reboot itself every now and again. The solution was (as you may have guessed by now) to clean every component thoroughly and replace the power supply. The "muck" on the components was actually able to conduct a small current. Sometimes that current would go where it wasn't wanted and zap!—a reboot. Also, the power supply fan is supposed to partially cool the insides of the computer. In this computer, it was actually detrimental to the computer since it got its cooling air from the shop floor, which contained diesel fumes, paint fumes, and other chemical fumes. Needless to say, those fumes aren't good for computer components.

Computers are like human beings. They have similar tolerances to heat and cold (although computers like the cold better than we do). In general, anything comfortable to us is comfortable to a computer. They need lots of clean, moving air to keep them functioning. They don't, however, require food or drink (except maybe a few RAM chips now and again!). Keep food and drink away from the computer.

The worst thing you can do is eat or smoke around your computer. The smoke particles contain tar that can get inside the computer and cause similar problems to those I've described earlier.

One way to ensure that the environment has the least possible effect on your computer is to always leave the "blanks" in the empty slots on the back of your box. These pieces of metal are designed to keep dirt, dust, and other foreign matter from the inside of the computer. They also maintain proper airflow within the case to ensure that the computer does not overheat.

FRUs

When a component has been deemed to be "bad," it needs to be replaced. That's where the FRU comes in. FRU stands for *field replaceable unit*.

FRUs can be individual parts (such as gears, springs, and shafts) or whole assemblies (like monitors, power supplies, and keyboards). In most cases you don't (or can't) replace individual parts. Most companies have gone to the strategy of using whole assemblies for FRUs. For example, you can't order a #2415 capacitor for a Compaq power supply from Compaq anymore. Instead you order a #A5123G power supply assembly. The individual assembly costs more, but there is less labor involved in replacing a whole power supply than a single capacitor, so it's actually cheaper for the customer as well as the service centers.

When you have determined that a particular component needs to be replaced, you will look in some kind of catalog (usually produced by the manufacturer) for the particular part number of the FRU that you need. These catalogs may also indicate the FRU's cost and shipping information. Some FRUs require an exchange of the old, broken component (called a "core" or "exchange" FRU). In this case, the catalog will indicate two prices: one for the FRU alone, and another for the FRU with an exchange. The price of the single FRU is usually double (sometimes triple) the price of a core FRU.

Printer Troubleshooting

Other than the monitor, the most popular peripheral purchased for computers today is the printer. They are also the most complex peripheral, as far as troubleshooting is concerned. In this section, we will cover the most common types of printer problems you will run into. We will break the section into three areas, for the three different types of printers that exist.

Dot Matrix Printer Problems

Dot matrix printers are relatively simple devices. Therefore there are only a few problems that usually arise. We will cover the most common problems and their solutions here.

Low Print Quality

Problems with print quality are easy to identify. When the printed page comes out of the printer, the characters are too light or have dots missing from them. Table 10.4 details some of the most common print quality problems, their causes, and their solutions.

TABLE 10.4   Common Dot Matrix Print Quality Problems

Characteristics	Cause	Solution
Consistently faded or light characters	Worn-out print ribbon	Replace ribbon with a new, vendor-recommended ribbon.
Print lines that go from dark to light as the print head moves across the page	Print ribbon advance gear slipping	Replace ribbon advance gear or mechanism.
A small, blank line running through a line of print (consistently)	Print head pin stuck inside the print head	Replace the print head.
A small, blank line running through a line of print (intermittently)	A broken, loose, or shorting print head cable	Secure or replace the print head cable.
A small, dark line running through a line of print	Print head pin stuck in the "out" position	Replace the print head. (Pushing the pin in may damage the print head.)
Printer makes printing noise, but no print appears on page	Worn, missing, or improperly installed ribbon cartridge	Replace ribbon cartridge correctly.
Printer prints "garbage"	Cable partially unhooked, wrong driver selected, or bad printer control board (PCB)	Hook up cable correctly, select correct driver, or replace PCB (respectively).

Printout Jams Inside the Printer (a.k.a. "The Printer Crinkled My Paper")

Printer jams are very frustrating because they always seem to happen more than halfway through your 50-page print job, requiring you to take time to remove the jam before the rest of your pages can print. A paper jam happens when something prevents the paper from advancing through the printer evenly. Print jobs jam for two major reasons: an obstructed paper path and stripped drive gears.

Obstructed paper paths are often difficult to find. Usually it means disassembling the printer to find the bit of crumpled-up paper or other foreign substance that's blocking the paper path. A very common obstruction is a piece of the "perf"—the perforated sides of tractor-feed paper—that has torn off and gotten crumpled up and then lodged into the paper path. It may be necessary to remove the platen roller and feed mechanism to get at the obstruction.

Use extra caution when printing peel-off labels in dot matrix printers. If a label or even a whole sheet of labels becomes misaligned or jammed, *DO NOT* roll the roller backward to realign the sheet. The small plastic paper guide that most dot matrix printers use to control the forward movement of the paper through the printer will peel the label right off its backing if you reverse the direction of the paper. And once the label is free, it can easily get stuck under the platen, causing paper jams. A label stuck under the platen is almost impossible to remove without disassembling the paper feed assembly. If a label is misaligned, try realigning the whole sheet of labels *slowly* using the *feed roller,* with the power off, moving it in very small increments.

Stepper Motor Problems

A *stepper motor* is a motor that can move in very small increments. Printers use stepper motors to move the print head back and forth as well as to advance the paper (these are called the *carriage motor* and *main motor,* respectively). These motors get damaged when they are forced in any direction while the power is on. This includes moving the print head over to install a printer ribbon as well as moving the paper feed roller to align paper. These motors are very sensitive to stray voltages. And, if you are rotating one of these motors by hand, you are essentially turning it into a small generator, damaging it!

A damaged stepper motor is easy to detect. Damage to the stepper motor will cause it to lose precision and move farther with each "step." Lines of print will be unevenly spaced if the main motor is damaged (which is more likely). Characters will be "scrunched" together if the print head motor goes bad. In fact, if the motor is bad enough, it won't move at all in any direction. It may even make high-pitched squealing noises. If any of these symptoms show themselves, it's time to replace one of these motors.

Stepper motors are usually expensive to replace. They are about half the cost of a new printer! Damage to them is very easy to avoid, using common sense.

And Now for the Real World...

If I had a wish for the service department I worked in, I would wish that all the dot matrix printers ever bought would be made by Okidata. Okidata dot matrix printers are a technician's dream machine. With nothing but a flat-bladed screwdriver and your hands, you can completely disassemble an Okidata dot matrix printer in less than 10 minutes. Replacing parts on them is just as easy. All parts "snap" into place, including the covers. They also have an excellent reputation. If a customer asks you for a recommendation when buying a dot matrix printer, you can't go wrong recommending an Okidata.

Bubble-Jet Printers

Bubble-jet printers are the most commonly sold printers for home use. For this reason, you need to understand the most common problems with bubble-jet printers so your company can service them effectively. Let's take a look at some of the most common problems with bubble-jet printers and their solutions.

Print Quality

The majority of bubble-jet printer problems are quality problems. Ninety-nine percent of these can be traced to a faulty ink cartridge. With most bubble-jet printers, the ink cartridge contains the print head and the ink. The major problem with this assembly can be described by "If you don't use it, you lose it." The ink will dry out in the small nozzles, blocking them if they are not used at least once a week.

An example of a quality problem is when you have thin, blank lines present in every line of text on the page. This is caused by a plugged hole in at least one of the small, pinhole ink nozzles in the print cartridge. Replacing the ink cartridge solves this problem easily.

Some people will try to save a buck by refilling their ink cartridge when they need to replace it. If you are one of them, STOP IT! Don't refill your ink cartridges! Almost all ink cartridges are designed *not* to be refilled. They are designed to be used once and thrown away! By refilling them, you make a hole in them, and ink can leak out and the printer will need to be cleaned. Also, the ink will probably be of the wrong type, and print quality can suffer. Finally, a refilled cartridge may void the printer's warranty.

If an ink cartridge becomes damaged, or develops a hole, it can put too much ink on the page and the letters will smear. Again, the solution is to replace the ink cartridge. (You should be aware, however, that a very small amount of smearing is normal if the pages are laid on top of each other immediately after printing.)

One final print quality problem that does not directly involve the ink cartridge occurs when the print goes from dark to light quickly, then prints nothing. As we already mentioned, ink cartridges dry out if not used. That's why the manufacturers included a small suction pump inside the printer that "primes" the ink cartridge before each print cycle. If this "priming pump" is broken or malfunctioning, this problem will manifest itself and the pump will need to be replaced.

If the problem of the ink going from dark to light quickly and then disappearing ever happens to you, and you really need to print a couple of pages, try this trick I learned from a fellow technician: Take the ink cartridge out of the printer. Squirt some window cleaner on a paper towel and gently tap the print head against the wet paper towel. The force of the tap plus the solvents in the window cleaner should dislodge any dried ink, and the ink will flow freely again.

Paper Jams

Bubble-jet printers usually have very simple paper paths. Therefore, paper jams due to obstructions are less likely. They are still possible, however, so an obstruction shouldn't be overlooked as a possible cause of jamming.

Paper jams in bubble-jet printers are usually due to one of two things:

- A worn pickup roller
- The wrong type of paper

The pickup roller usually has one or two D-shaped rollers mounted on a rotating shaft. When the shaft rotates, one edge of the "D" rubs against the paper, pushing it into the printer. When the roller gets worn, it gets smooth and doesn't exert enough friction against the paper to push it into the printer.

If the paper used in the printer is too smooth, it causes the same problem. Pickup rollers use friction, and smooth paper doesn't offer much friction. If the paper is too rough, on the other hand, it acts like sandpaper on the rollers, wearing them smooth. Here's a rule of thumb for paper smoothness: Paper slightly smoother than a new one-dollar bill will work fine.

Laser and Page Printers

I've got good news and bad news. The bad news is that laser printer problems are the most complex, because the printer is the most complex. The good news is that most problems are easily identifiable and have specific fixes. Most of the problems can be diagnosed with knowledge of the inner workings of the printer and a little common sense. Let's discuss the most common laser and page printer problems and their solutions.

Paper Jams

Laser printers today run at copier speeds. Because of this, their most common problem is paper jams. Paper can get jammed in a printer for several reasons. First of all, feed jams happen when the paper feed rollers get worn (similar to feed jams in bubble-jet printers). The solution to this problem is easy: Replace the worn rollers.

If your paper feed jams are caused by worn pickup rollers, there is something you can do to get your printer working while you're waiting for the replacement pickup rollers. Scuff the feed roller(s) with a Scotch-Brite® pot-scrubber pad (or something similar) to roughen up the feed rollers. This trick only works once. After that, the rollers aren't thick enough to touch the paper.

Another cause of feed jams is related to the drive of the pickup roller. The drive gear (or clutch) may be broken or have teeth missing. Again, the solution is to replace it. To determine if the problem is a broken gear or worn rollers, print a test page, but leave the paper tray out. Look into the paper feed opening with a flashlight and see if the paper pickup roller(s) are turning evenly and don't "skip." If they turn evenly, the problem is more than likely worn rollers.

Worn exit rollers can also cause paper jams. These rollers guide the paper out of the printer into the paper-receiving tray. If they are worn or damaged, the paper may "catch" on its way out of the printer. These types of jams are characterized by a paper jam that occurs just as the paper is getting to the exit rollers. If the paper jams, open the rear door and see where the paper is. If the paper is very close to the exit roller, the exit rollers are probably the problem.

The solution is to replace all the exit rollers. You must replace all of them at the same time since even one worn exit roller can cause the paper to jam. Besides, they're cheap. Don't be cheap and skimp on these parts if you need to have them replaced.

And Now for the Real World...

I was in our local hospital ER recently having my hand looked at (I had cut it pretty badly on some glass). The receptionist who examined me asked me a few questions and filled out a report in the medical database on her computer. When she had finished asking me questions, she got up to get the printout from her laser printer.

I was shocked to see what she did next. When the paper starting coming out of the laser printer, she grabbed it and "ripped" it from the printer like you might do if the paper were in an old typewriter! The printer's exit rollers complained bitterly and made a noise that made me cringe. I don't know what hurt worse, my hand or my ears. She did this for every sheet of paper that she printed. I didn't say anything, since my health was of primary concern at the time.

The following week I noticed a familiar laser printer come in for service from that very same hospital. As the technician started to work on it, I sauntered over and said, "I bet you 20 dollars it's the exit rollers." He said, "You're on!" Needless to say, I had a really good steak dinner that night with my wife.

I had a word with the person in charge of computer repair at that hospital the next day. They were surprised at what I had told them, but glad that I pointed it out. I saved them from many future repairs, and they were very grateful. As far as I know, the ER receptionist doesn't rip the pages from the printer anymore, since we haven't seen that printer back in for service in a while.

Paper jams can actually be the fault of the paper. If your printer consistently tries to feed multiple pages into the printer, the paper isn't dry enough. If you live in an area with high humidity, this could be a problem. I've heard some solutions that are pretty far out, but that work (like keeping the paper in a Tupperware-type of airtight container or microwaving it to remove moisture). The best all-around solution, however, is humidity control and to keep the paper wrapped until it's needed. Keep the humidity around 50 percent or lower (but above 25 percent if you can, in order to avoid problems with electrostatic discharge).

Finally, there is a metal, grounded strip called the static eliminator strip inside the printer that drains the corona charge away from the paper after it has been used to transfer toner from the EP cartridge. If that strip is missing, broken, or damaged the charge will remain on the paper and may cause it to stick to the EP cartridge, causing a jam. If the paper jams after reaching the corona assembly, this may be the cause.

Blank Pages

There's nothing more annoying than printing a 10-page contract and receiving 10 pages of blank paper from the printer. Blank pages are a somewhat common occurrence in laser and page printers. Somehow, the toner isn't being put on the paper. There are three major causes of blank pages:

- The toner cartridge
- The corona assembly
- The high-voltage power supply (HVPS)

Toner Cartridge

As we have already discussed in Chapter 7, "How Printers Work," the toner cartridge is the source for most quality problems, because it contains most of the image-formation pieces for laser and page printers. Let's start with the obvious. A blank page will come out of the printer if there is no toner in the toner cartridge. I know it sounds simple, but some people think these things will last forever. It's very easy to check: just open the printer, remove the toner cartridge, and shake it. You will be able to hear if there's toner inside the cartridge. If it's empty, replace it with a known, good, manufacturer-recommended toner cartridge.

Another problem that crops up rather often is the problem of using refilled or reconditioned toner cartridges. During their recycling process, these cartridges may get filled with the wrong kind of toner (for example, one with an incorrect charge). This may cause toner to be repelled from the EP drum instead of attracted to it. Thus, there's no toner on the page because there was no toner on the EP drum to begin with. The solution once again is to replace the toner cartridge with the type recommended by the manufacturer.

A third problem related to toner cartridges happens when someone installs a new toner cartridge and forgets to remove the sealing tape that is present to keep the toner in the cartridge during shipping. The solution to this problem is as easy as it is obvious. Just remove the toner cartridge from the printer, remove the sealing tape, and reinstall the cartridge.

Corona Assembly

The second cause of the "blank page" problem is a damaged or missing corona wire. If there is a lost or damaged wire, the developed image won't transfer from the EP drum to the paper. Thus, no image appears on the printout. To determine if this is causing your problem, do the first half of the self-test (described later in this chapter). If there is an image on the drum, but not on the paper, you will know that the corona assembly isn't doing its job.

To check if the corona assembly is causing the problem, open the cover and examine the wire (or roller, if your printer uses one). The corona wire is hard to see, so you may need a flashlight. You will know if it's broken or missing just by looking (it will either be in pieces or just not there). If it's not broken or missing, the problem may be related to the HVPS.

The corona wire (or roller) is a relatively inexpensive part and can be easily replaced with the removal of two screws and some patience.

High-Voltage Power Supply (HVPS)

The HVPS supplies high-voltage, low-current power to both the charging and transfer corona assemblies in laser and page printers. If it's broken, neither will work properly. If the self-test shows an image on the drum but none on the paper, and the corona assembly is present and not damaged, then the HVPS is at fault.

All Black Pages

Only slightly less annoying than 10 blank pages is 10 black pages. This happens when the charging unit (the charging corona wire or charging corona roller) in the toner cartridge malfunctions and fails to place a charge on the EP drum. Because the drum is grounded, it has no charge. Anything with a charge (like toner) will stick to it. As the drum rotates, all the toner will be transferred to the page and a black page is formed.

This problem wastes quite a bit of toner, but can be fixed easily. The solution (again) is to replace the toner cartridge with a known, good, manufacturer-recommended one. If that doesn't solve the problem, then the HVPS is at fault (it's not providing the high voltage that the charging corona needs to function).

Repetitive Small Marks or Defects

Repetitive marks occur frequently in heavily used (as well as older) laser printers. The problem may be caused by toner spilled inside the printer. It can also be caused by a crack or chip in the EP drum (this mainly happens with recycled cartridges). These cracks can accumulate toner. In both cases, some of the toner will get stuck onto one of the rollers. Once this happens, every time the roller rotates and touches a piece of paper, it will leave toner smudges spaced a roller circumference apart.

The solution is relatively simple: Clean or replace the offending roller. To help you figure out which roller is causing the problem, the service manuals contain a chart like the one in Figure 10.4. To use the chart, place the printed page next to the chart. Align the first occurrence of the "smudge" with the top arrow. The next smudge will line up with one of the other arrows. The arrow it lines up with tells which roller is causing the problem.

Remember that the chart in Figure 10.4 is only an example. Your printer may have different-sized rollers (and thus need a different chart). Check your printer's service documentation for a chart like this. It is valuable in determining which roller is causing a smudge.

Vertical Black Lines on Page

A groove or scratch in the EP drum can cause the problem of vertical black lines running down all or part of the page. Since a scratch is "lower" than the surface, it doesn't receive as much (if any) of a charge as the other areas. The result is that toner will stick to it as though it were discharged. Since the groove may go around the circumference of the drum, the line may go all the way down the page.

FIGURE 10.4 Laser printer roller circumference chart

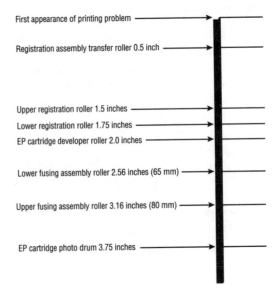

Another possible cause of vertical black lines is a dirty charge corona wire. A dirty charge corona will prevent a sufficient charge from being placed on the EP drum. Since the EP drum will be almost zero, toner will stick to the areas that correspond to the dirty areas on the charge corona.

The solution to the first problem is, as always, to replace the toner cartridge (or EP drum if your printer uses a separate EP drum and toner). You can also solve the second problem with a new toner cartridge, but in this case that would be an extreme solution. It's easier to clean the charge corona with the brush supplied with the cartridge.

Vertical White Line on Page

Vertical white lines running down all or part of the page are relatively common problems on older printers, especially ones that don't see much maintenance. They are caused by some foreign matter (more than likely toner) caught on the transfer corona wire. The dirty spots keep the toner from being transmitted to the paper (at those locations, that is), with the result that streaks form as the paper progresses past the transfer corona wire.

The solution is to clean the corona wires. LaserJet Series II printers contain a small corona wire brush to help in this procedure. It's usually a small, green-handled brush located near the transfer corona wire. To use it, remove the toner cartridge and run the brush in the charge corona groove on top of the toner cartridge. Replace the cartridge and use the brush to brush away any foreign deposits on the transfer corona. Be sure to put it back in its holder when you're finished.

Image Smudging

If you can pick up a sheet from a laser printer, run your thumb across it, and have the image come off on your thumb, you have a fuser problem. The fuser isn't heating the toner and fusing it into the paper. This could be caused by a number of things—but all of them would be taken care of with a fuser replacement. For example, if the halogen light inside the heating roller has burned out, that would cause the problem. The solution is to replace the fuser. The fuser can be replaced with a rebuilt unit, if you prefer. Rebuilt fusers are almost as good as new fusers, and some even come with guarantees. Plus, they cost less.

The whole fuser may not need to be replaced. Fuser components can be ordered from parts suppliers and can be rebuilt by you. For example, if the fuser has a bad lamp, you can order a lamp and replace it in the fuser.

Another problem similar to this is when there are small areas of smudging that repeat themselves down the page. Dents or "cold spots" in the fuser heat roller cause this problem. The only solution is to replace either the fuser assembly or the heat roller.

"Ghosting"

"Ghosting" is what you have when you can see light images of previously printed pages on the current page. This is caused by one of two things: bad erasure lamps or a broken cleaning blade. If the erasure lamps are bad, the previous electrostatic discharges aren't completely wiped away. When the EP drum rotates towards the developing roller, some toner will stick to the slightly discharged areas. A broken cleaning blade, on the other hand, causes old toner to build up on the EP drum and consequently present itself in the next printed image.

Replacing the toner cartridge solves the second problem. Solving the first problem involves replacing the erasure lamps in the printer. Since the toner cartridge is the least expensive cure, you should try that first. Usually, replacing the toner cartridge will solve the problem. If it doesn't, you will then have to replace the erasure lamps.

Printer Prints Pages of Garbage

This has happened to everyone at least once. You print a one-page letter and ten pages of what looks to be garbage come out of the printer. This problem comes from one of two different sources: the print driver software or the formatter board.

Printer Driver

The correct printer driver needs to be installed for the printer you have. For example, if you have a HP LaserJet III, then that is the driver you need to install. Once the driver has been installed, it must be configured for the correct page description language: PCL or PostScript. Most HP LaserJet printers use PCL (but can be configured for PostScript). Determine what page description your printer has been configured for and set the print driver to the same setting. If this is not done, you will get garbage out of the printer.

Most printers that have LCD displays will indicate that they are in PostScript mode with a "PS" or "PostScript" somewhere in the display.

If the problem is the wrong driver setting, the "garbage" that the printer prints will look like English. That is, the words will be readable, but they won't make any sense.

Formatter Board

The other cause of several pages of garbage being printed is a bad formatter board. This circuit board takes the information that the printer receives from the computer and turns it into commands for the various components in the printer. Usually problems with the formatter board produce wavy lines of print or random patterns of dots on the page.

It's relatively easy to replace the formatter board in a laser printer. Usually this board is installed underneath the printer and can be removed by loosening two screws and pulling the board out. Typically, replacing the formatter board also replaces the printer interface; another possible source of "garbage" printouts.

HP LaserJet Testing

Now that we've defined some of the possible sources of problems with laser printers, let's discuss a few of the testing procedures that you use with them. We'll discuss HP LaserJet laser printers since they are the most popular type of laser printer, but the topics covered here can be applied to other types of laser printers as well.

When you troubleshoot laser printers, there are three tests you can perform to narrow down which assembly is causing the problem. (These tests are internal diagnostics for the printers and are included with most laser printers.) The three tests are the engine self-test, the engine half self-test, and the secret self-test.

Self-Tests

There are three significant printer "self-tests"—tests that the printer runs on its own (albeit when directed by the user). These are the engine self-test, the print engine half self-test, and the secret self-test.

Engine Self-Test   The engine self-test tests the print engine of the LaserJet, bypassing the formatter board. This test will cause the printer to print a single page with vertical lines running its length. If an engine self-test can be performed, you will know that the laser print engine can print successfully. To perform an engine self-test, you must press the printer's self-test button, which is hidden behind a small cover on the side of the printer (see Figure 10.5). The location of the button varies from printer to printer, so you may have to refer to the printer manual. Using a pencil or probe, press the button and the print engine will start printing the test page.

Half Self-Test   A print engine half self-test is performed the same as the self-test, but you interrupt it halfway through the print cycle by opening the cover. This is useful in determining which part of the print process is causing the printer to malfunction. If you stop the print process and there is part of a developed image on the EP drum and part has been transferred to the paper, you know that the pickup rollers, registration rollers, laser scanner, charging roller, EP drum, and transfer roller are all working correctly. You can stop the half self-test at various points in the print process to determine the source of a malfunction.

FIGURE 10.5 Print engine self-test button location. (Location may vary on different printers.)

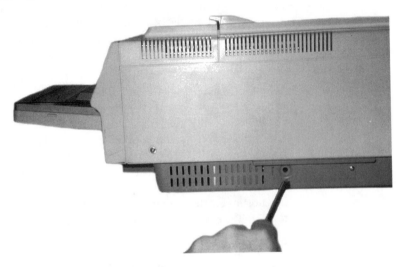

Secret Self-Test   To activate this test you must first put the printer into service mode. To accomplish this, you must first turn the printer on while simultaneously holding down the On Line, Continue, and Enter buttons (that's the first secret part, because nobody knows it unless somebody tells them). When the screen comes up blank, release the keys and press, in order, Continue, then Enter. The printer will perform an internal self-test, then display "00 READY." At this point you are ready to initiate the rest of the secret self-test by taking the printer offline and pressing the Test button on the front panel and holding it until you see the "04 Self Test" message. When you see this message, release the Test button. This will cause the printer to print one self-test page. (If you want a continuous printout, then instead of releasing the Test button at the "04 Self Test" message, keep holding the Test button down until the message "05 Self Test" is displayed. The printer will print continuous self-test pages until you power off the printer or hit On Line, or until the printer runs out of paper.)

Error Codes

In addition to the self-tests, you have another tool for troubleshooting HP laser printers. Error codes are a way for the LaserJet to tell the user (and a service technician) what's wrong. Table 10.5 details some of the most common codes displayed on an HP LaserJet.

TABLE 10.5 HP LaserJet Error Messages

Message	Description
00 Ready	The printer is in standby mode and ready to print.
02 Warming Up	The fuser is being warmed up before the 00 Ready state.
05 Self-Test	Full self-test has been initiated from the front panel.
11 Paper Out	The paper tray sensor is reporting that there is no paper in the paper tray. Printer will not print as long as this error exists.
13 Paper Jam	A piece of paper is caught in the paper path. To fix, open the cover and clear the jam (including all pieces of the jam). Close the cover to resume printing. Printer will not print as long as this error exists.
14 No EP Cart	There is no EP cartridge (toner cartridge) installed in the printer. Printer will not print as long as this error exists.
15 Engine Test	An engine self-test is in progress.
16 Toner Low	The toner cartridge is almost out of toner. Replacement will be necessary soon.
50 Service	A fuser error has occurred. Most commonly caused by fuser lamp failure. Power off the printer and replace the fuser to solve. Printer will not print as long as this error exists.
51 Error	Laser scanning assembly problem. Test and replace, if necessary. Printer will not print as long as this error exists.
52 Error	The scanner motor in the laser scanning assembly is malfunctioning. Test and replace as per service manual. Printer will not print as long as this error exists.
55 Error	Communication problem between formatter and DC controller. Test and replace as per service manual. Printer will not print as long as this error exists.

Troubleshooting Tips for HP LaserJet Printers

There is a set of troubleshooting steps that are usually used by printer technicians to help them solve HP LaserJet printing problems. Let's detail each of them to bring our discussion of laser printer troubleshooting to a close.

1. **Is the exhaust fan operational?** This is the first component to receive power when the printer is turned on. If you can feel air coming out of the exhaust fan, this confirms that AC voltage is present and power is turned on, that +5Vdc and +24Vdc are being generated by the AC power supply (ACPS), and that the DC controller is functional. If there is no power to the printer (no lights, fan not operating), the ACPS is at fault. Replacement involves removing all printer covers and removing four screws. You can purchase new ACPS modules, but it is usually cheaper to replace it with a rebuilt unit.

If you are into electronics, you can probably rebuild the ACPS yourself simply and cheaply. It's usually the main rectifier that fails in these units; it can easily be replaced if you know what you're doing.

2. **Do the control panel LEDs work?** This means that the formatter board can communicate with control panel. If the LEDs do not light, it could mean that the formatter board is bad, the control panel is bad, or the wires connecting the two are broken or shorting out.

3. **Does the main motor rotate at power up?** Turn the power off. Remove the covers from the side of the printer. Turn the printer back on and carefully watch and listen for main motor rotation. If you see and hear the main motor rotating, this indicates that toner cartridge is installed, all photosensors are functional, all motors are functional, and the printer can move paper (assuming there are no obstructions).

4. **Does the fuser heat lamp light up after the main motor finishes its rotation?** You will need to have the covers removed to notice. The heat lamp should light after the main motor rotation and stay lit until the control panel says "00 Ready."

5. **Can the printer perform an engine test print?** A sheet of vertical lines indicates that the print engine works. This test print bypasses the formatter board and will indicate if the print problem resides in the engine or not. If the test print is successful, the engine can be ruled out as a source of the problem. If the test print fails, you will have to further troubleshoot the printer to determine which engine component is causing the problem.

6. **Can the printer perform a control panel self-test?** This is the final test to ensure printer operation. If you can press the "Test Page" control panel button and receive a test printout, this means the entire printer is working properly. The only possibilities for problems would be outside the printer (i.e., interfaces, cables, and software problems).

Top 10 Troubleshooting Steps

Just as every artist has their own style, every technician has their own way to troubleshoot. Some people use their instincts; others use advice from other people. I have condensed the most common troubleshooting tips into a 10-step process. You try each step, in order. If that step doesn't narrow the problem down, you move on to the next step.

Step 1: Define the Problem

If you can't define the problem, you can't begin to solve it. You can define the problem by asking questions of the user. Here are a few questions to ask the user to aid in determining what exactly the problem *is*:

Can you show me the problem?   This question is one of the best. It allows the user to show you exactly where and when they experience the problem.

How often does this happen?   This question establishes whether or not this problem is a one-time occurrence (usually indicating a "soft" memory error or the like) that can be solved with a reboot, or whether the problem has a specific sequence of events that cause it to happen (usually indicating a more serious problem that may require software installation or hardware replacement).

Has any new software been installed recently?   New software can mean incompatibility problems with existing problems. This is especially true for Windows programs. A new Windows program can overwrite a required DLL file with a newer version of the same name, which an older program may not find useful.

Have any other changes been made to the computer recently?   If the answer is "Yes," ask if they can remember approximately when the change was made. Then ask them approximately when the problem started. If the two dates seem related, there's a good chance that the problem is related to the change. If it's a new hardware component, check to see that the hardware component was installed correctly.

Step 2: Check the Simple Stuff First

This step is the one that most experienced technicians overlook. Often, computer problems are the result of some simple problem. The technician will overlook them because they are so simple that they assume they *couldn't* be the problem. Some examples of simple problems are

Is it plugged in?   And on both ends? Cables must be plugged in on *both ends* in order to function correctly. Cables can be easily tripped over and inadvertently pulled from their sockets.

Is it turned on?   This one seems the most obvious, but we've all fallen victim to it at one point or another. Computers and their peripherals must be turned on in order to function. Most have power switches that have LEDs that glow when the power is turned on.

Is the system ready?   Computers must be ready before they can be used. "Ready" means that the system is ready to accept commands from the user. An indication that a computer is ready is when the operating system screens come up and the computer presents you with a menu or a command prompt. If that computer uses a graphical interface, the computer is ready when the mouse pointer appears. Printers are ready when the "On Line" or "Ready" light on the front panel is lit.

Reseat chips and cables.   You can solve some of the strangest problems (random hang-ups or errors) by opening the case and pressing down on each socketed chip. This remedies the chip creep problem mentioned earlier in the book. In addition, you should also reseat any cables to make sure that they are making good contact.

Step 3: Check to See If It's User Error

One of the more common errors that technicians run into is the "EEOC error" (Equipment Exceeds Operator Capability). This error is common, but preventable. The indication that a problem is due to user error is when a user says they can't perform some very common computer task—i.e., "I can't print," "I can't save my file," "I can't run my favorite application," etc. As soon you hear these words, you should start asking questions of the user to determine if it is EEOC or a real problem. A good question to ask following their statement of the problem would be, "Were you *ever* able to perform that task?" If they answer no to this question, it means they are probably doing the procedure wrong—EEOC. If they answer yes, you must move on to another set of questions.

This doesn't mean you should assume "the user is always wrong." An attitude like that can come across on the phone, and in person, as arrogance.

The Social Side of Troubleshooting

A few years ago, I attended troubleshooting courses from two different major vendors (who shall remain nameless) in two back-to-back weeks. In the first course, the instructor opened by saying "I'm now going to give you the secret to successful troubleshooting....Users Lie!" Of course, we were all shocked to hear this from a representative of a major software vendor, but he was right. Consider the typical answers to the following questions:

1. Question: So what were you doing when it broke?

   Answer: Nothing.

2. Question: What have you changed recently?

   Answer: Nothing.

3. When was the last time it worked?

   Answer: The last time I touched anything.

The truth is, users *DO* lie—not intentionally, but the result is the same. As troubleshooters, our job is to drag the truth out of them.

The second class opened with the instructor saying "I'm going to clue you in to the secret of successful troubleshooting....Troubleshooting is more social than technical." All of the computer geeks in the room gasped to hear someone belittle the value of their technical knowledge. Bottom line, though, the instructor was right. A problem isn't "fixed" until the user believes it is fixed!

When you combine those two "secrets," you get to the heart of troubleshooting. As technicians we need to be able to communicate clearly, use less intimidating questioning techniques (notice the questions above all seem to imply that the user was at fault), and reassure the user that the problem has been corrected.

When looking for clues to the nature of a problem no one can give you more information than the person who was there when it happened. They can tell you what led up to the problem, what software was running, the exact nature of the problem ("It happened when I tried to print"), and can help you recreate the problem, if possible.

Use questioning techniques that are neutral in nature. Instead of "What were you doing when it broke?" be more compassionate and say, "What was going on when the computer decided not to work?" It sounds silly, but these types of changes can make your job a lot easier!

Step 4: Reboot the Computer

It is amazing how often a simple computer reboot can solve a problem. Rebooting the computer clears the memory and starts the computer with a "clean slate." Whenever I perform phone support, I always ask the customer to reboot the computer and try again. If rebooting doesn't work, try powering down the system completely, and then powering it up again. More often than not, that will solve the problem.

Step 5: Determine If the Problem Is Hardware or Software Related

This step is an important one because it determines what part of the computer you should focus your troubleshooting skills on. Each part requires different skills and different tools.

To determine if a problem is hardware or software related, you could do a few things to narrow the problem down. For instance, does the problem manifest itself when you use a particular piece of hardware (a modem, for example)? If it does, the problem is more than likely hardware related.

This step relies on personal experience more than any of the other steps do. You will without a doubt run into several strange software problems. Each one has a particular solution. Some may even require reinstallation of the software or the entire operating system.

Step 6: If the Problem Is Hardware Related, Determine Which Component Is Failing

Hardware problems are pretty easy to figure out. If the modem doesn't work, and you know it isn't a software problem, it's pretty safe to say that the modem is probably the piece of hardware that needs to be replaced.

With some of the newer computers, several components are integrated onto the motherboard. If you troubleshoot the computer and find a hardware component to be bad, there's a good chance that the bad component is integrated into the motherboard (for example, the parallel port circuitry) and the whole motherboard must be replaced. An expensive proposition, to be sure.

Step 7: If the Problem Is Software Related, Boot "Clean"

If you are experiencing software problems, a common troubleshooting technique with DOS-based computers is to boot "clean." This means starting the computer with a bootable diskette that uses a CONFIG.SYS and AUTOEXEC.BAT with no third-party drivers in it (for example, no drivers for sound card, CD-ROM, or network). If the software that's experiencing the problem is incompatible with something in these clean CONFIG.SYS or AUTOEXEC.BAT files, this will indicate it. Once you have determined that there's an incompatibility, you can further determine what your chances are for fixing the problem by using the "REM" techniques presented earlier in this chapter.

Step 8: Check Service Information Sources

As you may or may not have figured out by now, I'm fond of old sayings. There's another old saying that applies here: "If all else fails, read the instructions." The service manuals are your "instructions" for troubleshooting and service information. Almost every computer and peripheral made today has a set of service documentation in the form of books, service CD-ROMs, and Web sites. The latter of the three seem to be growing in popularity as more and more service centers get connections to the Internet.

Step 9: If It Ain't Broke...

When doctors take the Hippocratic oath, they promise to not make the patient any sicker than they already were. Technicians should take a similar oath. It all boils down to, "If it ain't broke, don't fix it." When you troubleshoot, make one change at a time. If the change doesn't solve the problem, change it back to its original state before making a different change.

Step 10: Ask for Help

If you don't know the answer, ask one of your fellow technicians. They may have run across the problem you are having and know the solution.

This solution does involve a little humility. You must admit that you don't know the answer. It is said that the beginning of wisdom is, "I don't know." If you ask questions, you will get answers, and you will learn from the answers. Making mistakes is valuable as well, as long as you learn from them.

Summary

This book can give you the basic knowledge you need to be a good troubleshooter, but not the instinct you need to be a great one. There are very few people who have mastered the art of troubleshooting. The reason this is true is that troubleshooting *is* an art. And just as with any art, excellence comes only through experience. The best way to get experience is through reading, practice, and asking questions.

While experience is key, there are still basic resources and procedures that can help you troubleshoot while you are gaining that experience. In this chapter we presented a few of those tools.

We started the chapter with a discussion of some of the intellectual resources that are available. Product documentation, the Internet, and other technicians can often be used to answer questions based on your description of a problem. In the next section we covered the basics of hardware and software utilities that can be used to help troubleshoot.

We then moved to troubleshooting software issues. Starting with DOS and moving to Windows, we discussed common configuration files and techniques that can be used to test their validity.

The next section concentrated on hardware troubleshooting techniques. We discussed the POST routine (what it is and how it warns you of problems), motherboard problems, hard disk issues, keyboard and mouse problems, display system troubleshooting, BIOS issues, power supply problems, and a few other miscellaneous hardware problems.

We followed with a discussion of one of the most common troubleshooting tasks in the computer industry—troubleshooting printer problems. We discussed dot matrix, bubble-jet, and laser printers—their components and some of the most common problems with each technology.

Finally, we presented our top 10 troubleshooting steps. Following the steps should lead you to a satisfactory conclusion of your troubleshooting process.

Key Terms

backup	initialization command
bootable diskette	main motor
bubble-jet printer	network client
carriage motor	power on self-test
dot matrix printer	Registry
field replacement unit	REM statement
Field Replacement Unit (FRU)	resource discovery expansion card
Frequently Asked Questions (FAQ)	revision number
General Protection Fault (GPF)	stepper motor
INI file	system resources

Review Questions

1. A customer complains that his hard disk is making lots of noise. After examining the computer and hearing the noise for yourself, you notice that the high-pitched noise seems to be coming from the fan in the power supply. Which component(s) should be replaced? (Select all that apply.)

   A. Hard disk

   B. Power supply

   C. Motherboard

   D. Nothing. This is a software problem.

2. When you try to turn the computer on, you notice that the computer will not activate. The monitor is blank and the fan on the power supply is not active. Turning the switch off and then back on makes no difference. What is the most likely cause of this problem?

   A. The computer is unplugged.

   B. The BIOS on the motherboard needs to be upgraded.

   C. The monitor is malfunctioning.

   D. Both the fan on the power supply and the video card are bad.

   E. The power supply is bad.

   F. None of the above

3. A laser printer is printing pages that are all black. Replacing the toner cartridge has no effect. What are some possible causes of this problem? (Select all that apply.)

   A. The high voltage power supply (HVPS) is bad.

   B. The transfer corona assembly is damaged.

   C. The main motor assembly is bad.

   D. The laser scanner assembly is damaged.

   E. The EP cartridge is damaged.

   F. The printer has bad feed rollers.

4. What part of an HP LaserJet printer is malfunctioning if you receive a "50 Service" error?

   A. Toner cartridge

   B. Laser scanner assembly

   C. Fuser

   D. AC power supply

5. A paper jam on a dot matrix printer can be caused by _____.

   A. An obstructed paper path

   B. The wrong kind of paper

   C. A malfunctioning print head assembly

   D. The wrong ribbon is installed

6. A customer complains that they can't get their computer to work. When they turn it on, they get no video and hear a series of beeps. The beeps are in the sequence of one long beep, then two short beeps. You tell the customer to bring the machine in. Upon further examination you are able to reproduce the problem. What is your next step?

   A. Upgrade the PC's BIOS to the newest version.

   B. Replace the motherboard.

   C. Replace the video card.

   D. Replace the RAM.

   E. Upgrade the BEEP.COM file.

   F. Boot "clean" to a bootable floppy disk.

7. An HP LaserJet III printer isn't printing at all. The computer indicates that the "device on LPT1 isn't ready." You perform a service self-test on the printer and it prints the page of vertical lines with no problems. The front panel self-test doesn't work, however. Which component do you suspect is giving you the problem?

   A. Fuser

   B. DC controller

   C. AC power supply

   D. Main motor

   E. Formatter

   F. Toner cartridge

   G. Transfer corona

8. A "201" error at system startup means what?

   A. Bad floppy drive

   B. Bad system board

   C. Bad hard disk system

   D. Bad memory

   E. Bad keyboard

9. Which Windows error is caused by an application being "greedy" and taking memory away from other programs?

   A. General System Error

   B. General Protection Fault

   C. System Fault

   D. Memory Protection Fault

10. A 2GB FAT32 partition will have a cluster size of _____ KB?

   A. 4

   B. 16

   C. 32

   D. 64

11. What two files are used by DOS to configure a computer?

   A. INI files

   B. AUTOEXEC.BAT

   C. CONFIG.BAT

   D. CONFIG.SYS

12. A computer is experiencing random reboots and "phantom" problems that disappear after reboot. What should you do?

   A. Tell the customer that it's normal for the computer to do that.

   B. Replace the motherboard.

   C. Boot "clean."

   D. Replace the power supply.

   E. Open the cover and reseat all cards and chips.

13. A bubble-jet printer produces output that is acceptable. But after an ink cartridge replacement, the ink smears and generally looks "heavier" than normal. What is the problem?

   A. The ink cartridge from the factory is bad.

   B. A refilled ink cartridge has been used.

   C. The printer's controller circuitry is bad.

   D. The paper is too thin.

   E. None of the above.

14. A company that hires you to do service for them has just purchased a new laser printer. After two months and 3,000 copies, "ghosts" of previous pages appear on the printout. What action will solve the problem?

    A. Replace the toner cartridge.

    B. Replace the fuser.

    C. Replace the transfer corona assembly.

    D. Clean the transfer corona assembly.

    E. None of the above.

15. What is the largest cause of computer problems?

    A. Hardware failure

    B. Software failure

    C. ESD

    D. Technician inexperience

    E. User error

16. A user is getting a "301 error" when they turn on the computer. What is a possible cause?

    A. A virus on the boot sector of the hard disk

    B. User error

    C. Dust and dirt on the power supply fan

    D. A book lying on the keyboard during system start-up

17. You install a newly purchased sound card into your computer, but upon rebooting you find that the new device is not recognized by the system. Moreover, your modem, which has always worked perfectly, has stopped functioning. What is probably the problem?

    A. The sound card and modem are using the same slot on the motherboard.

    B. The drivers for the sound card need to be updated.

    C. The sound card is using the same IRQ as the modem.

    D. The modem is 16-bit and the sound card is 32-bit, meaning that they cannot both be used in the same system.

18. An HP LaserJet starts printing blank pages after you cleaned all of the internal parts. What is the most probable cause?

    A. You broke the transfer corona wire.

    B. There is no toner in the toner cartridge.

    C. The HVPS is not functioning.

    D. The fuser is still dirty.

19. What is the most probable cause of a defect that repeats itself on the page?

   A. Bad toner cartridge

   B. Bad fuser roller

   C. Any dirty or scratched roller

   D. Dirty or broken corona wire

   E. None of the above.

20. When troubleshooting a software problem, which of the following items is the easiest to check first?

   A. Non-DOS items in the configuration files

   B. System resources

   C. Hard drive

   D. Perform a clean boot

Answers to Review Questions

1. B. The first logical choice, since the noise is coming from the power supply, is to check the power supply.

2. A. Since turning the switch on and off makes no difference, the first item to check is to see if the computer is properly plugged in.

3. A, E. Since the laser printer is printing pages that are all black and replacing the toner cartridge has no effect, the probable cause of this problem is the high-voltage power supply (HVPS) is bad.

4. C. The part of an HP LaserJet printer that is malfunctioning if you receive a "50 Service" error is the fuser.

5. A. Leftover pieces of paper or other debris that have fallen into the printer can be the cause of an obstructed paper path and manifest as a paper jam.

6. C. When a computer is turned on and there is no video and a series of beeps, and the beeps are in the sequence of one long beep, then two short beeps, it means there is something wrong with the video card. Check first to see that it is seated properly and in the proper slot for its bus type. If this checks out fine, replace it with a known good card and turn the machine back on. If this solves the problem, then the issue was a bad card and it needs to be permanently replaced.

7. E. If after completing the above tests, it fails the self-test, then most likely the formatter is the problem.

8. D. Most error codes that begin with a 2 indicate a memory error of some sort.

9. B. While there are other factors that might contribute, most General Protection Fault errors are generated when an application either monopolizes too much memory or attempts to access inappropriate memory addresses.

10. A. FAT32 uses smaller cluster sizes on large drives and, therefore, is able to more efficiently store files.

11. B, D. The two files that are used by DOS to configure a computer are AUTOEXEC.BAT and CONFIG.SYS. In general, the CONFIG.SYS file sets up the operating system environment, and the AUTOEXEC.BAT file sets up the user environment.

12. E. When a computer is experiencing random reboots and "phantom" problems that disappear after reboot, you should open the cover and reseat all cards and chips. Most likely there are some components that have experienced chip creep.

13. B. Generally, this is the mark of a refilled ink cartridge. Most cartridges are not designed to be reused, as they contain the print head as well as the ink supply. Each is rated to last a certain number of copies. After that number, they need to be replaced to be able to produce the level of quality intended. Because of this, you should not use refilled cartridges.

14. A. Replacing the toner cartridge will solve the problem of "ghosts" of previous pages appearing on the printout. This is caused by either the drum not being charged properly or, more likely, not being cleaned correctly.

15. E. Unfortunately, the largest cause of computer problems is user error. These errors have the potential to be the most difficult to troubleshoot. A technician must have very good diplomatic skills to obtain all the answers necessary to fix the problem.

16. D. Errors that begin with 3 are typically keyboard errors. Common suspects to look for are a keyboard that is not properly connected, or a key that is stuck in the depressed position; in this case, because a book was lying on the keyboard.

17. C. When two otherwise healthy devices both are malfunctioning, there is a good chance that they are both trying to use the same system resources, and the IRQ and DMA settings are the most common culprits.

18. A. If, after cleaning all the internal components of a printer, it starts printing blank pages, most likely the transfer corona wire is damaged. Care must be taken when cleaning this, as it is a delicate component.

19. C. The most probable cause of a defect that repeats itself on the page is any dirty or scratched roller leaving a mark on the paper every time the drum rotates.

20. A. The non-DOS items can always be taken out or REMmed out to see if the machine is operating properly without that statement placed in the configuration files.

A+: Operating System Technologies Exam

Chapter 11

Introduction to Computer Operating Systems

"I think there is a world market for maybe five computers."

Thomas Watson
Chairman of IBM, 1943

n previous chapters we have looked at the hardware that composes a personal computer's physical components. Hardware is only half of the story though. When poor Mr. Watson made his prediction 60 years ago, he was looking at a very different machine from the ones we have today. At that time computers were bulky—as in room-sized—slow and difficult to use. As recently as the 1970s most machines were still using punch cards as a primary data input tool, and anyone wanting to use a computer had to navigate a complex, uninviting interface with only a keyboard to help them. In such an environment, Watson probably was correct to believe that few people would go through the time, effort, and expense to use computers.

As computer technology has evolved towards smaller, more powerful machines, the personal computer has made significant strides towards Microsoft's grandiose stated goal of "a computer in every home." The incredible global computer revolution is not due just to hardware, though. In many ways the acceleration of computer usage over the last decade has more to do with the ever-improving operating systems that humans use to interact with these machines. Computers require programmed code (called software) to run, and they require an input-output mechanism to allow users to give the machine instructions and view the results of those commands. The operating system is the primary software used to achieve these ends, and the evolution of more powerful and user-friendly operating systems has made computers less difficult to use and more enjoyable.

In order to understand the emergence of modern personal computer operating systems, you should know about the technologies that led to our present systems and about the critical relationship between hardware and software over the course of the PC's development. Graphics, speed, GUI interfaces, and multiple programs running concurrently are all made possible by software designers taking full advantage of the hardware for which they are designing their software. Because of this, we will see that as computer hardware has improved, software has improved with it. Because the operating system is the platform on which all other software builds, it is generally the development of a new operating system that drives the development of other software. This chapter is therefore the story of that very special, and crucial, type of software—the personal computer operating system. This chapter is spent looking at where operating systems have been, and we will focus the rest of the book looking at where they are currently by focusing on Microsoft's Windows 95/98 and Windows 2000 operating systems.

Types of Software

There are a number of different types of personal computer software, and each has a specific role in the operation of the machine. Among these are the following major distinctions:

Operating System (OS)   Provides a consistent environment for other software to execute commands. The OS gives users an interface with the computer so they can send commands to (input) and receive feedback or results back (output). To do this the operating system must communicate with the computer hardware to perform the following tasks:

- Disk and file management
- Device access
- Memory management
- Output format

Once the operating system has organized these basic resources, users can give the computer instructions through input devices (such as a keyboard or a mouse). Some of these commands are built into the operating system, while others are issued through the use of applications. The OS becomes the center through which the system hardware, other software, and the user communicate, and all the rest of the components of the system work together through the OS, which coordinates their communication.

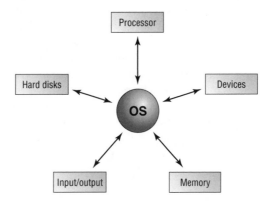

Network Operating System (NOS)   Similar to a standard operating system, except that the NOS is optimized to provide services to other machines on the network. NOS software is examined briefly in Part II, Chapter 18, "Configuring Network Software," but is discussed in-depth in Sybex's *Network+ Study Guide*.

Application   Used to accomplish a particular task, an application is software that is written to supplement the commands available to a particular operating system. Each application is specifically compiled (configured) for the operating system it is going to run on. For this reason, the application relies on the OS to do many of its basic tasks. Examples of an application might include complex programs, such as Microsoft Word or Netscape Navigator, or simple programs, such as a command line FTP program. Either way, when accessing devices and memory the programs can simply request that the OS do it for them. This arrangement saves substantially on programming overhead, as much of the executable code is "shared," meaning that it is written into the operating system and can therefore be used by multiple applications running on that OS.

Driver   Extremely specific software written for the purpose of instructing a particular OS on how to access a piece of hardware. Each modem or printer has unique features and configuration settings, and the driver allows the OS to properly understand how the hardware works and what it is able to do.

Types of PC Operating Systems

This chapter will introduce a few of the major operating systems of the past 20 years and will briefly describe how they work. These are not the only operating systems out there but are simply the ones that were accepted by a large enough segment of the PC market to become *de facto* standards. As you read about these different software products, try to think about the ways they differ from one another and the reasons they were designed in the fashion they were. The A+ exam focuses only on OS options available on Intel, and it will be those systems that are given the most time in this chapter. Although Macintosh, for instance, has a strong following in certain niche markets, it is little used in corporate settings. Intel/Windows machines dominate the corporate market almost completely. By knowing some of the OS options available to you, it will be easier to decide which operating system will work best in a particular situation and you can be better prepared to recommend a particular OS to your customers. The following OSs will be will be discussed over the course of the chapter:

- CP/M
- DOS

- Windows (1–3.*x*)
- OS/2
- Windows 95
- Windows NT Workstation
- Linux
- Macintosh OS 9

To understand the emergence of modern graphical operating systems, you should know about the technologies that led to our present systems and about the critical relationship between hardware and software. Graphics, speed, GUI interfaces, and multiple programs running concurrently are all made possible by software designers taking full advantage of the hardware for which they are designing their software.

Operating System Terms and Concepts

Before we actually get too far into our discussion of PC operating systems, it may be useful to define a few key terms. Below are some terms you will come across as you study this chapter, and visit with people in the computer industry.

Version   A version is a particular revision of a piece of software, normally described by a number, which tells you how new the product is in relation to other versions of the product. MS-DOS, for instance, is currently in its sixth major version. Major revisions are distinguished from minor ones in this manner: DOS 5.0 to 6.0 was a major revision, while 6.0 to 6.2 was a minor revision. This way of marking changes is now relatively standard in marking changes in other OS and application software. Additionally, very minor revisions are indicated with an additional decimal point. Upgrading from DOS version 6.21 to 6.22 involved only a few new files, but it was still an upgrade.

Source   The actual code that defines how a piece of software works. Computer operating systems can be "open source," meaning that the OS can be examined and modified by users, or it can be "closed source," meaning users cannot modify or examine the code.

Shell   A shell is a program that runs "on top of" the operating system and allows the user to issue commands through a set of menus or some other graphical interface. Shells make using an operating system easier to use by changing the user interface. The two shells we will be looking at most closely are Microsoft's DOS Shell (a menuing system) and Windows (a fully graphical user interface).

Graphical user interface (GUI)   The user interface is the method by which a person communicates with a computer. GUIs use a mouse, touch pad, or another mechanism (in addition to the keyboard) to interact with the computer to issue commands.

Network   A network is any group of computers that have a physical communication link between them. Networks allow computers to share information and resources quickly and securely.

Cooperative multitasking   A multitasking method that depends on the application itself to be responsible for using and then freeing access to the processor. This is the way that Windows 3.1 managed multiple applications. If any application locked up while using the processor, the application was unable to properly free the processor to do other tasks, and the entire system locked, usually forcing a reboot.

Preemptive multitasking   A multitasking method in which the operating system allots each application a certain amount of processor time and then forcibly takes back control and gives another application or task access to the processor. This means that if an application crashes, the operating system takes control of the processor away from the locked application and passes it on to the next application, which should be unaffected. Although unstable programs still lock, only the locked application will stall, not the entire system.

Multithreading   The ability of a single application to have multiple requests in to the processor at one time. This results in faster application performance, because it allows a program to do many things at once. Only 32-bit or higher operating systems support multithreading.

"Classic" Operating Systems

The word "classic" sounds so much better than "obsolete", doesn't it? Still, this isn't exactly the type of heading that makes you want to take notes, is it? That's the point, in a lot of ways, as the material in this chapter is not going to be on the A+ exam. Then why, you may ask, is it in the *A+ Complete Study Guide* at all? Two reasons, really. The first is that it is easier to understand the modern OS versions you will be tested on if you understand where they come from. The second is that being a technician isn't just about passing a test, and these systems will come up in discussions all through your career, as someone reminisces about the "good old days" of DOS or OS/2. It is important that we know where we have been and how we have gotten to where we are. Knowing this background is an essential part of being an informed and effective computer-support person or service technician and certainly is in accordance with the overall goals of certification. Customers and clients will be more confident of your abilities when you can show that you have a solid understanding of your industry. That said, those of you obsessed with certification can skip ahead a few pages to the "Current Operating Systems" section while the rest of us take a stroll down memory lane on the 16-bit bus.

CP/M

The *Control Program for Microcomputer (CP/M)* is an operating system you may never have heard of because it is not in use on modern PCs. Gary Kildall wrote this OS in 1973, using his PL/M programming language. It initially ran on the Intel 8008. It was later ported to the 8080 chip and was, in many ways, very similar in function to DOS. As a matter of fact, it looks quite similar to DOS, as you can see in Figure 11.1.

FIGURE 11.1   Control Program for Microcomputer (CP/M)

```
Z80 C>SUBMIT AUTOEXEC.Z80
Z80 C>set_bdos min
Z80 C>set_cpmecho off
Z80 C>set_cpmlist lpt1
Z80 C>set_cpmpun com1
Z80 C>set_cpmrdr com1
Z80 C>set_cpu z80
Z80 C>set_fake off
Z80 C>set_illop fault
Z80 C>set_iobase 400
Z80 C>set_mask on
Z80 C>set_source z80
Z80 C>set_term h19
Z80 C>set_vars on
Z80 C>coldboot
Z80 C>
Z80 C>
```

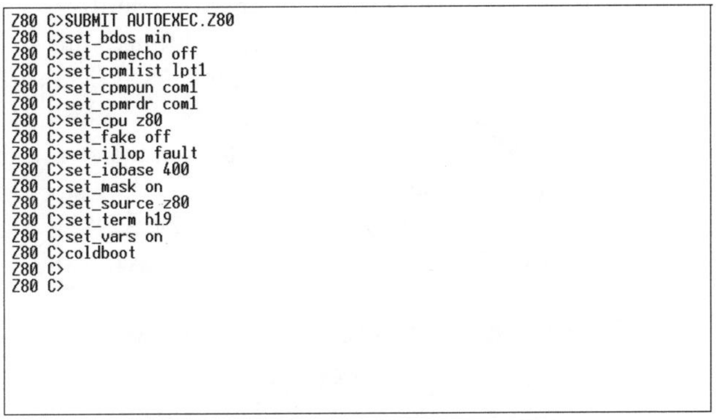

The following bit of computer folklore, which, despite questionable authenticity, has become well known in the industry, underscores the relationship between CP/M and DOS: In 1981, IBM decided to begin marketing machines to home users and small offices. They decided that, for reasons of time and efficiency, they would simply license an operating system rather than develop and support one of their own. To that end, they scheduled a meeting with Gary Kildall. The IBM representative arrived for the meeting at Kildall's house, but Gary wasn't there; he was out flying his plane. After an unsuccessful meeting with Kildall's wife and lawyer, the IBM representative left without an OS. Not long after, IBM found a different system, entering into a contract with Bill Gates by which Gates' fledgling company Microsoft (you may have heard of them) agreed to license their DOS operating system to IBM. Kildall says that this story is not accurate and, in fact, claims that Bill Gates was the first to tell the apocryphal story. One way or the other, the fact remains that Kildall's OS lost a huge opportunity. At the time that IBM allegedly came calling, CP/M was in fact the industry standard for low-cost computers on the Intel platform. Within a few years of losing the IBM contract, it was nothing but a memory.

A copy of CP/M itself is as hard to find these days as a baby sauropod, but the good folks at ZDNet have a great emulator called 22Nice available for download if you are interested in digging into computer history. Go out to zdnet.com.au/swlib/ Utilities/System_Utilities/0000CB.html to read more about it. Warning: Downloading and using command line operating systems will quickly earn you the "geek" label.

MS-DOS and PC-DOS

In the 1980s or early 1990s, the operating system that shipped with most PCs was a version of the *Disk Operating System (DOS)* created by Microsoft: *MS-DOS*. (There were a number of manufacturers of DOS, but most of them produced similar versions—they differed only in syntax and a few utilities. The important differences among DOS variants are to be found from one chronological version to the next, not among manufacturers.)

In next section, you will look at the origins of DOS and the way it has evolved, version by version, over time. After the history lesson, we will also examine some of the commands and syntax of the DOS OS, as you will need some knowledge of command line syntax before taking the A+ exam.

The Origins of DOS

The story behind MS-DOS is one of the most often told of all computer fables. But the intrigue goes further than the mystery of why Gary Kildall missed his meeting with IBM. As noted, Microsoft contracted with IBM to write the operating system for their new Intel-based microcomputer project. Although Bill Gates and his partner, Paul Allen, were both experienced programmers, they had gained their success through the creation of programming languages, not operating systems.

Gates and Allen had created the BASIC language in 1976 and had also released versions of COBOL and FORTRAN for Intel-based machines. However, they had never created an operating system from scratch, which is exactly what they promised to do for IBM. In an interesting twist, just as Seattle-based Microsoft was finishing up a very secretive deal with IBM, Tim Patterson of Seattle Computer Products began writing an operating system specifically for use with the 8086-based computer. Patterson was dissatisfied with how long it was taking for an x86 version of CP/M to be released, so he named his operating system *Quick-and-Dirty Disk Operating System (QDOS)*, and showed it to Microsoft, even as they were in the middle of talks with IBM. Paul Allen soon contracted with Seattle Computer Products to purchase QDOS to then sell to an unnamed client (IBM, of course). The purchase price of around $100,000 bought Microsoft an operating system, and a few months later, Patterson followed his operating system—he quit SCP and took a job with Gates and Allen. Microsoft soon acquired all rights to QDOS and renamed it MS-DOS.

From there, MS-DOS was modified for use with the new IBM minicomputer, and in the fall of 1981, IBM announced the IBM 5150 PC Personal Computer. The 5150 had a 4.77MHz Intel 8088 CPU, 64KB RAM, 40KB ROM, one 5.25-inch floppy drive, color graphics capability, and an OS called *PC-DOS 1.0*. PC-DOS, of course, was simply IBM's moniker for the MS-DOS they were licensing from Microsoft.

Before the PC, most computers were sold as kits. This meant that the customer had to assemble the machine, install the OS, etc. IBM debuted their IBM PC as a machine that anyone could use, because it was "ready to go" right out of the box.

Gates and Allen had contracted to allow IBM to *use* their operating system, rather than allowing IBM to *buy* it outright. Moreover, IBM had not been granted any type of exclusivity over DOS, hence Microsoft was also able to license versions of DOS to other companies, allowing the creation of what were originally called "IBM clone" machines. These machines ran on the same Intel chip as the IBM PC and used a similar version of the operating system. From 1981 on, the future of the personal computer was to be largely determined by the increasingly powerful processors created by Intel and the increasingly sophisticated operating systems Microsoft wrote to take advantage of Intel's enhancements.

MS-DOS Versions

Next we will look at the evolution of the MS-DOS operating system and will examine the major changes in microcomputer architecture and standards that are reflected in each revision. Smaller revisions—1.0 to 1.1, 6.0 to 6.1—are not enumerated, but their changes are included in the overall enhancements made to the overall version.

You will notice as you read about and use DOS that most of the versions of this operating system are very similar, as the OS proved to be very stable in its original design. Although various enhancements or features may or may not be available to you, depending on the version you are using, in a general sense you can trust that if you learn one version, you can probably use any of them.

MS-DOS 1

The original version of MS-DOS was, to put it mildly, a "no-frills" operating system. It had no provisions for networking, did not include any sort of graphical shell program, and had limited ability to manage system resources. Approximately a year after the release of DOS 1.0, a revision—DOS 1.1—added support for double-sided 320KB floppy drives. Double-sided disks were important, as they effectively doubled the machine's storage and retrieval capacity. It is difficult to grasp this concept today, when a 10- or 20-gigabyte hard drive is standard on most new desktop machines, but in 1981 internal hard drives were neither easily available nor supported by DOS. Users generally had only a single 5.25" drive, so the OS, any programs the users wanted to run, and any data they wanted to retrieve all had to be accessed through the 5.25" floppies!

MS-DOS 2

In early 1983, IBM introduced the IBM PC XT. The XT featured a 10MB hard drive, a serial interface, and three additional expansion slots. It also had 128KB of RAM and a 360KB floppy drive (40KB more capacity than that of single-sided floppies on the previous PC) and could support a 10MB internal hard drive. Users of this new PC needed an operating system that would allow them to take advantage of this new hardware, and Microsoft did not disappoint them.

MS-DOS 3

With DOS 3.0, released in summer 1984, Microsoft continued to include additional DOS features and to support more powerful hardware. DOS 3.0 supported hard drives larger than 10MB, as well as enhanced graphics formats. Three revisions—3.1, 3.2, and 3.3—provided additional innovations. The IBM PC AT was the first machine shipped with DOS 3. It had 256KB of RAM, an Intel 80286 processor (6 MHz!), and a 1.2MB 5.25~IN floppy drive. A 20MB hard drive and color video card were also available. Later upgrades to version 3 of MS-DOS included support for networking and 32MB partition sizes, as well as 1.44MB floppy drives.

Version 3.1 was notable because it featured the first DOS support for networking. The IBM PC Network was a simple local area network structure that was similar to today's workgroup networks.

DOS 3.2 introduced the XCOPY command, enabling the user to identify more than one file at a time to be copied, and it made important modifications to other DOS commands. It was also the first version to support IBM's Token Ring network topology and the first to allow for 720KB 3.5~IN floppies. Version 3.3, introduced in 1987, offered additional enhancements to numerous existing commands and introduced support for 1.44MB floppy disks. Logical partition sizes could be up to 32MB, and a single machine could support both a primary and a secondary partition on each disk. It is important to note that DOS 3 was released in 1984, the same year as Apple's infamous "1984" ad aired during the Super Bowl, marking the release of the Apple Macintosh. IBM had a great thing going with the PC, but they had gotten lazy and just made occasional improvements to DOS as needed, rather than really trying to make significant changes to it. As the challenge came in from Apple, whose graphical Macintosh

OS was clearly superior to DOS, Microsoft and IBM announced the creation of a second PC operating system, OS/2. Unfortunately, "announcing" and "delivering" are very different things, and the story of OS/2's production problems is a long one. We will look at both Apple and OS/2 later in the chapter.

MS-DOS 4

By 1988 it was apparent that the wave of the future was the graphical interface, and DOS 4 provided users with the DOS Shell, a utility much like the Windows File Manager. Actually, DOS Shell was simply a scaled-down version of Windows (which we will look at in a minute) that allowed users to manage files, run programs, and do routine maintenance, all from a single screen. The DOS Shell even supported a mouse. (That's right, there was no ability to use a mouse within DOS before this version. Oh, how Mac lovers must have mocked Microsofties back in the dark days of '88!)

MS-DOS 5

There were several important features introduced in the 1991 release of DOS 5.0. First of all, the ability to load drivers into reserved (upper) memory was a relief to those people who were constantly running out of conventional memory. This feature allowed more complex DOS programs (that took up more conventional memory) to be developed.

In addition to this feature, several software utilities made their debut. The most commonly used utility introduced at this time was EDIT.COM. This ASCII text editor has since become one of the most popular text editors for simple text files (and a welcomed relief from the single-line view of EDLIN.COM—previously the only choice for a text editor). Also added in DOS 5 were QBASIC.EXE, DOSKEY, UNFORMAT, and UNDELETE.

MS-DOS 6

Released in 1993 to excellent sales (and a lawsuit for patent infringement), DOS 6.0 offered a number of new commands and configurable options. Another enhancement in DOS 6.0 was EMM386.EXE, which allowed the system to pool extended and expanded memory. DOS 6.0 has subsequently been revised a number of times—once (DOS 6.2 to 6.21) because of a court order. Microsoft was found to have violated Stac Electronics' patent rights in the creation of the DoubleSpace utility for 6.0 and 6.1, and the only real difference between 6.2 and 6.21 is that DoubleSpace is removed. Never to be denied, Microsoft soon released DOS 6.22 with a disk compression program called DriveSpace.

As of this writing, DOS 6.22 is the most current MS-DOS version available as a stand-alone operating system. Microsoft has included certain DOS-style command line utilities for use within Windows 95, Windows NT and Windows 2000, but these are actually Windows programs that simply mimic the familiar, old command-prompt environment of DOS.

Microsoft Windows

Any real understanding of the success of DOS after 1987 requires knowledge of Windows. In the early years of its existence, Microsoft's DOS gained great acceptance and became a standard as a PC operating system. Even so, as computers became more powerful and programs more complex, the limitations of the DOS command-line interface were becoming apparent (as well as the aforementioned conventional memory limitation).

The solution to the problem was to make the operating system easier to navigate, more uniform, and generally more "friendly" to the user. IBM had understood that the average user did not want to receive their computer in pieces but preferred to have it ready-to-go out of the box. Oddly, they did not understand that the same user who wanted their *hardware* to be ready-to-go also wanted their *software* to be the same way. They did not want to edit batch files or hunt through directories using CD or DIR commands either. Because of this, when Microsoft came to IBM with a graphical user interface (GUI) based on groundbreaking work done by Xerox labs, IBM was not interested, preferring to go onward with the development of OS/2, a project it had already started with Microsoft.

The Xerox Corporation maintained a think-tank of computer designers in Palo Alto, California called the Palo Alto Research Center (PARC). One of the results of their work was the Alto workstation, which is generally thought to be the forerunner of all modern graphical operating systems. The Alto had a mouse and a GUI interface, and it communicated with other stations via Ethernet. Oh, and it was finished in 1974! Although it was never promoted commercially, both Microsoft and Apple viewed the Alto and incorporated its technology into their own systems. The accomplishments of the PARC lab in laying the groundwork for modern graphical computing systems simply cannot be overstated. Check out www.parc.xerox.com for more information on PARC past and present.

Regardless of IBM's interest, Microsoft continued on its own with its development of the GUI—which it named *Windows* after its rectangular work areas—and released the first version to the market in 1985. Apple filed a lawsuit soon after, claiming that the Microsoft GUI had been built using Apple technology, but the suit was dismissed. Apple's Macintosh and Microsoft's DOS-with-Windows combo have both continued to evolve, but until a recent deal between Apple and Microsoft, tensions have always been high. Mac and PC *users*, of course, still remain adamantly chauvinistic about their respective platforms.

Oh, the stories that have been told around the glow of a monitor about Gates vs. Jobs. Even so, one of the easiest ways to get a bit of the flavor of the struggle is through a recent movie called "Pirates of the Silicon Valley," in which Anthony Michael Hall of "The Breakfast Club" plays Gates and Noah Wyle of "ER" fame plays Jobs. More info at tnt.turner.com/movies/tntoriginals/pirates.

The Windows interface to MS-DOS is really just a shell program that allows users to issue DOS commands through a graphical interface—a prettier extension of Microsoft's earlier DOS Shell work. The integration of a mouse for nearly all tasks—a legacy of the Xerox Alto computer on which both the Macintosh and Windows GUIs are based—further freed users from DOS by allowing them to issue common commands without using the keyboard. Word processors, spreadsheets, and especially games were revolutionized as software manufacturers happily took advantage of the ease of use and flexibility that Windows added to DOS.

Windows Versions

After the development of Windows, many of the enhancements made to subsequent versions of DOS were designed to help free up and reallocate resources to better run Windows and Windows-based applications. Similarly, PC hardware continued to evolve far past the limits of DOS's ability to effectively use the power available to it, and later versions of Windows would be designed to hide and overcome the limitations of the operating system. The combination of MS-DOS and its Windows shell would make Microsoft the industry leader, and spurred the PC movement to new heights in the early 1990s. Following is a brief examination of the development of the Windows shell and a look at its different versions.

Windows 1

Version 1 of Windows featured the tiling windows, mouse support, and menu systems that still drive next-generation operating systems such as Windows 98, Windows CE, and Windows 2000. It also offered "cooperative multitasking," meaning that more than one Windows application could run concurrently. This was something that MS-DOS, up to this point, could not do.

Windows 1 was far from a finished product. For one thing, it didn't use icons, and it had few of the programs we have come to expect as Windows standards. Windows 1 was basically just an updated, more graphical version of the DOS SHELL.EXE program.

Windows 2

Version 2, released in 1987, added icons and allowed application windows to overlap each other, as well as tile. Support was also added for PIFs (program information files), which allowed the user to configure Windows to run their DOS applications more efficiently.

Windows 3.*x*

Windows 3.0 featured a far more flexible memory model, allowing it to access more memory than the 640KB limit normally imposed by DOS. It also featured the addition of the File Manager and Program Manager, allowed for network support, and could operate in "386 Enhanced mode." 386 Enhanced mode used parts of the hard drive as "virtual memory" and was therefore able to use disk memory to supplement the RAM in the machine. Windows today, in fact, is still quite similar to the Windows of version 3.0.

In 1992, a revision of Windows 3, known as Windows 3.1, provided for better graphical display capability and multimedia support. It also improved the Windows error-protection system and let applications work together more easily through the use of object linking and embedding (OLE).

Windows after the introduction of version 3.1 took a marked turn for the better, because Microsoft started making a serious effort to change to a full 32-bit application environment. With version 3.11, also known as Windows for Workgroups, Windows could offer support for both 16-bit and 32-bit applications. (Windows 3.1 could only support 16-bit applications.) Significant progress on the 32-bit front was not to be made, however, until very late in 1995, when Microsoft introduced Windows 95. Since that time the venerable DOS/Windows team has been largely replaced by newer, more advanced systems. You may occasionally still run into a Windows 3.1 machine, but it is not a common occurrence.

With the introduction of Windows for Workgroups, people speaking generically about the two "flavors" of Windows—3.1 and 3.11—started referring to them collectively as *Windows 3.x*, as in the heading of this section.

OS/2

Even as Windows 3.1 was in development, Microsoft was participating in a joint effort with IBM to create a next-generation operating system for use with 286 and higher processors. This operating system was to be IBM/Microsoft's second generation OS, or OS/2, intended to replace DOS. Differing goals for the design of the new system caused a number of disagreements, though, and the partnership soon broke up. IBM continued the development of OS/2 on their own, while Microsoft took their part of the technology and began to develop LAN Manager, which would eventually lead to the development of Windows NT.

With the second version, IBM made OS/2 a 32-bit system that required at least a 386 processor to run. Although this made it vastly more stable and powerful than Windows 3.1, both it and Microsoft's NT product had a problem finding a market. The main reason for this was probably that most users simply did not have powerful enough computers to properly use the system, and few pieces of software were available that leveraged the new architecture and OS properly.

With version 3 (OS/2 Warp), IBM created a multitasking, 32-bit OS that required a 386 but preferred a 486. Warp also required a ridiculous 4MB of RAM just to load. With a graphical interface and the ability to do a great deal of self-configuration, the Warp OS was a peculiar cross between DOS and a Macintosh. Warp featured true preemptive multitasking, did not suffer from the memory limitations of DOS, and had a desktop similar to the Macintosh.

For all of its tremendous features, OS/2 Warp had a funny name and was badly marketed. It never really established a wide user base. Nonetheless, until Windows NT 3.51 was released in 1995, OS/2 was the operating system of choice for high-end workstations, and up until recently the OS retained a small but faithful following. The last year or so has been harsh on OS/2 fans, though, as IBM has essentially abandoned the high-end desktop market to Windows NT, Windows 2000, and Linux. OS/2 has been largely forgotten, and IBM now ships Windows 2000 Professional with its own desktops. When even the company that makes an OS stops pushing it, it drops into the "obsolete" section real quick. For more info on OS/2, including current support options, go out to IBM's OS/2 information page at www-4.ibm.com/software/os/warp.

Windows 95

Although it dominated the market with its DOS operating system and its add-on Windows interface, Microsoft found that the constraints of DOS were rapidly making it difficult to take full advantage of rapidly improving hardware and software developments. The future of computing was clearly a 32-bit, preemptively multitasked system such as IBM's OS/2, but many current users had DOS-based software or older hardware that was specifically designed for DOS and would not operate outside of its Windows 3.1, cooperatively multitasked environment.

Because of this problem, in the fall of 1995 Microsoft released a major upgrade to the DOS/Windows environment. Called Windows 95, the new product integrated the operating system and the shell. Where previous versions of Windows simply provide a graphic interface to the existing DOS OS, the Windows 95 graphical interface *is* part of the OS. Moreover, Windows 95 was designed to be a hybrid of the features of previous DOS versions and newer 32-bit systems. To this end, it is a preemptively multitasked system that is able to emulate and support cooperative multitasking for programs that require it. It also supports both 32-bit and 16-bit drivers as well as DOS drivers, although the 32-bit drivers are strongly recommended over the DOS ones, as they are far more stable and faster.

Among the most important of the other enhancements debuted by Microsoft with Windows 95 was support for the Plug-and-Play standard (PnP). This meant that if a device was designed to be plug-and-play, a technician could install the device into the computer, start the machine, and have the device automatically recognized and configured by Windows 95. This was a major advance, but unfortunately for Plug and Play to work properly, three things had to be true:

1. The OS had to be PnP compatible.

2. The computer motherboard had to support PnP.

3. All devices in the machine had to be PnP compatible.

Unfortunately, at the time Windows 95 came out many manufacturers were creating their hardware for use in DOS/Windows machines, and DOS did not support PnP, so most pre-1995 computer components were not PnP compliant. Because of this, these components—generally referred to as "legacy" devices—often interfered with the Plug-and-Play environment. Legacy devices are sound cards, modems, etc. that do not support the Plug-and-Play standard. Such devices are not able to dynamically interact with newer systems. They therefore require manual configuration or must be replaced by newer devices, which don't usually need manual configuration. Due to problems managing legacy hardware under Windows 95, many people soured on PnP technology. Worse, they blamed Windows 95 for their problems, not the old hardware. "It worked fine in DOS" was the standard logic! Now, half a decade later, nearly all PC components are PnP compliant, and configuring computer systems is far easier than it was under DOS.

The foibles of PnP aside, to say that the new system was a success would be a major understatement. Within just a few years of its release, the Windows 95–style GUI had won over nearly all Windows users, and the more resilient architecture of 95 had won over network administrators and computer technicians. While it was far from perfect, Windows 95 was a tremendous advance out of the DOS age. Perhaps the only ones not thrilled were the folks at Apple, who continued to make a cottage industry out of starting lawsuits against Microsoft. This time Apple was contending that the Windows 95 interface itself was stolen from the Macintosh. While it is undeniable that the 95 interface is an evil twin of the Mac interface, it turned out that Apple themselves had gotten their GUI from somewhere else...the PARC Alto! Unbelievably, Xerox had evidently not only designed the first computer GUI, but they had created an interface that could not be significantly improved upon in over 20 years of OS development, and which both Apple and Microsoft settled on as the basis for their GUIs! All subsequent versions of Windows (98, NT, and 2000) use an interface essentially identical to the Windows 95 GUI.

Part II, Chapter 12, "Introduction to the Windows Interface," goes into depth on the nature of the Windows 95/98/NT/2000 interface, and overall Windows 95 OS is only marginally different from its Windows 98 upgrade, which is one of the operating systems you will be tested on during the A+ exam. As such, Windows 95 will be grouped with 98 for the rest of the book, and we will be more concerned with the differences between Windows 9*x* and Windows 2000 than we will be by differences between Windows 95 and Windows 98.

Other Current Operating Systems

And then there were only five. As this book is written, the desktop operating system market is dominated by one operating system, while four others are viable options...or pretenders to the throne. Clearly, Windows 95/98 is the primary desktop OS in the world, with a stranglehold on the desktops of the corporate environment and a strong lead in the home market. It is not, though, the only OS you may run across, and many high-end workstations are running one of the other options listed below. Without further ado, the five current OS options are

- Windows 98
- Windows NT Workstation
- Windows 2000 Professional
- Linux (all distributions)
- Mac OS 9

We will be talking about Windows 98 and Windows 2000 in depth throughout the rest of the study guide, as they are the two operating systems that you will be tested on. As such, the remainder of this chapter will focus on the other OS options available to the daring PC owner.

On the horizon: Microsoft released Windows Me just as the A+ test objectives were being finalized. Because of the timing of its debut, Me will not be part of the exam. Me is an upgrade to Windows 98 and is expected to be the last version of the Windows 95/98/Me architecture. Plans are for future releases of Microsoft's home/low-end desktop product to be based on the more stable Windows 2000 architecture instead of on the Windows 95 architecture.

Windows NT Workstation

As previously noted, Windows 98 is currently the most common PC operating system on the market. Still, for users who need more power, other options are available. One of these is the Windows NT operating system. NT (which unofficially stands for New Technology) is an OS that was designed to be far more powerful than any previous Windows version. It uses an architecture based entirely on 32-bit code and is capable of accessing up to four gigabytes (4,000 megabytes) of RAM.

Windows NT can support huge drive sizes and more than one processor, and has numerous advantages over Windows 95 and DOS. NT comes in two varieties—Workstation and Server, each intended for a particular role. NT Server is designed as the centerpiece of a network and is able to carry out numerous tasks for organizing and managing networked computers. Windows NT Workstation, on the other hand, is intended for users who work with large files or complex programs. CAD (computer-aided design) programs are a good example of the sort of applications that run better under NT than under other versions of Windows.

Windows NT also allows for better security than previous versions of Windows and is more stable. Naturally, each version of NT that has come out has been more expensive than the current version of Windows 3.*x* or 95 and needed a significantly more powerful machine to run well. A quick rundown of the evolution of NT follows.

Windows NT Workstation 3.*x*

Windows NT was first released in 1993, under the title of *Windows NT 3.1*. Where, you may ask, were Windows NT 1.0 and 2.0? Perhaps in the same closet at Microsoft where all of the copies of Word 5.0 are hidden....NT was essentially a reworking of the LAN Manager software which had come out of Microsoft's aborted OS/2 partnership with IBM, but part of the "New Technology" (hence NT) offering was a workstation option that had not been available on LAN Manager. Windows NT 3.1 debuted at the familiar 3.1 version number to stay in line with the rest of the 3.*x* Windows family. It was subsequently upgraded to 3.5 and then to 3.51.

In 1993 Windows NT 3.1 was definitely a step up from DOS/Windows and was adopted in many CAD and number-crunching environments. When Windows NT 3.51 arrived in the fall of 1995, it featured a number of improvements, such as a fully 32-bit OS, file-level security, support for more RAM, and support for multiple processors.

Windows NT Workstation 4.0

With the release in 1996 of Windows NT 4.0, the NT platform was given a facelift and now sported the popular Windows 95 GUI. (NT 3.*x* had used the Windows 3.*x* Program Manager GUI.) This and the increasing availability of NT-compatible application software allowed NT 4.0 Workstation to solidify its place in the market as a high-end desktop. NT was positioned directly against its cousin, OS/2 Warp. With the 95 GUI and the power of Microsoft marketing, NT quickly took over most of the "power user" market. NT workstations are excellent for any of the following tasks:

- Database client
- Graphics station
- CAD station

Probably the only real problem that the Windows NT system had when compared to Windows 95 was that both NT 3.*x* and NT 4.0 lacked plug-and-play capabilities, a fact that would irritate many a technician over the next few years.

LINUX

Over the past couple of years the "open-source" movement has been rallying around Linus Torvalds and his Linux OS. Linux is a Unix-type operating system that has been released into the public domain and is being developed as an operating system standard, much as TCP/IP is a protocol standard. There are a number of computer users who are uncomfortable with Microsoft's dominance of the crucial OS market, and, as a result, Linux has been positioned as an excellent alternative to the Microsoft juggernaut. There were suspicions that CompTIA would be adding Linux questions into the A+ exam, but in the end it was decided that Linux' time had not yet come.

This was probably the right decision, for two reasons. The first of these is that while it is making inroads with knowledgeable home users and is even being used as a server in many corporate environments, Linux has simply not been able to break into the mass home or corporate desktop markets that the A+ objectives prepare you to serve. The second reason follows from this. Because most Linux users are computer junkies themselves, few of them will be taking their computers in for professional (i.e., paid) configuration or support. As an A+ certified tech, you will be working for the people who will pay you, and most of them are still running Windows.

That said, Linux is a nifty idea. The theory behind it is to make core operating system code available to anyone who wants it, so that the code can then be explored and enhanced by users. Those who choose to can even create a full Unix-type OS from the Linux source code, modify it as they see fit, and release it to the world as a Linux "distribution." Distributions are similar to versions, but where versions are chronological enhancements to a single company's OS, distributions are variations on a single OS theme. For a list of Linux distributions, refer to www.linux.org/dist/english.html.

The architecture of Linux is based on Unix, the OS used in mainframes and other high-end computers, and it is extremely powerful and stable. Linux also is commonly used as a Web server or e-mail server on the Internet, and can function as either a network operating system or a desktop operating system, just as Windows NT can.

There are few creatures more rabid in defense of their cause than Linux fans, and for good reason. The basic philosophy of Linux is that the people who use an operating system are the ones who know best what needs to be improved on it and that user feedback should be respected and acted upon. Linux has not always been an OS for the masses, as early distributions were complex to install and had little application support, but through a small army of users sending suggestions it has improved markedly.

The Linux vs. Microsoft debate is an interesting one in the computer world, as it is a face-off between idealism and corporate power, open-source and proprietary code. It is a battleground where we will eventually see whether users prefer a system which gives them power (but requires a bit more work) or one that makes everything easy (but gives them fewer choices). Should be fun to watch, if nothing else.

For detailed information of the world of Linux, two Web sites are obvious starting points: www.linux.org and www.linux.com. Linux.org is probably the better of the two for those interested in simply learning about what Linux is, and it has a great online course called "Getting Started with Linux."

Macintosh OS 9

Finally, we come to the venerable old man of the graphical operating system world, the Apple Macintosh. Apple was founded by Steve Jobs and Steve Wozniak. Wozniak built the first Apple, and was the technical wizard. Jobs was the sales and marketing guy, and together they built and marketed the Apple II, which Jobs dubbed "the computer for the rest of us." The Apple II was an immediate success, as it had color graphics, and useful applications such as Visicalc were available for it. For 1977, it was quite a spiffy machine.

The Apple was a relatively simple computer, though, and was operated via an OS like CP/M or BASIC. In 1984 all that changed, as Apple unveiled the Macintosh, a new machine with a revolutionary graphic user interface. Or at least an interface revolutionary to everyone outside the PARC labs. The original Mac had its faults—it was too expensive, it didn't have a hard drive, etc.—but nonetheless it laid the groundwork for many Macs (and Windows enhancements) to come. The Mac II came out in 1987, and included color support (the original Mac was b/w), but overall the Macintosh was undermined by problems within Apple (that caused Steve Jobs to be forced out) and limited Macintosh software development. The Apple philosophy was always one of producing both the hardware and the software for their machines and not licensing anyone else to do either. Eventually this backfired, as consumers chose cheaper and better-supported Intel/Microsoft options instead.

Fast forward to 2000, and the Macintosh is relatively popular again after nearly a decade of decline. A good part of this renaissance is due to the extremely successful iMac line, and the continuing success of the PowerBook (a Macintosh notebook). Mac computers are often found in artsy places—design houses, marketing departments, etc.—and are still the choice of people who want their computer to be simple to use and pretty to look at. Mind you, there's nothing wrong with that, but thank heavens we aren't tested on these things.

Choosing an Operating System

Now that we have sampled the variety of PC operating systems, it is time to take a more in-depth look at the two systems that dominate the current environment: Windows 95/98 and Windows 2000.

If you have users who have older hardware, Windows 95 may be the best bet, simply because of its low resource usage. Most other home users will be happiest with Windows 98 (or now Windows Me), and corporate users are generally divided between Windows 98/Me and Windows NT Workstation/Windows 2000 Professional. As we will see, users who need higher performance or strong security should be nudged toward NT or 2000 Professional. Really, the choices that you will probably be dealing with come down to the two OS options dealt with in-depth in the following chapters: Windows 98 for home/casual users and Windows NT for high-end systems.

Now that we have discussed the various types of PC operating systems, it is time to take a quick look at which ones you may want to recommend for users who are looking to upgrade. First off, Macintosh and Linux are sort of off on their own. The Mac OS runs on a different processor than Intel PCs, so if you own an Apple machine, you will be running the Mac OS on it. Linux is a great system, but is only for the adventurous at this time and is generally not something you want to recommend to the casual user. Linux will certainly work for anyone, but experienced computer users will be happier with it than novices will. That leaves us with the Microsoft family of products. If you have users who have older hardware, Windows 95 may be the best bet, simply because of its low resource usage. Most other home users will be happiest with Windows 98 or Windows Me, and corporate users are generally divided between Windows 98/Me and Windows NT Workstation/Windows 2000 Professional. Users who need higher performance or strong security should be nudged toward NT or 2000 Pro.

Summary

In this chapter we have looked at the evolution of the personal computer and how it has changed over the past two decades. The PC and especially its ever-improving operating systems have revolutionized the way that computing is done. From the Xerox Alto GUI to DOS to Macs and Windows, a number of different solutions have been found to the problem of allowing humans to communicate with machines. Over the rest of this book, we will leave behind most of the operating systems, just as CompTIA has done, and focus on just two platforms—Windows 98 and Windows 2000. The choices that you will probably face come down to the two OS options dealt with in-depth in the following chapters, where we will explore Windows 98 for home/casual users and Windows NT for high-end systems.

Key Terms

Before you take the exam, be certain you are familiar with the following terms:

Control Program for Microcomputer (CP/M)

PC-DOS 1.0

co-operative multitasking

preemptive multitasking

Disk Operating System (DOS)

Quick-and-Dirty Disk Operating System (QDOS)

graphical user interface (GUI)

shell

MS-DOS

source

multithreading

version

network

Review Questions

1. All of the following are important developments in Intel platform PC operating systems except _____.

   A. CP/M

   B. MS-DOS and PC-DOS

   C. Windows Interfaces to DOS

   D. OS/1

2. CP/M stands for _____.

   A. Control Processing Management

   B. Control Program for Microcomputer

   C. Control Power for Microcomputer

   D. Control Processing Microcomputer

3. What was the original version of MS-DOS?

   A. MS-DOS 2

   B. MS-DOS 3

   C. MS-DOS 1

   D. MS-DOS 5

4. What was the major innovation that came after MS-DOS -1?

   A. The 5.25" disk drive

   B. The 3.5" disk drive

   C. Double-sided 3.35" disks were created

   D. Double-sided 320K floppy drives were created

5. In early 1983 IBM introduced the IBM PC-XT. The PC-XT featured all of the following except _____.

   A. DOS 1.25 was the operating system

   B. 10MB hard drive

   C. Serial interface

   D. Three additional expansion slots

   E. 128K of RAM

6. The XT shipped with which version of DOS?

   A. MS-DOS 3

   B. MS-DOS 2

   C. MS-DOS 4

   D. MS-DOS 1

7. All of the following were features of MS-DOS 3 except _____.

    A. Supported hard drives larger than 10MB

    B. Enhanced graphics formats

    C. Support for networking

    D. Could support 1.44MB floppy drives

8. The IBM PC-AT introduced in 1984 featured all but which the following?

    A. 128KB RAM

    B. An Intel processor 80286

    C. 1.25MB floppy drive

    D. 20MB hard drive

9. What was the first graphical interface that was introduced with MS-DOS 4?

    A. GUI

    B. DOSwin

    C. DOS Shell

    D. DOSini

10. The XCOPY command was introduced with which DOS version?

    A. DOS version 3.2

    B. DOS Version 3.1

    C. DOS Version 3.0

    D. DOS Version 4

11. All of the following were features introduced by MSDOS-5 except _____.

    A. The ability to load drivers into reserved or upper memory

    B. EDIT.COM utility

    C. EDLIN.COM

    D. QBASIC.EXE

12. What version of MS-DOS was DOSKEY.COM and UNDELETE.EXE introduced?

    A. MS-DOS version 6

    B. MS-DOS version 5

    C. MS-DOS version 4

    D. MS-DOS version 3

13. The ability to pool EMS and XMS memory using EMM386.EXE was introduced in which version of DOS?

A. MS-DOS 5

B. MS-DOS 4

C. MS-DOS 6

D. MS-DOS 3

14. Windows featured tiling windows, mouse support, and menu systems in which versions?

A. Windows 1

B. Windows 2

C. Windows 3

D. Windows 95

E. All of the Above

15. What was the first Windows version that allowed more memory than the 640KB limit normally imposed by DOS?

A. Windows 1

B. Windows 2

C. Windows 3

D. Windows 95

16. What was the first 32-bit preemptive multitasking system?

A. Windows 2

B. Windows 3

C. Windows 1

D. Windows 95

17. _____ is the best of these Microsoft operating system for users needing to deal with large files or complex programs.

A. Windows NT

B. Windows 95

C. Windows 3.11

D. Windows 2

18. What was the minimum processor that version 2 of OS/2, a 32-bit system, required?

A. 486

B. 586

C. 686

D. 386

19. Which Windows operating system would provide high performance and file security?

A. Windows 95

B. Windows 98

C. Windows NT

D. Windows Me

20. Which of these "classic" operating systems can be looked at as the model on which modern graphical systems such as Windows 2000 and the Apple Macintosh are based?

A. Windows 1.0

B. OS/2

C. CP/M

D. Alto

Answers to Review Questions

1. D. CP/M, MS-DOS and PC-DOS, and Windows Interfaces are all are important developments in Intel platform PC operating systems.

2. B. This OS was written in 1973 by Gary Kildall, using Kildall's PL/M programming language, and it initially ran on the Intel 8008. It was later ported to the 8080 chip and was in many ways very similar in function to DOS.

3. C. This DOS version had a "no-frills" operating system. It had no provisions for networking, did not include any sort of graphical shell program, and had limited ability to manage system resources.

4. D. Double-sided 320K floppy drives were created was the major innovation that came after MS-DOS -1. At the time, hard drives were not easily available; therefore, all information was stored on 5.25" floppy disk.

5. A. The XT featured a 10MB hard drive, a serial interface, and three additional expansion slots. It also had 128KB of RAM and a 360KB floppy drive.

6. B. The XT shipped with MS-DOS 2.0, a revision of the DOS operating system that had to be redone almost from the ground up. It closely fit the machine it was built for, and it supported 10MB hard drives and the new 360KB floppy disks.

7. D. MS-DOS 3 could not support 1.44MB floppy drives. MS-DOS used 5.25" floppy drives.

8. A. The IBM PC-AT introduced in 1984 did not feature 128KB RAM. The IBM PC-AT was the first machine shipped with DOS 3. It had 256KB of RAM, an Intel 80286 processor (6 MHz!), and a 1.2MB, 5.25" floppy drive. A 20MB hard drive and color video card were also available.

9. C. MS-DOS 4 introduced the first graphical interface, which was called DOS Shell. The DOS Shell was simply a scaled-down version of Windows that allowed users to manage files, run programs, and do routine maintenance all from a single screen. The DOS Shell even supported a mouse.

10. A. The XCOPY command was introduced with DOS version 3.2. The XCOPY command enables the user to identify more than one file at a time to be copied. It also copies file attributes.

11. C. MS-DOS introduced all of the features listed except EDLIN.COM which was introduced in MS-DOS 3.0 and is a line editor.

12. B. DOSKEY.COM and UNDELETE.EXE were introduced in MS-DOS version 5. The DOSKEY.COM command loads the DOSKEY program into memory. DOSKEY is a program that runs in the background of other programs. The UNDELETE.EXE command makes it possible to recover a deleted file if the space on the disk has not been written over by a new file.

13. C. The ability to pool EMS and XMS memory using EMM386.EXE was introduced in MS-DOS 6. EMS stands for Expanded Memory Specification and provides access for the microprocessor to the upper memory area. XMS is Extended Memory Specification and is loaded by HIMEM.SYS.

14. B, C, D. Windows featured tiling windows, mouse support, and menu systems in all Windows versions from Windows 1 through Windows 95.

15. C. Windows 3 substantially increased the size and complexity of programs that could be executed under DOS/Windows and was a crucial step in making Windows a viable product.

16. D. The first 32-bit preemptive multitasking system was Windows 95. Windows 95 is a preemptively multitasked system that is able to emulate and support cooperative multitasking for programs that require it. It also supports both 32-bit and 16-bit drivers as well as DOS drivers, although the 32-bit drivers are strongly recommended over the DOS ones, as they are far more stable and are faster.

17. A. Support for large files or complex programs was the specialty of Windows NT, and its mantle has now been passed to Windows 2000. These operating systems are designed to support more and faster hardware and to provide greater stability and security.

18. D. IBM made version 2 of OS/2 a 32-bit system that required at least a 386 processor to run. This made it immensely more stable and powerful.

19. C. Windows NT is a 32-bit OS that offers file-level security and support for multiple processors.

20. D. Although all of these systems have had some effect on the composition of modern GUIs, it was the Xerox Alto that was first with many of the innovations that we now look at as the basis of a GUI system, including the mouse and windowing capability.

Chapter

12

Using the Microsoft Operating System GUI

THE FOLLOWING OBJECTIVES ARE COVERED IN THIS CHAPTER:

✓ 1.1 Identify the operating system's functions, structure, and major system files to navigate the operating system and how to get to needed technical information.

   Content may include the following:

- Major operating system functions
  - Create folders
  - Checking OS version
- Major operating system components
  - Explorer
  - My Computer
  - Control Panel
- Contrasts between Windows 9x and Windows 2000
- Major system files: what they are, where they are located, how they are used, and what they contain:

   System, configuration, and user interface files

- IO.SYS
- BOOT.INI
- WIN.COM
- MSDOS.SYS
- AUTOEXEC.BAT
- CONFIG.SYS
- Command line prompt

   Memory management

- Conventional
- Extended/upper memory
- High memory
- Virtual memory

- HIMEM.SYS
- EMM386.EXE

Windows 9*x*

- IO.SYS
- WIN.INI
- USER.DAT
- SYSEDIT
- SYSTEM.INI
- MSCONFIG (98)
- COMMAND.COM
- REGEDIT.EXE
- SYSTEM.DAT
- Run command
- Command line prompt

Windows 2000

- Computer management
- BOOT.INI
- REGEDT32
- REGEDIT
- RUN CMD
- NTLDR
- NTDETECT.COM
- NTBOOTDD.SYS

Command prompt procedures (command syntax)

- DIR
- Attrib
- VER
- MEM
- SCANDISK
- DEFRAG
- EDIT
- XCOPY
- COPY
- SETVER
- SCANREG

As mentioned in the previous chapter, the Windows 95 graphical user interface (GUI) has been incredibly successful since its debut. Because of this, all Microsoft operating system GUIs since then have drawn heavily from Windows 95. Among these are both Windows 98 and Windows 2000, the two key operating systems you will need to know for the A+ operating systems exam.

For complete coverage of objective 1.1, please also see Chapter 14. For coverage of the Memory management subobjectives of objective 1.1, refer back to Part I, Chapter 3.

The development of the graphical user interface from the Alto to Windows 2000 was discussed in Chapter 11, "An Introduction to Computer Operating Systems," and made out to be a major reason the personal computer industry has taken off in the last decade or two. What exactly is it all about, though? In this chapter, we will look at the post-Windows 95 Microsoft GUI from the ground up, beginning with a detailed look at its key components and ending with an exploration of basic tasks common to both Windows 98 and Windows 2000. The following general topics will be covered:

- Windows GUI components
- Using Windows Explorer and Internet Explorer
- Using Control Panel
- The command prompt

The Windows 9x/2000 Interface

When you look at the monitor of a machine running Windows 98 and then look at the monitor of a machine running Windows 2000, it is difficult to tell the two apart. If you look closely, you will notice that the names of some icons have changed, but for the most part the two are identical and look very much like the screen in Figure 12.1.

FIGURE 12.1 The Windows interface

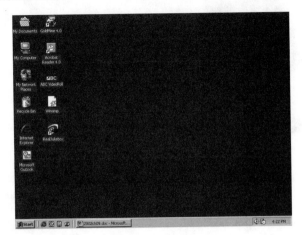

As a technician, you will quickly realize that this is very good for you! Because of Microsoft's standardization of a single graphical interface for all of its operating systems, most basic tasks are accomplished in identical fashion on everything from a Windows 95 workstation computer to a Windows 2000 Advanced Server computer. Also, while the tools that are used often vary between Windows 98 and 2000, the way you use those tools remains remarkably consistent across *platforms*.

We will begin by taking an overview look at the common elements of the Windows GUI. We will then look at some tasks that are similar across Windows 98 and 2000. If you have a copy of Windows 9x or Windows NT4/2000 available, you may want to follow along by exploring each of the elements as they are discussed. If you are able to follow along, you may also notice that there are numerous additional icons and options we are not mentioning. Some of these will be covered in later chapters, so for now simply ignore them, or browse through them on your own and then return to the text.

The Desktop

The Desktop, simply put, is the virtual desk upon which all of your other programs and utilities run. By default it contains the *Start menu*, the *Taskbar*, and a number of *icons*. The Desktop can also contain additional elements, such as Web page content, through the use of the Active Desktop option. Because it is the base on which everything else sits, how the Desktop is configured can have a major effect on how the GUI looks and how convenient it is for users.

You can change the Desktop's background patterns, screen saver, color scheme, and size by right-clicking any area of the Desktop that doesn't contain an icon. The menu that appears allows you to do several things, such as creating new Desktop items, changing how your icons are arranged, or selecting a special command called Properties, as shown in Figure 12.2.

FIGURE 12.2   The Desktop right-click

The Three Clicks in Windows

- Primary mouse click. A single click used to select an object or place a cursor.

- Double-click. Two primary mouse clicks in quick succession. Used to open a program through an icon or for other specific application functions.

- Secondary mouse click. Most mice have two buttons. Clicking once on the secondary button (usually the one on the right side, although that can be modified) is interpreted differently from a left mouse click. Generally in Windows this displays a context-sensitive menu from which you are given the ability to perform tasks or view object properties.

When you right-click the Desktop and choose Properties, you will see the Display Properties screen shown in Figure 12.3. From this screen you can click the various tabs at the top to move to the different screens of information about the way Windows looks. Tabs are similar to index cards, in that they are staggered across the top so you can see and access large amounts of data within a single small window. Each Properties window has a different set of tabs. Among the tabs in the Display Properties are the following:

Background   Used to select an HTML document or a picture to display on the desktop.

Screen Saver   Sets up an automatic screen saver to cover your screen if you have not been active for a certain period of time. Originally used to prevent "burned" monitors, they are now generally used for entertainment or to password-protect user's desktops. The Screen Saver tab also contains other power settings.

Appearance Used to select a color scheme for the Desktop or to change the color or size of other Desktop elements.

Effects Contains numerous options best described as "assorted visual options."

Web Allows for configuration of Active Desktop settings.

Settings Used to set color depth or screen size. Also contains the Advanced button, which leads to graphics driver and monitor configuration settings.

FIGURE 12.3 The Display Properties screen

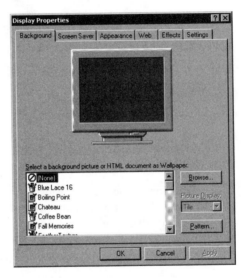

 You can also access the Display Properties settings by using the Display Control Panel under Start ➢ Settings ➢ Control Panel.

EXERCISE 12.1

Changing a Screen Saver

To change the Windows screen saver on Windows 98 or Windows 2000, perform the following steps:

1. Right-click the Desktop.

2. Choose Properties from the context menu.

3. Click the Screen Saver tab.

4. Choose Starfield Simulation. Click Preview to see the new screen saver. Move the mouse to cancel the screen saver and return to your Desktop.

5. Click the OK or the Apply button. (OK performs two tasks: Apply and Exit window, while Apply leaves the window open.)

The Taskbar

The Taskbar (see Figure 12.4) is another standard component of the Windows interface. It contains two major items: the Start menu and the System Tray. The Start menu is on the left side of the Taskbar and is easily identifiable by the fact that it is a button that has the word "Start" on it. The System Tray is located on the right side of the Taskbar and contains only a clock by default, but other Windows utilities (for example, screen savers or virus-protection utilities) may put their icons here when running to indicate that they are running and to provide the user with a quick way to get access to their features.

FIGURE 12.4   The Taskbar

Besides the Start button and the System Tray, the middle area of the Taskbar is also used by Windows. Whenever you open a new window or program, it gets a button on the Taskbar with an icon that represents the window or program. To bring that window or program to the front (or to maximize it if it was minimized), click its button on the Taskbar. As the middle area of the Taskbar fills up with buttons, the buttons become smaller in order to display all of them.

You can increase the size of the Taskbar by moving the mouse pointer to the top of the Taskbar and pausing until the pointer turns into a double-headed arrow. Once this happens, you can click the mouse and move it up to make the Taskbar bigger. Or, you can move it down to make the Taskbar smaller. You can also move the Taskbar to the top or sides of the screen by clicking the Taskbar and dragging it to the new location.

EXERCISE 12.2

Hiding the Taskbar

You can make the Taskbar automatically hide itself when not being used (thus freeing up that space for use by the Desktop or other Windows):

1. Right-click the Taskbar.

2. Choose Properties, which will bring up the Taskbar Properties screen.

3. Check the Auto Hide option on the General tab.

4. Click OK.

5. Move your mouse to the top of the Desktop. The Taskbar will retract off the screen.

6. Move the mouse pointer back to the bottom of the screen, and the Taskbar will pop up and can be used as normal.

The Start Menu

When Microsoft officially introduced Windows 95 to the world, it bought the rights to use the Rolling Stones' song "Start Me Up" in its advertisements and at the introduction party. They chose that particular song because the Start menu was the central point of focus in the new Windows interface, and it has been in all subsequent versions.

To display the Start menu, click the Start button in the Taskbar, as shown in Figure 12.5. From the Start menu, you can select any of the various options the menu presents. An arrow pointing to the right means that there is a submenu. To select a submenu, move the mouse pointer over the submenu title and pause. The submenu will then appear; you don't even have to click. (You have to click to choose an option *on* the submenu, though.) We'll discuss each of the default Start menu's submenu options and how to use them momentarily.

FIGURE 12.5 The Start menu

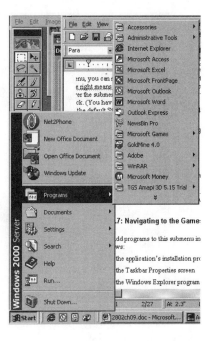

One handy feature of the Start menu is that it usually displays the name of the operating system type along its side when you activate it. This provides an excellent way to quickly see whether you are on Windows 95, 98, NT, or 2000. You can also check which operating system you are using by right-clicking the My Computer icon on the Desktop and selecting Properties. The operating type and version will be displayed on the first tab.

Programs Submenu

The Programs submenu holds the program groups and program icons that you can use. When you select this submenu, you will be shown yet another submenu, with a submenu for each program group (see Figure 12.6). You can navigate through this menu and its submenus and click the program you wish to start.

FIGURE 12.6 Navigating to the Games program group

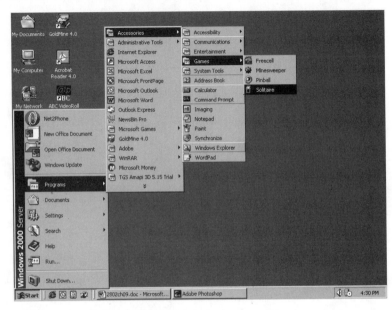

You can add programs to this submenu in many ways. The three most popular ways are as follows:

- Using the application's installation program
- Using the Taskbar Properties screen
- Using the Windows Explorer program

The first (and simplest) way is to use the application's installation program. The installation program will not only copy the files for the program, but it will also automatically make a program group and shortcuts for the programs under the Programs submenu.

You can add shortcuts to the top of the Start menu (above the Programs submenu) by clicking a program or shortcut and dragging it onto the Start menu. A shortcut for that item will then appear in the Start menu above a divider between Programs and the new shortcut.

Another way to add programs to the Programs submenu is to use the Taskbar Properties screen. To get to this screen, right-click the Taskbar and choose Properties. When the Taskbar Properties screen appears, click the Start Menu Programs tab to bring it to the front. You will then see the screen shown in Figure 12.7. From here, you can click Add to add a new program or Remove to remove one. A *Wizard* (a special sequence of screens designed to walk you through the necessary steps to accomplish certain tasks) will help you create or delete the shortcut(s).

FIGURE 12.7   Use the Taskbar Properties screen to add and remove programs from the Programs submenu.

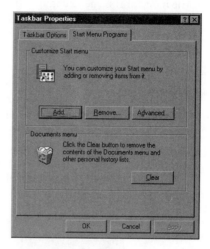

Finally, you can add programs to the Programs submenu on Windows 98 or Windows 2000 by using another new component introduced in Windows 95: Windows Explorer (EXPLORER.EXE). We will talk more about using Explorer later in the chapter.

Documents Submenu

The Documents submenu has one and only one function: to keep track of the last 15 data files you opened. Whenever you open a file, a shortcut to it is automatically made in this menu. To open the document again, just click the document in the Documents menu to open it in its associated application.

If you want to clear the list of documents shown in the Documents submenu, go to the Taskbar Properties screen. Then click the Clear button within the Documents Menu section.

Settings Submenu

The Settings submenu provides easy access to the configuration of Windows. There are numerous submenus to the Settings submenu including Control Panel, Printers, and Taskbar & Start Menu. Additional menus are available depending on which version of Windows you are using. These submenus give you access to the Control Panel, printer driver, and Taskbar configuration areas, respectively. You can also access the first two areas from the My Computer icon; they are placed here together to provide a common area to access Windows settings.

Search (Find) Submenu

The name of this menu changes between Windows 98 and Windows 2000, but the purpose doesn't. The Windows 98 Find submenu is used to locate information on your computer or on a network. The Search menu of Windows 2000 has the same functionality.

To find a file or directory, select the Find or Search submenu and then select Files or Folders (see Figure 12.8). In the Named field in this dialog box, simply type in the name of the file or directory you are looking for and click Find Now. Windows will search whatever is specified in the Look In parameter for the file or directory. Matches will be listed in a window underneath the Find window. You can use wildcards (* and ?) to look for multiple files and directories. You can also click the Advanced tab to further refine your search. This will be discussed in more detail later in the chapter in the "File Management" section.

FIGURE 12.8   Options in the Find submenu

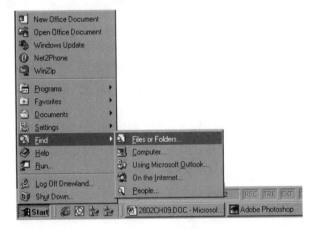

Help Command

Windows includes a *very* good help system. Not only is it arranged by topic, but it is fully indexed and searchable. Because of its usefulness and power, it was placed into the Start menu for easy access. When you select this command, it will bring up the Windows Help screen (see Figure 12.9). From this screen, you can double-click a manual to show a list of subtopics and then click a subtopic to view the text of that topic.

FIGURE 12.9   Windows 98 Help screen

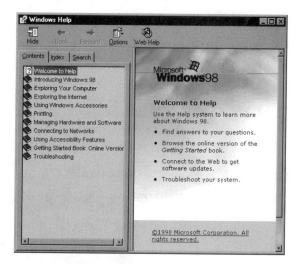

Or, you can click the Index tab to show an alphabetic listing of topics (see Figure 12.10). To select a topic, type the first few letters of the topic (for example, type **print** to move to the section that talks about printing), then click Display to display the text on the topic.

FIGURE 12.10   The Index tab on the Help screen

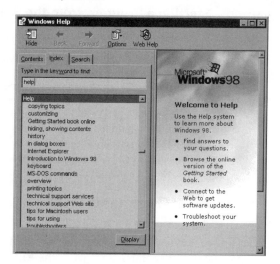

You can also click the Search tab to find any text you want in the help files. Simply type the text. As you type, Help will display a list of topics that contain the characters you are typing. You will see the list of topics get shorter as you type, because the more you type the more you are narrowing down your search.

When the topic you want appears in the list, click the one(s) you want to read about, then click Display.

Run Command

The Run command can be used to start programs if they don't have a shortcut on the Desktop or in the Programs submenu. When you choose Run from the Start menu, the screen in Figure 12.11 appears. To execute a particular program, just type its name and path in the Open field. If you don't know the exact path, you can browse to find the file by clicking the Browse button. Once you have typed in the executable name and path, click OK to run the program.

FIGURE 12.11   The Start menu's Run command

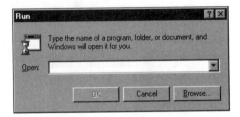

EXERCISE 12.3

Starting a Program from the Run Window

1. Click Start ➢ Run.

2. In the Open window, type **notepad**.

3. Click OK. Notepad will open up in a new window.

If the program you want to run has been run from the Run window before, you can find it on the Open field's drop-down list. Click the down arrow to display the list, then select the program you want by clicking its name and then clicking OK. More about starting and using applications later.

Shut Down Command

Windows 9x and 2000 are very complex operating systems. At any one time, there are several files open in memory. If you accidentally hit the power switch and turn the computer off while these files are open, there is a good chance these files will be corrupted. For this reason, Microsoft has added the Shut Down command under the Start menu. When you select this option, Windows presents you with three choices, as shown in Figure 12.12.

FIGURE 12.12   Shut Down command options

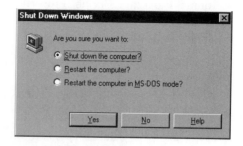

The three Shut Down choices are as follows:

Shut Down the Computer   This option will write any unsaved data to disk, close any open applications, and get the computer ready to be powered off. When you see a black screen with the message `It's now safe to turn off your computer` in orange text, it is, in fact, safe to power off the computer. You can also hit Ctrl+Alt+Del to reboot the computer at this point.

Restart the Computer   This option works the same as the first option but instead of shutting down completely, it will automatically reboot the computer with a warm reboot.

Restart the Computer in MS-DOS Mode (Windows 9x only)   This option is special. It does the same tasks as the previous options, except upon reboot, Windows 9x will execute the command prompt only and will not start the graphic portion of Windows 9x. You can then run DOS programs as though the machine were a DOS machine. When you are finished running these programs, type **exit** to reboot the machine back into the "full" Windows 9x with the GUI.

Icons

Icons are not nearly as complex as windows can be, but they are very important nonetheless. Icons are shortcuts that allow a user to open a program or a utility without knowing where that program is or how it needs to be configured. Icons consist of four elements:

- Icon label
- Icon graphic
- Program location
- Working directory location

The label and graphic simply tell the user the name of the program and give a visual hint as to what that program does. Solitaire, for instance, is labeled Solitaire, and its icon graphic is a deck of cards. By right-clicking an icon once, you make that icon the active icon, and a drop-down menu appears. One of the selections is Properties. Clicking Properties will bring up the attributes of an icon (see Figure 12.13) and is the only way to see exactly which program an icon is configured to start.

FIGURE 12.13   The Properties window with its icon to the left

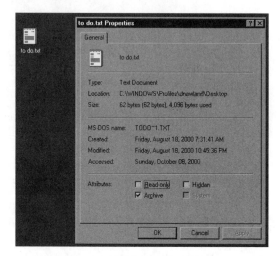

The *working directory* simply tells Windows where to save documents created through this icon. This is default and can be over-ridden.

Standard Desktop Icons

In addition to the options in your Start menu, there are a number of icons that are placed directly on the Desktop. Two of the most important icons are My Computer and the Recycle Bin.

The My Computer Icon

If you double-click the My Computer icon, it will display all the disk drives installed in your computer as well as the Control Panel and Printers folders (see Figure 12.14), which can be used to configure the system. If you double-click a disk drive, you will see the contents of that disk drive.

FIGURE 12.14   Using My Computer to open folders

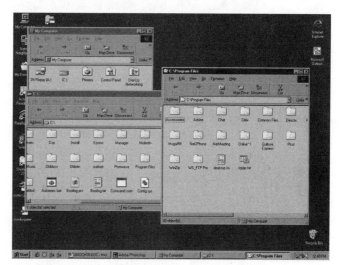

You can delve deeper into each disk drive and open a window for each sub-directory by double-clicking it. You can also copy and move files between drives and between directories using these windows.

In addition to allowing you access to your computer's files, the My Computer icon allows you a view of your machine's configuration and hardware, also called the System Properties, as shown in Figure 12.15. The following exercise shows you how to view these properties.

FIGURE 12.15   System Properties screen

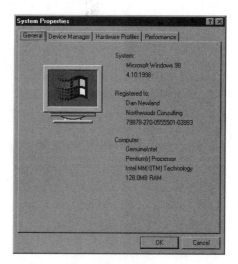

EXERCISE 12.4

Viewing System Properties

1. Right-click the My Computer icon.

2. Choose Properties.

3. On the System Properties screen, look to see what type of processor your computer uses and how much RAM is installed. It also will tell you what version of Windows is being used.

The Recycle Bin

All files, directories, and programs in Windows are represented by icons and are generally referred to as objects. When you want to remove an object from Windows, you do so by deleting it. Deleting doesn't only remove the object, though. It also removes the ability of the system to access the information or application that the object represents. Because of this, Windows includes a special directory where all deleted files are placed: the Recycle Bin. This Recycle Bin holds the files until it is emptied and allows users the opportunity to recover files that they deleted accidentally.

You can retrieve a file that you have deleted by opening the Recycle Bin icon, then dragging the file from the Recycle Bin back to the disk it came from. To permanently erase the file, you need to empty the Recycle Bin, thereby permanently deleting any items in it and freeing up the hard drive space they took up. If the Recycle Bin has files in it, its icon will look like the full trash can shown on the left of Figure 12.16; after it is emptied, its icon will reflect this, as shown on the right.

Deleting a file from the Recycle Bin frees up space on the drive by simply deleting the file's record from the drive's File Allocation Table (FAT). The information in the file will actually remain on the drive until it has been overwritten by new information.

FIGURE 12.16 A full (left) and empty (right) Recycle Bin

EXERCISE 12.5

Emptying the Recycle Bin

1. Right-click the Recycle Bin.

2. Choose Empty Recycle Bin.

3. A window appears asking if you are certain you want to permanently delete the objects. Click Yes.

What's in a Window?

We have now looked at the nature of the Desktop, the Start menu, and the Taskbar. Each of these was created for the primary purpose of making access to user applications easier, and these applications are in turn used and managed through the use of windows, the rectangular application environments for which the Windows family of operating systems is named. We will now examine how windows work and what they are made of.

Program Windows

A program *window* is a rectangular area created on the screen when an application is opened within Windows. This window can have a number of different forms, but most windows include at least a few basic elements. Figure 12.17 shows the Control box, Title bar, Minimize button, Restore button, Close button, and resizable border in a text editor called Notepad (NOTEPAD.EXE) that has all of the basic window elements and little else!

FIGURE 12.17   The basic elements of a window

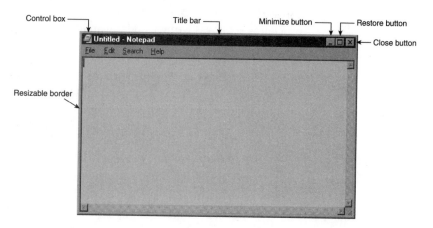

Elements of a Window

Control box   In the upper-left corner of the window. Used to control the state of the application. It can be used to maximize, minimize, and close the application. Clicking it once brings into view a selection menu. Double-clicking it closes the window and shuts down the application.

Minimize and Restore buttons   Used to change the state of the window on the Desktop. They will be discussed in the "States of a Window" section later in this chapter.

Close button   Used to easily end a program and return any resources it was using to the system. It essentially does the same thing as double-clicking the control box, but with one less click.

Title bar   The area between the Control box and the Minimize button. It simply states the name of the program and in some cases gives information as to the particular document being accessed by that program. The color of the Title bar indicates whether or not a particular window is the active window.

Menu bar   Used to present useful commands in an easily accessible format. Clicking one of the menu choices will display a list of related options you may choose from.

Active window   The window that is currently being used. It has two attributes: first, any keystrokes that are entered are directed there by default. Second, any other windows that overlap the active window will be pushed behind it.

Border   A thin line that surrounds the window in its restored state that allows it to be widened and shortened.

These elements are not all found on every window, as programmers can choose to eliminate or modify them. Still, in most cases these will be constant, with the rest of the window filled in with menus, toolbars, a workspace or other application-specific elements. For instance, Microsoft Word, the program with which this book was written, adds an additional control box and minimize and maximize buttons for each document. It also has a menu bar, a number of optional toolbars, scroll bars at the right and bottom of the window, and a status bar at the very bottom. Application windows can become very cluttered.

Notepad is a very simple Windows program. It has only a single menu bar and the basic elements seen previously in Figure 12.17. Figure 12.18 shows a Microsoft Word window. Both Word and Notepad are used to create and edit documents, but Word is far more configurable and powerful and therefore has many more optional components available within its window.

FIGURE 12.18   A window with more components

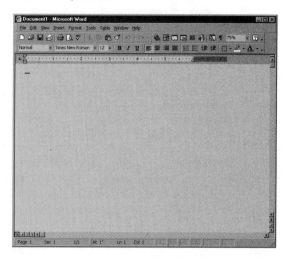

States of a Window

There is more to the Windows interface than the physical parts of a window itself, though. Windows also are movable, stackable, and resizable, and they can be hidden behind other windows (often unintentionally!).

When an application window has been launched, it will exist in one of three states:

Maximized   A maximized window is one that takes up all available space on the screen. When it is in front of the other programs, it is the only thing visible—even the Desktop is hidden. In Figure 12.19, note that Microsoft Word is maximized; it takes up the entire space of the Desktop, and the middle button in the upper-right corner displays two rectangles rather than one. The sides of the window no longer have borders. The window is flush with the edges of the screen. Maximizing a window provides the maximum workspace possible for that window's application, and the window can be accessed actively by the user. In general, maximized mode is the preferred window size for most word processing, graphics creation, and other user applications.

Restored   A restored window is one that can be used interactively and is identical in function to a maximized window, with the simple difference that it does not necessarily take up the entire screen. Restored windows can be very small, or they can take up almost as much space as maximized windows. Generally, how large the restored window becomes is the user's choice. Restored windows display a restore box (the middle button in the upper-right corner) with a single rectangle in it; this is used to maximize the window. Restored windows have a border. Figure 12.19 shows an example of Notepad in a restored state.

Minimized   The last window state is minimized. Minimized program windows are represented by nothing but an icon on the Taskbar, and they are not usable until they have been either maximized or restored. The only difference between a minimized program and a closed program is that a minimized program is out of the way but is still taking up resources and is therefore ready to use if you need it. It will also leave the content of the window in the same place when you return to it as when you minimized it. In Figure 12.19, Adobe Photoshop is minimized.

When a program is open and you need to open another program (or maybe need to stop playing a game because your boss has entered the room), you have two choices. First, you can close the program and reopen it later. If you do this, however, your current game will be lost and you will have to start over. Minimizing the game window, on the other hand, will remove the open window from the screen and leave the program open but display nothing more than an icon in the lower-left corner of the Taskbar, as with my Photoshop icon in Figure 12.19. Later, you can restore the window to its previous size and finish the game in progress.

FIGURE 12.19   Windows in different states

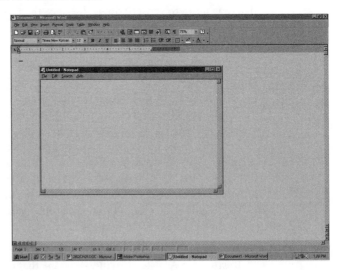

Using the Command Prompt

The Microsoft Disk Operating System, or MS-DOS, was never meant to be extremely friendly. It had its roots in CP/M, which, in turn, had its roots in UNIX. Both of these older operating systems were command line–based, and so was MS-DOS. In other words, they all used long strings of commands typed in at the computer keyboard to perform operations. This type of interaction with the computer is preferred by some people, most often folks with technical backgrounds (including yours truly). Although Windows has now left the full command-line interface behind, there is still a bit of DOS in Windows, and the way to get to it is through the command prompt.

We will look at a number of graphical utilities in the next few chapters and, believe it or not, the command prompt is one of them. Although you can't tell from looking at it (see Figure 12.20), the crazy thing about the Windows command prompt is that it is actually a 32-bit Windows program that is intentionally *designed* to have the look and feel of a DOS command line!

Because it is, despite its appearance, a Windows program, the command prompt provides all of the stability and configurability that you would expect from Windows.

FIGURE 12.20 The Windows command prompt

Running a Utility or Program from the Command Prompt

Windows includes a number of command-line utilities. Among these is the IPCONFIG utility of Windows 2000. If you are running Windows 2000, this is the utility that allows you to check on the TCP/IP settings of the machine. (TCP/IP is the protocol which allows networked computers to use the Internet, and as such is something you will probably see a lot of. It will be discussed further in Chapter 18, "Configuring Network Software.")

Other than that, there are very few actual text-based applications in newer versions of Windows. For a bit of a taste of the old days, though, check out the EDIT program (See Figure 12.21), still provided free of charge with both Windows 98 and Windows 2000. EDIT is still often used to modify batch files and text configuration files.

FIGURE 12.21 The EDIT program

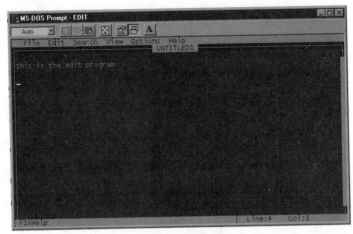

EXERCISE 12.6

Using the EDIT Program

1. Open a command prompt. To do this in Windows 98, click Start ➢ Programs ➢ MS-DOS Prompt. In Windows 2000, click Start ➢ Programs ➢ Accessories ➢ Command Prompt.

2. Type **EDIT**.

3. The **EDIT** utility will open. In the text area, type **hello**.

4. To save the file, press Alt+F. This brings up the File menu. From this, press A.

5. In the Save As window, type **hello.txt** and click OK.

6. To exit from **EDIT**, press ALT+F and press X for Exit.

Issuing Text Commands

In general, Windows 98 uses more text-based commands than Windows 2000, and a number of standard commands are stored in the Windows 98 command directory. This can be found in whichever directory (usually Windows) that Windows 98 is installed into. See Table 12.1 for a list of Windows text commands, some of which are available only in Windows 98, while others are available in Windows 2000 as well.

TABLE 12.1 Windows Text Commands

Command	Purpose
ATTRIB	Allows the user to set or remove file attributes.
CD	Changes your current folder to another folder.
CHECKDSK	Examines the hard drives of the machine.
COPY	Copies a file into another directory.
DEFRAG	Used to defragment (reorganize) the files on your machine's hard drives, which can result in better performance.
DEL	Deletes a file from the folder.
DELTREE	Deletes files and subdirectories. A more powerful extension of the DEL command.
DIR	Displays the contents of the current folder.
DISKCOPY	Duplicates floppy disks.
DOSKEY	Lists recently issued commands with a prompt session.
FDISK	Creates, deletes, and manages hard disk partitions.
FORMAT	Prepares a drive for use.
MD	Creates a new folder.
MEM	Provides information on how much memory is available to the system.
MOVE	Moves files from one folder to another.
MSCDEX	Accesses CD-ROMs.
REN	Renames a file.
SCANDISK	Similar to CHECKDSK.
SCANREG	Scans the Registry by starting a Windows application that checks for errors and allows you to back up the Registry files.

TABLE 12.1 Windows Text Commands *(continued)*

Command	Purpose
SETVER	Sets the version and reports version numbers of DOS utilities.
SYS	Prepares a drive to be used to start a computer.
VER	Checks the current version of the operating system.
XCOPY	Duplicates files and subdirectories. An extension of the COPY command.

To issue a command from the command prompt, you need to know the structure that the command uses, generally referred to as its *syntax*. The following exercise shows how to learn about a command and then run that command. The command in the exercise is ATTRIB, which is used to allow a user to set one of four attributes on a file: Read Only, Archive Needed, System, or Hidden.

If you don't know the options for a DOS command, you can usually find them out using the online help for that command. Simply type the command followed by a forward slash (/) and a question mark (?). This will display all the options for that command and how to use them properly, as in Figure 12.22.

FIGURE 12.22 Options available for ATTRIB.EXE

EXERCISE 12.7

Changing a File Attribute on Windows 98

1. Open a command prompt. To do this, click Start ➤ Programs ➤ MS-DOS Prompt.

2. Type `CD C:\` and press Enter.

3. Type `DIR` and press Enter. A list of all the files in the root of C: will be shown.

4. Type `ATTRIB /?` and press Enter.

5. Type `ATTRIB autoexec.bat`. The current attributes of the file will be displayed.

6. Type `ATTRIB autoexec.bat +R`.

7. Repeat step 5 to view the changed attribute, and then repeat step 6 with a `-R` to return the file to its original attributes.

Windows Configuration

Simply navigating the Start menu and running EDIT does not an A+ certified tech make! Most of the tasks that you will be called on to deal with are more complex than minimizing a window. The Windows OS provides numerous utilities to aid you in changing system configuration elements or identifying and diagnosing problems. Many of these are specific to the particular operating system, but nonetheless their location and general usage is similar on both Windows 98 and Windows 2000. Because of this, system management in Windows can be loosely grouped into the following areas:

- File management
- System tools
- Control Panel programs
- The Registry Editor

File Management

File management is the process by which a computer stores data and retrieves it from storage. The process of actually preparing drives for storage, called *disk management*, is significantly different on Windows 98 and Windows 2000 and will be dealt with in later chapters. The process of managing files, though, is similar across both platforms.

Files and Folders

For a program to run, it must be able to read information off of the disk and write information back to it. In order to be able to organize and access information—especially in larger new systems that may have thousands of files—it is necessary to have a structure and an ordering process.

Windows provides this process by allowing you to create *directories*, also known as folders, in which to organize files. Windows also regulates the way that files are named and what the properties of the file are. Each file created in Windows has to follow certain rules, and any program that accesses files through Windows must comply with these rules. Files created on a Windows system will follow these rules:

- It will have a filename of up to 256 characters.

- Certain characters such as a period (.) and a slash (\ or /) are prohibited in the filename.

- An optional extension (generally three or four characters) can be added to identify the file's type.

The Windows file system is arranged like a filing cabinet. In a filing cabinet, paper is placed into folders, which are inside dividers, which are in a drawer of the filing cabinet. In the DOS file system, individual files are placed in subdirectories that are inside directories, which are stored on different disks. Windows also protects against duplicate filenames, as no two files on the system can have exactly the same name and *path*. A path indicates the location of the file on the disk; it is composed of the logical drive letter the file is on, and if the file is located in a directory or subdirectory, the names of those directories. For instance, a file named AUTOEXEC.BAT is located in the root of the C: drive—meaning it is not within a directory—so the path to the file is simply C:\AUTOEXEC.BAT. Another important file, FDISK.EXE, is located in the Command directory under Windows under the root of C:, so the path to FDISK is therefore C:\WINDOWS\COMMAND\FDISK.EXE.

The *root directory* of any drive is simply the place where the hierarchy of that drive begins. On a C: drive, for instance, C:\ is the root directory of the drive.

Capabilities of the Windows Explorer

Although it is technically possible to simply use the command-line utilities provided within the command prompt to manage your files, this generally is not the most efficient way to accomplish most tasks. The ability to use drag-and-drop techniques and other graphical tools to manage the file system makes the process far simpler, and the Windows Explorer is a utility that allows the user to accomplish a number of important file-related tasks from a single graphical interface, as shown in Figure 12.23.

FIGURE 12.23 The Windows Explorer program

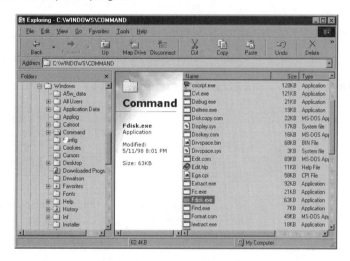

Some of the tasks you can accomplish using the Explorer include:

- Viewing files and directories
- Opening programs or data files
- Creating directories and files
- Copying objects (files or directories) to other locations
- Moving objects (files or directories) to other locations
- Deleting or renaming objects (files or directories)
- Searching for a particular file or type of file
- Changing file attributes
- Formatting new disks (such as floppy disks)

Navigating and Using the Explorer

Using the Windows Explorer is actually pretty simple. Just a few basic instructions will be all you will need to start working with it. First off, the Explorer interface itself has a number of parts, each of which serves a specific purpose. The top area of the Explorer is dominated by a set of menus and toolbars that allow easy access to common commands. The main section of the window is divided into two panes. The left pane displays the drives and folders available to the user, while the right pane displays the contents of the currently selected folder. Along the bottom of the window, the Status Bar displays information about the used and free space on the current directory. Some common actions in Explorer include:

Expanding a folder   You can double-click a folder to expand the folder (i.e., show its subfolders in the left panel) and display the contents of the folder in the right pane. Simply clicking the "+" sign to the left of a folder will expand the folder without changing it (see Figure 12.24).

Collapsing a folder   Clicking the "−" sign next to a folder will unexpand it.

FIGURE 12.24   The Expand and Collapse symbols

Selecting a file   If you click the file in the right pane , Windows will highlight the file by marking it with a darker color.

Selecting multiple files   The Ctrl and Shift keys allow you to select multiple files at once. Holding down Ctrl while clicking individual files will select each new file while leaving the currently selected file or files selected as well. Holding down Shift while selecting two files will select both of them and all files in between.

Opening a file   Double-clicking a file in the right pane will open the program if it is an application; if it is a file, it will open it using whichever file extension is configured for it.

Changing the view type   There are four different primary view types: Large Icons, Small Icons, List, and Details. You can move between these views by clicking the View menu and selecting the view you prefer.

Finding specific files   This is accessed under View ➢ Find in Windows 98 or by using the Search button in Windows 2000. Either way, you can search for files based on their name, file size, file type, and other attributes, as shown in Figure 12.25.

FIGURE 12.25 Searching for a file in Windows

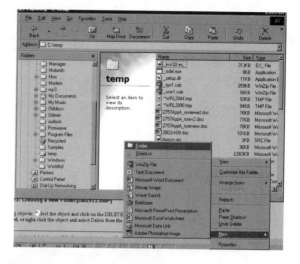

EXERCISE 12.8

Searching for a Type of File

1. In Windows 98, click Tools ➤ Find ➤ Files or Folders. In Windows 2000, simply click the Search button on the toolbar.

2. Either the Search window (Windows 98) or Search pane (Windows 2000) will appear. You will be prompted for the Search information.

3. Type ***.TXT** in the Named field.

4. In the Look In field, enter **C:**, and click Find Now.

5. Make sure the Include Subfolders check box is checked, and click OK.

6. Windows will now search the C: drive and will eventually display a Search Results window with all of the files it has found.

When searching, wildcards can also be used. Wildcards are characters which act as placeholders for a character or set of characters, allowing, for instance, a search for all files with text (TXT) extensions. To perform such a search, you'd type an asterisk (*) as a stand-in for the filename: ***.TXT**. Asterisks are used to take the place of any number of characters in a search, while question marks (?) are used to take the place of a single number or letter, for example, AUTOEX??.BAT would return the file AUTOEXEC.BAT as part of its results.

Creating new objects   To create a new file, folder, or other object, navigate to the location where you want to create the object, and then right-click in the right pane. In the menu that appears, select New and then choose the object you want to create, as shown in Figure 12.26.

FIGURE 12.26   Creating a new folder

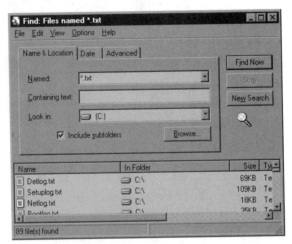

Deleting objects   Select the object and press the Del key on the keyboard, or right-click the object and select Delete from the menu that appears.

The simplicity of deleting in Windows makes it very likely that you or one of the people you support will delete or misplace a file or a number of files that are still needed. In such a case the Recycle Bin (mentioned earlier) is a lifesaver!

EXERCISE 12.9

Using Windows Explorer

1. Open the Windows Explorer. In Windows 98, click Start ➢ Programs ➢ Windows Explorer. In Windows 2000, click Start ➢ Programs ➢ Accessories ➢ Windows Explorer.

2. To see what applications are installed in the Program Files directory, navigate the hierarchy from My Computer to C: to Program Files. You may need to click the "+" sign next to one or more of the folders to expand them and see their contents.

3. Navigate back to the root of C: and right-click in the right pane. Select New ➢ Folder and type **TEST** as the name of the folder.

4. Double-click the new **TEST** folder, and examine the right pane after its contents are displayed. As the folder was just created, it is empty. Right-click in the right pane and select New ➢ Text Document. Give the file the name **NEW.TXT**.

5. To delete the file you just created, select it by clicking it once and then right-click it. Choose Delete. You are asked whether you are sure you want to send the file to the Recycle Bin. Click Yes.

Besides simplifying most file management commands as shown above, the Explorer also allows you to easily complete a number of disk management tasks. Floppy disks can be formatted and labeled and the Windows system files can be copied to a floppy so that a disk may be used to boot a machine.

Disk management will be covered more fully in Chapters 13 and 14, "Windows 95/98" and "Windows 2000," respectively.

System Tools

Windows 98 and Windows 2000 also include a number of applications that a user can run to check on the health and performance of their computer. Windows 98 undoubtedly has more of these gadgets, but Windows 2000 has a good number of them as well. In both cases, these utilities, if installed, can be found in the same folder on the Start menu: Start ➢ Programs ➢ Accessories ➢ System Tools, as shown in Figure 12.27. The programs in this folder can be very useful to a technician. Some common Windows 98 utilities found there, along with their purpose, are listed in Table 12.2. Some, but not all, of these tools are also available on Windows 2000.

FIGURE 12.27 The System Tools program group

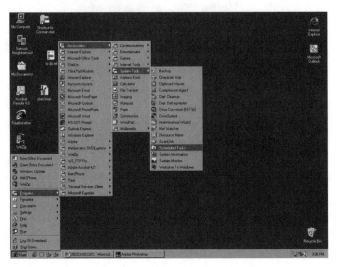

TABLE 12.2 System Tools

System Tool	Function
Backup	Makes archival copies of important files.
Character Map	Determines which type of letters, numbers, and nonalphanumeric characters the machine will use.
Clipboard Viewer	Allows you to see what has been copied onto the system clipboard.
Drive Space 3	Allows you to compress the files on a drive to get more information onto it (although compressing files makes them slower to access).
Compression Agent	Used with Drive Space 3. Allows you to set up parameters for automatically determining which files to compress.
Disk Cleanup	A utility which goes through the system and deletes unneeded files to free up drive space.

TABLE 12.2 System Tools *(continued)*

System Tool	Function
Disk Defragmenter	Arranges data on the computer's disk drives so that it will be more easily available.
Maintenance Wizard	Sets up a system maintenance plan.
Net Watcher	Checks the performance of the network.
Resource Meter	Gives a quick, graphical display of how heavily basic system resources are being used.
Scandisk	Checks a disk drive for errors or problems
Scheduled Tasks	Enables the running of recurring tasks automatically.
System Information	Finds information on the hardware and software installed on a PC.
System Monitor	A more complex version of Resource Meter. Monitors specific resources and watches how they are used in real time.

Windows 2000 also has a folder called Administrative Tools where many of its system configuration utilities are kept. Many of these tools are available in both Windows 98 and Windows 2000 but by different names or in different locations. For instance, Windows 98's System Monitor is expanded into a more powerful tool in Windows 2000 called Performance, which you can access by clicking Start ➤ Control Panel ➤ Administrative Tools folder.

EXERCISE 12.10

Scheduling a Disk Cleanup Task

1. Click Start ➤ Programs ➤ Applications ➤ System Tools ➤ Scheduled Tasks.

2. In the Scheduled Tasks window that appears, double-click the Add a Scheduled Task icon.

3. Read the introduction screen, then click Next. (After filling out any screen in a Wizard, you must click Next to continue. At the end of a Wizard, you will need to click Finish.) In the next screen, choose Disk Cleanup as the application to run, as shown in the graphic.

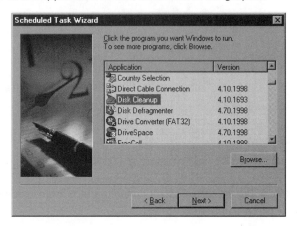

4. Choose to run it monthly.

5. Click the Day radio button and accept the default times.

6. Choose to view advanced properties and click Finish.

7. Under the Settings tab, check the Wake the Computer to Run This Task option and click OK. Your task will now run on the first day of each month with the options you have selected.

8. If you do not want to keep this task, simply delete it.

The Control Panel

Although for the most part the Windows system is functional from the time it is first installed, Microsoft realized that if someone were going to be using computers regularly, they would probably want to be able to customize their environment so that it would be better suited to their needs—or at least more fun to use. Because of this, the Windows environment has a large number of utilities that are intended to give the user control over the look and feel of the Desktop.

This is, of course, an excellent idea. It is also a bit more freedom than some less-than-cautious users seem to be capable of handling, and you will undoubtedly serve a number of customers who call you in to restore their configuration after botched attempts at changing one setting or another.

More than likely, you will also have to reinstall Windows yourself a few times because of accidents that occur while you are studying or testing the system's limits. This is actually a good thing since no competent computer technician can say that they have never had to reinstall because of an error. You can't really know how to fix Windows until you are experienced at breaking it. Because of this, it is extremely important to experiment and find out what can be changed in the Windows environment, what results from those changes, and how to undo any unwanted results. To this purpose, we will be examining the most common configuration utility in Windows: the Control Panel.

The Control Panel is the graphical entryway to the heart of Windows' configurable settings. One of the few applications in Windows that contains icons of its own, the Control Panel utility houses a number of separate configuration options. Some standard Control Panel icons are shown in Figure 12.28, but various applications and add-on products can add others. We will be taking only a brief look at the uses of these panels, but many of them are worth exploring closely on your own. Table 12.3 lists a number of common Control Panel options and what they are used for.

FIGURE 12.28 The Control Panel interface

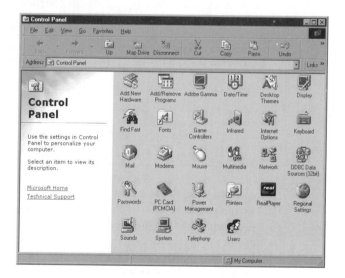

TABLE 12.3 Selected Windows Control Panel Programs (Windows 2000 Names)

Program Name	Function
Add/Remove Hardware	Adds and configures new hardware.
Add/Remove Programs	Changes, adds, or deletes software.

TABLE 12.3 Selected Windows Control Panel Programs (Windows 2000 Names) *(continued)*

Program Name	Function
Date/Time	Sets the system time and configures options such as time zone.
Display	Configures screen savers, colors, display options, and monitor drivers.
Fonts	Adds and removes fonts.
Internet Options	Sets a number of options which are discussed in more detail in Chapter 18, "Configuring Network Software."
Multimedia	Configures audio and video options. Discussed in more detail in Chapter 16, "Using and Configuring Additional Peripherals."
Network (Network and Dial-up Connections)	Sets options for connecting to other computers. Discussed further in Chapter 18.
Modems (Phone and Modem Options)	Sets options for using phone lines to dial out to a network or the Internet. Again, see Chapter 18.
Printers	Configures printer settings and print defaults.
System	Allows you to view and configure various system elements. Very different in Windows 98 and Windows 2000.

For a quick look at how the Control Panel programs work, the following exercise looks at some of the settings in the Date/Time program. The Date/Time program is used to configure the system time, date, and time zone settings, which can be important for files that require accurate timestamps or to users who don't have a watch. Because it is a very simple program, it's a perfect example to use. Date/Time includes only two sets of tabs: Date & Time and Time Zone, and only includes one option, to use Daylight Savings or not.

EXERCISE 12.11

Changing the Time Zone

1. Click Start ➢ Settings ➢ Control Panel.

2. From Control Panel, double-click the Date/Time icon (by default, the programs are listed alphabetically).

3. Click the Time Zone tab and use the drop-down menu to select (GMT –03:30) Newfoundland, as shown in the graphic.

4. Hop a plane to Newfoundland, secure in the knowledge that you will know what time it is once you get there.

5. If you skipped step 4, change the time zone back to where it should be before closing the window.

The Registry Editor

Configuration information is also stored in a special configuration database known as the *Registry*. This centralized database contains environmental settings for various Windows programs. It also contains what is known as *registration* information, which details which types of file extensions are associated with which applications. So, when you double-click a file in Windows Explorer, the associated application runs and opens the file you double-clicked.

The Registry was introduced with Windows 95 and is a database of configuration information. Most operating systems up until Windows 95 were based on text files, which can be edited with almost any text editor. However, the Registry database is contained in special binary file which can be edited only with the special Registry Editor provided with Windows. The Registry Editor program is called **REGEDIT.EXE**, and its icon is not typically created during Windows installation—you must create the icon manually. You can also run the program manually by selecting Start ➤ Run, typing **REGEDIT**, and clicking OK.

Windows 2000 has two applications which can be used to edit the Registry, REGEDIT and REGEDT32 (with no /). Both work similarly, but each has slightly different options for navigation and browsing.

The Registry is broken down into a series of separate areas called hives (see Figure 12.29). These keys are divided into two basic sections—user settings and computer settings. In Windows 9x, Registry information is stored in the user .dat and system.dat files, while in Windows 2000 a number of files are created corresponding to each of the different hives. The basic hives of the Registry include:

HKEY_CLASSES_ROOT This hive includes information about which file extensions map to particular applications.

HKEY_CURRENT_USER This hive holds all configuration information specific to a particular user, such as their desktop settings and history information.

HKEY_LOCAL_MACHINE This hive includes nearly all configuration information concerning the actual computer hardware and software.

HKEY_USERS This hive includes information on all users who have logged on to the system. The HKEY_CURRENT_USER hive is actually a subkey of this hive.

HKEY_CURRENT_CONFIG This hive provides quick access to a number of commonly needed keys that are otherwise buried deep in the HKEY_LOCAL_MACHINE structure.

Modifying a Registry Entry

If you find it is necessary to modify the Registry, you can modify the values in the database, or can even create new entries or keys. You will find the options for adding a new element to the Registry under the Edit menu. To edit an existing value, simply double-click the entry and modify it as needed. On Windows 2000 systems, you will need administrative-level access to modify the Registry.

Windows extensively uses the Registry to store all kinds of information. Indeed, it holds most, if not all, of the configuration information for Windows 98 and 2000. It is a potentially dangerous task to modify the Registry in Windows. The reason that the Control Panel and other configuration tools are provided for you is so that you will have graphical tools for modifying system settings. Directly modifying the Registry can have unforeseen—and unpleasant—results. You should only modify the Registry when told to do so by an extremely trustworthy source.

FIGURE 12.29 The Registry Editor

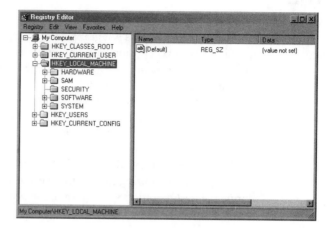

Restoring the Registry in Windows 9*x*

As you may have noticed, the Registry is extremely important to the functioning of Windows. Because of this, any problems with the Registry can cause system-wide trouble. If your Windows 9*x* Registry files (system.dat or user.dat) become corrupted, there are two primary ways for them to be repaired:

Automatically Windows keeps backups of each of your Registry files and checks the current Registry for errors each time you boot the system. If errors are found, the backup copy of the Registry will be located and will be used to replace the corrupt Registry. As long as you have not purposely deleted the Windows backup files, this works fine.

Manually If the Registry backups are damaged or lost, you will then need to use a different plan. In Windows 95, you can manually restore the Registry by simply replacing the system.dat or user.dat file with the system.da0 or user.da0 files that hold Windows 95's Registry backup. Windows 98 stores the Registry backups differently, and manual restores require that files be backed up previously using a backup program.

Restoring the Registry in Windows 2000

Windows 2000 also stores Registry information in files on the hard drive. These can be restored through the use of the Last Known Good Configuration, which restores the Registry to a backup of its last functional state. To use this option, simply click F8 during startup, and then select Last Known Good Configuration from the menu that appears. The Registry files can also be backed up to the systemroot\repair directory by using the Windows 2000 Backup program, or can be saved to tape during a normal backup. To repair the Registry from a backup simply overwrite the Registry files in systemroot\system32\config.

Summary

Because Windows is a graphical system, the key to success in learning to use it is to click every option and examine every window. By exploring the system to find out what it can do, you will be better prepared to later decipher what a user has done. Moreover, remember that when you are first learning Windows, the solution to a support issue is most often found through your eyes, not your memory. If you have a problem to troubleshoot, begin by looking in all of the windows you can find that may have settings relating to the problem. Often, the answer actually is staring you in the face!

With the basic knowledge gained in this chapter, we are now ready to look at installing and configuring each of the specific applications you will be tested on during the A+ Operating System exam: the Windows 95/98 and Windows 2000 chapters are next!

Key Terms

Before you take the exam, be certain you are familiar with the following terms:

directories	syntax
icons	tabs
path	Taskbar
platforms	window
Registry	Wizard
root directory	working directory
Start menu	

Review Questions

1. What is the Desktop?

   A. The top of the desk where the computer sits

   B. The virtual desk upon which all of your other programs and utilities run

   C. It keeps track of all the data on disk

   D. Where all of a computer's memory is stored

2. When you right-click on the desktop with the mouse, a menu appears. This menu allows you to do all of the following except:

   A. Create new icons

   B. Create new directories

   C. Change the TCP/IP address

   D. Arrange icons

3. The screen saver can be changed in the Display _____ dialog box.

   A. Properties

   B. Taskbar

   C. Menu Bar

   D. Shortcut Menu

4. There are three types of mouse clicks in Windows. What are they?

   A. Primary click, triple-click, and right-left click

   B. Double-click, right-left click, and primary click

   C. Primary click, left-right click, and triple-click

   D. Secondary click, primary click, and double-click

5. The Taskbar can be increased in size by:

   A. Right-clicking the mouse and dragging the Taskbar to make it bigger

   B. Left-clicking the mouse and double-clicking the Taskbar

   C. Moving the mouse pointer to the top of the Taskbar and pausing until the pointer turns into a double-headed arrow

   D. Highlighting the Taskbar and double-clicking in the center

6. Which submenu holds the program groups and program icons that you can use?

   A. Programs

   B. Document

   C. Settings

   D. Find

7. What tool is used to check a machine for hard drive errors?

A. Disk Cleanup

B. Disk Fragmenter

C. SCANDISK

D. System Monitor

8. The Windows Explorer Program can be accessed by: (Select all that apply.)

A. Selecting Start ➤ Run ➤ Programs

B. Selecting Start ➤ CMD ➤ Programs

C. Selecting Start ➤ Programs ➤ Explorer

D. Right-clicking My Computer with the mouse and selecting Explore

9. C:\ and D:\ are both examples of what?

A. Network drives

B. Root directories

C. Share points

D. Drive menus

10. Which submenu keeps track of the last 15 data files that you opened?

A. Programs

B. Taskbar

C. Settings

D. Documents

11. Which submenu provides you with easy access to the configuration of Windows 9x?

A. Settings

B. Programs

C. Documents

D. Find

12. What are three submenus of the Settings submenu?

A. Control Panel, Printers, Start

B. Control Panel, Printers, Taskbar

C. Control Panel, Taskbar, Help

D. Find, Printers, Taskbar

13. You can start programs if they don't have a shortcut on the Desktop or in the Programs submenu by:

   A. Using the Shut Down command

   B. Typing **cmd** in the Start Run box

   C. Using the Run command and typing in the name of the program

   D. Typing **cmd** in the Start box and then the program name

14. The My Computer icon will display all of the following except:

   A. All the disk drives installed in your computer

   B. Control Panel

   C. Dial-up Networking

   D. Printers

   E. Modems

15. Icons consist of which elements?

   A. Icon label, icon graphic, program location, working directory location

   B. Working directory location and program assistance

   C. Programming, working directory, and program location

   D. Programming, program assistance, and program location

16. In Windows 9x, a deleted file can be retrieved using the:

   A. My Computer icon

   B. Recycle Bin

   C. Control Panel

   D. Settings panel

17. To turn off a Windows 9x machine you should:

   A. Run Shut Down

   B. Turn off the switch and unplug the machine

   C. Press Ctrl+Alt+Del

   D. Select Start ➢ Shut Down, choose Shut Down and turn the computer off

18. The Control Panel in Windows 9x is accessed by: (Select all that apply.)

   A. Selecting ➢ Start ➢ Settings ➢ Control Panel

   B. Selecting Start ➢ Control Panel

   C. Selecting Start ➢ Programs ➢ Control Panel

   D. Double-clicking My Computer and double-clicking the Control Panel icon

19. How can you find files in Windows 9*x*?

    A. Through the Program Manager

    B. By selecting Start ➢ Find

    C. By using `FINDFILE.EXE`

    D. You cannot search for files in Windows 9*x*.

20. What file is needed to enable CD-ROM support under MS-DOS?

    A. `CDLDR`

    B. `MSCDEX.EXE`

    C. `CDLRD.EXE`

    D. `CDEX.EXE`

Answers to Review Questions

1. B. By default, the Desktop contains the Start menu, the Taskbar, and a number of icons. Because it is the base on which everything else sits, how the Desktop is configured can have a major effect on how the GUI looks and how convenient it is for users.

2. C. The menu that appears when you right-click a mouse allows you to: create new icons, create new directories, and arrange icons.

3. A. The screen saver can be changed in the Properties dialog box. To access the Properties dialog box, you can either right-click anywhere on the Desktop and choose Properties from the menu that appears or go to the Control Panel and click Display.

4. D. There are three mouse clicks in Windows. A primary click is used to select an object or place a cursor. A double-click is used to open a program through an icon or for other specific application functions. A secondary click (usually a click on the right mouse button, although that can be modified) is interpreted differently than a left mouse click. In Windows, it generally displays a context-sensitive menu from which you are given the ability to perform tasks or view object properties.

5. C. The Taskbar can be increased in size by moving the mouse pointer to the top of the Taskbar and pausing until the pointer turns into a double-headed arrow.

6. A. When you select the Programs submenu, you will be shown yet another submenu, with a submenu for each program group. You can navigate through this menu and its submenus and click the program you wish to start.

7. C. SCANDISK examines the drives on a machine both for file errors and physical defects in the drive itself.

8. C, D. The Windows Explorer program can be accessed by clicking Start ➢ Programs ➢ Explorer or right-clicking My Computer and selecting Explore.

9. B. The top of any drive hierarchy is referred to as its root directory.

10. D. Whenever you open a file, a shortcut is automatically made to the file in the Documents menu. To open the same document again, just click on its name in the Documents menu.

11. A. The Settings submenu provides you with easy access to the configuration of Windows 9x. To open it, select Start ➢ Settings.

12. B. In Windows 2000, Network and Dial-Up Connections is also a submenu of Settings.

13. C. To run any program, select Start ➢ Run and type in the name of the program in the Open field. If you don't know the exact path to the program, you can find the file by clicking the Browse button. Once you have typed in the executable name and path, click OK to run the program.

14. E. To locate your modems, you must go into Control Panel and click the Modems icon.

15. A. The label and graphic tell the user the name of the program and give a visual hint as to what that program does. By right-clicking an icon once, you make that icon the active icon, and a drop-down menu appears. One of the selections is Properties. Clicking Properties will bring up the attributes of an icon and is the only way to see exactly which program an icon is configured to start.

16. B. The Recycle Bin is where all deleted files are placed. Deleted files are held here until the Recycle Bin is emptied. Users can easily recover accidentally deleted files from the Recycle Bin.

17. D. To turn off a Windows 9x machine, select Start ➢ Shut Down, choose Shut Down and turn the computer off.

18. A, D. Control Panel in Windows 9x can be accessed by either selecting Start ➢ Settings ➢ Control Panel or by double-clicking My Computer and double-clicking the Control Panel icon.

19. B. Files can be found in Windows 9x by selecting Start ➢ Find and selecting the appropriate drive.

20. B. MSCDEX.EXE, along with the drivers for the particular device, is used to access a CD-ROM drive from DOS.

Chapter 13

Installing and Using Windows 95/98

THE FOLLOWING OBJECTIVES ARE COVERED IN THIS CHAPTER:

✓ **2.1 Identify the procedures for installing Windows 9x, and Windows 2000 for bringing the software to a basic operational level.**

    Content may include the following:

- Start Up
- Partition
- Format drive
- Loading drivers
- Run appropriate set up utility

✓ **2.2 Identify steps to perform an operating system upgrade.**

    Content may include the following:

- Upgrading Windows 95 to Windows 98
- Upgrading Windows NT Workstation 4.0 to Windows 2000
- Replacing Windows 9x with Windows 2000
- Dual boot Windows 9x/Windows NT 4.0/2000

✓ **2.3 Identify the basic system boot sequences and boot methods, including the steps to create an emergency boot disk with utilities installed for Windows 9x, Windows NT, and Windows 2000.**

    Content may include the following:

- Startup disk
- Safe Mode
- MS-DOS mode
- NTLDR (NT Loader), BOOT.INI
- Files required to boot
- Creating emergency repair disk (ERD)

✓ **2.4 Identify procedures for loading/adding and configuring application device drivers, and the necessary software for certain devices.**

Content may include the following:

- Windows 9x Plug and Play and Windows 2000

- Identify the procedures for installing and launching typical Windows and non-Windows applications (Note: there is no content related to Windows 3.1.)

- Procedures for set up and configuring Windows printing subsystem.

  - Setting Default printer

  - Installing/Spool setting

  - Network printing (with help of LAN admin)

Over the past two years, Windows 98 has become the operating system of choice for thousands of users. Most people who have computers today have upgraded to Windows 98 so that they can take advantage of its many features. There is still a significant user base for Windows 95 as well, though, and as such this section details the steps needed to install Windows 95 on a computer, as well as the steps needed to upgrade to Windows 98 from an existing Windows 95 system.

In this chapter, we will therefore take a look at what sort of hardware is required to install Windows 95 and Windows 98 (referred to generically as Windows 9x hereafter), what you need to know to get each installed and running, and what some of the major files and boot processes are for each.

> **NOTE** For additional coverage of objective 2.1, please see Chapter 14. Additional coverage of objective 2.2 can be found in Chapter 14. Objective 2.3 is also covered in Chapters 14 and 17, and there is additional coverage of objective 2.4 in Chapters 14, 15, and 16.

Installation Prerequisites

Although they are very similar operating systems, Windows 95 and Windows 98 do have some significant differences. For instance, whereas Windows 95 can be installed from either floppy disks or from CD-ROM, Windows 98 is an extremely large operating system and is generally installed either from CD-ROM or over a network connection. (It is also technically possible to install Windows 98 using floppy disks, but at over 70 disks, you simply don't want to go there.)

Hardware Requirements

In an earlier edition of this book, published in 1997, we referred to Windows 95 by saying, "Let there be no doubt about it, Windows 95 is a resource hog." Ah, how times change. Although it's true that Windows 95 requires substantially more RAM, hard disk space, and processor speed than any of its predecessors, compared to the requirements of Windows 98 and Windows 2000, it seems extremely compact. As a reference, Table 13.1 lists the hardware requirements for installing each of the Windows $9x$ platforms.

TABLE 13.1 Windows Hardware Prerequisites

Hardware	95 Requirement	98 Requirement
Processor	386DX or higher processor (486 recommended).	386DX or higher processor (Pentium recommended).
Memory	4MB (8MB recommended).	8MB (16–32MB recommended).
Free hard disk space	50–55MB for typical install (40MB if upgrading from a previous version of Windows). Could go as high as 85MB for a custom install with all options.	120MB for typical install. Could go as high as 250MB for a custom install with all options.
Floppy disk	One 3½-inch disk drive (if doing installation from floppy disks).	One 3½-inch disk drive (if doing installation from floppy disks).
CD-ROM	Required if installing from CD (preferred method).	Required if installing from CD (preferred method).
Video	VGA or better.	VGA or better.
Mouse	Required.	Required.
Keyboard	Required.	Required.

The installation needs of Windows 2000 will be examined in Chapter 14.

If there is one thing to be learned from Table 13.1, by the way, it is that Microsoft is nothing if not optimistic. For your own sanity, though, we *strongly* suggest that you do not try to run Windows 98 on a 386DX machine with 8MB of RAM. Windows 95 seems to perform acceptably—in our opinion—if the machine has a Pentium-class processor and at least 16MB of RAM, but Windows 98 has a few more built-in gizmos and normally should be run on a 200+ megahertz machine with at least 32MB of RAM. As this book is being written, machines of that description can be purchased on eBay for about $75 (with shipping), or less than the price of a copy of the Windows 98 upgrade. If someone comes to you with a 486/33 and 8MB of RAM wanting to upgrade to Windows 98, do them—and yourself—a favor and direct them to a hardware upgrade first! Also, anyone who does have better hardware but is still running Windows 95 should seriously consider upgrading. Windows 98 is better supported by software vendors, and its ability to support more powerful memory and storage make it preferable on new machines.

Other hardware—sound cards, network cards, modems, video cards, and so on—may or may not work with Windows 95 or Windows 98. If the device is fairly recent, you can be relatively certain that it was built to work with Windows 9*x*, but if it is older, you may need to find out who made the hardware and check their Web site to see if they have Windows 9*x* drivers. If they don't, you can also use DOS 16-bit "real-mode" drivers, but this should be done only as a last resort because they are more difficult to configure and are less effective than Windows 9*x* 32-bit drivers. We will talk more about this distinction in the discussion of the hardware detection phase of setup later in this chapter, and in the chapters on multimedia (Chapter 15) and networking (Chapter 18) later on.

Briefly, a real-mode driver is one that directly accesses hardware, as was the standard in DOS; 32-bit Windows drivers work through the Windows system, allowing Windows to optimize and control hardware access. Although they are slow, real-mode drivers will usually work with Windows 9*x* if you cannot obtain updated drivers for your hardware. Before using an old driver, always search vendor Web sites for updated versions.

Preparing the Computer for Installation

Once you have verified that the machine on which you are planning to install Windows 9*x* is capable of running it properly and that all hardware is supported, you will need to make certain that the system is ready for the install. The primary question here is whether you are planning to perform a fresh install of Windows or whether you are going to be upgrading an existing system. Upgrading will be dealt with later in the chapter; for now, we'll focus on new installations.

The Windows Startup Disk

If you are installing Windows $9x$ onto a system that does not already have a functioning operating system, you have a bit of work to do before you get to the installation itself. New disk drives need to have two critical functions performed on them before they are able to be used—partitioning and formatting:

Partitioning   The process of assigning part or all of the drive for use by the computer

Formatting   The process of preparing the partition to store data in a particular fashion

These two procedures are dealt with in Windows $9x$ by using the FDISK.EXE and FORMAT.EXE commands. Running any sort of command on a machine that has no operating system is, well, impossible, though, so in order to do this, you need to boot the computer using a floppy disk that is bootable to MS-DOS or the Windows $9x$ command line. Windows $9x$ solves this problem through the use of a startup disk that allows you to boot a computer and run these and other basic commands. It should be included in the Windows 95/98 package you are installing from, but if it is not, you will need to make one.

Neither the Windows 95 nor the Windows 98 CD-ROM is bootable, which is why the startup disk is so crucial, however, Windows 98 Second Edition is bootable.

In a paradox every bit as difficult to resolve as the chicken-or-egg debate, you are only able to make the startup disk (a) during setup or (b) once 95/98 is installed. If you have lost your startup disk and need to prepare a new drive, your best bet is to find a machine with an existing installation of Windows 95 or 98 and an create a startup disk off of it. To do this, go to Start ➤ Settings ➤ Control Panel and double-click the Add/Remove Programs icon. Within Add/Remove Programs is a tab called Startup Disk (Figure 13.1).

FIGURE 13.1   The Windows 98 Startup Disk tab

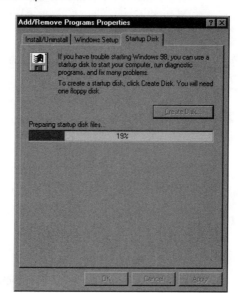

Click the Startup Disk tab to bring it to the front. Click the Create Disk button to start the startup disk creation process. You will need a single floppy disk for this, and all information on it will be deleted and replaced. If you can't find a floppy disk and even a single machine already running Windows 9*x*, well, you may be in the wrong business....

If you are performing the installation via CD, you must also make certain that the startup disk is capable of accessing the CD-ROM drive on your machine. In Windows 98, the startup disk automatically loads standard CD-ROM drivers and presents you with an option to load CD-ROM support on startup. Some Windows 95 startup disks also have this, but if not, you can modify the AUTOEXEC.BAT and CONFIG.SYS to load a CD-ROM driver. The exact modifications you will need to make depend on the type and manufacturer of your CD-ROM drive, but a sample CONFIG.SYS and AUTOEXEC.BAT follow:

```
CONFIG.SYS:
      Files=25
      Buffers=9,256
      DEVICE=C:\PANCD.SYS /B:25 /N:PANCD001

AUTOEXEC.BAT
      PATH=C:\;C:\DOS
      MSCDEX.EXE /D:PANCD001 /L:D /M:100
```

Notice that these aren't big changes, but they are crucial to make the CD-ROM functional under DOS; once Windows 95 or 98 is loaded, these files won't be needed because Windows has its own drivers for accessing the CD drive, and they will be loaded during the install. These lines can be added to and later removed from AUTOEXEC.BAT and CONFIG.SYS using any text editor.

Once you have a basic Windows startup disk, you will want to continue to make other small improvements upon it as well by adding tools to allow you to perform common tasks more easily. SMARTDRV.EXE and XCOPY.EXE are two we recommend adding. Smart drive (SMARTDRV.EXE) increases file copy speed, and XCOPY.EXE allows you to copy multiple files and directories easily.

Partitioning Using a Windows 95 Boot Disk

Once you have a DOS or Windows startup disk, it is time to boot the computer and prepare it for the Windows installation. When the computer first boots up, the Windows 95 boot disk will simply bring you to an A:\> prompt.

Partitioning refers to establishing large allocations of hard drive space. A partition is a continuous section of sectors that are next to each other. In DOS and Windows, a partition is referred to by a drive letter, such as C: or D:. Partitioning a drive into two or more parts gives it the appearance of being two or more physical hard drives.

When a drive is partitioned in DOS, the first partition you create will be a *primary partition*, which is marked *active*. The active partition is the location of the boot-up files for DOS or Windows. If there is more than one partition, the second and remaining DOS partitions are found inside of another partition type called an *extended partition*. An extended partition contains one or more *logical partitions*; it is the logical partitions that have drive letters associated with them. Only one primary and one extended partition can be created per disk using the Windows 95 disk utility, which is called FDISK. This two-partition limit is a characteristic of Windows 95, not a limitation of the hard drive.

When FDISK is executed, a screen appears that gives four or five options (Figure 13.2 shows the screen with four options). The fifth option, which allows you to select a hard drive, appears only when there is more than one physical hard drive. FDISK will only partition one hard drive at a time.

FIGURE 13.2 The introductory screen in FDISK.EXE

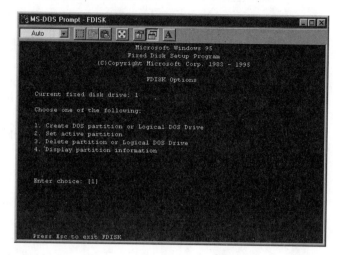

With FDISK, you can create partitions, delete partitions, mark a partition as active, or display available partitioning information. You must create a primary partition before you can create any other partitions. If space is still available on the drive, then a second, extended partition may be created. No drive letter is assigned to the extended partition. One or more logical partitions must be defined within the extended partition, and they can then have drive letters attached to them so users can access them.

It is possible for no partitions to be marked active on a particular drive. In this case, the machine will not be able to boot to the drive. If this is the case, you must use FDISK to set an active partition before you will be able to properly install Windows 9x. One and only one partition can be marked active.

FDISK creates a start and an end to a section of hard drive space. At the beginning of that space, it creates a special file called the Master Boot Record, or MBR. The MBR contains the partition information about the beginning and end of the primary and extended partitions. At the beginning of the partitions, this record is called the DOS Volume Boot Sector.

The size of a partition will determine certain aspects of a file pointer table called the *file allocation table*, or *FAT* for short. The larger the drive partition, the more space will be wasted on the drive.

Formatting

The next step in management of a hard drive is formatting, initiated by the FOR-MAT command. Technically the sort of formatting that we are talking about is high-level formatting. This should not be confused with low-level formatting, although it can be just as destructive to information on the hard drive. High-level formatting is, these days, normally the only formatting a technician will do. When high-level formatting is performed, the following actions take place:

- The surface of the hard drive platter is briefly scanned to find any possible bad spots, and the areas surrounding a bad spot are marked as bad sectors.

- Magnetic tracks are laid down in concentric circles. These tracks are where information is eventually encoded. These tracks, in turn, are split into pieces of 512 bytes called sectors. Some space is reserved in between the sectors for error correction information, referred to as CRC, or Cyclic Redundancy Check, information. The operating system may use CRC information to re-create data that has been partially lost from a sector.

- Additionally, a file allocation table (FAT) is created. This table will contain information about the location of files as they are placed onto the hard drive. The FAT has a limited number of entries. Therefore, the space allocated for the partition may need to be divided into clusters of sectors, where a sector is the smallest part of a hard drive.

Low-level formatting is the first step in preparing to install an operating system into a computer. It is the process of getting the surface material of the hard drive platters prepared to accept information. Low-level formatting creates the tracks and sectors that higher-level processes look for. This formatting process destroys any information that is already present on the hard drive. For this reason, low-level formatting is rarely used on IDE hard drives, which contain some special information written at the factory. SCSI hard drives will occasionally be low-level formatted; on very rare occasions, an IDE drive will also be low-level formatted. Fortunately, these days hard drives are usually low-level formatted at the factory and never need to have this done to them again. For most technicians, this is just a historical fact of past times.

Optimization

Each FAT has a set number of entries; the number depends on the size of the hard drive. On a very small hard drive, the FAT could theoretically be large enough to track all the sectors, but in practice this never occurs. Only high-density floppy disks have FATs that track individual sectors. Sectors on hard drives will be clumped together in what is called a *cluster* or *allocation unit*. In general, as the drive or drive partition increases in size, the number of sectors per cluster increases.

A drive between 16MB and 128MB will have four sectors per cluster. A larger drive of up to 256MB will have eight sectors per cluster. In fact, every time you double the hard drive size, you double the number of sectors per cluster. Thus, drives of up to 512MB will have 16 sectors per cluster, drives of up to 1024MB will have 32 sectors per cluster, and so on. Clusters of 32 sectors are 16KB in size.

Allocation units may not be used by two different files, thus any empty space in an allocation unit (any space not filled by the file assigned to that allocation unit) is wasted. Many files almost fill the last cluster allocated to them, but many files barely use this last allocated cluster. On the average, files use half of the last cluster allocated to them.

Imagine large clusters with one cluster per file being only half filled. If these clusters are 16KB and there are 5,000 files, then roughly 40MB of hard drive space is designated but unused. For example, if a hard drive has almost 25,000 files on one partition, that translates to 200MB of wasted space.

One solution to optimizing hard drive space is to set up multiple partitions that are smaller in size and therefore use smaller clusters. It is not unusual for a 1GB drive to regain 200MB or more when split into two partitions. You should also avoid partition sizes that are just over the limit for cluster sizes. A 528MB partition has less available space on it than a 512MB partition does, simply because the clusters are large enough to waste more than the extra space on the larger partition. As new drives get larger, though, the difference between 528MB and 512MB becomes largely irrelevant. Because of this, a new file system—FAT32—solves many of these problems (and will be discussed later).

EXERCISE 13.1

Preparing a New Disk for Windows 95

1. Insert the Windows 95 boot disk and start the computer.

2. At the prompt, type **FDISK**.

3. In the main FDISK screen, select option 4, Display partition information.

4. If the drive is already partitioned properly, the partitions and their sizes will be listed.

5. Return to the main screen by clicking the ESC key on your keyboard. If the partitions were properly created already, click ESC again to leave FDISK.

6. If the disk is not yet partitioned, select 1, Create DOS partition or logical DOS drive.

EXERCISE 13.1 *(continued)*

7. Click 1, Create a primary DOS partition. You will be asked if you want to use the maximum space available and make the partition startable. In most cases, this is best, but if you wish to make the partition a particular size, you can do so. *IMPORTANT: If there are partitions on the disk already, you must delete them to create new ones. If you do this, all information currently on those partitions will be lost!*

8. After you have created the new C: partition, click ESC until you are asked to reboot.

9. Reboot, and again use the startup disk to start the system. At the A: prompt, type **FORMAT C:** to format the drive with the standard FAT file system.

10. You will be warned that all information on the drive will be deleted. Type **Y** to confirm, and the format will begin. This can take some time. When the format is completed, you may begin the installation of Windows. You do not need to reboot after a format.

Using the Windows 98 Boot Disk

If you are using a Windows 98 boot disk to prepare a drive, you will notice that a few things are different. First, when the machine first starts up, you will be presented with two options: boot with CD-ROM support or boot without it. The default is to boot with CD support. If you are planning to install from CD-ROM, this makes life easy because most supported CD drives are simply loaded automatically.

Second, as you start the Windows 98 FDISK program, you will be presented with the message about working with large hard drives. Standard FAT (FAT16) has problems dealing with large drives, both due to its maximum partition size of 4GB and because it uses extremely large cluster sizes for large partitions. As the size of computer hard drives increased, this became a serious problem, so Microsoft added support for a second format type—FAT32. Earlier versions of the file allocation tables are known as FAT12 and FAT16 (because the size of the FAT entries are 12 bits and 16 bits respectively). First implemented in Windows 95 "Revision B," FAT32 support became standard in later versions of Windows—98 and 2000. As a comparison of how the new system saves you space, a 2GB drive with FAT16 has clusters of 32KB; with FAT32, the cluster sizes are 4KB. Because of this, if you save a 15KB file, FAT will need to allocate an entire 32KB cluster. FAT32 would use four 4KB clusters, for a total of 16KB. FAT32 wastes an unused 1KB, while FAT wastes 15 times as much!

The disadvantage of FAT32 is that it is not compatible with older DOS, Windows 3.*x*, and Windows 95 operating systems. This means that when you boot a Windows 95 Rev B. or Windows 98 FAT32–formatted partition with a DOS boot floppy, you can't read the partition.

NOTE

FAT32 supports drives of up to 2 terabytes. If you have a disk that is over 2,000GB in size, you will have to create multiple partitions on it.

Starting a Windows 9*x* Installation

Once you have the drive prepared, you are ready to start the Windows install process. To do this, boot to the startup disk and put either the CD-ROM or the first setup disk into the machine.

The program that performs the installation is called SETUP.EXE, and it's located either in the root directory of Disk 1 of the set of installation floppies or in the WIN95/WIN98 directory of the installation CD-ROM. It examines your hard disk and makes sure there is enough room to install Windows 95, then copies a few temporary files to your hard disk. These temporary files are the components of the Installation Wizard that will guide you through the installation of Windows 9*x*.

There are a few options that you can use with the Setup program. To use them, you place them after the SETUP at the command line, separated by a single space. Table 13.2 details these Setup startup switches.

TABLE 13.2 Windows 95 SETUP Command-Line Options

Option	Function
/d	Tells Setup to ignore your existing copy of Windows. It only applies during an upgrade.
<filename>	Used without the < and >, specifies the preconfigured setup file that Setup should use (e.g., SETUP MYFILE.INI causes Setup to run with the settings contained in MYFILE.INI).
/id	Tells Setup to skip the disk space check.
/iq	Tells Setup to skip the test for cross-linked files.
/is	Tells Setup to skip the routine system check.
/it	Tells Setup to skip the check for Terminate and Stay Resident programs (TSRs) that are known to cause problems with Windows 95 Setup.

TABLE 13.2 Windows 95 SETUP Command-Line Options *(continued)*

Option	Function
/l	Enables a Logitech mouse during setup.
/n	Causes Setup to run without a mouse.
/p	Tells Setup to skip the check for any Plug-and-Play devices.
/T:C:\tmp	Specifies which directory (C:\tmp in this case) Setup will copy its temporary files to. If this directory doesn't exist, Setup will create it.

In this portion of the chapter, we will look at the Windows 95 setup specifics. To start the installation, you simply change to the drive letter where the installation files are and type **SETUP** (with the appropriate startup switches), like so:

```
C:>D:
D:>SETUP
```

Setup will tell you that it's going to check your system and that you must press Enter to continue. If you want to cancel the installation without continuing, you can press Esc. When you press Enter, Setup copies a very basic Windows system to your computer from the CD and starts it. Setup then executes in a Windows environment and welcomes you to the installation (Figure 13.3).

FIGURE 13.3 Windows 95 Setup Welcome screen

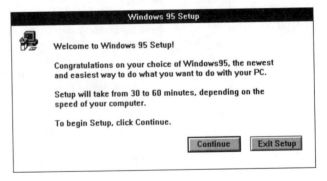

Because Windows may need these files later, it is often a good idea to simply copy all of the needed files (the `Win95` directory on the CD or all of the files on each setup disk) to a directory on the local drive of the machine. Some folks use a directory called `C:\disks` for this purpose.

To begin the installation, click Continue. Setup will then copy some more files your to computer while it builds the Setup Wizard. The Windows 95 Setup Wizard guides you through the installation step by step. At each step, you will be asked questions about how you would like Windows 95 configured. Then you simply click the Next or Continue button.

The Setup Wizard will ask you questions about three main categories:

- Gathering information
- Copying files to your computer
- Finishing the installation

These three general steps will be presented to you when you begin the installation and at various times during the installation.

After the Welcome screen, Setup will present you with the text of the license agreement. The Windows 95 license agreement basically says that you are being sold a copy of this software for use on one computer and that you won't give it away or sell it to anyone else for a profit. There's a bunch more to it, so you should read the entire agreement. When you've read it, click Yes to accept the agreement and move on. If you click No, you are telling Setup (and Microsoft) that you don't agree to the terms of the contract. This will cancel the installation.

Step 1: Collecting Information about Your Computer

Next you'll be presented with the screen in Figure 13.4. This screen gives you the basic outline of the Windows 95 Installation process. In the first step, Setup asks you questions about how your computer is currently configured and which options you would like to install.

FIGURE 13.4 Windows Setup start screen

From this point in the setup process on, the Setup screens will have a Back button and a Cancel button. You click the Back button to go back to the preceding screen, and click the Cancel button to completely exit the installation. If you exit the installation before it's completely finished, Setup will restore your system to its former state.

To begin the gathering of information, click the Next button (or press Enter).

Choosing the Windows Installation Directory

Setup will allow you to choose where you would like to install Windows 95. Setup chooses C:\WINDOWS by default. However, if you want to have both Windows 3.*x* and Windows 95 on the same system, you should install Windows 95 to a directory other than C:\WINDOWS. To do so, click the Other Directory radio button and then click Next. Setup will then ask you which directory you want to put Windows 95 in.

For most installations, you will want to install Windows 95 to the C:\WINDOWS directory. If this is the case, leave C:\WINDOWS checked and click the Next button to continue. Setup will check to see if you have enough disk space and memory to install Windows 95. If either of these two requirements are below the recommendations, Setup will issue an error and quit. If they pass, Setup will continue to the next step, choosing the type of setup you want to perform.

Choosing the Setup Options

The screen shown in Figure 13.5 allows you to select which type of installation you want. There are four options, outlined in Table 13.3.

FIGURE 13.5 Selecting the type of setup you want to perform

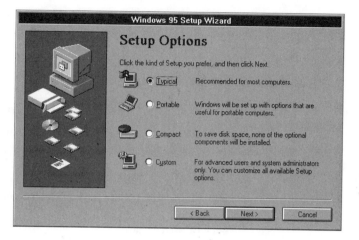

TABLE 13.3 Windows 95 Setup Types

Setup Option	Description
Typical	Allows Setup to choose the most popular features during the rest of the setup process.
Portable	Sets up the most common applications and utilities for portable computers. This option will install PCMCIA support and Advanced Power Management (APM).
Compact	Installs the minimum components Windows 95 needs to function.
Custom	Allows you to choose which components to install. If you select this option, Setup will present you with a list of utilities and programs to install. This option allows you to make the most choices about how Windows 95 gets installed. This is the method most commonly used by technicians to install Windows 95.

Because it's the most popular option for technicians, select the Custom radio button. Then click Next to continue the installation.

Entering User Information

In the next screen, you enter information about yourself and your company (if applicable). This information will be used when you install most other Microsoft applications. Simply start typing your name in the Name field. Then press the Tab key to move to the next field, Company. Type in your company name (or the name of the company that owns the computer) and click Next to continue.

Entering the Product Identification Number

The product identification number helps to ensure that you aren't illegally installing Windows 95 from a pirated copy. The number you must enter is usually found on the back cover of the CD case (look for a yellow sticker with the words *CD KEY*). It might also be found on the warranty registration card. You should send this card in so that you can receive technical support if you ever need it. From this screen (Figure 13.6), simply type in the number *exactly* as it appears on the back of the CD case.

FIGURE 13.6 Entering the product identification number

After you finished typing the number, you can click Next. If you type the wrong number, Setup will tell you and ask you to enter it again.

Analyzing Your Computer and Setting Up Hardware

Setup is now ready to start looking for the hardware devices it needs to install drivers for. To let Setup search for the devices, select the Yes (Recommended) option in the screen that appears. To specify all the hardware that your computer has manually, select the No, I Want to Modify the Hardware List option. Windows 95 does a pretty good job of detecting hardware in the computer and installing device drivers for those devices. For most computers, you'll want to select the Yes option and click Next.

After you click Next, Setup will present you with a screen like the one shown in Figure 13.7. If you have a network adapter, sound card, or CD-ROM drive, mark the appropriate check box(es). A check box will appear to tell Setup to install drivers and software for those items. When you have finished selecting hardware drivers from this screen, click Next to continue the installation and begin the hardware detection process.

FIGURE 13.7 Choosing special setup options

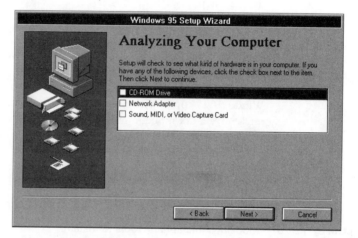

The hardware detection process may take several minutes. During this time, you will see a screen like the one in Figure 13.8 and you will hear the hard drive searching for files (or at least you'll see the hard drive light flash madly). When Setup finds a piece of hardware, it will make a note of which driver to install; if it finds something it doesn't have a driver for, it will ask you whether you want to provide one or not install the device at all.

FIGURE 13.8 Analyzing the computer's hardware to determine which drivers to install

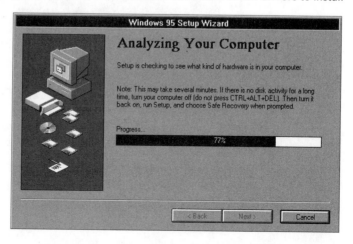

If the progress bar stops moving for more than 10 minutes and there is no hard disk activity, more than likely the machine is locked up. Reboot the computer and rerun Setup. Setup will detect that a previous installation wasn't completed and it will try to resume where it left off. Neat, huh?

After the hardware detection is finished, Setup will automatically move on to the next step.

Choosing E-Mail and Fax Software to Install

Windows 95 comes with several pieces of software to get you connected to the rest of the world. From the screen shown in Figure 13.9, you can choose to install Microsoft's online service, the Microsoft Network (MSN). In addition, Windows 95 comes with the software to send and receive faxes (although you must have a fax modem installed in your computer to use it). This software is called Microsoft Fax and it's integrated into Windows 95's Universal Mailbox called the Exchange Client (meaning you must have the Exchange Client installed to use MS Fax). The Exchange Client is actually called Microsoft Mail in the Setup window. This name, although confusing, stems from the fact that this mail client has its roots in the old MS Mail software.

FIGURE 13.9 Choosing which online tools to install

If you want to install any of these components, check the appropriate box. When you're finished selecting items, click Next to continue.

These check boxes just tell Setup whether you want the e-mail and fax software installed. Setup doesn't let you configure these components until after Windows 95 is installed.

Choosing Which Windows 95 Components You Want Installed

If you choose a Standard installation type, Setup will ask you whether you want it to choose all the components automatically or see a list of components. If you choose the latter, the screen in Figure 13.10 appears. If you chose a Custom installation type, Setup will automatically present you with the screen in Figure 13.10.

FIGURE 13.10 Custom setup component selection

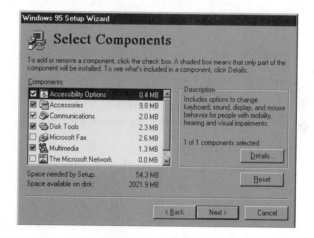

If a check box is gray with a check mark in it, that means that not all the components of that category are going to be installed. If you highlight the category that has the gray check box and click the Details button, a screen will appear that will allow you to select or deselect additional components. Figure 13.11 shows the screen that appears when you highlight Accessories and click Details. Notice that Games is not checked by default. If you want Solitaire installed (and most people do), click the check box next to Games and click OK.

FIGURE 13.11 Adding or removing components from an installation group

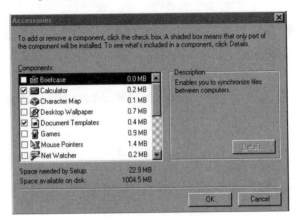

Once you have selected all the components you want installed, accept all selections by clicking OK until you get back to the screen shown in Figure 13.10. Then, click the Next button to continue the installation.

If you make a mistake selecting items, you can click the Reset button (see Figure 13.10) to reset the selections to the Setup defaults. However, be aware that the selections made in the e-mail/fax section of the installation will also be reset to their defaults, which is that they are not installed.

Network Configuration

The next step in the installation of Windows 95 shows up only if there is a network card installed in the machine. From this screen (Figure 13.12), you can customize which networking components are installed and how they are configured. Click Next to continue this installation.

FIGURE 13.12 The Network Configuration screen

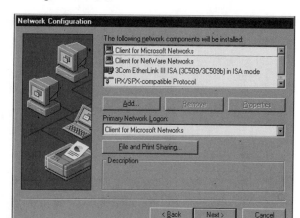

Because Windows 95 Networking configuration is covered in Chapter 18, we won't cover it again here. Refer to Chapter 18 for information about the details of configuring the Network Configuration screen.

If you have networking installed, the next screen you will see will be the computer identification screen. This only applies if you have the Client for Microsoft Networks installed because, on Microsoft networks, each computer has to have a name and should belong to a workgroup (these concepts will also be discussed in Chapter 18). After entering the information for Computer Name and Workgroup parameters, click Next to continue to the next step in the installation.

Verifying Computer Settings

Now that Setup has detected all the hardware in your machine in a Custom setup, the Setup Wizard will present you with a list of the hardware (Figure 13.13) that it found and allow you to modify which driver Windows 95 will use. If any of the drivers in the list are incorrect or have the word *Unknown* next to them, click the driver description, then click the Change button. Setup will present you with a list of alternatives. If none of the alternatives fit, leave the driver unchanged and install a new one after the installation.

FIGURE 13.13 Verifying computer settings

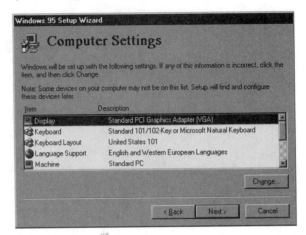

Once you have verified that all hardware drivers are correct, click Next to continue.

Installing and updating drivers for peripheral hardware is covered in Chapter 16, and updating current drivers is covered later in this chapter.

Creating a Startup Disk

The next step in the Windows 95 installation is to decide whether you want a startup disk (see Figure 13.14). This is the same disk we discussed earlier. You can choose to make one at this time (the Yes option) or to make one at a later time (the No option). Most technicians make their own Windows 95 startup disk, copy all their diagnostic utilities to it, and never use this option again. Because you booted using the one you created earlier, select No and click Next to continue the installation.

FIGURE 13.14   Choosing not to create a startup disk

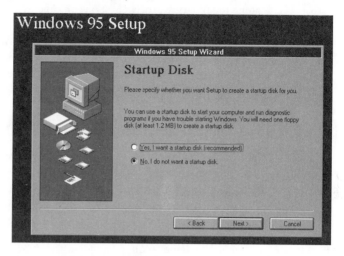

Step 2: Copying Files to Your Computer

At this point, you have given the Setup Wizard all the information it needs to begin installing Windows 95. It will present you with a screen (Figure 13.15) telling you this and giving you one last chance to cancel before copying files to your computer. If you think you made any mistakes, you can click the Back button. You can also click Cancel to abort the entire installation. If you believe you have entered all information correctly, click Next to start the file copy.

FIGURE 13.15   Starting the file copy

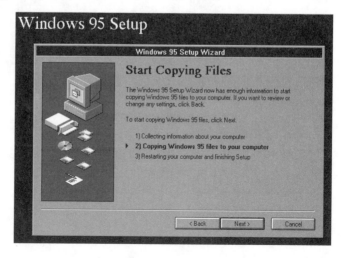

The bottom of the next screen displays a progress bar to indicate how far along the file copy process is. You can cancel the file copy at any time by clicking the Exit button in the lower-right corner of the screen or by pressing the F3 key on your keyboard. The file copy may take several minutes, depending on the speed of your computer. The nice part is, you don't have to watch a boring, blue bar go across the screen. Instead, you get to read several screens that give you information about the features of Windows 95.

Step 3: Restarting the Computer and Finishing Setup

When the file copy is finished, you will see a screen like the one in Figure 13.16. This screen is telling you that the majority of the installation is finished. You just need to reboot the computer and customize the way Windows 95 operates. To restart the computer and run Windows 95, remove any disks from their respective disk drives and click Finish. This will cause the computer to reboot.

FIGURE 13.16   Finishing the installation

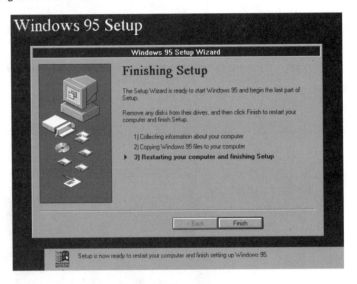

Upon rebooting, you'll see a blue screen with the message `Getting ready to run Windows 95 for the first time...` in red at the bottom of the screen.

If you have a network client installed, you may see a network login screen. The first time you run Windows 95, you won't be able to use your network connection anyway, so click Cancel for any screens you see that deal with network logins.

Setting Up Hardware and Software After Installation

The next screen you will see will tell you that Windows 95 is setting up hardware and any Plug-and-Play devices you might have (Figure 13.17). If there are any devices for which Windows 95 can't determine the settings (or find drivers), it will pop up a screen asking you to specify them. It will then pop up another screen telling you what settings it is configuring. It will automatically continue to the next screen.

FIGURE 13.17 Setting up hardware

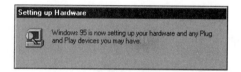

Briefly, a *driver* is a small program or piece of program code that runs in the background and translates the information going to and from an application and a piece of hardware. For example, a program such as WordPerfect doesn't keep track of all the different types of printers that are available; instead, it uses a printer driver. (Windows 95 and DOS applications use their own specific printer drivers.) WordPerfect is loaded into memory along with a printer driver that is specific to the user's printer. If a different printer is attached to that system, then a different printer driver may be required.

Setting the Date/Time Properties

After you set the hardware and software parameters, Windows 95 will present you with a screen that will allow you to set the date, time, and time zone (Figure 13.18) of the computer.

FIGURE 13.18 The Time Zone tab of the Date/Time property box

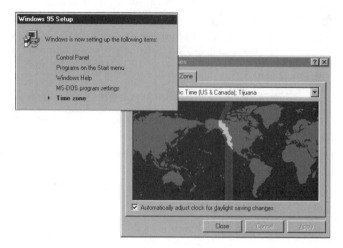

There are two tabs at the top of the window:

- In the Time Zone tab, you can click a map to set your time zone (click your current location on the map and it will set the time zone to the correct zone automatically, or if you know it, you can select your time zone from a drop-down list). You can click the check box next to Automatically Adjust Clock for Daylight Saving Changes and Windows 95 will set the clock automatically forward or backward on the appropriate day.

- The other tab is the Date & Time tab. From here you can set the current date and time by clicking the appropriate date in the calendar. You move to different months by selecting them from the drop-down list. If you need to move forward or backward a year, click the up or down arrows that are to the right of the year. To change the time, click the area that indicates the time and use the arrows to the right to move the hours, minutes, and seconds forward or backward.

When you've finished setting the date, time, and time zone, you can click OK to continue the installation.

Setting Up Your Universal Inbox

If you chose to install either Microsoft Mail or Microsoft Fax, Windows 95 will ask you to install Microsoft Exchange using the Inbox Setup Wizard. This wizard will guide you through the setup of the e-mail and fax services. If you have a modem installed in your computer, the wizard will help you configure it to work with these services. Because this material isn't covered on the exam, we'll refer you to the Windows 95 Help file that comes on the installation CD.

Setting Up a Printer

The final step to configuring Windows 95 is setting up a printer. To do this, Windows 95 starts up the Add Printer Wizard. This wizard is designed to guide you through the installation of a printer. We will cover this in more detail in Chapter 18, so we won't devote a great deal of time to discussing it here. If you don't want to install a printer now (or don't have one connected to your computer), click Cancel.

Final Installation Steps

After you configure a printer, Windows 95 is finally fully configured and will present you with a screen instructing you that it will reboot one final time. To reboot your computer and bring up Windows 95, click OK. Windows 95 is installed!

Once Windows 95 opens for the first time (without any wizards), you can start using it. You can also further customize the interface using the techniques discussed in Chapter 12 or those covered in "Configuring Windows 9x Software" later in this chapter.

Upgrading to Windows 98 from Windows 95

If you are currently running Windows 95 and want to upgrade to Windows 98, you're not alone. Most corporate and many home users have upgraded to Windows 98 at the time this book is being written in late 2000. This is due, in part, to some of the features that Windows 98 added to enhance Windows 95. It can also be attributed to the fact that the upgrade process is very easy (almost painless, in fact) and to the fact that the Microsoft marketing machine did a great job of selling it as a significant upgrade. Some of the major enhancements with Windows 98 include the following:

- Better Internet support through the integration of Internet Explorer
- Year 2000 fixes
- Support for newer hardware, such as USB, AGP, and DVD
- FAT32
- DOS 7 (16-bit) is replaced by DOS32 (32-bit)
- Enhancements for MMX processors, better use of RAM and disk resources

In truth, Windows 98 is a relatively basic upgrade. Besides the fact that most of the changes were relatively modest, most of them were generally also available to interested Windows 95 users through free Internet updates. As you will see, for most configuration and troubleshooting tasks, Windows 95 and 98 are identical.

Still, time marches on, and if you are asked to upgrade a machine from Windows 95 to Windows 98, the procedure is relatively straightforward. Let's run through a typical upgrade.

Starting the Upgrade

For the most part, the major steps that you need to follow when upgrading from an earlier version of Windows to Windows 98 are the same steps used to install Windows 98 on a machine without an operating system. These are divided by Setup into the following areas:

1. Preparing to run Windows 98 setup

2. Collecting information about your computer

3. Copying Windows 98 files to your computer

4. Restarting your computer

5. Setting up hardware and finalizing settings

The Windows 98 installation program, SETUP.EXE, performs these steps. In order to start the upgrade, you need to start the SETUP.EXE program. If you are upgrading to Windows 98 using a CD-ROM with a working installation of Windows 95, things couldn't be much simpler. Insert the disk into the CD drive and a window similar to the one in Figure 13.19 appears. In addition to this window, a box will appear noting that you are using an earlier version of Windows and offering to upgrade you to Windows 98.

FIGURE 13.19 The Windows 98 Autorun window

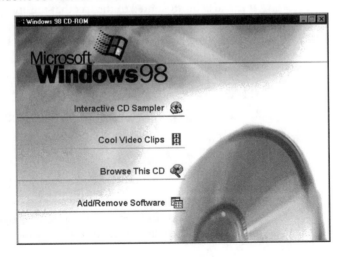

Simply click Yes, and the SETUP.EXE program will load. You will be able to see the progress of the setup process along the left side of the window as the Setup program shows you which part of the install you are in and approximately how much time is remaining.

Preparing to Run Windows 98 Setup

The first part of the setup routine is pretty basic. All that happens during the initial preparation is that the drives are given a quick examination and the files needed to run the setup are loaded. There are a couple of things that Windows checks for at this time, such as whether you have enough free drive space for the install and whether you have any programs running that may interfere with the upgrade.

During a system upgrade, you will generally want to shut down all nonessential programs, including those that are sitting in your system tray. This will help avoid conflicts and make it more likely that the install will go smoothly.

Collecting Information about Your Computer

Once the Setup program is convinced that you are ready to install, it will begin to gather the details needed for this install. A wizard appears and goes through the following screens:

License agreement   This is where you give Bill your firstborn. Few people bother to read these, and fewer still understand them. The most important thing that you need to remember is that if you don't accept the license agreement, you can't complete the install. That simple.

Product Key   These just keep getting longer, and more annoying. Microsoft keys have gone from 10 keys in Windows 95 to 25 in Windows 98. Remember that if a user has purchased the software, you need to put in their actual key, not just any one you have handy.

Install Directory   Here you enter the directory in which the Windows 98 files will be stored. By default, this is the same directory that the current version of Windows is in—generally C:\WINDOWS. You can change this directory, but if you do, the upgrade will no longer migrate existing programs and you will have to install all programs and drivers over again (as in a new install).

At this point, Setup does some system checks and again checks for drive space. It also looks at the install directory you have specified. If you are upgrading over an existing Windows install, you're given the option to save your existing system files so that you can revert back if you have problems with Windows 98. If you decide to save these files, they will be saved at this point.

To save the files needed to revert back to Windows 95, you must have about 50MB of extra disk space. In most cases, you will not need these files and will choose not to save them. If you have any doubt about the compatibility of the hardware or software on the machine, though, this is a reassuring option.

Next you are presented with choices as to which Windows components you wish to install. There are four basic installation types, each of which gives you a different set of components:

Typical   If you are installing a system for someone else, and are not sure which options to install, this is a good base install of most elements.

Portable   This type installs fewer components, but it includes a number of communication tools left out of the typical install, including Dial-Up Networking.

Compact   The no-frills install. It installs a minimal set of options.

Custom   The technician's special. It allows you to go in and choose exactly which components you want and which you don't from the component groups. Each group generally has a number of options included with it, and you can choose to install all, some, or none of any component group. The component groups are Accessibility (used to install options for those with mobility, hearing, or visual impairments), Accessories, Communications, Desktop Themes, Internet Tools, Microsoft Outlook Express, Multilanguage Support, Multimedia, Online Services, System Tools, and Web TV for Windows.

If a box is checked, all components for that group will be installed. If it is clear, none will be. If the box is gray, only some of the components will be installed. To see exactly which components are selected, use the Details button (see Figure 13.20).

FIGURE 13.20 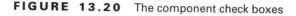 The component check boxes

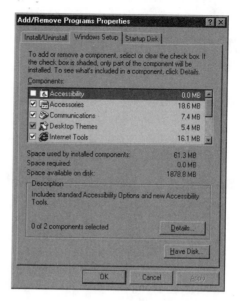

Once you have selected your components, you will be asked for a computer name, a workgroup, and a description of the machine. The computer name can be up to 15 characters with no spaces, as can the workgroup name. The Description field can be longer and can include spaces. Their functions are as follows:

Computer Name   Used to uniquely identify the machine on a Microsoft network. This name cannot be the same as any other machine's computer name.

Workgroup   Used to organize computers, a workgroup is a group of machines that participate in a loose grouping on the network. If your workgroup name is different than everyone else's, you will be the only person in that workgroup.

Description   Simply a text field in which you can describe what the machine is, where the machine is, or why the machine is. It can also be left blank.

Once these fields have been filled in, Setup confirms keyboard layout and regional settings, as well as country or regional information. You are then given the opportunity to make a Windows 98 startup disk. As this is an upgrade, you may not have a Windows 98 startup disk, and this is an excellent time to create one. Click Next past the first screen, and then either OK or Cancel, depending on whether you need a 98 startup disk or not. If you choose to create one, place a floppy into the A: drive. Any data already on this disk will be completely erased.

After you have completed the startup disk screens, the "collecting information about your computer" phase of the installation is over. The next phase of the install begins immediately.

Copying Windows 98 Files to Your Computer

Not a lot happens during this phase, at least as far as user interaction. Files will copy from the CD to the hard drive, and during this time, Microsoft marketing information about various Windows 98 features will be displayed to keep you occupied. This is an excellent time to wander off and make coffee.

Restarting Your Computer

Once the file copy is complete, you will be asked to reboot the machine. If you are off making coffee, as recommended, the Setup program will simply reboot for you after a 15-second delay.

Setting Up Hardware and Finalizing Settings

During the reboot, Windows collects information about the hardware installed in the machine, exactly as it did during an installation under Windows 95. Plug-and-Play devices are listed and activated if possible. Setup will load and test drivers to detect other hardware.

Once your hardware has been detected, you will be given the chance to specify driver locations for any devices that are not supported out of the box by Windows 98.

If you are upgrading, Windows 98 will generally find and use the device drivers that were in use under Windows 95. This is good, in that it makes for an easy install, but you should check vendor Web sites to see if they have updated Windows 98 drivers. If so, you will need to upgrade to the new driver.

Once Windows has detected and installed drivers for all of the hardware it can find, it will reboot a second time in order to initialize the new configuration and present your Desktop.

Windows 98 Setup

After the reboot, you're almost there. You can be pretty sure that you are nearing the end of the setup when you see in the Windows 98 Setup window that the basic settings for each of the following are being configured:

Control Panel

Programs on the Start Menu

Windows Help

MS-DOS Program Settings

Tuning up Application Start

System Configuration

These are user-based settings that are configured for each user the first time they use Windows 98. Windows 98 sets up the Desktop and other user-specific system elements according to the system defaults, after which point you are presented with a Windows 98 Desktop.

That didn't hurt at all, now, did it? Of course, the setup was completed without any problems, too, which always helps. For more information about what to do when the setup doesn't go so well, check out Chapter 19.

If the computer seems to start up fine but Windows 9x doesn't function properly, try rebooting in *Safe mode*. This mode of operation loads Windows 98 with a minimal set of drivers and can help you determine if the problem is hardware or software related. To boot the computer, turn it on and press the F8 key when you see the words *Starting Windows 98*. Doing so will present you with a list of boot-up choices, the third of which is Boot Computer in Safe Mode. Select this option (number 3) and press Enter. When Windows 98 comes up, it will be running in Safe mode, indicated by the words *Safe Mode* in all four corners of the screen. You can then check on drivers, conflicts, and so on and make changes to the configuration as needed. To exit Safe mode, restart the computer. If you have fixed the problem, upon reboot, the computer will be operating normally. For more on Safe mode, see Chapter 19 on troubleshooting.

Configuring Windows 9x Software

Once you have the system up and running, you may want to know just what you have installed. Windows 95 and Windows 98 are pretty much identical under the hood, so we will simply look at this as a 9x discussion.

Because Windows 9x is a very different operating system than Windows 3.x (which it replaced), most of its configuration is done using different tools than were used in Windows 3.x. Even so, Windows 9x shares a few configuration similarities with its ancestors (Windows 3.x and DOS) for compatibility's sake. The AUTOEXEC.BAT and CONFIG.SYS are used to a limited extent, but they're not needed and remain only for older hardware and software compatibility. Additionally, INI files are still used for some Windows programs (generally, older 32-bit apps) to hold configuration settings.

The Registry was completely overhauled between Windows 3.1 and Windows 95 and has taken the place of most INI files. In addition to software extension information, it also contains software configuration information and hardware configuration information. Generally speaking, most of the Windows 9x settings that were previously stored in INI files are now stored in the Registry.

Let's discuss some Windows 9*x* configuration files and the tools used to edit them.

Important System Files

There are a number of files stored in the root of C:, as well as in the WINDOWS directory, which can be used to modify your system's configuration and affect how your computer works. Some of the files listed in the following subsections are critical to the functioning of a Windows 9*x* computer, whereas others are simply holdovers from earlier operating systems.

Due to the fact that the Registry actually handles most of the startup tasks in Windows 9*x*, many system files are there mostly for compatibility with older programs. Because of that, you may never use them. Regardless, many of these obsolete files are listed in CompTIA's test objectives, so you need to know about them!

Examining the Windows 9*x* Boot Process

First, let's look at the process you use when you boot the system. When Windows 9*x* first starts up, it goes through a number of steps before presenting you with a Desktop. The basic elements of a Windows 9*x* startup are as follows:

- *System self-checks and enumerates hardware resources.* Each machine has a different startup routine, called the POST (power on self-test), which is executed by the commands written to the motherboard of the computer. Newer Plug-and-Play boards not only check memory and processors, they also poll the systems for other devices and peripherals.

- *MBR loads and finds the boot sector.* Once the system has finished with its housekeeping, the master boot record is located on the first hard drive and loaded into memory. The MBR finds the bootable partition and searches it for the boot sector of that partition. Information in the boot sector allows the system to locate the root directory of C: and to find and load into memory the IO.SYS file located there.

- *IO.SYS loads into memory and starts the processor in real mode.* The IO.SYS file performs a number of tasks, each of which is done in real mode. Real mode is simply a method of accessing the processor in 16-bit mode. Drivers loaded through the CONFIG.SYS file therefore can continue to function in real mode even after the next step, unless they are replaced by 32-bit Windows drivers. The IO.SYS file performs the following tasks:
  - Provides basic file system access to allow the rest of the boot files to be found
  - Accesses the MSDOS.SYS file to obtain boot configuration parameters

- Loads LOGO.SYS (Windows bitmap display) and DRVSPACE.BIN (compressed drive access) if they are present and needed
- Loads the Registry file SYSTEM.DAT into memory, but does not access it
- Selects a hardware profile (or allows the user to)
- Processes the commands in the CONFIG.SYS and AUTOEXEC.BAT files if they are present

- *WIN.COM loads and transfers the processor to protected mode.* Once the AUTOEXEC.BAT file is parsed and processed, the WIN.COM file is automatically executed. This file then loads various drivers as instructed by the Registry. It also examines the SYSTEM.INI and WIN.INI files to obtain additional configuration information. Once the Registry files have been loaded, the processor is transferred into 32-bit protected mode.

- *Virtual device drivers, the Windows kernel, and the GDI load.* Once the system is in 32-bit mode, various 32-bit virtual device drivers load to manage hardware resources, often replacing 16-bit real-mode drivers. The Windows kernel, which controls access to the processor from Windows 9*x*, is loaded into memory, and once the graphical display interface (GDI) loads to manage screen I/O, the system is ready to accept customers.

- *The Explorer shell loads and the user is presented with a Desktop.* The last part of the boot process is the loading of the "shell" program: EXPLORER.EXE. The Explorer is the program that manages the graphical interface—the toolbar, the Desktop, and the Start menu. Once this loads, network connections are restored and programs in the STARTUP folder are run, all of which is determined by settings read out of the USER.DAT Registry settings for that user.

Listing the Important Files

Among the things you will have to be familiar with in preparation for the A+ exam are the startup and system files used by Windows 9*x*. We will now look at each of these individually, but Windows makes nosing around in the startup environment difficult, and as such there is a change you'll need to make first.

To protect them from accidental deletion, and to simply get them out of the way of the average user, Windows 9*x* system files are hidden from the user by default. Because of this, many of the files we are about to talk about will not be visible to you. To change this, you will need to change the display properties of the Windows Explorer. To do so, follow these steps:

1. Open the Windows Explorer.

2. Browse to the root of the C: drive. Look for the IO.SYS system file. It should be hidden and will not appear in the file list.

3. Choose View ➢ Folder Options. The Folder Options window opens.

4. Select the View tab, and scroll until you find the Hidden Files option (see Figure 13.21).

FIGURE 13.21 The Explorer View options

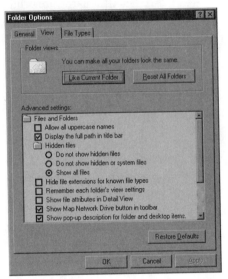

5. Select Show All Files.

6. Also uncheck the Hide File Extensions for Known File Types box.

7. Click OK. You will now be able to see the IO.SYS file and the others discussed in the following sections. For security, you should set these attributes back after you've read this chapter.

Startup Files

We discussed a number of files in the section "Examining the Windows 9x Boot Process." Now we will take a minute to explain each one further (there is an asterisk next to the names of the files that are required to boot Windows 9x):

MSDOS.SYS* Functions primarily to handle disk I/O, hence the name *disk operating system (DOS)*. Just like IO.SYS, MSDOS.SYS is loaded into memory at bootup and remains in memory at all times.

EMM386.EXE Provides the operating system with a mechanism to see additional memory. The memory space that EMM386.EXE controls has come to be known as *upper memory*, and the spaces occupied by programs in that region are known as *upper memory blocks (UMBs)*.

HIMEM.SYS Used to access upper memory.

IO.SYS* Allows the rest of the operating system and its programs to interact directly with the system hardware and the system BIOS. IO.SYS includes hardware drivers for common hardware devices. It has built-in drivers for such things as printer ports, serial or communication ports, floppy drives, hard drives, auxiliary ports, console I/O (input and output), and so on.

WIN.INI Sets particular values corresponding to the Windows environment. It's used extensively by 16-bit Windows 3.x applications; it's almost entirely replaced by the Registry for Windows 9x 32-bit apps.

WIN.COM* Initiates the Windows 9x protected load phase.

SYSTEM.INI Used in DOS and Windows 3.1 to store information specific to running the operating system. This and other INI files were used to configure 16-bit DOS and Windows apps.

COMMAND.COM Called the *DOS shell* or the *command interpreter*. It provides the command-line interface that the DOS user sees. This is usually, but not always, the C:\> prompt.

CONFIG.SYS Loads device drivers and uses the information from the AUTOEXEC.BAT to configure the system environment. Memory management tools and DOS peripheral drivers can be added here.

AUTOEXEC.BAT Used to run particular programs during startup. Also declares variables (such as search paths).

A batch file, named with a .bat extension, is simply a set of commands that Windows can execute or run. These commands may run utilities, or they may point toward full-blown applications. The AUTOEXEC.BAT is a batch file that is automatically executed when the system starts up.

Startup Files Configuration Tools

There are a number of ways to modify the INI files on a Windows 9x machine. First, you can open up a copy of Notepad, or the text editor of your choice, and go to town. This is still probably the most common method of modifying INI configuration files. If you prefer to have things a bit easier, though, there are a couple of tools provided with Windows 9x for dealing with these files. Both Windows 95 and Windows 98 allow you to use a tool called SYSEDIT.EXE to modify certain files, and Windows 98 has added MSCONFIG.EXE as well.

SYSEDIT

To run SYSEDIT, choose Start ➢ Run and type **SYSEDIT** at the prompt. You will see a window with a number of key configuration files open, as shown in Figure 13.22.

FIGURE 13.22 Main SYSEDIT window

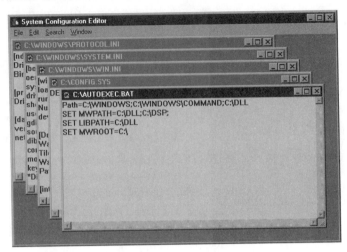

From here, you can examine, compare, and if needed, modify any of these files. All that the SYSEDIT program really does is open multiple text editors, each of which has one of the key text files in it.

SYSEDIT can be used to view and edit the PROTOCOL.INI, SYSTEM.INI, WIN.INI, CONFIG.SYS, and AUTOEXEC.BAT files.

MSCONFIG

Provided as a new addition to Windows 98, the System Configuration Utility is accessed by opening a Run window and typing **MSCONFIG**. The System Configuration Utility has a number of tabs, each of which has specific options you can manage (see Figure 13.23).

FIGURE 13.23   The System Configuration Utility

The thing that makes the System Configuration Utility different is that it lets you use your mouse to browse and modify settings that previously were accessible only through manual text configuration. You can also enable or disable Windows 98–specific elements, such as those shown in Figure 13.24. The MSCONFIG utility therefore merges Windows 98 configuration info with a way for non–DOS savvy users to work with DOS-era configuration files. Table 13.4 lists the tabs on the System Configuration Utility window.

FIGURE 13.24   The Advanced window from the SCU's General tab

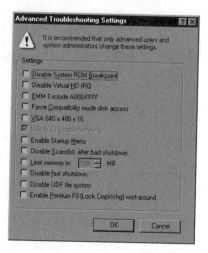

TABLE 13.4 System Configuration Utility Tabs

Tab	Function
General	Used to set startup options, as well as to determine which files to load during startup
Config.sys	Used to graphically view and edit the CONFIG.SYS file
Autoexec.bat	Used to graphically view and edit the AUTOEXEC.BAT file
System.ini	Allows you to modify the SYSTEM.INI file using a Registry-type interface
Win.ini	Allows you to modify the WIN.INI file using a Registry-type interface
Startup	Can be used to enable or disable particular startup options

Note that in the copy of Notepad in Figure 13.25, the contents of the AUTOEXEC.BAT file are displayed. The Autoexec.bat tab of the System Configuration Utility shows the same information. If you uncheck the last item and then reopen the AUTOEXEC.BAT file, the REM statement is added to block the execution of a line without actually deleting the command, in case you need it again later (Figure 13.26). This is very useful for troubleshooting.

FIGURE 13.25 The AUTOEXEC.BAT file before modification

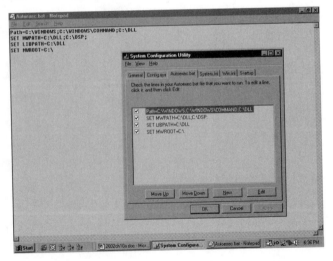

FIGURE 13.26   The AUTOEXEC.BAT file after modification

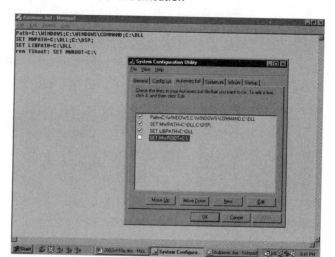

The Windows 9x Registry

The two major types of configuration files are the INI files and the Registry. The INI files are still used in Windows 9x, but as previously mentioned, they have less responsibility. The Registry, on the other hand, is used almost exclusively for holding configuration settings. It holds them not only for applications, but also for the system itself. Additionally, it contains different settings for different users.

The Windows 9x Registry is a database that is made up of two files: USER.DAT and SYSTEM.DAT. USER.DAT contains environmental settings for each user who logs in to Windows 9x. SYSTEM.DAT contains information about the hardware configuration of the computer that Windows is running on.

You can also create a third file—CONFIG.POL—which you can configure to specify particular security settings for a particular user or group of users. This file is used to "lock down" the Windows 9x interface so a user can't change it (useful if you have a user who is constantly changing their settings and messing up their computer). The CONFIG.POL file is created and edited with a utility called the Policy Editor, which is available on the Windows 95 and 98 installation CD-ROM. Normally you do not need to modify the system using the Policy Editor unless you are managing a network environment.

USER.DAT and SYSTEM.DAT cannot be edited with a text editor because they aren't ASCII text files (like AUTOEXEC.BAT, CONFIG.SYS, or the INI files). To edit the Windows 95 Registry, you need to use a tool specifically designed for that purpose: the aptly named Registry Editor (REGEDIT.EXE).

To start the editor, choose Start ➤ Run and type **REGEDIT**. Click OK and the Registry Editor will open, allowing you to view the Registry. The screen shown in Figure 13.27 shows a typical Registry. On the left side of this screen you will see the areas of the Registry. Each area (called a *key*) contains different types of settings. Table 13.5 explains these six keys and their functions.

FIGURE 13.27   A typical REGEDIT screen

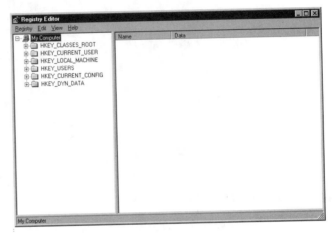

 If you make changes to the Registry, you will have to reboot your computer to have them take effect. The Registry is loaded into memory at start up.

TABLE 13.5   Registry Keys and Their Functions

Key	Description
HKEY_CLASSES_ROOT	Contains file extension associations. This tells Windows when a file with a particular extension should be opened in a particular application. Much of the data in this key is duplicated in the HKEY_LOCAL_ MACHINE key.

TABLE 13.5   Registry Keys and Their Functions *(continued)*

Key	Description
HKEY_CURRENT_USER	Contains user profile information for the person currently logged in to Windows. It contains the preferences for color settings and Desktop configuration. It is a subset of the HKEY_USERS key (described below).
HKEY_LOCAL_MACHINE	Contains settings and information for the hardware that is installed in the computer. When troubleshooting hardware issues, you might make changes to this section.
HKEY_USERS	Contains the default user profile and the profile for the current user (HKEY_CURRENT_USER, described above).
HKEY_CURRENT_CONFIG	Contains the current hardware configuration. This key is a subset of the HKEY_LOCAL_MACHINE (described above).
HKEY_DYN_DATA	Contains the dynamic settings for any Plug-and-Play devices in your computer. This setting is kept in RAM and doesn't require a reboot when changes are made to it.

Whenever you need to make changes to the Registry, open REGEDIT. The next step is to locate the subkey (the folders underneath the keys shown) that contains the setting you want to change. You can find it two ways. You can browse to it by clicking the plus sign (+) next to a folder to display the subkeys inside. Keep clicking until you find the subkey you're looking for. This can take a while because there may be several hundred folders to browse through. The other method is much more logical. In REGEDIT, select Edit ➢ Find (Figure 13.28). Then type in the string of characters you are looking for and click Find Next. REGEDIT will search the database until it comes across a string that matches what you typed in. If it isn't the entry you are looking for, press F3 to find the next entry that contains the string.

FIGURE 13.28 Performing a Find in REGEDIT

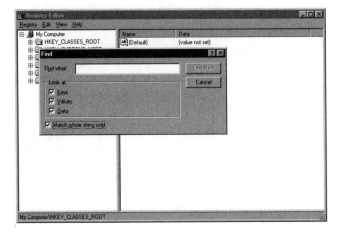

Thankfully, there aren't many times you need to go into the Registry to make changes. Most often, when you use the Windows 9*x* configuration utilities to make changes, changes will be made to the Registry as well. Let's discuss three of the tools that allow you to make these changes: the Properties menu option, the Control Panels, and the Device Manager.

And Now for the Real World...

If it's not apparent by now, the Registry is very important for correct Windows 9*x* operation. That's why every time Windows 9*x* successfully loads the Registry, it makes a backup of the two Registry files: USER.DAT and SYSTEM.DAT. These backup files are called USER.DA0 and SYSTEM.DA0, respectively, and can be used to restore a good Registry over one that's broken. In case of a Registry corruption, boot in Safe Mode Command Line by pressing F8 at system start up and choosing Safe Mode Command Line. Or boot to a Windows 9*x* startup disk. Then change the extension of the Registry files from .dao to .dat and reboot the computer. The Registry will be current as of the last successful boot.

Managing Hardware in Windows 9*x*

Configuring your software is just half of the work you have to deal with when working on Windows 9*x*. The system's hardware can also be configured, and there are a number of tools and options for letting you install, update, and configure your system. We will first look at how you can examine the hardware that is installed on your machine, and then we'll examine how to install a new device.

Device Manager

The *Device Manager* is a graphical view of all the hardware installed in your computer that Windows 9x has detected. You can open it by right-clicking My Computer, choosing Properties, then clicking the Device Manager tab. Or you can open the System Control Panel program (from Start ➢ Settings ➢ Control Panel) and choose Device Manager. In either case, you will see a screen similar to the one in Figure 13.29.

FIGURE 13.29   An example of a Device Manager screen

As you can see, one of the devices (COM 2) is marked with a red *X*. That is because the COM 2 port needed to be disabled so that the modem (which is installed to use COM 2) can use it.

The Device Manager is used to display all the hardware that Windows 9x "knows about" and to configure the hardware settings of those devices. If you click the plus sign (+) next to a category of devices, it will "tree out" that category and allow you to see the devices in the category. If you then click a device and click Properties, you can view the information about that device. Figure 13.30 shows the result of selecting a network card and clicking Properties. Notice that there are three tabs: General, Driver, and Resources. Most devices will have these tabs (although some devices may have only one or two). The General tab (shown in Figure 13.30) shows general information about the device and status information. It also allows you disable the device in the current hardware profile.

FIGURE 13.30 Displaying the properties of a device in the Device Manager

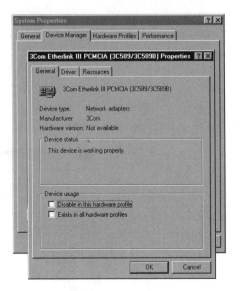

 For more information about hardware profiles, refer to either the Windows 95 or 98 Help file or the Windows 95 (or 98) Resource Kit by Microsoft. Don't worry, hardware profiles aren't covered on the exam.

Updating a Device's Properties or Driver

The next tab is usually the Driver tab (Figure 13.31). This tab allows you to see the driver name for the device as well as the driver version, if available. You can see in the figure that no drivers have been loaded for this device, or the drivers specified for the device are not compatible. If you need to load a driver (or update a driver), click the Update Driver button. Windows $9x$ will present you with a list of drivers to select from or allow you to install your own from floppy disk or CD-ROM. If you have upgraded to Windows 98 from Windows 95, you may find that a number of updated Windows 98 drivers are available on vendor Web sites.

FIGURE 13.31   The Driver tab of a device in the Device Manager

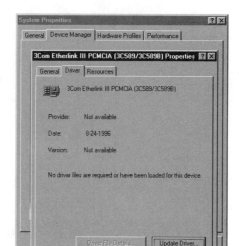

 To add drivers available on the Web, you usually must download the compressed driver files and then expand them onto a floppy disk or into a hard drive folder. At that point, you can run the update, and point to the location you extracted the files to. My personal favorite is www.windrivers.com.

The rightmost tab is usually Resources. From this tab, you can view and configure the system resources that the device is using (Figure 13.32). Most often, the check box next to Use Automatic Settings is checked, meaning that Windows 9x Plug-and-Play has determined the settings for the device and is managing it. However, if the device is not a Plug-and-Play device and needs to be configured manually, simply uncheck the Use Automatic Settings check box. You can then select the setting (for example, the Interrupt Request) and click the Change Setting button to pick the correct setting from a list. When you configure settings manually, Windows 9x will let you know if the setting you have chosen conflicts with another device. However, if you are in Safe mode, this feature can't be used and Windows 9x will not tell you.

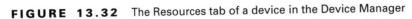

FIGURE 13.32 The Resources tab of a device in the Device Manager

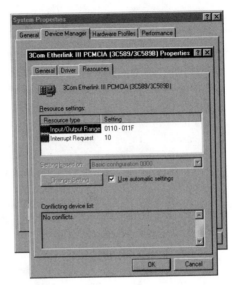

 Occasionally, Windows will not automatically detect a device that you have installed. In such a case, you will have to install the device manually. To learn about more complex peripheral device installs, refer to Chapter 16.

Windows 9*x* Management

Once you have the system configured and running, you may also want to go in and optimize certain settings. We will be focusing on three areas in which you can view and modify the Windows system to (potentially!) improve performance:

- Disk management
- Resource monitoring
- DOS application management

Disk Management

Several configuration settings that previously had to be manually adjusted are now automatic with Windows 9*x*. Among the most notable of these settings are the swap file and disk drive caching. There are essentially just three resources that a computer operating system needs to manage: processor, memory, and disk drives. Two of these three are managed completely automatically in Windows 9x. The third, disk drives, affects how both of the others perform, though, and can be configured in a number of ways.

Virtual Memory

The swap file is used to provide "virtual memory" to the Windows 9x system. What this means is that the swap file is hard drive space that idle pieces of programs are placed in, while other active parts of programs are kept in or swapped into main memory. The programs running within Windows believe that their information is still in RAM, but Windows has simply moved it into "near-line" storage on the hard drive. When the application needs the information again, it is "swapped" back into RAM so that it can be used by the processor. When you are working in your office and need a document, you may have to walk over to a file cabinet to get it. You then return to your seat and read the document. When you have finished and need to go on with another task, you need to put down the current document. If you don't need it again in the near future, you should get up and put it back in the file cabinet. If you will be needing it again, though, you may just set it on your desk for easier access. As with a document, though, when you need it again you do still have to pick it back up (unless you can remember what it said without looking again). Generally, you can think of a computer's disk drive as the file cabinet and virtual memory as the desk. Real memory (RAM) is the computer's memory. The more RAM you put into the machine, the more things it is able to remember without looking anything up. The larger the swap file, the fewer times it has to do intensive drive searches.

The moral of the story: As with most things virtual, a swap file is not nearly as good as actual RAM, but it is better than nothing!

As shown Figure 13.33, the default behavior for virtual memory is that Windows 9x simply handles it for you. This is a good thing, and unless you have a particular need to modify the file, you are best served by letting the computer handle it. If a particular application does require extensive virtual memory, you can modify it easily, though. To find the Virtual Memory button, choose Start ➤ Settings ➤ Control Panel. Double-click the System icon and select the Performance tab. The Virtual Memory button is along the bottom of the window.

FIGURE 13.33   The Windows 98 Virtual Memory window

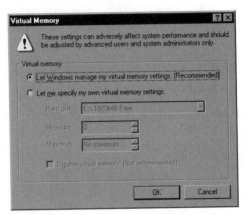

Locate the swap file on a drive with plenty of empty space. As a general rule, try to keep 20 percent of your drive space free for the overhead of various elements of the operating system, like the swap file.

Do not set the swap file to an extremely low size. Another general rule would be that the swap file should be at least as big as the amount of RAM in the machine. If you make the swap file too small, the system can become unbootable, or at least unstable.

Disk Caching

Disk caching in Windows 9x is no longer handled by SMARTDRIVE, as it was in earlier versions of Windows. Instead, Windows 9x uses a 32-bit caching program called VCACHE, originally introduced with Windows 3.11. This protected-mode driver runs more efficiently than its real-mode predecessor, SMARTDRIVE. It uses a more efficient set of rules for predicting the needed hard drive data. Further, it caches data from the network and from the CD-ROM; thus it is able to speed up the access to data from these devices.

Disk Conversion

Because many users upgraded their systems to Windows 98 from Windows 3.1 or Windows 95 Rev. A, they did not have the opportunity to choose between FAT16 and FAT32 because those earlier systems only supported FAT16. Because of this, you may want to convert their existing drives to the newer, faster file system using the Drive Converter utility. This utility is located in the Start ➤ Programs ➤ Accessories ➤ System Tools folder and will convert a partition from FAT16 to FAT32 without destroying the information that is on it.

Although conversion generally works without a hitch, a power outage or acciden- tal shutdown during the conversion could be *very* bad. Make sure to back up all crucial files before the conversion!

Disk Compression

The disk compression utility that comes with Windows 9x is still called DriveSpace, but unlike the earlier DriveSpace, it is now a protected-mode driver with faster performance. Older drives that have been doubled in space by using DriveSpace or DoubleSpace should be switched to the new protected-mode ver- sion. DriveSpace is automatically loaded, but not activated, when Windows 9x is installed.

Microsoft has been improving compression over time. Windows 95 used an awful system with a .CSV file and a host drive (usually H:) to compress information. Win- dows 98 does much the same, but uses an advanced utility called DriveSpace3 which allows you to set compression levels and to compress just parts of a drive. Both the Windows 95 and Windows 98 compression utilities work well enough, but they are difficult to understand and use and have limits. Only FAT16 drives can be compressed, and as FAT partitions under 9x can only be 2GB, that means any partition over 2GB cannot be compressed. Moreover, the FAT system itself is rel- atively inefficient because of its larger cluster sizes on bigger drives. Often a user can free up a lot of space on a FAT drive simply by converting it to FAT32. Refer to the next chapter for more advanced compression options in Windows 2000.

Resource Monitoring

Sometimes you just need to know a bit about what a machine is running, and what its current configuration settings are, before you start to reconfigure it. To do this, there are a couple of key utilities that you can gather information through.

Microsoft System Information

This is a great tool! It gives you a ton of information—everything from the user- name and swap file information to detailed displays of the exact resource usage of a particular device. You can't modify anything using this tool, so there isn't much else to say, but it is a great troubleshooting/configuration snooping utility (see Figure 13.34). The following categories are available for browsing:

- Hardware Resources
- Components
- Software Environment
- Applications

FIGURE 13.34 MS System Information Display info

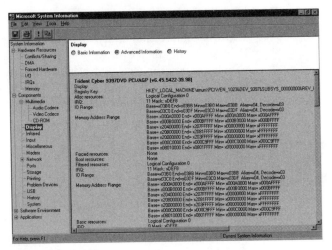

System Monitor

If you are interested in finding out what effect a particular application has on a Windows 9x system, you can use the System Monitor to plot key system resources in real time. Each resource you choose to monitor will be given a separate line that you can watch. In Figure 13.35, for instance, you can see that the Reads/second (in blue) spiked when a Word document was opened from the hard drive.

FIGURE 13.35 Watching resource usage with System Monitor

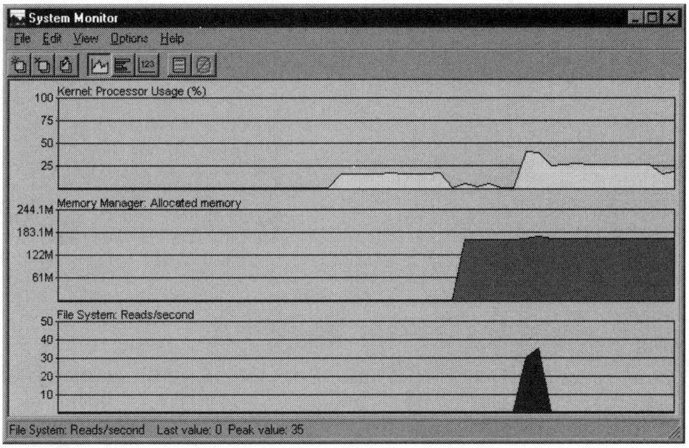

The general categories you can monitor include the following:

- Disk Cache
- File System
- Kernel
- Memory Manager
- Microsoft Network Client

Each of these categories then has specific counters beneath them that allow you to monitor particular elements. You can even change the polling interval from the default 5 seconds if you would like more specific results.

For a quick look at system resources, you can also just open up the Resource Meter (also in the SYSTEM TOOLS folder). It has just three counters—System resources, User resources, and GDI resources. Also, it shows you what is *free*, whereas the System Monitor shows you what is *used*. The Resource Meter is shown in Figure 13.36.

FIGURE 13.36   The Resource Meter

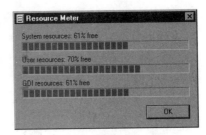

The Joy That Is Shareware

If, for some reason, you decide that the tools provided with Windows 9x simply aren't right for the exact problem you are having, it's no one's fault but your own if you don't find a better utility. The unending river of free or inexpensive utilities available is actually enough to dwarf all but the most active imaginations. If you need it, head out to www.download.com or www.tucows.com, and it's probably there. Rarely are any of us blessed with a truly unique problem, and there are lots of folks out there producing nifty solutions to your problems.

DOS Optimization

Compatibility with older programs is important because people have a significant investment in the money spent on their programs and in their time learning how to use them. Microsoft built a number of features into Windows 9x that allow previous users of DOS and Windows 3.x to capitalize on their investment and that allow technicians access to DOS-based troubleshooting.

According to Microsoft (see, for example, the Microsoft Windows 95 Resource Kit), memory management for conventional memory while running the Windows 9x operating system is the same as for MS-DOS 6.x. This applies to the management of conventional memory only because all other memory management in Windows 9x is essentially automatic. If 16-bit DOS and 16-bit Windows 3.x programs are not even going to be used, then these techniques are not necessary.

If you do need to use DOS/Windows 3.1 "real-mode" programs, you have three options:

- The user can initiate a DOS shell from inside of Windows 9x. This Virtual DOS Machine (VDM) is actually a 32-bit Windows application that emulates a DOS environment.

- The user can exit from Windows 9x into DOS mode. To do this, simply choose Start ➢ Shut Down ➢ Restart in MS-DOS Mode. Any programs you are currently running will be shut down and a DOS session will be opened. The advantage of this is that some DOS applications require actual control of the computer, and will not work through a VDM.

- In some cases, the user can boot the computer straight into DOS. This requires having a copy of MS-DOS installed on the machine and using a dual-boot scenario, with Windows 9*x* installed and DOS coexisting as a totally different, stand-alone system.

In any of these cases, special configuration tasks can potentially make DOS/3.1 programs function more efficiently. To maximize available memory for real-mode programs, load the extended memory manager, HIMEM.SYS, and the expanded memory manager, EMM386, in the CONFIG.SYS file. If possible, remove the real-mode drivers from the AUTOEXEC.BAT file and utilize the protected-mode drivers that are built into Windows 9*x*. You should not load SMARTDRIVE because the VCACHE disk caching that comes with Windows 9*x* is superior and does not detract from conventional memory.

MEMMAKER, which came with DOS 6.2*x*, is found on the Windows 9*x* CD in the directory OTHER\OLDDOS. MEMMAKER may be used to optimize the CONFIG.SYS and AUTOEXEC.BAT files for conventional memory.

 If you want to dual-boot to DOS, you must use the FAT file system and keep your C: partition below 2GB; FAT32 and partition sizes over 2GB are not supported by DOS. Don't worry about this too much, though, because finding a machine that is still running DOS 6.*x* or lower is extremely rare. Because Windows 95 (DOS 7) and 98 (DOS32) support DOS applications well enough in most cases and have far more functionality, "real" 6.*x* and earlier DOS has largely gone the way of the Atari 2600 and laserdiscs.

Summary

So that was Windows 9*x* in a nutshell. We have looked at the hardware requirements of Windows 95 and 98, how they are installed, and what is involved in an upgrade. We have also examined the Windows 9*x* boot process, and the files needed to start the system. Past that, we looked at the tools provided by Microsoft to view and configure Windows 9*x* and the hardware of the computer it is running on.

Installing Windows 9*x* starts with creating a startup disk and preparing the drive using the FDISK and FORMAT commands. At that point, you boot to the CD (or the network) and run the SETUP.EXE program that starts the Windows 9*x* install routine. You then work through the interactive Setup Wizard and provide information as needed.

Upgrading to Windows 98 from Windows 95 is pretty straightforward and usually involves little more than putting the CD into a CD-ROM drive and running Setup. You will be presented with a wizard that allows you to keep your current configuration even as you upgrade to the newer OS and update your file system to FAT32.

Understanding the boot process is crucial to knowing what is going on if errors occur during start up, and as such, we looked at the files needed for a Windows 9*x* machine to start and how system start up occurs, including what some of those files are and what they do.

Once the machine is up and running, getting it to run better, or to support certain applications, may require additional configuration. Tools such as the Registry Editor and Device Manager facilitate this, as do configuration options such as the Virtual Memory settings.

Last, some older DOS/Windows 3.1 programs require additional support, such as DOS mode. These applications often use configurations that must be specifically customized for them.

With this chapter, we have looked at one of the big two Microsoft operating systems. Next up is Windows 9*x*'s younger—and stronger—brother, Windows 2000.

Key Terms

Before you take the exam, be certain you are familiar with the following terms:

Active Directory	extended partition
allocation unit	File Allocation Table (FAT)
cluster	key
Device Manager	logical partitions
disk operating system (DOS)	primary partition
DOS shell	Safe mode
driver	upper memory blocks (UMBs)

Review Questions

1. Which of the following is not a requirement of installing Windows 95?

    A. 386DX or higher processor

    B. 2MB of memory

    C. 50–55MB free hard disk space

    D. One 3½-inch disk drive

    E. VGA video card or better

    F. Mouse and keyboard

2. Which of the following is not a requirement to install Windows 98?

    A. 486 or higher processor; Pentium recommended

    B. 8MB of memory; 16 to 32MB recommended

    C. 120MB free hard disk space

    D. One 3½-inch disk drive

    E. CD-ROM

    F. VGA or better video card

    G. Mouse and keyboard is required

3. A real-mode driver is one that _____ .

    A. Directly accesses hardware

    B. Indirectly accesses hardware

    C. Is software configurable

    D. Is a 32-bit Windows driver

4. What is the first step when installing Windows 9x onto a system that doesn't already have a functioning operating system?

    A. Formatting

    B. Partitioning

    C. Redirecting

    D. Installing the operating system

5. The DOS command that partitions the hard drive is called what?

    A. FORMAT.EXE

    B. XCOPY.EXE

    C. FDISK.EXE

    D. FDISK.COM

6. When a drive is partitioned, what is the first partition that is created called?

   A. Secondary partition

   B. Extended partition

   C. Expanded partition

   D. Primary partition

7. How many partitions can be created on a single drive using Windows 95's FDISK program?

   A. Two

   B. Three

   C. One

   D. Four

8. Which option on the FDISK utility allows you to select the hard drive and appears only when there is more than one physical hard drive?

   A. First option

   B. Second option

   C. Third option

   D. Fifth option

9. Which of the following is not performed by formatting the hard drive?

   A. Formatting scans the surface of the hard drive platter to find bad spots and marks the areas surrounding a bad spot as bad sectors.

   B. High-level formatting lays down magnetic tracks in concentric circles.

   C. The tracks are split into pieces of 512 bytes called sectors.

   D. Low-level formatting creates a file allocation table that contains information about the location of files.

10. A 2GB FAT32 partition will have a cluster size of _____ KB?

    A. 4

    B. 16

    C. 32

    D. 64

11. A 2GB FAT partition will have a cluster size of _____ KB.

    A. 4

    B. 16

    C. 32

    D. 64

12. When you use a Windows 98 boot disk when the machine first starts up, what is the first option?

   A. Boot with CD-ROM support or without it.

   B. Boot from a floppy disk.

   C. Boot from the hard drive.

   D. Format the hard drive.

13. What is the disadvantage of FAT32?

   A. It supports drives up to 2 terabytes.

   B. It's not compatible with older versions of DOS or with Windows 3.x and Windows 95 operating systems.

   C. It is compatible with all versions of DOS and other operating systems.

   D. You don't have to create multiple partitions.

14. The program that performs the Windows 9x installation is called _____ .

   A. INSTALL.BAT

   B. SETUP.DAT

   C. SETUP.EXE

   D. INSTALL.DAT

15. Which switch tells Windows 95's Setup program to ignore settings from your current copy of Windows?

   A. /is

   B. /it

   C. /id

   D. /d

16. Which switch causes Setup to run without a mouse?

   A. /n

   B. /l

   C. /p

   D. iq

17. The Setup Wizard will ask questions about how many main categories?

   A. One

   B. Two

   C. Three

   D. Four

18. Which of the following is not a category Setup asks questions about?

   A. Gathering information

   B. Networking information

   C. Copying files to your computer

   D. Finishing the installation

19. How many different types of installations are there?

   A. One

   B. Two

   C. Three

   D. Four

20. Which installation type allows Setup to choose the most popular options?

   A. Typical

   B. Portable

   C. Compact

   D. Custom

Answers to Review Questions

1. B. Windows 95 requires 4MB memory (and recommends 8MB).

2. A. To install Windows 98, you must have a 386DX or higher processor; Pentium is recommended.

3. A. A real-mode driver is one that directly accesses hardware, as was the standard in DOS. 32-bit Windows drivers work through the Windows system to access hardware, allowing Windows to optimize and control hardware access.

4. B. New disk drives or PCs with no operating system need to have two critical functions performed on them before they are able to be used: partitioning and formatting. These two functions are performed by using two commands, `FDISK.EXE` and `FORMAT.EXE`, which can be copied to a bootable floppy.

5. C. FDISK is usually performed on a computer that has no operating system or has a new hard drive. FDISK creates a start and an end to a section of hard drive space. At the beginning of that space, it creates a special file called the Master Boot Record, or MBR. The MBR contains the partition information about the beginning and end of the primary and extended partitions.

6. D. When a drive is partitioned, the first partition that is created is called the primary partition. The primary partition must be named drive C:, must contain the system files, and must be marked active for the system to boot up.

7. A. FDISK is a DOS-derived utility, and DOS only can access two partitions per drive. Other disk utilities allow up to four partitions per drive.

8. D. The fifth option on the FDISK utility allows you to select the hard drive and appears only when there is more than one physical hard drive. The fifth option is Select Hard Drive.

9. D. The file allocation table is created by high-level formatting, not low-level formatting.

10. A. FAT32 uses smaller cluster sizes on large drives and, therefore, is able to more efficiently store files.

11. C. FAT was designed for small drives (as small as 16MB), and as drive size increases, FAT handles it relative inefficiently.

12. A. When you use a Windows 98 boot disk when the machine first starts up, the first option is whether to boot with CD-ROM support or without it. The default is to boot with CD-ROM support.

13. B. The disadvantage of FAT32 is that it's not compatible with older versions of DOS or with Windows 3.x and early Windows 95 operating systems.

14. C. The program that performs the Windows 9x installation is called SETUP.EXE. You cannot boot from the CD-ROM to install Windows 9x.

15. D. The /d switch in Windows 95 ignores the setup of your existing copy of Windows. The /id switch tells Setup to skip the disk space check, /it tells it to skip the check for Terminate and Stay Resident programs (TSR) that are known to cause problems with Windows 95 Setup, and /is skips the routine system check.

16. A. The /n switch causes Setup to run without a mouse. Use /l if you have a Logitech mouse and want it enabled during setup. The /p switch tells Setup to skip the check for any Plug-and-Play devices, and /iq tells Setup to skip the test for cross-linked devices.

17. C. The Setup Wizard will ask questions about three main categories. The three main categories are gathering information, copying files to your computer, and finishing the installation.

18. B. Setup does not ask questions about networking.

19. D . Windows 95 has four different types of setups: Typical, Portable, Compact, and Custom.

20. A. The Typical option allows Setup to choose the most popular options.

Chapter

14

Installing and Using Windows 2000 Professional

THE FOLLOWING OBJECTIVES ARE COVERED IN THIS CHAPTER:

✓ **1.1 Identify the operating system's functions, structure, and major system files to navigate the operating system and how to get to needed technical information.**

Content may include the following:
- Major operating system functions
  - Create folders
  - Checking OS version
- Major operating system components
  - Explorer
  - My Computer
  - Control Panel
- Contrasts between Windows 9x and Windows 2000
- Major system files: what they are, where they are located, how they are used, and what they contain:

  System, configuration, and user interface files
- IO.SYS
- BOOT.INI
- WIN.COM
- MSDOS.SYS
- AUTOEXEC.BAT
- CONFIG.SYS
- COMMAND LINE PROMPT

  Memory management
- Conventional
- Extended/upper memory
- High memory

- Virtual memory
- HIMEM.SYS
- EMM386.exe

Windows 9x

- IO.SYS
- WIN.INI
- USER.DAT
- SYSEDIT
- SYSTEM.INI
- MSCONFIG (98)
- COMMAND.COM
- REGEDIT.EXE
- SYSTEM.DAT
- RUN COMMAND
- COMMAND LINE PROMPT

Windows 2000

- Computer Management
- BOOT.INI
- REGEDT32
- REGEDIT
- RUN CMD
- NTLDR
- NTDETECT.COM
- NTBOOTDD.SYS

Command Prompt Procedures (Command syntax)

- DIR
- ATTRIB
- VER
- MEM
- SCANDISK
- DEFRAG
- EDIT
- XCOPY
- COPY
- SETVER
- SCANREG

✓ **1.2 Identify basic concepts and procedures for creating, viewing, and managing files, directories, and disks. This includes procedures for changing file attributes and the ramifications of those changes (for example, security issues).**

Content may include the following:

- File attributes—Read Only, Hidden, System, and Archive attributes
- File naming conventions (most common extensions)
- Windows 2000 COMPRESS, ENCRYPT
- IDE/SCSI
- Internal/External
- Backup/Restore
- Partitioning/Formatting/File System
  - FAT
  - FAT16
  - FAT32
  - NTFS4
  - NTFS5
  - HPFS

Windows-based utilities

- ScanDisk
- Device Manager
- System Manager
- Computer Manager
- MSCONFIG.EXE
- REGEDIT.EXE (View information/backup Registry)
- REGEDT32.EXE
- ATTRIB.EXE
- EXTRACT.EXE
- DEFRAG.EXE
- EDIT.COM
- FDISK.EXE
- SYSEDIT.EXE
- SCANREG
- WSCRIPT.EXE
- HWINFO.EXE
- ASD.EXE (Automatic Skip Driver)
- Cvt1.EXE (Drive Converter FAT16 to FAT32)

✓ **2.1 Identify the procedures for installing Windows 9***x* **and Windows 2000 for bringing the software to a basic operational level.**

Content may include the following:
- Start Up
- Partition
- Format drive
- Loading drivers
- Run appropriate set up utility

✓ **2.2 Identify steps to perform an operating system upgrade**

Content may include the following:
- Upgrading Windows 95 to Windows 98
- Upgrading Windows NT Workstation 4.0 to Windows 2000
- Upgrading Windows 9*x* with Windows 2000
- Dual boot Windows 9*x*/Windows NT 4.0/2000

✓ **2.3 Identify the basic system boot sequences and boot methods, including the steps to create an emergency boot disk with utilities installed for Windows 9x, Windows NT, and Windows 2000.**

Content may include the following:
- Startup disk
- Safe Mode
- MS-DOS mode
- NTLDR (NT Loader), BOOT.INI
- Files required to boot
- Creating emergency repair disk (ERD)

✓ **2.4 Identify procedures for loading/adding and configuring application device drivers and the necessary software for certain devices.**

Content may include the following:
- Windows 9*x* Plug and Play and Windows 2000
- Identify the procedures for installing and launching typical Windows and non-Windows applications (Note: there is no content related to Windows 3.1)
- Procedures for set up and configuring Windows printing subsystem.
  - Setting Default printer
  - Installing/Spool setting
  - Network printing (with help of LAN admin)

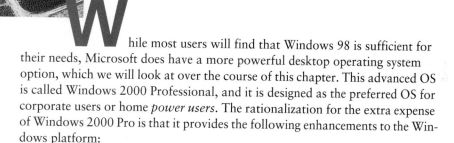

hile most users will find that Windows 98 is sufficient for their needs, Microsoft does have a more powerful desktop operating system option, which we will look at over the course of this chapter. This advanced OS is called Windows 2000 Professional, and it is designed as the preferred OS for corporate users or home *power users*. The rationalization for the extra expense of Windows 2000 Pro is that it provides the following enhancements to the Windows platform:

- Advanced security
- Support for more hardware
- Greater application stability

For complete coverage of objective 1.1, please also see Chapter 12. For complete coverage of objective 2.1, please also see Chapters 13 and 16. For complete coverage of objective 2.2, please also see Chapter 13. For complete coverage of objective 2.3, please also see Chapters 13 and 17. For complete coverage of objective 2.4, please also see Chapters 13, 15 and 16.

For coverage of the Memory management subobjectives of objective 1.1, please refer back to Part I, Chapter 3.

Over the course of this chapter we will look at these enhancements, along with examining the basic steps needed to install and configure Windows 2000 Professional. In the process, we will also look at a number of the critical files used to start and run Windows 2000.

Although the A+ objectives talk almost exclusively about Windows 9x and Windows 2000, you may see exam questions on Windows NT as well. Because NT and 2000 are very similar in their architecture and key files, you should be able to answer most NT questions by simply providing the answer that would be appropriate in Windows 2000. This is not always the case, however. To cover all your bases (for the exam and in the real world), you may want to read up on Windows NT a bit more before the test.

Installing Windows 2000

Windows 9x and Windows 2000 may look a lot alike when they are running, but one of the most important concepts you will have to deal with in becoming a computer technician is that no two operating systems are completely alike. As such, the installation process we used for Windows 9x is completely different than the installation process for Windows 2000. We will begin this chapter by looking into the 2000 installation process and, in doing so, cover the following topics:

- Installation requirements
- Accessing the Setup files
- Running the Setup program
- Partitioning
- Formatting
- Customizing Setup

Installation Prerequisites

As with last chapter, we will start off by looking at what you will need to consider before installing or upgrading to Windows 2000. Because of the fact that it is a "power workstation," the hardware requirements for Windows 2000 are higher than that of Windows 9x, and it also is less forgiving of older, less efficient software.

Hardware Requirements

The hardware requirements to install Windows 2000 Professional are actually rather low—a Pentium 133 and 64MB of RAM. Almost any machine that is still being used in a corporate environment will meet these basic requirements. More than any other OS we have looked at, though, more is better for Windows 2K, and as such your clients will be far happier with their system performance if you ensure that they have PII-class machines with 64MB–128MB of RAM.

NOTE The "recommended" levels are simply a guideline from Microsoft. Remember the hardware levels in the first column of Table 14.1 are the ones you need for the test!

TABLE 14.1 Windows 2000 Hardware Prerequisites

Hardware	Required	Recommended
Processor	Pentium 133	Pentium II or higher
Memory	64MB	128MB or higher
Free hard disk space	2GB	2GB plus what is needed for your applications and storage
Floppy disk	Required only if installing from the boot disks	Yes
CD-ROM	Required only if installing from CD	Yes
Video	VGA	SVGA
Mouse	Yes	Yes
Keyboard	Yes	Yes

Once you have found hardware that you feel is going to run Professional acceptably, your next step is to determine whether this hardware is compatible with the OS. There are a number of ways to do this, but probably the most dependable is to go to www.microsoft.com/windows2000 to download a copy of the most recent *Hardware Compatibility List (HCL)*. This list will tell you which hardware has been tested with Windows 2000 and should run properly. If your hardware is not on the HCL, contact your vendor for compatibility information and updated Windows 2000 drivers. Many Windows NT drivers will work with 2000, while Windows 95 or 98 drivers will NOT work!

Most hardware on the HCL also has drivers that ship with Windows 2000, so the hardware should be installed and configured automatically with the new drivers by plug-and-play during setup. If your hardware is extremely new or if your vendor did not submit the hardware to Microsoft for testing, you may find that you need to supply your own drivers.

Accessing the Setup Files

Unlike Windows 9x Setup, which must run from a functioning operating system (an earlier version of DOS or Windows or a boot disk), Windows 2000 will generally be a breeze to install on a machine. To start the install process, simply place the Windows 2000 Professional CD into the CD-ROM drive and restart the computer. After the POST routine for the computer has completed, a message will appear that says, "Press any key to boot from CD…" Hit a key, any key, and the Windows 2000 Setup program will start.

That is a "perfect world" situation, and sometimes reality intrudes. If the message discussed above does not appear, that generally means that your PC is not configured to boot from CD-ROM or does not have that capability. In such a case, you will need to do one of two things:

1. Go into the BIOS to set the machine to boot to its CD drive. Consult your computer's user guide for more information on examining and making changes to the BIOS.

2. Create and use Windows 2000 boot disks to start the setup.

The Windows 2000 Boot Disks

Although most modern machines support booting from CD-ROM, you may occasionally need to use a boot disk to start Setup. This disk can either be a Windows Boot Disk with CD-ROM support or the startup disk set that can be made from the Windows 2000 CD. To create the 2000 boot disks, you will need access to the Windows 2000 CD and a computer with a CD-ROM drive. There is a directory on the CD called BOOTDISK. In this directory is an executable file called MAKEBOOT, which is used to make Windows 2000 startup disks from any version of DOS or Windows.

The above information should be only informational, as starting Setup from boot disks is slow and requires changing disks. If you need to use a boot disk, use a Windows 98 startup disk with the CD-ROM support option, and then run SETUP from the root of the CD or WINNT from the i386 directory.

Starting a Windows 2000 Installation

The startup options listed above all eventually lead you to the same point: executing the setup routine for Windows 2000 Professional. Professional has two different executables used to start Setup, depending on the OS you are using to start the install. These executables are WINNT (used from DOS or Windows *9x*) and WINNT32 (used from Windows NT or 2000). These commands have various options associated with them, as shown in Tables 14.2 and 14.3.

TABLE 14.2   Common WINNT.EXE Options

Option	Function
/s:*sourcepath*	Allows you to specify the location of the Windows 2000 source files.
/t:*tempdrive*	Allows you to specify the drive the setup uses to store temporary installation files.
/u:*answer file*	Used in an unattended installation to provide responses to questions the user would normally be prompted for.
/udf:*id* [,UDB_*file*]	If you are installing numerous machines, each must have a unique computer name. This setting lets you specify a file with unique values for these settings.
/e:*command*	Allows you to add a command (such as a batch script) to execute at the end of Setup.
/a	Tells Setup to enable accessibility options.

TABLE 14.3   Common WINNT32.EXE Options

Option	Function
/s:*sourcepath*	Allows you to specify the location of the Windows 2000 source files.
/tempdrive: *drive_letter*	Allows you to specify the drive Setup uses to store temporary installation files.
/unattend	Used to run install without user intervention.
/unattend[*num*]: [*answer_file*]	Allows you to specify custom settings for machines during an unattended installation.

TABLE 14.3 Common WINNT32.EXE Options *(continued)*

Option	Function
/cmd: *command_line*	Executes a command (such as a batch file at the end of Setup).
/debug[*level*]: [*filename*]	Used to troubleshoot problems during an upgrade.
/udf:*id* [,*UDB_file*]	Allows certain values that need to be unique to be set separately for each machine installed.
/checkupgradeonly	Performs all the steps of an upgrade, but only as a test. The results are saved to an upgrade.txt file that can be examined for potential problems.
/makelocalsource	Specifies that the i386 installation directory from the CD should be copied to the hard drive, allowing for easier updates later.

If you simply start the install from CD-ROM or create the Windows 2000 boot disks, WINNT.EXE will start the install by loading a number of files, and then present you with a screen that says, "Welcome to Setup."

If you use a Windows 98 boot disk, change to the i386 directory and run WINNT from that directory.

Partitioning the Drive

To start Setup, click Enter at the welcome screen, and you will be shown a list of the partitions currently configured on the machine. If one of these is acceptable, simply select that partition, then click Enter. If you wish to create a new partition, you can do so using the Setup program itself, which replaces FDISK as a way to set up the system's hard drive(s).

To delete an existing partition, highlight the partition and press D. You will be asked to confirm your choice and will be reminded that all information on the partition will be lost. If the disk is new or if the old information is no longer needed, this is fine.

If you are not sure what is on the drive, find out before you repartition it!

To create a new partition, highlight some free space, and click C. You will be asked how big you want the partition to be. Remember that Windows 2000 Professional wants you to have about 2GB as a minimum, but can be as large as the entire drive.

Formatting

Once you have created or decided on a partition to use, you will be asked to format that partition. In doing so, you will need to choose between the NTFS file system and the FAT file system. FAT is the file system of DOS, and its advantages include the following:

- Compatible with DOS and Windows 9*x* dual-boot configurations
- Excellent speed on small drives
- Accessible and modifiable with many standard DOS disk utilities

The *NTFS* file system, as one might expect, comes from Windows NT and is a more sophisticated file system that has a number of enhancements that set it apart from FAT:

- Supports larger partition sizes than FAT
- Allows for file-level security to protect system resources
- Supports compression, encryption, disk quotas, and file ownership

In most cases, you will find that it will be better to go with the newer and more advanced NTFS system.

When you choose one of the format options, the machine will go out and format the installation partition. This generally takes a few minutes, even on a fast PC.

Advanced Attributes

NTFS gives you a number of options that are not available on FAT or FAT32 drives. A number of these are implemented through the use of the Advanced Attributes window, shown in Figure 14.1. To reach these options, simply right-click the folder or file you wish to modify and select Properties from the menu. On the main properties page of the folder or file, click the Advanced button in the lower right corner.

FIGURE 14.1 The Advanced Options window

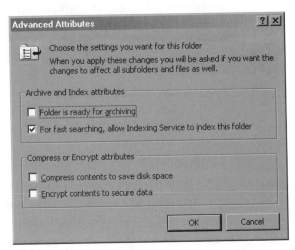

On the Advanced Attributes screen you will have access to the following settings:

Archiving Identical to the Archive attribute on a FAT or FAT32 drive. This tells the system whether the file has changed since the last time it was backed up. Technically it is known as the "Archive Needed" attribute; if this box is selected, the file should be backed up. If it is not selected, a current version of the file is already backed up.

Indexing Windows 2000 implements an Index Service to catalog and improve the search capabilities of your drive. Once files are indexed you can search them more quickly by name, date, or other attributes. Setting the index option on a folder will cause a prompt to appear, asking whether you want the existing files in the folder to be indexed as well. If you choose to do this, Windows 2000 will automatically reset this attribute on subfolders and files. If not, only new files created in the directory will be indexed.

Compression Windows 2000 supports advanced compression options first introduced in Windows NT. NTFS files and folders can be dynamically compressed and uncompressed, often saving a great deal of space on the drive. As with Indexing, turning on Compression for a folder will result in your being prompted as to whether you want the existing files in the folder to be compressed. If you choose to do this, Windows 2000 will automatically compress the subfolders and files. If not, only new files created in the directory will be compressed.

Compression works best on files such as word processing documents and uncompressed images. Word files or MS Paint bitmaps can be compressed to up to 80 percent using compression. Files that are already packed well do not compress as effectively; EXE and Zip files generally compress only about 2 percent. Similarly GIF and JPG images are already compressed (which is why they are used in Internet Web pages), so they compress little or not at all.

Encryption   This last advanced attribute is totally new to Windows 2000. Encryption allows a user to secure their files against anyone else being able to view them by actually encoding the files with a key that only the user has access to. This can be useful for those who are worried about extremely sensitive information, but in general, encryption is not necessary on the network. NTFS local file security is usually enough to provide users access to what they need and prevent others from getting to what they shouldn't. If users do want to encrypt a file, they simply go through the same process as they would in indexing or compressing.

If a user forgets their password or is unable to access the network to authenticate their account, they will not be able to open encrypted files. If the user's account is lost or deleted, the only other user who is able to decrypt the file is the Administrator account.

Yet another file type—HPFS—is mentioned in the exam objectives. HPFS is the advanced file system for OS/2, and, due to Microsoft's desire to replace OS/2 in the market, they added support for HPFS into Windows NT. Windows 2000 no longer supports HPFS, though.

Installing Windows 2000

After the installation partition is formatted, the system checks the new partition for errors, and then begins to copy files.

While the files are being copied, a progress indicator will display on the screen showing you how far along the process is. Windows will install files into temporary installation folders on the drive and will ask you to reboot once the copy is complete. If you do not reboot within 15 seconds of the end of the file copy, the system will automatically reboot for you.

If Setup detects any problems during the partition check, it will attempt to fix the problem and will immediately ask you to reboot. At that point the install will need to start over. If problems are found, this can often be an indicator that there are problems with the hard drive, and you may want to run a full scandisk before returning to the install.

The Graphical Phase of Setup

When Windows 2000 Professional reboots, it will automatically bring you into a graphical setup, which resembles a massive Windows wizard (as shown in Figure 14.2). This is generally referred to as the "graphical phase" of Windows 2000 Setup. This is due to the contrast between this phase and the earlier blue-background and text "non-graphical" phase where we configured partitions and copied temporary files.

FIGURE 14.2 The Windows 2000 Setup Wizard

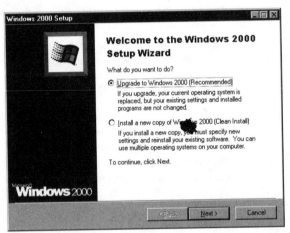

During this phase Windows will attempt to identify and configure the hardware in the computer, which may take a few minutes. One of the more unsettling parts of Setup occurs during this time, as the screen flickers—and often goes completely black—while monitor detection occurs.

Windows 2000 comes packaged with an impressive array of drivers and is able to identify and load most modern hardware. Still, not all devices have compatible drivers on the Windows 2K CD-ROM, so if your hardware is not detected during startup, you can install additional device drivers after Setup completes, as shown later in the chapter.

After hardware detection is completed, the ever-polite Windows 2000 Setup Wizard welcomes you once again. To move through the wizard, simply click on the Next and Back buttons along the bottom of the window. The screens of the setup process are as follows:

Regional Settings   The first screen rarely needs to be modified if you are configuring the machine for use in the U.S., but users in other countries will find that this is where they can change keyboard and language settings.

Personalize Your Software   This is used to enter the name (required) and organization (optional) of the person to whom the software is registered. Both fields are just text boxes. Enter any values that apply.

Computer Name and Administrator Password   The *computer name* is the name by which a machine will be known if it participates on a network. This name is generally 15 characters or less. The administrator password is used to protect access to the powerful Administrator account. Unlike Windows *9x*, where usernames and password security is optional, all users must log on with a username and password to use a Windows 2000 Professional desktop.

Modem Dialing Information   If a modem has been detected, you will be asked for country, area code, and dialing preference information. If you do not have a modem, this screen will be skipped.

Date and Time Settings   The Date and Time dialog box also has time zone and daylight savings time information. Any data on this screen can easily be changed later as well.

Networking Settings/Installing Components   After the date and time, you will be waiting for a minute or two as Windows 2K installs any networking components that it has found and prepares to walk you through the configuration of the network. As you are waiting, you will see which components are being installed in the Status area.

Performing Final Tasks   Once you have made it through the component install, the setup process is in the home stretch. The Final Tasks page reports on the setup's progress while it does the following:

Installs Start menu items   This is where shortcuts are created to the applications and options installed during the setup.

Registers components   The Registry is updated with setup information.

Saves settings   Configuration information is saved to disk, and other defaults and user selections are applied (such as area code, time zone, etc.).

Removes any temporary files used   The temporary files saved to the hard drive at the start of Setup and used to install Windows are removed to free drive space.

This last screen can take quite a long time to complete, and in general the install of Windows 2000 takes about twice as long as an install of Windows 9x.

Eventually, the wizard will complete, and you will be asked to reboot by clicking the Finish button. When the system restarts, Windows 2000 Professional Setup will be complete, and the standard 2000 boot process will initiate.

Upgrading to Windows 2000

If the machine that you want to install Windows 2000 on already has Windows 9x or Windows NT up and running, you may want to upgrade to the advanced security and performance of Windows 2000 without losing your installed programs or system configuration. Windows 2000 allows for this by providing a very sophisticated upgrade mechanism that can check your hardware and software, and then update an existing Windows 9x install while preserving the look, feel, and functionality of your current environment.

Windows 2000 can not upgrade Windows 3.1 or DOS systems to 2000 Professional. Most machines running 3.1 or DOS probably will be running older hardware, but if you do want to upgrade such a system, you will need to perform a new full install rather than an upgrade. All programs or drivers that were installed on DOS or Windows 3.x will then need to be reinstalled under 2000.

Starting Setup

Compared to the work involved in setting up a new Windows 2000 install, running the 2000 upgrade is almost completely effortless. The basic requirements are the same for an upgrade as they are for a new install, and again you will have the option of either doing a CD-based install or a network-based install.

Generally, the simplest option is to place the Windows 2000 Professional disk into the CD-ROM drive of the machine to be upgraded. A window (see Figure 14.3) should automatically appear asking if you want to upgrade to Windows 2000.

FIGURE 14.3   The Windows 2000 Upgrade Autorun screen

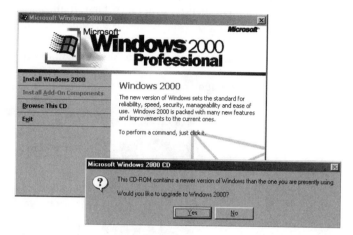

 When a compact disc is inserted into a drive, it often automatically starts a program, such as an install routine. This is done through the *Autorun* option.

 Upgrading to Windows 2000 Professional from Windows 9*x* and Windows NT Workstation is essentially the same process. Just pop the disk in and go. One of the big advantages of the Windows NT upgrade is that because it is a very similar OS to Windows 2000, you should have fewer compatibility issues. Also, Windows NT drivers can be used in Windows 2000, where Windows 9*x* drivers cannot, meaning more hardware may be automatically detected and installed.

If you click Yes to accept the offered upgrade, the Windows 2000 Setup Wizard will begin. This wizard will perform a number of pre-upgrade tasks and will then start the upgrade itself. The screens you may see during the Upgrade Wizard include the following:

Welcome to the Windows 2000 Setup Wizard   The first choice of the wizard is also probably the most important. The screen (shown in Figure 14.4) is where you decide whether to perform an upgrade to your existing system or to simply install a fresh copy of Windows 2000 onto the drive. Both of these have their advantages.

Upgrade to Windows 2000 (Recommended)   The upgrade allows you to keep your existing programs, but it also retains any existing *problems*. Because of this, any system configuration glitches or files that are no longer used will continue to plague you in the new install, just like they had in Windows 9*x*.

Install a new copy of Windows 2000 (Clean Install) A clean install has two major advantages. First, it allows you to start fresh without the baggage of your Windows 9x Setup. Second, it allows you to "dual boot" back to your original Windows 9x OS. The disadvantage, of course, is that you will have to re-install all of your programs in this scenario.

FIGURE 14.4 The Upgrade or Install Option

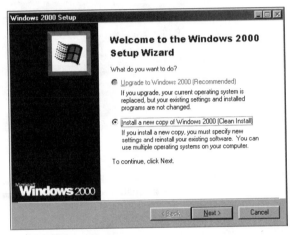

Windows 2000 and Windows 9x can't exist on the same partition in a dual-boot scenario, since certain drive locations (such as the location of Internet Explorer) are hard-wired to the same directory for both. To install a new copy of Windows 2000 and dual-boot to Windows 9x, you need to have a second partition on your disk or a second disk. Windows 9x should be installed on the C partition first, and then Windows 2000 can be installed afterwards on the D partition. The installation of Windows 9x *after* Windows 2000 is not supported as a dual-boot scenario.

If you choose to upgrade, you will continue through the wizard. If you choose to install a new copy of the OS, you will be immediately funneled into the process described in the "Installing Windows 2000" section.

In most cases, I use upgrades as an opportunity to clean up a system. In order to do this I generally back up any needed data and then simply reformat the machine's drives and start over from ground zero. It takes a bit more time, but it is often worth it. Before doing this, though, make sure you still have installation disks for all of the applications and other software you will need to reinstall.

License Agreement and Product Key   Assuming you have continued the upgrade, you're required to complete the next two screens, License Agreement and Product Key. They allow you to accept the Microsoft licensing terms and ask you for a Windows 2000 *product key*. As with the regular install, this key is an obscene 25 characters in length and can usually be found on the case of the CD.

Preparing to Upgrade to Windows 2000   With the bookkeeping out of the way, you can now get down to the business of the upgrade itself. Before you start copying files, the Upgrade Wizard will examine your existing configuration to see whether there are any problems that will make upgrading difficult. Figure 14.5 illustrates this. The Upgrade Wizard provides a link to Microsoft's Windows Compatibility Web site for product updates and compatibility information.

FIGURE   14.5   Preparing to Upgrade to Windows 2000

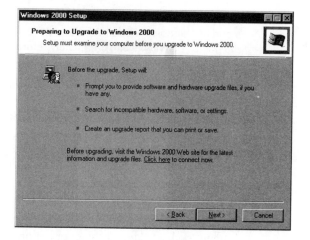

 During the upgrade, Setup will try to contact Microsoft's site for information and updates, including the upgrade packs it's looking for on the next page of the wizard. If you do not have a connection to the Web as you are upgrading, you will be asked to connect, but you can choose to continue to work offline. If you do work offline, any updates must be applied manually later. If you have an Internet connection, it is recommended to go out to the Web site and look for updates.

Provide Upgrade Packs   If you do work offline, one of the things you may need to provide are application upgrade packs. Most 32-bit applications will continue to function without any problems. If you have any 16-bit DOS or Windows 3.*x* applications, though, they may not work. Also, any new or odd hardware may not be upgraded properly, as we will see in the next section. If you have been out to the Microsoft upgrade site of a vendor site and have obtained updated files for 2000, you may add them now by choosing the Yes, I Have Upgrade Packs option. If not, simply select the No, I Don't Have Any Upgrade Packs option. In such a case you can still apply upgrades later if applications do not function after the upgrade.

Upgrading to the Windows 2000 NTFS File System   Another upgrade option you will be given is to upgrade your drive's file system to Windows 2000's advanced NTFS. The upgrade to NTFS enables increased file security, disk quotas, and disk compression. NTFS also makes better use of large drives by using a more advanced method of saving and retrieving data.

To enable NTFS and sever all ties to Windows 9x, select the Yes, Upgrade My Drive option. To retain your links to the past and allow for dual-boot scenarios, select the No, Do Not Upgrade My Drive option.

While upgrading to NTFS has a number of advantages, the file system is only understood by Windows NT and Windows 2000. If you want to reinstall Windows 9x on the drive, you will have to completely reformat.

Preparing an Upgrade Report   Once you have made your choices, Setup will finally go through and examine your system for compatibility issues. This involves checking all hardware and software that is currently installed can be found, and it also involves creating a detailed upgrade report. Once it is finished you will be allowed to do two things: provide updated files for any incompatible hardware and view a report of what the compatibility check has found.

Provide Updated Plug-and-Play Files   In upgrading any system there is a chance that incompatible hardware may be found. In upgrading certain systems, such as older machines or laptops, the chances are even greater. IBM's ThinkPad series, for example, has hardware support for DVD playback available through an MPEG-2 Decoder Card. This is an optional piece of hardware which is specifically built by IBM for IBM, and as such it is not common enough to be recognized by the setup process. In order for this device to work, updated files must be obtained from IBM.

If you don't have updated files at present for any unsupported hardware, you can still continue with the install but will have to update the files before the hardware will function under Windows 2000. If the functioning of the hardware is essential to the operation of the system (network card, video card, etc.) you may want to stop the install and get the new drivers before continuing. For non-essential hardware such as a DVD decoder, you can continue and simply fix the problem later, but it is a good idea to at least verify that the hardware is compatible with Windows 2000, just so you won't be surprised later.

As noted earlier, you cannot use the same Windows 9x or Windows NT drivers that are currently installed.

Upgrade Report   Once you have added any plug-and-play drivers, the Setup Wizard will provide you with a detailed report (see Figure 14.6) of what it thinks may cause you "issues" as you upgrade. The following topics are included:

Hardware   Any devices that cannot be confirmed as compatible with Windows 2K will be listed here.

FIGURE 14.6   The completed upgrade report

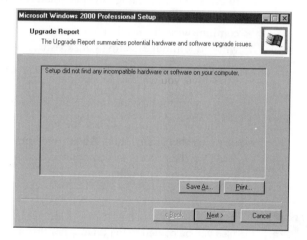

Software   Programs that do not work with Windows 2K are listed here. The ThinkPad upgrade, for instance, found that not only was the DVD decoder not supported, but the installed DVD player also will not work. In these cases you are directed to uninstall the program before the upgrade, because it will not function and may not uninstall properly after the upgrade.

This particular IBM DVD player should be expected to fail, as it was designed to link directly to the IBM DVD decoder card. Such direct access of hardware is explicitly restricted in Windows NT and 2000, and as such this software will be prevented from executing without an acceptable Windows 2000 driver.

Program Notes   Besides incompatibilities, some programs simply need to be reconfigured to work with Windows 2000. The Program Notes area details some of these known issues, such as how Microsoft Outlook 2000 works with Windows 2000 but must be reinstalled after the upgrade.

General Information This section details information best described as "other." Some of the upgrade issues that came up during a recent upgrade included notes on issues concerning hardware profiles, backup files, and the recycle bin.

If you wish to save the upgrade report information for later use, you have two options: print it or save it to a file. If you feel that the machine has major compatibility issues, you should probably save or print the report, and visit the www.microsoft.com/windows2000/compatible and www.hardwareupdate.com for information or updates.

Once you have checked out the upgrade report, you have to choose whether to proceed with the upgrade immediately or to exit from the upgrade in order to regroup and obtain needed updates. If you are ready to proceed, click Next to continue with the install. If you would rather wait, click Cancel, and the upgrade will end without affecting your existing Windows 9x or NT install.

Ready to Install Windows 2000 If you have made it this far, the tough part is now over. As the wizard states, "This process is completely automatic, and you will not have to answer any additional questions."

All you need to do is click the Next button and head off to get some coffee, or preferably some lunch. About one hour and three restarts later you should find that the process has completed, and a Windows 2000 logon screen should be waiting for you when you return.

After the first reboot the existing Windows install will be deleted, and Windows 2000 files will be copied to the drive. After that a second graphical setup will start, and your settings from Windows 9x or NT will be automatically reapplied.

Logging On to Windows 2000

As shown in Figure 14.7, users are presented with a number of options when they start Windows 2000. The user logon system comes up immediately at the end of the Windows 2000 startup process, and the system requires, at the very least, a username and password, but it allows for other choices. This is due to the fact that its security structure requires that every user on a Windows 2000 Professional system have a unique name and password to identify them and their configuration.

FIGURE 14.7   The Windows 2000 Logon screen

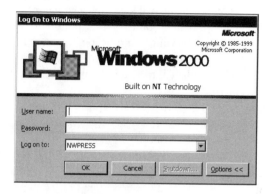

The options available on this screen include the following:

Username   The *username* is the name that defines a particular individual on the computer. Each user has their own desktop and personal settings and can be given or restricted from particular files or tasks. This field displays your letters as you type them and is not case sensitive.

Password   A *password* is a personal identifier that is used to verify that the user is who they say they are. Without a verified username and password set, a user cannot log onto a Windows 2000 Professional workstation. The password field displays only asterisk (*) characters as you type, and the field is case sensitive.

From   This allows the user to set the security context from which they will be authenticated. Windows 2000 Professional workstations have their own user database, but they can also authenticate using a shared database, such as the Windows 2000 Server Active Directory. You cannot type new information into the From field, but if you have multiple authentication options configured, you will be able to select from among them using the down arrow.

Logon using Dial-Up Networking   Allows a user to establish a dial-up connection to a remote network, and then authenticate against a database over that connection. This option is rarely used, but it may be needed in high-security environments.

For now we will only discuss logging on to the local computer. In Chapter 18, "Configuring Network Software," we will look into other logon options during an examination of Windows 2000 Professional networking options.

In order to log on you will need to enter valid credentials. You may have created an administrator account and password during the setup, or you may need to get this information from a network administrator.

Once you have entered your credentials, Windows 2000 will configure your desktop and will load any personal settings and any user policy settings associated with your account. At that point you will be able to begin using Windows 2000.

If it is your first time logging on to the system as a particular user, it may take a minute or two for your initial system environment to be set up. A number of wizards will run and an introduction screen will be displayed, as in Figure 14.8.

FIGURE 14.8 The Getting Started screen

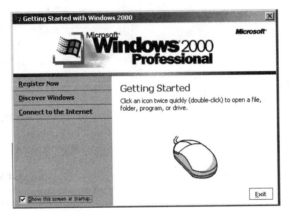

Windows 2000 System Information

Once you have completed the upgrade, you will immediately notice that Windows 2000 has some differences from Windows 9x. Windows 2K uses different startup procedures and different startup files. In this section we will discuss how Windows 2000 boots and what files are needed to keep it healthy and happy.

Key Boot Files

Almost all of the files needed to boot Windows 3.1 or 9x are unnecessary for Windows 2000. Windows 2K requires, in fact, only a very few files, each of which performs specific tasks:

NTLDR This file "bootstraps" the system. In other words, it is the file that starts the loading of an operating system on the computer.

BOOT.INI Holds information about what operating systems are installed on the computer.

BOOTSECT.DOS In a dual-boot configuration this keeps a copy of the DOS or Windows 9x boot sector so that the Windows 9x environment can be restored and loaded as needed.

NTDETECT.COM   Parses the system for hardware information each time Windows 2000 is loaded. This information is then used to create dynamic hardware information in the Windows 2000 Registry.

NTBOOTDD.SYS   On a system with a SCSI boot device, this file is used to recognize and load the SCSI interface. On EIDE systems this file is not needed and is not even installed.

System files   Besides the previously listed files, all of which are located in the root of the C partition on the computer, Windows 2000 also needs a number of files from its system directories, including the hardware abstraction layer (HAL.DLL) and the Windows 2000 command file (WIN.COM).

Numerous other DLL (dynamic link library) files are also required, but usually the lack or corruption of one of these will simply produce a non-critical error, while the absence of WIN.COM or HAL.DLL will cause the system to be nonfunctional.

The Boot Process

When Windows 2000 starts, the computer's BIOS performs a number of system checks, and then it looks for an operating system to load. What it finds is Windows 2000's NTLDR (NT loader) file, which is then read into memory. The NTLDR prepares the system for the boot process and invokes a rudimentary file system access that allows it to read the BOOT.INI file in the root of C. This file is then used to construct a menu from which a user may select an operating system. If Windows 2000 is the only OS installed on the machine, the choice is moot, but if the system dual-boots, you may choose your OS at this point and boot directly into your selected OS. You may also make additional selections by pressing the F8 key.

The system waits a predetermined amount of time for a user choice, and then simply loads the default OS. Both the default option and the time can be configured in Windows 2K's System properties.

Using the F8 Options

In most cases you will be able to just boot into Windows 2000 without worrying about the advanced options. Occasionally, though, problems may arise. If you have a problem which makes it difficult to get 2000 up and running, the advanced options offer a number of useful tools.

Safe Mode   Starts Windows 2000 using only basic files and drivers (mouse, except serial mice; monitor; keyboard; mass storage; base video; default system services; and no network connections). Once in Safe Mode, you can restore files that are missing or fix a configuration error.

Safe Mode with Networking Same as Safe Mode, but tries to load networking components as well.

Safe Mode with Command Prompt Similar to Safe Mode, but doesn't load the Windows GUI. Presents the user with a Windows 2000 command prompt interface.

Enable Boot Logging Logs all boot information to a file called ntbtlog.txt. This file can be found in the \WINNT directory. You can then check the log for assistance in diagnosing system startup problems.

Enable VGA Mode Starts Windows 2000 using the basic VGA driver, but loads the rest of the system as normal. If you happen to install an incorrect video driver or a video driver corrupts, this allows you to get into the system to fix the problem.

Last Known Good Configuration This option is useful if you have changed a configuration setting in the Registry, which then causes the system to have serious problems. LKGC will not save you from a corrupt file or a deleted file error.

Debugging Mode A sort of advanced boot logging, Debugging Mode requires that another machine be hooked up to the computer through a serial port. The debug information is then passed to that machine during the boot process. This is rarely used and should not be bothered with in most cases. If it comes to this, reinstalling is far faster!

For more on Safe Mode and Windows troubleshooting, refer to Chapter 19, "Software Troubleshooting."

Starting Windows 2000

Once you have chosen to start Windows 2000 Professional, NTLDR will invoke NTDETECT.COM to check the system's hardware, and will load NTBOOTDD.SYS if the system uses a SCSI boot device. Once this is complete, NTLDR will then pass control of the system to WIN.COM, and the graphical phase of startup will begin.

During this time you will be presented with a series of screens that show the system's progress during startup; the interface is initiated and network connections and computer policies (if present) are loaded. Once this has completed, Windows 2000 presents you with a Logon screen as discussed earlier, (see Figure 14.7), and you can now start to use the system.

If you choose to boot back to a previous OS, NTLDR will immediately pass control to BOOTSECT.DOS, and the other files mentioned will not be used.

Modifying Windows 2000 Settings

Once Windows 2000 Professional is up and running, you probably will have relatively few additional configuration options that need to be set, but there are a few things that may need to be done. With Windows 2000 Professional, Microsoft has provided a one-stop shopping environment for finding system information in the Computer Management tool, while most system-wide configuration changes are made using the System icon in the Control Panel. In this section we will look at each of these.

The 2000 Professional Administrative Tools

Windows 2000 includes a number of tools for administration and management of the system. These can be found in the *Administrative Tools* icon in the Control Panel, which has a number of utilities. Component Services, Data Sources, and Telnet Server Administration are beyond the scope of this book, as is the local security policy. The rest of these tools are available through Computer Management, and that is where we will examine them.

Computer Management

The Computer Management tool (see Figure 14.9) is new to Windows 2000, and combines many Windows-based administrative tools into a single interface. There are three basic classes of tasks available from this console:

- System Tools
- Storage
- Services and Applications

FIGURE 14.9   The Computer Management interface

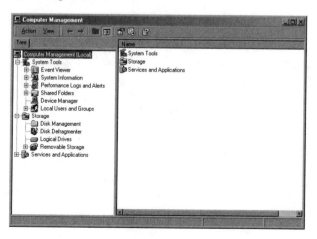

System Tools

The System Tools area provides access to a number of different utilities, many of which are also available elsewhere on the system. Even so, this provides a central interface for the following information:

Event Viewer   Logs data about the computer. It is also accessible through Computer Management.

System Information   Allows you to poll the system to find out information on installed hardware and software.

Performance Logs and Alerts   Used to monitor system resource usage in real time or to log performance.

Shared Folders   A place to get a quick look of what is being shared on your computer. Sharing will be discussed more fully in Part II, Chapter 18, "Configuring Network Software."

Device Manager   Used to view and modify information about system hardware. We will look at this more in the "Hardware" section.

Local Users and Groups   As the Windows 2000 Professional station maintains its own list of security accounts, this is where those accounts are stored and modified. For a user to log onto a Windows 2000 station, they must have a user account defined in the Local Users and Groups utility or they must use a *network security provider*, such as a Windows 2000 Active Directory or Novell's NetWare Directory Services.

Storage

The storage tools are used to manage and maintain the hard drives and other storage devices on your machine.

Disk Management   Known as Disk Administrator in Windows NT 4, Disk Management is Windows 2000's replacement for FDISK. You can use it to create or delete partitions and even modify drive types.

Windows 2000 includes an enhanced disk type called a "dynamic disk." Dynamic disks can be used to create additional partitions and can also allow you to create advanced disk configurations. Dynamic disks can only be used by Windows 2000 machines, so this change should only be made if Windows 2K is the only OS that will be running on the machine.

Disk Defragmenter   Nearly identical to the Disk Defragmenter program in Windows 9*x*, this checks the drive for errors, and rearranges (defragments) files so that they are more efficiently arranged on the drive.

Removable Storage   This option allows you to manage a backup tape drive or a ZIP-type removable disk drive with your system. It also is the place where you can go to check up on your CD-ROM or DVD drive, as they are also considered to be removable storage.

Services and Applications

The last of the options, the Services and Applications tree, contains only one option that most of you will use, that being the Services option. WMI Control and Indexing Service almost never need to be modified.

WMI Control   Used to configure and control the Windows Management Instrumentation service.

Services   Used to start and stop services that are on the machine. A *service* is simply an application or a function that the computer runs in the background. Services are also accessible through Computer Management. If a service is unable to start, any of a number of things could be the problem. For more on this refer to Part II, Chapter 19, "Software Troubleshooting."

Indexing Service   In order to speed searches of your drives or information, the Indexing Service keeps an index of your drive. From this location, you can configure how the Indexing Service is carried out.

We simply don't have the time to go into each of these in great depth, but if you have access to a Windows 2000 Professional machine, I highly recommend that you go through and examine each of these tools.

The System Properties Icon

While many of the tools in Computer Management are informational, the System Properties control panel (see Figure 14.10) is nearly all business. From within this one relatively innocuous panel you can make 90+ percent of all configuration changes that need to be done to a Windows 2000 Professional machine. The System Properties panel is divided into five tabs: General, Network Identification, Hardware, User Profiles, and Advanced. The General tab simply gives you an overview of the system, such as OS version, registration information, and basic hardware levels (Processor and RAM). For the rest of the tabs, we will look a bit more closely at their functionality.

FIGURE 14.10   The System Properties window

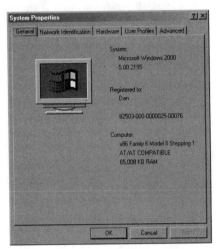

Network Identification

This tab is used to define whether the machine is in a workgroup or a domain environment. We will talk more about networking in Part II, Chapter 18, "Configuring Network Software," but in general terms, the difference between a workgroup and a domain is this:

Workgroup   Loosely associated computers, each of which is their own security authority.

Domain   A group of computers that is tightly connected, due to the fact that they have a single authority (called a domain controller) which manages security for all of them.

As a trainer, I am always looking for analogies to help explain things, and it seems that the best way to think of this is in relation to the difference between the United States and Europe. In the U.S. a single authority (the Federal Government) controls our military and has a strong degree of control over the individual states of the Union. In Europe, the European Union is a far weaker bond, and each country in the EU still maintains their own armies and more independent governments. The EU, essentially, is a workgroup model; the US Federal system is a domain model, at least it has been since the Civil War. But that is a completely different argument...

Hardware

This tab includes a number of tools, all of which allow you to change how the hardware on your machine is used. Because Windows 2000 is a plug-and-play system, it does many hardware-related functions similarly to Windows 9x. As it is a more advanced system, though, certain things are different.

Hardware Wizard

The Hardware Wizard is used, as it says, to "install, uninstall, repair, unplug, eject, and configure" hardware in the system. What this essentially means is that if you want to add a new device into the system or to uninstall drivers that are already there, this is the place to go. You can also use this to temporarily eject *PC Card* devices or other removable components.

Even in a plug-and-play system, it is important to properly unplug a device if you wish to remove it while the system is running. If you don't do this, nothing may go wrong at all, but you can sometimes damage the device or cause the system to become unstable.

Driver Signing

This is an option new to Windows 2000. In order to minimize the risks involved with adding third-party software to your Windows 2000 Professional machine, Microsoft has come up with a technique called *driver signing* (see Figure 14.11). Installing new hardware drivers onto the system is a situation in which both viruses and badly written software can threaten your system's health. To minimize the risks of this, you can choose to only use drivers which have been "signed." The signing process is meant to ensure that you are getting drivers that have been checked with Windows 2000 and that those drivers have not been modified maliciously.

FIGURE 14.11 Driver signing options

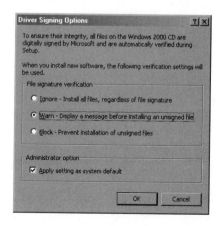

Device Manager

Although many hardware changes can be made through the Hardware Wizard, it is often easier to use the Device Manager, which provides a very simple and well-organized method to manage hardware in the system. In Figure 14.12, for instance, a modem can be disabled or uninstalled simply through a right-click.

FIGURE 14.12   Device Manager

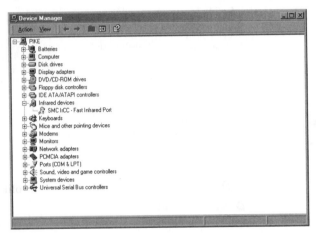

You can also go into a device's properties and modify other information, including the device's software drivers. If a new driver is made available for a device, you will want to update your existing driver to the newer (and purportedly better) software.

UPDATING DRIVERS

If you have upgraded to Windows 2000 from Windows NT this can be especially important, as 2000 can use Windows NT drivers, but prefers drivers specifically written for it. If you are upgrading, you should collect as many Windows 2000–specific drivers as possible and upgrade them either during or soon after the upgrade. To upgrade an existing driver, simply open the Device Manager and find the hardware you want to update drivers for. Right-click the device and select Properties from the menu. On the Properties window that appears, select the Drivers tab, and you should see an Update Drivers button. Clicking it will start the Update Device Driver Wizard, which will then require that you provide the location of the new Windows 2000 drivers for the device.

Hardware Profiles

A hardware profile is used to allow you to start the computer with different hardware configurations. This is most useful on laptops, which often have docking stations, or at the very least are moved from place to place often. These are very similar (i.e., exactly the same) as the hardware profiles discussed for Windows 9x.

User Profiles

Unlike Windows 9x, where *user profiles* are an optional setting, in Windows 2000 every user will automatically be given a user profile when they log on to the workstation. This profile is stored in the Documents and Settings folder on the drive that 2000 is installed on, and it contains information about the user's settings and preferences. Although this does not happen often, occasionally a user profile will become corrupt or will need to be destroyed. Alternatively, if a particular profile is set up exceptionally well, you can copy it so that it is available for other users as well. To do either of these, use the User Profiles tab (as shown in Figure 14.13) to select the user profile that you want to work with. At that point you will be given three options:

Delete   Use this to remove the user's profile entirely. When that user logs on again they will be given a fresh profile taken from the system default. Any settings that they have added will be lost, as will any profile-related problems that they have caused themselves.

FIGURE 14.13   The User Profiles tab

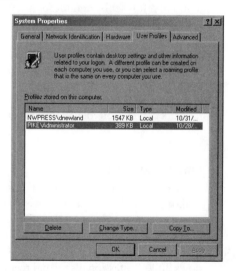

Change Type   This is used to configure a profile as local (the default) or roaming. In a standard Windows 2000 Professional Setup, if a user works at two machines, each of them will use a different profile. Updates to one machine will not be reflected on the other. If you have a network, though, roaming profiles can be configured to allow a user to have a single profile anywhere on the network. Getting into this any further is beyond the scope of this book.

Copy To   Used to copy a profile from one user to another. Often the source profile is a template set up to provide a standard configuration.

Advanced

Finally we arrive at the Advanced tab, which has three subheadings, each of which can be configured separately. This could also be called the "Etc." tab rather than the Advanced tab. Among its options are the following:

- Performance
- Environment Variables
- Startup and Recovery

Performance

Although it is hidden away in the backwaters of Windows 2000's system configuration settings, the Performance button holds some of the most important settings you may need to configure on a 2000 Professional system. Among the settings in the Performance window are the size of your virtual memory and the maximum size of the Registry.

The initial Performance window has two options: application response and virtual memory. Application response is normally not something you will need to modify. It is set by default to optimize the system for foreground applications, making the system most responsive to the user who is running programs. This is generally best, but it does mean that any applications (databases, network services, etc.) that are run by the system are given less time by the system.

If the Windows 2000 Professional machine is going to be primarily working as a network server, you may want to change this to background services. Otherwise leave it as is.

VIRTUAL MEMORY

The virtual memory settings (see Figure 14.14) tell you how much hard drive space is allocated to the system as a swap file. For a review of what *virtual memory* is, return to Part II, Chapter 13, "Windows 95/98." Windows 2000 recommends a particular virtual memory level, but you can add to or subtract from this as you need. Often, certain applications (SQL Server for instance) will need to have Windows 2000 Professional's virtual memory limit raised in order to work properly. Graphics and CAD applications also require raising the virtual memory level, but if this is the case, the setup instructions for the application will generally tell you what modifications need to be made.

Adding to the pagefile size is not always helpful and can sometimes actually slow down the system. Only modify this setting if you have been instructed to or if you are testing to see whether the change speeds up or slows down the computer. Reducing the pagefile size is generally not recommended and can have serious consequences on performance.

FIGURE 14.14 The Virtual Memory window

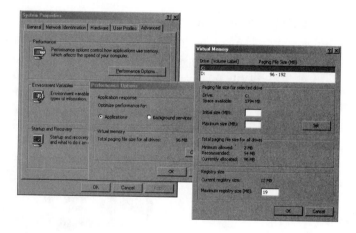

REGISTRY SIZE

Another option that is available in the Virtual Memory window is the ability to change the maximum Registry size. In most cases the default size is fine, but if a number of users are on a machine each of their settings must be stored separately, and the Registry can fill up. To prevent this, you can allow the Registry to continue to grow using this setting.

Letting the Registry fill up is a serious problem. If you think this may happen, you should change this option. An extra 10MB today could save a lot of pain tomorrow....

Environment Variables

There are two types of *environment variables*, and each can be added through the Environmental Variables button.

User Variables   These specify settings that are specific to an individual user, and do not affect others who log on to the machine.

System Variables These are set for all users on the machine. System variables are used to provide information needed by the system when running applications or performing system tasks.

System and user variables were extremely important in DOS and Windows 3.1. If you are going to try to run DOS/Win3.1 applications on Windows 2000, you will likely have to add additional variables in this window to support those applications.

Startup and Recovery

The Windows 2000 Startup and Recovery options are relatively straightforward (Figure 14.15). They involve two areas: what to do during system startup and what to do in case of unexpected system shutdown.

FIGURE 14.15 The Startup and Recovery window

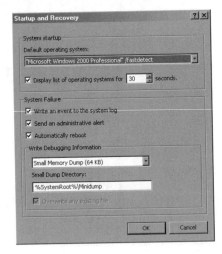

System Startup

The System Startup option defaults to Windows 2000 Professional when you install Windows 2000 Professional, but you can change this default behavior if you would like. Unless you are *dual-booting*, there is only one option available, but if you have another OS installed, you can change the Windows 2000 boot manager to load that as the default. You can also reduce the time that the menu is displayed or remove the menu entirely.

If you choose to completely disable the menu on a dual-boot system, you will find that this may cause you annoyance in the future when you want to boot into a different OS but no longer have a choice to do so. Even if you almost always boot into Professional, you will still want to let the boot menu appear for at least 2–5 seconds if you are dual booting.

System Failure

A number of options are available in the Startup and Recovery screen for use in the case of problems as well. These include writing an event about the problem, sending out an alert of the network, and saving information about the problem to disk. These options only come into play in case of a major system problem, though.

Your options for handling system failures will be covered along with the troubleshooting information in Part II, Chapter 19, "Software Troubleshooting."

Summary

Although similar in many ways to Windows 9*x*, Windows 2000 is also very different in significant ways. The installation process for Windows 2000 is far more straightforward, as it allows booting to set up directly from the CD and integrates disk preparation tools into the setup process.

Upgrading from Windows 9*x* to Windows 2000 is, similarly, a relatively simple task, although you will have to take into account that not all applications that run on Windows 9*x* will also run on 2000, and hardware may need to be pumped up a bit for the newer OS.

In this chapter, we looked at how you will soon find that, once you have installed Windows 2000 Professional, the startup process, the logon process, and the process of changing settings are different in 2000 than in 9*x*. Also, we looked at additional features that are available in 2000, such as the Administrative Tools.

Key Terms

Before you take the exam, be certain you are familiar with the following terms:

Administrative Tools	password
Autorun	PC card
computer name	power users
driver signing	product key
dual-booting	service
environment variables	user profiles
Hardware Compatibility List (HCL)	username
network security provider	virtual memory
NTFS	

Review Questions

1. What three basic classes of tasks are available in the Computer Management tool in Windows 2000? (Select all that apply.)

    A. Storage

    B. Network

    C. System Tools

    D. Services and Applications

2. When installing Windows 2000, you realize that you need to create a new partition. What would your next step be?

    A. Exit Setup, reboot the computer with a system disk, and use the DOS program FDISK to create your partition.

    B. Exit Setup, open the control panel of your current operating system, click the device applet, and choose the Disk Partition option.

    C. Create new partitions from within the Setup program itself.

    D. There is nothing that can be done. Once Setup has begun, there is no stopping it.

3. You want to change the size of your virtual memory and the maximum size of the Registry. Within Windows 2000, how can you accomplish your goal?

    A. You can change the size of virtual memory and the maximum size of the Registry by accessing the Control Panel, clicking System Panel, selecting the Advanced tab, clicking the Performance button, and making your changes.

    B. You can change the size of virtual memory and the maximum size of the Registry by accessing the Control Panel and clicking the Virtual Memory icon. Registry size may also be changed within that option.

    C. Virtual memory and Registry size are changed during the setup process. From that point on, they automatically change based upon the user profile.

    D. Virtual memory and Registry size should not be modified.

4. Which of the following is NOT required hardware for Windows 2000?

    A. Pentium 133

    B. 64MB of RAM

    C. 2GB hard drive

    D. SVGA video

5. You have successfully completed the installation of Windows 2000 Professional on a machine with minimum hardware requirements. Upon accessing one of your older graphics programs and opening a large BMP file, your computer seems sluggish and it takes many seconds for the image to be displayed. What can you do to improve performance?

   A. Nothing, short of adding more RAM.

   B. Open the Control Panel, click the System Panel button, select the Advanced tab, click the Performance button, and then increase the size of your virtual memory.

   C. Open the Control Panel, select the Hardware tab, and then change the size of your virtual memory.

   D. Reinstall the graphics program.

6. You successfully install Windows 2000 Professional and want to check your drives for errors. What is one way this can be accomplished?

   A. Open the Control Panel, click Administrative Tools, click Computer Management, and within the Storage tab, click Disk Defragmenter.

   B. Open the Control Panel, click Administrative Tools, click Computer Management, and within the Storage tab, click Disk Management.

   C. Open the Control Panel, select the Systems tab, and click Device Manager.

   D. Type `C:\defragment` at the DOS prompt.

7. The Hardware Compatibility List (HCL) lists hardware that has been tested with Windows 2000. If your hardware is NOT on the HCL, what should you do?

   A. Reload your Windows 95 or 98 drivers.

   B. Reinstall the device. The correct driver will load automatically.

   C. Contact the vendor and get updated Windows 2000 drivers.

   D. Download an updated HCL from Microsoft, which will then include the drivers for any device on your PC.

8. You want to set up a dual-boot scenario between Windows 98 and Windows 2000. Which option would work?

   A. Install Windows 2000 in the same partition as Windows 98 for efficient use of disk space.

   B. Partition your hard drive. Install Windows 2000 first. Once it is working, install Windows 98 in a second partition.

   C. Partition your hard drive. Install Windows 98 first. Then install Windows 2000 in a second partition.

   D. It is not possible to set up a dual-boot between Windows 98 and Windows 2000.

9. During Setup, all system hardware and software is tested. When the test is complete, a detailed upgrade report is generated. Which of the following topics are included as part of the upgrade report? (Select all that apply.)

   A. Hardware

   B. Software

   C. Program Notes

   D. General Information

10. Windows 2000 was installed and running on a PC. After making a change in the Registry, the system failed to reboot properly. Which troubleshooting option would work best?

   A. Reboot the computer using the F8 option, choose Safe Mode, reopen the Registry, and try to undo your change.

   B. Reboot the computer using the F8 option, choose the Last Known Good Configuration option, and complete the boot sequence.

   C. Reboot the computer using the F8 option, choose the Debugging Mode option, and complete the boot sequence. The system will debug itself.

   D. Reinstall your operating system. Any change made to the Registry is irreversible.

11. Logging onto a Windows 2000 system requires, at the very least, which of the following? (Select all that apply.)

   A. A username

   B. The Windows 2000 product key

   C. A password

   D. A remote access account

12. During the Windows 2000 Setup, you are asked to choose between the NTFS file system and the FAT file system. Which of the following is NOT an advantage of NTFS?

   A. NTFS supports compression, encryption, disk quotas, and file ownership.

   B. NTFS can be accessed and modified with standard DOS disk utilities.

   C. NTFS supports larger partitions than FAT.

   D. NTFS allows for file-level security.

13. What does the parameter /checkupgradeonly do?

   A. It instructs the Setup program that the procedure is an upgrade, not a full installation.

   B. It checks the computer for upgrade compatibility with Windows 2000 and generates a report.

   C. There is no such a command.

   D. It instructs the Setup program to thoroughly scan the hard drive only during the upgrade process.

14. During a routine installation of Windows 2000, Setup detected a problem during the partition check. After rebooting and reattempting setup, the problem continues. What should you do?

   A. Nothing, Windows 2000 Setup is designed to fix any problem encountered.

   B. Reboot the computer, access the system BIOS, change the boot sequence to boot from the CD-ROM, and reboot. The problem will go away.

   C. Install Windows 2000 to an alternate partition.

   D. Terminate Setup and run a full scandisk.

15. After a successful upgrade to Windows 2000, what should you do with the temporary files generated during the setup process?

   A. Nothing, all temporary files saved to your hard drive and used during setup are automatically removed.

   B. Nothing, these temporary files are actually needed, as they contain all user settings from the previous operating system.

   C. Emptying your Recycle Bin will remove these temporary files from your hard drive.

   D. If you install Windows 2000 from a CD-ROM, no temporary files are created, so there is nothing to delete.

16. You are preparing a computer for a dual-booting between Windows 98 and Windows 2000. Your drive is partitioned, and Windows 98 is already installed. Which of the following must you also consider?

   A. You must choose NTFS for the Windows 2000 partition for file-level security.

   B. You must choose FAT for the Windows 2000 partition. NTFS is not compatible with Windows 98 dual-boot configurations.

   C. Choose either FAT or NTFS, as long as you install Windows 2000 into a different partition than Windows 98.

   D. You cannot create a dual-boot configuration between Windows 98 and Windows 2000.

17. Which of the following is NOT a part of the graphical phase of Windows 2000 Setup?

   A. Date and Time settings

   B. Partitioning the hard drive

   C. Networking Setting/Installing Components

   D. Regional Setting

18. Driver Signing is an option new to Windows 2000. What exactly does driver signing do?

A. It controls access to the Internet.

B. It minimizes the risk involved with installing new hardware drivers.

C. It has to do with the pre-determined times certain system tasks are performed, such as disk defragmenting, virus checking, and so on.

D. It has to do with which folder drivers are stored.

19. What is the key difference between a workgroup and a domain, as defined in this chapter?

A. A workgroup consists of several computers sharing a single security authority. A domain allows each computer to handle its own security.

B. A workgroup and a domain handle security in much the same way. There is no difference.

C. In a workgroup, each computer is responsible for security. In a domain, there is a single authority for managing security.

D. A workgroup can only include Windows 9x machines, while a domain can include Windows 2000 workstations.

20. Which of the following is not a Windows 2000 Key Boot file?

A. AUTOEXEC.BAT

B. NTLDR

C. BOOTSECT.DOS

D. BOOT.INI

Answers to Review Questions

1. A, C, D. Windows 2000 includes the Computer Management tool, which combines many Windows-based administrative tools into a single interface. The three basic classes of tasks available from the Computer Management console are System Tools, Storage, and Services and Applications.

2. C. During the Windows 2000 Setup, you are shown a list of current partitions. If you wish to create a new partition, you can do so from within the Setup program. There is no need to exit Setup.

3. A. There are three subheadings under the Advanced tab: Performance, Environment Variables, and Startup and Recovery. The Performance button allows you to change the size of your virtual memory and Registry.

4. D. A Pentium 133, 64MB of RAM, and a 2GB hard drive are minimum hardware requirements for the installation of Windows 2000. However, VGA is the minimum for video. While SVGA will enhance the performance of Windows 2000, it is only recommended.

5. B. The virtual memory settings tell the user how much hard drive space is allocated to the system as a swap file. With minimum RAM on the system illustrated in this question, this setting may need to be modified.

6. A. The Disk Defragmenter is located within the Storage tab. This program checks for drive errors, as well as defragmenting the hard drive.

7. C. The Hardware Compatibility List (HCL), while comprehensive, does not include every legacy driver ever made. It may thus be necessary to contact the vendor for compatibility information.

8. C. Windows 2000 cannot exist in the same partition as Windows 98. It is thus necessary to partition the hard drive, install Windows 98 first, and then Windows 2000. Installing Windows 98 after Windows 2000 is not supported as a dual-boot option.

9. A, B, C, D. Setup performs a thorough check, or test of all hardware and software. The upgrade report details those issues that may require upgrading. Hardware, Software, Program Notes, and General Information are the four topics listed.

10. B. There are several advanced boot options available when pressing F8 during the boot process. Last Known Good Configuration works when a configuration setting in the Registry is changed, causing a problem. This option will not restore a corrupt or deleted file, however.

11. A, C. While there are other login options available for logging into a Windows 2000 system, at the very least, a user needs a username and a password.

12. B. NTFS is a more sophisticated file system. However, it is not compatible with DOS.

13. B. There are many Setup commands with various options associated with them. /checkupgradeonly does exactly what it says it does. It checks a computer for upgrade compatibility with Windows 2000 and generates either a .log or a .txt report.

14. D. Although Setup will detect and attempt to fix any problem encountered during installation, persistent drive problems need to be fixed before installation can be continued.

15. A. One of the final tasks performed by the Setup program is the removal of any temporary file saved to the hard drive at the start of the setup.

16. C. The C drive with Windows 98 must remain FAT, but the Windows 2000 partition can be FAT, FAT32, or NTFS.

17. B. The graphical phase of Windows 2000 Setup begins after the hard drive is formatted and/or partitioned. Thus, partitioning the hard drive occurs before the graphical phase begins.

18. B. Installing new hardware drivers can cause system problems. To minimize this, Windows 2000 has pre-tested most drivers. Thus, you can install only those drivers that have "signed" or screened for reliability.

19. C. A domain is a group of tightly connected computers managed by a domain controller that handles security for the entire group. In a workgroup, however, each computer is responsible for its own security.

20. A. Almost all of the files needed to boot Windows 3.1 or 9x are unnecessary for Windows 2000. Thus, AUTOEXEC.BAT is not a key Windows 2000 boot file.

Chapter

15

Application Installation and Configuration

THE FOLLOWING OBJECTIVES ARE COVERED IN THIS CHAPTER:

✓ **2.4 Identify procedures for loading/adding and configuring application device drivers and the necessary software for certain devices.**

   Content may include the following:

- Windows 9x Plug and Play and Windows 2000
- Identify the procedures for installing and launching typical Windows and non-Windows applications. (Note: there is no content related to Windows 3.1.)
- Procedures for setup and configuring Windows printing subsystem.
  - Setting default printer
  - Installing/spool setting
  - Network printing (with help of LAN admin)

Buying a computer back in the 1980s was sort of like buying a DVD player when they came out a couple of years ago. It was so amazing that you just had to have one, but then once you had it, you rapidly discovered the fact that you had no movies to play on it (or at least very few). When I plunked down my hard-earned dollars for a Commodore 64 or an IBM PC, about all I got along with it was a manual. Because of this, one of the most under-appreciated elements of Windows is that the system comes prepackaged with a number of useful—and entertaining—applications. From the Address Book to WordPad, you can find all sorts of good stuff already installed when you first start using a Windows 9*x* or 2000 machine.

NOTE For complete coverage of objective 2.4, please also see Chapters 13, 14, and 16.

In most cases, though, users aren't satisfied to only use the tools that are provided with Windows. Either a particular tool they need isn't included (for example, Microsoft didn't put a spreadsheet application into Windows), or they need a more sophisticated version of a particular application—Wordpad and Word 2000 are both word processors, but that's about where the similarity ends. This demand has led to a booming software industry, and there are literally thousands of applications available that users can install and use with Windows. Because of this, installing and maintaining programs on user's computers is a big part of a technician's job. In order to prepare you for this task, we will discuss the following topics in this chapter:

- Comparing Windows 9*x* to Windows 2000 for application support and install methods
- Common application types
- Installing an application with a simple setup routine
- Installing a more complex program using the new Windows Installer
- Repairing and modifying installed applications
- Uninstalling applications
- Dealing with the issue of old DOS applications

Application Basics

In general, any computer program that is not essential to the operation of the operating system can be thought of as an application. *Applications* are program code designed with a particular purpose in mind, and generally fall into one of a few broad categories:

Utilities These are programs which accomplish certain tasks. The Backup or Task Scheduler programs are good examples of *utilities* that come with Windows. Other common utilities include WinZip (for compressing and uncompressing files) or McAfee's VirusScan software, which helps protect a computer from malicious attack.

Productivity tools These are applications that help users get their work done. Simple *productivity tools* such as WordPad and the Calculator are included with Windows; we will also be looking at Microsoft Office (the mother of all productivity tools) later in this chapter. Other common applications that fit into this category are the Lotus SmartSuite (which has word processing and spreadsheet components, among others) and Intuit's Quicken for managing finances.

Entertainment Well, here we have it. As noted, there are thousands of programs available for Windows, and probably 90 percent of them are games or multimedia tools. This category of application provides special challenges and can often be among the most vexing to install and configure. Fortunately, these are also the applications that are the least likely to be brought to a technician to work on, because most service work is done for corporate accounts—and corporations are unlikely to pay you to figure out why Age of Kings won't install properly! Unfortunately, this doesn't mean you are out of the woods, since once you become a "computer geek," every friend and relative will soon be asking you why their new game doesn't work.

Comparing Windows 9*x* to Windows 2000 for Application Support and Install Methods

When you start looking at installing applications on a Windows machine, the first thing to note is that the installation is generally pretty similar regardless of whether the program is installed on Windows 9*x* or Windows 2000. Even so, there are a number of differences in applications, and as such you should take these into account. Here are a few key things to look for.

Application Architecture

One of the first things you will want to look for when getting ready to install a new application is what type of operating systems are supported by the product.

Not all programs install on all operating systems, and the following sections detail the key questions you will want to ask.

Is It a DOS or a Windows Application?

In order to make it easier for third-party vendors to write applications for Windows, Microsoft provides *APIs (application programming interfaces)* for Windows 3.*x*, 9*x*, and 2000. These APIs allow programmers to write applications more easily because Windows itself provides much of the functionality. For instance, when a programmer wants to write a routine that prints out a result, they can simply call printing APIs, instead of writing out the entire print process. This does two things. First, it makes programming more simple and second, it standardizes the way that certain tasks are performed. Almost all print or file save screens in Windows, for example, look about the same because all of them use a standardized API set.

If a program is written for Windows, it should run on either 9*x* or 2000. We will see in the next section that it may not run optimally, but generally, it will work. If the application was written for DOS, though, it could be a different story. Windows 9*x* provides an environment that allows you to use older DOS applications, but Windows 2000 does not. Most non-Windows applications will fail if you attempt to run them on Windows 2000! We will deal with how Windows 9*x* runs DOS applications later in the chapter.

There are, of course, applications written for many operating systems other than Windows and DOS. Most of them will not run on either Windows 9*x* or Windows 2000. Macintosh applications, Linux applications, and C/PM applications, for instance, will all error if you try to use them on a Windows machine.

Is It a 32-Bit or 16-Bit Windows Application?

Windows-based applications that are written for older versions of Windows are referred to as *16-bit applications* or *Windows 3.x applications*. Newer applications written specifically for Windows 9*x* or Windows 2000 are designed for use on more modern hardware and take advantage of the fact that Windows 9*x* and 2000 are 32-bit operating systems. Although both 16-bit and 32-bit Windows applications will generally run on either of the 32-bit Windows platforms, 32-bit applications are faster and more stable and should be used whenever possible.

Does the Application Use Any Non-Standard Windows APIs?

As I just mentioned, most 16-bit and 32-bit Windows applications will run on either Windows 98 or Windows 2000. Unfortunately, though, this is a guideline, not a rule. Because of the fact that there are Windows APIs which are supported by Windows 9*x* but not by Windows 2000, and vice versa, you will occasionally find that a 32-bit Windows application will work only on the *9x* or the 2000 platform.

Microsoft has developed a standard for easily identifying whether an application is compatible with a particular version of Windows. Most software written for Windows now comes with a graphic that declares which systems it is verified to run on.

Because they are very similar architecturally, applications written for Windows 95 will work with Windows 98, and those written for Windows NT will work with Windows 2000. Those written for the newer systems, however, are not always backward compatible.

Other Considerations

Aside from architecture, there are a couple of other things you should be aware of when installing applications.

Beta Code

Pioneered by Netscape, which was one of the first companies to use the Internet as its primary software distribution channel, the popularity of *beta* applications has added an entire new chapter to the book of technician headaches. When an application is in development, its *alpha* phase is the time during which the application is being created and tested in-house. Once the application is thought to be ready, a number of companies have taken to releasing a presales version of the application on the Internet as a way of testing consumer response. Later versions of the beta product are generally released as well, and eventually a "release version" of the software is completed. Because beta software is generally released on an as-is basis, you should avoid using this on production systems. Most beta software is not eligible for technical support and is generally less stable than the later release version of the software.

Licensing Issues

As the great Napster controversy of 2000 has shown, the Internet is a place where many of the rules that govern property rights have gone out the window. In your role as a technician, though, you are a part of the computer industry, and protecting the copyrights and intellectual property of software developers is part of that job. As such, you will need to familiarize yourself with licensing issues and make certain that you don't end up installing programs for which you don't have a license.

What you do at home is your own business, but if you are being paid to install a piece of software, the people who wrote it should be getting paid, too. If a user buys one copy of Microsoft Word from you and asks you to install it on 10 machines, that is a clear violation of the licensing agreement. This is a difficult situation, as you don't want to aggravate the customer, but you also can't ethically do what they are asking. Get ready to deal with this issue, by the way, because it almost certainly will come up eventually. Figure 15.1 shows an example of licensing information.

FIGURE 15.1 MS Word licensing info

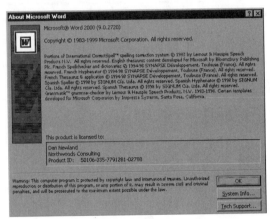

Installing Applications

Once you have determined that an application is able to run on your Windows machine (or you think it will!) you need to transfer the files and settings for that application onto the computer. In Windows, this is generally done through the use of a Setup program, although, as you will see with Windows 2000, Microsoft has debuted a new way of installing and managing applications that could mean the end of setup as we know it. Because of this, the installation information in this chapter is divided into two sections: the first describes a standard application setup, and the second describes a setup using the *Windows Installer* (*MSI*) files. We will not divide this up in a Windows 9x/Windows 2000 fashion because they are identical in the way they handle each setup.

Because it is the application that controls the setup procedures, both Windows 9x and Windows 2000 machines will be able to use the new setup method of Office 2000.

Running a Basic Setup Program

In preparing for the A+ exams, one thing you are nearly certain to need is a copy of the objectives, as laid out on the CompTIA Web site. It isn't just as simple as going out and reading them, though, as the objectives are saved on the site in

Adobe Acrobat format. Acrobat is a great utility that allows you to save documents in exactly the form they are produced and distribute them for viewing. The only disadvantage to this is that in order for a user to see the document, they must have a special piece of software called the Adobe Acrobat Reader. In this first section, I will show you how to obtain the reader installation software and run its setup routine.

Getting the Files

Applications are really nothing more than software code installed onto the hard drive of your machine. Because of this, it shouldn't be a big surprise to know you have to obtain a copy of the software installation files before running setup. The most common installation methods today are as follows:

CD-ROM   Most programs are sold on CD-ROM. To install them, you simply put the disk into the disk drive, and an install routine should start up. If it doesn't, you may have to browse to the setup file.

Network   In organizations where network installations are available, they are generally preferred to CD-ROM installs because there is no need to carry around the disk (or in my case, to *find* the disk I need). Network installs are also generally faster than CD-ROM installs.

Internet   Installing software that is downloaded directly over the Internet is becoming increasingly popular because of its convenience and flexibility.

Installing applications acquired from the Internet can also be dangerous to the health of your machine. Most viruses and other malicious problems are passed on through opening and using executable files, and SETUP.EXE is one such file. Only download and use content direct from vendor sites or respected mirror sites.

For Acrobat Reader, the best place to go is www.adobe.com, the home page of the company that makes the Acrobat software. At Adobe you can download a copy of the Reader for free simply by registering and providing some marketing info; on Adobe's Web site, just look for the icon shown in Figure 15.2.

FIGURE 15.2   The Acrobat icon

The marketing info is, unfortunately, pretty standard, as everyone wants your name, e-mail address, and a short biography before they give you their stuff. Once you get through this, you will come to a screen from which you are able to download a file that has all of the setup information wrapped up inside it, as shown in Figure 15.3.

FIGURE 15.3 The File Download window

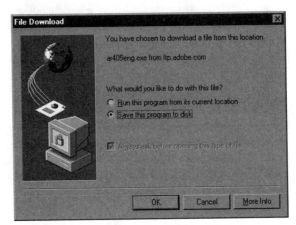

Generally, you will save this file to a directory on your hard drive and then run it from there.

Starting the Install

Once you have the installation CD or have downloaded the files you need, find the installation file—it will usually be SETUP.EXE or INSTALL.EXE. In this case, though, the file is called A40ENG.EXE. Start the setup program by double-clicking A40ENG.EXE. The Acrobat icon will unpack the file and then start the setup program, as shown in Figure 15.4.

FIGURE 15.4 Unpacking the Acrobat files

 Nonstandard setup filenames are relatively common among software distributed over the Internet. In this case, it simply reflects that this is the Acrobat **4.05 ENG**lish version. As updates become available and the version number changes, so will the filename. If the numbers in the download file are higher than 405, the application has probably been updated, and a newer version is being distributed.

Once setup begins, you will usually be presented with a number of questions given sequentially by a setup Wizard (Figure 15.5). Your answers to one question may determine what pages you see later in setup.

FIGURE 15.5 Choosing a destination for the Acrobat files

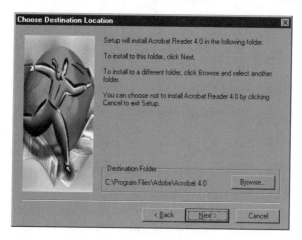

Once the setup routine has completed (Figure 15.6), you will find that a number of changes have been made to your system. First, there are changes to the GUI consisting of a new group of icons in Start ➢ Programs ➢ Adobe Acrobat 4.0, and there is an icon on the Desktop as well.

FIGURE 15.6 A note that the install is done

In addition to these changes, the setup file also makes changes under the hood. A number of files are installed onto the hard drive in C:\PROGRAM FILES\ ADOBE\ACROBAT 4.0. These files consist of DLLs (which are code libraries) and other informational and executable files, but there are no configuration files such as INI text files. Rather, configuration elements are set by adding a number of entries to the Registry, which can be found (among other places) in HKEY_LOCAL MACHINE\SOFTWARE\ADOBE.

I have used Acrobat for years and never had to modify its Registry settings (although it *is* technically possible to do so). The same can be said for most other simple programs. Install them and upgrade them when a new version comes out—you are generally best off if you simply leave their innards alone!

Installing Microsoft Office 2000 Using the New Windows Installer

Most programs use a setup program similar to the one we saw with the Acrobat Reader install. There are some significant limitations to these setup programs, though, and Microsoft recently began using a new method of setting up applications called the *Windows Installer*. The installer has the following advantages over traditional installation methods:

- The ability to logically group application elements for installation
- The ability to install components only when they are needed, through the Install on First Use option
- The ability to automatically detect and restore deleted or corrupt files (!)
- Easier customization through the use of MST files, which are used to save customized installation options for reuse

As an example of how these features work, let's run through an upgrade install of one of the most popular application suites, Microsoft Office 2000.

 Office has a number of versions—it is not really a program so much as it is a collection of programs, or *suite*. Office Standard includes Word (word processing), Excel (spreadsheet), Outlook (personal information manager), and PowerPoint (presentation). Office Professional adds Access, which is a database, and Office Premium adds the FrontPage Web editor and a number of other tools.

As with other programs, Microsoft Office has a SETUP.EXE file that it uses to start its installation routine. To start the install, simply insert the Office 2000 disk into your disk drive. Setup will begin automatically and will install Windows Installer onto your machine. If you already have a current version of the MS Installer software, the install continues, as in Figure 15.7. If not, an update will occur, and you may need to reboot and restart the install.

FIGURE 15.7 The Installer starting setup

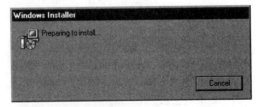

After this, you will be asked for a CD key, and you will need to agree to the license agreement. Once you have typed in the ridiculously long 25-digit key and have signed away your organs to Microsoft, you will be presented with a choice of a standard or a custom install.

Choose the custom choice and leave the default location. On the Selecting Features screen, you will be asked to not only decide which options you want, but also how you want them to be installed. In Figure 15.8, for instance, Microsoft Word Help is selected to run from CD, Wizards and Templates will not be installed, and Text with Layout Converter will be installed only if it is used. The Address Book and Page Border Art are the only optional Word components that will actually be written to the disk as part of this installation. These installation options are available because of the flexibility of the Windows Installer program, which actually stays on your hard drive and can start a small install any time you need it, as when someone wants to use the Text with Layout converter. Not all programs support these options yet, but many more will in the coming years.

FIGURE 15.8 The Selecting Features screen for Office 2000

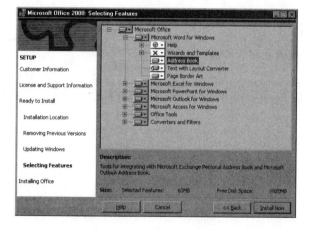

Once you have selected the options you need, click the Install Now button, and the setup program will configure your setup. Figure 15.9 displays the indicator that shows you how the installation is progressing.

FIGURE 15.9 Setup verifying tasks

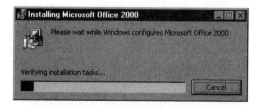

Once setup has completed, the Installer presents you with a parting gift in the form of a restart notification. This is because new information has been written to the Registry and may not be properly read until the system is reinitialized.

Some programs, such as Acrobat, do not need to reboot. Others do, though, and generally it is best to restart immediately if asked (Figure 15.10).

FIGURE 15.10 Windows completing the install and asking if you want to restart

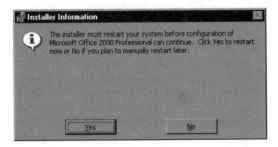

Repairing or Uninstalling Applications

Once an application is installed, it is generally pretty stable as long as one of two things does not happen. The basic categories of application problems can be categorized as follows:

File corruption   This can be caused by failing hard drives, power failures, viruses, or even poorly written programs

User error   Users... You gotta love 'em, because without them we would make a lot less money. Users may delete critical application files, shut down the system improperly, or introduce beta software onto the system that causes problems to other applications, among other things.

Between them, these two problems account for pretty much all problems with software applications. Generally, an application that has gone bad can be dealt with by either repairing or reinstalling it. If an application is badly written or is functioning perfectly but you no longer need it, you can also *uninstall* it, which removes it completely.

Repairing an Application

For most Windows programs, *file corruption* or deletion is best dealt with by running the setup program over again or by using the Add/Remove Programs Control Panel program. In such a case, you normally have to just reinstall the application with the same options as before, and the files will be recopied. Some programs, such as Internet Explorer 5, will even allow you to run a limited recopy that looks at your previous install and repairs it by recopying any files that are missing or corrupt. The IE options are shown in Figure 15.11.

Corrupt files can usually be detected by the repair process because their size changes due to the corruption.

FIGURE 15.11 The Repair Internet Explorer option

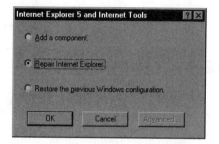

Microsoft Office is able to repair itself as well because it uses the Windows Installer (as does Internet Explorer). If Office or Internet Explorer has a problem, the Installer is able to review the installation and either download the needed replacement files or ask the user to install a CD with the files on it, as in Figure 15.12.

FIGURE 15.12 The Office Maintenance Mode window with Repair, Add, or Remove options

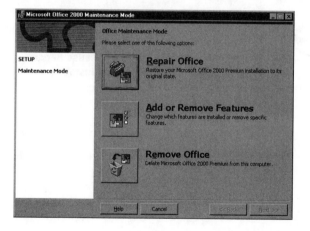

Windows Update

As more and more users are getting online and as bandwidth is becoming cheaper and more available, many software companies are making software updates available online. Some companies send out an e-mail to registered users noting that an updated version of the software is available for download, while others have mechanisms built into the software that can automatically update the software as new versions or patches are available. Because of the security issues involved in having new software installing itself on a PC without user knowledge or consent, this sort of update is currently rather uncommon, but it is definitely on the rise! As part of this, Microsoft now allows users to automatically update Windows OS components, as well as other Microsoft applications using Windows Update. We won't look at this as it is not generally something techs need to deal with, but you may run across it, so it's good to know about.

Uninstalling an Application

Occasionally, you will install an application on a PC and then decide that you no longer need it. In order to free up hard drive space, you may then want to remove that application from the PC. This is done through a process called *uninstalling*. The uninstall feature, which completely removes a program from the computer, also goes into the Registry and other system areas and removes references to the application. To access the uninstall feature for an application in Windows, you generally have one of two options (or sometimes both):

- Use the Uninstall icon from the application's program group
- Use Add/Remove Programs and choose to remove all or uninstall, depending on what terminology the program uses.

It is crucial to the health of your system that you do not simply go into the Windows Explorer and delete the files for an application. Removing the files without performing an uninstall will cause Registry problems and other difficulties, and may even make the system unstable.

We'll use Adobe Acrobat as an example of a program to uninstall.

The Uninstall Option in Its Program Group

Not all applications provide you with this handy tool, but most of the good ones do. On the Start menu, simply click Programs ➤ Adobe Acrobat 4.0 ➤ Uninstall Adobe Acrobat 4.0 (Figure 15.13), and the program removes the software icons and files and cleans up after itself in the Registry as well.

FIGURE 15.13 The Uninstall option for Acrobat

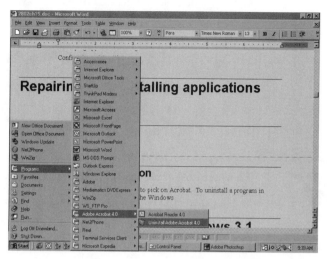

The Add/Remove Programs Control Panel Program

With this Control Panel program, you can add and remove Windows components and third-party software. To uninstall an option, open the Control Panel, click Add/Remove Programs, select the program you wish to uninstall , and click the Add/Remove button, as shown in Figure 15.14. Windows will look for uninstall information for the application and begin the uninstall process.

FIGURE 15.14 The Windows Add/Remove Programs Control Panel program

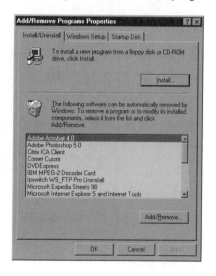

Once you have chosen to uninstall a program, you will be presented with the Confirm File Deletion dialog box as displayed in Figure 15.15.

FIGURE 15.15   The Confirm File Deletion dialog box

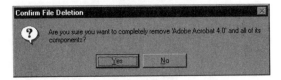

Some applications, such as Office, have literally hundreds of possible components. These larger applications usually present an intermediate screen asking whether you want to add or remove particular components or whether you wish to completely uninstall the product. Acrobat has very few options and simply starts the uninstall routine immediately.

If you select Yes, the Remove Programs from Your Computer window, as shown in Figure 15.16, shows you which components are being removed, including Registry information. Some programs are better at this than others, but it is important to remember that few programs ever remove all of the files that they install. There are other third-party applications (such as CleanSweep) that go out and find leftover elements of deleted applications, but generally the uninstall feature does a good enough job. Once the uninstall routine completes, you will see the Uninstall successfully completed message.

FIGURE 15.16   Completing the uninstall

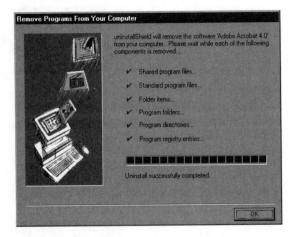

In the case of Acrobat, for instance, a post-uninstall Registry and drive search shows that the files have all been removed properly, but a few references to Acrobat remain in the Registry. If I wanted to, I could manually search and destroy these as well, but it is rarely worth it to be that compulsive. For general intents and purposes, the application is completely uninstalled.

Sometimes you need to uninstall an older (or beta) version of an application before reinstalling a newer or full version of the product. In such cases, the setup routine for the newer application may search the Registry for earlier installations of the product, and you may have to physically delete leftover Registry information before your reinstall will work properly.

Dealing with Older DOS/Windows 3.*x* Applications

There are two ways to install DOS programs onto a Windows 9*x* machine. Many older DOS programs can simply be copied; newer, more complex DOS programs will have to be installed with a setup routine specific to that application. In either case, Windows 9*x* has the ability to let you configure the DOS environment to allow DOS applications to run as well as, well, a DOS application is going to run.

The process for installing and using DOS applications is the same in Windows 2000 as it is in Windows 9*x*. That said, there is one critical difference: DOS applications generally run pretty well under Windows 9*x* and generally won't run at all under Windows 2000. If you are thinking of installing a 16-bit DOS application on Windows 2000 Professional, you need to test it carefully to make certain it will function properly.

Windows 3.*x* 16-bit applications setup routines look similar to the Windows 32-bit applications we looked at earlier except that they use INI and other configuration files and are generally completely ignorant of the Registry.

Installing an Application by Copying

Many years ago, DOS applications were simple executable COM or EXE files that could be run from a floppy. Copying these files to the hard drive was a common practice (if the computer had a hard drive) because programs run faster from a hard drive than they do from a floppy drive. As programs became larger, with many pieces and added-in drivers, it became more than just practical to copy the files to the hard drive; it became necessary.

Figure 15.17 shows a list of files on a floppy disk being copied to a directory on the hard drive. Two of these files are DOS executables, INTERLNK.EXE and INTERSVR.EXE. (These files are required to establish an interlink connection between two computers.)

FIGURE 15.17   Copying DOS program files

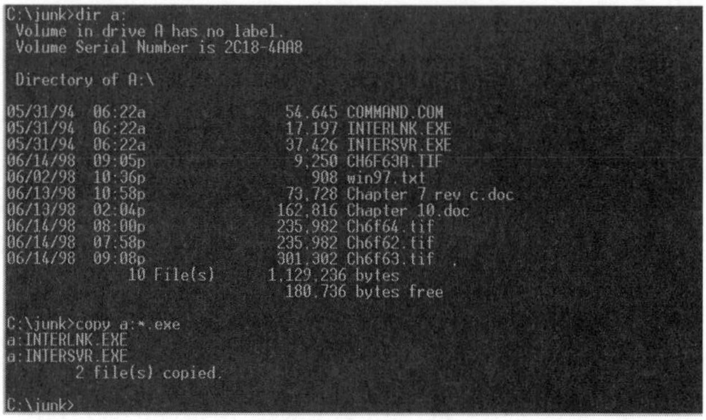

Installing an Application with a Setup Routine

More complex DOS programs need to be installed, rather than just copied, to work properly. One example is PC Tools from Central Point Software. PC Shell is a DOS shell with a bit of a graphical look and feel that can be used for file management. It's made up of a collection of files that fit onto several floppies but can work together only on a larger drive. Some of the utilities included in this suite can be run from the floppy, but others require the presence of overlay files and device drivers that span more than one floppy disk.

Although PC Tools (in its early versions, at least) *can* be copied onto the hard drive, it comes with an installation program that aids in the copying process by locating or creating a subdirectory for the files to be copied to. The install program also prompts you to insert each floppy disk as it is needed.

More complex programs require a more intricate installation procedure, usually meaning that you'll have to make decisions throughout the setup process. DOS programs generally use device drivers that are specific to that program, so when you load WordPerfect for DOS, you'll need to select a printer, even though you may have already selected the printer for Lotus 1-2-3. Likewise, you may have to select a display driver for fitting more text or typed data on a screen.

As shown in Figure 15.18, early installation routines primarily copy files and offer a few options on how to configure the files and computer after the application has been installed. Notice that this screen is a little bit graphical but not to the extent that modern Windows screens are. This PC Tools installation screen is actually built up out of DOS ASCII characters.

FIGURE 15.18   Installing PC Tools version 6

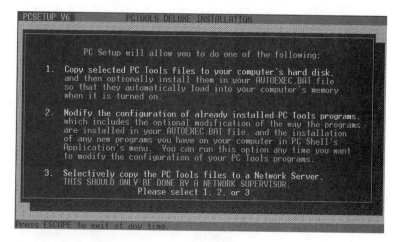

 If you have questions about installing a DOS-based programs in a DOS environment, refer to the user guide that comes with the software.

Launching an Application

Launching an application in DOS usually means typing in its name or the name of its main executable file at a DOS command prompt. For example, you could start the Central Point Software program PC Shell by typing **pcshell** at the DOS command prompt. Generally, programs are put into their own subdirectories, so a path must exist pointing to that subdirectory, or you must already be in that subdirectory.

Alternatives include typing the complete path at the command prompt along with the startup command or launching the application with a batch file that has the complete path as part of the startup command. For example, an AUTOEXEC.BAT file could include the following command line in order to start the PC Tools shell when the computer starts up:

C:\PCTOOLS6\PCSHELL6

The PC Shell utility provides file list and directory tree windows similar to Windows File Manager (in Windows 3.x) or Windows Explorer (in Windows 9x or 2000).

Uninstalling an Application

With DOS programs, the uninstall process is the reverse of copying: you simply erase all the files associated with the program.

Of course, sometimes an installation will have made modifications to the CONFIG.SYS and AUTOEXEC.BAT files. Depending on the nature of these configuration modifications, there may be no side effects to the removal of a program, or there may be some error messages about files not being found.

Rarely are these configuration changes harmful if left in, although many times the changes will leave extra and unneeded drivers loaded or memory configurations that are not optimized for the applications left on the hard drive. If you edit the CONFIG.SYS and the AUTOEXEC.BAT files, remarking out suspicious statements, it will usually fix things up.

Summary

In this chapter, we looked at how you can extend the functionality of a Windows-based computer by installing additional software on it. The installation and configuration of applications and utilities is a big part of a technician's daily work.

We looked at the different types of software available and at the different ways in which that software can be obtained and installed. We also looked at removing programs that are no longer used and examined the increasingly uncommon case of installing DOS/Windows 3.*x* applications on a Windows 9*x* or 2000 machine.

Key Terms

Before you take the exam, be certain you are familiar with the following terms:

alpha	productivity tool
beta	uninstall
file corruption	Windows Installer

Review Questions

1. Programs that are used to accomplish certain tasks are referred to as:

   A. Utilities

   B. Productivity tools

   C. Entertainment

   D. Control panels

2. Common examples of a utility program are: (Select all that apply.)

   A. WinZip

   B. Backup

   C. Virus scan software

   D. WordPad

   E. Calculator

3. Applications that help users get their work done are referred to as:

   A. Utilities

   B. Productivity tools

   C. Entertainment

   D. Control panels

4. When purchasing an application, which of the following would be listed as logical questions to ask? (Select all that apply.)

   A. Is the application a DOS or a Windows application?

   B. Is it a 32-bit or 16-bit application?

   C. Is it a third-party or first-party vendor?

   D. Does the application use any nonstandard Windows APIs?

5. If a program is written for Windows it should run on either:

   A. Windows 9*x* or Windows 2000

   B. Windows 2.*x* or Windows 95

   C. Windows 3.*x* or Windows NT

   D. Windows 3.*x* or Windows 98

6. APIs allow programmers to do all of the following except:

   A. Write applications more easily

   B. Accept nonstandard applications

   C. Standardize the way certain tasks are performed

   D. Make programming more simple

7. Windows 9*x* and Windows 2000 are what type of operating systems?

   A. 12-bit operating systems

   B. 8-bit operating systems

   C. 16-bit operating systems

   D. 32-bit operating systems

8. Applications written for Windows 95 will work with which operating systems?

   A. Only Windows 98

   B. Windows 98, Windows NT, Windows 2000

   C. Windows 98 and Windows NT

   D. Windows 98 and Windows 2000

9. Applications written for Windows 2000 are pretty certain to run on which of these operating systems? (Select all that apply.)

   A. Windows 95

   B. Windows 98

   C. Windows NT

   D. Windows 2000

   E. All of the above

10. When an application is in the early stages of development, it's referred to as being in the _____ phase:

    A. Alpha

    B. Beta

    C. Testing

    D. Developmental

11. Protecting the copyrights and intellectual properties of software developers is referred to as:

    A. Coding

    B. Licensing

    C. Copying

    D. Developing

12. Windows Installer files can be easily identified by the extension:

    A. EXE

    B. BAT

    C. MSI

    D. DAT

13. Applications can be installed from all of the following devices except:

    A. Backup drives

    B. CD-ROM

    C. Network

    D. Internet

14. In starting the installation you must activate the installation file. Most installation files have which extension? (Select all that apply.)

    A. EXE

    B. BAT

    C. DAT

    D. TMP

15. Which of the following is not an advantage of the Windows Installer over traditional installing methods?

    A. The ability to individualize application elements for installation

    B. The ability to install components only when they are needed

    C. The ability to detect and restore deleted or corrupt files

    D. Easier customization through the use of MST files

16. Which is the recommended choice for install for new beginners?

    A. Custom

    B. Typical

    C. Express

    D. Advanced

17. The basic categories of application problems can be categorized as: (Select all that apply.)

    A. File corruption

    B. User error

    C. Application error

    D. Program error

18. How many options are there to uninstall an application?

    A. One

    B. Two

    C. Three

    D. Four

19. The Windows 98 Add/Remove Programs icon is located in:

    A. Control Panel

    B. Network Neighborhood

    C. My Computer

    D. The Recycle Bin

20. DOS applications generally run under all of the following except:

    A. Windows 95

    B. Windows 98

    C. Windows NT

    D. Windows 2000

    E. Both C and D

Answers to Review Questions

1. A. Utilities provide a way for a user to control the provisions and use of hardware resources and are a subcategory of system software designed to enhance the operating system.

2. A, B, C. Utility programs, when activated, accomplish specific tasks. For Example, Norton Utilities troubleshoots problems with a computer's disk drives, makes data more secure by encrypting it, and helps to retrieve data from damaged disks.

3. B. A productivity tool is a graphical user interface. Tools help users get their work done by making it easier for users to interact with a software program.

4. A, B. Whether it's a first- or third-party vendor usually doesn't matter. The main issue when purchasing an application is compatibility. Most software written for Windows now comes with a graphic declaring which systems it is verified to run on; this is an easy way to identify whether an application is compatible with a particular version of Windows.

5. A. If a program is written for Windows, it should run on either $9x$ or 2000—it may not run optimally, but generally it will work. However, most non-Windows applications will fail if you attempt to run them on Windows 2000.

6. B. APIs allow programmers to write applications more easily because Windows itself provides much of the functionality. For instance, when a programmer wants to write a routine that prints out a result, they can simply call printing APIs, instead of writing out the entire print process. This makes programming simpler and standardizes the way that certain tasks are performed.

7. D. Although both 16-bit and 32-bit Windows application will generally run on either of the 32-bit Windows platforms, 32-bit applications are faster and more stable and should be used whenever possible.

8. A. Because the operating systems are very similar architecturally, applications written for Windows 95 will work with Windows 98. Those written for newer systems, however, are not always backward compatible.

9. D. Although Windows 2000 applications may run well on Windows NT or Windows $9x$ as well as on 2000, this is not always the case and should be verified, not assumed.

10. A. When an application is in development, its *alpha* phase is the time during which the application is being created and tested in-house.

11. B. Protecting the copyrights and intellectual properties of software developers is referred to as licensing. A software license is a legal contract that defines the ways in which you may use a computer program.

12. C. The Windows Installer service has files with the extensions MSI and MST.

654 Chapter 15 · Application Installation and Configuration

13. A. Backup brings back files from an existing install. It cannot be used to perform an initial installation.

14. A, B. Most installation files have the file extension EXE and BAT. EXE stands for execution; BAT stands for *batch*.

15. A. Windows Installer has the ability to logically group application elements for installation, install components only when they are needed though the Install on First Use option, and automatically detect and restore deleted or corrupt files. The Installer also provides easier customization through the use of MST files, which are used to save customized installation options for reuse.

16. B. It is recommended that beginners use the typical install because settings are chosen for them automatically, and the most commonly used options are installed.

17. A, B. File corruption and user error account for almost all of the problems with software applications. File corruption can be caused by failing hard drives, power failures, viruses, or even poorly written programs. Examples of user errors are deleting critical application files, shutting down the system improperly, or introducing beta software onto the system that causes problems with other applications.

18. B. To uninstall an application you can either uninstall from the application's program group or use Add/Remove Programs. It is crucial to the health of your system that you do not go into the Windows Explorer and delete the files for an application by hand. Removing the files without performing an uninstall will cause Registry problems and other difficulties and may even make the system unstable.

19. A. The Windows 98 Add/Remove Programs icon is located in Control Panel, which you can access either by selecting Start ➢ Settings ➢ Control Panel, or opening My Computer and double-clicking Control Panel.

20. E. DOS applications do not generally run under Windows NT and Windows 2000.

Chapter 16

Using and Configuring Additional Peripherals

THE FOLLOWING OBJECTIVES ARE COVERED IN THIS CHAPTER:

✓ **2.4 Identify procedures for loading/adding and configuring application device drivers and the necessary software for certain devices.**

Content may include the following:

- Windows 9*x* Plug and Play and Windows 2000
- Identify the procedures for installing and launching typical Windows and non-Windows applications. (Note: there is no content related to Windows 3.1)
- Procedures for set up and configuring Windows printing subsystem.
  - Setting Default printer
  - Installing/Spool setting
  - Network printing (with help of LAN admin)

Just as there are many different types of peripherals, there are many types of peripheral connection methods. The A+ exam will test your knowledge of these different types of methods, including

- Serial
- Parallel
- SCSI
- USB
- FireWire (IEEE 1394)

For complete coverage of objective 2.4, please also see Chapters 13, 14, and 15.

Peripheral Connection Methods

In this section, you'll learn about the different types of peripheral connection methods. You'll also learn how to differentiate them from one another by their properties.

Serial

Of all the peripheral connection methods, none is as popular as serial. It's a simple, effective way to connect a peripheral to a PC. It is also cheap to manufacture, which is probably the main reason it's so popular. *Serial* connections transfer data one bit at a time, one right after another. The maximum speed of a serial connection is 128Kbps, so it isn't good for large amounts of data transfer, but it works great for synchronizing two data sources. The most popular application of a serial connection is connecting an external modem to a PC.

Parallel

The next most popular peripheral connection method is parallel. *Parallel* connections transfer data 8 bits at a time as opposed to 1 bit at a time (as serial connections do). The most common peripheral connected via a parallel connection is a printer. Hence, parallel ports are often called printer ports. Additionally, newer parallel ports can connect devices like scanners and Zip drives to computers. Unfortunately, this doesn't work as well as other types of connection methods such as USB work because the parallel connection wasn't designed for connecting devices other than printing devices. Parallel was only designed to connect one peripheral at a time.

SCSI

The *Small Computer System Interface (SCSI)* is another method of connecting peripherals. It is the best choice for peripherals that require high-speed connections, as well as those that transfer large amounts of data, because it can transfer data either 16 or 32 bits at a time. For example, you could use a SCSI connection to connect a scanner, which might have to transfer megabytes of image data in a short period of time. The most popular use for SCSI is to connect disk drives to computers.

Although it is most often found in server systems, SCSI can be added to desktop systems through the use of an expansion card.

USB

In the last few years, a high-speed bus has been developed specifically for peripherals. That bus is the *Universal Serial Bus*, or *USB*. The serial bus could only connect a maximum of two external devices to a PC. USB, on the other hand, can connect a maximum of 127 external devices. Also, USB is a much more flexible peripheral bus than either serial or parallel. USB supports connections to printers, scanners, and many other input devices (such as joysticks and mice).

When connecting USB peripherals, you must connect them either directly to one of the USB ports on the PC or to a USB hub that is connected to one of those USB ports. Hubs can be chained together to provide multiple USB connections. Although you can connect up to 127 devices, it is impractical in reality. Most computers with will support around 12 USB devices.

Here are the steps to connect a USB digital camera to a PC to download the images from the camera:

1. With the PC powered on, connect the USB cable from a digital camera to an open USB port, either on a hub or a USB port on the back of the computer. Windows Plug and Play will recognize that there is a new device attached and will automatically start the Add New Hardware Wizard.

2. Follow the prompts on the screen to install the driver for your digital camera.

3. Install the image manipulation software that came with your digital camera.

As you can see, the combination of USB and Windows Plug and Play allows devices to be configured very easily.

FireWire (IEEE 1394)

With the advent of digital video, a new peripheral connection method was needed in order to download large video files into a PC. *IEEE-1394* was the standard developed to meet this need. This standard was developed from work done by Apple and others. The standard is more commonly known as *FireWire*, after the moniker given to it by Apple. FireWire was a leap in technology over USB because it could transfer data at a maximum of 400MB per second. It became the peripheral connection method of choice for connecting digital video cameras to PCs. IEEE 1394 ports can be found on many different types of computers, but they are most commonly found on Apple iMac computers. As a matter of fact, Apple has made a special version of the iMac, called the iMac DV, that is specifically set up for digital video.

Windows Printing Configuration

Probably the most troublesome aspect of a technician's job is configuring Windows printing properly. As such, the A+ exam will test your ability to do so. There are two ways to configure Windows printing: with a local printer or a network printer. In this section, you will learn about topics related to each.

When it comes to configuring a printer, the steps for both Windows 9*x* and 2000 are essentially the same.

Local Printing Configuration

One of the most common devices to add to computer system is a printer. Whether you are installing a dot-matrix printer or laser printer, the configuration is basically the same. In this section, we'll examine how to set up a Windows computer to print to a locally attached printer. Setting a workstation to print to a network printer is covered later in this chapter.

Adding a Printer

Microsoft was thoughtful enough to provide a wizard to help us install printers. The name of this wizard is the Add Printer Wizard (neat, huh?). It will guide you through the basic steps of installing a printer by asking you questions about how you would like the printer configured.

To start the Add Printer Wizard (APW for short), you must first open the PRINTERS folder by either going to Start ➤ Settings ➤ Printers or double-clicking the Printers icon in the Control Panel. Once you get to the PRINTERS folder, you can double-click the Add Printer icon. Doing so will display a screen that tells you the wizard is going to help you install your printer "quickly and easily." Let's hope so. Click Next to begin the configuration.

The first question the APW will ask you is where this printer is (Figure 16.1). If it is connected to the network, click the button next to Network Printer. If the printer is connected to your PC, click Local Printer. We will discuss using network printers later, so for right now, click Local Printer and click Next.

FIGURE 16.1 Telling the APW where the printer is

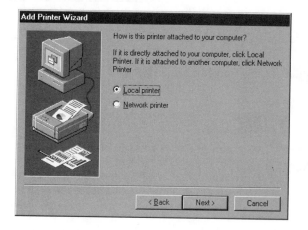

In Windows 2000, there is an extra option to allow Windows to automatically detect and install the printer for you. If you want, you can leave this option selected (which is the default), and Windows will automatically install the driver and configure the printer. The rest of these steps will then be moot.

The next screen that the APW presents allows you to choose the driver for your printer by simply selecting the manufacturer from the list on the left and the model from the list that appears on the right (Figure 16.2). You may need to scroll on either side because the lists can get rather long. If your printer is not listed, or if you would like to install a more current driver, you can click the Have Disk button and

APW will prompt you to insert the disk and type in the path to the directory where the driver is located. Either way, select your driver and click Next.

FIGURE 16.2 Selecting a printer driver to install

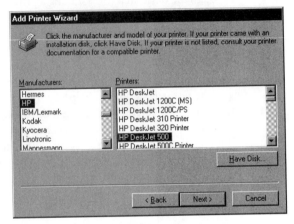

Make sure you select the correct driver for your model of printer. Most printing problems can be traced to a corrupt or out-of-date printer driver.

Some printer drivers can't be installed using the Add Printer Wizard. You must run SETUP or INSTALL from the disk to install the printing software. These programs will not only install the correct printer drivers, they will also set up the printer for use with Windows. In this case, you won't have to run the APW (in fact, it won't work because you can't select the right driver).

The next screen (Figure 16.3) allows you to choose which port the printer is hooked to. It will present you with a list of ports that Windows knows about, including parallel (LPT), serial (COM), and infrared (IR) ports, and ask you to choose which port the printer is hooked to. Simply click the port name on the list and click Next. If necessary, you can click Configure Port to configure any special port settings the printer may require.

FIGURE 16.3   Picking the printer port

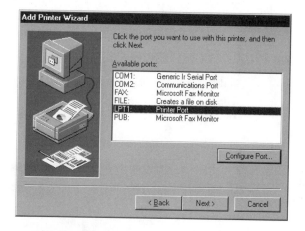

In the next step, APW asks you to give the printer a name (Figure 16.4) so that you can choose the printer by name when you select Print from any program. By default, the APW will supply the name of the print driver in this field. You can change it by simply clicking in the field and typing in a new name. Additionally, you can select whether or not you want this printer to be the default that Windows selects when you don't select a specific printer. If you want this printer to be the default, click the button next to Yes. If not, click No. When you're finished changing these settings, click Next.

FIGURE 16.4   Naming the printer

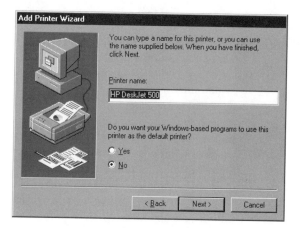

The final step in setting up a new printer is to indicate to the APW whether or not you'd like to print a test page (Figure 16.5). If you say Yes and click Finish, Windows will copy the driver and any support files and then try to print a test page. When the test page is printed, Windows will present you with a screen asking you if the page printed correctly. If you click Yes, the APW is finished and you know the printer works. If you select No, APW will launch Windows Help and bring you to the Printing Troubleshooting page. If you don't want to print a test page, select No (from the APW screen) and APW will simply copy the files and bring you back to the desktop.

FIGURE 16.5 Finishing setting up a printer

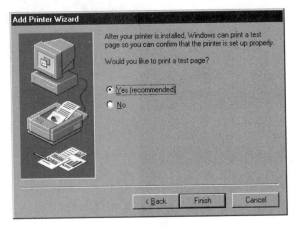

Managing an Existing Printer

If you have a printer installed on your Windows computer, there will be times where you need to change the way the printer functions. For this reason, you should know how to manage an existing printer under Windows. Managing a printer involves knowing how to configure the printer object after you have used the APW to set it up.

First, most of what you need to configure is centered around the printer icon (in the PRINTERS folder) that represents the printer you want to configure. You can configure most items from the property page of the printer by double-clicking the icon of the printer you want to configure.

If you right-click a printer's icon in the PRINTERS folder and choose Properties, you will see a screen similar to the one in Figure 16.6. There may be more options, depending on the type of printer it is. Each tab is used to configure different properties. Table 16.1 lists the tabs and a description of the function of each one.

You can print a test page from this page at any time by simply clicking the Print Test Page button.

FIGURE 16.6 The property page for a printer

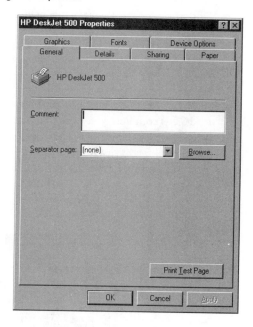

TABLE 16.1 Printer Properties Tabs and Functions

Tab	Description
General	Displays the printer's name as well as any comments you want to enter to describe the printer's functions (or eccentricities).
Details	Used to configure how Windows communicates with the printer.
Sharing	Used to share the printer on the network to which the machine is connected.
Paper	Used to configure what kind of paper the printer is using (size-wise) as well as its orientation when printing.

TABLE 16.1 Printer Properties Tabs and Functions *(continued)*

Tab	Description
Graphics	Used to configure the resolution of the printer. Lower resolutions use less toner.
Fonts	Displays the installed fonts. Also used to install other fonts.
Device Options	Changes depending on what kind of printer it is. Used to set the device-specific settings for the printer.

If you select the Details tab, you will see a screen similar to the one in Figure 16.7. From here you can configure how Windows communicates with the printer. For example, you can select a different port to print to for this printer. Additionally, you can install a new or updated driver from this screen. Simply click on the New Driver button. Windows will present you with a driver selection screen (similar to the one shown in Figure 16.2 earlier in this chapter).

FIGURE 16.7 The Details tab of the property page of a Windows 9*x* printer

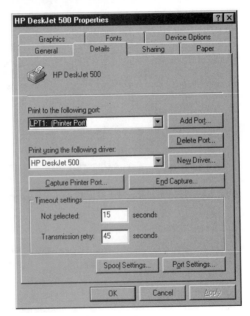

One of the most important options on this screen is the Spool Settings button. This button allows you to configure whether or not Windows will spool print jobs. If print jobs are spooled, every time you click Print in a program, the job is

printed to a spool directory (usually a subdirectory of the C:\WINDOWS\SPOOL directory) by a program called SPOOL32.EXE. Then the job is sent to the printer in the background while you continue to work. If you don't want print jobs to be spooled (it is the default), click the Spool Settings button. From the screen shown in Figure 16.8, you can choose either Spool Print Jobs... or Print Directly to the Printer. Choose the appropriate option and click OK. Once you have made changes to a printer, click OK on the property page to save them.

FIGURE 16.8   Changing a printer's spool settings

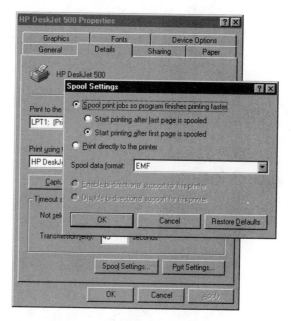

The other way to configure a printer is through the printer item in the System Tray (Figure 16.9). When you print a document, an icon of a printer will appear in the System Tray. By double-clicking it, you can open it so that you can manage the print jobs.

FIGURE 16.9   The printer icon in the System Tray

When you double-click the printer icon, you will see the screen shown in Figure 16.10. From here you can see any pending print jobs listed as well as their statistics. Notice that there is one print job currently being printed. If you want to stop the printer, you can choose Printer ➤ Pause Printing and Windows will stop sending print jobs to the printer. If you want to delete a job, click the job in the list of jobs and press the Delete key on your keyboard.

FIGURE 16.10 Printer job list

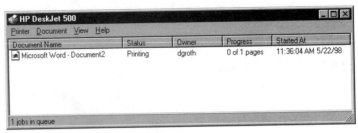

If you want to delete all jobs in this list, choose Purge Print Jobs from the Printer menu. All jobs that are currently spooled will be deleted.

Network Printing

Network printing is a lot like local printing except that with network printing, you are introducing a degree of separation between the computer and the printer. That degree of separation is a network. Configuring network printing is very similar to configuring local printing except you must configure the Windows printer driver to print to the network instead of to a local printer port. Usually, this involves installing network software that comes with the printer; the software will make a virtual printer port that points to the specified network printer.

For the A+ exam, you will not be expected to know everything about connecting network printers (after all, that is what the Network+ exam is for). However, you should know the basic steps.

Installing a Network Printer

To set up the printer on your workstation, you most likely will use the Point and Print option for Windows printing. This option allows you to click and drag a printer to the PRINTERS folder and run a shorter version of the Add Printer Wizard, which will set up the printer icon and set up the right drivers on your machine automatically. Follow these steps:

1. Browse to the computer that hosts the printer you want to set up and double-click the computer name. You'll see a window with a list of resources the computer is hosting.

2. Open up the PRINTERS folder (choose Start ➢ Settings ➢ Printers). Arrange these windows so you can see both at the same time (Figure 16.11).

FIGURE 16.11 Preparing for the Point-and-Print process

3. To start the Add Printer Wizard, drag the printer you want to set up from the list of resources the computer is hosting to the Printers window. As soon as you release the mouse button, you will see the wizard start, and it will display the window shown in Figure 16.12.

FIGURE 16.12 Starting the Add Printer Wizard

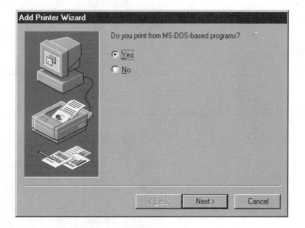

4. The wizard will ask you a series of questions that will help you to config-ure the printer. The first question it will ask you is "Do you print from MS-DOS–based programs?" The reasoning behind this question is similar to the reason we map drive letters. Most older DOS programs (and to a lesser extent, Windows programs) don't understand the UNC path syntax for access to a shared resource. Instead, they understand a name for a local hardware resource (like LPT1, for the first local parallel port). So, you must point a local printer port name out to the network in a process known as capturing. If you need to capture a printer port, answer "Yes"

to this question; otherwise leave it set to the default ("No"). For our example, click Yes and click Next to move to the next step of the wizard.

5. The next step in the Add Printer Wizard is to capture the printer port, assuming you chose Yes in the preceding step. If you did, you will see the screen in Figure 16.13. This screen allows you to capture a printer port so that DOS programs can print to the network printer. Click the Capture Printer Port button to bring up the screen (shown in Figure 16.14) that allows you to choose which local port you want to capture.

FIGURE 16.13 Capturing a printer port

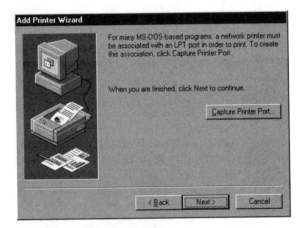

FIGURE 16.14 Picking which local port to capture

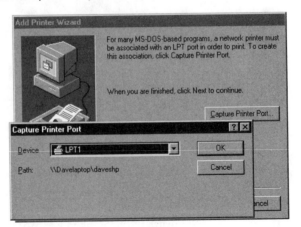

6. From the drop-down list shown, choose the local port you want to capture (any port from LPT1 to LPT9). Remember two things about capturing ports:

   - The port doesn't physically have to be installed in your computer in order to be captured. The capture process just associates a port name with a shared printer.

   - If the port you capture *is* installed in your computer and you capture it, all print jobs sent to that port name will be sent to the network printer, not out the local port (which is the way it is supposed to work). If you have a printer attached to that port, you would not be able to print to it.

7. Pick the LPT port you want to capture and click OK to accept the choice and return to the wizard screen. Then, click Next to continue running the wizard.

8. The next step is to give the printer instance a name. You should give a network printer a name that reflects what kind of printer it is and which machine is hosting it. In this example, the printer is labeled HP LaserJet III (the default name of the driver), but it could have been named Laser on Bob's PC. Type in the name that makes sense to you in the screen that the wizard presents (Figure 16.15). You also have the choice as to whether or not you want the printer to be the default printer that gets used by all Windows applications.

FIGURE 16.15   Naming the printer

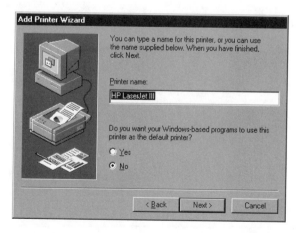

From here on, printer installation is exactly the same as installing a local printer. We covered this earlier, so we won't discuss it further here.

Installing and Configuring Peripheral Drivers

In order to make Windows recognize a particular piece of hardware, you must install a driver for it. Each driver is written for the hardware it supports. Not only do you need to install the driver for it, it must be the correct driver. It *is* possible to install a similar driver that may function but is not the correct one. In this section, you will learn how to install a piece of hardware in both Windows 9*x* and 2000.

Windows 95/98

Adding new hardware devices is very simple under Windows. When you start Windows after installing a new hardware device, it will normally detect the new device using Plug and Play and automatically install the software for it. If not, you need to run the Add New Hardware Wizard.

To start adding the new device, double-click the My Computer icon. Then double-click the Control Panel. To start the wizard, double-click Add New Hardware icon in the Control Panel window (Figure 16.16).

FIGURE 16.16 The Control Panel window

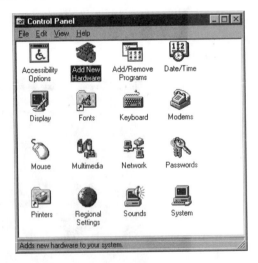

 You can also bring up this window by choosing clicking the Start ➢ Settings ➢ Control Panel.

Once you have started the Add New Hardware Wizard, you will see a screen similar to the one in Figure 16.17. This is the introduction to the wizard. To start the configuration of the new hardware, click Next.

FIGURE 16.17 Add New Hardware Wizard

The next screen that is presented (Figure 16.18) allows you to select whether the wizard will search for the hardware. If you choose Yes, then in the next step, Windows will search for the hardware and install the drivers for it automatically. It is the easiest method (especially if the hardware is Plug and Play compliant) and is the least complex. If you choose No, the wizard will present a screen from which you will have to select the type, brand, and settings for the new hardware. For our example, choose Yes and click Next.

FIGURE 16.18 Telling Windows to search for the new hardware

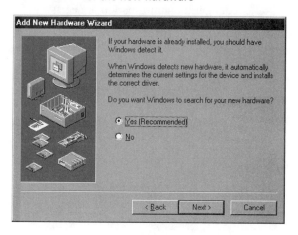

The next screen will tell you that Windows is ready to search for the new hardware. To begin the detection, click Next again. Windows will make an intensive scan of the hardware (you should notice that the hard disk light will be on almost constantly and you will hear the hard disk thrashing away during the detection). During this scan, you will see a progress bar at the bottom of the screen (Figure 16.19) that indicates Windows's progress with the detection. You can stop the detection at any time by clicking the Cancel button.

FIGURE 16.19   Detecting new hardware

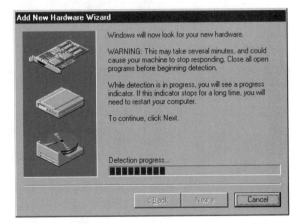

When the progress indicator gets all the way to the right, Windows will tell you that it found some hardware that it can install (Figure 16.20). You can see which hardware it found by clicking the Details button. To finish the setup of the new hardware, click the Finish button. Windows will copy the drivers from the installation disks or CD for the device. Once it has done that, it may ask you for configuration information, if necessary. To finish the hardware setup, it will ask you to reboot Windows so that the changes take effect and Windows can recognize (and use) the new hardware.

FIGURE 16.20 Finishing new hardware installation

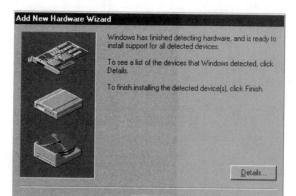

Windows 2000

Again, just like adding printers, there are very few differences between adding a new piece of hardware in Windows 9x and in Windows 2000. However subtle the differences, though, they are important to note. First, Windows 2000 relies very heavily on Plug and Play. Installing a piece of hardware in a Windows 2000 computer basically involves physically installing the device, booting the computer, and letting Windows 2000 automatically install the driver for that device. If it can't find the driver, it will ask you for the location. Additionally, the screens have the Windows 2000 "look and feel." Finally, you can use the Add New Hardware Wizard to both add new hardware and update drivers for existing hardware.

Just as with Windows 9x, you can begin the by double-clicking the Add New Hardware icon (found in Start ➤ Settings ➤ Control Panel). This will start the Add New Hardware Wizard, which is similar to the one in Windows 9x. However, after clicking Next past the first screen, you will be asked if you want to either add/troubleshoot a device or uninstall/unplug a device. The latter choice will allow you to prepare Windows to completely remove a device or temporarily disable a device. To continue adding a hardware device, choose Add/Troubleshoot a Device and click Next.

At this point, Windows 2000 will try to search for any uninstalled Plug and Play devices. It will also search for a list of currently installed devices that may or may not need new drivers. The wizard will then present you with a list of devices so that you can choose which device you want to install a new driver for (either a new device or an existing one), as shown in Figure 16.21. If you are installing a new device, choose Add a New Device. If you are updating a driver for an existing device, choose the device you want to update the driver for. When you've made your choice, click Next.

FIGURE 16.21   Choosing a device to install a driver for

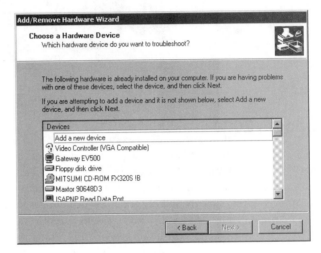

From this point on, the Add New Hardware Wizard works almost exactly the same as the Windows 9x wizard. You choose whether you want Windows to search for the hardware or whether you'll select from a list. The wizard will then install the hardware driver or ask you for the appropriate driver and the installation will be finished.

One final difference between installing new hardware on 9x and installing it on 2000 is that, if the device driver can't be found or won't install correctly, Windows 2000 will start a troubleshooting wizard to help you finish installing the new hardware.

Summary

In this chapter, you learned how to use and configure additional peripherals. A peripheral is any device that is not part of the computer itself. Examples of peripherals include modems, printers, scanners, and so on.

In the first section of this chapter, you learned about the most popular methods of connecting peripherals to host computers. These methods include serial, parallel, USB, FireWire, and SCSI. We discussed the advantages and disadvantages of each connection method as well as the best application for each.

In the final section, you learned about the proper methods of setting up Windows printing for both locally connected printers and network-connected printers. We showed you how to use the Add Printer Wizard to connect both of these types of printers as well as how to add printer drivers and configure printing properties for each type of printer.

Key Terms

Before you take the exam, be certain you are familiar with the following terms:

FireWire

IEEE-1394

Small Computer System Interface (SCSI)

Universal Serial Bus (USB)

Review Questions

1. You've successfully completed an upgrade to Windows 2000 Professional. Several days later, you add your old printer, using the driver that originally came with it. Now the printer, which has never had a problem, won't print. What do you need to do to fix the problem?

   A. Older printers are often not compatible with Windows 2000. You may need to replace the printer.

   B. Your printer driver is out-of-date. Contact the vendor or visit its Web site for an updated driver.

   C. Uninstall, then reinstall the printer using the original driver.

   D. None of the above.

2. You've set up a network printer. However, you cannot print from your DOS-based programs. What did you do wrong during printer setup?

   A. Nothing. You cannot print from DOS-based programs within Windows 2000.

   B. You have an incorrect printer driver and need an update.

   C. During setup, you did not "capture" the printer port. Rerun the Add Printer Wizard and make the appropriate changes.

   D. Run the Add Printer Wizard again and accept all defaults.

3. When you print in Windows 2000, you cannot perform any other task until the print job is complete. What can you do?

   A. Your printer driver is corrupt. Replace it.

   B. There is nothing you can do. That is the normal printing mode.

   C. Change your printer settings back to the default mode.

   D. Your computer needs more RAM.

4. Which of the following methods correctly adds new hardware to a Windows 9x system if Plug and Play does not work? (Select all that apply.)

   A. Choose Start ➤ Settings ➤ Control Panel and then click the Add New Hardware icon.

   B. Exit to DOS and use the software that came with the device to run the installation.

   C. If Plug and Play does not work, there is no way to get the hardware working in the Windows 9x environment.

   D. On the desktop, double-click the My Computer icon, double-click the Control Panel icon, then double-click the Add New Hardware icon.

5. The most popular connection method is serial. Which of the following are characteristics of a serial connection? (Select all that apply.)

A. Transfer rate of one data bit at a time.

B. Maximum speed of 128Kbps.

C. Though popular, it is expensive to manufacture.

D. All of the above.

6. Which of the following is a difference between installing new hardware on a Windows 9x system versus a Windows 2000 system?

A. There is no difference.

B. With Windows 9x, if the proper device driver cannot be found or won't install properly, a troubleshooting wizard helps finish the task.

C. With Windows 2000, if the proper device driver cannot be found or won't install properly, a troubleshooting wizard helps finish the task.

D. With Windows 9x, if the proper device driver cannot be found or won't install properly, then the device cannot be installed at all.

7. The Small Computer System Interface (commonly known as SCSI) is yet another method for connecting peripherals. Which of the following are characteristics of SCSI? (Select all that apply.)

A. SCSI is the best choice for high-speed connectivity.

B. SCSI, when properly linked, can support up to 127 peripheral devices.

C. SCSI can transfer either 16 or 32 bits of data at a time.

D. SCSI can be added to desktop systems with an expansion card.

8. Which of the following are peripheral connection methods for Windows 9x and Windows 2000? (Select all that apply.)

A. Parallel

B. Serial

C. SCSI

D. USB

E. IEEE 1394

9. You're using your USB port for your scanner. What is the preferred method for swapping your scanner with a previously configured digital camera?

   A. Shut the computer down, disconnect the scanner, connect the digital camera, and then turn your computer back on.

   B. With USB, you can hot-swap devices. Therefore, just disconnect the scanner, hook up the digital camera, and you're done.

   C. Turn off the scanner and disconnect it. Connect the digital camera. Reboot. You can now use your digital camera.

   D. None of the above. Digital cameras will not work on a USB port.

10. Which of the following are accepted methods for initiating the Add Printer Wizard (APW, for short)? (Select all that apply.)

    A. Choose Start ➢ Settings ➢ Printers and double-click the Add Printer icon.

    B. Type **APW.EXE** at the DOS prompt.

    C. Double-click the Printers icon in the Control Panel and double-click the Add Printer icon.

    D. Choose Start ➢ Run, type **APW.EXE**, and click OK.

11. Serial connections are very popular. One of the most popular applications of a serial connection is _____ .

    A. Synchronize two data sources

    B. Link multiple peripherals

    C. Transfer large amounts of data at high speeds

    D. All of the above

12. What is the final step in setting up a newly installed printer?

    A. Configure the port settings.

    B. Create a unique printer identification name.

    C. Configure the Graphics setting.

    D. Print a test page.

13. FireWire, or IEEE 1394, is a relatively new peripheral connection method. What is FireWire used for?

    A. It is primarily used to download large video files to a PC.

    B. It is the preferred method for linking multiple peripherals.

    C. It provides direct access to the Internet, bypassing the modem.

    D. It is used to activate explosives via computer.

14. A previously installed Windows *9x* printer needs to be modified for higher resolution. How can this be accomplished?

    A. Uninstall, then reinstall the printer, making your changes during the installation process.

    B. Right-click the printer icon, choose Properties, click the Graphics tab, and make your changes.

    C. Right-click the printer icon, choose Change Graphics, and make your changes.

    D. Right-click the printer icon, choose Properties, click Change Graphics, click Resolution, and make your changes.

15. One of the most popular connection methods is parallel. Which of the following are characteristics of a parallel connection? (Select all that apply.)

    A. Transfer rate of 8 data bits at a time

    B. Usually used to connect printers

    C. New parallel ports can connect scanners and Zip drives

    D. Can connect multiple devices at the same time

16. Plug and Play includes a troubleshooting wizard on which operating system?

    A. Windows 95

    B. Windows 98

    C. Windows NT

    D. Windows 2000

17. Which icon will allow you to manage print jobs as well as printer properties?

    A. PRINTERS folder

    B. Printer icon in PRINTERS folder

    C. Printer icon in System Tray

    D. Spooler control panel

18. In addition to the Add Printer Wizard, which other method(s) can be used to configure a printer? (Choose all that apply.)

    A. Copy the new driver to the `C:\WINDOWS\PRINTERS` directory

    B. INSTALL on manufacturer's disk

    C. PSETUP in `C:\WINDOWS` directory

    D. SETUP on manufacturer's disk

    E. Choose all that apply

19. The Universal Serial Bus, or USB, is a relatively new connection device. Which of the following are characteristics of USB?

   A. Can connect a maximum of 127 external devices

   B. Supports printers, scanners, joysticks, digital cameras, and mice

   C. Faster data transfer rate than a serial port

   D. All of the above

20. You've installed a printer for network use, but no one on the network is able to print to it. Which of the following would be a viable solution to fixing the problem?

   A. Right-click the Printer icon, click Network, and configure the printer as needed.

   B. Right-click the Printer icon, click Properties, click the Sharing tab, and configure the printer as needed.

   C. Open the Control Panel, double-click the Printer icon, click Network, and configure the printer as needed.

   D. Only a reinstall of the printer will enable it for network use.

Answers to Review Questions

1. B. When installing a printer, you must always be sure to have an updated driver. Many printing problems originate with out-of-date printer drivers.

2. C. During setup, you must point a local printer port name out to the network. This process is known as capturing. During normal setup, the default to capture a printer port is No. If the Add Printer Wizard is run again and the answer to the Capture Printer Port question is changed to Yes, your printer should then be able to print from DOS-based programs.

3. C. The default setting for printing enables a program called SPOOL32.EXE. That program allows your printing to be done in the background while you can work on other tasks. Spool Print Jobs is a property of most printers.

4. A, D. Plug and Play will automatically detect new hardware and install the proper software. If it is not successful, the Add New Hardware program can be used. That program can be accessed by the methods indicated in answers A and D.

5. A, B. Serial connections have a transfer rate of one data bit at a time, a maximum speed of 128Kbps, and are very inexpensive to manufacture.

6. C. One major difference between installing new hardware on a Windows 9x system versus a Windows 2000 system is that, if the proper device driver cannot be found or won't install properly, a Windows 2000 troubleshooting wizard helps to finish the task.

7. A, C, D. SCSI offers an array of benefits, including high speeds, 16- or 32-bit data transfer rates, and ease of use via an expansion card, but it cannot support 127 peripheral devices. Only USB can do that.

8. A, B, C, D, E. All of the options are peripheral connection methods.

9. B. With USB, you can hot-swap devices. With the PC powered on, disconnect the scanner from the USB cable and connect the cable to the digital camera. There is no need to shut the computer down or reboot.

10. A, C. As with most functions within Windows, there is more than one way to accomplish a task. To initiate the Add Printer Wizard, options A and C are equally correct.

11. A. Serial connections are popular because they are so inexpensive to manufacture. But their transfer rate is slow and only one peripheral can be connected to a serial port. They are, however, an excellent way to synchronize two data sources.

12. D. Option D, print a test page, is the final step in setting up a new printer.

13. A. With a maximum data transfer rate of 400MB per second, FireWire is primarily used to download large video files.

14. B. It is relatively easy to make changes to installed printers. Right-clicking the printer icon and choosing Properties opens a series of printer property pages and functions. Thus, B is the correct answer.

15. A, B, C. Parallel connections have a transfer rate of 8 data bits, they are primarily used to connect printers, and new parallel ports can connect other devices. However, they can connect only one device at a time.

16. D. When Plug and Play does not work, Windows 2000 has a troubleshooting wizard to assist the user. Also, the Add New Hardware Wizard in Windows 2000 can be used to add new hardware and update drivers for existing hardware.

17. C. While a document is printing, a printer icon will appear in the System Tray. By double-clicking it, you can open it and manage your print jobs as well as the printer properties from menus within it.

18. B, D. There are printers for which the APW does not work. In such instances, you will need to run SETUP or INSTALL from the vendor printer disk to install the appropriate printing software.

19. D. The Universal Serial Bus (USB) connects up to 127 external devices, supports most peripherals (including printers, scanners, digital cameras, mice, etc), and provides a high data transfer rate.

20. B. One of the tabs on the printer property page is Sharing. That tab is used to share the printer on the network. The Sharing function can be accessed as indicated in option B.

Preventative Maintenance

THE FOLLOWING OBJECTIVES ARE COVERED IN THIS CHAPTER:

✓ **2.3 Identify the basic system boot sequences and boot methods, including the steps to create an emergency boot disk with utilities installed for Windows 9*x*, Windows NT, and Windows 2000.**

Content may include the following:

- Startup disk
- Safe Mode
- MS-DOS mode
- NTLDR (NT Loader), BOOT.INI
- Files required to boot
- Creating emergency repair disk (ERD)

✓ **3.2 Recognize common problems and determine how to resolve them.**

Content may include the following:

- Eliciting problem symptoms from customers
- Having customer reproduce error as part of the diagnostic process
- Identifying recent changes to the computer environment from the user
- Troubleshooting Windows-specific printing problems
  - Print spool is stalled
  - Incorrect/incompatible driver for print
  - Incorrect parameter

Other Common problems

- General Protection Faults
- Illegal operation
- Invalid working directory
- System lock up

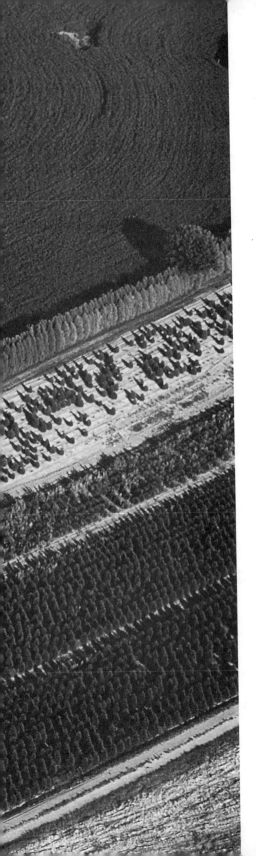

- Option (Sound card, modem, input device) or will not function
- Application will not start or load
- Cannot log on to network (option—NIC not functioning)
- TSR (Terminate Stay Resident) programs and virus
- Applications don't install
- Network connection

Viruses and virus types

- What they are
- Sources (floppy, e-mails, etc.)
- How to determine presence

Because of their very nature, computers can and do fail. *Preventative maintenance* involves performing certain practices on a computer so that the computer will function reliably and not fail as often.

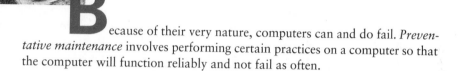For complete coverage of objective 2.3, please also see Chapters 13 and 14. For complete coverage of objective 3.2, please also see Chapter 19.

Thankfully, Microsoft has included a few pieces of software with their operating systems that allow us to perform preventative maintenance fairly easily. No fuss, no muss. The three preventative maintenance procedures we're going to discuss in this chapter are:

- Backing up your data
- Guarding against virus attacks
- Creating and using an emergency disk

With these procedures, you should be able to recover most of the common problems.

Backing Up Your Data

A *backup* is a duplicate copy of all the files and software on your hard disk. This copy is usually stored in a safe place (like a safe) in case of a system failure. When a system failure occurs, the backup can be copied back onto the system, restoring the system to the state it was in at the time of the last backup. This process of restoring the system is known as a *restore*.

Most backups are done the same way: select what you want to back up, then select where you want to back up to, then finally begin the backup. The files and directories you want to back up (and, subsequently, the drive they are stored on) are called the *backup source*. The device that you are backing up to is called the *backup target*. Once you have selected these items, some backup software will let you save these selections in a file known as a *backup set* so that you can reselect them later for restore by simply retrieving the backup set file from the backup media.

Backup Devices

There are several pieces of backup hardware that are currently available. You can back up your information to magnetic tape, Digital Audio Tape (DAT), Digital Linear Tape (DLT), optical disk, removable hard disk, and many other removable media. The key here is that all of these media can be removed from the drive and stored in a safe place.

It's a common misconception that if you back up your data to a second, non-removable hard disk in your computer, your data is safe. But what happens if your computer is in a fire? What happens is that you lose your data. On the other hand, if the backup media are stored in a fireproof safe, you can purchase a new computer (assuming you have insurance), restore the data from the backup, and be working again in a short time.

Of all the backup media that are available, the most popular is magnetic tape (including reel-to-reel, DAT, DLT, and any backup system that uses a magnetic tape in a cartridge). There are a few reasons it is the most popular:

- First, it's inexpensive. Magnetic tape costs around $.01 to $.02 per MB (around $30 to $40 to back up 2GB), and the price is going down.

- Second, magnetic tapes are small and each holds several hundred MB of data.

- Finally, it's reliable. Magnetic tape is a proven technology that has been around for several years and will continue to expand in capacity and speed in the future.

Backup Types

There are four major types of backup that most backup software will use when backing up files. The four types are Full, Differential, Incremental, and Custom. Each type differs in the amount that it backs up, the time it takes to perform the backup and the time it takes to restore the system to its pre-backup condition.

Full Backup

A Full backup, as its name suggests, backs up everything on the entire disk at once. It simply copies everything from the disk being backed up to the backup device. The backup takes a long time to perform (relative to the other types of backup), but the advantage is that the backup (and, subsequently, the restore) will use only one tape (assuming the tape capacity is large enough to handle backing up the hard disk in one shot).

Full backups are most often performed on systems that require that there be very little down time. Insurance computer systems are one such example. Their administrators will perform a Full backup every night so that if there is a failure, the system can be brought up quickly and the data will be as current as the time of the last backup.

Differential

A Differential backup backs up the files on a disk that have changed since the last Full backup, regardless of whether a Differential or Incremental backup has been done since the last Full backup. The Full backup is done usually once a week (i.e., on Friday) and copies all the files from the disk to the backup device. The Differential backup is done every day.

The size of a Differential backup increases every day following the Full backup. For example, if you do a Full backup on Friday night, then start your Differential backups on Monday, the Monday Differential tape will only have a small amount of information on it. When you get to Thursday, the Thursday tape will have all of the information on the disk that has changed since last Friday (including Monday, Tuesday, Wednesday, and Thursday's information).

The advantage to a Differential backup style is that during the week, the backups don't take very long (although the time it takes to back up increases as the week goes on). In addition, you don't have to buy many backup tapes or media. You can use the same backup media you use for the Differential backup (not the one for the Full backup) over and over again each day.

When you restore from a Differential backup, you will need two tapes: the Full backup from the previous week and the current Differential backup. You will need to restore the Full backup first, then restore the Differential backup to restore the changes made since the last Full backup.

Incremental

What kind of backup strategy would you use with a terabyte (1,024 gigabytes) of data? A Full backup every day would be impractical because it would take too long and use several tapes. A Differential backup would use even more tapes. Given these limitations, an Incremental backup would be the best choice.

The Incremental backup works similarly to the Differential backup but uses fewer tapes in a large backup situation. An Incremental backup does a Full backup once a week, then the backup software backs up all the files that have changed since the *previous* backup (not necessarily the last *Full* backup). Each day the backup software backs up a different amount of data, depending on the amount of data that was created that day.

The upside to the Incremental backup is that only the files that have changed that day will be backed up. If only three files changed today, then only three files will be backed up. Incremental backups tend to be very quick. Additionally, there is very little wasted effort because you aren't backing up files that haven't changed since you last backed them up. The downside to Incremental backups is the number of tapes needed for a restore. To restore from an Incremental backup, you need the last Full backup tape and all the Incremental backup tapes from the day of the failure back to the day of the last Full backup.

Custom

The last type of backup that is performed is the Custom backup. A Custom backup is any combination of the above three types. A Custom backup involves selecting the files you want backed up as well as when you want them backed up. Most backup software programs have the ability to perform this type of backup. An example of a time when you might need to perform a Custom backup is the end of the year. Accountants will need to back up the previous year's accounting data before finishing the year's accounting, just in case they make any mistakes and need to restore and start over.

And Now for the Real World...

There are some computer systems that can't afford any "down time" (i.e., banking, flight control, and certain high-volume sales systems). These systems back up all the data in real time and are called "high-availability data solutions." They will use various techniques to ensure that as soon as the data is written to disk, another copy is written to a second disk. If the system goes down, the backup system takes over automatically.

As you can imagine, these systems are usually impractical for home users, but they are found quite commonly in the network world on servers.

Backing Up in MS-DOS: Using MSBACKUP.EXE

Because of the importance of backing up your data, there are many different backup programs to choose from. Microsoft has ensured that you will have one to use by including one with each of its major operating systems: DOS, Windows 3.*x* and Windows 95 (a backup utility is also included with Windows 98, NT, and 2000).

 We will assume that you will be backing up to floppy for these examples, but it should be noted that most computers can be fitted with tape drives that can be used by some of these programs (the Windows 9*x*/NT/2000 Backup, for example). If you have a tape drive in your computer and want to use the following guidelines to back up your data, just ignore the steps where you need to swap disks.

The MS-DOS backup program MSBACKUP is a very simple, very powerful program. It can be run in either command line mode or with a menu-driven interface. In either mode it can copy files to any DOS device (including floppy drives and redirected network drives—tape drives aren't supported). It can perform any of the types of backups including Full, Incremental, and Differential (and Custom is an option if you select specific files to back up).

MSBACKUP uses special settings files called SET files to store the settings for how it should run. The default SET file is called DEFAULT.SET and, if unmodified by the user, will allow a user to back up their entire hard drive by simply starting the backup program and pressing *B* for Backup and *S* for Start Backup.

To start MSBACKUP, simply type **C:\>MSBACKUP** at the DOS command line and press Enter. MSBACKUP will start and present you with a menu giving you five choices: Backup, Restore, Compare, Configure, or Quit. Because the A+ Exam doesn't have too many questions about this menu, we'll just give a summary of each of these options.

If you have never run MSBACKUP before, it will present you with a screen that asks you to configure it. You will need to enter some settings and test MSBACKUP to make sure that backups are reliable.

Configure

Because MSBACKUP is a DOS program, you may need to configure the hardware it's using. When you select the Configure button from the main menu, you will be presented with a screen where you can configure the video settings (like what resolution and which colors you want to use), mouse settings (important if you want the mouse to work properly in this program), and which backup devices MS Backup is going to use (not really necessarily if you are backing up to floppy).

The final option on this screen is the Compatibility Test. This test ensures that your system is able to backup files reliably. The test is automated (you must specify which drive you are using to back up to), but you will need to have a disk available so that it can do a test backup. Click the button to perform this compatibility test. If it finishes with no errors, you can begin your backup.

You cannot perform a backup until you run a compatibility test!

Backup

To use the Backup option:

1. Click the Backup button (assuming your mouse is set up to work under DOS) or type **B**. When you select this option, a menu will appear.

2. At the top of this menu, you will see a file name under "Setup File." This is the name of the SET file that MSBACKUP gets its settings from. If you

have saved previously configured settings, choose this option and pick the SET file that contains the details of how backup should run. Otherwise, leave this option set to DEFAULT.SET.

3. You can then click the Backup From box and choose which files you want to back up. Click the drive(s) that you want to back up or use the Select Files button underneath this window to pick specific files you want to back up. Remember that the more you choose to back up, the longer the backup will take and the more media (disks) you will use.

4. Choose the drop-down list under Backup To to pick which drive letter you want to back the files up to. If you pick a floppy disk drive (A or B in most systems), MSBACKUP will copy as many files as it can to the disk, then ask for a new, blank disk when it is full.

As you remove disks or other backup media that are full from a drive, label them immediately. That way you won't lose them or get them out of order.

5. After you have chosen where you are backing up to, you should choose whether to do a Full, Differential, or Incremental backup. (Custom backups simply involve changing the settings for any of the other types.) The default type is Full, but you can change this option by clicking on the drop-down menu and selecting Differential or Incremental.

6. When you have finished setting up the backup, you can click Start Backup. During the backup, MSBACKUP will display how long the backup will take, how many disks it will take, and how much data is being backed up. When the backup is complete, it will display a screen telling you all the statistics about the backup that was performed, including any files that were skipped and the speed (in KB per minute) at which the backup took place.

Compare

Once you have performed a backup, you should use the Compare option on the MS Backup main menu to compare the files you just backed up to the originals that are currently on the disk. This option, when selected, will allow you to perform one of two operations:

- You can check the integrity of the current backup.
- You can check to see how many files have changed on your computer since the backup was performed.

The second of these two operations is useful before performing an Incremental or Differential backup because it will give you an idea of how many files have changed and thus of how many will be backed up during either an Incremental or Differential.

Restore

Hopefully, you will never need to restore. If you have to restore, that usually means there was a disk failure of some kind and you've lost some (or all) of your data. Before you can restore, you must have DOS, as well as the MSBACKUP program installed on the computer. Then, follow these steps:

1. Run MSBACKUP and select Main ➤ Restore.

2. Place the backup media that contains the files you want restored into its appropriate drive.

3. Choose the location you want to restore from by clicking Restore From and choosing the drive letter of the disk you are restoring from.

4. Select Restore To ➤ Original Locations so that the files will be restored along with the directories they came from.

5. Next, you *must* choose which files to restore (you can't proceed with the restore otherwise):

   - To restore the entire backup of the drive, just make sure that [-C-] All Files is selected in the Restore Files window.

   - If you want to restore a particular file or files, choose Select Files and pick the file(s) you want to restore.

6. When you are finished with your selections, click the Start Restore button to begin the restoration. During the restoration, MS Backup will ask you for several disks, in the same order it did when you performed the backup. Insert each disk when MS Backup asks for it.

When the restore is finished, you will see a status screen informing you of how long it took and how many files were restored.

Quit

Select this option when you have finished performing your backup, configure, or restore. When selected, this option will exit the program and leave you at a DOS prompt.

Backing Up in Windows 3.x: Using MWBACKUP.EXE

Now that we have discussed the MSBACKUP program for DOS, we need to discuss the available, built-in backup for Windows 3.x. There is a Windows version of MSBACKUP.EXE that comes with MS-DOS. It is called MWBACKUP.EXE, and it runs basically the same as the MS-DOS version, except all screens now have the Windows "look and feel" to them. Additionally, the main menu has been replaced by a menu bar at the top of the Microsoft Backup window. The four buttons are the same choices you have with the DOS version, and they perform the same functions.

Using the Microsoft Backup for Windows is basically the same as using the DOS version. This is mainly because they are based on the same backup engine. Generally speaking, you can follow the same steps to back up with Microsoft Backup for Windows that you did with MSBACKUP.EXE for DOS. The only difference is that you will see Windows windows and menus instead of DOS windows and menus.

Backing Up in Windows 95: Using Backup for Windows 95

The third backup utility we're going to discuss is Microsoft Backup for Windows 95. It is basically the old Microsoft Backup, with a new interface and a few new features. It can support backing up to both floppies and other types of backup devices (like tape drives). However, the types of tape drives it can use are somewhat limited. Table 17.1 lists the tape drives that are compatible with Windows 95 and the ones that aren't.

TABLE 17.1 Windows 95 Backup Tape Drive Compatibility Chart

Tape Drive	Compatible
Archive (any)	No
QIC 40	Yes
QIC 80	Yes
QIC 3010	Yes
QIC 40, 80, and 3010	Yes
Irwin (any)	No
Mountain (any)	No
QIC Wide	No
QIC 3020	No
SCSI tape drives (any)	No
Summit (any)	No
Travan (any)	No
Wangtek (QIC 40, 80, and 3010)	Yes

As you can see, basically only a QIC 40, 80, or 3010 tape drive will really work properly with Backup for Windows 95 (as well as any floppy drive).

Installing Windows 95 Backup

In Windows 95, Backup can sometimes be found under Start ➤ Programs ➤ Accessories ➤ System Tools. I say "sometimes" because it is not installed by default. You must specifically install it (either after Windows 95 has been installed or during a custom install) in order to use it.

To install Backup after Windows 95 has been installed, follow these steps:

1. Proceed to the Windows 95 Control Panel under Start ➤ Settings ➤ Control Panel.

2. Select Add/Remove Programs and choose the Windows Setup tab (Figure 17.1).

3. Click the check box next to Disk Tools. Doing so will tell the Windows 95 Setup program that you want to install the disk tools (including Backup).

4. To finish the installation, click OK.

Windows will copy the files from the installation location (either floppy or CD-ROM) and update the System Tools program group with an icon for Backup.

FIGURE 17.1   Installing Windows 95 Backup using Add/Remove Programs

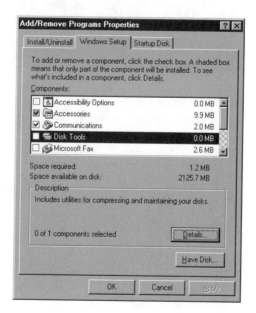

Starting Backup

To start the Windows 95 Backup, choose Start ≻ Programs ≻ Accessories ≻ System Tools ≻ Backup. The first time you run Backup, you will see a screen similar to the one shown in Figure 17.2. As you can see, this window explains, in a very broad sense, how to use Backup to back up your files. If you haven't used Backup before, you might want to click the Help button. This will bring up a Windows Help screen that will allow you to browse and search for help on how to use Backup. Once you have read the help file, or if you already know how to use Backup, you can click OK.

FIGURE 17.2 You will see this screen the first time you run Backup.

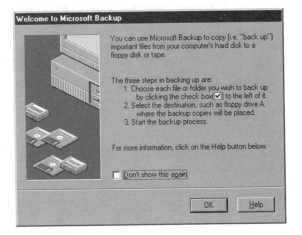

 If you don't want to see this screen again, check the box next to Don't Show This Again.

The nice thing about the Windows 95 Backup program is that it automatically makes a backup set for you, to get you started. This backup set is a full backup of the hard disk, including the Registry files (which some backup programs can't back up). After you click OK to the screen in Figure 17.2, Backup will present you with the screen shown in Figure 17.3, which tells you it has made this backup set and what you can use it for.

 Do not use this backup set (called Full System Backup) to base your Incremental or Differential backups on. They may not work correctly if based on this particular backup set.

FIGURE 17.3 Backup automatically creates a backup set called Full System Backup for you the first time you run it.

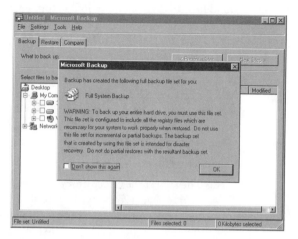

To start using Backup, mark the check box (if you don't want to see this warning again) and click OK.

Layout of Backup

Backup is a rather simple yet powerful program. There are two panes in the main window (Figure 17.4). These two panes work very similarly to the Windows Explorer program. If you double-click on an item in the right pane, it will open and allow you to see what's inside. You can also use the right pane and click on the + signs next to items to "tree them out" and show the directory structure. These two panes allow you to select items to be backed up or restored depending on which tab is selected above. In Figure 17.4, the Backup tab is forward, meaning that selections you make will be for files and directories to be backed up.

FIGURE 17.4 The Windows 95 Backup main window

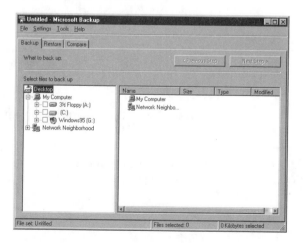

In addition to the two panes, you will notice that there are menus at the top of the screen. The most important of these menus is Help. If you don't understand how to do something in Backup, press the F1 key or choose Help ➤ Help Topics. Doing so will open the Windows 95 Help topics for Backup.

Backing Up Files

Backing up files in Windows 95 Backup works very similarly to the Windows MWBACKUP.EXE program. First you select what you want to back up, then where to want to back up those files and directories to, and then you initiate the backup:

1. To start the backup process, select the Backup tab (if it's not already selected).

2. Then select the directories you want to back up by clicking the check boxes next to them (you may need to click the + sign next to a directory if the subdirectory you want is inside it). If you want to back up the entire C drive, simply click the check box next to the drive icon labeled "C:" When you make a selection, a window will appear that shows you it is counting the files and determining how much space they will take up (Figure 17.5).

FIGURE 17.5 Selecting files to back up

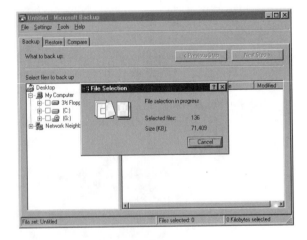

3. Once Backup finishes counting files, you will be able to click the button marked Next Step to start the Backup Wizard.

If you make an icon on your desktop for Backup and you have a preconfigured backup set (SET file), you can start the backup by dragging the SET file onto the Backup icon.

4. The next step in the backup process involves selecting where you want to back the files up to (Figure 17.6).

- If you have a compatible tape drive installed, it will show up in the list on the left. You can then select it as the target device and click Start Backup to begin the backup.

- If you don't have a tape drive (or don't want to use it), you can select one of the floppy drives as the target device by clicking on its name. The name of the device will appear under Selected Device or Location as the device that has been specified as the target. In either case, select the device you want to back up to and click Start Backup to continue.

FIGURE 17.6 Selecting a backup target device

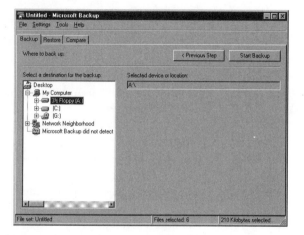

5. Now that you have selected what you want to back up, chosen the target backup device, and begun the backup, Backup will ask you what you want to call the backup set (Figure 17.7). Type in a name that describes what you are backing up. You can use any character except \, /, :, or > in the backup set name. For example, if you are backing up the entire C drive, you might call the backup of the C drive "Full Backup." To start the backup, type the name of the backup set, then click OK.

FIGURE 17.7 Entering a backup set name

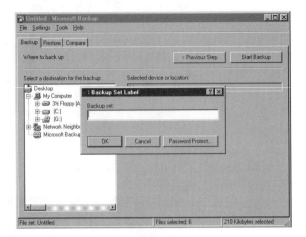

You can protect sensitive backup data by entering a password for the backup set. Simply click the Password Protect button to enter a password. This password will be required during the restore process in order to restore the data.

6. As soon as you click OK, Backup will present you with a screen similar to the one shown in Figure 17.8. As you can see, this screen shows you how many files it is backing up, how much space they occupy, and how far along the backup is. When the backup is finished, it will present you with a screen telling you that the backup is finished (Figure 17.9). Click OK to acknowledge this screen, and you will see the backup statistics screen that shows you how many files were backed up, how much data (in KB) was backed up, and how long it took. Click OK and you are finished with the backup.

FIGURE 17.8 Backup progress screen

FIGURE 17.9 The Backup Finished window

Restoring Files

It's amazing: There are some customers I've done work for who have had a computer company come in, set up their backup system for them, and only show them how to change tapes! When the customers have a problem, they feel helpless and don't know if their backup is any good until the computer company comes in and does their restore for them.

In order to ensure that your backups are good, you should perform a test restore every once in a while. If you used the Windows 95 backup program to back up your files, you will need to know how to use it to restore, as well:

1. To begin a restore, run Backup and insert the first disk (or tape) of the backup into the drive.

2. Once Backup is up and running, you must click on the Restore tab to start the restore process.

3. In the screen that appears (Figure 17.10), you will see a list of the possible backup devices on the left. From this list, you must select the device you want to restore from by clicking on it.

4. Once you select a backup device, a list of the backup sets on that device will appear in the right-hand window. To continue, you must select the backup set that contains the files you want to restore and click Next Step.

5. If there is a password on the backup set, Backup will prompt for it. You must enter the correct password before Backup will let you continue with the restore.

FIGURE 17.10   The Windows 95 Backup Restore window

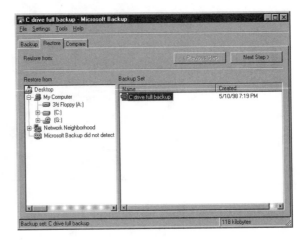

6. The next step in the restore is to select the files and directories you want to restore. The screen shown in Figure 17.11 works the same as the file selection screen for backing up files earlier in the chapter: simply place a check mark next to the file(s) you want to restore and click Start Restore. On the other hand, if you want to restore the whole backup set, click the check box next to the name of the backup set in this window. All files from the backup set will be restored with this selection.

FIGURE 17.11   Selecting files to restore

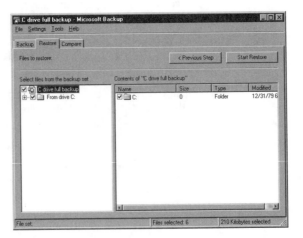

Once you have clicked Start Restore, Backup will review the backup set and count how many files there are to restore. It will then display a status window (very similar to the backup progress window in Figure 17.8) that will show how far along the backup is. (See Figure 17.12.) This screen will display how many files have been restored (out of the total number of files to be restored), how long you have been restoring files, and how much data has been restored (in KB).

FIGURE 17.12   Restore progress screen

When Backup finishes restoring all the files you have selected, it will present you with a summary of the restore (Figure 17.13) detailing how much data was restored and how long it took. Click OK to complete the restore and return to the Backup main screen.

FIGURE 17.13   Restore summary screen

And Now for the Real World...

In most situations, the backup software that comes with most operating systems is adequate. However, you can buy backup software that has more features than the included software. Some of those features include data compression, backup scheduling, and greater hardware device support.

For home computers, the Microsoft backup products are more than adequate. However, for business users, I would recommend looking at products like Norton Backup or Central Point backup. The features they add will make a computer administrator much happier in the end.

Guarding against Virus Attacks

A computer *virus* is a small, deviously genius program that replicates itself to other computers, generally causing the computers to behave abnormally. Generally speaking, a virus's main function is to reproduce. A virus attaches itself to files on a hard disk and modifies the files. When these files are accessed by a program, the virus can "infect" the program with its own code. The program may then, in turn, replicate the virus code to other files and other programs. In this manner, a virus may infect an entire computer.

When an infected file is transferred to another computer (via disk or modem download), the process begins on the other computer. Because of the frequency of downloads from the Internet, viruses can run rampant if left unchecked. For this reason, anti-virus programs were developed. They check files and programs for any program code that shouldn't be there and either eradicate it or prevent the virus from replicating. An anti-virus program is generally run in the background on a computer and examines all the file activity on that computer. When it detects a suspicious activity, it will notify the user of a potential problem and ask them what to do about it. Some anti-virus programs can also make intelligent decisions about what to do as well. The process of running an anti-virus program on a computer is known as *inoculating* the computer against a virus.

For a listing of most of the viruses that are currently out there, refer to Symantec's Anti-Virus Research Center (SARC) at www.symantec.com/avcenter/index.html.

There are two real categories of viruses, benign and malicious. The benign viruses don't do much besides replicate themselves and exist. They may cause the occasional problem, but it is usually an unintentional side effect. Malicious viruses, on the other hand, are designed to destroy things. Once a malicious virus (i.e., the Michelangelo virus) infects your machine, you can usually kiss the contents of your hard drive goodbye.

> **But Where Do I Stick the Needle?**
>
> You may notice that a lot of the language surrounding computer viruses sounds like language we use to discuss human illness. The moniker "virus" was given to these programs because a computer virus functions much like a human virus, and the term helped to anthropomorphize the computer a bit. Somehow, if people can think of a computer as getting "sick," it breaks down the computer phobia that many people have.

Anti-Virus Software

Wouldn't it be nice if Microsoft included an anti-virus program with their operating systems? They did, but only with MS-DOS. MS-DOS 6.22 comes with anti-virus software that lets you detect viruses on your computer as well as clean any infected files. This software is called Microsoft Anti-Virus and has been included with DOS since version 6.0. The same program contains files to allow it to work with Windows.

Using Microsoft Anti-Virus for DOS

To use Microsoft Anti-Virus for DOS:

1. Type **C:\>MSAV** at the MS-DOS command line. From the main menu on the screen that appears, you can check for viruses on any disk drive as well as remove them if any are present. In the lower-right corner of this screen, you can see which drive you are currently scanning for viruses.

2. From the main menu, you have five options: Detect, Detect & Clean, Select New Drive, Options, and Exit. Choose Select New Drive. This option allows you to pick which drive you want to scan. You can select from any of the disk drives you have installed in your system.

You don't necessarily have to scan the drive letters for CD-ROM drives. CD-ROMs are read-only so viruses can't be transferred to them from your machine. On the other hand, you may want to scan them anyway because viruses can be burned onto CDs if the machine doing the burning has a virus.

3. Back at the Main menu, you have two options if you want to see if you have a virus on your computer. You can use the Detect option or the Detect & Clean option. Choose either one and MS Anti-Virus will check the entire disk to find any viruses that it knows about.

   - If it detects a virus and you have Detect & Clean selected, it will present you with a screen that allows you to choose whether or not you want MS Anti-Virus to try and clean the virus from the disk or to ignore it (Figure 17.14).

- If MS Anti-Virus finds a virus and you have Detect selected, the program will simply tell you which files are afflicted.

FIGURE 17.14 MS Anti-Virus finds a virus

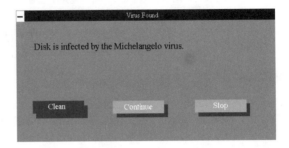

4. When it has finished scanning the disk, MSAV will present you with a list of the disks it has scanned, the file types it has scanned, the number of viruses found on the disks, and the number of files cleaned. If it hasn't found any viruses, select OK to return to the main menu. Then select Exit to quit MSAV. If it did find a virus or two, select OK and return to the main menu, then re-run the Detect & Clean process just to make sure the virus is gone.

There are two options left on the main menu to discuss: Options and Exit. Both are pretty much self-explanatory. The Options menu allows you to change how aggressively MSAV checks for viruses. The Exit menu completely exits you from the MSAV program.

Using Microsoft Anti-Virus for Windows

If you want to use Microsoft Anti-Virus for Windows, simply open the Microsoft Tools program group and double-click the Microsoft Anti-Virus icon. In the window that appears, select which disk (or disks) you want to scan from the list at the left side, then click the Detect button or the Detect & Clean button to start the scanning for viruses.

During detection MSAV will display a screen showing which files it's scanning and the progress. If it finds a file infected with a virus, it will display a warning and give you the same options it does under MS-DOS.

Finally, once MSAV is finished running, it will present you with a status screen that gives you a list of the number of files it scanned, the number that were infected, and the time it took the scan (similar to the status screen for the DOS version).

> ### And Now for the Real World...
>
> There are several commercial anti-virus programs available. One of the best and most widely used is Symantec Anti-Virus (SAM). It has a memory resident component to constantly look for viruses, as well as an executable component for scanning for viruses. SAM is available for Macintosh, Windows 3.*x*, Windows 9*x*, Windows NT, Windows 2000, UNIX, and a few other platforms.
>
> There are also programs like Norton Anti-Virus and Central Point Anti-Virus available if the Symantec product isn't your bag. And you can always just use the ones that come with DOS and Windows (unless you have Windows 95, which doesn't come with one).

Creating and Using an Emergency Disk

What happens when your Windows computer has a problem so severe the computer won't boot? Often times, if the Registry is corrupt, the Windows interface won't come up—not even in Safe Mode. All versions of Windows after 95 come with a utility that allows you to create a disk that can be used to fix Windows. This disk is often called the Windows Emergency Repair Disk (ERD). It contains enough of the Windows startup files to boot the computer. The disk also contains files and utilities to examine (and possibly fix) the machine, utilities like FDISK, SCANDISK, EDIT, ATTRIB, FORMAT, DEBUG, CHKDSK, and UNINSTAL.EXE.

Windows 9*x* Startup Disk

The Windows 9*x* emergency disk is a simple bootable disk that contains some basic utilities, like FDISK, ATTRIB, CHKDSK, DEBUG, EDIT, FORMAT, RESTART, SCANDISK, and SYS. These files are used to correct basic disk problems as well as file boot problems. However, the Windows 9*x* emergency disk CANNOT be used to restore a corrupt Registry (apart from copying the USER.DAT and SYSTEM.DAT files from their backup locations).

Creating a Windows 9*x* Startup Disk

To create a Windows 9*x* startup disk, select Start ➢ Settings ➢ Control Panel, double-click Add/Remove Programs, and select the Startup Disk tab (see Figure 17.15). When you are ready to create a startup disk, insert a blank floppy disk in your A drive and click the Create Disk icon. Windows 9*x* will format the disk and make it bootable (see Figure 17.16). It will then copy the aforementioned utilities to it so that you can use them to fix Windows 9*x*.

When Windows 9x finishes copying files to the disk, remove the disk from the drive, label it "Windows 9x Emergency Startup Disk," and put it in a safe place so that you can get to it easily if there is ever a problem.

FIGURE 17.15 The Startup Disk tab of the Add/Remove Programs control panel

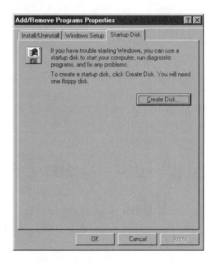

FIGURE 17.16 Creating a new startup disk

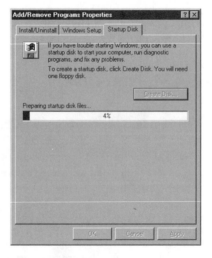

Using the Windows 9x Repair Disk

If you have a problem with your Windows installation and you suspect the disk has a problem, you can boot to the repair disk and try to repair the hard disk.

Simply insert the floppy you made into your floppy drive and boot to it. This startup disk will create a small, virtual disk drive (usually labeled D or something similar) with all the repair utilities installed on it. You can then use these utilities to repair the disk or files. Additionally, since you are booted up to a command line, you can copy new files over old, corrupt ones, if necessary.

Windows NT Emergency Repair Disk (ERD)

When compared to Windows 9*x*, Windows NT is a much more advanced operating system that relies much more on the Registry than any of its predecessors did. The Windows NT Emergency Repair Disk (ERD) is a special disk you can create in Windows NT that can be used to repair the Registry as well as startup files. One important difference between the NT ERD and the Windows 9*x* Startup Disk is that the NT ERD contains only information—it is NOT a bootable disk. You must use some other method of booting NT (usually a startup disk set or the NT installation CD itself).

The Windows NT ERD typically contains the following files:

- System Registry hive (SYSTEM._)
- Software Registry hive (SOFTWARE._)
- The Security Account Manager (SAM) and Security database Registry hives (SAM._ and SECURITY._)
- Default user profile (default._)
- New user profile (ntuser.da_) Windows NT version 4.0 only
- The SETUP.LOG file
- The AUTOEXEC.NT file
- The CONFIG.NT file

These files can be used to restore a Windows NT system to proper operation.

An explanation of these files can be found in Part II, Chapter 14, "Windows 2000."

Creating a Windows NT ERD

To create a Windows NT Emergency Repair Disk, you must use the RDISK utility. This utility is installed with the default installation of Windows NT and by default is installed to the C drive in the WINNT\SYSTEM32 directory. To create the NT ERD using RDISK, follow these steps:

1. Go to Start ➤ Run and type **RDISK**.

2. The graphic below will display. At this screen, click the Create Repair Disk button.

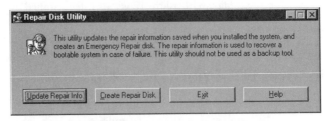

3. RDISK will prompt you to insert a disk. Insert a blank diskette (or one that is okay to format) and click OK.

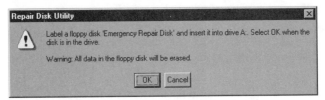

4. RDISK will format the diskette and copy the configuration files to it. RDISK will present progress bars as it does so to let you know how far along the process is.

5. When it has finished creating the disk and copying files to it, it will present a screen telling you that this disk contains security sensitive data and to store it only in a safe location. Click OK to finish creating the disk.

6. When RDISK returns to the initial screen, click the Exit button to exit the program. Remove the diskette from your floppy drive and label it as Windows NT ERD. You will also want to label that disk as being only for that particular Windows NT machine.

Using the Windows NT ERD

To use the ERD, you must first boot the NT computer using either an NT Setup Boot Disk set or the Windows NT CD-ROM. Once you get to the screen that asks you to "Press Enter to install Windows NT or press R to repair a damaged installation", go ahead and press R. Insert the ERD in your floppy drive when prompted by the setup program. Once you have started the emergency repair, you will have four options:

- Inspect Registry files
- Inspect startup environment
- Verify Windows NT system files
- Inspect Boot Sector

Which option(s) you choose will depend on what you suspect is wrong with your computer. To choose an option, navigate to it using the arrow keys and select or clear the check boxes using the Enter key.

Windows 2000

In Windows 2000, if your system won't start and either Safe Mode or the Recovery Console hasn't helped, you may need to use the emergency repair disk option. Unlike previous versions of Windows, the "Create Emergency Repair Disk" option is part of the Windows 2000 backup program. This program includes a wizard to help you create a disk to repair your system. Then, like with Windows NT, you can start the machine with either the startup disks or Setup CD-ROM and use the ERD to restore the system files.

Creating a Windows 2000 ERD

To create an emergency repair disk in Windows 2000, use the following steps:

1. Insert a blank, formatted 1.44MB floppy disk into your floppy disk drive.
2. Select Start ➤ Programs ➤ Accessories ➤ System Tools ➤ Backup.
3. From the Welcome tab, click Emergency Repair Disk.

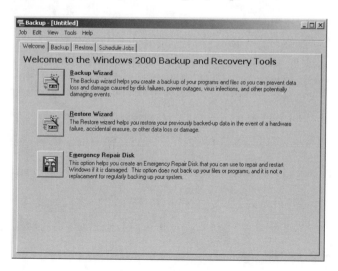

4. Backup prompts you to insert a disk, which you have already done. There is a check box on this screen that, when selected, will put a copy of the Registry in the `C:\WINNT\REPAIR` directory (assuming Windows 2000 was installed to `C:\WINNT`).

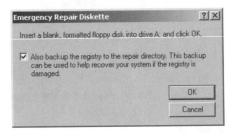

 When you finish installing Windows 2000 successfully, information about the setup is stored in the *systemroot*\Repair folder on the system partition. DO NOT DELETE THIS FOLDER. It contains the information necessary to use the ERD to restore your system to its original state.

5. Click OK to start copying ERD files. Backup will display a progress bar as the files copy.

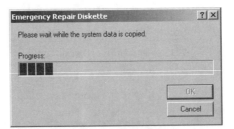

6. When finished, Backup will display a message that the disk was created successfully. Remove the disk, label it as your Windows 2000 ERD and include the name of the computer it was created for. Put it in a safe place so it will be available when your computer has a problem.

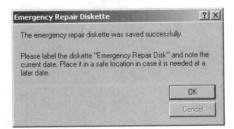

Using a Windows 2000 ERD

If you want to use or test your newly created ERD, follow the following steps:

1. Boot to either the Windows 2000 Startup floppy disks or the Windows 2000 CD-ROM.

2. When prompted, choose the Repair option by pressing R.

3. When prompted, choose the emergency repair process by pressing R. You can additionally choose to either run a manual repair (by selecting M) or a fast repair (by selecting F).

4. Follow the prompts. During this process, the backup files of the C:\WINNT\Repair directory are restored to the setup of Windows 2000.

5. The system will restart automatically when the repair is successfully completed.

Summary

Preventative maintenance is a set of practices that you do to prevent problems from happening (or to prevent them from happening frequently). In this chapter, you learned several preventative maintenance techniques to aid you in keeping your computer functional. Some of these techniques include backing up, anti-virus software use and installation, and making an emergency repair disk.

In this first section, you learned about the proper procedures for protecting your data by copying it to a backup media. You learned about the different methods of backing up (Full, Differential, and Incremental) as well as how to perform these backups using the built-in backup software of DOS, Windows, and Windows 9x.

In addition to protecting your data by backing up, you learned how to protect your computer from malicious programs known as viruses. In the next section, you learned about the built-virus protection programs, how to use them to protect against viruses, and how to eliminate any existing virus.

On occasion, your Windows software will become damaged so badly that it can't be booted. When that happens, you can fixed your damaged Windows installation by booting an Emergency Repair Disk (ERD). This disk will allow you to boot your machine. Additionally, it contains utilities to help you fix these problems. Some of these utilities include FDISK, FORMAT, COPY, and ATTRIB.

Key Terms

Before you take the exam, be certain you are familiar with the following terms:

backup	preventative maintenance
backup set	restore
backup source	target
inoculating	virus

Review Questions

1. Which type of backup copies all files that have changed since the last full backup, regardless if they have been backed up since then?

   A. Full

   B. Incremental

   C. Differential

   D. Custom

2. A computer virus is _____.

   A. A small program

   B. A small living organism

   C. Something that makes you sick

   D. A type of word processing software

3. What is one of the main functions of all viruses?

   A. Party

   B. Reproduce

   C. Destroy files

   D. Make strange things happen to your computer

4. To start the Windows 95 backup program the correct sequence is_____.

   A. Choose Start ➤ Programs ➤ Accessories ➤ System Tools ➤ Backup.

   B. Choose Programs ➤ Start ➤ Accessories ➤ System Tools ➤ Backup.

   C. Choose Backup ➤ Start ➤ Programs ➤ Accessories ➤ System Tools.

   D. Choose Accessories ➤ Start ➤ Programs ➤ System Tools ➤ Backup.

5. If you backed up 60MB of data using the full backup technique, how many tapes are required to restore from a full backup (generally speaking)?

   A. 4

   B. 2

   C. 7

   D. 1

6. What is the name of the executable for Microsoft Backup for DOS?

   A. MSBKUP.EXE

   B. MSBACKUP.EXE

   C. BACKUP.EXE

   D. MWBACKUP.EXE

7. What is the name of the executable for Microsoft Backup for Windows 3.*x*?

    A. MSBKUP.EXE

    B. MSBACKUP.EXE

    C. BACKUP.EXE

    D. MWBACKUP.EXE

8. What kind of backup strategy would you use with a terabyte of data?

    A. Full

    B. Differential

    C. Incremental

    D. Custom

9. What would you type at a DOS command line to start the Microsoft Anti-Virus?

    A. AV

    B. MSANTIVI

    C. MSAV

    D. ANTIVIRU

10. Which program in the Control Panel can be used to create a startup disk?

    A. System

    B. Add New Hardware

    C. Add/Remove Programs

    D. Startup

11. Which type of backup involves selecting the files you want backed up as well as when you want them backed up?

    A. Full

    B. Differential

    C. Incremental

    D. Custom

12. There are several pieces of backup hardware that are currently available. Of the following, which are NOT valid backup hardware?

    A. Digital audio tape

    B. Digital linear tape

    C. Optical disk

    D. Stationary hard disk

13. Which type of backup backs up files on a disk that has changed since the last full backup?

   A. Differential

   B. Incremental

   C. Full

   D. Custom

14. The final option in the Configure Screens menu is _____.

   A. Selecting the type of backup

   B. Selecting the device you are backing up to

   C. The compatibility test

   D. Selecting the backup option

15. The MSBACKUP program in DOS receives its settings from what file?

   A. DAT file

   B. BAK file

   C. TDR file

   D. SET file

16. Once the backup has been performed, what is the next step?

   A. Compare

   B. Restore

   C. Quit

   D. Reboot

17. The main menu of the Microsoft Anti-Virus program has how many options?

   A. One

   B. Two

   C. Five

   D. Three

18. The five options on the main menu for the Microsoft Anti-Virus program contain all of the following except _____.

   A. Detect

   B. Detect & Clean

   C. Erase

   D. Select New drive

   E. Exit

19. The Windows 95 Emergency Repair Disk should contain all of the following files and utilities except:

   A. CHKDSK

   B. UNINSTALL.EXE

   C. REGEDIT

   D. MSAV

20. What is the company most readily identified with anti-virus software?

   A. Symantec

   B. Microsoft

   C. Macintosh

   D. Novell

Answers to Review Questions

1. C. The differential type of backup copies all files that have changed since the last full backup, regardless if they have been backed up since then.

2. A. A computer virus is a small program that, if left unattended, can destroy an entire hard drive and all files on the hard drive.

3. B. One of the main functions of all viruses is to reproduce and that means to duplicate all files on the hard drive, thus taking up all hard drive space. Although some viruses do destroy files, that is not their main function.

4. A. To start the Windows 95 backup program the correct sequence is: Start ➤ Programs ➤ Accessories ➤ System Tools ➤ Backup.

5. D. To back up 60MB of data, one tape is required to restore from a Full backup, as opposed to Differential or Incremental backups, which require multiple tapes.

6. B. The name of the executable for Microsoft Backup for DOS is MSBACKUP.EXE.

7. D. The name of the executable for Microsoft Backup for Windows 3.x is MWBACKUP.EXE.

8. C. The Incremental backup is best suited for this situation because an Incremental only backs up the daily changed information. A Full backup every day would be impractical, because it would take too long and use several tapes. A Differential backup would use even more tapes. Given these situations, an Incremental backup would be the best choice.

9. C. The command to type at a DOS command line to start the Microsoft Anti-Virus is MSAV.

10. C. The Add/Remove Programs in the Control Panel can be used to create a Startup Disk.

11. D. Custom is the type of backup that involves selecting the files you want backed up as well as when you want them backed up.

12. D. Of the items listed, the following are valid backup hardware: digital audio tape, digital linear tape, and optical disk. Because hard disks are more failure-prone than the other types listed, they make a poor backup medium.

13. A. The Differential type of backup backs up files on a disk that have changed since the last Full backup.

14. C. The final option in the Configure Screens menu is the compatibility test.

15. D. The MSBACKUP program in DOS receives its settings from the SET file.

16. A. Once the backup has been performed, the next step is to select the Compare option to compare the files you just backed up to the originals that are currently on the disk. That way, you know if the ones backed up are the same as the ones on the disk and that the backup was successful.

17. C. The main menu of the Microsoft Anti-Virus program has five options.

18. C. The five options on the main menu for the Microsoft Anti-Virus program contain all of the options listed except Erase.

19. D. To have an effective emergency repair disk, the ERD should contain all of the files listed above except MSAV.

20. A. The company most readily identified with anti-virus software is Symantec.

Chapter

18

Configuring Network Software

THE FOLLOWING OBJECTIVES ARE COVERED IN THIS CHAPTER:

✓ **4.1 Identify the networking capabilities of Windows, including procedures for connecting to the network.**

    Content may include the following:

- Protocols
- IPCONFIG.EXE
- WINIPCFG.EXE
- Sharing disk drives
- Sharing print and file services
- Network type and network card
- Installing and Configuring browsers
- Configure OS for network connection

✓ **4.2 Identify concepts and capabilities relating to the Internet and basic procedures for setting up a system for Internet access.**

    Content may include the following:

    Concepts and terminology

- ISP
- TCP/IP
- IPX/SPX
- NetBEUI
- E-mail
- PING.EXE
- HTML
- HTTP://
- FTP
- Domain Names (Web sites)
- Dial-up networking
- TRACERT.EXE

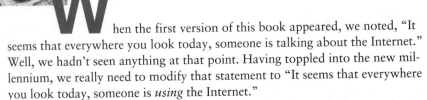

When the first version of this book appeared, we noted, "It seems that everywhere you look today, someone is talking about the Internet." Well, we hadn't seen anything at that point. Having toppled into the new millennium, we really need to modify that statement to "It seems that everywhere you look today, someone is *using* the Internet."

In the space of just a few years, computer networking has gone from an obscure technology to a part of everyday life. Computers are being connected to networks and to each other at a flabbergasting rate, and as a computer professional, one of your primary jobs over the next decade may be to connect your clients' PCs to a network or to manage their access resources on their local network or the Internet.

Just look at the preponderance of Web site addresses on radio and television commercials today. The Web has become a "hot button" that advertising companies love to exploit. But very few people realize what the Internet actually is. Some people think it's a public thoroughfare for information (hence the moniker "information superhighway"). Others believe it to be some kind of new high-tech toy. In reality, however, the *Internet* is just a mesh of interconnected private networks that spans the globe. Whether it is the Internet or a local network at your school or place of work, the basic concepts remain the same. Because of this, to understand the Internet, you really must understand its underlying infrastructures: networks.

Simply put, a *network* is a number of devices (not just computers) connected together for the purpose of sharing resources, such as printers or disk space. Networks provide the physical path upon which computers communicate. When two networks connect to each other, they then form a single larger network called an *internetwork*. The largest of these internetworks is the Internet, which spans the globe and reaches into nearly every major business in the world, as well as into millions of homes. Networking software is written to be used by several people at once and to perform a variety of functions such as e-mail, collaboration, and business management, whereas networking hardware includes the machines that make that collaboration possible.

The A+ exam includes information about basic networking concepts, the Internet, and setting up computers to access both regular business networks and the Internet. We will discuss the installation and configuration of connecting to local area networks (LANs) and to the Internet from both Windows 9*x* and Windows 2000. Luckily, much of this information is similar in both systems, but as always, there are some significant differences.

In the networking software business, there are quite a few major players (like Novell, Microsoft, IBM, and Seagate). However, there are clearly two leaders in the game: Novell (whose company headquarters is in Provo, UT) and Microsoft (headquartered in Redmond, WA). Each company produces several software products for networks, but in the following sections, we'll focus on the different ways that Windows 98 and Windows 2000 connect to the networking operating systems (NOSs) made by these two companies.

Even as Microsoft was creating both clients and servers, other companies were specializing in one or the other. One of the most successful was Novell (www.novell.com), who has been a market leader in providing networking and network management software for the last decade. Novell has developed a NOS called NetWare (currently at version 5.1). NetWare has been the 800-pound gorilla of the networking world for over a decade, but Microsoft's Windows 2000 Server is following on the heels of the immensely successful Windows NT 4 Server and has made substantial gains over the last few years. Both NetWare and Windows 2000 Server are extremely common at this time. Other systems, such as Sun's Solaris or the open-source Linux variants, will not be specifically discussed.

The Internet is still very much a Unix world, though, so in fact our discussion of how to access the Internet is in some ways a look at how to attach to everything that isn't NetWare or Windows.

Except that you have to know what they are, we won't be dealing with the NOS servers themselves. Rather, we will be looking at how Windows 98 and Windows 2000 implement various networking elements and examine their networking capabilities when they're hooked up to other systems. Also, because the A+ exam deals only with the client side of networking (i.e., getting to resources that are already on the network), we won't be dealing extensively with how Windows 98 or Windows 2000 works as a network server. Nonetheless, both operating systems can act as servers, and if you are interested in learning more about this refer to *Network+ Study Guide* (Sybex, 2001).

Microsoft Networking Basics

When MS-DOS was developed, it was designed to be a simple, stand-alone, operating system. To that end, it didn't contain any network software, except SHARE.EXE. SHARE.EXE was designed as an add-on to popular networking software that allowed two users to edit the same file at the same time on a network. Without SHARE.EXE, when a second user tried to open a file that the first user had opened, they got an error message. With SHARE.EXE installed, when the second user tried to open the file, they received a message saying that the file was being used by someone else and offering to provide a copy of the file.

Another aspect of networking with MS-DOS is that DOS can run client software for Novell and Microsoft networks. Most client software for DOS (and Windows 3.*x*) falls into the category of redirection software. This software redirects requests bound for *local resources* out to network resources (Figure 18.1). For example, with network client software installed, you could point a DOS drive letter to some disk space on the network. When you saved a file to that drive letter, you were really saving that file to a server. But, as far as DOS was concerned, it was accessing a local drive letter.

FIGURE 18.1 Network client software redirects local requests to the network.

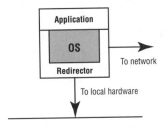

 With *client software*, a computer can connect to a server and access the network resources hosted by that server.

As discussed earlier, Windows 3.1 was little more than a pretty face sitting on top of the MS-DOS OS, and because of this, Windows 3.1 networking was every bit as limited as DOS networking. In an effort to help, Microsoft brought out Windows 3.11, which has an add-on called Windows for Workgroups. This add-on allows a machine running DOS and Windows 3.11 to participate in a peer-to-peer network and share its files and any local printers with the rest of the network. Windows for Workgroups also allowed a user to add 32-bit TCP/IP networking. While far better than before, though, even Windows 3.11 was relatively limited in its networking capacities.

Microsoft was not only working on its clients, though. The Redmond Fun Bunch had also released Microsoft LAN Manager, a relatively primitive network server that would allow users to access centralized resources on the network. LAN Manager then evolved into Windows NT, and as part of that evolution, the LAN Manager networking software was integrated into the Windows NT Workstation client as well, giving Microsoft its first really effective network client.

Servers are computers that offer up resources (files, printers) or services (name resolution, time synchronization) to other machines on the network. They use special software to detect and respond to client requests.

Windows 95 and Beyond

When Windows 95 was released in late 1995, it wasn't the first Microsoft operating system to contain built-in networking. Both the Windows NT operating system and, to a lesser extent, Windows for Workgroups already had provided networking functionality. However, Windows 95 was similar to the "Monolith" of 2001 in that it issued in a new age of PC networking by providing easy-to-use-and-configure built-in networking. Suddenly, normal people could actually get their modems to work, corporate users could actually use the network without constantly getting sharing errors (SHARE.EXE was no more!), and improved support for all phases of the networking process rounded out the package.

Installing Networking Hardware and Software

Before you can begin with the configuration of your network, you must have a network card installed in the machine. Installing a network card is a fairly simple task if you have installed any expansion card before; a network interface card (NIC) is just a special type of expansion card. To install an NIC, follow these steps:

1. First move jumpers or flip DIP switches on the expansion card to set it to the correct IRQ/DMA/IO port settings as per the factory instructions. If the card uses a software set program, you can ignore this step. Most newer NICs do not have jumpers and are entirely software configured.

2. Next, power off the PC, remove the case, and insert the expansion card into an open slot.

3. Secure the expansion card with the screw provided.

4. Put the case back on the computer and power it up (you can run software configuration at this step, if necessary). If there are conflicts, change any parameters so that the NIC doesn't conflict with any existing hardware.

5. The final step in installing an NIC is to install a driver for the NIC for the type of operating system that you have. Windows should auto-detect the NIC and install the driver automatically. It may also ask you to provide a

copy of the necessary driver if it does not recognize what type of NIC you have installed. If the card is not detected at all, run the Add New Hardware Wizard by double-clicking Add New Hardware in the Control Panel.

6. After installing an NIC, you must hook the card up to the network using the cable supplied by your network administrator. You will need to attach this "patch cable" to the connector on the NIC and to a port in the wall, thus connecting your PC to the rest of the network.

Sometimes older NICs can conflict with newer Plug-and-Play (PnP) hardware. Additionally, some newer NICs with PnP capability don't like some kinds of networking software. To resolve a PnP conflict of the latter type, disable PnP on the NIC either with a jumper or with the software setup program. In this chapter, we will assume that your NIC is installed and the drivers are loaded. For more information on resolving hardware issues, refer to Chapter 16.

Configuring Windows 9*x* as a Network Client

The configuration of Windows 9*x* networking centers on the Control Panel's Network program. From this one interface, you configure client software, protocols, network interface cards (NICs), and the network services you want this machine to perform. To access the Network program, select Start ➢ Settings ➢ Control Panel and double-click Network in the Control Panel window that appears. Windows 9*x* will display the Network window. The Network window has three areas of interest: the components list, the primary logon list, and the File and Print Sharing button.

If you already have some networking components installed, you can simply right-click the Network Neighborhood icon on your desktop and choose Properties from the pop-up menu.

Network Components

First, let's review the four basic types of networking components that can be added in the Network panel, as shown in Figure 18.2. This screen can be reached by clicking Add on the Configuration tab.

FIGURE 18.2 The Select Network Component Type window

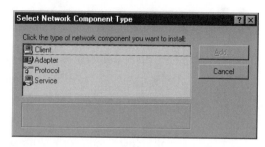

The networking components are as follows:

Client   As mentioned before, the client is software that allows your machine to talk to servers on the network. Each server vendor uses a different way of designing its network access, though, so if a computer needs to get to both a Novell and a Microsoft network, the computer must have two pieces of client software installed, one for each type of server. The three network client groups supported by Windows 9x are for Microsoft, Novell, and Banyan servers.

Adapter   The *adapter* is technically the peripheral hardware that installs into your computer, but in this case, it refers to the software that defines how the computer talks to that hardware. If you do not have the proper adapter software installed, your PC will not be able to talk properly to the NIC and you will not be able to access the network until you change the adapter to one that is compatible with the hardware. It is often best to simply think of an adapter as a network driver, which is what it is. A long list of adapters are supported by Windows 95, and Windows 98 supports even more, with support for more recent hardware. Adapter drivers can also be downloaded from most NIC vendors' Web sites.

Protocol   Once the client service and the adapter are installed, you have cleared a path for communication from your machine to network servers. The *protocol* is the computer language that you use to facilitate communication between the machines. If you want to talk to someone, you have to speak their language. Computers are no different. Among the languages available to Windows 98 are NetBEUI, NWLink, and *TCP/IP*.

Service   A *service* is a component that gives a bit back to the network that gives it so much. Services add functionality to the network by providing resources or doing tasks for other computers. In Windows 98, services include file and printer sharing for Microsoft or Novell networks.

Installing Components

Let's suppose you want to connect to Microsoft servers on your network (including Windows 2000 Server, 2000 Professional, or Windows 9x with sharing enabled). To connect to this network, you must have at least three components (no services, the fourth component, are required at this point):

- A client, such as Client for Microsoft Networks
- A protocol (whichever protocol is in use on the network; generally TCP/IP)
- An adapter (whatever is in the PC)

To install a client and protocol for use with your network adapter, follow these steps:

1. Click the Add button toward the bottom of the Network window. This will display the screen shown in Figure 18.2.

2. In this screen you can choose what type of item you are going to install. In this example, we're installing the Client for Microsoft Networks, so click Client and then click Add.

3. You will see a screen similar to the one in Figure 18.3. This screen is the standard "pick your component" screen that Windows 95 uses. On the left, select the company whose software (or driver) you want to install (in this example, Microsoft). When you have selected a manufacturer, a list of the software that Windows 95 can install from that company appears on the right.

FIGURE 18.3 Selecting the software you want to install

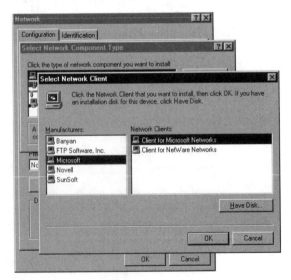

4. Click Client for Microsoft Networks when it appears in the right pane, then click OK. Windows 9*x* will bring you back to the Configuration tab of the Network program.

5. Once you have a client installed, you can verify that the protocol you need is present. TCP/IP generally installs by default, but this is not always so. If it is not present, click Add on the Configuration tab. In the Select Network Component Type window, select Protocol and then click Add. In the Select Network Client window, select Microsoft in the Manufacturers list and TCP/IP in the Network Protocols list. Click OK to complete the installation.

When it is first installed, TCP/IP is configured to expect that a special server, called a *Dynamic Host Configuration Protocol (DHCP)* server, is available on the network to provide it with information about the network. If a DHCP server is not available, the protocol will not function properly. Consult your administrator to see whether the network uses DHCP or static addressing. In static addressing, all TCP/IP settings must be manually added, and in this case, you will need additional information from the administrator. TCP/IP will be discussed in more detail later in this chapter.

The list of components should reflect your additions and show which network components are currently installed on this machine. If there are a number of components, a scroll bar appears on the right-hand side. The scroll bar allows you to see all the clients, network adapters, protocols, and services that might be installed. Once the client and protocol are installed, you will have all the software you need to connect to the network. At that point, just a few choices remain. Don't close that Network program yet!

Primary Logon

A Windows 9*x* workstation can support multiple simultaneous network types. For example, a user can log in to both Novell and Microsoft networks, assuming they have both network clients installed and configured correctly. The Primary Network *Logon* drop-down list determines which network type you will log on to first. If you have not yet installed a network client, this list will only give you one option: Windows Logon.

We have installed a Microsoft network client, so select the Client for Microsoft Networks as the primary logon, as displayed in Figure 18.4.

FIGURE 18.4 Choosing a Primary Network Logon

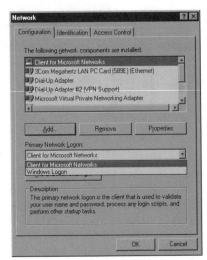

Once you have made this selection, click the OK button. The Network program will close, and you will be asked to restart the computer so that the new settings can take effect. Until you reboot, the network will not function. When the machine restarts, the network should be available.

Configuring Windows 2000 Professional as a Network Client

For the most part, the concepts behind configuring Windows 9x are the same as the concepts for configuring in Windows 2000. You still need a client, a protocol, and an adapter, for instance. The difference is in how they are configured because Microsoft has changed a few things in Windows 2000.

First, the Network program is now called Network and Dial-up Connections (NDC hereafter) and is organized differently. When you first access the NDC window, you will see that instead of a list of all components, you are greeted simply by a Make New Connection icon and a Local Area Connection icon, as shown in Figure 18.5.

FIGURE 18.5 The Network and Dial-up Connections window

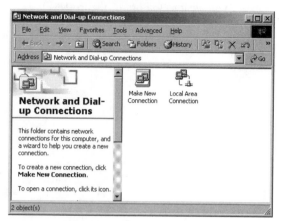

If you do not see a local area connection, your NIC or modem is not present or is not functioning properly. If you see more than one LAN connection, it means you have multiple NICs installed (Windows 2000 can support multiple NICs).

To add client software and protocols, right-click the LAN connection and select Properties. You should find that everything you need is in place because the MS client and IP are installed by default on the LAN adapter.

File and Printer Sharing for Microsoft Networks is also installed by default. To disable it, click the check mark next to the service. To remove it completely, click Uninstall.

You can also add additional clients, protocols, and services. Windows 2000 supports the same components Windows 9*x* supports, plus some new additions (the only component not supported in 2000 that is in 9*x* is the Banyan client). Once you have verified that the Client for Microsoft Networks and TCP/IP are installed, click OK. You should not have to reboot after making changes to the network settings in Windows 2000.

Configuring Clients for NetWare Network Access

Both Windows 9*x* and Windows 2000 handle the addition of a network client for NetWare in similar ways. Add (9*x*) or install (2000) the client, and it will automatically install the NetWare-compatible NWLink protocol for you as well (Figure 18.6). Once you have these, you will be presented with a NetWare logon option screen on startup, where you can choose which NetWare server or tree you wish to log on to (Figure 18.7).

FIGURE 18.6 NDC with the NetWare client and NWLink installed

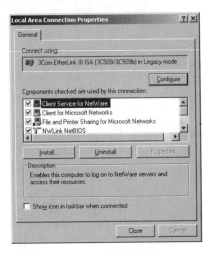

FIGURE 18.7 The NetWare default server/tree option screen

The tree is a group of machines that share security and configuration information. Both Novell's NetWare and Microsoft's Active Directory use tree structures to store information and authenticate users. To access the NetWare tree more efficiently, frequent NetWare users should download the newest version of NetWare's own client software for 9x/2000. It is available at www.novell.com/download/index.htm.

Configuring Windows to Share Files and Printers

As noted before, it is possible to set up both Windows 9*x* and Windows 2000 Professional to share files and printers with other users on the network. Networking in which users share each other's resources is called *peer-to-peer networking*, where each computer acts as both a client and a server.

We have already completed the client configuration. This is a must, actually, because file and printer sharing is only possible if the proper client and protocol are already set up. Now they are, so all you need to do is turn on file and print sharing and then specify which resources you wish to share. Even after file and printer sharing is enabled, you must specifically share any directory or printer that you want to make available on the network.

Enabling File and Printer Sharing on Windows 9*x*

To add file and printer sharing services, perform the following steps:

1. Open the Network program and click the File and Print Sharing button. You will see a screen that will allow you to select which services you want to share (Figure 18.8).

FIGURE 18.8 Enabling file and printer sharing

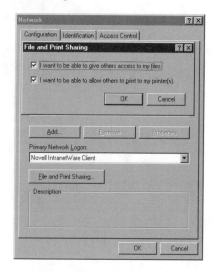

2. Click the box next to the top option (I Want to Be Able to Give Others Access to My Files) if you want to share files on your machine with someone

else on the network. If you want others to be able to print to a printer hooked to your machine, click the box next to the bottom option, I Want to Be Able to Allow Others to Print to My Printer(s). A check mark will appear in the box next to an option when it is enabled. To disable an option, simply click in the box again and the check mark will disappear.

3. Once you have enabled file and printer sharing, the service called File and Printer Sharing for Microsoft Networks will appear in the list of installed network components. In addition to specifying what you are going to share, you must specify how security is going to be handled. There are two options: Share-Level Access Control and User-Level Access Control. With share-level control, you supply a username, password, and security settings for each resource that you share. With user-level control, there is a central database of users (usually administrated by the network administrator) that Windows 9*x* can use to specify security settings for each shared resource. Most of the time, share-level access control is fine. There are only a few cases where user-level control is needed (such as in a network where the administrator has said you will do it this way). To specify these settings, choose the Access Control tab in the Network window (Figure 18.9) and choose the appropriate option.

FIGURE 18.9 Specifying the access control method

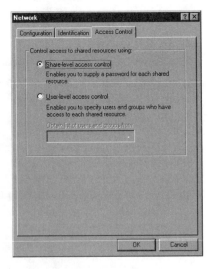

4. Click OK to save all of these new settings.

5. Windows 9x will copy some files and ask you to reboot (big surprise, huh?). Reboot your computer to start sharing files and printers.

As described earlier, Windows 2000 automatically starts and installs File and Printer Sharing when a network connection is created. Unless you have disabled it, no additional configuration is required to begin sharing resources!

Sharing Folders

If you have a folder on your machine that contains information that everyone should be able to see, you will need to enable *file sharing*. Sharing is generally enabled through Windows Explorer.

Any folder can be shared (including the root of the C: drive). When you share a folder, the person you share it with will be able to see not only the folder you've shared but also any folders inside that folder. Therefore, you should be certain that all subfolders under a share are intended to be shared as well. If they are not, move them out of the share path.

Once you have decided what to share, simply right-click the folder that will be the start of the share and choose Sharing from the menu that pops up. This option will bring up the Properties window of that folder with the Sharing tab in front.

You can also access the Sharing tab by right-clicking a folder, choosing Properties, and clicking the tab.

To start the share, click the Shared As radio button. Two previously grayed-out fields will become visible (Figure 18.10). The first field is Share Name. The name you enter here will be used to access this folder. It should be something that accurately represents what you are sharing. The second field allows you to enter a description of the share as a comment that will help identify the contents of the share to users. The share name is required, and the comment is optional.

FIGURE 18.10 Enabling a share

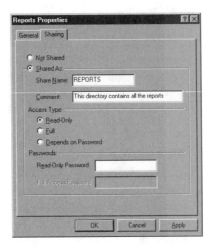

Finally, you may specify the access rights and password(s) for the share. There are three options for access rights when you're using the share-level security scheme. Click the radio button next to the option you want to use:

Read-Only With this option selected, anyone accessing the share will only be able to open and read the files inside the folder and any subfolders. You must specify a password that users can use to access the share in read-only mode.

Full In full access mode, everyone accessing the share has the ability to do anything to the files in the folder as well as any subfolders. This includes being able to delete those files. You must specify a password that the users will use to access this share.

Depends on Password This option is probably the best option of the three. With this option, users can use one password to access the share in read-only mode and a different password to access it in full access mode. You can give everyone the read-only password so they can view the files and give the full access password only to users who need to change the files.

By default, the share is a full control share in Windows NT/2000. This means that anyone on the network can come in and view, modify, or even delete the files in the share. Often this is just a bit too dangerous, and as such, you will probably want to use a read-only or a depends-on password security setting. (A Windows 9x share is read-only by default. Anyone on the network can view files in the share.)

Once you have specified the share name, comments, and access rights, click OK to share the folder. Notice that the folder now has a hand underneath it, indicating that it is being shared (Figure 18.11).

FIGURE 18.11 The REPORTS folder after being shared

 In Windows 2000, sharing is enabled in exactly the same way as in Windows 9*x*. The only difference is that in 2000, you can enable the NTFS file system and use it to secure files and folders. At that point, all you have to do is create a share on Windows 2000 Professional to the directories you wish to allow the network access to and the permissions set at the file level will be enforced.

Sharing Printers

Sharing printers is similar to sharing folders. First, you must have the printer correctly set up to print on the machine that will be "hosting" it. Second, you need to right-click on a printer in the PRINTERS folder and click Sharing. The printer property page will appear with the Sharing tab selected to allow you to share the printer.

To share the printer, simply click Shared As and specify a name for the share (Figure 18.12). The name will default to a truncated version of the printer name you gave it when you installed it. Notice in Figure 18.12 that Windows 95 truncated the name HP LaserJet III to HP. The name you give this share (called the *share name*) should be something that everyone will recognize when they see it on the network and that accurately describes the printer. This one is called DavesHP so people will know that it's next to Dave's workstation and that it's an HP printer.

FIGURE 18.12 Sharing a printer

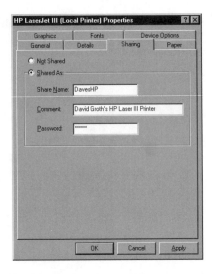

In addition to specifying the name of the printer share, you can enter a comment that describes the printer accurately. Finally, you should specify a password that users must enter in order to install this printer on their workstations (they won't have to enter it every time they print).

To finish sharing the printer, click OK. Windows 95 will prompt you for the password again, just to verify that you know what it is and that you didn't misspell it. Retype the password in the box that appears and click OK and the share will be active. Notice that the printer in the PRINTERS folder in Figure 18.13 has a hand under it, indicating that it is shared.

FIGURE 18.13 The printer is now shared.

Using Shared Resources

To access shared folders and printers, we'll turn to the Network Neighborhood icon. When you double-click this icon, you can browse the network for resources. Figure 18.14 shows an example of a Network Neighborhood browse window. As you can see, there are several entities on this network. The little icons that look like computers are just that, computers on the network. However, there isn't a different icon for a Novell server, an NT server, or a Windows 95 machine sharing out part of its hard disk. They all look the same to Windows 95. The one that looks like a tree is in fact an NDS tree for a Novell network.

FIGURE 18.14   A sample Network Neighborhood window

Through this screen, you can double-click any computer to see the resources that are hosted by that computer. Once you have found the share you require, using a shared folder is just like using any other folder on your computer, with one or two exceptions: First, the folder exists on the network, so you have to be connected to the network to use it. Second, for some programs to work properly, you must map a local drive letter to the network folder. This is because the Windows 9x reference to a share on the network uses the Universal Naming Convention path (or UNC path). The UNC path uses the format *machinename**share**path*\. So, a directory called JULY98 underneath a share called REPORTS on a machine called DAVELAPTOP would be written as \\DAVELAPTOP\REPORTS\JULY98.

In Windows 9x, if you do know the name of the computer that hosts the resource you are looking for, you can use the Find command instead of browsing. Just go to Start ➤ Find ➤ Computer and type in the name of the computer preceded by two backslashes (the beginning of a UNC path).

If there is a space in the name of any item, be careful. Some DOS utilities can't interpret spaces.

To connect to a network folder share, simply double-click the computer that's hosting it to view the list of shares (Figure 18.15). Notice that both the folder and printer that were shared in the previous examples are there. Because we want to use the folder share, we can just double-click it to see its contents (and copy files to and from it if necessary). Or, we can map a drive letter so that all our applications will be able to use it.

FIGURE 18.15 Viewing the resources a computer is hosting

Now that you see all the resources the computer is hosting, you can map a drive letter to it by right-clicking the folder (REPORTS in this case) and choosing Map Network Drive. This will cause the screen shown in Figure 18.16 to appear. You must pick a drive letter (one that is not being used) and click OK to map the drive. Remember that most Windows applications can use UNC paths and don't need drive mappings, but even some newer applications still require a drive letter.

FIGURE 18.16   Mapping a drive letter to a network share

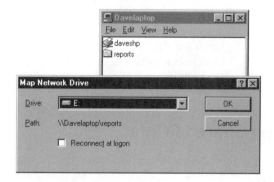

Now that you have a drive mapped, you can use the files and directories in the share that you mapped to.

Sharing Options with Windows 2000

Windows 2000 is very similar to Windows 9x when it comes to accessing network resources, but there are just a few modifications. First, Network Neighborhood is renamed My Network Places in Windows 2000. Second, to search for computers by name, you no longer go to the Find menu (now renamed Search, anyhow). Instead, when you double-click My Network Places, you will have the Search for Computers and Search for Files or Folders options in the left part of the window (Figure 18.17). Click the Entire Contents link on the left, and the network contents will be displayed. At that point, everything will be displayed as it is in Windows 9x and you can view and map network drives.

FIGURE 18.17   The initial Entire Network window

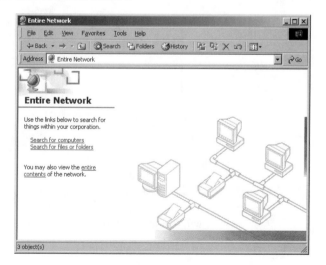

Another option for mapping a drive in 9*x* and 2000 is to use the Windows Explorer. In Explorer, click the Tools menu, and select Map Network Drive. You will need to either enter the UNC path (\\server\share) or navigate to the folder using the Browse button. Drives can be disconnected using the Tools ➢ Disconnect Network Drive option.

Using a Shared Printer

In this section, we'll discuss the way to set up a Windows 9*x* or 2000 client to print to a shared printer. Accessing shared printers is very similar to accessing shared resources; in both cases, you are accessing a resource that has been shared on the host computer. Additionally, in both cases, you are pointing a local resource (in this case a printer icon) to a network resource (a shared printer).

To set up the printer on your workstation, you most likely will use the Point and Print option for Windows 9*x* and 2000 printing. This option allows you to click and drag a printer to the PRINTERS folder and run the Add Printer Wizard, which will set up the printer icon and set up the right drivers on your machine. Follow these steps:

1. Browse to the computer that hosts the printer you want to set up and double-click the computer name so you can see the printer you want to install.

2. Open up the PRINTERS folder under Start ➢ Settings ➢ Printers. Arrange these windows so you can see both at the same time (Figure 18.18).

FIGURE 18.18 Preparing to configure the Point and Print option

3. To start the Add Printer Wizard, drag the printer you want to set up from the list of resources the computer is hosting to the Printers window. As soon as you release the mouse button, you will see the wizard start, and it will display the window shown in Figure 18.19.

FIGURE 18.19 Starting the Add Printer Wizard

4. The wizard will ask you a series of questions that will help you to configure the printer. If you are using Windows 9*x*, the wizard will ask "Do you print from MS-DOS–based programs?" The reasoning behind this question is similar to the reason we map drive letters. Most older DOS programs (and to a lesser extent, Windows programs) don't understand the UNC path syntax for access to a shared resource. Instead, they understand a name for a local hardware resource (like LPT1: for the first local parallel port). So, you must point a local printer port name out to the network in a process known as capturing. If you need to capture a printer port, answer "Yes" to this question, otherwise leave it set to the default ("No"). For our example, click Yes and click Next to move to the next step of the wizard.

Although Windows 2000 allows you to map LPT: ports, 2000 does not have much interest in DOS, and so it does not make any special mention of it.

5. If you chose Yes in the preceding step, the next step is to capture the printer port. You will see the screen in Figure 18.20. This screen allows you to capture a printer port so that DOS programs can print to the network printer. Click the Capture Printer Port button to bring up the screen (Figure 18.21) that allows you to choose which local port you want to capture. Select a port (generally LPT:1).

FIGURE 18.20 Capturing a Printer port

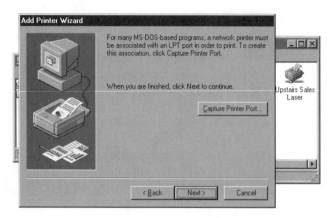

FIGURE 18.21 Picking which local port to capture

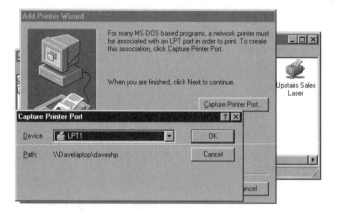

6. The next step is to give the printer instance a name. You should give a network printer a name that reflects what kind of printer it is and which machine is hosting it. In this example, the printer is labeled HP LaserJet III (the default name of the driver), but we could have named it Laser on Bob's PC. Whatever name makes sense to you, type in the name that you want to call the printer in the screen that the wizard presents (Figure 18.22). You also have the choice as to whether or not you want the printer to be the default printer that gets used by all Windows applications.

FIGURE 18.22 Naming the printer

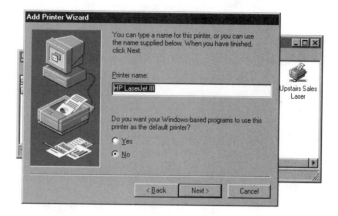

From here on, printer installation is exactly the same as installing a local printer (covered in Chapter 16).

Networking and the Internet

One of the most oft-performed procedures by today's technicians is setting up a computer to connect to the Internet. The Internet is no longer just a buzzword, it's a reality. It has been estimated that over 50 percent of the homes in America have computers and that over 50 percent of those computers are connected to the Internet. It's is no wonder that most computers come with software to connect them to the Internet.

Before we can discuss connecting Windows to the Internet, we need to discuss the Internet itself. There are some common terms and concepts every technician must understand about the Internet. First of all, the Internet is really just a bunch of private networks connected together using public telephone lines. These private networks are the access points to the Internet and are run by companies called Internet Service Providers (ISPs). They will sell you a connection to the Internet for a monthly service charge (kind of like your cable bill or phone bill). Your computer talks to the ISP using public phone lines, or even using new technologies such as cable or wireless.

Types of Connections

There are several designations and types of public phone lines that range in speeds from 56Kbps to several Megabits per second (Mbps) and that your computer might use to talk to an ISP. Remember that these same types of phone lines connect the ISPs to each other to form the Internet. Table 18.1 details a few of the more common connection types and speeds.

TABLE 18.1 Common Connection Types and Speeds

Designation	Speed Range	Description
POTS	2400bps to 115Kbps	Plain Old Telephone System. Your regular analog phone line.
ISDN	64Kbps to 1.554Mbps	Integrated Services Digital Network. Popular for home office Internet connection.
Frame Relay	56Kbps to 1.554Mbps	Cheap, simple connection where you share bandwidth with several other people.
56K Point-to-Point	56Kbps	A direct connection between two points at a guaranteed bandwidth.
T1	1.554Mbps	A direct connection between two points at a guaranteed bandwidth.
T3	44Mbps	A direct connection between two points at a guaranteed bandwidth. Extremely fast.
DSL	256Kbps to ?	Digital Subscriber Line. Shares existing phone wires with voice service.
ATM	155Mbps	Asynchronous Transfer Mode. Fiber-optic ring network. Extremely fast.

The majority of home Internet connections use POTS (Plain Old Telephone System) and a modem. Most ISPs connect with each other using phone lines of T1 speeds (1.554Mbps) or faster. Certain ISPs that make up the backbone of the Internet use technologies like SONET that can get the data moving at gigabit speeds.

Connection Protocols

Whichever connection type is used, there must be a plan for how to transmit data across a network's lines. Network connection types also use different protocols to communicate, just as computers do, and because of this we also need to mention these connection protocols. For instance, TCP/IP Internet traffic runs over two different analog connection protocols: Serial Line Internet Protocol (SLIP) and Point-to-Point Protocol (PPP). Both work to get you on the Internet, but PPP is more commonly used because it is more easily configured; it's also more stable because it includes enhanced error-checking capabilities. Other common connection protocols include X.25 and ATM (the name is used for both the network and the connection protocol controlling traffic across it).

A TCP/IP Primer

Regardless of which network type you choose, you will probably be running Transmission Control Protocol/Internet Protocol (TCP/IP) over the top of it. Because the Internet is a network, everyone on it needs to be running the same protocol in order to communicate. The protocol of the Internet is TCP/IP, and increasingly, the protocol of the Internet is becoming the primary protocol of all networks. Named for two of its most commonly used components, TCP/IP is actually a suite of protocols rather than just being a single monolithic creation.

Created in 1969 as a part of DARPAnet (the Defense Advanced Research Projects Administration Network), TCP/IP evolved over time. The DARPAnet evolved also, eventually moving out of government hands and becoming the Internet that we know and love. Currently the Internet is managed by the Internet Society (`www.isoc.org`), which develops new standards for the Internet and for the TCP/IP suite.

When starting to work with TCP/IP, the first thing to note is that it is generally managed by using two independent hierarchical structures. The first is the IP address hierarchy. Each computer that runs TCP/IP must have a unique IP address assigned to it, and that address must fall within a specific range. IP addresses are composed of a set of four numbers, each of which must be from 0 to 255. The IP address can either be automatically assigned to the machine or an administrator can specifically assign it. Aside from its IP address, a machine will also have a *host name*, which identifies it on the network. Host names are friendly names by which computers can be more easily located, and they are managed using a worldwide naming system called the *Domain Name System (DNS)*. DNS allows a user to type in http://www.yahoo.com and be taken directly to a computer hundreds or thousands of miles away. The same user could have used an IP address such as http://200.50.172.14, (not Yahoo!'s actual address), but most people find that the domain name (yahoo.com) is far easier to remember! Table 18.2 includes a list of other common Internet terms with which you will want to be familiar.

TABLE 18.2 Internet Terminology

Term	What It does
ISP	Internet Service Provider. A company that provides access to the Internet.
Host	A computer on a TCP/IP network such as the Internet.
WWW	A graphical extension of the Internet, the World Wide Web (or just the Web) allows users to search for and view information easily through the use of a browser. Users navigate the Web by jumping from one page to the next through hyperlinks.
Hyperlink	Text or an image on a Web page that, when clicked, takes the user to another place on the page or to a different page.
Browser	Software made to understand and interpret HTTP content.
HTTP	A TCP/IP protocol which defines how World Wide Web content is downloaded and displayed in your browser. HTTP stands for Hypertext Transfer Protocol.
FTP	Another TCP/IP protocol. The File Transfer Protocol is used to transfer large files over the Internet. Users can use either a graphical client or a command line.
E-mail	Electronic mail is a way of sending and receiving messages over the Internet.
DHCP	The Dynamic Host Configuration Protocol. This is used to automatically configure TCP/IP information for hosts on the network.
WINS	Windows Internet Name Service. Manages Microsoft NetBIOS-based names and makes It easier to find resources on a Microsoft network.
DNS	The Domain Name System manages Internet host and domain names and makes it easier to find resources on TCP/IP networks.

Computer Name Resolution

This isn't something that is in the objectives, so you can take it or leave it, but it is incredibly important to understanding how machines communicate on Microsoft networks. When Microsoft first started producing network-capable operating systems, such as DOS with networking, LanManager and Windows NT 3.1, the

Internet was nothing but a group of mainframe computers connecting selected military and university campuses. At that time, it seemed that the thing to do when you created network software was to also create your own proprietary protocol and assume that no one would ever connect to any network but yours. Novell had IPX/SPX, Apple had AppleTalk, and Microsoft, sadly, came up with NetBEUI.

The NetBEUI protocol is insufficient on so many levels that discussing its faults is too big a job for this chapter. Nonetheless, it is an extremely fast protocol for allowing a few computers on a single network to communicate. It just doesn't scale very well, which has doomed it as networks grew and started to interconnect.

The death knell of NetBEUI wasn't a problem, because TCP/IP and other protocols were ready to take over. The one thing that has continued to cause confusion and trouble, though, is that NetBEUI was based on another Microsoft protocol called NetBIOS, which has been far more difficult to replace.

NetBEUI and NetBIOS

NetBEUI and NetBIOS are obviously similar-looking terms, and unfortunately, there has been a certain amount of confusion surrounding them. Here is a brief explanation of what each does:

- NetBEUI is a transport protocol. It is responsible for how data is transmitted between two computers. It is not routable and is rarely used in modern computing.

- NetBIOS is a name resolution system. It allows a computer to search for another computer on the network by its Microsoft computer name. It must be used on every Microsoft-based network up to Windows 2000.

Computer Names and Host Names

The continuing presence of NetBIOS makes for some interesting confusion in that a Microsoft 9x machine with TCP/IP installed actually has two distinct names. Its NetBIOS computer name is set in the Identification tab of the Network program (Figure 18.23), whereas its host name is set in the TCP/IP DNS Configuration tab (Figure 18.24). In the figures, both names are set to COYOTE, and usually the computer and host name will be the same because they are set that way by default. If you are having trouble reaching a 9x or NT machine, though, you may want to check this setting.

FIGURE 18.23 The NetBIOS computer name

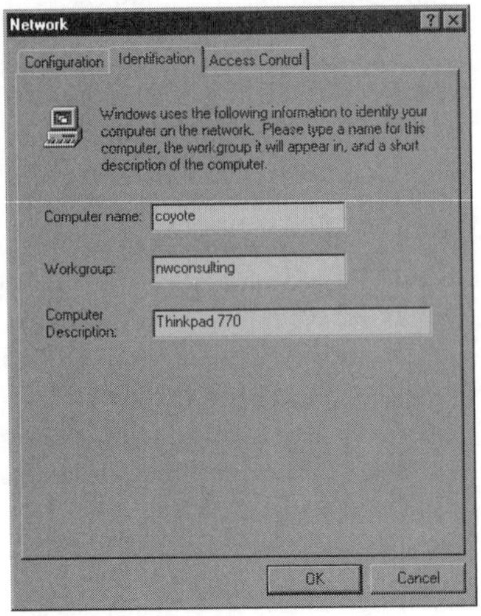

FIGURE 18.24 The TCP/IP host name

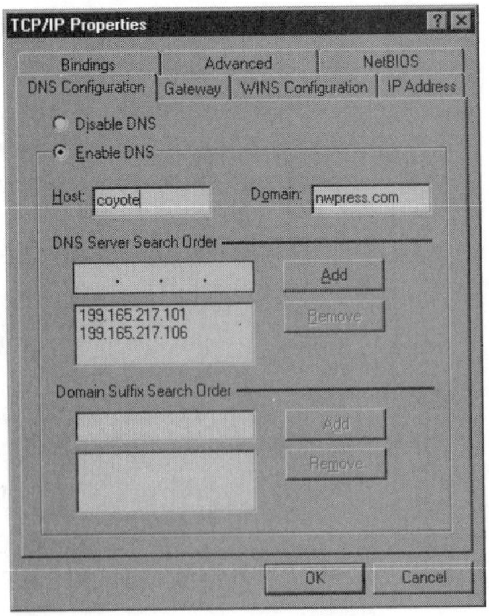

In Windows 2000, Microsoft has finally started to make a break from this non-sense. Computer and host names in 2000 must be the same, and NetBIOS name resolution has largely been replaced with DNS naming resolution.

So What Is Resolution?

In order for a computer to talk to another computer, it must be able to access it using an IP address. Computers speak in numbers, not letters! Because of this, the "friendly" names that we use to make computers easy to remember and find must be *resolved* to find out what IP address the machine is using. There are a number of methods of doing this, but WINS servers and DNS servers are the most common. WINS resolves NetBIOS computer names to IP addresses, and DNS does so for host names. More on this in a minute.

Another way of resolving names is to use either the LMHOSTS file (computer names) or the HOSTS file (host names). These are text files into which you can put entries that specifically tell your machine what the address of another machine is, as in the following line:

```
192.168.1.250                    NTSERVER
```

Although these files work fine, they require a lot of maintenance and are not used regularly in modern networking.

Configuring TCP/IP

NetBEUI and NWLink are protocols that need little tuning. You can pretty much install them and go, without needing to configure anything. Not so with TCP/IP, which has a number of settings that must be configured so you can access network resources.

First, there are two settings that are absolutely crucial. Without an IP address and a subnet mask, TCP/IP will not function. In addition, a number of other settings may also be needed, depending on what you are planning to access. The settings are listed in Table 18.3 (settings needed for Internet access are marked with an asterisk).

TABLE 18.3   TCP/IP Configuration Settings

Setting	Example	Purpose
IP address*	192.168.1.75	Uniquely identifies the computer on the network.

TABLE 18.3 TCP/IP Configuration Settings *(continued)*

Setting	Example	Purpose
Subnet mask*	255.255.255.0	Used to determine whether other IP addresses are on the same network or on another network. Sadly, there is no easy explanation for subnet masks. Suffice it to say that you need it, and it has to be right! The network administrator should give you the subnet mask setting (and all other necessary info).
Default gateway*	192.168.1.1	The address of the router your machine will use to access the outside world.
Host	Coyote	The name that the machine is referred to in DNS.
Domain	Sybex.com	The name of the organization you are in. Similar to a workgroup, but for TCP/IP.
DNS server*	192.168.1.250	The machine that resolves names for the network. This machine will answer a question such as "What IP address does coyote.sybex.com have?" with an answer of "192.168.1.75."
WINS server	192.168.1.250	Serves the same purpose as DNS, but deals with computer names, not host names. Answers questions such as "What IP address does COYOTE have?"

Managing TCP/IP

There are two ways to manage TCP/IP. The manual way involves going to each machine and setting upward of 10 separate values for TCP/IP. This would also be known as the "hard way" of configuring IP. Another possibility is the use of DHCP. If your network is using DHCP, all you have to do is install IP and reboot. A special server called a DHCP server will then provide your machine with all the values it needs when it starts up again. Machines are given "leases" to the IP addresses that the server manages and must periodically renew these leases. If you are using DHCP, your TCP/IP settings in the Network program should be grayed out, as shown in Figure 18.25.

FIGURE 18.25 TCP/IP auto-configured by DHCP

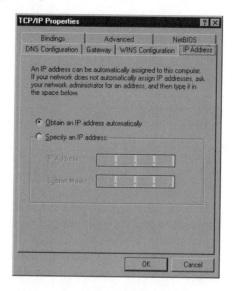

If you are wondering what the IP settings for a machine are, there are a number of utilities you can use. The primary options, though, are listed in Table 18.4.

TABLE 18.4 TCP/IP Utilities

Protocol	Function
WINIPCFG	A graphical utility on Windows 9x that allows you to get information about your IP configuration. It also allows you to release a DHCP lease and request a new one.
IPCONFIG	Does the same thing as WINIPCFG, but for Windows NT and 2000. IPCONFIG is also different in that it is a command-line utility.
PING	The PING command allows you to test connectivity with another host by just typing **PING www.sybex.com** or **PING 192.168.1.250**.
Tracert	This trace route utility allows you to watch the path that information takes getting from your machine to another one.

Using these utilities is pretty straightforward. For an example, follow these steps to view TCP/IP information on Windows 2000:

1. Choose Start ➢ Run.

2. Type **CMD** and press Enter. This will bring up a command prompt.

3. At the prompt, type **IPCONFIG**. Basic information about your TCP/IP configuration will be displayed.

4. Type **IPCONFIG** again, this time adding the /A switch: **IPCONFIG /A**. The /ALL switch tells the system to display additional information. Other options can be found using the IPCONFIG /? Command. The additional options are also run using switches, and are run in the same fashion as the /A switch, by typing them in after the command.

Configuring Internet Access Software

If you want to connect your Windows 95 machine to the Internet, the first step is to get an account with an Internet Service Provider. They will give you a sheet with all the information you need to connect your machine, or in some cases, they will give you a disk with a preconfigured connection and browser so all you have to do is install the software and you'll be ready to connect to the Internet. A browser is a piece of software used to access the World Wide Web, and a Dial-Up Networking (DUN) connection holds the settings needed to access an ISP. In this section, we will look at how to install and use each of these.

Although in most cases you need to make a Dial-Up Networking connection to use the Internet, it is important to note that some service providers, such as AOL or Prodigy, create their own connections. Don't try to make the connection for them, and don't delete them!

Some connections, such as cable or DSL, do not use a modem and as such are configured through the use of network cards and standard network clients. Configuring Internet access for DSL is very similar to configuring access on a company network. You simply install TCP/IP, configure it properly, and then skip ahead to "Connecting to the Internet." You will need information from the ISP when configuring these systems.

Creating a Windows 9*x* DUN Connection

To create a new DUN connection, open the Dial-Up Networking folder under Start ➢ Programs ➢ Accessories. This will open a window that shows all the DUN connections that are configured. You must create a new one to connect to the

Internet. To do so, double-click the item in this folder called Make New Connection. This will bring up the screen shown in Figure 18.26. From this screen, you can give the connection a name. As with other names in Windows 9x, use one that reflects what it is (in this case, a connection to the Internet). Additionally, this screen will allow you to select which modem you want to use to dial this connection (if you only have one configured in Windows 9x, it will default to that one).

FIGURE 18.26 Making a new connection and naming it

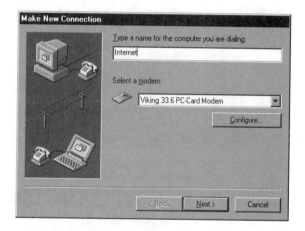

The next step is to enter the phone number of the system you are dialing (Figure 18.27). Simply type in the area code and phone number of your ISP and click Next to continue. When it dials, Windows 9x will determine if it's a long-distance number automatically and either add or omit the 1 plus the area code.

FIGURE 18.27 Entering the ISP's phone number

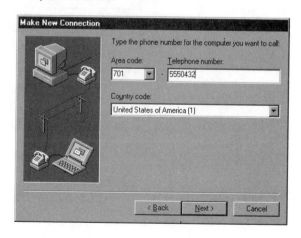

> If you live in another country, select your country under Country Code to change how Windows 95 interprets phone number syntax.

Finally, you are presented with the final screen that tells you that you are basically finished setting up the connection. All you have to do is click the Finish button to finish creating the connection.

Configuring the Properties of a Windows 9x DUN Connection

Now that you have a DUN connection, you need to configure the settings specific to your Internet connection. Simply right-click the connection in the Dial-Up Networking folder (Figure 18.28). From the menu that appears, you can choose to use the connection to connect (the Connect option), or you can choose the Properties option to configure it. Because you aren't ready to connect yet, choose the Properties item from the menu.

FIGURE 18.28   Choosing the DUN connection to configure

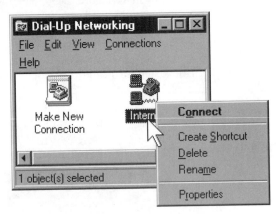

You should now see a screen similar to the one in Figure 18.29. From this screen, you can configure the same properties you configure in the Make New Connection Wizard (i.e., telephone number, connection name, and modem). This screen has two more tabs that you can use to configure the other properties (such as protocol settings).

FIGURE 18.29 Properties of the Internet DUN connection

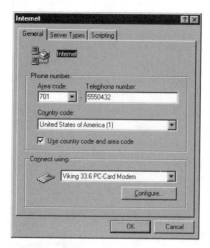

If you click the Server Types tab, you will see the settings for the type of server you are dialing in to (Figure 18.30). For an Internet connection, this is usually set to PPP: Windows 95, Windows NT 3.5, Internet (unless your ISP instructs you to use another setting). Notice also that there are check boxes for several other settings, including which protocol(s) this dial-up connection will use. TCP/IP must be selected in order for an Internet connection to work. Configure these settings according to your ISP's instructions and click OK to accept them.

FIGURE 18.30 Configuring the Server Types parameter

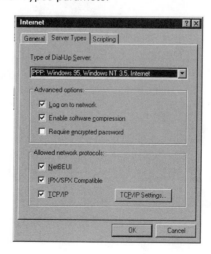

The Scripting tab is used if your ISP doesn't support any type of automatic user-name and password authentication protocol like *Password Authentication Protocol (PAP)* or *Challenge Handshake Authentication Protocol (CHAP)*. If in doubt, ask your ISP. This tab allows you to specify a file that will automatically enter your username and password. The Windows 95 Help file documents how to use this feature.

You can also configure DUN parameters in the Connect screen of the Internet connection. To access this area, double-click the connection. You will see a screen similar to the one in Figure 18.31. In this screen, you enter the username and password that your ISP has assigned you. Additionally, double-check the phone number you entered to make sure it's correct. Once you've finished configuring the phone number, you're ready to connect to the Internet.

FIGURE 18.31 The Connect screen

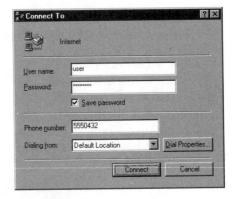

If you want to save the password so you don't have to type it in every time, click the check box next to Save Password. Be careful, though. If you save your password, anyone can get onto the Internet from your computer (using your user-name) without having to enter a password.

Installing DUN on Windows 2000

With Windows 2000, wizards are used everywhere, including the creation of a dial-up networking connection:

1. Choose Start ➤ Settings➤ Network and Dial-up Connections.

2. In the window that appears, double-click Make New Connection.

3. If this is the first time you have created a network connection, the Location Information window appears. You cannot escape this window without entering an area code, so enter it and click OK. You will get another location screen as well. Click OK again and the Network Connection Wizard appears.

4. In the Network Connection Wizard, choose Dial Up to the Internet and the Welcome to the Internet Connection Wizard (ICW) window appears (Figure 18.32). That makes three nested wizards. A bit extreme, no?

FIGURE 18.32 The first screen of the Internet Connection Wizard

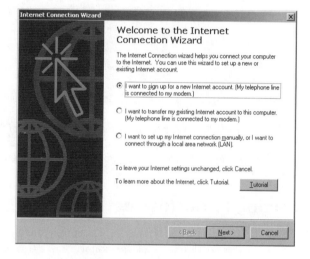

5. In the ICW, you will be led through a long series of choices. Click through and enter the values that apply to your Internet setup. You will be asked what type of device (modem or network) you are using, what number you need to dial, and what your username and password are. At the end, you can even set up your mail account, and the wizard offers to connect you when you are finished.

6. A new icon will appear in the Network and Dial-Up Connections window showing that your new connection has been added (Figure 18.33). You can view the status of a connection by double-clicking it or change its settings by right-clicking and selecting Properties.

FIGURE 18.33 The finished dial-up connection

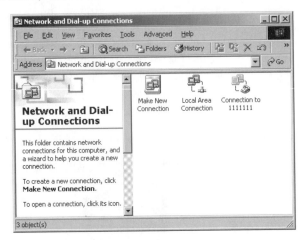

 The Windows 2000 Internet setup is typical of the sort of straightforward, easy-to-use tools that we as technicians have to hope do not become common. If everything gets this easy, it's going to be tough to make a living in this business!

Connecting to the Internet

Connecting to the Internet is simple once you get the connection configured. Simply double-click the connection, enter the password (unless you chose the Save Password button previously), and click Connect. A window will appear that allows you to follow the status of the connection (Figure 18.34). You should hear the modem dial and then connect. When it connects, the status screen will say, "Verifying Username and Password," and then "Connected." Once you are connected, the status screen will go away and you will see an icon on the taskbar (the same icon that's on the status screen). At this point, you are connected to your ISP and, through it, to the rest of the world. You can then fire up your favorite Web browser and start surfin'.

FIGURE 18.34 Connection status screen

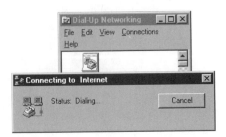

If you are configuring the system for someone who just wants to click and go, you can also right-click the Internet Explorer icon on the desktop and use the Connection tab of the Internet Settings window to configure auto-dial. Set the connection you have created as the default and specify that the system should "Always dial my default connection." Any time an application needs to access the Internet, it can simply initiate the DUN connection automatically.

Browsers

The first, and probably the most important, thing you'll need is a Web browser. This piece of software will allow you to view Web pages from the Internet. The two browsers with the largest market share are Netscape Navigator and Microsoft Internet Explorer (also known as IE). Both work equally well for browsing the Internet. Microsoft includes its browser, IE (Figure 18.35), with both Windows 98 and Windows 2000, whereas Netscape Navigator (Figure 18.36), which is free, must be downloaded separately.

FIGURE 18.35 The main window of Microsoft Internet Explorer

FIGURE 18.36 The main window of Netscape Navigator

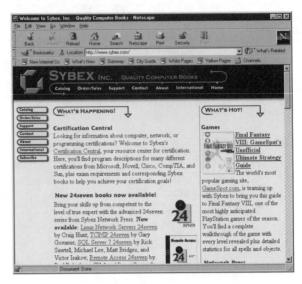

If you are looking for a newer version of Internet Explorer, you can go to Microsoft's Web site, `www.microsoft.com/windows/ie`. For Navigator, go to `www.netscape.com`. Once you are there, select the version you want and specify what type of machine you will be using it on. You can then download and install the software.

Besides a browser, you will probably need to use at least two other critical Internet functions: FTP and e-mail. Both are supported natively in Windows 9*x* and Windows 2000.

FTP

The File Transfer Protocol is available to you either through the command-line FTP client or through your browser. To access the Microsoft FTP site through the command prompt, open a prompt and type **FTP ftp.microsoft.com**. The site will respond with a request for your e-mail address, and you will then be given access. You can use standard DOS navigation commands to move between directories, and you can retrieve or send files using the GET *<filename>* or PUT *<filename>* commands. When you are finished with your session, simply type **QUIT**.

Internet Explorer also supports FTP. To go to Microsoft's Web site, you can simply type in **http://www.microsoft.com** and you will be taken to a Web page.

If you change the first part of the name to ftp://, though, the system knows to look for an FTP resource instead. Typing **ftp://ftp.microsoft.com** will also take you to the Microsoft Web site, and you can then use all of the standard Explorer GUI file management techniques, just as you would if you were connecting to any other network drive.

Because Microsoft's FTP site is a public site, it allows you to use a special anony-mous account that provides access. If you go to a site where that account has been disabled, you will need to provide another username and password, which should be provided by the site's administrator, or you will not be allowed into the site. Also, most FTP sites only allow visitors to download data, so PUT commands generally will be rejected unless you have a real (non-anonymous) account on the server.

E-Mail

Another common use of the Internet is to send and receive electronic mail. E-mail allows you to quickly and inexpensively transfer messages to other people. To send and receive e-mail, you need to have only two things: an e-mail account and an e-mail client. The account can be provided by a company, or it can be asso-ciated with your ISP account. Either way, you will have an address that looks like username@domain.com.

The last part of this address (after the @) identifies the domain name of the company or ISP that provides you with your e-mail account. The part before the @ is your username. A username must be unique on each domain. Two Bill the Cat users on a single network, for instance, might be billthecat@domain.com and billthecat1@domain.com.

As with other TCP/IP services, e-mail needs to be configured. Nothing in TCP/IP networking ever just works, it seems. Still, Windows provides a service called *Messaging Application Programming Interface (MAPI)* to make configuring e-mail easier, and overall, configuring e-mail is relatively straightforward.

Your MAPI settings can be defined in Control Panel's Mail program. Fig-ure 18.37 shows just a few of the many Internet e-mail settings you can define. Among these are the *Post Office Protocol v 3 (POP3)* and *Simple Mail Transport Protocol (SMTP)* server settings, which you will need to be given by an administrator. A POP3 server is a machine on the Internet that accepts and stores Internet e-mail and allows you to retrieve that mail when you are online. An SMTP server is a server that accepts mail you want to send, and forwards it to the proper user. In order to send and receive mail, you need both!

FIGURE 18.37   Internet E-mail properties

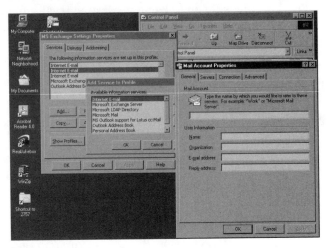

Once you have the settings configured, you will need to simply install an e-mail client or use the built-in client included with Windows 98 and 2000. That client is called Outlook Express, and it's a good basic e-mail application.

Monitoring and Disconnecting from the Internet

To see information (such as speed and quantity) about the data you have transferred during your Internet session, you can double-click the connection icon in the system tray (lower-right portion of the screen) to bring up a status window. From this window, you can see the number of bytes sent and received, and you can disconnect from the Internet. You can also do disconnect by simply right-clicking the connection icon itself and choosing Disconnect.

Summary

At one time, computer repair technicians and computer network engineers had distinctly different job descriptions, and techs rarely needed to deal with network issues at all. As documents become larger, and networking and the Internet become a more basic part of both home and office computer use, understanding networking is no longer an optional part of a computer technician's job description. Whether you need to access drivers on the Internet or set up a client's machine to share files on the network, PC techs now need to learn about networking.

In this chapter, we looked at a number of the basic issues you may come across, including how to set up a Windows machine to use a particular protocol and client software. We also looked at how a Windows client can access file or print resources on the network and how a Windows 9x or 2000 machine can also be configured to provide file or print services to other machines on the network.

Last, we looked at the special case of the TCP/IP protocol, and the Internet, because configuring TCP/IP and installing and using Internet applications are crucial tasks for both network and Internet configurations.

Key Terms

Before you take the exam, be certain you are familiar with the following terms.

browser	Logon
client software	Messaging Application Programming Interface (MAPI)
default gateway	network
domain	network adapter
Domain Name System (DNS)	peer-to-peer networking
Dynamic Host Configuration Protocol (DHCP)	PING
e-mail	Post Office Protocol v 3 (POP3)
file sharing	protocol
File Transfer Protocol (FTP)	Servers
host	share name
host name	Simple Mail Transport Protocol (SMTP)
Hypertext Transfer Protocol (HTTP)	subnet mask
Internet	TCP/IP
Internet Service Provider (ISP)	Tracert
internetwork	Windows Internet Name Service (WINS)
IP address	WINIPCFG
IPCONFIG	World Wide Web (WWW)
local resources	

Review Questions

1. Using either a Windows 9x or Windows 2000 workstation, which of the following components do you need to connect to a Microsoft network server? (Select all that apply.)

   A. Protocol

   B. Client

   C. Adapter

   D. Sharing

2. Which of the following are common Internet connection types. (Select all that apply.)

   A. ISDN

   B. POTS

   C. T1

   D. DSL

   E. All of the above

3. Transmission Control Protocol/Internet Protocol (TCP/IP) is a collection of protocols that help manage Internet communication. Each computer running TCP/IP must have a unique IP address assigned to it. Which of the following statements best describes an IP address?

   A. An IP address is no more than your dial-up telephone number.

   B. An IP address is a set of four numbers, each of which must be from 0 to 255. These numbers can be automatically provided or assigned by a system administrator.

   C. An IP address is a set of three numbers, each of which must be from 0 to 255. An IP address is a unique name that identifies the computer within a network. This name can be automatically provided or assigned by a system administrator.

   D. IP addresses are composed of four numbers, each of which is between 1 and 256. These numbers can be automatically provided or assigned by a system administrator.

4. You've enabled file and printer sharing on your Windows 9x system. You must now specify how security will be handled. What are your options? (Select all that apply.)

   A. Share-Level Access Control

   B. System-Wide Access Control

   C. Remote-Access Control

   D. User-Level Access Control

5. TCP/IP is installed on each PC within a network. You can communicate within the network but are unable to access the Internet. Which of the following TCP/IP settings must be properly configured for Internet access? (Select all that apply.)

   A. IP Address

   B. Subnet Mask

   C. Default Gateway

   D. DNS Server

6. A Windows 9*x* workstation includes default support for which of the following network types? (Select all that apply.)

   A. Microsoft's Windows Networking

   B. Sun's Solaris

   C. Novell's NetWare

   D. Apple's Macintosh Networking

7. You've installed an older NIC in a Windows 9*x* system. During the Plug-and-Play (PnP) process, you encounter a conflict. Which of the following methods would you use to resolve the conflict?

   A. Disable PnP on the NIC either with a jumper or with the software setup program.

   B. Run PnP again. The conflict should be resolved the second time around.

   C. Older NICs are prone to this problem. Remove the older NIC and buy a new one.

   D. None of the above.

8. Configuring a Windows 2000 system as a network client requires three elements: a client, an adapter, and _____ .

   A. A host name

   B. An IP address

   C. A protocol

   D. A gateway

9. You've set up a network whereby each computer acts as a client and a server and in which each user shares each other's resources, including printers. What is the correct term for such an arrangement?

   A. Enterprise Services

   B. Sharing & Caring

   C. Server-client linking

   D. Peer-to-peer networking

10. In a Windows 9*x* system, which of the following statements involving NetBEUI and NetBIOS is true?

    A. NetBEUI is a name resolution system, whereas NetBIOS is a transport protocol.

    B. NetBEUI and NetBIOS are subprotocols of TCP/IP.

    C. NetBEUI is a transport protocol, and NetBIOS is a name resolution system.

    D. NetBEUI and NetBIOS are not used within a Windows 9*x* system.

11. Sending and receiving electronic mail (e-mail) is a common benefit of the Internet. Assuming a user has access to the Internet on a properly configured PC, which of the following items are required before a user can begin using e-mail?

    A. An e-mail account and a domain

    B. An e-mail account and an e-mail client

    C. An e-mail account and e-mail permissions

    D. None of the above

12. You can map a network drive in both Windows 9*x* and 2000 using which of the following commands?

    A. Map Network Drive

    B. Connect to Network Share

    C. Connect Network Share

    D. Map Network Share

13. You've been granted the right to use a shared folder and printer in a Windows 9*x* system. What do you need to do to gain access to them?

    A. From the desktop, double-click the Network icon. Click the Shared Resources tab. Any resources you have access to will be listed.

    B. Double-click the My Computer icon on your desktop. Click Web Folders. Your shared resources will be listed.

    C. From the desktop, double-click the Network Neighborhood icon, which will allow you to browse for shared resources.

    D. Open the Control Panel and click on the Network Neighborhood icon. Browse for shared resources.

14. Computers communicate using IP addresses. The address can be a series of numbers or a host name such as Bob's PC. Obviously, it is easier for humans to remember the host name, but computers communicate with numbers. Which of the following methods help locate a computer's numeric IP address when a human searches for it using only the host name? (Select all that apply.)

A. NRP (Name Resolution Protocol)

B. WINS (Windows Internet Name Service)

C. DNS (Domain Name System)

D. None of the above

15. Which of the following types of networking components can be added in the Network program on a Windows 9x system? (Select all that apply.)

A. Protocol

B. Adapter

C. Client

D. Service

16. Which of the following is the correct way to use the protocol utility IPCONFIG in a Windows 2000 environment?

A. IPCONFIG does not work with Windows 2000.

B. Choose Start ➤ Run and type **IPCONFIG**.

C. Open a browser window and type **IPCONFIG** in the address line.

D. Choose Start ➤ Run, type **CMD**, and press Enter. At the command prompt, type **IPCONFIG**.

17. What would you need to do to create a new Dial-Up Networking (DUN) connection within a Windows 9x system?

A. Open the Control Panel and click the Dial-Up Networking icon. Click Make New Connection. Choose a name for your connection. Select which modem you are using. Enter the dial-in telephone number. Click the Finish button.

B. Choose Start ➤ Programs ➤ Accessories. Choose Dial-Up Networking. This will open a window that shows all current DUN connections. Double-click Make New Connection. Choose a name for your connection. Select which modem you are using. Enter the dial-in telephone number. Click the Finish button.

C. Open the Control Panel and click the Make New Connection icon. Choose a name for your connection. Select which modem you are using. Enter the dial-in telephone number. Click the Finish button.

D. None of the above.

18. Networks that transmit data use protocols to make communication possible. TCP/IP, for example, uses two different analog connection protocols: Serial Line Internet Protocol (SLIP) and Point-to-Point Protocol (PPP). PPP is the more common of the two protocols for which of the following reasons? (Select all that apply.)

    A. PPP is easier to configure.

    B. PPP broadcasts all data requests, increasing the chances of a response.

    C. PPP uses enhanced error-checking, making it more stable.

    D. All of the above.

    E. Choose all that apply.

19. In a Windows 9*x* environment, if you don't know the name of the computer that is acting as the host for a resource you are looking for, you can use the _____ command.

    A. Map

    B. Run

    C. Find

    D. Search

20. You have just granted someone share-level access to a folder in your Windows 9*x* system. What are the three access rights available? (Select all that apply.)

    A. Full Access

    B. Depends on Password

    C. Depends on IP Address

    D. Read-Only

Answers to Review Questions

1. A, B, C. Using either Windows 9*x* or 2000, three initial components— Adapter, Client, and Protocol—are required to connect to a Microsoft network server.

2. E. Most home Internet connections use POTS (Plain Old Telephone System). Other options include fiber optics (ATM), digital phone technology (DSL), T1 and T3, digital phone line (ISDN), Frame Relay, and 56K point-to-point.

3. B. Every computer running TCP/IP must have a unique IP address, and that address is in the format *x.x.x.x*, where *x* is a number from 0 to 255. These numbers can be automatically provided or assigned by a system administrator. The machine will also have a host name, which identifies the machine on the network.

4. A, D. There are two security options in a Windows 9*x* system. Share-Level Access Control involves supplying a username, password, and security setting for each shared resource. User-Level Access Control means there is a central database of users that Windows 9*x* uses to specify security settings for each shared resource.

5. A, B, C, D. A proper IP address and subnet mask are essential for any sort of network communication. However, to reach the Internet, a default gateway, which is the IP address of the router your machine uses to access the Internet, must be configured. You also need the Domain Name System (DNS) server, so you can type **www.yahoo.com** instead of having to remember the numeric IP address.

6. A, C. Within a Windows 9*x* workstation, clients are provided for both Microsoft and Novell networks.

7. A. Conflicts between older NICs and the Plug-and-Play installation process can occur. However, as indicated in option A, if PnP is disabled either with a jumper or with the software program, the device can be successfully installed.

8. C. Both Windows 2000 and Windows 9*x* require three elements: a client, an adapter, and a protocol. How each element is configured is slightly different between the two operating systems, however. Host names, IP addresses, and gateways may also be necessary, but only if the chosen protocol is TCP/IP.

9. D. Networking in which users share each other's resources, is called peer-to-peer networking.

10. C. NetBEUI is a transport protocol, managing data transmission between two computers. NetBIOS is a name resolution system, allowing a computer to search for another computer on a network by its Microsoft computer name.

11. B. To send and receive e-mail, all that is required is an e-mail account and an e-mail client.

12. A. This is one of those "technicality" questions, but knowing proper terminology is important when taking technical exams, and questions like this crop up regularly.

13. C. The Network Neighborhood icon, located on the Desktop, provides easy access to any shared resources. Network Neighborhood is not accessible from the Control Panel or from My Computer.

14. B, C. Although there are a number of services available for resolving names, the most common are WINS and DNS. WINS resolves NetBIOS computer names to the appropriate IP address, while DNS does the same for host names.

15. A, B, C, D. There are four basic types of networking components in a Windows 9x system. They are protocol, adapter, client, and service.

16. D. As indicated in option D, the IPCONFIG protocol utility is a good way to find basic information about your TCP/IP configuration. It can be used at the command prompt. If you type **IPCONFIG /A**, the system will display additional information.

17. B. You can create a new DUN as indicated in option B. The Dial-Up Networking icon can also be accessed by double-clicking My Computer from the desktop.

18. A, C. As indicated, what makes Point-to-Point the more popular analog connection protocol is the fact that it is easy to configure, and due to its error-checking capabilities, it is more stable.

19. C. The Find command can be used to search your machine for files or the network for other machines. Search is used on Windows 2000 to do the same tasks.

20. A, B, D. Read-Only, Full Access, and Depends on Password are the three options for access rights. These options are accessible by right-clicking the shared folder and choosing Sharing.

Chapter 19

Windows and Application Troubleshooting

THE FOLLOWING OBJECTIVES ARE COVERED IN THIS CHAPTER:

✓ **1.2 Identify basic concepts and procedures for creating, viewing, and managing files, directories, and disks. This includes procedures for changing file attributes and the ramifications of those changes (for example, security issues).**

Content may include the following:

- File attributes—Read Only, Hidden, System, and Archive attributes
- File naming conventions (most common extensions)
- IDE/SCSI
- Internal/External
- Backup/Restore
- Partitioning/Formatting/File System
  - FAT
  - FAT16
  - FAT32
  - NTFS4
  - NTFS5
  - HPFS

Windows-based utilties:

- SCANDISK
- Device Manager
- System Manager
- Computer Manager

- MSCONFIG.EXE
- REGEDIT.EXE (View information/Backup registry)
- REGEDT32.EXE
- ATTRIB.EXE
- EXTRACT.EXE
- DEFRAG.EXE
- EDIT.COM
- FDISK.EXE
- SYSEDIT.EXE
- SCANREG
- WSCRIPT.EXE
- HWINFO.EXE
- ASD.EXE (Automatic Skip Driver)
- Cvt1.EXE (Drive Converter FAT16 to FAT32)

✓ **3.1 Recognize and interpret the meaning of common error codes and startup messages from the boot sequence, and identify steps to correct the problems.**

Content may include the following:

- Safe Mode
- No operating system found
- Error in CONFIG.SYS line XX
- Bad or missing COMMAND.COM
- HIMEM.SYS not loaded
- Missing or corrupt HIMEM.SYS
- SCSI
- Swap file
- NT boot issues
- Dr. Watson
- Failure to start GUI
- Windows Protection Error
- Event Viewer—Event log is full
- A device referenced in SYSTEM.INI, WIN.INI, Registry is not found

✓ **3.2 Recognize common problems and determine how to resolve them.**

Content may include the following:

- Eliciting problem symptoms from customers
- Having customer reproduce error as part of the diagnostic process
- Identifying recent changes to the computer environment from the user
- Troubleshooting Windows-specific printing problems
  - Print spool is stalled
  - Incorrect/incompatible driver for print
  - Incorrect parameter

Other common problems:

- General Protection Faults
- Illegal operation
- Invalid working directory
- System lock up
- Option (sound card, modem, or input device) will not function
- Application will not start or load
- Cannot log on to network (option—NIC not functioning)
- TSR (Terminate Stay Resident) programs and virus
- Applications don't install
- Network connection

Viruses and virus types:

- What they are
- Sources (floppy, e-mails, etc.)
- How to determine presence

roubleshooting involves asking a lot of questions of yourself and of other people. Beginners (and yes, I was a beginner once upon a time) like the trial and error method of fixing things, but in the long run, a methodological approach will work better. The reason that beginners often choose a trial and error approach is that they don't yet have a good enough background to analyze the problem.

NOTE For complete coverage of objective 1.2, please also see Chapter 14. For complete coverage of objective 3.2, please also see Chapter 17.

NOTE Analysis is the act of breaking down a structure or system into its component parts and their relationships.

More than occasionally, a technician will unwittingly create new problems in an attempt to fix a real problem. For example, if a program will not run and displays an Out of Memory error, it might seem logical to add more memory.

But certain types of memory currently on the market will not work in older 486 computers—what happens if the memory the technician installs is the wrong type for the computer? Now there are two problems.

And what if the computer with the mismatched memory actually starts up but eventually locks up because of the memory problem? The lock-ups could create an interruption in writing information to the hard drive, and a program could become corrupted. That would make three problems total.

Once the technician has sorted out all the problems, it's time to actually repair whatever went wrong. In the above example, it is quite likely that the source of the original Out of Memory error was really some corrupted program code. Many times, a Windows program with some damage to one or more components will cause exactly that error to be displayed.

Troubleshooting Steps

In a computer system, there are at least four main parts to be considered, each of which is in turn made up of many pieces:

1. There is a collection of hardware pieces that are integrated into a working system. As you know, the hardware can be quite complex, what with motherboards, hard drives, video cards, etc. Software can be equally perplexing.

2. There is an operating system that in turn is dependent on the hardware. Remember that the DOS and Windows operating systems have kernels, internal commands, and external commands, which may interact with the hardware in different ways.

3. There is an application or a software program that is supposed to do something. Programs such as Microsoft Word and Excel are now bundled with a great many features.

4. There is a computer user, ready to take the computer system to its limits (and beyond). A technician can often forget that the customer user is a very complex and important part of the puzzle.

Effective troubleshooting will require some experience just for the background required to analyze the problem at hand, but there are also some other logical steps that need to be remembered. Ask yourself the question, "Is there a problem?" Perhaps it is as simple as a customer expecting too much from the computer. If there is a problem, is it just one problem?

Step 1: Talk to the Customer

Talking to the user is an important first step. Your first contact with the computer that has a problem will usually be through the customer, either directly or by way of a work order that contains the user's complaint. Often, the complaint will be something straightforward, such as, "There's a disk stuck in the floppy drive." At other times, the problem will be complex and the customer will not have mentioned everything that has been going wrong.

The act of diagnosis starts with the art of customer relations. Go to the customer with an attitude of trust: *believe* what the customer is saying. At the same time, go to the customer with an attitude of hidden skepticism, meaning *don't* believe that the customer has told you everything. This attitude of hidden skepticism is not the same as distrust. Most customers are not going to lie, but they may inadvertently forget to give some crucial detail.

For example, a customer once complained that his CD-ROM drive didn't work. What he failed to say was that it had never worked and that he had installed it himself. It turned out that he had mounted it with screws that were too long and that these prevented the tray from ejecting properly.

The most important part of this step is to have the customer show you what the problem is. The best method I've seen of doing this is to ask them, "Show me what 'not working' looks like." That way, you see the conditions and methods under which the problem occurs. The problem may be a simple matter of an improper method. The user may be doing an operation incorrectly or doing the steps in the wrong order. During this step, you have the opportunity to observe how the problem occurs, so pay attention.

Step 2: Gather Information

The user can give you vital information. The most important question is "what changed?" Problems don't usually come out of nowhere. Was a new piece of hardware or software added? Did the user drop some equipment? Was there a power outage or a storm? These are the types of questions that you can ask a user in trying to find out what is different.

If nothing changed, at least outwardly, then what was going on at the time of failure? Can the problem be reproduced? Can the problem be worked around? The point here is to ask as many questions as you need to in order to pinpoint the trouble.

Step 3: Eliminate Possibilities

Once the problem or problems have been clearly identified, your next step is to isolate possible causes. If the problem cannot be clearly identified, then further tests will be necessary. A common technique for hardware and software problems alike is to strip the system down to bare-bones basics. In a hardware situation, this could mean removing all interface cards except those absolutely required for the system to operate. In a software situation, this may mean booting up with the CONFIG.SYS and AUTOEXEC.BAT files disabled.

Generally, then, you can gradually rebuild the system toward the point where it started. When you reintroduce a component and the problem reappears, then you know that component is the one causing the problem.

Step 4: Document Your Work

One last point needs to be made in this brief introduction to troubleshooting: you should document your work. If the process of elimination or the process of questioning the user goes beyond two or three crucial elements, start writing it down. Nothing is more infuriating than knowing you did something to make the system work but not being able to remember what it was.

Windows File-Related Problems

Many problems in Windows can be traced to missing, corrupt, or misconfigured files. They can cause consternation to no end because they can be troublesome to fix. Thankfully, they usually give indications of which file is the problem in the error message.

In this section, you will learn about some of the various file-related problems that can be found in Windows as well as their solutions. The problems you will learn about in this section can be categorized into four main areas:

- System files not found
- Config file issues
- Swap file issues
- NT boot issues

Since the most easily fixed problems are related to missing system files, that's the next topic we'll cover.

System Files Not Found

Every operating system or operating environment (such as Windows 9*x* or Windows NT) has certain key system files that must be present in order for it to function. If these files are missing or corrupt, the operating system will cease to function properly. Files can be deleted by accident rather easily, so it's important to know what these system files are, where they are located, and how to replace them.

Windows 9*x* system files are covered in Chapter 13, "Windows 95/98," and Windows 2000 system files are covered in Chapter 14, "Windows 2000."

When you boot Windows 9*x* or Windows NT, the presence of the system files (e.g., HIMEM.SYS, COMMAND.COM, etc.) is checked, and each file is loaded. If you'll remember, the computer's BIOS first checks the hardware of the PC, then looks for a boot sector on one of the disks and loads the operating system found in that boot sector. However, if the computer can't find a boot sector with an operating system installed on any of the disks, it will display an error similar to the following:

```
No operating system found
```

This error means that the computer's BIOS checked all the drives it knew about and couldn't find any disk with a bootable sector. This could be for any number of reasons, including:

- An operating system wasn't installed.
- The boot sector has been corrupted.
- The boot files have been corrupted.

Thankfully, there are a couple of solutions to these problems. First of all, if the file or files are simply missing, just copy them from the original setup diskettes or CD-ROM, or copy them from a backup (assuming you have one). The same holds true if you have a corrupt file, except you must delete the corrupt file(s) first, then replace them with new copies.

 When deleting and/or replacing system files, you must use the ATTRIB command to remove the hidden, system, and read-only attributes before you replace these files.

These same concepts hold true for other system file–related problems, such as:

Bad or missing COMMAND.COM

HIMEM.SYS not loaded

Missing or corrupt HIMEM.SYS

These errors just mean that the specified (e.g., COMMAND.COM, HIMEM.SYS) files are either missing or corrupt. Just replace them with fresh copies. The error should go away, and the computer will function properly.

Configuration File Issues

As discussed in Chapters 13 and 14, Windows 9x and Windows NT contain several files that hold configuration data for the Windows, such as the Registry, SYSTEM.INI, WIN.INI, and the CONFIG.SYS. Because these files can be edited by a user, the possibility for introduction of invalid configurations is more likely. Additionally, most of the software installation programs modify these files when a new program is installed. These files are modified so often, in fact, that it is a wonder they aren't corrupted more often.

Some of the more commonly seen errors in Windows that are related to configuration files are:

A device referenced in SYSTEM.INI can not be found

A device referenced in WIN.INI can not be found

A device referenced in the Registry can not be found

Error in CONFIG.SYS line XX

These errors are basically the same error and mean that an item that refers to a piece of hardware or software that wasn't installed was placed into a configuration file. The difference is which file the error is contained in. Again, with missing stuff, the solution is very simple: just add the missing item. In fact, in `Error in CONFIG.SYS line xx`, the error message actually tells you which line has the error in it. You can then go directly to that line and fix the problem. With the `SYSTEM.INI` and `WIN.INI` file errors, you must search through the files using your favorite text editor to try and find the invalid line. It may be something as hard to find as an additional backslash put in the wrong place, or as easy to find as a string of corrupt characters.

That process is the same for the Registry except that you must use the Registry Editor (`REGEDIT.EXE` or `REGEDT32.EXE`, for Windows 9*x* and Windows NT/2000, respectively) to search for corrupt or invalid entries. You will learn more about the Registry later in this chapter.

Swap File Issues

As mentioned in earlier chapters, Windows uses swap files (called page files in Windows NT) to increase the amount of usable memory it has by using hard disk space as memory. However, sometimes problems can occur when a computer doesn't have enough disk space to make a proper swap file. Because Windows relies on swap files for proper operation, if a swap file isn't big enough, Windows will slow down and start running out of usable memory. All sorts of memory-related problems can stem from incorrect or too small swap files. Symptoms of swap file problems include an extremely slow system speed and a disk that is constantly being accessed. This condition is known as hard disk *thrashing* and occurs because Windows doesn't have enough memory to contain all the programs that are running, and there isn't enough disk space for a swap file to contain them all. This causes Windows to swap between memory and hard disk.

The solution to this problem is to first free up some disk space. With IDE hard disk sizes at tens of gigabytes for around $100, the easiest thing to do is install a bigger hard disk. If that solution isn't practical, you must delete enough unused files so that the swap file can be made large enough to be functional.

Windows NT Boot Issues

Troubleshooting Windows NT boot issues is another type of Windows trouble-shooting that is commonly performed. To understand Windows NT boot issues, you must first understand the NT boot process, which is as follows:

1. The POST routine examines the boot sector and loads the Master Boot Record (MBR).

2. The boot sector is loaded from the active partition.

3. NTLDR is loaded from the boot sector and initialized.

4. NTLDR loads the appropriate minifile drives for the type of file system on the boot partition (e.g., FAT or NTFS).

5. NTLDR reads the BOOT.INI file and looks for the list of operating systems installed on the computer. Windows NT is one of the choices, along with any other operating system that was installed over when Windows NT was installed.

6. A user selects an operating system to boot to.

7. If Windows NT is selected, NTLDR runs NTDETECT.COM to detect new hardware.

8. NTLDR then loads the kernel file (NTOSKRNL.EXE), hardware abstraction layer (HAL), and the Registry, as well as any device drivers found there.

9. NTLDR finally passes control to NTOSKRNL.EXE. At this point, the boot process is finished and NTOSKRNL can start loading other files.

As you can see, NTLDR is heavily relied upon during the boot process. If it is missing or corrupted, Windows NT will not be able to boot and you'll get an error similar to Can't find NTLDR.

On the other hand, if you get an error such as NTOSKRNL.EXE missing or corrupt on bootup, it may be an error in the BOOT.INI file. This is a common occurrence if you have improperly used the multi(0)disk(0)rdisk(0)partition(1)\ WINNT="Windows NT Server" syntax entries. If these entries are correct, the NTOSKRNL.EXE file may be corrupt or missing. Boot to a startup disk and replace the file from the setup disks or CD-ROM.

Windows Printing Problems

If a printer is not printing at all, then you should start with the DOS troubleshooting method. First, reboot the computer in Safe Mode DOS Prompt. (See the section "Windows-Based Utilities" for more information on Safe Mode.) Then copy a file or a directory listing to the printer port. If the file or directory listing doesn't print, the cause is most likely a hardware failure or loose cable. If it *does* print, then you can assume the printing problems are associated with the Windows printer drivers.

One common source of printer driver errors is corruption of the driver. If a printer doesn't work, you can delete the printer from the printer settings window and reinstall it. If this method fails, the problem may be that related printer files were not replaced. Delete all printers from the computer and reinstall them. If this second method fails, then the printer driver is not compatible with Windows 9x or with the printer, and you will need to obtain an updated driver.

A quick way to test the printer functionality is to use the Print Test Page option. This option is presented to you as the last step when setting up a new printer in Windows. Always select this option when you're setting up a new printer so you can test its functionality. To print a test page for a printer that's already set up, look for the option on the Properties menu for the particular printer.

After the test page is sent to the printer, the computer will ask if it printed correctly. For the first few times, you'll probably want to answer No and use the troubleshooting Wizard that appears, but after you have troubleshot a few printer problems, you may prefer to answer Yes and bypass the Wizard, which is rather simplistic and annoying.

Other Common Problems

Some common Windows problems don't fall into any great category other than "common Windows problems". Some of these problems include:

General Protection Faults (GPFs)   Probably the most common and most frustrating error. A *General Protection Fault (GPF)* happens in Windows when a program accesses memory that another program is using or when a program accesses a memory address that doesn't exist. Generally, GPFs are the result of sloppy programming. To fix this type of problem, a simple reboot will usually clear memory. If they keep occurring, check to see which software is causing the GPF. Then, find out if the manufacturer of the software has a patch to prevent it from GPFing.

Windows protection error   A Windows protection error is a condition that usually happens on either startup or shutdown. Protection errors occur because Windows 9*x* could not load or unload a virtual device driver (VxD) properly. Thankfully, this error usually tells which VxD is experiencing the problem so you can check to see if the specified VxD is missing or corrupt. If it is, you can replace it with a new copy. If it is one of the Windows 9*x* built-in VxDs, you must re-run Windows 9*x* SETUP.EXE with the /p I option.

Illegal operation   Occasionally, a program will quit for apparently no reason and present you with a window that says This program has performed an illegal operation and will be shut down. If the problem persists, contact the program vendor. An *illegal operation error* usually means that a program was forced to quit because it did something Windows didn't like. It then displays this error window. The name of the program that quit will appear at the top of the window along with three buttons: OK, Cancel, and Details. The OK and Cancel buttons do the same thing: they both dismiss the window. The Details button will open the window a little farther and show the details of the error. The details of the error include which module experienced the problem, the memory location being accessed at the time, and the registers and flags of the processor at the time of the error.

System lock-up   It is obvious when a system lock-up occurs. The system simply stops responding to commands and stops processing completely. System lock-ups can occur when a computer is asked to process too many instructions at once with too little memory. Usually, the cure for a system lock-up is to simply reboot. If the lock-ups are persistent, it may be a hardware-related problem instead of a software problem.

Dr. Watson   Windows NT 4 includes a special utility known as Dr. Watson. This utility intercepts all error conditions and, instead of presenting the user with a cryptic Windows error, presents the user with a slew of information that can be used to troubleshoot the problem. Additionally, Dr. Watson logs all errors to log files stored in the WINDOWS\DRWATSON directory.

Failure to start GUI   Occasionally, the GUI of Windows won't appear. The system will hang just before the GUI appears. Or, in the case of Windows NT, the *Blue Screen of Death (BSOD)*—not a technical term, by the way—will appear. The BSOD is another way of describing the blue screen error condition that occurs when Windows NT fails to boot properly or quits unexpectedly. In Windows 9x, instead of a BSOD, you will simply get a black screen (usually with a blinking cursor in the upper left corner) that indicates there is a problem. Because it is at this stage that the device drivers for the various pieces of hardware are installed, if your Windows GUI fails to start properly, more than likely the problem is related to a misconfigured driver or misconfigured hardware. Try booting Windows in Safe Mode to bypass this problem. (See the section "Windows-Based Utilities" for more information on Safe Mode.)

If you happen to get a Blue Screen of Death (BSOD) with a "Fatal Exception error 0D," chances are that the culprit is a problem relating to the video card.

Option (sound card, modem, SCSI card, or input device) will not function   When you are using Windows, you are constantly interacting with some piece of hardware. Each piece of hardware has a Windows driver that must be loaded in order for Windows to be able to use it. Additionally, the hardware has to be installed and functioning properly. If the device driver is not installed properly or the hardware is misconfigured, the device won't function properly.

TSR (Terminate and Stay Resident) programs and viruses   In the days of DOS, there was no easy way of running a utility program in the background while you ran an application. Because necessity is the mother of invention, programmers came up with Terminate and Stay Resident (TSR) programs. These programs were loaded from the AUTOEXEC.BAT and stayed resident in memory until called for by some key combination. Unfortunately, while that worked for DOS, Windows 95 had its own method for using background utilities. If any DOS TSR programs are in memory when Windows 9x is running, the TSR(s) can interfere with the proper operation of Windows programs. Before you install Windows 9x, make sure that any DOS TSRs are disabled in the AUTOEXEC.BAT.

Cannot log on to network (option—NIC not functioning)   If your computer is hooked up to a network (and more and more computers today are), you need to know when your computer is not functioning on the network properly and what to do about it. In most cases, the problem can be attributed to either a malfunctioning Network Interface Card (NIC) or improperly installed network software. The biggest indicator in Windows that some component of the network software is nonfunctional is that you can't log on to the network or access any network service. To fix this problem, you must first fix the underlying hardware problem (if one exists), then properly install or configure the network software.

 Networking software is covered in Chapter 18, "Configuring Network Software."

Applications don't install   We've all experienced this frustration. You are trying to install the coolest new program and, for whatever reason, it just won't install properly. It may give you one of the above-mentioned errors or a cryptic installation error. If a software program won't install and it gives you any previously mentioned errors (e.g., GPF or Illegal Operation), use the solutions for those errors first. If the error that occurs during install is unique to the application being installed, check the application manufacturer's Web site for an explanation or update. These errors generally occur when you're trying to install over an application that already exists, or when you're trying to replace a file that already exists but that another application has in use. When installing an application, it is extremely important that you quit all running programs before installing so that the installer can replace any files it needs to.

Application will not start   Once you have an application successfully installed, you may run across a problem getting the application to start properly. This problem can come from any number of sources, including an improper installation, software conflict, and system instability. If your application was installed incorrectly, the files required to properly run the program may not be present and the program can't function without them. If a shared file that's used by other programs is installed, it could be a different version from what should be installed that causes conflicts with other already-installed programs. Finally, if one program GPFs, it can cause memory problems that can destabilize the system and cause other programs to crash. The solution to these problems is to reinstall the offending application, first making sure that all programs are closed.

Invalid working directory   Some Windows programs are extremely processing intensive. These programs require an area on the hard disk to store their temporary files while they work. This area is commonly known as a *working directory*, and the location of it is usually specified during that program's installation. However, if that directory changes after installation and the program still thinks its working directory is in the same location, the program will receive an error that says something such as `Invalid working directory`. The solution is to reinstall the program with the correct parameters for the working directory.

It is for this reason that many programs use the Windows TEMP directory as their working directory. You will only see this error if the programmer chose to use a user-settable working directory.

Bad Network Connection   When troubleshooting network problems, as with other problems, never fail to check the simple stuff. Although it could be something difficult like weird driver conflicts, more often than not, problems sending and receiving data with the network can often be attributed to bad physical connections. Bad network connections are the result of some problem with the cabling system and its connections. Things to check when looking for cable problems include:

- Broken or loose connectors
- Wires pulled free from connector
- Kinked wires
- Unplugged patch cables

Remember that there are two universal solutions to Windows problems: rebooting and obtaining an update from the software manufacturer.

Windows-Based Utilities

In addition to learning about the many common problems and troubleshooting techniques for Windows, you should know about the different resources that Microsoft provides with Windows to troubleshoot Windows. These resources are the best to use if you have no other troubleshooting tools available. They can also be used as a starting point for troubleshooting a computer. The built-in Windows tools that the A+ exam tests you on, include:

- Safe Mode
- SCANDISK
- Device Manager
- System Manager

- Computer Manager
- MSCONFIG.EXE
- REGEDIT.EXE (view information/back up Registry)
- REGEDT32.EXE
- ATTRIB.EXE
- EXTRACT.EXE
- DEFRAG.EXE
- EDIT.COM
- FDISK.EXE
- SYSEDIT.EXE
- SCANREG
- WSCRIPT.EXE
- HWINFO.EXE
- ASD.EXE (Automatic Skip Driver)
- CVT1.EXE (Drive Converter FAT16 to FAT32)
- Event Viewer—Event log is full

Safe Mode

When Windows won't start properly, it is probably due to a driver or some piece of software that's not loading correctly. To fix problems of this nature, you should boot Windows in *Safe Mode*. In Safe Mode, Windows loads a minimal set of drivers (including a VGA-only video driver) so that you can disable an offending driver. To start Windows in Safe Mode, press the F8 key when you see the Starting Windows display during Windows bootup. This will bring up a menu that will allow you to choose to start Windows in Safe Mode. Once booted in Safe Mode, you can uninstall any driver you suspect is causing a Windows boot problem. Upon reboot, the system should go back to normal operation (non-Safe Mode).

You can also use the F8 menu to select other boot options, such as logging all messages to a log file during boot, booting to a command prompt, or starting Windows in Safe Mode with network support.

SCANDISK

You can use the Windows SCANDISK utility to correct corrupt file problems or disk errors, like cross-linked files (which CHKDSK can't do). There are two ways you can use SCANDISK. First, if you suspect a particular hard disk is having problems or you have a corrupt file on a particular disk, you can manually start SCANDISK by right-clicking the problem disk and selecting Properties. This will bring up the Properties window for that disk, which shows the current status of the selected disk drive, as shown here.

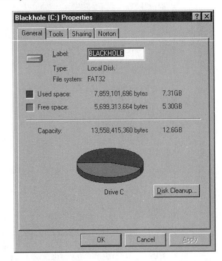

Click the Tools tab at the top of the screen, then click the Check Now button in the Error-Checking Status section to start SCANDISK, as shown here.

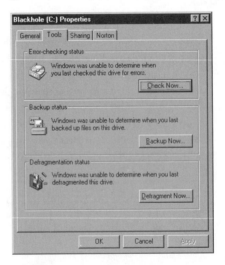

Once you start SCANDISK, you start the scanning process by selecting the type of scan you want to perform (Standard or Thorough) and clicking Start.

SCANDISK will scan the disk looking for corrupt files and fix or delete them, as shown here. Additionally, if you choose the Thorough option, SCANDISK will scan the surface of the disk for defects and mark them as unusable.

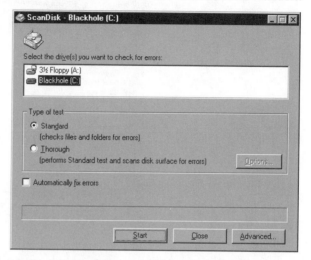

You can also run SCANDISK automatically. When you turn off a Windows computer without choosing the Shut Down command, Windows 95 OSR2 and Windows 98 will automatically run SCANDISK when the computer is restarted. SCANDISK will check to see if any of the Windows files are corrupt so that Windows can be started.

Device Manager

With Windows 9x, Microsoft provides the Device Manager, a tool that will analyze hardware-related problems. The Device Manager displays all of the devices installed in a computer (as shown in Figure 19.1). If a device is malfunctioning, a yellow triangle with an exclamation point inside it is displayed (as with the Iomega Parallel Port Interface in Figure 19.1).

FIGURE 19.1 The Windows 9x Device Manager

With this utility, you can not only view the devices installed in a system and any of those devices that are failing, but you can also double-click on a device and view and set its properties (as shown in Figure 19.2). On the General tab, you will see the status of the device (i.e., whether its working or not). The other tabs are used for configuring the individual devices, adding or updating drivers, and verifying the version of drivers installed.

FIGURE 19.2 Properties of a network card

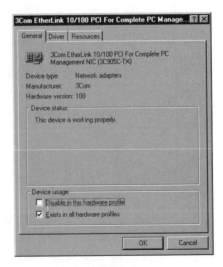

When troubleshooting a specific Windows-related hardware problem, you can access the Device Manager in two different ways. First and quickest, you can right-click on the My Computer icon and choose Properties. This brings up the General tab by default. To access the Device Manager from here, click on the Device Manager tab. You can then use the Device Manager to troubleshoot your system.

System Manager

You may be asking yourself, what is a System Manager? We asked ourselves the same question when we looked at the CompTIA A+ objectives. There are several options, but at the time of this writing we could find none that referred to Windows 9*x*, NT, or 2000. As the A+ operating system technology evolves, perhaps we will see a more definitive explanation as to why CompTIA included System Manager in their objectives.

Computer Manager

Windows 2000 includes a new piece of software to manage computer settings, the Computer Manager. Since Windows 2000 is more advanced as a platform, the Computer Manager can manage more than just the installed hardware devices. In addition to a Device Manager that functions almost identically to the one in Windows 9*x*, Computer Manager can also manage all the services running on that computer. It contains an Event Viewer to show all the system errors and events that show up, as well as methods to configure the software components of all the computer's hardware. Figure 19.3 shows an example of the Computer Manager running on Windows 2000.

FIGURE 19.3   Windows 2000 Computer Manager

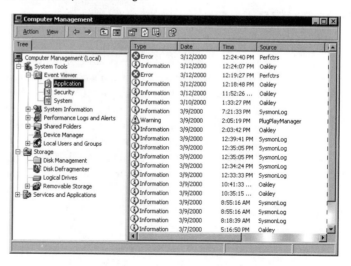

To access the Computer Manager, go to Start ➤ Programs ➤ Administrative Tools ➤ Computer Manager. You will see all of the computer management tools, including the Device Manager. You can then use Computer Manager to manage hardware devices and software services.

Event Viewer

Windows NT, like other network operating systems, employs comprehensive error and informational logging routines. Every program and process theoretically could have its own logging utility, but Microsoft has come up with a rather slick utility, Event Viewer, which, through log files, tracks all events on a particular Windows NT computer. Normally, though, you must be an administrator or a member of the Administrators group to have access to Event Viewer.

To start Event Viewer, log in as an administrator (or equivalent) and go to Start ➤ Programs ➤ Administrative Tools ➤ Event Viewer. From here you can view the System, Application, and Security log files. The System log file displays alerts that pertain to the general operation of Windows. The Application log file logs server application errors. The Security log file logs security events such as login successes and failures. These log files can give a general indication of a Windows computer's health.

One situation that does occur with the Event Viewer is that the Event Viewer log files get full. Although it isn't really a problem, it can make viewing log files confusing because there are many entries. Even though each event is time- and date-stamped, you should clear the Event Viewer every so often. To do this, open the Event Viewer and choose Clear All Events from the log menu. This will erase all events in the current log file, allowing you to see new events easier when they occur.

MSCONFIG.EXE

With the introduction of Windows 98, a new utility was introduced, MSCONFIG.EXE (a.k.a. System Configuration Utility) that allows a user to manage their computer system's configuration. MSCONFIG.EXE (shown in Figure 19.4) allows a user to boot Windows 98 in diagnostic mode, in which a user can select which drivers to load interactively. If you suspect a certain driver is causing problems during boot, you can use MSCONFIG.EXE to prevent that driver from loading. Additionally, each of the major configuration files (CONFIG.SYS, AUTOEXEC.BAT, WIN.INI, SYSTEM.INI) and the programs loaded at startup can be reconfigured and reordered using a graphical interface.

FIGURE 19.4   MSCONFIG.EXE Screen

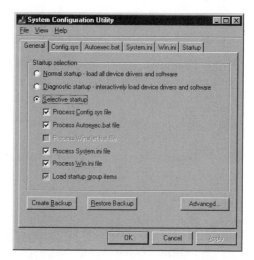

If you want to prevent a particular driver from loading, you can go to the tab that represents the file from which the driver is loaded and uncheck the box in front of the driver you want to eliminate. Or, from the General tab, you can check Diagnostic Startup in the Startup Selection area and then reboot the computer. Upon reboot, as each driver loads, you will be able to choose whether or not a particular driver loads or not during this boot cycle.

REGEDIT.EXE

The most flexible (and possibly the most dangerous) utility in the Windows troubleshooting arsenal is the Registry Editor, also known by its executable names REGEDIT.EXE (for Windows 9x) and REGEDT32.EXE (for Windows NT and 2000). The Registry stores all Windows configuration information. If you edit the Registry, you are essentially changing the configuration of Windows. The Registry Editor is used to manually change settings that are usually changed by other means (such as through Setup programs and other Windows utilities).

In addition to changing Windows settings, you can use REGEDIT to back up and restore the Registry. To back up the Registry, choose the Export Registry File command under the Registry menu. This command will allow you to save the Registry file to some kind of backup media. You can restore it later by choosing the Import Registry File command under the Registry menu.

ATTRIB.EXE

Every operating system since DOS provides four attributes that can be set for files to modify their interaction with the system. These attributes are as follows:

Read-only   Prevents a file from being modified, deleted, or overwritten.

Archive   Used by backup programs to determine whether the file has changed since the last backup and needs to be backed up.

System   Used to tell the OS that this file is needed by the system and should not be deleted.

Hidden   Used to keep files from being seen in a normal directory search. This is useful to prevent system files and other important files from being accidentally moved or deleted.

Attributes are set for files using an external DOS command called `ATTRIB.EXE`, which uses using the following syntax:

`ATTRIB <filename> [+ or -][attribute]`

To set the read-only attribute on the file `TESTFILE.DOC`, use the following series of commands:

`ATTRIB TESTFILE.DOC +r`

Occasionally, it is necessary to remove various attributes and replace them again. To do this, use the `ATTRIB` command.

EXTRACT.EXE

All Windows setup files come compressed in Cabinet (CAB) files. These files are extracted during the Windows Setup process by the `EXTRACT.EXE` utility. This utility can also be used to extract one or multiple files from a CAB file to replace a corrupt file. If you have one Windows file that is corrupt, you can extract a replacement from the Windows setup CAB files. If you don't know which CAB file a particular Windows system file is contained in, you can look it up in the `CABS.TXT` file

For example, to extract the `UNIDRV.DLL` file from the `Win95_10.CAB` file on a CD-ROM in drive D: to the `C:\WINDOWS\SYSTEM` directory, use the following command syntax:

`EXTRACT D:\WIN95_10.CAB UNIDRV.DLL /L C:\WINDOWS\SYSTEM`

The new file will be extracted to the new location and replace the old corrupt version in that location.

DEFRAG.EXE

When Windows is installed on a new disk, all the full clusters are contiguous. That is, they are located one after another rotationally on the disk. However, as files and programs get installed and deleted, the blocks of disk space get less and less contiguous. This can hinder Windows performance as it has to constantly go looking for more sections of different files.

To solve this problem, Microsoft has included a utility with Windows known as DEFRAG.EXE that is used to reorganize, or *defragment* the hard disk. You can access this program from the properties of the disk drive you want to fragment (it's found on the same option page as SCANDISK). Or, you can run it using the Start ➢ Run command and type in DEFRAG. Finally, you can run it by going to Start ➢ Programs ➢ Accessories➢ System Tools ➢ Disk Defragmenter.

The utility will ask you which disk you want to defragment. Choose the appropriate disk from the drop-down list and click OK. Defrag will start defragmenting the drive. This process may take several minutes or several hours, depending on how badly the drive is fragmented.

Defragmenting a drive will increase the system's performance because file access times will be faster.

EDIT.COM

Occasionally, you need to quickly edit a configuration file or other text file (such as the CONFIG.SYS or AUTOEXEC.BAT). For this, a simple editor named EDIT.COM has been included with all Microsoft operating systems since DOS version 6. To edit a file, start a command line session and type in the following:

    EDIT <filename>

Replace *<filename>* with the name of the file you wish to edit. Once EDIT comes up, it works like any other word processor or text editor. When you are finished editing the file, save it, and it will be saved as a standard ASCII text file.

FDISK.EXE

If you have already installed the disk drives and now need to configure unused space on your drive for use, you will need to use the FDISK command. FDISK.EXE is a DOS program that allows you to access and modify information about your fixed disks (hence the name). It is used for four major tasks:

- Viewing the current partition configuration
- Creating DOS partitions or logical DOS drives
- Setting active partitions
- Deleting partitions or logical DOS drives

These functions can be used on any of the physical disks in your machine, as long as those disks are considered to be permanent, that is, fixed, drives. Hard drives, whether they are SCSI, IDE, or EIDE, are all fixed. Once installed, they are expected to be permanently attached to the system, and if one is removed, extensive reconfiguration may need to be done on the system. Floppy drives and

CD-ROM drives are designed to support removable, interchangeable media, and as such are not configurable under FDISK.

To run the FDISK utility, boot to a bootable disk and type **FDISK**.

You must run FDISK from a bootable disk, NOT from within a command prompt within Windows. This is because Windows may not represent the disk drives correctly.

Following the prompts on screen, you can then view, add, or delete partitions.

SYSEDIT.EXE

The System Editor (SYSEDIT.EXE) is a holdover from Windows 3.*x*. With this utility, you can view and edit the CONFIG.SYS, AUTOEXEC.BAT, WIN.INI, SYSTEM.INI, PROTOCOL.INI, and MSMAIL.INI. Although it is not as efficient as MSCONFIG.EXE, you can still use SYSEDIT to edit these files quickly and to easily remove an offending driver entry or software configuration. To run this program in Windows 9*x*, go to Start ➢ Run and type in SYSEDIT. This will bring up the window shown in Figure 19.5 from which you can click on a window and edit any of the particular files just as if you were using EDIT.COM. You can then save the changes and restart the computer to make them take effect.

FIGURE 19.5 SYSEDIT screen

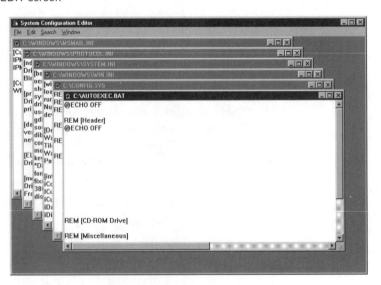

SCANREG.EXE

The Windows Registry Checker, SCANREG.EXE is a quick and simple utility that you can use to check the Registry for consistency and to make a backup of the Registry. To start SCANREG, go to Start ➢ Run, type **SCANREG**, and click OK. This will start SCANREG, which will initiate an immediate scan and fix the Registry (Figure 19.6).

FIGURE 19.6   SCANREG.EXE screen

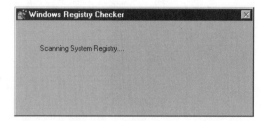

After the Registry scan is complete, SCANREG will prompt you to back up your Registry. You can use this backup to restore the Registry in case of a problem.

WSCRIPT.EXE

The Windows Scripting Host (WSCRIPT.EXE) is a service that allows programmers to write Windows scripts that can perform any number of automated tasks. Unfortunately, because WSCRIPT can also work with Internet Explorer, if it's allowed to run unchecked it is a major security hole that can potentially allow malicious scripts to be run without the user's knowledge.

This tool is responsible for the propagation of weird Microsoft-only bugs such as the fairly recent I Love You virus. If you see WSCRIPT present in the task list on Windows NT, make sure it is supposed to running. Or, if you are sure you won't need it for any scripts of any kind, completely delete it.

HWINFO.EXE

Windows 9x and above includes a utility that can give a text report of all the hardware configuration information for Windows. It includes the driver name, version, company name, Registry information, and other file-related information for the driver. You can then save or print this text report for later reference on this system.

To view this file, you must start the HWINFO.EXE utility by selecting Start ➢ Run, typing **HWINFO /UI**, and clicking OK. This will run the HWINFO utility and produce a report similar to the one in Figure 19.7. You can then either save this file as an ASCII text file or print the file to a printer by using either the Save or Print command, respectively, under the File menu.

FIGURE 19.7 The HWINFO Screen

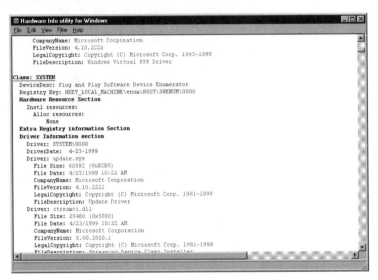

This utility is useful when trying to track down a hardware problem you suspect may be due to an outdated driver. You can examine the file this utility produces for the versions of all drivers and compare them to the newest possible drivers on the hardware vendors' Web sites.

ASD.EXE (Automatic Skip Driver)

It never fails: eventually, you will have a driver that hangs the system on bootup. We've already discussed several methods for troubleshooting this problem, and this is yet another one. The Automatic Skip Driver (ASD.EXE) utility is used to automatically skip loading a driver during boot that failed to load at the last boot.

To use ASD, go to Start ➢ Run, type **ASD**, and click OK. This will bring up the ASD utility (Figure 19.8). From this screen, you can see which tasks failed to respond. If you check a box next to a particular task, the next time you boot Windows, that task won't load. In this way, ASD can prevent lockups during boot.

FIGURE 19.8   ASD.EXE main screen

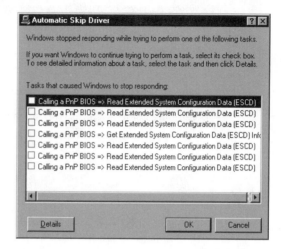

CVT1.EXE

With the release of Windows 95 OSR2 came a new feature: a new 32-bit FAT table, also known as FAT32. Up until that point, the FAT system was a 16-bit system (now known as FAT16). The new FAT32 system allowed for faster access and larger drive sizes. With newly installed systems, FAT32 was the FAT type of choice. However, older systems still used FAT16. The FAT32 Upgrade Wizard, also known as CVT1.EXE, allows you to convert a FAT16 disk system to a FAT32 system. To do this, you must first run the Drive Converter by clicking Start ➤ Run, typing in **CVT1.EXE**, and clicking OK. This will start the Driver Converter Wizard (Figure 19.9). From this Wizard, you follow the prompts and continue clicking Next to convert your drive from FAT16 to FAT32.

FIGURE 19.9   FAT32 Convert Wizard

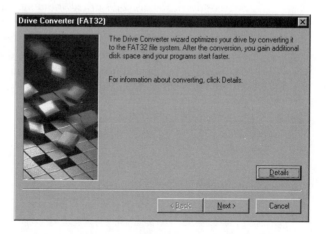

A Few Warnings about Converting to FAT32

- Once you convert to FAT32, you can't go back to FAT16.

- You may not be able to convert a compressed drive.

- Removable disks formatted with FAT32 may not work with other systems.

- Dual-boot to older systems will not be possible after a conversion to FAT32.

Summary

In this chapter, you were given some tips for troubleshooting the Windows environment. Just as with troubleshooting hardware, it is important that you know how to troubleshoot software problems. However, troubleshooting software is actually more difficult because the problems can appear to be more "phantom."

In the first section, you learned the basic steps to troubleshooting software problems. You also learned how to apply these troubleshooting steps to problems. These steps are:

1. Talk to the customer.

2. Gather information.

3. Eliminate possibilities.

4. Document the solution.

In the next section, you learned how to troubleshoot file-related problems. You learned some of the more common file-related problems and their solutions. Some of the problems you learned about include missing or corrupt system files, missing application DLL files, Windows NT boot problems, and swap file issues.

In the next section, you learned about some of the printing problems that are commonly found in the Windows environment (e.g., wrong driver installed). You learned how to use the Windows printing troubleshooting utilities (Print Test Page and the Troubleshooting Wizard) to troubleshoot these problems.

Because Windows has some problems that don't fall into any particular category, you learned in the next section how to troubleshoot problems that don't fall into any particular category. Some of these problems include General Protection Faults, Invalid Page Faults, and applications that won't install. You learned how to recognize the symptoms of each of these problems and how to solve them when they occur.

Finally, you learned how to use the various built-in Windows troubleshooting utilities. You learned what each utility is for and how to use it. You also learned when to apply a particular utility to a problem and when NOT to use a utility.

Key Terms

Before you take the exam, be certain you are familiar with the following terms:

Blue Screen of Death (BSOD)	Safe Mode
defragmentation	thrashing
General Protection Fault (GPF)	working directory
illegal operation error	

Review Questions

1. All of the following are considered to be Windows-based utilities except:

   A. SYSEDIT

   B. PSCRIPT

   C. HWINFO.EXE

   D. ASD.EXE

   E. CVT1.EXE

2. Some of the common problems faced in troubleshooting Windows and applications are all of the following except:

   A. General Protection Faults

   B. Valid working directory

   C. System lock-up

   D. Application will not start or load

3. The first step in the troubleshooting process is:

   A. Talk to the customer

   B. Gather information

   C. Eliminate possibilities

   D. Document your work

4. Windows file-related problems include all of the following except:

   A. System files not found

   B. Config file issues

   C. AUTOEXEC.BAT issues

   D. Swap file issues

   E. NT boot issues

5. The files that are checked upon bootup of Windows 9x or Windows NT are:

   A. Config files

   B. AUTOEXEC.BAT files

   C. System files

   D. Swap files

6. The `No Operating System Found` error message means that the computer's BIOS checked all the drives it knew about and couldn't find any disk with a bootable sector. This could occur because of all of the following reasons except:

   A. An operating system wasn't installed

   B. There is no problem with the boot sector

   C. The boot files have been corrupted

   D. The boot sector has been corrupted

7. Some of the commonly seen errors in Windows that are related to configuration files include all of the following except:

   A. `Device referenced in Info.INI file cannot be found`

   B. `Device referenced in WIN.INI cannot be found`

   C. `Device referenced in the Registry cannot be found`

   D. `Error in CONFIG.SYS line XX`

8. In order to delete and/or replace system files, which command must you use to remove the hidden, system, and read-only attributes on the file before you replace the file?

   A. `UNDELETE`

   B. `ERASE`

   C. `ATTRIB`

   D. `DELETE`

9. Symptoms of swap file problems include extremely slow system speed and a disk that is constantly being accessed, which is referred to as:

   A. Clocking

   B. Thrashing

   C. Booting

   D. Filtering

10. The solution to thrashing is: (Select all that apply.)

    A. Formatting the disk

    B. Buying a new hard disk

    C. Freeing up disk space

    D. Deleting all files

11. All of the following are a part of the NT boot process except:

    A. The `POST` routine examines the boot sector and loads the MBR.

    B. The boot sector is loaded from the extended partition.

    C. `NTLOADER` is loaded from the boot sector and initialized.

    D. `NTLDR` reads the `BOOT.INI` file and looks for the list of operating systems installed on the computer.

12. The solution to a corrupt `NTOSKRNL.EXE` file is to:

   A. Reinstall Windows NT

   B. Replace the corrupt file with a new one

   C. Delete the `NTOSKRNL.EXE` file and modify the `BOOT.INI` file

   D. Boot to a startup disk and replace the file from the setup disks or CD-ROM

13. After connecting to a printer and installing the print drivers, what is the best way to test its functionality? (Select all that apply.)

   A. Go to Word and print a document

   B. Print a test page from Printer Properties

   C. Go to the printer and run diagnostics

   D. Wait until someone prints a document and complains

14. One of the most frustrating sets of problems for Windows is:

   A. Hardware problems

   B. Software problems

   C. Printing problems

   D. Windows operating system problems

15. The most common Windows printing problems are: (Select all that apply.)

   A. Print spool is stalled

   B. Incompatible printer model

   C. Incorrect/incompatible driver for print

   D. Incorrect parameter

16. A condition that usually happens on either startup or shutdown and results because Windows 9x could not load or unload a virtual device driver properly is called:

   A. General Protection Fault (GPF)

   B. Windows protection error

   C. Illegal operation

   D. System lock-up

17. The most common error that happens in Windows when a program accesses memory that another program is using or when a program accesses a memory address that doesn't exist is called:

   A. General Protection Fault

   B. Windows protection error

   C. Illegal operation

   D. System lock-up

18. Which Windows error message is displayed when a program is forced to quit because it did something Windows didn't like?

    A. General Protection Fault

    B. Windows protection error

    C. Illegal operation

    D. System lock-up

19. What error occurs when the system stops responding to commands and stops processing completely?

    A. General Protection Fault

    B. Windows protection error

    C. Illegal operation

    D. System lock-up

20. What error occurs when the GUI of Windows won't appear?

    A. Illegal operation

    B. Dr. Watson

    C. Failure to start GUI

    D. Option sound card, modem, SCSI card, or input device will not function

Answers to Review Questions

1. B. PSCRIPT is not considered to be a Windows-based utility. SYSEDIT, HWINFO.EXE, ASD.EXE, and CVT1.EXE are all utilities used to troubleshoot Windows.

2. B. Valid working directory is not a common problem faced in troubleshooting Windows and applications.

3. A. The first step in the troubleshooting process is to talk to the customer. It is best to obtain as much information as possible from the user so you have an idea of where to begin your troubleshooting.

4. C. Windows file-related problems do not include AUTOEXEC.BAT issues. AUTOEXEC.BAT is a DOS batch file that is automatically executed during boot-up if the file is present.

5. C. The files that are checked upon bootup of Windows 9x and Windows NT are the system files. Every operating system or operating environment has certain key system files that must be present in order for it to function.

6. B. The No Operating System Found error means that an operating system wasn't installed, the boot sector has been corrupted, or the boot files have been corrupted.

7. A. Some of the commonly seen errors in Windows that are related to configuration files include all of the following except Device referenced in Info.INI file cannot be found.

8. C. In order to delete and/or replace system files you must use the ATTRIB command to remove the hidden, system, and read-only attributes on the file.

9. B. Thrashing means an extremely slow system speed and a disk that is constantly being accessed. This condition occurs because Windows doesn't have enough memory to contain all the programs that are running.

10. B, C. The solution to thrashing is to free up some disk space. However, with IDE hard disk sizes at tens of gigabytes available for around $100, the easiest thing to do is install a bigger hard disk. If that solution isn't practical, you must delete enough unused files so that the swap file can be made large enough to be functional.

11. B. The boot sector is always loaded from the active partition, not the extended partition.

12. D. The solution to a corrupt NTOSKRNL.EXE file is to boot to a startup disk and replace the file from the setup disks or CD-ROM.

13. A, B, D. You should go to Word and print a document, print a test page in Printer Properties, or wait until someone prints a document and complains. Printing diagnostics only tests whether the printer is able to print if it is connected to a device with the correct drivers.

14. C. One of the most frustrating set of problems for Windows is printing problems.

15. A, B, C. The most common Windows printing problems are that the print spool is stalled, there's an incorrect/incompatible driver for print, or there's an incorrect parameter. Windows will support almost any type of printer model.

16. B. A condition that usually happens on either startup or shutdown and results because Windows 9x could not load or unload a virtual device driver properly is called a Windows protection error.

17. A. The most common error that happens in Windows when a program accesses memory that another program is using or when a program accesses a memory address that doesn't exist is called a General Protection Fault. Generally, GPFs are the result of sloppy programming and can often be fixed by clearing the memory with a simple reboot.

18. C. Illegal operation is the Windows error message displayed when a program is forced to quit because it did something Windows didn't like. The details of the error include which module experienced the problem, the memory location being accessed at the time, and the registers and flags of the processor at the time of the error.

19. D. The system lock-up error occurs when the system stops responding to commands and stops processing completely. System lock-ups can occur when a computer is asked to process too many instructions at once with too little memory. Usually, the cure for a system lock up is to simply reboot. If the lock-ups are persistent, it may be a hardware-related problem.

20. C. If your Windows GUI fails to start properly, more than likely the problem is related to a misconfigured driver or misconfigured hardware.

A+ Complete Glossary

386 enhanced mode   In Microsoft Windows, the most advanced and complex of the different operating modes, 386 enhanced mode lets Windows access the protected mode of the *80386* (or higher) processor for extended memory management and multitasking for both Windows and non-Windows application programs.

802.3   An IEEE standard that defines a bus topology network that uses a 50-ohm coaxial baseband cable and carries transmissions at 10Mbps. This standard groups data bits into frames and uses the Carrier Sense Multiple Access with Collision Detection (CSMA/CD) cable access method to put data on the cable.

802.5   The IEEE 802.5 standard specifies a physical star, logical ring topology that uses a token-passing technology to put the data on the cable. IBM developed this technology for their mainframe and minicomputer networks. IBM's name for it was Token Ring. The name stuck, and any network using this type of technology is called a Token Ring network.

80286   Also called the 286. A 16-bit microprocessor from Intel, first released in February 1982 and used by IBM in the IBM PC/AT computer. Since then it has been used in many other IBM-compatible computers. The 80286 uses a 16-bit data word and a 16-bit data bus, and it uses 24 bits to address memory.

80287   Also called the 287. A floating-point processor from Intel, designed for use with the 80286 CPU chip. When supported by application programs, a floating-point processor can speed up floating-point and transcendental math operations by 10 to 50 times. The 80287 conforms to the IEEE 754-1985 standard for binary floating-point operations, and it is available in clock speeds of 6, 8, 10, and 12MHz.

80386DX   Also called the 80386, the 386DX, and the 386. A full 32-bit microprocessor introduced by Intel in October 1985 and used in many IBM and IBM-compatible computers. Available in 16-, 20-, 25-, and 33MHz versions, the 80386 has a 32-bit data word, can transfer information 32 bits at a time over the data bus, and can use 32 bits in addressing memory. The 80386 is equivalent to about 275,000 transistors, and can perform 6 million instructions per second. The floating-point processor for the 80386DX is the 80387.

80386SX   Also called the 386SX. A lower-cost alternative to the 80386DX microprocessor, 80386SX was introduced by Intel in 1988. Available in 16-, 20-, 25-, and 33MHz versions, the 80386SX is an 80386DX with a 16-bit data bus. This design allows systems to be configured using cheaper 16-bit components, leading to a lower overall cost. The floating-point processor for the 80386SX is the 80387SX.

80387   Also called the 387. A floating-point processor from Intel, 80387 was designed for use with the 80386 CPU chip. When supported by application programs, a floating-point processor can speed up floating-point and transcendental math operations by 10 to 50 times. The 80387 conforms to the IEEE 754-1985 standard for binary floating-point operations and is available in speeds of 16, 20, 25, and 33MHz.

80486DX   Also called the 486 or i486. 80486DX is a 32-bit microprocessor introduced by Intel in April 1989. The 80486 represents the continuing evolution of the 80386 family of microprocessors and adds several notable features, including on-board cache, built-in floating-point processor and memory management unit, as well as certain advanced provisions for multiprocessing. Available in 25-, 33-, and 50MHz versions, the 80486 is equivalent to 1.25 million transistors and can perform 20 million instructions per second.

80486DX2   Also known as the 486DX2. A 32-bit microprocessor introduced by Intel in 1992. It is functionally identical to and 100 percent compatible with the 80486DX, but it has one major difference: the DX2 chip adds what Intel calls speed-doubling technology—meaning that it runs twice as fast internally as it does with components external to the chip. For example, the DX2-50 operates at 50MHz internally but at 25MHz while communicating with other system components, including memory and the other chips on the motherboard, thus maintaining its overall system compatibility. 50- and 66MHz versions of the DX2 are available. The 486DX2 contains 1.2 million transistors and is capable of 40 million instructions per second.

80486SX   Also called the 486SX. A 32-bit microprocessor introduced by Intel in April 1991. The 80486SX can be described as an 80486DX with the floating-point processor circuitry disabled. Available in 16-, 20-, and 25MHz versions, the 80486SX contains the equivalent of 1.185 million transistors and can execute 16.5 million instructions per second.

80487   Also called the 487. A floating-point processor from Intel, designed for use with the 80486SX CPU chip. When supported by application programs, a floating-point processor can speed up floating-point and transcendental math operations by 10 to 50 times. The 80487 is essentially a 20MHz 80486 with the floating-point circuitry still enabled. When an 80487 is added into the coprocessor socket of a motherboard running the 80486SX, it effectively becomes the main processor, shutting down the 80486SX and taking over all operations. The 80487 conforms to the IEEE 754-1985 standard for binary floating-point operations.

8086   This 16-bit microprocessor from Intel was first released in June 1978, and it is available in speeds of 4.77MHz, 8MHz, and 10MHz. The 8086 was used in a variety of early IBM-compatible computers as well as the IBM PS/2 Model 25 and Model 30. The 8086 uses a 16-bit data word and a 16-bit data bus. The 8086 contains the equivalent of 29,000 transistors and can execute 0.33 million instructions per second.

8088   This 16-bit microprocessor from Intel was released in June 1978, and it was used in the first IBM PC, as well as the IBM PC/XT, Portable PC, PCjr, and a large number of IBM-compatible computers. The 8088 uses a 16-bit data word, but transfers information along an 8-bit data bus. Available in speeds of 4.77MHz and 8MHz, the 8088 is approximately equivalent to 29,000 transistors and can execute 0.33 million instructions per second.

8-bit bus   The type of expansion bus that was used with the original IBM PC. The bus can transmit 8 bits at a time.

Accelerated Graphics Port (AGP) bus   A type of 32-bit expansion bus that runs at 66MHz. It is a very high-speed bus that is used primarily for video expansion cards and can transfer data at a maximum throughput 508.6MBps.

access time   The period of time that elapses between a request for information from disk or memory and the information arriving at the requesting device. Memory access time refers to the time it takes to transfer a character from memory to or from the processor, while disk access time refers to the time it takes to place the read/write heads over the requested data.

Active Directory   The Active Directory, a new feature of Windows 2000, stores information about users, computers, and network resources. The Active Directory is stored in databases on special Windows 2000 Server computers called Domain Controllers.

Active hubs   A type of hub that uses electronics to amplify and clean up the signal before it is broadcast to the other ports.

active matrix   A type of liquid crystal display that has a transistor for each pixel in the screen.

active-matrix screen   An LCD display mechanism that uses an individual transistor to control every pixel on the screen. Active-matrix screens are characterized by high contrast, a wide viewing angle, vivid colors, and fast screen refresh rates, and they do not show the streaking or shadowing that is common with cheaper LCD technology.

actuator arm   The device inside a hard disk drive that moves the read/write heads as a group in the fixed disk.

address bus   The internal processor bus used for accessing memory. The width of this bus determines how much physical memory a processor can access.

address   The precise location in memory or on disk where a piece of information is stored. Every byte in memory and every sector on a disk have their own unique addresses.

Administrative Tools   In Windows 2000 Professional, this is the group of utilities used to manage many common configuration and maintenance tasks.

allocation unit   An allocation unit is a portion of the hard drive that is used by the computer when saving information to the drive. Smaller allocation units are generally more efficient, because they result in less wasted space.

alpha   Extremely early versions of computer software are called "alpha code." Alpha code is generally incomplete and unusable, and it is almost never released to the public.

analog   Describes any device that represents changing values by a continuously variable physical property such as voltage in a circuit, fluid pressure, liquid level, and so on. An analog device can handle an infinite number of values within its range.

anti-static bag   A bag designed to keep static charges from building up on the outside of a computer component during shipping. The bag will collect some of the charges, but does not drain them away as ESD mats do.

anti-static wrist strap (ESD strap)   A specially constructed strap worn as a preventive measure to guard against the damages of ESD. One end of the strap is attached to an earth ground and the other is wrapped around the technician's wrist.

anti-virus program   An application program you run to detect or eliminate a computer virus or infection. Some anti-virus programs are terminate-and-stay-resident programs that can detect suspicious activity on your computer as it happens, while others must be run periodically as part of your normal housekeeping activities.

Application layer   The seventh, or highest, layer in the International Organization for Standardization's Open Systems Interconnection (ISO/OSI) model for computer-to-computer communications. This layer uses services provided by the lower layers, but is completely insulated from the details of the network hardware. It describes how application programs interact with the network operating system, including database management, e-mail, and terminal emulation programs.

ASCII   Acronym for American Standard Code for Information Interchange. A standard coding scheme that assigns numeric values to letters, numbers, punctuation marks, and control characters, to achieve compatibility among different computers and peripherals.

asynchronous   Describes a type of communication that adds special signaling bits to each end of the data. The bit at the beginning of the information signals the start of the data and is known as the start bit. The next few bits are the actual data that needs to be sent. Those bits are known as the data bits. Stop bits indicate that the data is finished. Asynchronous communications have no timing signal.

AT bus   Another name for the ISA bus. See also *ISA*.

ATA version 2 (ATA-2) The second version of the original IDE (ATA) specification that allowed drive sizes of several gigabtyes and overcame the limitation of 528MB. It is also sometimes generically known as Enhanced IDE (EIDE).

Attached Resource Computer Network (ARCNet) A network technology that uses a physical star, logical ring and token passing access method. It is typically wired with coaxial cable.

AUTOEXEC.BAT A contraction of AUTOmatically EXECuted BATch. AUTOEXEC.BAT is a special DOS batch file, located in the root directory of a startup disk, and it runs automatically every time the computer is started or restarted.

auto-ranging multimeters A multimeter that automatically sets its upper and lower ranges depending on the input signal. These multimeters are more difficult to damage by choosing the wrong range setting. See also *multimeter*.

Autorun On a CD-ROM, the Autorun option allows the CD to automatically start an installation program or a menu screen when it is inserted into the CD-ROM drive.

"baby" AT A type of motherboard form factor where the motherboard is smaller than the original AT form factor.

backup A duplicate copy made to be able to recover from an accidental loss of data.

backup set A related collection of backup media.

backup software Program that is used to back up a small amount of data.

backup source The device or data being backed up.

bandwidth In communications, the difference between the highest and the lowest frequencies available for transmission in any given range. In networking, the transmission capacity of a computer or a communications channel stated in megabits or megabytes per second; the higher the number, the faster the data transmission takes place.

basis weight A measurement of the "heaviness" of paper. The number is the weight, in pounds, of 500 17" × 22" sheets of that type of paper.

batch file File with a .bat extension that contains other DOS commands. By typing the name of the batch file and pressing Enter, DOS will process all of the batch file commands, one at a time, without need for any additional user input.

baud rate In communications equipment, a measurement of the number of state changes (from 0 to 1 or vice versa) per second on an asynchronous communications channel.

Berg connector A type of connector most commonly used in PC floppy drive power cables; it has four conductors arranged in a row.

Berg connectors A type of power connector that is used on floppy drives.

beta Beta code is software that has reached the stage where is usable and generally stable, but it is not completely finished. Beta code is often released to the public for testing on an "as is" basis, and user comments are then used to finish the release version of the product.

bias voltage The high-voltage charge applied to the developing roller inside an EP cartridge.

binary Any scheme that uses two different states, components, conditions, or conclusions. In mathematics, the binary (base-2) numbering system uses combinations of the digits 0 and 1 to represent all values.

BIOS (basic input/output system) The ROM-based software on a motherboard that acts as a kind of "interpreter" between an operating system and a computer's hardware.

BIOS CMOS setup program Program that modifies BIOS settings in the CMOS memory. This program is available at system startup time by pressing a key combination such as Alt+F1 or Ctrl+F2.

BIOS shadow A copy of the BIOS in memory.

bit Contraction of BInary digiT. A bit is the basic unit of information in the binary numbering system, representing either 0 (for off) or 1 (for on). Bits can be grouped together to make up larger storage units, the most common being the 8-bit byte. A byte can represent all kinds of information including the letters of the alphabet, the numbers 0 through 9, and common punctuation symbols.

bit-mapped font A set of characters in a specific style and size, in which each character is defined by a pattern of dots. The computer must keep a complete set of bitmaps for every font you use on your system, and these bitmaps can consume large amounts of disk space.

Blue Screen of Death (BSOD) A typical way of describing the blue screen error condition that occurs when Windows NT fails to boot properly or quits unexpectedly.

boot The loading of an operating system into memory, usually from a hard disk, although occasionally from a floppy disk. This is an automatic procedure begun when you first turn on or reset your computer. A set of instructions contained in ROM begin executing, first running a series of power on self-tests (POSTs) to check that devices, such as hard disks, are in working order, then locating and loading the operating system, and finally passing control of the computer over to that operating system.

bootable disk   Any disk capable of loading and starting the operating system, although most often used when referring to a floppy disk. In these days of larger and larger operating systems, it is less common to boot from a floppy disk. In some cases, all of the files needed to start the operating system will not fit on a single floppy disk, which makes it impossible to boot from a floppy.

BPS (bits per second)   A measurement of how much data (how many bits) is being transmitted in one second. Typically used to describe the speed of asynchronous communications (modems).

bridge   This type of connectivity device operates in the Data Link layer of the OSI model. It is used to join similar topologies (Ethernet to Ethernet, Token Ring to Token Ring) and to divide traffic on network segments. This device will pass information destined for one particular workstation to that segment, but it will not pass broadcast traffic.

broadcasting   Sending a signal to all entities that can listen to it. In networking, it refers to sending a signal to all entities connected to that network.

brouter   In networking, a device that combines the attributes of a bridge and a router. A brouter can route one or more specific protocols, such as TCP/IP, and bridge all others.

brownout   A short period of low voltage often caused by an unusually heavy demand for power.

browser   A piece of software used to access the Internet. Common browsers are Netscape's Navigator and Microsoft's Internet Explorer.

bubble-jet printer   A type of sprayed ink printer, this type uses an electric signal that energizes a heating element, causing ink to vaporize and get pushed out of the pinhole and onto the paper.

bug   A logical or programming error in hardware or software that causes a malfunction of some sort. If the problem is in software, it can be fixed by changes to the program. If the fault is in hardware, new circuits must be designed and constructed. Some bugs are fatal and cause the program to hang or cause data loss, others are just annoying, and many are never even noticed.

bug-fix   A release of hardware or software that corrects known bugs but does not contain additional new features. Such releases are usually designated only by an increase in the decimal portion of the version number; for example, the revision level may advance from 2 to 2.01 or 2.1, rather than from 2 to 3.

bus   A set of pathways that allow information and signals to travel between components inside or outside of a computer.

bus clock   A chip on the motherboard that produces a type of signal (called a clock signal) that indicates how fast the bus can transmit information.

bus connector slot   A slot made up of several small copper channels that grab the matching "fingers" of the expansion circuit boards. The fingers connect to copper pathways on the motherboard.

bus mastering   A technique that allows certain advanced bus architectures to delegate control of data transfers between the Central Processing Unit (CPU) and associated peripheral devices to an add-in board.

bus mouse   A mouse connected to the computer using an expansion board plugged into an expansion slot, instead of simply connected to a serial port as in the case of a serial mouse.

bus topology   Type of physical topology that consists of a single cable that runs to every workstation on the network. Each computer shares that same data and address path. As messages pass through the trunk, each workstation checks to see if the message is addressed for itself. This topology is very difficult to reconfigure, since reconfiguration requires you to disconnect and reconnect a portion of the network (thus bringing the whole network down).

byte   Contraction of BinarY digiT Eight. A group of 8 bits that, in computer storage terms, usually holds a single character, such as a number, letter, or other symbol.

cable access methods   Methods by which stations on a network get permission to transmit their data.

cache   Pronounced "cash." A special area of memory, managed by a cache controller, that improves performance by storing the contents of frequently accessed memory locations and their addresses. When the processor references a memory address, the cache checks to see if it holds that address. If it does, the information is passed directly to the processor; if not, a normal memory access takes place instead. A cache can speed up operations in a computer in which RAM access is slow compared with its processor speed, because the cache memory is always faster than normal RAM.

cache memory   Fast SRAM memory used to store, or cache, frequently used instructions and data.

capacitive keyboard   Keyboard designed with two sheets of semi-conductive material separated by a thin sheet of Mylar inside the keyboard. When a key is pressed, the plunger presses down and a paddle connected to the plunger presses the two sheets of semi-conductive material together, changing the total capacitance of the two sheets. The controller can tell by the capacitance value returned which key was pressed.

capacitive touch screen Type of display monitor that has two clear plastic coatings over the screen, separated by air. When the user presses the screen in a particular spot, the coatings are pressed together and the controller registers a change in the total capacitance of the two layers. The controller then determines where the screen was pressed by the capacitance values and sends that information to the computer in the form of x,y coordinates.

capacitor An electrical component, normally found in power supplies and timing circuits, used to store electrical charge.

card services Part of the software support needed for PCMCIA (PC Card) hardware devices in a portable computer, controlling the use of system interrupts, memory, or power management. When an application wants to access a PC Card, it always goes through the card services software and never communicates directly with the underlying hardware.

carpal tunnel syndrome A form of wrist injury caused by holding the hands in an awkward position for long periods of time.

carriage motor Stepper motor used to move the print head back and forth on a dot-matrix printer.

cathode-ray tube See *CRT*.

CCD (charge-coupled device) A device that allows light to be converted into electrical pulses.

CCITT Acronym for Comité Consultatif Internationale de Téléphonie et de Télégraphie. An organization, based in Geneva, that develops worldwide data communications standards. CCITT is part of the ITU (International Telecommunications Union). The organization has been renamed ITU-T (ITU Telecommunications Standardization Sector).

CD-ROM Acronym for compact disc read-only memory. A high-capacity, optical storage device that uses compact disc technology to store large amounts of information, up to 650MB (the equivalent of approximately 300,000 pages of text), on a single 4.72" disk.

Central Processing Unit (CPU) The computing and control part of the computer. The CPU in a mainframe computer may be contained on many printed circuit boards, the CPU in a mini computer may be contained on several boards, and the CPU in a PC is contained in a single extremely powerful microprocessor.

centralized processing A network processing scheme in which all "intelligence" is found in one computer and all other computers send requests to the central computer to be processed. Mainframe networks use centralized processing.

Centronics parallel interface   A standard 36-pin interface in the PC world for the exchange of information between the PC and a peripheral, such as a printer, originally developed by the printer manufacturer Centronics, Inc. The standard defines eight parallel data lines, plus additional lines for status and control information.

CGA   Acronym for Color/Graphics Adapter. CGA is a video adapter that provided low-resolution text and graphics. CGA provided several different text and graphics modes, including 40- or 80-column by 25-line, 16-color text mode, and graphics modes of 640 horizontal pixels by 200 vertical pixels with 2 colors, or 320 horizontal pixels by 200 vertical pixels with 4 colors. CGA has been superseded by later video standards, including EGA, VGA, SuperVGA, and XGA.

Charge-coupled device   See *CCD (charge-coupled device)*.

charging corona   The wire or roller that is used to put a uniform charge on the EP drum inside a toner cartridge.

checksum   A method of providing information for error detection, usually calculated by summing a set of values.

checksumming   An error checking routine that runs a mathematical equation against a set of data and comes up with a result, called a checksum. The data is then transmitted, and the receiver then runs the same formula against the data transmitted and compares the result to the checksum. If they are the same, the transmission is considered successful.

chip creep   The slow self-loosening of chips from their sockets on the system board as a result of the frequent heating and cooling of the board (which causes parts of the board—significantly, the chip connector slots—to alternately expand and shrink).

chip puller   A tool that is used on older (pre-386) systems to remove the chips without damaging them.

cleaning step   The step in the EP print process where excess toner is scraped from the EP drum with a rubber blade.

client   A network entity that can request resources from the network or server.

client computers   A computer that requests resources from a network.

client software   Software that allows a device to request resources from a network.

clock doubling   Technology that allows a chip to run at the bus's rated speed externally, but still be able to run the processor's internal clock at twice the speed of the bus. This technology improves computer performance.

clock rate   See *clock speed*.

clock signal   Built-in metronome-like signal that indicates how fast the components can operate.

clock speed   Also known as clock rate. The internal speed of a computer or processor, normally expressed in MHz. The faster the clock speed, the faster the computer will perform a specific operation, assuming the other components in the system, such as disk drives, can keep up with the increased speed.

clock tripling   A type of processor design where the processor runs at one speed externally and at triple that speed internally.

cluster   The smallest unit of hard disk space that DOS can allocate to a file, consisting of one or more contiguous sectors. The number of sectors contained in a cluster depends on the hard disk type.

CMOS   Acronym for Complementary Metal Oxide Semiconductor. An area of nonvolatile memory that contains settings that determine how a computer is configured.

CMOS battery   A battery used to power CMOS memory so that the computer won't lose its settings when powered down.

COMMAND.COM   Takes commands issued by the user through text strings or click actions and translates them back into calls that can be understood by the lower layers of DOS. It is the vital command interpreter for DOS.

Complementary Metal Oxide Semiconductor   See *CMOS*.

computer name   The name by which a Microsoft computer is known on the network. This is a NetBIOS name (up to 15 characters in length) which must be unique on the network. In Windows 2000, the computer name is always the same as the machine's host name, while in Windows 9*x* the two can be different.

conditioning step   The step in the EP print process where a uniform charge is applied to the EP drum by the charging corona or charging roller.

conductor   Any item that permits the flow of electricity between two entities.

CONFIG.SYS   In DOS and OS/2, a special text file containing settings that control the way that the operating system works. CONFIG.SYS must be located in the root directory of the default boot disk, normally drive C, and is read by the operating system only once as the system starts running. Some application programs and peripheral devices require you to include special statements in CONFIG.SYS, while other commands may specify the number of disk-read buffers or open files on your system, specify how the disk cache should be configured, or load any special device drivers your system may need.

connectivity devices   Any device that facilitates connections between network devices. Some examples include hubs, routers, switches, and gateways.

Control Program for Microcomputer (CP/M)   A computer operating system that was an early competitor of Microsoft's DOS system. CP/M was a command-line system that was developed by Gary Kildall.

conventional memory   The amount of memory accessible by DOS in PCs using an Intel processor operating in real mode, normally the first 640K.

cooperative multitasking   A form of multitasking in which all running applications must work together to share system resources.

corona roller   Type of transfer corona assembly that uses a charged roller to apply charge to the paper.

corona wire   Type of transfer corona assembly. Also, the wire in that assembly that is charged by the high voltage supply. It is narrow in diameter and located in a special notch under the EP print cartridge.

CPU (Central Processing Unit)   See *Central Processing Unit (CPU)*.

CPU clock   Type of clock signal that dictates how fast the CPU can run.

crosstalk   Problem related to electromagnetic fields when two wires carrying electrical signals run parallel and one of the wires induces a signal in the second wire. If these wires are carrying data, the extra, unintended signal can cause errors in the communication. Crosstalk is especially a problem in unshielded parallel cables that are longer than 10 feet.

CRT   Acronym for cathode-ray tube. A display device used in computer monitors and television sets. A CRT display consists of a glass vacuum tube that contains one electron gun for a monochrome display, or three (red, green, and blue) electron guns for a color display. Electron beams from these guns sweep rapidly across the inside of the screen from the upper-left to the lower-right of the screen. The inside of the screen is coated with thousands of phosphor dots that glow when they are struck by the electron beam. To stop the image from flickering, the beams sweep at a rate of between 43 and 87 times per second, depending on the phosphor persistence and the scanning mode used—interlaced or non-interlaced. This is known as the refresh rate and is measured in Hz. The Video Electronics Standards Association (VESA) recommends a vertical refresh rate of 72Hz, non-interlaced, at a resolution of 800 by 600 pixels.

cylinder   A hard disk consists of two or more platters, each with two sides. Each side is further divided into concentric circles known as tracks, and all the tracks at the same concentric position on a disk are known collectively as a cylinder.

daisy-chaining   Pattern of cabling where the cables run from the first device to the second, second to the third, and so on. If the devices have both an "in" and an "out," the in of the first device of each pair is connected to the out of the second device of each pair.

daisy-wheel printer   An impact printer that uses a plastic or metal print mechanism with a different character on the end of each spoke of the wheel. As the print mechanism rotates to the correct letter, a small hammer strikes the character against the ribbon, transferring the image onto the paper.

DAT   See *digital audio tape (DAT)*.

data bits   In asynchronous transmissions, the bits that actually comprise the data; usually 7 or 8 data bits make up the data word.

data bus   Bus used to send and receive data to the microprocessor.

data compression   Any method of encoding data so that it occupies less space than in its original form.

data encoding scheme (DES)   The method used by a disk controller to store digital information onto a hard disk or floppy disk. DES has remained unbroken despite years of use; it completely randomizes the information so that it is impossible to determine the encryption key even if some of the original text is known.

Data Link layer   The second of seven layers of the International Standards Organization's Open Systems Interconnection (ISO/OSI) model for computer-to-computer communications. The Data Link layer validates the integrity of the flow of data from one node to another by synchronizing blocks of data and by controlling the flow of data.

data set ready   See *DSR*.

data terminal equipment   See *DTE*.

data terminal ready   See *DTR*.

data transfer rate   The speed at which a disk drive can transfer information from the drive to the processor, usually measured in megabits or megabytes per second.

daughter board   A printed circuit board that attaches to another board to provide additional functions.

DB connector   Any of several types of cable connectors used for parallel or serial cables. The number following the letters DB (for data bus) indicates the number of pins that the connector usually has.

de facto   Latin translation for "by fact". Any standard that is a standard because everyone is using it.

de jure Latin translation for "by law". Any standard that is a standard because a standards body decided it should be so.

debouncing A keyboard feature that eliminates unintended triggering of keystrokes. It works by having the keyboard controller constantly scan the keyboard for keystrokes. Only keystrokes that are pressed for more than two scans are considered keystrokes. This prevents spurious electronic signals from generating input.

decimal The base-10 numbering system that uses the familiar numbers 0–9.

dedicated server The server that is assigned to perform a specific application or service.

default gateway If a user needs to communicate by TCP/IP with a computer that is not on their subnet (the local network segment) the computer needs to use a gateway to access this remote network. The default gateway is simply the path that is taken by all outgoing traffic unless another path is specified.

defragmentation The process of reorganizing and rewriting files so that they occupy one large continuous area on your hard disk rather than several smaller areas.

DES See *data encoding scheme (DES)*.

Desktop Contains the visible elements of Windows and defines the limits of the graphic environment.

Desktop Control Panel Windows panel that is used to configure the system so it is more easily usable. This control panel contains the settings for the background color and pattern as well as screen saver settings.

developing roller The roller inside a toner cartridge that presents a uniform line of toner to help apply the toner to the image written on the EP drum.

developing step The step in the EP print process where the image written on the EP drum by the laser is developed, that is, it has toner stuck to it.

device driver A small program that allows a computer to communicate with and control a device.

Device Manager A utility in Windows 9*x* and Windows 2000 that allows the user to view and modify hardware settings. Device drivers can be installed or upgraded, and problems with devices can be found and dealt with here.

DEVICE= Command found in the DOS CONFIG.SYS that tells DOS which driver to find and load into memory at boot time.

DEVICEHIGH= Command that is used to load the device drivers into upper memory blocks, thereby freeing up space in conventional memory.

diagnostic program   A program that tests computer hardware and peripherals for correct operation. In the PC, some faults are easy to find, and these are known as "hard faults"; the diagnostic program will diagnose them correctly every time. Others, such as memory faults, can be difficult to find; these are called "soft faults" because they do not occur every time the memory location is tested, but only under very specific circumstances.

differential backup   Backs up files that have changed since the last full backup.

digital audio tape (DAT)   A method of recording information in digital form on a small audio tape cassette. Many gigabytes of information can be recorded on a cassette, and so a DAT can be used as a backup medium. Like all tape devices, however, DATs are relatively slow.

digital signal   A signal that consists of discrete values. These values do not change over time; in effect, they change instantly from one value to another.

DIMM (Dual Inline Memory Module)   Memory module that is similar to a SIMM (Single Inline Memory Module), except that a DIMM is double-sided. There are memory chips on both sides of the memory module.

DIN-*n*   Circular type of connector used with computers. (The *n* represents the number of connectors.)

DIP (Dual Inline Package)   A standard housing constructed of hard plastic commonly used to hold an integrated circuit. The circuit's leads are connected to two parallel rows of pins designed to fit snugly into a socket; these pins may also be soldered directly to a printed-circuit board. If you try to install or remove dual inline packages, be careful not to bend or damage their pins.

DIP switch   A small switch used to select the operating mode of a device, mounted as a Dual Inline Package. DIP switches can be either sliding or rocker switches and are often grouped together for convenience. They are used on printed circuit boards, dot-matrix printers, modems, and other peripherals.

direct memory access   See *DMA (direct memory access)*.

directory   Directories are used to organize files on the hard drive. Another name for a directory is a folder. Directories created inside or below others are called "subfolders" or "subdirectories."

Direct Rambus   A memory bus that transfers data at 800MHz over a 16-bit memory bus. Direct Rambus memory models (often called *RIMMs*), like DDR SDRAM, can transfer data on both the rising and falling edges of a clock cycle.

direct-solder method   A method of attaching chips to the motherboard where the chip is soldered directly to the motherboard.

disk cache   An area of computer memory where data is temporarily stored on its way to or from a disk. A disk cache mediates between the application and the hard disk, and when an application asks for information from the hard disk, the cache program first checks to see if that data is already in the cache memory. If it is, the disk cache program loads the information from the cache memory rather than from the hard disk. If the information is not in memory, the cache program reads the data from the disk, copies it into the cache memory for future reference, and then passes the data to the requesting application.

disk-caching program   A program that reads the most commonly accessed data from disk and keeps it in memory for faster access.

disk controller   The electronic circuitry that controls and manages the operation of floppy or hard disks installed in the computer. A single disk controller may manage more than one hard disk; many disk controllers also manage floppy disks and compatible tape drives.

disk drive   A peripheral storage device that reads and writes to magnetic or optical disks. When more than one disk drive is installed on a computer, the operating system assigns each drive a unique name—for example A and C in DOS, Windows, and OS/2.

disk duplexing   In networking, a fault-tolerant technique that writes the same information simultaneously onto two different hard disks. Disk duplexing is offered by most of the major network operating systems and is designed to protect the system against a single disk failure; it is not designed to protect against multiple disk failures and is no substitute for a well-planned series of disk backups.

diskette   An easily removable and portable "floppy" disk that is 3.5" in diameter and enclosed in a durable plastic case that has a metal shutter over the media access window.

diskless workstation   A networked computer that does not have any local disk storage capability.

disk mirroring   In networking, a fault-tolerant technique that writes the same information simultaneously onto two different hard disks, using the same disk controller. In the event of one disk failing, information from the other can be used to continue operations. Disk mirroring is offered by most of the major network operating systems and is designed to protect the system against a single disk failure; it is not designed to protect against multiple disk failures and is no substitute for a well-planned series of disk backups.

Disk Operating System   See *DOS*.

distributed processing   A computer system in which processing is performed by several separate computers linked by a communications network. The term often refers to any computer system supported by a network, but more properly refers to a system in which each computer is chosen to handle a specific workload and the network supports the system as a whole.

DIX Ethernet   The original name for the Ethernet network technology. Named after the original developer companies, Digital, Intel, and Xerox.

DMA (direct memory access)   A method of transferring information directly from a mass-storage device such as a hard disk or from an adapter card into memory (or vice versa), without the information passing through the processor.

DMA channels   Dedicated circuit pathways on the motherboard that make DMA possible.

docking station   A hardware system into which a portable computer fits so that it can be used as a full-fledged desktop computer. Docking stations vary from simple port replicators (that allow you access to parallel and serial ports and a mouse) to complete systems (that give you access to network connections, CD-ROMs, even a tape backup system or PCMCIA ports).

domain   1. The security structure for Windows NT Server and Windows 2000 Active Directory.
2. The namespace structure of TCP/IP's DNS structure.

Domain Name System (DNS)   DNS allows TCP/IP-capable users anywhere in the world to find resources in other companies or countries by using their domain name. Each domain is an independent namespace for a particular organization, and DNS servers manage requests for information about the IP addresses of particular DNS entries. DNS is used to manage all names on the Internet.

dongle   A special cable that provides a connector to a circuit board that doesn't have one. For example, a motherboard may use a dongle to provide a serial port when there is a ribbon cable connector for the dongle on the motherboard, but there is no serial port.

dongle connection   A connector on a motherboard where a dongle will connect.

DOS   1. Acronym for Disk Operating System, an operating system originally developed by Microsoft for the IBM PC. DOS exists in two very similar versions; MS-DOS, developed and marketed by Microsoft for use with IBM-compatible computers, and PC-DOS, supported and sold by IBM for use only on computers manufactured by IBM.
2. A DOS CONFIG.SYS command that loads the operating system into conventional memory, extended memory, or into upper memory blocks on computers using the Intel 80386 or later processor. To use this command, you must

have previously loaded the HIMEM.SYS device driver with the DEVICE command in CONFIG.SYS.

DOS Environment Variables   Variables that specify global things like the path that DOS searches to find executables.

DOS extender   A small program that extends the range of DOS memory. For example, HIMEM.SYS allows DOS access to the memory ranges about 1024K.

DOS prompt   A visual confirmation that DOS is ready to receive input from the keyboard. The default prompt includes the current drive letter followed by a right angle bracket (for example, C>). You can create your own custom prompt with the PROMPT command.

DOS shell   An early graphic user interface for DOS that allowed users to manage files and run programs through a simple text interface and even use a mouse. It was soon replaced by Windows.

dot-matrix printer   An impact printer that uses columns of small pins and an inked ribbon to create the tiny pattern of dots that form the characters. Dot-matrix printers are available in 9-, 18-, or 24-pin configurations.

dot pitch   In a monitor, the vertical distance between the centers of like-colored phosphors on the screen of a color monitor, measured in millimeters (mm).

dots per inch (dpi)   A measure of resolution expressed by the number of dots that a device can print or display in one inch.

double-density disk   A floppy disk with a storage capacity of 360KB.

DRAM   See *dynamic RAM (DRAM)*.

drawing tablet   Pointing device that includes a pencil-like device (called a stylus) for drawing on its flat rubber-coated sheet of plastic.

drive bay   An opening in the system unit into which you can install a floppy disk drive, hard disk drive, or tape drive.

drive geometry   Term used to describe the number of cylinders, read/write heads, and sectors in a hard disk.

drive hole   Hole in a floppy disk that allows the motor in the disk drive to spin the disk. Also known as the hub hole.

drive letter   In DOS, Windows, and OS/2, the drive letter is a designation used to specify a particular hard or floppy disk. For example, the first floppy disk is usually referred to as drive A, and the first hard disk as drive C.

driver   See *device driver*.

driver signing In order to prevent viruses and poorly written drivers from damaging your system, Windows 2000 uses a process called driver signing that allows companies to digitally sign their device software, and it also allows administrators to block the installation of unsigned drivers.

driver software See *device driver*.

D-Shell See *DB connector*.

DSR Abbreviation for data set ready. A hardware signal defined by the RS-232-C standard to indicate that the device is ready.

D-Sub See *DB connector*.

DTE Abbreviation for data terminal equipment. In communications, any device, such as a terminal or a computer, connected to a communications channel or public network.

DTR Abbreviation for data terminal ready. A hardware signal defined by the RS-232-C standard to indicate that the computer is ready to accept a transmission.

dual-booting If a single machine must be used for many tasks, it may be necessary for it to have multiple operating systems installed simultaneously. To do this a boot manager presents the user with a choice of which operating system to use at startup. To use a different OS the user would have to shut down the system, restart it, and select the other OS.

Dual Inline Memory Module See *DIMM (Dual Inline Memory Module)*.

Dual Inline Package See *DIP (Dual Inline Package)*.

dumb terminal A combination of keyboard and screen that has no local computing power, used to input information to a large, remote computer, often a minicomputer or a mainframe. This remote computer provides all the processing power for the system.

duplex In asynchronous transmissions, the ability to transmit and receive on the same channel at the same time; also referred to as full duplex. Half-duplex channels can transmit only or receive only. Most dial-up services available to PC users take advantage of full-duplex capabilities, but if you cannot see what you are typing, switch to half duplex. If you are using half duplex and you can see two of every character you type, change to full duplex.

duplex printing Printing a document on both sides of the page so that the appropriate pages face each other when the document is bound.

dynamic electricity See *electricity*.

Dynamic Host Configuration Protocol (DHCP)   DHCP manages the automatic assignment of TCP/IP addressing information (such as the IP address, subnet mask, default gateway and DNS server). This can save a great deal of time when configuring and maintaining a TCP/IP network.

Dynamic Link Library (DLL) files   Windows component files that contain small pieces of executable code that are shared between multiple Windows programs. They are used to eliminate redundant programming in certain Windows applications. DLLs are used extensively in Microsoft Windows, OS/2, and in Windows NT. DLLs may have filename extensions of `.dll`, `.drv`, or `.fon`.

dynamic RAM (DRAM)   A common type of computer memory that uses capacitors and transistors storing electrical charges to represent memory states. These capacitors lose their electrical charge, and so they need to be refreshed every millisecond, during which time they cannot be read by the processor. DRAM chips are small, simple, cheap, easy to make, and hold approximately four times as much information as a static RAM (SRAM) chip of similar complexity. However, they are slower than static RAM. Processors operating at clock speeds of 25MHz or more need DRAM with access times of faster than 80 nanoseconds (80 billionths of a second), while SRAM chips can be read in as little as 15 to 30 nanoseconds.

Each operating system contains a standard set of device drivers for the keyboard, the monitor, and so on, but if you add specialized peripherals (such as a CD-ROM disk drive) or a network interface card, you will probably have to add the appropriate device driver so that the operating system knows how to manage the device. In DOS, device drivers are loaded by the DEVICE or DEVICEHIGH commands in CONFIG.SYS.

edge connector   A form of connector consisting of a row of etched contacts along the edge of a printed circuit board that is inserted into an expansion slot in the computer.

EDO (Extended Data Out) RAM   A type of DRAM that increases memory performance by eliminating wait states.

EEPROM   Acronym for Electrically Erasable Programmable Read-Only Memory. A memory chip that maintains its contents without electrical power, and whose contents can be erased and reprogrammed either within the computer or from an external source. EEPROMs are used where the application requires stable storage without power but may have to be reprogrammed.

EGA   Acronym for Enhanced Graphics Adapter. A video adapter standard that provides medium-resolution text and graphics. EGA can display 16 colors at the same time from a choice of 64, with a horizontal resolution of 640 pixels and a vertical resolution of 350 pixels. EGA has been superseded by VGA and SVGA.

EISA Acronym for Extended Industry Standard Architecture. A PC bus standard that extends the traditional AT-bus to 32 bits and allows more than one processor to share the bus. EISA has a 32-bit data path and, at a bus speed of 8MHz, can achieve a maximum throughput of 33 megabytes per second.

EISA Configuration Utility (EISA Config) The utility used to configure an EISA bus expansion card.

Electrically Erasable Programmable Read-Only Memory See *EEPROM*.

electricity The flow of free electrons from one molecule of substance to another. This flow of electrons is used to do work.

electromagnetic drawing tablets Type of drawing tablet that has grids of wires underneath the rubberized surface. The stylus contains a small sensor that is sensitive to electromagnetic fields. At timed intervals, an electromagnetic pulse is sent across the grid. The sensor in the stylus picks up these pulses.

electromagnetic interference (EMI) Any electromagnetic radiation released by an electronic device that disrupts the operation or performance of any other device.

electron gun The component of a monitor that fires electrons at the back of the phosphor-coated screen.

electrostatic discharge (ESD) When two objects of dissimilar charge come in contact with one another, they will exchange electrons in order to standardize the electrostatic charge between the two objects. This exchange, or discharge, can sometimes be seen as a spark or arc of electricity. Even when it cannot be seen it is damaging to electronic components.

e-mail Electronic mail is generally sent across the Internet using protocols named SMTP (for sending) and POP3 (for receiving).

EMI See *electromagnetic interference (EMI)*.

EMM386.EXE Reserved memory manager that emulates Expanded Memory in the Extended Memory area (XMS) and provides DOS with the ability to utilize upper memory blocks to load programs and device drivers.

encoding Process by which binary information is changed into flux transition patterns on a disk surface.

Enhanced Graphics Adapter See *EGA*.

enhanced keyboard A 101- or 102-key keyboard introduced by IBM that has become the accepted standard for PC keyboard layout. Unlike earlier keyboards, it has 12 function keys across the top, rather than 10 function keys in a block on the left side, has extra Ctrl and Alt keys, and has a set of cursor control keys between the main keyboard and the numeric keypad.

Enhanced Small Device Interface (ESDI)   A popular hard-disk, floppy-disk, and tape-drive interface standard, capable of a data transfer rate of 10 to 20 megabits per second. ESDI is most often used with large hard disks.

environment variables   These are used to set certain system-wide parameters that can then be used by applications running on the system. For instance, a system's temporary directory can be set to a specific location using an environment variable.

EP drum   Device that is coated with a photosensitive material that can hold a static charge when not exposed to light. The drum contains a cleaning blade that continuously scrapes the used toner off the photosensitive drum to keep it clean.

EP print process   Six-step process an EP laser printer uses to form images on paper. In order, the steps are charging, exposing, developing, transferring, fusing, and cleaning.

EP printer (electrophotographic printer)   Printer that uses high voltage, a laser, and a black carbon toner to form an image on a page.

EPROM   Acronym for erasable programmable read-only memory. A memory chip that maintains its contents without electrical power, and whose contents can be erased and reprogrammed by removing a protective cover and exposing the chip to ultraviolet light.

ergonomics   Standards that define the positioning and use of the body to promote a healthy work environment.

ESD   See *electrostatic discharge (ESD)*.

ESD mat   Preventive measure to guard against the effects of ESD. The excess charge is drained away from any item that comes in contact with it.

Ethernet   A network technology based on the IEEE 802.3 CSMA/CD standard. The original Ethernet implementation specified 10MBps, baseband signaling, coaxial cable, and CSMA/CD media access.

even parity   A technique that counts the number of 1s in a binary number and, if the number of 1s total is not an even number, adds a digit to make it even. (See also *parity*).

exit roller   Found on laser and page printers, the mechanism that guides the paper out of the printer into the paper-receiving tray.

expanded memory page frame   See *page frame*.

expanded memory specification (EMS)   The original version of the Lotus-Intel-Microsoft Expanded Memory Specification (LIM EMS) that lets DOS applications use more than 640KB of memory space.

expansion bus An extension of the main computer bus that includes expansion slots for use by compatible adapters, such as memory boards, video adapters, hard disk controllers, and SCSI interface cards.

expansion card A device that can be installed into a computer's expansion bus.

expansion slot One of the connectors on the expansion bus that gives an adapter access to the system bus. You can add as many additional adapters as there are expansion slots inside your computer.

extended DOS partition A further optional division of a hard disk, after the primary DOS partition, that functions as one or more additional logical drives. A logical drive is simply an area of a larger disk that acts as though it were a separate disk with its own drive letter.

Extended Graphics Array See *XGA*.

Extended Industry Standard Architecture See *EISA*.

extended memory manager A device driver that supports the software portion of the extended memory specification in an IBM-compatible computer.

Extended Memory System (XMS) Memory above 1,024KB that is used by Windows and Windows-based programs. This type of memory cannot be accessed unless the HIMEM.SYS memory manager is loaded in the DOS CONFIG.SYS with a line like DEVICE=HIMEM.SYS.

extended partition If all of the space on a drive is not used in the creation of the drive's primary partition, a second partition can be created out of the remaining space. Called the extended partition, this second partition can hold one or more logical drives.

external bus An external component connected through expansion cards and slots allows the processor to talk to other devices. This component allows the CPU to talk to the other devices in the computer and vice versa.

external cache memory Separate expansion board that installs in a special processor-direct bus that contains cache memory.

external commands Commands that are not contained within COMMAND .COM. They are represented by a .COM or .EXE extension.

external hard disk A hard disk packaged in its own case with cables and an independent power supply rather than a disk drive housed inside and integrated with the computer's system unit.

external modem A stand-alone modem, separate from the computer and connected by a serial cable. LEDs on the front of the chassis indicate the current modem status and can be useful in troubleshooting communications problems.

An external modem is a good buy if you want to use a modem with different computers at different times or with different types of computer.

FAQ   Acronym for Frequently Asked Question. A document that lists some of the more commonly asked questions about a product or component. When researching a problem, the FAQ is usually the best place to start.

FAT   See *file allocation table (FAT)*.

fax modem   An adapter that fits into a PC expansion slot and provides many of the capabilities of a full-sized fax machine, but at a fraction of the cost.

FDDI   See *fiber distributed data interface (FDDI)*.

FDISK.EXE   The DOS utility that is used to partition hard disks for use with DOS.

feed roller   The rubber roller in a laser printer that feeds the paper into the printer.

fiber distributed data interface (FDDI)   A specification for fiber-optic networks transmitting at a speed of up to 100 megabits per second over a dual, counter-rotating, Token Ring topology. FDDI is suited to systems that require the transfer of very large amounts of information, such as medical imaging, 3D seismic processing, oil reservoir simulation, and full-motion video.

fiber optic cable   A transmission technology that sends pulses of light along specially manufactured optical fibers. Each fiber consists of a core, thinner than a human hair, surrounded by a sheath with a much lower refractive index. Light signals introduced at one end of the cable are conducted along the cable as the signals are reflected from the sheath.

field replacement unit   See *FRU (field replacement unit)*.

file allocation table (FAT)   A table maintained by DOS or OS/2 that lists all the clusters available on a disk. The FAT includes the location of each cluster, as well as whether it is in use, available for use, or damaged in some way and therefore unavailable. FAT also keeps track of which pieces belong to which file.

file compression program   An application program that shrinks program or data files, so that they occupy less disk space. The file must then be extracted or decompressed before you can use it. Many of the most popular file compression programs are shareware, like WinZIP, PKZIP, LHA, and StuffIt for the Macintosh, although utility packages like PC Tools from Central Point Software also contain file compression programs.

file corruption   Occasionally an improper shutdown, a virus, or a random problem will cause a file's information to become unreadable. This unreadable file is referred to as "corrupt" and it must be either repaired or replaced.

file locking   A feature of many network operating systems that prevents more than one person from updating a file at the same time by "locking" the file.

File Manager   Windows utility that allows the user to accomplish a number of important file-related tasks from a single interface. This is a Windows 3.*x* feature only; Window 9*x* uses Explorer.

file server   A networked computer used to store files for access by other client computers on the network. On larger networks, the file server may run a special network operating system; on smaller installations, the file server may run a PC operating system supplemented by peer-to-peer networking software.

file sharing   In networking, the sharing of files via the network file server. Shared files can be read, reviewed, and updated by more than one individual. Access to the file or files is often regulated by password protection, account or security clearance, or file locking, to prevent simultaneous changes from being made by more than one person at a time.

File Transfer Protocol (FTP)   FTP is used to transfer large files across the Internet or any TCP/IP network. Special servers, called FTP servers, store information and then transfer it back to FTP clients as needed. FTP servers can also be secured with a username and password to prevent unauthorized downloading (retrieval of a file from the server) or uploading (placing of a file on the server).

FireWire   See *IEEE-1394*.

firmware   Any software stored in a form of read-only memory—ROM, EPROM, or EEPROM—that maintains its contents when power is removed.

fixed disk   A disk drive that contain several disks (also known as platters) stacked together and mounted through their centers on a small rod. The disks rotate as read/write heads float above the disks that make, modify, or sense changes in the magnetic positions of the coatings on the disk.

fixed resistor   Type of resistor that is used to reduce the current by a certain amount. Fixed resistors are color coded to identify their resistance values and tolerance bands.

flash memory   A special form of non-volatile EEPROM that can be erased at signal levels normally found inside the PC, so that you can reprogram the contents with whatever you like without pulling the chips out of your computer. Also, once flash memory has been programmed, you can remove the expansion board it is mounted on and plug it into another computer if you wish.

flatbed scanner   An optical device used to digitize a whole page or a large image.

flat-panel display   In laptop and notebook computers, a very narrow display that uses one of several technologies, such as electroluminescence, LCD, or thin film transistors.

floating-point calculation   A calculation of numbers whose decimal point is not fixed but moves or floats to provide the best degree of accuracy. Floating-point calculations can be implemented in software, or they can be performed much faster by a separate floating-point processor.

floating-point processor   A special-purpose, secondary processor designed to perform floating-point calculations much faster than the main processor.

floppy disk   A flat, round, magnetically coated plastic disk enclosed in a protective jacket. Data is written onto the floppy disk by the disk drive's read/write heads as the disk rotates inside the jacket. It can be used to distribute commercial software, to transfer programs from one computer to another, or to back up files from a hard disk. Floppy disks in personal computing are of two physical sizes, 5.25" or 3.5", and a variety of storage capacities. The 5.25" floppy disk has a stiff plastic external cover, while the 3.5" floppy disk is enclosed in a hard plastic case. IBM-compatibles use 5.25" and 3.5" disks, and the Macintosh uses 3.5" disks.

floppy disk controller   The circuit board that is installed in a computer to translate signals from the CPU into signals that the floppy disk drive can understand. Often it is integrated into the same circuit board that houses the hard disk controller; it can, however, be integrated into the motherboard in the PC.

floppy disk drive   A device used to read and write data to and from a floppy disk. Floppy disk drives may be full-height drives, but more commonly these days they are half-height drives.

floppy drive cable   A cable that connects the floppy drive(s) to the floppy drive controller. The cable is a 34-wire ribbon cable that usually has three connectors.

floppy drive interfaces   A connector on a motherboard used to connect floppy drives to the motherboard.

floptical disk   A removable optical disk with a recording capacity of between 20 and 25 megabytes.

flux transition   Presence or absence of a magnetic field in a particle of the coating on the disk. As the disk passes over an area the electromagnet is energized to cause the material to be magnetized in a small area.

footprint   The amount of desktop or floor space occupied by a computer or display terminal. By extension, also refers to the size of software items such as applications or operating systems.

FORMAT.COM External DOS command that prepares the partition to store information using the FAT system as required by DOS and Windows 9x.

formatter board Type of circuit board that takes the information the printer receives from the computer and turns it into commands for the various components in the printer.

formatting 1. To apply the page-layout commands and font specifications to a document and produce the final printed output.
2. The process of initializing a new, blank floppy disk or hard disk so that it can be used to store information.

form factors Physical characteristics and dimensions of drive styles.

form feed (FF) A printer command that advances the paper in the printer to the top of the next page by pressing the FF button on the printer.

fragmentation A disk storage problem that exists after several smaller files have been deleted from a hard disk. The deletion of files leaves the disk with areas of free disk space scattered throughout the disk. The fact that these areas of disk space are located so far apart on the disk causes slower performance because the disk read/write heads have to move all around the disk's surface to find the pieces of one file.

free memory An area of memory not currently in use.

Frequently Asked Question See *FAQ*.

friction feed A paper-feed mechanism that uses pinch rollers to move the paper through a printer, one page at a time.

FRU (field replacement unit) The individual parts or whole assemblies that can be replaced to repair a computer.

"full" AT A type of motherboard form factor where the motherboard is the same size as the original IBM AT computer's motherboard.

full-duplex communications Communications where both entities can send and receive simultaneously.

function keys The set of programmable keys on the keyboard that can perform special tasks assigned by the current application program.

fuser Device on an EP Printer that uses two rollers to heat the toner particles and melt them to the paper. The fuser is made up of a halogen heating lamp, a Teflon-coated aluminum fusing roller, and a rubberized pressure roller. The lamp heats the aluminum roller. As the paper passes between the two rollers, the rubber roller presses the paper against the heated roller. This causes the toner to melt and become a permanent image on the paper.

fusing assembly   See *fuser*.

fusing step   The step in the EP process where the toner image on the paper is fused to the paper using heat and pressure. The heat melts the toner and the pressure helps fuse the image permanently to the paper.

game port   A DB-15 connector used to connect game devices (like joysticks) to a computer.

gateway   In networking, a shared connection between a local area network and a larger system, such as a mainframe computer or a large packet-switching network. Usually slower than a bridge or router, a gateway typically has its own processor and memory and can perform protocol conversions. Protocol conversion allows a gateway to connect two dissimilar networks; data is converted and reformatted before it is forwarded to the new network.

GDI.EXE   Windows core component that is responsible for drawing icons and windows in Windows 3.*x*.

General Protection Fault (GPF)   A Windows error that typically occurs when a Windows program tries to access memory currently in use by another program.

gigabyte   One billion bytes; however, bytes are most often counted in powers of 2, and so a gigabyte becomes 2 to the 30th power, or 1,073,741,824 bytes.

GPF   See *General Protection Fault (GPF)*.

graphical user interface (GUI)   A graphics-based user interface that allows users to select files, programs, or commands by pointing to pictorial representations on the screen rather than by typing long, complex commands from a command prompt. Application programs execute in windows, using a consistent set of pull-down menus, dialog boxes, and other graphical elements such as scroll bars and icons.

graphics accelerator board   A specialized expansion board containing a graphics coprocessor as well as all the other circuitry found on a video adapter.

graphics mode   A mode of a video card that allows the video card to display graphics.

group icons   A type of Windows icon that groups Windows program icons together in the Program Manager.

GUI   See *graphical user interface (GUI)*.

half-duplex communications   Communications that occur when only one entity can transmit or receive at any one instant.

half-height drive   A space-saving drive bay that is half the height of the 3" drive bays used in the original IBM PC. Most of today's drives are half-height drives.

hand-held scanner   Type of scanner that is small enough to be held in your hand. Used to digitize a relatively small image or artwork, it consists of the controller, CCD, and light source contained in a small enclosure with wheels on it.

hard disk controller   An expansion board that contains the necessary circuitry to control and coordinate a hard disk drive. Many hard disk controllers are capable of managing more than one hard disk, as well as floppy disks and even tape drives.

hard disk drive   A storage device that uses a set of rotating, magnetically coated disks called platters to store data or programs. A typical hard disk platter rotates at up to 7200rpm, and the read/write heads float on a cushion of air from 10 to 25 millionths of an inch thick so that the heads never come into contact with the recording surface. The whole unit is hermetically sealed to prevent airborne contaminants from entering and interfering with these close tolerances. Hard disks range in capacity from a few tens of megabytes to several gigabytes of storage space; the bigger the disk, the more important a well thought out backup strategy becomes.

hard disk interfaces   A connector on a motherboard that makes it possible to connect a hard disk to the motherboard.

hard disk system   A disk storage system containing the following components: the hard disk controller, hard disk, and host adapter.

hard memory error   A reproducible memory error that is related to hardware failure.

hard reset   A system reset made by pressing the computer's reset button or by turning the power off and then on again.

hardware   All the physical electronic components of a computer system, including peripherals, printed-circuit boards, displays, and printers.

Hardware Compatibility List (HCL)   An HCL is a list (that is maintained and regularly updated by Microsoft for each of its Windows OSs) of all hardware currently known to be compatible with a particular operating system. Windows 98, NT, and 2000 all have their own HCL.

hardware interrupt   An interrupt or request for service generated by a hardware device such as a keystroke from the keyboard or a tick from the clock. Because the processor may receive several such signals simultaneously, hardware interrupts are usually assigned a priority level and processed according to that priority.

hardware ports   See *I/O address*.

head   The electromagnetic device used to read from and write to magnetic media such as hard and floppy disks, tape drives, and compact discs. The head converts the information read into electrical pulses sent to the computer for processing.

header   Information that is attached to the beginning of a network data frame.

heat sink   A device that is attached to an electronic component that removes heat from the component by induction. It is often a plate of aluminum or metal with several vertical fingers.

hertz   Abbreviated Hz. A unit of frequency measurement; 1 hertz equals one cycle per second.

hexadecimal   Abbreviated hex. The base-16 numbering system that uses the digits 0 to 9, followed by the letters A to F (equivalent to the decimal numbers 10 through 15). Hex is a very convenient way to represent the binary numbers computers use internally, because it fits neatly into the 8-bit byte. All of the 16 hex digits 0 to F can be represented in 4 bits, and so two hex digits (one digit for each set of 4 bits) can be stored in a single byte. This means that 1 byte can contain any one of 256 different hex numbers, from 0 through FF. Hex numbers are often labeled with a lowercase *h* (for example, 1234h) to distinguish them from decimal numbers.

high-density disk   A floppy disk with more recording density and storage capacity than a double-density disk.

high-level format   The process of preparing a floppy disk or a hard disk partition for use by the operating system. In the case of DOS, a high-level format creates the boot sector, the file allocation table (FAT), and the root directory.

high memory area (HMA)   In an IBM-compatible computer, the first 64K of extended memory above the 1MB limit of 8086 and 8088 addresses. Programs that conform to the extended memory specification can use this memory as an extension of conventional memory although only one program can use or control HMA at a time.

high-voltage power supply (HVPS)   Provides the high voltages that are used during the EP print process. This component converts house AC currents into higher voltages that the two corona assemblies can use.

high-voltage probe   A device used to drain away voltage from a monitor before testing. It is a pencil shaped device with a metal point and a wire lead with a clip.

HIMEM.SYS   The DOS and Microsoft Windows device driver that manages the use of extended memory and the high memory area on IBM-compatible computers. HIMEM.SYS not only allows your application programs to access extended memory, it oversees that area to prevent other programs from trying to use the same space at the same time. HIMEM.SYS must be loaded by a DEVICE command in your CONFIG.SYS file; you cannot use DEVICEHIGH.

HMA   See *high memory area (HMA)*.

home page   On the Internet, an initial starting page. A home page may be related to a single person, a specific subject, or a corporation and is a convenient jumping-off point to other pages or resources.

host   The central or controlling computer in a networked or distributed processing environment, providing services that other computers or terminals can access via the network. Computers connected to the Internet are also described as hosts, and can be accessed using FTP, Telnet, Gopher, or a browser.

host adapter   Translates signals from the hard drive and controller to signals the computer's bus can understand.

host name   The name by which a computer is known on a TCP/IP network. This name must be unique within the domain that the machine is in. In Windows 2000 the computer name is always the same as the machine's host name, while in Windows 9x the two can be different.

hub   A connectivity device used to link several computers together into a physical star topology. They repeat any signal that comes in on one port and copies it to the other ports.

HVPS   See *high-voltage power supply (HVPS)*.

hybrid topology   A mix of more than one topology type used on a network.

Hypertext Transfer Protocol (HTTP)   HTTP is the protocol of the World Wide Web, and is used to send and receive Web pages and other content from an HTTP server (Web server). HTTP makes use of linked pages, accessed via hyperlinks, which are words or pictures that, when clicked on, take you to another page.

I/O address   Lines on a bus used to allow the CPU to send instructions to the devices installed in the bus slots. Each device is given its own communication line to the CPU. These lines function like one-way (unidirectional) mailboxes.

I/O ports   See *I/O address*.

laser printer   A generic name for a printer that uses the electrophotographic (EP) print process.

IBM-compatible computer   Originally, any personal computer compatible with the IBM line of personal computers. With the launch of IBM's proprietary micro channel architecture in the PS/2 line of computers, which replaced the AT bus, two incompatible standards emerged, and so the term became misleading. Now, it is becoming more common to use the term "industry-standard computer" when referring to a computer that uses the AT or ISA bus, and the term "DOS computer" to describe any PC that runs DOS and is based on one of the Intel family of chips.

IBM PC A series of personal computers based on the Intel 8088 processor, introduced by IBM in mid-1981. The PC was released containing 16K of memory, expandable to 64K on the motherboard, and a monochrome video adapter incapable of displaying bit-mapped graphics. The floppy disk drive held 160K of data and programs. There was no hard disk on the original IBM PC; that came later with the release of the IBM PC/XT.

IBM PS/2 A series of personal computers using several different Intel processors, introduced by IBM in 1987. The main difference between the PS/2 line and earlier IBM personal computers was a major change to the internal bus. Previous computers used the AT bus, also known as industry-standard architecture, but IBM used the proprietary micro channel architecture in the PS/2 line instead. Micro channel architecture expansion boards will not work in a computer using ISA. See *IBM-compatible computer*.

IC See *integrated circuit (IC)*.

Icons On-screen graphics that act as doors through which programs are started and therefore used to spawn windows. They are shortcuts that allow a user to open a program or a utility without knowing where that program is or how it needs to be configured.

IDE Acronym for integrated drive electronics. A hard disk technology that can connect multiple drives together. These drives integrate the controller and drive into one assembly. This makes them very inexpensive. Because of this, IDE drives are the most commonly used disk technology installed in computers today.

IEEE-1394 A high-speed digital interface most commonly used to transfer data between computers and digital video cameras. It has a maximum data transfer rate of over 400MBps.

illegal operation error A Windows error that occurs when a program does something that Windows wasn't expecting or doesn't know how to do.

impact printer Any printer that forms an image on paper by forcing a character image against an inked ribbon. Dot-matrix, daisy-wheel, and line printers are all impact printers, whereas laser printers are not.

In a virtual memory system, programs and their data are divided up into smaller pieces called pages. At the point where more memory is needed, the operating system decides which pages are least likely to be needed soon (using an algorithm based on frequency of use, most recent use, and program priority), and it writes these pages out to disk. The memory space that they used is now available to the rest of the system for other application programs. When these pages are needed again, they are loaded back into real memory, displacing other pages.

incremental backup A backup of a hard disk that consists of only those files created or modified since the last backup was performed.

industry-standard architecture   See *ISA*.

INI file   Text file that is created by an installation program when a new Windows application is installed. INI files contain settings for individual Windows applications as well as for Windows itself.

initialization commands   A set of commands sent to a modem to prepare it to function.

inoculating   The process of protecting a computer system against virus attacks by installing antivirus software.

input/output addresses   See *I/O address*.

integrated circuit (IC)   Also known as a chip. A small semiconductor circuit that contains many electronic components.

integrated drive electronics   See *IDE*.

Integrated Services Digital Network   See *ISDN*.

integrated system boards   A system board that has most of the computer's circuitry attached, as opposed to having been installed as expansion cards.

Intel OverDrive   OverDrive chips boost system performance by using the same clock multiplying technology found in the Intel 80486DX-2 and DX4 chips. Once installed, an OverDrive processor can increase application performance by an estimated 40 to 70 percent.

intelligent hub   A class of hub that can be remotely managed on the network.

interface   Any port or opening that is specifically designed to facilitate communication between two entities.

interface software   The software for a particular interface that translates software commands into commands that the printer can understand.

interlacing   A display technique that uses two passes over the monitor screen, painting every other line on the screen the first time and then filling in the rest of the lines on the second pass. It relies on the physiological phenomenon known as persistence of vision to produce the effect of a continuous image.

interleaving   Interleaving involves skipping sectors to write the data, instead of writing sequentially to every sector. This evens out the data flow and allows the drive to keep pace with the rest of the system. Interleaving is given in ratios. If the interleave is 2:1, the disk skips 2 minus 1, or 1 sector, between each sector it writes (it writes to one sector, skips one sector, then writes to the next sector following). Most drives today use a 1:1 interleave, because today's drives are very efficient at transferring information.

International Standards Organization (ISO)   An international standard-making body, based in Geneva, that establishes global standards for communications and information exchange.

Internet   The Internet (Net) is the global TCP/IP network that now extends into nearly every office and school. The World Wide Web is the most visible part of the Internet, but e-mail, newsgroups, and FTP (to name just a few) are also important parts of the Internet.

Internet address   An IP or domain address which identifies a specific node on the Internet.

Internet Protocol   See *IP*.

Internet Service Provider (ISP)   An ISP is a company that provides Internet access for users. Generally ISPs are local or regional companies that provide Internet access and e-mail addresses to users.

internetwork   Any TCP/IP network that spans router interfaces is considered to be an internetwork. This means that anything from a small office with two subnets to the Internet itself can be described as an internetwork.

interrupt   A signal to the processor generated by a device under its control (such as the system clock) that interrupts normal processing. An interrupt indicates that an event requiring the processor's attention has occurred, causing the processor to suspend and save its current activity and then branch to an interrupt service routine. This service routine processes the interrupt (whether it was generated by the system clock, a keystroke, or a mouse click) and when it's complete, returns control to the suspended process. In the PC, interrupts are often divided into three classes: internal hardware, external hardware, and software interrupts. The Intel 80x86 family of processors supports 256 prioritized interrupts, of which the first 64 are reserved for use by the system hardware or by DOS.

interrupt request (IRQ)   A hardware interrupt signals that an event has taken place that requires the processor's attention, and may come from the keyboard, the input/output ports, or the system's disk drives. In the PC, the main processor does not accept interrupts from hardware devices directly; instead interrupts are routed to an Intel 8259A Programmable Interrupt Controller. This chip responds to each hardware interrupt, assigns a priority, and forwards it to the main processor.

interrupt request (IRQ) lines   Hardware lines that carry a signal from a device to the processor.

IP   Abbreviation for Internet Protocol. The underlying communications protocol on which the Internet is based. IP allows a data packet to travel across many networks before reaching its final destination.

IP address In order to communicate on a TCP/IP network, each machine must have a unique IP address. This address is in the form $x.x.x.x$ where x is a number from 0 to 255.

IPCONFIG Used on Windows 2000 to view current IP configuration information and to manually request updated information from a DHCP server.

IRQ See *interrupt request (IRQ)*.

ISA Abbreviation for industry-standard architecture. The 16-bit bus design was first used in IBM's PC/AT computer in 1984. ISA has a bus speed of 8MHz and a maximum throughput of 8 megabytes per second. EISA is a 32-bit extension to this standard bus.

ISDN Abbreviation for Integrated Services Digital Network. A worldwide digital communications network emerging from existing telephone services, intended to replace all current systems with a completely digital transmission system. Computers and other devices connect to ISDN via simple, standardized interfaces, and when complete, ISDN systems will be capable of transmitting voice, video, music, and data.

joystick port See *game port*.

jumper A small plastic and metal connector that completes a circuit, usually to select one option from a set of several user-definable options. Jumpers are often used to select one particular hardware configuration rather than another.

kernel file Windows core component that is responsible for managing Windows resources and running applications.

kilobit Abbreviated Kb or Kbit. 1024 bits (binary digits).

kilobits per second Abbreviated Kbps. The number of bits, or binary digits, transmitted every second, measured in multiples of 1024 bits per second. Used as an indicator of communications transmission rate.

kilobyte Abbreviated K, KB, or Kbyte. 1024 bytes.

L1 Cache Any cache memory that is integrated into the CPU.

L2 Cache Any cache memory that is external to the CPU.

LAN See *local area network (LAN)*.

laser scanner The assembly in an EP process printer that contains the laser. This component is responsible for writing the image to the EP drum.

latency The time that elapses between issuing a request for data and actually starting the data transfer. In a hard disk, this translates into the time it takes to position the disk's read/write head and rotate the disk so that the required sector or cluster is under the head. Latency is just one of many factors that influence disk access speeds.

LCD   See *liquid crystal display (LCD)*.

LCD monitor   A monitor that uses liquid crystal display technology. Many laptop and notebook computers use LCD displays because of their low power requirements.

least significant bit (LSB)   In a binary number, the lowest-order bit. That is, the rightmost bit. So, in the binary number 0001, the 1 is the least significant bit.

LED page printer   A type of EP process printer that uses a row of LEDs instead of a laser to expose the EP drum.

legacy   A component that is still functional but is out of date.

letter quality (LQ)   A category of dot-matrix printer that can print characters that look very close to the quality a laser printer might produce.

liquid crystal display (LCD)   A display technology common in portable computers that uses electric current to align crystals in a special liquid. The rod-shaped crystals are contained between two parallel transparent electrodes, and when current is applied, they change their orientation, creating a darker area. Many LCD screens are also backlit or side-lit to increase visibility and reduce the possibility of eyestrain.

local area network (LAN)   A group of computers and associated peripherals connected by a communications channel capable of sharing files and other resources between several users.

local bus   A PC bus specification that allows peripherals to exchange data at a rate faster than the 8 megabytes per second allowed by the ISA (Industry Standard Architecture) and the 32 megabytes per second allowed by the EISA (Extended Industry Standard Architecture) definitions. Local bus can achieve a maximum data rate of 133 megabytes per second with a 33MHz bus speed, 148 megabytes per second with a 40MHz bus, or 267 megabytes per second with a 50MHz bus.

local resources   Files or folders that are physically located on the machine the user is sitting at are referred to as local to that user. Windows 2000 has the ability to enforce local security, while Windows 9*x* does not.

logic board   The sturdy sheet or board to which all other components on the computer are attached. These components consist of the CPU, underlying circuitry, expansion slots, video components, and RAM slots, just to name a few. Also known as a motherboard or planar board.

logical drive   Created within an extended partition, a logical drive is used to organize space within the partition, which can be accessed through the use of a drive letter.

logical memory   The way memory is organized so it can be accessed by an operating system.

logical topology   Topology that defines how the data flows in a network.

logon   The process of logging on submits your username and password to the network and gives you the network credentials you will use for the rest of that session. Users can either log on to a workgroup or to a network security entity (such as the Active Directory).

low-level format   The process that creates the tracks and sectors on a blank hard disk or floppy disk; sometimes called the physical format. Most hard disks are already low-level formatted; however, floppy disks receive both a low- and a high-level format (or logical format) when you use the DOS or OS/2 command FORMAT.

LPTx ports   In DOS, the device name used to denote a parallel communications port, often used with a printer. DOS supports three parallel ports: LPT1, LPT2, and LPT3, and OS/2 adds support for network ports LPT4 through LPT9.

magneto-optical (MO) drives   An erasable, high-capacity, removable storage device similar to a CD-ROM drive. Magneto-optical drives use both magnetic and laser technology to write data to the disk and use the laser to read that data back again. Writing data takes two passes over the disk, an erase pass followed by the write pass, but reading can be done in just one pass and, as a result, is much faster.

main motor   A printer stepper motor that is used to advance the paper.

master drive   The primary drive in an IDE master/slave configuration.

math coprocessor   A processor that speeds up the floating decimal point calculations that are needed in algebra and statistical calculations.

MCA   MCA is incompatible with expansion boards that follow the earlier 16-bit AT bus standard, physically because the boards are about 50 percent smaller and electronically as the bus depends on more proprietary integrated circuits. MCA was designed for multiprocessing, and it also allows expansion boards to identify themselves, thus eliminating many of the conflicts that arose through the use of manual settings in the original bus.

Megabit (Mbit)   Usually 1,048,576 binary digits or bits of data. Often used as equivalent to 1 million bits.

megabits per second (Mbps) A measurement of the amount of information moving across a network or communications link in 1 second, measured in multiples of 1,048,576 bits.

Megabyte (MB) Usually 1,048,576 bytes. Megabytes are a common way of representing computer memory or hard-disk capacity.

Megahertz (MHz) One million cycles per second. A processor's clock speed is often expressed in MHz. The original IBM PC operated an 8088 running at 4.77MHz, while the more modern Pentium processor runs at speeds of up to 1000MHz and higher.

memory The primary random access memory (RAM) installed in the computer. The operating system copies application programs from disk into memory, where all program execution and data processing takes place; results are written back out to disk again. The amount of memory installed in the computer can determine the size and number of programs that it can run, as well as the size of the largest data file.

memory address The exact location in memory that stores a particular data item or program instruction.

memory map The organization and allocation of memory in a computer. A memory map will give an indication of the amount of memory used by the operating system and the amount remaining for use by applications.

memory optimization The process of making the most possible conventional memory available to run DOS programs.

memory refresh An electrical signal that keeps the data stored in memory from degrading.

mesh topology Type of logical topology where each device on a network is connected to every other device on the network. This topology uses routers to search multiple paths and determine the best path.

Messaging Application Programming Interface (MAPI) The MAPI interface is used to control how Windows interacts with messaging applications such as e-mail programs. MAPI makes most of the functions of e-mail transparent and allows programmers to just write the application, not the whole messaging system.

MFM encoding See *modified frequency modulation (MFM) encoding*.

Microsoft Diagnostics See *MSD (Microsoft Diagnostics)*.

Microsoft Disk Operating System See *MS-DOS*.

modem   Contraction of modulator/demodulator, a device that allows a computer to transmit information over a telephone line. The modem translates between the digital signals that the computer uses and analog signals suitable for transmission over telephone lines. When transmitting, the modem modulates the digital data onto a carrier signal on the telephone line. When receiving, the modem performs the reverse process and demodulates the data from the carrier signal.

modified frequency modulation (MFM) encoding   The most widely used method of storing data on a hard disk. Based on an earlier technique known as frequency modulation (FM) encoding, MFM achieves a two-fold increase in data storage density over standard FM recording, but it is not as efficient a space saver as run-length limited encoding.

Molex connector   See *standard peripheral power connector*.

monitor   A video output device capable of displaying text and graphics, often in color.

monochrome monitor   A monitor that can display text and graphics in one color only. For example, white text on a green background or black text on a white background.

most significant bit (MSB)   In a binary number, the highest-order bit. That is, the leftmost bit. In the binary number 10000000, the 1 is the most significant bit.

motherboard   The main printed circuit board in a computer that contains the central processing unit, appropriate coprocessor and support chips, device controllers, memory, and also expansion slots to give access to the computer's internal bus. Also known as a logic board or system board.

mouse   A small input device with one or more buttons used as for pointing or drawing. As you move the mouse in any direction, an on-screen mouse cursor follows the mouse movements; all movements are relative. Once the mouse pointer is in the correct position on the screen, you can press one of the mouse buttons to initiate an action or operation; different user interfaces and file programs interpret mouse clicks in different ways.

MSBACKUP   A DOS program that allows the user to make backup copies of all the programs and data stored on the hard disk. This program is menu-driven and allows the user to set up options that can be used each time you back up the hard drive.

MSD (Microsoft Diagnostics)   Program that allows the user to examine many different aspects of a system's hardware and software setup.

MS-DOS   Acronym for Microsoft Disk Operating System. MS-DOS, like other operating systems, allocates system resources (such as hard and floppy disks, the monitor, and the printer) to the applications programs that need them. MS-DOS is a single-user, single-tasking operating system, with either a command-line interface or a shell interface.

multimedia   A computer technology that displays information by using a combination of full-motion video, animation, sound, graphics, and text with a high degree of user interaction.

multimeter   Electronic device used to measure and test ohms, amperes, and volts.

multiplexer   A network device that combines multiple data streams into a single stream for transmission. Multiplexers can also break out the original data streams from a single, multiplexed stream.

multipurpose server   A server that has more than one use. For example, a multi-purpose server can be both a file server and a print server.

multistation access unit (MAU)   The central device in a Token Ring network that provides both the physical and logical connections to the stations.

multisync monitor   A monitor designed to detect and adjust to a variety of different input signals. By contrast, a fixed-frequency monitor must receive a signal at one specific frequency.

multitasking   A feature of an operating system that allows more than one program to run simultaneously.

multithreading   The ability of a program to send multiple tasks to the processor at the same time. This allows an application to execute more quickly, but it requires the support of a multithreaded operating system.

near letter quality (NLQ)   A category of dot-matrix printer that can come close to the quality of a laser printer, but still is lacking somewhat in print quality.

NetBEUI   Abbreviation for NetBIOS Extended User Interface. A network device driver for the transport layer supplied with Microsoft's LAN Manager.

NetBIOS   Acronym for Network Basic Input/Output System. In networking, a layer of software, originally developed in 1984 by IBM and Sytek, that links a network operating system with specific network hardware. NetBIOS provides an application program interface (API) with a consistent set of commands for requesting lower-level network services to transmit information from node to node.

NetBIOS Extended User Interface   See *NetBEUI*.

network   A group of computers and associated peripherals connected by a communications channel capable of sharing files and other resources between several users. A network can range from a peer-to-peer network (that connects a small number of users in an office or department) to a local area network (that connects many users over permanently installed cables and dial-up lines) or to a wide area network (that connects users on several different networks spread over a wide geographic area).

network adapter   In order to access network resources, a physical connection to the network must be made. This is generally done through the network adapter, which is expansion hardware designed to interface with the network.

Network Basic Input/Output System   See *NetBIOS*.

network client software   The software that enables a computer to communicate on the network.

network interface card (NIC)   In networking, the PC expansion board that plugs into a personal computer or server and works with the network operating system to control the flow of information over the network. The network interface card is connected to the network cabling (twisted-pair, coaxial or fiber-optic cable), which in turn connects all the network interface cards in the network.

Network layer   The third of seven layers of the International Standards Organization's Open Systems Interconnection (ISO/OSI) model for computer-to-computer communications. The Network layer defines protocols for data routing to ensure that the information arrives at the correct destination node.

network security provider   In a network environment, it is often easier to manage the network by having centralized user ID and password storage. Examples of this type of centralized system are Windows 2000's Active Directory or NetWare's NDS.

NIC   See *network interface card (NIC)*.

node   In communications, any device attached to the network.

noncoductor   Any material that does not conduct electricity.

nondedicated server   A computer that can be both a server and a workstation. In practice, by performing the functions of both server and workstation, this type of server does neither function very well. Nondedicated servers are typically used in peer-to-peer networks.

nonintegrated system boards   A type of motherboard where the various subsystems (video, disk access, etc.) are not integrated into the motherboard, but rather placed on expansion cards that can be removed and upgraded.

non-interlaced   Describes a monitor in which the display is updated (refreshed) in a single pass, painting every line on the screen. Interlacing takes two passes to paint the screen, painting every other line on the first pass, and then sequentially filling in the other lines on the second pass. Non-interlaced scanning, while more expensive to implement, reduces unwanted flicker and eyestrain.

NOS (Network Operating System)   Software that runs on the server and controls and manages the network. The NOS controls the communication with resources and the flow of data across the network.

notebook computer   A small portable computer, about the size of a computer book, with a flat screen and a keyboard that fold together. A notebook computer is lighter and smaller than a laptop computer. Some models use flash memory rather than conventional hard disks for program and data storage, while other models offer a range of business applications in ROM. Many offer PCMCIA expansion slots for additional peripherals such as modems, fax modems, or network connections.

NTFS   The NT File System was created to provide enhanced security and performance for the Windows NT operating system, and it has been adopted and improved upon by Windows 2000. NTFS provides Windows 2000 with local file security, file auditing, compression, and encryption options. It is not compatible with Windows 9x or DOS.

null modem   A short RS-232-C cable that connects two personal computers so that they can communicate without the use of modems. The cable connects the two computers' serial ports, and certain lines in the cable are crossed over so that the wires used for sending data by one computer are used for receiving data by the other computer and vice versa.

numeric keypad   A set of keys to the right of the main part of the keyboard, used for numeric data entry.

odd parity   A technique that counts the number of 1s in a binary number and, if the number of 1s total is not an odd number, adds a digit to make it odd. See also *parity*.

ohm   Unit of electrical resistance.

Open Systems Interconnection (OSI) model   See *OSI (Open Systems Interconnection) model*.

operating system (OS)   The software responsible for allocating system resources, including memory, processor time, disk space, and peripheral devices such as printers, modems, and the monitor. All application programs use the operating system to gain access to these system resources as they are needed. The operating system is the first program loaded into the computer as it boots, and it remains in memory at all times thereafter.

optical disk   A disk that can be read from and written to, like a fixed disk but, like a CD, is read with a laser.

optical drive   A type of storage drive that uses a laser to read from and write to the storage medium.

optical mouse   A mouse that uses a special mouse pad and a beam of laser light. The beam of light shines onto the mouse pad and reflects back to a sensor in the mouse. Special small lines crossing the mouse pad reflect the light into the sensor in different ways to signal the position of the mouse.

optical scanner   See *scanner*.

optical touch screen   A type of touch screen that uses light beams on the top and left side and optical sensors on the bottom and right side to detect the position of your finger when you touch the screen.

option diskette   A diskette that contains the device-specific configuration files for the device being installed into a MCA bus computer.

opto-mechanical mouse   Type of mouse that contains a round ball that makes contact with two rollers. Each roller is connected to a wheel that has small holes in it. The wheel rotates between the arms of a U-shaped mechanism that holds a light on one arm and an optical sensor on the other. As the wheels rotate, the light flashes coming through the holes indicate the speed and direction of the mouse, and these values are transmitted to the computer and the mouse control software.

OSI (Open Systems Interconnection) model   A protocol model, developed by the International Standards Organization (ISO), that was intended to provide a common way of describing network protocols. This model describes a seven-layered relationship between the stages of communication. Not every protocol maps perfectly to the OSI model, as there is some overlap within some the layers of some protocols.

page description language   Describes the whole page being printed. The controller in the printer interprets these commands and turns them into laser pulses or firing print wires.

page frame   The special area reserved in upper memory that is used to swap pages of memory into and out of expanded memory.

page printers   Type of printer that handles print jobs one page at a time instead of one line at a time.

pages   16K chunks of memory used in expanded memory.

paging   The process of swapping memory to an alternate location, such as to and from a page frame in expanded memory or to and from a swap file.

paper pickup roller   A D-shaped roller that rotates against the paper and pushes one sheet into the printer.

paper registration roller   A roller in an EP process printer that keeps paper movement in sync with the EP image formation process.

paper transport assembly   The set of devices that moves the paper through the printer. It consists of a motor and several rubberized rollers that each perform a different function.

parallel port   An input/output port that manages information 8 bits at a time, often used to connect a parallel printer.

parallel processing   A processor architecture where a processor essentially contains two processors in one. The processor can then execute more than one instruction per clock cycle.

parity   Parity is a simple form of error checking used in computers and telecommunications. Parity works by adding an additional bit to a binary number and using it to indicate any changes in that number during transmission.

partition   A portion of a hard disk that the operating system treats as if it were a separate drive.

partition table   In DOS, an area of the hard disk containing information on how the disk is organized. The partition table also contains information that tells the computer which operating system to load; most disks will contain DOS, but some users may divide their hard disk into different partitions, or areas, each containing a different operating system. The partition table indicates which of these partitions is the active partition, the partition that should be used to start the computer.

passive hub   Type of hub that electrically connects all network ports together. This type of hub is not powered.

passive-matrix screen   An LCD display mechanism that uses a transistor to control every row of pixels on the screen. This is in sharp contrast to active-matrix screens, where each individual pixel is controlled by its own transistor.

password   In order to identify themselves on the network, each user must provide two credentials—a username and a password. The username says, "This is who I am," and the password says, "And here's proof!" Passwords are case sensitive and should be kept secret from other users on the network.

path   When referring to a file on a computer's hard drive, the path is used to describe where it exists within the directory structure. If a file is on the D drive in a folder named TEST, its path is `d:\test\`.

PC Card   A PC Card, also known as a PCMCIA card or a "credit card adapter" is a peripheral device that uses the PCMCIA specification. These have the advantage of being small, easy to use and fully plug-and-play compliant.

PC Card slot   An opening in the case of a portable computer intended to receive a PC Card; also known as a PCMCIA slot.

PC Card Socket Services   See *socket services*.

PCB   See *printed-circuit board (PCB)*.

PC-DOS 1.0   Microsoft's Disk Operating System is generally referred to as MS-DOS. When it was packaged with IBM's personal computers, though, DOS was modified slightly and was called PC-DOS.

PCI   Abbreviation for Peripheral Component Interconnect. A specification introduced by Intel that defines a local bus that allows up to 10 PCI-compliant expansion cards to be plugged into the computer. One of these 10 cards must be the PCI controller card, but the others can include a video card, network interface card, SCSI interface, or any other basic input/output function. The PCI controller exchanges information with the computer's processor as 32- or 64-bits and allows intelligent PCI adapters to perform certain tasks concurrently with the main processor by using bus mastering techniques.

PCMCIA   Abbreviation for PC Memory Card International Association. Expansion cards developed for this standard are now called PC Cards.

peer-to-peer network   Network where the computers act as both workstations and servers and where there is no centralized administration or control.

Pentium   The Pentium represents the evolution of the 80486 family of microprocessors and adds several notable features, including 8K instruction code and data caches, built-in floating-point processor and memory management unit, as well as a superscalar design and dual pipelining that allow the Pentium to execute more than one instruction per clock cycle.

Pentium Pro   The 32-bit Pentium Pro (also known as the P6) has a 64-bit data path between the processor and cache and is capable of running at clock speeds up to 200MHz. Unlike the Pentium, the Pentium Pro has its secondary cache built into the CPU itself, rather than on the motherboard, meaning that it accesses cache at internal speed, not bus speed.

peripheral   Any hardware device attached to and controlled by a computer, such as a monitor, keyboard, hard disk, floppy disk, CD-ROM drives, printer, mouse, tape drive, and joystick.

Peripheral Component Interconnect   See *PCI*.

permanent swap file　A permanent swap file allows Microsoft Windows to write information to a known place on the hard disk, which enhances performance over using conventional methods with a temporary swap file. The Windows permanent swap file consists of a large number of consecutive contiguous clusters; it is often the largest single file on the hard disk, and of course this disk space cannot be used by any other application.

PGA (Pin Grid Array)　A type of IC package that consists of a grid of pins connected to a square, flat package.

photosensitive drum　See *EP drum.*

Physical layer　The first and lowest of the seven layers in the International Standards Organization's Open Systems Interconnection (ISO/OSI) model for computer-to-computer communications. The Physical layer defines the physical, electrical, mechanical, and functional procedures used to connect the equipment.

physical topology　A description that identifies how the cables on a network are physically arranged.

pickup roller　See *paper pickup roller.*

Pin Grid Array　See *PGA (Pin Grid Array).*

PING　PING is a utility used to send a short message to another computer on a TCP/IP network. PING can be useful to test connectivity between networks or to see if a particular machine is communicating with the network.

pixel　Contraction of picture element. The smallest element that display software can use to create text or graphics. A display resolution described as being 640×480 has 640 pixels across the screen and 480 down the screen, for a total of 307,200 pixels. The higher the number of pixels, the higher the screen resolution. A monochrome pixel can have two values, black or white, and this can be represented by 1 bit as either 0 or 1. At the other end of the scale, true color, capable of displaying approximately 16.7 million colors, requires 24 bits of information for each pixel.

planar board　See *motherboard.*

platform　An operating system (OS) is the basic software that runs on a computer, and it is the base on which all other software sits. As such the OS is the "platform" that applications and utilities run on.

Plug and Play (PnP)　A standard that defines automatic techniques designed to make PC configuration simple and straightforward.

POST　See *power on self-test (POST).*

Post Office Protocol v 3 (POP3)   POP3 is used to accept and store e-mail and to allow users to connect to their mailbox and access their mail. SMTP is used to send mail to the POP3 server.

PostScript   A page-description language used when printing high-quality text and graphics. Desktop publishing or illustration programs that create PostScript output can print on any PostScript printer or imagesetter, because PostScript is hardware-independent. An interpreter in the printer translates the PostScript commands into commands that the printer can understand.

potentiometer   See *variable resistor*.

power on self-test (POST)   A set of diagnostic programs, loaded automatically from ROM BIOS during startup, designed to ensure that the major system components are present and operating. If a problem is found, the POST software writes an error message in the screen, sometimes with a diagnostic code number indicating the type of fault located. These POST tests execute before any attempt is made to load the operating system.

power supply   A part of the computer that converts the power from a wall outlet into the lower voltages, typically 5 to 12 volts DC, required internally in the computer.

power surge   A brief but sudden increase in line voltage, often destructive, usually caused by a nearby electrical appliance (such as a photocopier or elevator) or when power is reapplied after an outage.

power users   A power user is someone who either does administrative-level tasks on their machine or needs to have additional access to the system to do their work. The Power Users group on a Windows 2000 Professional station has abilities somewhere between normal users and administrators.

preemptive multitasking   A form of multitasking where the operating system executes an application for a specific period of time, according to its assigned priority and need. At that time, it is preempted and another task is given access to the CPU for its allocated time. Although an application can give up control before its time is up, such as during input/output waits, no task is ever allowed to execute for longer than its allotted time period.

Presentation layer   The sixth of seven layers of the International Standards Organization's Open Systems Interconnection (ISO/OSI) model for computer-to-computer communications. The Presentation layer defines the way that data is formatted, presented, converted, and encoded.

preventative maintenance   The process of performing various procedures on a computer to prevent future data loss or system downtime.

primary DOS partition   In DOS, a division of the hard disk that contains important operating system files. A DOS hard disk can be divided into two partitions, or areas: the primary DOS partition and the extended DOS partition. If you want to start your computer from the hard disk, the disk must contain an active primary DOS partition that includes the three DOS system files: MSDOS.SYS, IO.SYS, and COMMAND.COM. The primary DOS partition on the first hard disk in the system is referred to as drive C. Disk partitions are displayed, created, and changed using the FDISK command.

print consumables   Products that a printer uses in the print process that must be replaced occasionally. Examples include toner, ink, ribbons, and paper.

printed-circuit board (PCB)   Any flat board made of plastic or fiberglass that contains chips and other electronic components. Many PCBs are multilayer boards with several different sets of copper traces connecting components together.

printer control assembly   Large circuit board in the printer that converts signals from the computer into signals for the various parts in the laser printer.

printer ribbon   A fabric strip that is impregnated with ink and wrapped around two spools encased in a cartridge. This cartridge is used in dot-matrix printers to provide the ink for the print process.

printhead   That part of a printer that creates the printed image. In a dot-matrix printer, the printhead contains the small pins that strike the ribbon to create the image, and in an ink-jet printer, the printhead contains the jets used to create the ink droplets as well as the ink reservoirs. A laser printer creates images using an electrophotographic method similar to that found in photocopiers and does not have a printhead.

print media   Another name for the mediums being printed on. Examples include paper, transparencies, and labels.

product key   Software piracy is a serious problem in the industry, so many programs include a product key that must be typed in for the software to install properly. This key is then submitted if the user registers for technical support.

productivity tools   Any of a number of applications users depend on to do job-related tasks. Word processors and spreadsheets are common examples, but most companies have additional productivity tools as well.

Program Groups   See *group icons*.

Program Manager Group (GRP) Files   Files in the Windows 3.*x* directories that store information about which application icons are contained in which group icons.

Program Manager The primary interface to Windows that allows you to organize and execute numerous programs by double-clicking an icon in a single graphical window.

proprietary design A motherboard design that is unique to a particular manufacturer and is not licensed to other manufacturers.

protected mode A processor operating mode where every program's memory is protected from every other program so that if one program crashes, it doesn't bring down the other programs.

protocol In networking and communications, the specification that defines the procedures to follow when transmitting and receiving data. Protocols define the format, timing, sequence, and error-checking systems used.

protocol stack In networking and communications, the several layers of software that define the computer-to-computer or computer-to-network protocol. The protocol stack on a Novell NetWare system will be different from that used on a Banyan VINES network or on a Microsoft LAN Manager system.

PS/2 mouse interface A type of mouse interface that uses a round, DIN-6 connector that gets its name from the first computer it was introduced on, the IBM PS/2.

puck The proper name for the mouse-like device used with drawing tablets.

QSOP (Quad Small Outline Package) A type of IC package that has all leads soldered directly to the circuit board. Also called a "surface mount" chip.

Quick-and-Dirty Disk Operating System (QDOS) Created by Tim Patterson of Seattle Computer Products, QDOS was the basis of MS-DOS. QDOS was purchased by Microsoft and renamed MS-DOS.

radio frequency interference (RFI) Many electronic devices, including computers and peripherals, can interfere with other signals in the radio-frequency range by producing electromagnetic radiation; this is normally regulated by government agencies in each country.

RAM Acronym for random access memory. The main system memory in a computer, used for the operating system, application programs, and data.

RAM disk An area of memory managed by a special device driver and used as a simulated disk. Anything stored on a RAM disk will be erased when the computer is turned off; therefore, the contents must be saved onto a real disk.

Rambus Inline Memory Modules (RIMMs) A type of memory module that uses Rambus memory. See *Direct Rambus*.

random access memory See *RAM*.

rasterizing   The process of converting signals from the computer into signals for the various assemblies in the laser printer.

read-only memory   See *ROM (read-only memory)*.

read/write head   That part of a floppy- or hard-disk system that reads and writes data to and from a magnetic disk.

real mode   A processor operating mode whereby a processor emulates an 8086 processor.

reference disk   A special disk that is bootable and contains a program that is able to send special commands to MCA bus devices to configure their parameters.

refresh rate   In a monitor, the rate at which the phosphors that create the image on the screen are recharged.

registration roller   See *paper registration roller*.

Registry   The Registry is used in Windows 9*x*, NT, and 2000 to store configuration information about the machine. This includes information about both individual user settings and global system settings.

REM statement   A command placed in the beginning of a line in a DOS batch file to prevent that line from executing.

removable mass storage   Any high-capacity storage device inserted into a drive for reading and writing, then removed for storage and safekeeping.

removable media   Any storage media that can be removed from the system.

repeater   In networking, a simple hardware device that moves all packets from one local area network segment to another.

reserved memory   In DOS, a term used to describe that area of memory between 640K and 1MB, also known as upper memory. Reserved memory is used by DOS to store system and video information.

resistor   An electronic device used to resist the flow of current in an electrical circuit. See also *fixed resistor* and *variable resistor*.

resistor pack   A combination of multiple resistors in a single package. Often used for terminating SCSI buses.

resource   Anything on a network that clients might want to access or use.

restore   The process of getting data from a backup restored to the computer it originally came from.

RFI   See *radio frequency interference (RFI)*.

rheostat   See *variable resistor*.

ribbon cartridge   The container that holds the printer ribbon.

ring topology   Type of physical topology in which each computer connects to two other computers, joining them in a circle and creating a unidirectional path where messages move from workstation to workstation. Each entity participating in the ring reads a message, regenerates it, and then hands it to its neighbor.

RJ-11/RJ-45   A commonly used modular telephone connector. RJ-11 is a four- or six-pin connector used in most connections destined for voice use; it is the connector used on phone cords. RJ-45 is the eight-pin connector used for data transmission over twisted-pair wiring and can be used for networking; RJ-45 is the connector used on 10Base-T Ethernet cables.

RLL encoding   See *run-length limited (RLL) encoding*.

ROM (read-only memory)   A type of computer memory that retains its data permanently, even when power is removed. Once the data is written to this type of memory, it cannot be changed.

root directory   In a hierarchical directory structure, the directory from which all other directories must branch. The root directory is created by the FORMAT command and can contain files as well as other directories. This directory cannot be deleted.

router   In networking, an intelligent connecting device that can send packets to the correct local area network segment to take them to their destination. Routers link local area network segments at the network layer of the International Standards Organization's Open Systems Interconnect (ISO/OSI) model for computer-to-computer communications.

RS-232-C   In asynchronous transmissions, a recommended standard interface established by the Electrical Industries Association. The standard defines the specific lines, timing, and signal characteristics used between the computer and the peripheral device and uses a 25-pin or 9-pin DB connector. RS-232-C is used for serial communications between a computer and a peripheral such as a printer, modem, digitizing tablet, or mouse.

RS-232 cables   See *serial cables*.

RS-422/423/449   In asynchronous transmissions, a recommended standard interface established by the Electrical Industries Association for distances greater than 50 feet but less than 1000 feet. The standard defines the specific lines, timing, and signal characteristics used between the computer and the peripheral device.

RTS   Abbreviation for request to send. A hardware signal defined by the RS-232-C standard to request permission to transmit.

run-length limited (RLL) encoding   An efficient method of storing information on a hard disk that effectively doubles the storage capacity of a disk when compared to older, less efficient methods such as modified frequency modulation encoding (MFM).

Safe Mode   A Windows *9x* operating mode that only loads a basic set of drivers and a basic screen resolution. It can be activated using the F8 key at boot time.

scanner   An optical device used to digitize images such as line art or photographs, so that they can be merged with text by a page-layout or desktop publishing program or incorporated into a CAD drawing.

screen saver   Program originally designed to prevent damage to a computer monitor from being left on too long. These programs usually include moving graphics so that no one pixel is left on all the time. Screen savers detect computer inactivity and activate after a certain period.

SCSI   Acronym for small computer system interface. A high-speed, system-level parallel interface defined by the ANSI X3T9.2 committee. SCSI is used to connect a personal computer to several peripheral devices using just one port. Devices connected in this way are said to be "daisy-chained" together, and each device must have a unique identifier or priority number.

SCSI adapter   Device that is used to manage all the devices on the SCSI bus as well as to send and retrieve data from the devices.

SCSI address   A unique address given to each SCSI device.

SCSI bus   Another name for the SCSI interface and communications protocol.

SCSI chain   All the devices connected to a single SCSI adapter.

SCSI terminator   The SCSI interface must be correctly terminated to prevent signals echoing on the bus. Many SCSI devices have built-in terminators that engage when they are needed. With some older SCSI devices, you have to add an external SCSI terminator that plugs into the device's SCSI connector.

sector   The smallest unit of storage on a disk, usually 512 bytes. Sectors are grouped together into clusters.

seek time   Time it takes the actuator arm to move from rest position to active position for the read/write head to access the information. Often used as a performance gauge of an individual drive. The major part of a hard disk's access time is actually seek time.

semiconductors   Any material that, depending on some condition, is either a conductor or non-conductor.

serial cables   Cables used for serial communications. See *serial communications*.

serial communications   The transmission of information from computer to computer or from computer to a peripheral, one bit at a time. Serial communications can be synchronous and controlled by a clock or asynchronous and coordinated by start and stop bits embedded in the data stream.

serial mouse   A mouse that attaches directly to one of the computer's serial ports.

serial port   A computer input/output port that supports serial communications in which information is processed one bit at a time. RS-232-C is a common serial protocol used by computers when communicating with modems, printers, mice, and other peripherals.

serial printer   A printer that attaches to one of the computer's serial ports.

server   In networking, any computer that makes access to files, printing, communications, or other services available to users of the network. In large networks, a server may run a special network operating system; in smaller installations, a server may run a personal computer operating system.

service   A service is any program that runs in the background on a computer and performs some sort of task for that computer or other machines on the network.

Session layer   The fifth of seven layers of the International Standards Organization's Open Systems Interconnection (ISO/OSI) model for computer-to-computer communications. The Session layer coordinates communications and maintains the session for as long as it is needed, performing security, logging, and administrative functions.

share name   The share name is used to identify a network access point. Share names can be the same as the directory they are sharing or they can be different.

shell   Every operating system needs to have some sort of interface that allows users to navigate the system. The shell is the program that controls how this interface works. For MS-DOS, the Windows Program Manager was its most popular shell. For Windows 9*x* and 2000, Explorer (`explorer.exe`) is the standard shell program.

shielded twisted-pair   See *STP (shield twisted-pair)*.

Simple Mail Transport Protocol (SMTP)   SMTP is used to send mail from a client to an e-mail server. SMTP servers do not store mail for users to pick up; they simply send the mail out, and another server (such as a POP3 server) is used to store incoming mail.

Single Inline Memory Module (SIMM)   Individual RAM chips are soldered or surface mounted onto small narrow circuit boards called carrier modules, which can be plugged into sockets on the motherboard. These carrier modules are simple to install and occupy less space than conventional memory modules.

Single Inline Package (SIP)   A type of semiconductor package where the package has a single row of connector pins on one side only.

single-purpose server   A server that is dedicated to one purpose (e.g., a file server or a printer server).

site license   A software license that is valid for all installations at a single site.

slave drive   The secondary drive in a IDE master/slave disk configuration.

small computer system interface   See *SCSI.*

socket services   Part of the software support needed for PCMCIA hardware devices in a portable computer, controlling the interface to the hardware. Socket services is the lowest layer in the software that manages PCMCIA cards. It provides a BIOS-level software interface to the hardware, effectively hiding the specific details from higher levels of software. Socket services also detect when you insert or remove a PCMCIA card and identify the type of card it is.

software   An application program or an operating system that a computer can execute. Software is a broad term that can imply one or many programs, and it can also refer to applications that may actually consist of more than one program.

software driver   Software that acts as the liaison between a piece of hardware and the operating system and allows the use of a component.

solenoid   An electromechanical device that, when activated, produces an instant push or pull force.

source   All computer programs—operating system or application—are nothing but a collection of program code. This is the source code or "source" that defines what a program is and how it works. The open source movement is involved with allowing you to see and even modify this code.

spin speed   An indication of how fast the platters on a fixed disk are spinning.

spindle   The rod that platters are mounted on to in a hard disk drive.

SRAM   See *static RAM (SRAM).*

ST506 interface   A popular hard-disk interface standard developed by Seagate Technologies, first used in IBM's PC/XT computer and still popular today, with disk capacities smaller than about 40MB. ST506 has a relatively slow data transfer rate of 5 megabits per second.

stack   Another name for the memory map, or the way memory is laid out.

standard peripheral power connector   Type of connector used to power various internal drives. Also called a Molex connector.

star network A network topology in the form of a star. At the center of the star is a wiring hub or concentrator, and the nodes or workstations are arranged around the central point representing the points of the star.

start bit In asynchronous transmissions, a start bit is transmitted to indicate the beginning of a new data word.

Start menu As the main focus of the Windows 9x/NT/2000 user interface, the Start menu allows program shortcuts to be placed for easy and organized access.

static RAM (SRAM) A type of computer memory that retains its contents as long as power is supplied. It does not need constant refreshment like dynamic RAM chips.

static-charge eliminator strip The device in EP process printers that drains the static charge from the paper after the toner has been transferred to the paper.

stepper motor A very precise motor that can move in very small increments. Often used in printers.

stop bit(s) In asynchronous transmissions, stop bits are transmitted to indicate the end of the current data word. Depending on the convention in use, one or two stop bits are used.

STP (shield twisted-pair) Cabling that has a braided foil shield around the twisted pairs of wire to decrease electrical interference.

stylus A pen-like pointing device used in pen-based systems and personal digital assistants.

subnet mask The subnet mask is a required part of any TCP/IP configuration, and it is used to define which addresses are local and which are on remote networks.

superscalar See *parallel processing*.

SuperVGA (SVGA) An enhancement to the Video Graphics Array (VGA) video standard defined by the Video Electronics Standards Association (VESA).

surface mount See *Quad Small Outline Package (QSOP)*.

surge suppressor Also known as a surge protector. A regulating device placed between the computer and the AC line connection that protects the computer system from power surges.

SVGA See *SuperVGA (SVGA)*.

swap file   On a hard disk, a file used to store parts of running programs that have been swapped out of memory temporarily to make room for other running programs. A swap file may be permanent, always occupying the same amount of hard disk space even though the application that created it may not be running, or is temporary, only created as and when needed.

synchronization   The timing of separate elements or events to occur simultaneously.
1. In a multimedia presentation, synchronization ensures that the audio and video components are timed correctly, so they actually make sense.
2. In computer-to-computer communications, the hardware and software must be synchronized so that file transfers can take place.
3. The process of updating files on both a portable computer and a desktop system so that they both have the latest versions is also known as synchronization.

synchronous DRAM   A type of DRAM memory module that uses memory chips synchronized to the speed of the processor.

synchronous transmission   In communications, a transmission method that uses a clock signal to regulate data flow. Synchronous transmissions do not use start and stop bits.

syntax   Syntax is a term used to describe the proper way of forming a text command for entry into the computer. Many commands have a number of different options, each of which requires a particular format.

system attribute   Attribute of DOS that is used to tell the OS that this file is needed by the OS and should not be deleted. Marks a file as part of the operating system and will also protect the file from deletion.

system board   The sturdy sheet or board to which all other components on the computer are attached. These components consist of the CPU, underlying circuitry, expansion slots, video components, and RAM slots, just to name a few. Also known as a logic board, motherboard, or planar board.

system disk   A disk that contains all the files necessary to boot and start the operating system. In most computers, the hard disk is the system disk; indeed, many modern operating systems are too large to run from floppy disk.

SYSTEM.INI   In Microsoft Windows, an initialization file that contains information on your hardware and the internal Windows operating environment.

system resources   On a Windows 3.*x* or 95/98 machine, the system resources represent those components of the PC that are being used (memory, CPU, etc.).

system software   The programs that make up the operating system, along with the associated utility programs, as distinct from an application program.

tabs   On many windows you will find that, to save space, a single window will have many tabs, each of which can be selected to display particular information.

tape cartridge   A self-contained tape storage module, containing tape much like that in a video cassette. Tape cartridges are primarily used to back up hard disk systems.

tape drive   Removable media drive that uses a tape cartridge that has a long polyester ribbon coated with magnetic oxide and wrapped around two spools with a read/write head in between.

target   Another name for the backup media, it is the destination for the data being backed up. It is usually a tape drive or other backup device.

taskbar   The area of the Windows 9*x*/NT/2000 interface which includes the Start button and the System Tray, as well as icons for any open programs.

TCP/IP   Acronym for Transmission Control Protocol/Internet Protocol. A set of computer-to-computer communications protocols that encompass media access, packet transport, session communications, file transfer, e-mail, and terminal emulation. TCP/IP is supported by a very large number of hardware and software vendors and is available on many different computers from PCs to mainframes.

temporary swap file   A swap file that is created every time it is needed. A temporary swap file will not consist of a single large area of contiguous hard disk space, but may consist of several discontinuous pieces of space. By its very nature, a temporary swap file does not occupy valuable hard disk space if the application that created it is not running. In a permanent swap file the hard disk space is always reserved and is therefore unavailable to any other application program.

terminal   A monitor and keyboard attached to a computer (usually a mainframe), used for data entry and display. Unlike a personal computer, a terminal does not have its own central processing unit or hard disk.

Terminate and Stay Resident (TSR)   A DOS program that stays loaded in memory, even when it is not actually running, so that you can invoke it very quickly to perform a specific task.

terminator   A device attached to the last peripheral in a series or the last node on a network. A resistor is placed at both ends of a coax Ethernet cable to prevent signals from reflecting and interfering with the transmission.

text mode   A video display mode for a video card that allows it to only display text. When running DOS programs, a video card is in text mode.

The VL bus is a 32-bit bus, running at either 33 or 40MHz. The maximum throughput is 133 megabytes per second at 33MHz, or 148 megabytes per second at 40MHz. The most common VL bus adapters are video adapters, hard-disk controllers, and network interface cards.

thermal printer   A nonimpact printer that uses a thermal printhead and specially treated paper to create an image.

thick Ethernet   Connecting coaxial cable used on an Ethernet network. The cable is 1 cm (approximately 0.4") thick and can be used to connect network nodes up to a distance of approximately 3300 feet. Thick Ethernet is primarily used for facility-wide installations. Also known as 10Base5.

thin Ethernet   Connecting coaxial cable used on an Ethernet network. The cable is 5 mm (approximately 0.2") thick, and can be used to connect network nodes up to a distance of approximately 1000 feet. Thin Ethernet is primarily used for office installations. Also known as 10Base2.

thrashing   A slang term for the condition that occurs when Windows must constantly swap data between memory and hard disk. The hard disk spins continuously during this and makes a lot of noise.

token passing   A media access method that gives every NIC equal access to the cable. The token is a special packet of data that is passed from computer to computer. Any computer that wants to transmit has to wait until it has the token, at which point it can add its own data to the token and send it on.

Token Ring network   A local area network with a ring structure that uses token-passing to regulate traffic on the network and avoid collisions. On a Token Ring network, the controlling computer generates a "token" that controls the right to transmit. This token is continuously passed from one node to the next around the network. When a node has information to transmit, it captures the token, sets its status to busy, and adds the message and the destination address. All other nodes continuously read the token to determine if they are the recipient of a message; if they are, they collect the token, extract the message, and return the token to the sender. The sender then removes the message and sets the token status to free, indicating that it can be used by the next node in sequence.

tolerance band   Found on a fixed resistor, this colored band indicates how well the resistor holds to its rated value.

toner   Black carbon substance mixed with polyester resins and iron oxide particles. During the EP printing process, toner is first attracted to areas that have been exposed to the laser in laser printers and is later deposited and melted onto the print medium.

toner cartridge   The replaceable cartridge in a laser printer or photocopier that contains the electrically charged ink to be fused to the paper during printing.

topology A way of laying out a network. Can describe either the logical or physical layout.

touch screen A special monitor that lets the user make choices by touching icons or graphical buttons on the screen.

Tracert Used to trace the path of a packet across a TCP/IP network.

trackball An input device used for pointing, designed as an alternative to the mouse.

tracks The concentric circle unit of hard disk division. A disk platter is divided into these concentric circles.

transfer corona assembly The part of an EP process printer that is responsible for transferring the developed image from the EP drum to the paper.

transfer step The step in the EP print process where the developed toner image on the EP drum is transferred to the print media using the transfer corona.

transistor Abbreviation for transfer resistor. A semiconductor component that acts like a switch, controlling the flow of an electric current. A small voltage applied at one pole controls a larger voltage on the other poles. Transistors are incorporated into modern microprocessors by the million.

Transmission Control Protocol/Internet Protocol See *TCP/IP*.

Transport layer The fourth of seven layers of the International Standards Organization's Open Systems Interconnection (ISO/OSI) model for computer-to-computer communications. The Transport layer defines protocols for message structure and supervises the validity of the transmission by performing some error checking.

TSR See *Terminate and Stay Resident (TSR)*.

twisted-pair cable Cable that comprises two insulated wires twisted together at six twists per inch. In twisted-pair cable, one wire carries the signal and the other is grounded. Telephone wire installed in modern buildings is often twisted-pair wiring.

UART Acronym for Universal Asynchronous Receiver/Transmitter. An electronic module that combines the transmitting and receiving circuitry needed for asynchronous transmission over a serial line. Asynchronous transmissions use start and stop bits encoded in the data stream to coordinate communications rather than the clock pulse found in synchronous transmissions.

Ultra DMA IDE Also known as ATA version 4 (ATA-4), it can transfer data at 33Mbps, so it is also commonly seen in motherboard specifications as Ultra DMA/33, Ultra 66, or UDMA.

uninstall   To remove a program from a computer. This generally involves removing its configuration information from the Registry, its icons from the Start menu, and its program code from the file system.

Universal Serial Bus   See *USB*.

Unix   Pronounced "you-nix." A 32-bit, multiuser, multitasking, portable operating system.

upper memory area   See *reserved memory area*.

upper memory block (UMB)   Free areas of memory that can be used for loading drivers and programs into the upper memory area.

USB   Acronym for Universal Serial Bus. A technology used to connect peripheral devices to a computer. Each USB channel will support 127 devices and has a total transfer rate of up to 12Mbps.

USER.EXE   Windows core component that allows a user to interact with Windows. It is the component responsible for interpreting keystrokes and mouse movements and sending the appropriate commands to the other core components.

username   In order to identify themselves on the network, each user must provide two credentials—a username and a password. The username says, "This is who I am," and the password says, "And here's proof!" Each username must be unique on the network and is generally used by only one person.

user profiles   In order to allow each user to customize their Windows experience, user profiles save a particular user's desktop appearance and preferences so that when they log on, they will always have there own desktop, even if they share the machine with others.

utility program   A small program or set of small programs that support the operating system by providing additional services that the operating system does not provide.

UTP   Acronym for unshielded twisted-pair. A type of unshielded network cable that contains multiple conductors in pairs that are twisted around each other.

vaccine   An application program that removes and destroys a computer virus. The people who unleash computer viruses are often very accomplished programmers, and they are constantly creating new and novel ways of causing damage to a system. The antivirus and vaccine programmers do the best they can to catch up, but they must always lag behind to some extent.

vacuum tube   Electronic component that is a glorified switch. A small voltage at one pole switches a larger voltage at the other poles on or off.

variable resistor   A resistor that does not have a fixed value. Typically the value is changed using a knob or slider.

version   Each time that computer software is modified, new features are added and old problems are, hopefully, fixed. To tell these modified programs apart, computer programmers use versions. These are incremented by one digit (for example, from 1.0 to 2.0) for major revisions, or by a tenth of a digit (for example, from 2.0 to 2.1) for minor modifications. Higher version numbers mean newer versions.

VGA   Acronym for Video Graphics Array. A video adapter. VGA supports previous graphics standards, and provides several different graphics resolutions, including 640 pixels horizontally by 480 pixels vertically. A maximum of 256 colors can be displayed simultaneously, chosen from a palette of 262,114 colors. Because the VGA standard requires an analog display, it is capable of resolving a continuous range of gray shades or colors. In contrast, a digital display can only resolve a finite range of shades or colors.

video adapter   An expansion board that plugs into the expansion bus in a DOS computer and provides for text and graphics output to the monitor. The adapter converts the text and graphic signals into several instructions for the display that tell it how to draw the graphic.

Video Graphics Array   See *VGA*.

video RAM (VRAM)   Special-purpose RAM with two data paths for access, rather than just one as in conventional RAM. These two paths let a VRAM board manage two functions at once—refreshing the display and communicating with the processor. VRAM doesn't require the system to complete one function before starting the other, so it allows faster operation for the whole video system.

virtual memory   A memory-management technique that allows information in physical memory to be swapped out to a hard disk. This technique provides application programs with more memory space than is actually available in the computer. True virtual-memory management requires specialized hardware in the processor for the operating system to use; it is not just a question of writing information out to a swap file on the hard disk at the application level.

virus   A program intended to damage your computer system without your knowledge or permission. A virus may attach itself to another program or to the partition table or the boot track on your hard disk. When a certain event occurs, a date passes, or a specific program executes, the virus is triggered into action. Not all viruses are harmful; some are just annoying.

VL bus   Also known as VL local bus. Abbreviation for the VESA local bus, a bus architecture introduced by the Video Electronics Standards Association (VESA), in which up to three adapter slots are built into the motherboard. The VL bus allows for bus mastering.

VLSI (Very Large Scale Integration)   Technology used by chip manufacturers to integrate the functions of several small chips into one chip.

volts   Unit of electrical potential.

VRAM   See *video RAM (VRAM)*.

wait state   A clock cycle during which no instructions are executed because the processor is waiting for data from a device or from memory.

WAN (wide area network)   Network that expands LANs to include networks outside of the local environment and also to distribute resources across distances.

warm boot   Refers to pressing Control+Alt+Delete to reboot the computer. This type of booting doesn't require the computer to perform all of the hardware and memory checks that a cold boot does.

wide area network   See *WAN (wide area network)*.

window   In a graphical user interface, a rectangular portion of the screen that acts as a viewing area for application programs. Windows can be tiled or cascaded and can be individually moved and sized on the screen. Some programs can open multiple document windows inside their application window to display several word processing or spreadsheet data files at the same time.

Windows 95   Windows 95 is a 32-bit, multitasking, multithreaded operating system capable of running DOS, Windows 3.1, and Windows 95 applications; supports Plug and Play (on the appropriate hardware); and adds an enhanced FAT file system in the Virtual FAT which allows long filenames of up to 255 characters while also supporting the DOS 8.3 file-naming conventions.

Windows 98   The home PC operating system released by Microsoft, as the successor to their popular Windows 95 operating system. Basically the same as Windows 95, it offers a few improvements. For example, Windows 98 improves upon the basic "look and feel" of Windows 95 with a "browser-like" interface. It also contains bug-fixes and can support two monitors simultaneously. In addition to new interface features, it includes support for new hardware, including Universal Serial Bus devices.

Windows 2000   The newest Windows operating system that incorporates the "look and feel" of Windows 9*x* with the power of Windows NT.

Windows Desktop   See *Desktop*.

Windows Installer   A new method Microsoft is using to allow users to customize their application installations more easily. The Windows Installer also makes it easier for users to install approved software on secured workstations and can automatically repair damaged installs.

Windows Internet Name Service (WINS)   WINS provides a database for the storage and retrieval of NetBIOS computer names. Each client must register with the WINS server to be able to be added to and query the database.

Windows NT   A 32-bit multitasking portable operating system developed by Microsoft. Windows NT is designed as a portable operating system, and initial versions run on Intel 80386 (or later) processors and RISC processors, such as the MIPS R4000 and the DEC Alpha. Windows NT contains the graphical user interface from Windows 3.1, and can run Windows 3.1 and DOS applications as well as OS/2 16-bit character-based applications and new 32-bit programs specifically developed for Windows NT. Multitasking under Windows NT is preemptive, and applications can execute multiple threads. Security is built into the operating system at the U.S. Government–approved C2 security level. Windows NT supports the DOS FAT file system, the OS/2 HPFS, installable file systems such as CD-ROM systems, and a native file system called NTFS. Windows NT also supports multiprocessing, OLE, and peer-to-peer networking.

Windows Program Manager   Windows 3.*x* file that contains all of the program icons, group icons, and menus used for organizing, starting, and running programs.

WIN.INI   File that contains Windows environmental settings that control the environment's general function and appearance.

WINIPCFG   In Windows 9*x*, this is the utility that allows you to view your current TCP/IP configuration. It also allows a user to request a new IP configuration from a DHCP server.

wizard   Wizards are pre-programmed utilities that walk the user through a particular task. Each wizard generally includes a number of different pages, each of which allows you to enter information or choose particular options. At the finish of the wizard, the computer will then perform the requested task based on the information it has gathered.

word   In binary communications, multiple bytes associated together are usually called a *word*.

workgroup   A group of individuals who work together and share the same files and databases over a local area network. Special groupware such as Lotus Notes coordinates the workgroup and allows users to edit drawings or documents and update the database as a group.

working directory   Programs that need to save temporary files or configuration data while they are running do so within their working directory. Users can also have a working directory to save their temporary files.

workstation 1. In networking, any personal computer (other than the file server) attached to the network.

2. A high-performance computer optimized for graphics applications such as computer-aided design, computer-aided engineering, or scientific applications.

World Wide Web (WWW) This is the graphical extension of the Internet that features millions of pages of information accessed though the use of the Hypertext Transfer Protocol (HTTP).

write-protect To prevent the addition or deletion of files on a disk or tape. Floppy disks have write-protect notches or small write-protect tabs that allow files to be read from the disk, but prevent any modifications or deletions. Certain attributes can make individual files write-protected so they can be read but not altered or erased.

write-protect tab The small notch or tab in a floppy disk that is used to write-protect it.

writing step The step in the EP print process where the items being printed are written to the EP drum. In this step, the laser is flashed on and off as it scans across the surface of the drum. The area where the laser shines on is discharged to almost ground (-100 volts).

***x*86 series** The general name given to the Intel line of IBM-compatible CPUs.

XGA Acronym for Extended Graphics Array. XGA is only available as a micro channel architecture expansion board; it is not available in ISA or EISA form. XGA supports resolution of 1024 horizontal pixels by 768 vertical pixels with 256 colors, as well as a VGA mode of 640 pixels by 480 pixels with 65,536 colors, and like the 8514/A, XGA is interlaced. XGA is optimized for use with graphical user interfaces, and instead of being very good at drawing lines, it is a bit-block transfer device designed to move blocks of bits like windows or dialog boxes.

zero insertion force (ZIF) A type of processor socket where you don't have to "snap" the chip into the socket. Rather, you simply set the chip into the ZIF socket and push a bar down to secure it.

zero wait state Describes a computer that can process information without wait states. A wait state is a clock cycle during which no instructions are executed because the processor is waiting for data from a device or from memory.

ZIF socket Abbreviation for Zero Insertion Force socket. A specially designed chip socket which makes replacing a chip easier and safer.

Index

Note to the reader: Throughout this index **boldfaced** page numbers indicate primary discussions or definitions of a topic. *Italicized* page numbers indicate illustrations and tables.

F

G

P

From self-study guides to advanced computer-based training, simulated testing programs to last-minute review guides, Sybex has the most complete CompTIA training solution on the market.

Sybex® Covers
CompTIA.®
CERTIFICATION PROGRAMS

Study Guides

Designed for optimal learning, Sybex Study Guides provide you with comprehensive coverage of all exam objectives. Hands-on exercises and review questions help reinforce your knowledge.

STUDY

- In-depth coverage of exam objectives
- Hands-on exercises
- CD includes: test engine, flashcards for PCs and Palm devices, PDF version of entire book

Virtual Trainers™
software

Based on the content of the Study Guides, Sybex Virtual Trainers offer you advanced computer-based training, complete with animations and customization features.

- Customizable study planning tools
- Narrated instructional animations
- Preliminary assessment tests
- Results reporting

Virtual Test Centers™
software

Powered by an advanced testing engine, Sybex's new line of Virtual Test Centers give you the opportunity to test your knowledge before sitting for the real exam.

PRACTICE

- Hundreds of challenging questions
- Computer adaptive testing
- Support for drag-and-drop and hot-spot formats
- Detailed explanations and cross-references

Exam Notes™

Organized according to the official exam objectives, Sybex Exam Notes help reinforce your knowledge of key exam topics and identify potential weak areas requiring further study.

REVIEW

- Excellent quick review before the exam
- Concise summaries of key exam topics
- Tips and insights from experienced instructors
- Definitions of key terms and concepts

*Look to Sybex for exam prep materials on major CompTIA certifications, including A+™, Network+™, I-Net+™, and Server+™. For more information about CompTIA and Sybex products, visit **www.sybex.com.***

CompTIA.®
One Industry. One Voice.

SYBEX®
www.sybex.com

Sybex—The Leader in Certification

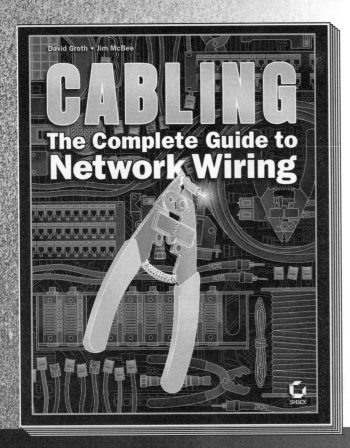

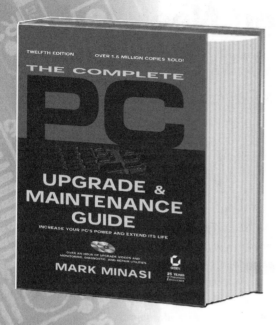

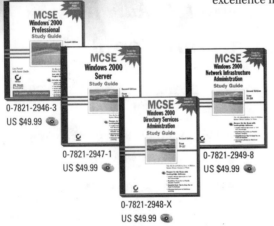